# The
# New Testament

## Of Our Lord and Savior

# Jesus Christ

## With the

# Book of Psalms

**An Inspired Revision of the
Authorized Version
By Joseph Smith, Junior**

*Inspired Version, 1991 Edition*

# TABLE OF CONTENTS

## THE BOOKS OF THE NEW TESTAMENT

| | | | |
|---|---|---|---|
| Matthew | 3 | I Timothy | 225 |
| Mark | 41 | II Timothy | 229 |
| Luke | 65 | Titus | 231 |
| John | 104 | Philemon | 233 |
| Acts | 132 | Hebrews | 234 |
| Romans | 167 | James | 244 |
| I Corinthians | 182 | I Peter | 248 |
| II Corinthians | 195 | II Peter | 252 |
| Galatians | 204 | I John | 254 |
| Ephesians | 209 | II John | 258 |
| Philippians | 214 | III John | 258 |
| Colossians | 217 | Jude | 259 |
| I Thessalonians | 220 | Revelation | 260 |
| II Thessalonians | 223 | | |

## THE BOOK OF PSALMS
283

The complete text of the Inspired Version of the Holy Scriptures (Old and New Testaments) is also available from Herald Publishing House.

Copyright © 1991
The Board of Publication of the Reorganized Church of Jesus
   Christ of Latter Day Saints
Published by Herald Publishing House
Independence, Missouri
ISBN 0-8309-0595-2

Printed in the United States of America

94 93 92 91    1 2 3 4

# THE NEW TESTAMENT
## The Testimony of St. Matthew

### CHAPTER 1

*Giving the genealogy from Abraham until the coming of Christ.*

1 The book of the generation of Jesus Christ, the son of David, the son of Abraham.

2 Abraham begat Isaac; and Isaac begat Jacob; and Jacob begat Judas and his brethren; and Judas begat Phares and Zara of Thamar; and Phares begat Esrom; and Esrom begat Aram; and Aram begat Aminadab; and Aminadab begat Naason; and Naason begat Salmon; and Salmon begat Booz of Rachab; and Booz begat Obed of Ruth; and Obed begat Jesse; and Jesse begat David the king.

3 And David the king begat Solomon of her whom David had taken of Urias; and Solomon begat Roboam; and Roboam begat Abia; and Abia begat Asa; and Asa begat Josaphat; and Josaphat begat Joram; and Joram begat Ozias; and Ozias begat Joatham; and Joatham begat Achaz; and Achaz begat Ezekias; and Ezekias begat Manasses; and Manasses begat Amon; and Amon begat Josias; and Josias begat Jechonias and his brethren, about the time they were carried away to Babylon.

4 And after they were brought to Babylon, Jechonias begat Salathiel; and Salathiel begat Zorobable; and Zorobable begat Abiud; and Abiud begat Eliakim; and Eliakim begat Azor; and Azor begat Sadoc; and Sadoc begat Achim; and Achim begat Eliud; and Eliud begat Eleazar; and Eleazar begat Matthan; and Matthan begat Jacob; and Jacob begat Joseph, the husband of Mary, of whom was born Jesus, as the prophets have written, who is called Christ.

5 So all the generations from Abraham to David, were fourteen generations; and from David until the carrying away into Babylon, were fourteen generations; and from the carrying away into Babylon until Christ, were fourteen generations.

### CHAPTER 2

*Giving a history of the birth of Christ.*

1 Now, as it is written, the birth of Jesus Christ was on this wise. After his mother, Mary, was espoused to Joseph, before they came together, she was found with child of the Holy Ghost.

2 Then Joseph, her husband, being a just man, and not willing to make her a public example, was minded to put her away privily.

3 But while he thought on these things, behold, the angel of the Lord appeared unto him in a vision, saying, Joseph, thou son of David, fear not to take unto thee Mary thy wife; for that which is conceived in her, is of the Holy Ghost.

4 And she shall bring forth a son, and thou shalt call his name Jesus; for he shall save his people from their sins.

5 Now this took place, that all things might be fulfilled, which were spoken of the Lord, by the prophets, saying,

6 Behold, a virgin shall be with child, and shall bring forth a son, and they shall call his name Emmanuel, (which, being interpreted, is, God with us).

7 Then Joseph, awaking out of his vision, did as the angel of the Lord had bidden him, and took unto him his wife;

8 And knew her not until she had brought forth her firstborn son; and they called his name Jesus.

### CHAPTER 3

*Joseph, being warned in a vision, flees to Egypt—John's mission—He baptizeth Jesus.*

1 Now when Jesus was born in Bethlehem of Judea, in the days of Herod the king, behold, there came wise men from the east to Jerusalem,

2 Saying, Where is the child that is born, the Messiah of the Jews? for we have seen his star in the east, and have come to worship him.

3 When Herod the king had heard of the child, he was troubled, and all Jerusalem with him.

4 And when he had gathered all the chief priests, and scribes of the people

3

together, he demanded of them, saying, Where is the place that is written of by the prophets, in which Christ should be born? For he greatly feared, yet he believed not the prophets.

5 And they said unto him, It is written by the prophets, that he should be born in Bethlehem of Judea, for thus have they said,

6 The word of the Lord came unto us, saying, And thou Bethlehem, which lieth in the land of Judea, in thee shall be born a prince, which art not the least among the princes of Judea; for out of thee shall come the Messiah, who shall save my people Israel.

7 Then Herod, when he had called the wise men privily, inquired of them diligently what time the star appeared.

8 And he sent them to Bethlehem, and said, Go and search diligently for the young child; and when ye have found the child, bring me word again, that I may come and worship him also.

9 When they had heard the king, they departed; and lo, the star which they saw in the east, went before them, until it came and stood over where the young child was.

10 When they saw the star, they rejoiced with exceeding great joy.

11 And when they were come into the house, they saw the young child, with Mary his mother, and fell down and worshiped him. And when they had opened their treasures, they presented unto him gifts; gold, and frankincense, and myrrh.

12 And being warned of God in a dream that they should not return to Herod, they departed into their own country another way.

13 And when they were departed, behold, the angel of the Lord, appeared to Joseph in a vision, saying, Arise and take the young child and his mother, and flee into Egypt, and tarry thou there until I bring thee word; for Herod will seek the young child to destroy him.

14 And then he arose, and took the young child, and the child's mother, by night, and departed into Egypt;

15 And was there until the death of Herod, that it might be fulfilled which was spoken of the Lord, by the prophet, saying, Out of Egypt have I called my Son.

16 Then Herod, when he saw that he was mocked of the wise men, was exceeding wroth; and sent forth and slew all the children that were in Bethlehem, and all the coasts thereof, from two years old and under, according to the time which he had diligently inquired of the wise men.

17 Then was fulfilled that which was spoken by Jeremiah the prophet, saying,

18 In Ramah there was a voice heard, lamentation, and weeping, and great mourning; Rachael weeping for the loss of her children, and would not be comforted because they were not.

19 But when Herod was dead, behold, an angel of the Lord appeared in a vision to Joseph in Egypt,

20 Saying, Arise, and take the young child and his mother, and go into the land of Israel; for they are dead who sought the young child's life.

21 And he arose, and took the young child and his mother, and came into the land of Israel.

22 But when he heard that Archelaus did reign in Judea, in the stead of his father Herod, he was afraid to go thither; but, notwithstanding, being warned of God in a vision, he went into the eastern part of Galilee;

23 And he came and dwelt in a city called Nazareth, that it might be fulfilled which was spoken by the prophets, He shall be called a Nazarene.

24 And, it came to pass that Jesus grew up with his brethren, and waxed strong, and waited upon the Lord for the time of his ministry to come.

25 And he served under his father, and he spake not as other men, neither could he be taught; for he needed not that any man should teach him.

26 And after many years, the hour of his ministry drew nigh.

27 And in those days came John the Baptist, preaching in the wilderness of Judea,

28 And saying, Repent ye; for the kingdom of heaven is at hand.

29 For I am he who was spoken of by the prophet Esaias, saying, The voice of one crying in the wilderness, Prepare ye the way of the Lord and make his paths straight.

30 And the same John had his raiment of camels' hair, and a leathern

girdle about his loins; and his food was locusts and wild honey.

31 Then went out to him Jerusalem, and all Judea, and all the region round about Jordan,

32 And many were baptized of him in Jordan, confessing their sins.

33 But when he saw many of the Pharisees and Sadducees come to his baptism, he said unto them, O, generation of vipers! who hath warned you to flee from the wrath to come?

34 Why is it that ye receive not the preaching of him whom God hath sent? If ye receive not this in your hearts, ye receive not me; and if ye receive not me, ye receive not him of whom I am sent to bear record; and for your sins ye have no cloak.

35 Repent, therefore, and bring forth fruits meet for repentance;

36 And think not to say within yourselves, We are the children of Abraham, and we only have power to bring seed unto our father Abraham; for I say unto you that God is able of these stones to raise up children into Abraham.

37 And now, also, the axe is laid unto the root of the trees; therefore every tree which bringeth not forth good fruit, shall be hewn down, and cast into the fire.

38 I indeed baptize you with water, upon your repentance; and when he of whom I bear record cometh, who is mightier than I, whose shoes I am not worthy to bear, (or whose place I am not able to fill,) as I said, I indeed baptize you before he cometh, that when he cometh he may baptize you with the Holy Ghost and fire.

39 And it is he of whom I shall bear record, whose fan shall be in his hand, and he will thoroughly purge his floor, and gather his wheat into the garner; but in the fullness of his own time will burn up the chaff with unquenchable fire.

40 Thus came John, preaching and baptizing in the river of Jordan; bearing record, that he who was coming after him had power to baptize with the Holy Ghost and fire.

41 And then cometh Jesus from Galilee to Jordan, unto John, to be baptized of him;

42 But John refused him, saying, I have need to be baptized of thee, and why comest thou to me?

43 And Jesus, answering, said unto him, Suffer me to be baptized of thee, for thus it becometh us to fulfill all righteousness. Then he suffered him.

44 And John went down into the water and baptized him.

45 And Jesus when he was baptized, went up straightway out of the water; and John saw, and lo, the heavens were opened unto him, and he saw the Spirit of God descending like a dove and lighting upon Jesus.

46 And lo, he heard a voice from heaven, saying, This is my beloved Son, in whom I am well pleased. Hear ye him.

## CHAPTER 4

*Christ led away by the Spirit—Tempted of the devil—The commencement of his ministry.*

1 Then Jesus was led up of the Spirit, into the wilderness, to be with God.

2 And when he had fasted forty days and forty nights, and had communed with God, he was afterwards an hungered, and was left to be tempted of the devil.

3 And when the tempter came to him, he said, If thou be the Son of God, command that these stones be made bread.

4 But Jesus answered and said, It is written, Man shall not live by bread alone, but by every word that proceedeth out of the mouth of God.

5 Then Jesus was taken up into the holy city, and the Spirit setteth him on the pinnacle of the temple.

6 Then the devil came unto him and said, If thou be the Son of God, cast thyself down, for it is written, He shall give his angels charge concerning thee, and in their hands they shall bear thee up, lest at any time thou dash thy foot against a stone.

7 Jesus said unto him, It is written again, Thou shalt not tempt the Lord thy God.

8 And again, Jesus was in the Spirit, and it taketh him up into an exceeding high mountain, and showeth him all the kingdoms of the world and the glory of them.

9 And the devil came unto him again, and said, All these things will I give unto thee, if thou wilt fall down and worship me.

10 Then said Jesus unto him, Get

5

thee hence, Satan; for it is written, Thou shalt worship the Lord thy God, and him only shalt thou serve. Then the devil leaveth him.

11 And now Jesus knew that John was cast into prison, and he sent angels, and, behold, they came and ministered unto him.

12 And Jesus departed into Galilee, and leaving Nazareth, in Zebulun, he came and dwelt in Capernaum, which is upon the seacoast, in the borders of Nephthalim,

13 That it might be fulfilled which was spoken by Esaias the prophet, saying,

14 The land of Zebulun, and the land of Nephthalim, in the way of the sea, beyond Jordan, Galilee of the Gentiles;

15 The people which sat in darkness saw a great light, and unto them that sat in the region and shadow of death, light is sprung up.

16 From that time, Jesus began to preach, and to say, Repent; for the kingdom of heaven is at hand.

17 And Jesus, walking by the sea of Galilee, saw two brethren, Simon, called Peter, and Andrew, his brother, casting a net into the sea; for they were fishers.

18 And he said unto them, I am he of whom it is written by the prophets; follow me, and I will make you fishers of men.

19 And they, believing on his words, left their nets, and straightway followed him.

20 And going on from thence, he saw other two brethren, James, and John his brother, the sons of Zebedee, in a ship with Zebedee their father, mending their nets; and he called them.

21 And they immediately left their father in the ship, and followed him.

22 And Jesus went about all Galilee teaching in their synagogues, and preaching the gospel of the kingdom; and healing all manner of sickness, and all manner of diseases among the people which believed on his name.

23 And his fame went throughout all Syria; and they brought unto him all sick people that were taken with divers diseases, and torments, and those who were possessed with devils, and those who were lunatic, and those that had the palsy; and he healed them.

24 And there followed him great multitudes of people from Galilee, and Decapolis, and Jerusalem, and Judea, and beyond Jordan.

## CHAPTER 5

*The commencement of Christ's teaching on the mount.*

1 And Jesus, seeing the multitudes, went up into a mountain; and when he was set down, his disciples came unto him;

2 And he opened his mouth, and taught them, saying,

3 Blessed are they who shall believe on me; and again, more blessed are they who shall believe on your words, when ye shall testify that ye have seen me and that I am.

4 Yea, blessed are they who shall believe on your words, and come down into the depth of humility, and be baptized in my name; for they shall be visited with fire and the Holy Ghost, and shall receive a remission of their sins.

5 Yea, blessed are the poor in spirit, who come unto me; for theirs is the kingdom of heaven.

6 And again, blessed are they that mourn; for they shall be comforted.

7 And blessed are the meek; for they shall inherit the earth.

8 And blessed are all they that do hunger and thirst after righteousness; for they shall be filled with the Holy Ghost.

9 And blessed are the merciful; for they shall obtain mercy.

10 And blessed are all the pure in heart; for they shall see God.

11 And blessed are all the peacemakers; for they shall be called the children of God.

12 Blessed are all they that are persecuted for my name's sake; for theirs is the kingdom of heaven.

13 And blessed are ye when men shall revile you, and persecute you, and shall say all manner of evil against you falsely, for my sake.

14 For ye shall have great joy, and be exceeding glad; for great shall be your reward in heaven; for so persecuted they the prophets which were before you.

15 Verily, verily, I say unto you, I give unto you to be the salt of earth; but if the salt shall lose its savor, wherewith shall the earth be salted? the salt shall thenceforth be good for

nothing, but to be cast out, and to be trodden under foot of men.

16 Verily, verily, I say unto you, I give unto you to be the light of the world; a city that is set on a hill cannot be hid.

17 Behold, do men light a candle and put it under a bushel? Nay, but on a candlestick; and it giveth light to all that are in the house.

18 Therefore, let your light so shine before this world, that they may see your good works, and glorify your Father who is in heaven.

19 Think not that I am come to destroy the law, or the prophets; I am not come to destroy, but to fulfill.

20 For verily I say unto you, Heaven and earth must pass away, but one jot or one tittle shall in no wise pass from the law, until all be fulfilled.

21 Whosoever, therefore, shall break one of these least commandments, and shall teach men so to do, he shall in no wise be saved in the kingdom of heaven; but whosoever shall do and teach these commandments of the law until it be fulfilled, the same shall be called great, and shall be saved in the kingdom of heaven.

22 For I say unto you, Except your righteousness shall exceed that of the scribes and Pharisees, ye shall in no case enter into the kingdom of heaven.

23 Ye have heard that it hath been said by them of old time that, Thou shalt not kill; and whosoever shall kill, shall be in danger of the judgment of God.

24 But I say unto you that whosoever is angry with his brother, shall be in danger of his judgment; and whosoever shall say to his brother, Raca, or Rabcha, shall be in danger of the council; and whosoever shall say to his brother, Thou fool, shall be in danger of hell fire.

25 Therefore, if ye shall come unto me, or shall desire to come unto me, or if thou bring thy gift to the altar, and there rememberest that thy brother hath aught against thee,

26 Leave thou thy gift before the altar, and go thy way unto thy brother, and first be reconciled to thy brother, and then come and offer thy gift.

27 Agree with thine adversary quickly, while thou art in the way with him; lest at any time thine adversary deliver thee to the judge, and the judge deliver thee to the officer, and thou be cast into prison.

28 Verily I say unto thee, Thou shalt by no means come out thence, until thou hast paid the uttermost farthing.

29 Behold, it is written by them of old time, that thou shalt not commit adultery.

30 But I say unto you that whosoever looketh on a woman to lust after her, hath committed adultery with her already in his heart.

31 Behold, I give unto you a commandment, that ye suffer none of these things to enter into your heart,

for it is better that ye should deny yourselves of these things, wherein ye will take up your cross, than that ye should be cast into hell.

32 Wherefore, if thy right eye offend thee, pluck it out and cast it from thee; for it is profitable for thee that one of thy members should perish, and not that thy whole body should be cast into hell.

33 Or if thy right hand offend thee, cut it off and cast it from thee; for it is profitable for thee that one of thy members should perish, and not that thy whole body should be cast into hell.

34 And now this I speak, a parable concerning your sins; wherefore, cast them from you, that ye may not be hewn down and cast into the fire.

35 It hath been written that, Whosoever shall put away his wife, let him give her a writing of divorcement.

36 Verily, verily, I say unto you that whosoever shall put away his wife, saving for the cause of fornication, causeth her to commit adultery; and whosoever shall marry her that is divorced, committeth adultery.

37 Again, it hath been written by them of old time, Thou shalt not forswear thyself, but shalt perform unto the Lord thine oaths.

38 But I say unto you, Swear not at all; neither by heaven, for it is God's throne; nor by the earth, for it is his footstool; neither by Jerusalem, for it is the city of the great King; neither shalt thou swear by thy head, because thou canst not make one hair white or black.

39 But let your communication be Yea, yea; Nay, nay; for whatsoever is more than these cometh of evil.

40 Ye have heard that it hath been

said, An eye for an eye, and a tooth for a tooth.

41 But I say unto you that ye resist not evil; but whosoever shall smite thee on thy right cheek, turn to him the other also.

42 And if any man will sue thee at the law, and take away thy coat, let him have it; and if he sue thee again, let him have thy cloak also.

43 And whosoever shall compel thee to go a mile, go with him a mile; and whosoever shall compel thee to go with him twain, thou shalt go with him twain.

44 Give to him that asketh of thee; and from him that would borrow of thee, turn not thou away.

45 Ye have heard that it hath been said, Thou shalt love thy neighbor, and hate thine enemy.

46 But I say unto you, Love your enemies; bless them that curse you; do good to them that hate you; and pray for them that despitefully use you and persecute you;

47 That ye may be the children of your Father who is in heaven; for he maketh his sun to rise on the evil and on the good, and sendeth rain on the just and on the unjust.

48 For if ye love only them which love you, what reward have you? Do not even the publicans the same?

49 And if ye salute your brethren only, what do ye more than others? Do not even the publicans the same?

50 Ye are therefore commanded to be perfect, even as your Father who is in heaven is perfect.

## CHAPTER 6

*Christ's teaching on the mount continued.*

1 And it came to pass that, as Jesus taught his disciples, he said unto them, Take heed that ye do not your alms before men, to be seen of them; otherwise ye have no reward of your Father who is in heaven.

2 Therefore, when thou doest alms, do not sound a trumpet before thee, as the hypocrites do, in the synagogues and in the streets, that they may have glory of men. Verily I say unto you, They have their reward.

3 But when thou doest alms, let it be unto thee as thy left hand not knowing what thy right hand doeth;

4 That thine alms may be in secret; and thy Father who seeth in secret, himself shall reward thee openly.

5 And when thou prayest, thou shalt not be as the hypocrites; for they love to pray standing in the synagogues and in the corners of the streets, that they may be seen of men; for, verily, I say unto you, They have their reward.

6 But thou, when thou prayest, enter into thy closet, and when thou hast shut the door, pray to thy Father who is in secret; and thy Father who seeth in secret shall reward thee openly.

7 But when ye pray, use not vain repetitions, as the hypocrites do; for they think that they shall be heard for their much speaking.

8 Therefore be ye not like unto them; for your Father knoweth what things ye have need of, before ye ask him.

9 Therefore after this manner shall ye pray, saying,

10 Our Father who art in heaven, Hallowed be thy name.

11 Thy kingdom come. Thy will be done on earth, as it is done in heaven.

12 Give us this day, our daily bread.

13 And forgive us our trespasses, as we forgive those who trespass against us.

14 And suffer us not to be led into temptation, but deliver us from evil.

15 For thine is the kingdom, and the power, and the glory, forever and ever, Amen.

16 For if ye forgive men their trespasses, who trespass against you, your heavenly Father will also forgive you; but if ye forgive not men their trespasses, neither will your heavenly Father forgive you your trespasses.

17 Moreover, when ye fast, be not as the hypocrites, of a sad countenance; for they disfigure their faces, that they may appear unto men to fast. Verily, I say unto you, They have their reward.

18 But thou, when thou fastest, anoint thy head and wash thy face, that thou appear not unto men to fast, but unto thy Father who is in secret; and thy Father who seeth in secret, shall reward thee openly.

19 Lay not up for yourselves treasure upon earth, where moth and rust doth corrupt, and where thieves break through and steal.

20 But lay up for yourselves treasures in heaven, where neither moth

nor rust doth corrupt, and where thieves do not break through nor steal.

21 For where your treasure is, there will your heart be also.

22 The light of the body is the eye; if therefore thine eye be single to the glory of God, thy whole body shall be full of light.

23 But if thine eye be evil, thy whole body shall be full of darkness. If therefore the light which is in thee be darkness, how great shall that darkness be.

24 No man can serve two masters, for either he will hate the one, and love the other; or else he will hold to the one and despise the other. Ye cannot serve God and Mammon.

25 And, again, I say unto you, Go ye into the world, and care not for the world; for the world will hate you, and will persecute you, and will turn you out of their synagogues.

26 Nevertheless, ye shall go forth from house to house, teaching the people; and I will go before you.

27 And your heavenly Father will provide for you, whatsoever things ye need for food, what ye shall eat; and for raiment, what ye shall wear or put on.

28 Therefore I say unto you, Take no thought for your life, what ye shall eat, or what ye shall drink; nor yet for your bodies, what ye shall put on. Is not the life more than meat, and the body than raiment?

29 Behold the fowls of the air, for they sow not, neither do they reap, nor gather into barns; yet your heavenly Father feedeth them. Are ye not much better than they? How much more will he not feed you?

30 Wherefore take no thought for these things, but keep my commandments wherewith I have commanded you.

31 For which of you by taking thought can add one cubit unto his stature?

32 And why take ye thought for raiment? Consider the lilies of the field, how they grow; they toil not, neither do they spin.

33 And yet I say unto you that even Solomon, in all his glory, was not arrayed like one of these.

34 Therefore, if God so clothe the grass of the field, which today is, and tomorrow is cast into the oven, how

much more will he not provide for you, if ye are not of little faith?

35 Therefore take no thought, saying, What shall we eat? or, What shall we drink? or, Wherewithal shall we be clothed?

36 Why is it that ye murmur among yourselves, saying, We cannot obey thy word because ye have not all these things, and seek to excuse yourselves, saying that, After all these things do the Gentiles seek.

37 Behold, I say unto you that your heavenly Father knoweth that ye have need of all these things.

38 Wherefore, seek not the things of this world but seek ye first to build up the kingdom of God, and to establish his righteousness, and all these things shall be added unto you.

39 Take, therefore, no thought for the morrow; for the morrow shall take thought for the things of itself. Sufficient unto the day shall be the evil thereof.

## CHAPTER 7

*Christ instructing his disciples what to teach unto the world.*

1 Now these are the words which Jesus taught his disciples that they should say unto the people.

2 Judge not unrighteously, that ye be not judged; but judge righteous judgment.

3 For with what judgment ye shall judge, ye shall be judged; and with what measure ye mete, it shall be measured to you again.

4 And again, ye shall shall say unto them, Why is it that thou beholdest the mote that is in thy brother's eye, but considerest not the beam that is in thine own eye?

5 Or how wilt thou say to thy brother, Let me pull out the mote out of thine eye; and canst not behold a beam in thine own eye?

6 And Jesus said unto his disciples, Beholdest thou the scribes, and the Pharisees, and the priests, and the Levites? They teach in their synagogues, but do not observe the law, nor the commandments; and all have gone out of the way, and are under sin.

7 Go thou and say unto them, Why teach ye men the law and the commandments, when ye yourselves are the children of corruption?

8 Say unto them, Ye hypocrites, first

cast out the beam out of thine own eye; and then shalt thou see clearly to cast out the mote out of thy brother's eye.

9 Go ye into the world, saying unto all, Repent, for the kingdom of heaven has come nigh unto you.

10 And the mysteries of the kingdom ye shall keep within yourselves; for it is not meet to give that which is holy unto the dogs; neither cast ye your pearls unto swine, lest they trample them under their feet.

11 For the world cannot receive that which ye, yourselves, are not able to bear; wherefore ye shall not give your pearls unto them, lest they turn again and rend you.

12 Say unto them, Ask of God; ask, and it shall be given you; seek, and ye shall find; knock, and it shall be opened unto you.

13 For every one that asketh, receiveth; and he that seeketh, findeth; and unto him that knocketh, it shall be opened.

14 And then said his disciples unto him, They will say unto us, We ourselves are righteous, and need not that any man should teach us. God, we know, heard Moses and some of the prophets; but us he will not hear.

15 And they will say, We have the law for our salvation, and that is sufficient for us.

16 Then Jesus answered, and said unto his disciples, Thus shall ye say unto them,

17 What man among you, having a son, and he shall be standing out, and shall say, Father, open thy house that I may come in and sup with thee, will not say, Come in, my son; for mine is thine, and thine is mine?

18 Or what man is there among you, who, if his son ask bread, will give him a stone?

19 Or if he ask a fish, will he give him a serpent?

20 If ye then, being evil, know how to give good gifts unto your children, how much more shall your Father who is in heaven give good things to them that ask him?

21 Therefore, all things whatsoever ye would that men should do to you, do ye even so to them; for this is the law and the prophets.

22 Repent, therefore, and enter ye in at the strait gate; for wide is the gate, and broad is the way that leadeth to destruction, and many there be who go in thereat.

23 Because strait is the gate, and narrow is the way that leadeth unto life, and few there be that find it.

24 And, again, beware of false prophets, who come to you in sheep's clothing; but inwardly they are ravening wolves.

25 Ye shall know them by their fruits; for do men gather grapes of thorns, or figs of thistles?

26 Even so every good tree bringeth forth good fruit; but a corrupt tree bringeth forth evil fruit.

27 A good tree cannot bring forth evil fruit; neither can a corrupt tree bring forth good fruit.

28 Every tree that bringeth not forth good fruit, is hewn down, and cast into the fire.

29 Wherefore by their fruits ye shall know them.

30 Verily I say unto you, It is not every one that saith unto me, Lord, Lord, that shall enter into the kingdom of heaven; but he that doeth the will of my Father who is in heaven.

31 For the day soon cometh, that men shall come before me to judgment, to be judged according to their works.

32 And many will say unto me in that day, Lord, Lord, have we not prophesied in thy name; and in thy name cast out devils; and in thy name done many wonderful works?

33 And then will I say, Ye never knew me; depart from me ye that work iniquity.

34 Therefore, whosoever heareth these sayings of mine and doeth them, I will liken him unto a wise man, who built his house upon a rock, and the rains descended, and the floods came, and the winds blew, and beat upon that house, and it fell not; for it was founded upon a rock.

35 And every one that heareth these sayings of mine, and doeth them not, shall be likened unto a foolish man, who built his house upon the sand; and the rains descended, and the floods came, and the winds blew, and beat upon that house, and it fell; and great was the fall of it.

36 And it came to pass when Jesus had ended these sayings with his disciples, the people were astonished at his doctrine;

37 For he taught them as one having

authority from God, and not as having authority from the scribes.

## CHAPTER 8

*Jesus comes down from the mountain—Does many mighty works—Sends the devils into the swine.*

1 And when Jesus was come down from the mountain, great multitudes followed him.

2 And, behold, there came a leper worshiping him, saying, Lord, if thou wilt, thou canst make me clean.

3 And Jesus put forth his hand and touched him, saying, I will; be thou clean. And immediately his leprosy was cleansed.

4 And Jesus said unto him, See thou tell no man; but go thy way and show thyself to the priest, and offer the gift that Moses commanded, for a testimony unto them.

5 And when Jesus was entered into Capernaum, there came unto him a centurion, beseeching him, and saying, Lord, my servant lieth at home sick of the palsy, grievously tormented.

6 And Jesus said unto him, I will come and heal him.

7 The centurion answered and said, Lord, I am not worthy that thou shouldest come under my roof; but speak the word only, and my servant shall be healed.

8 For I am a man under authority, having soldiers under me; and I say to this man, Go, and he goeth; and to another, Come, and he cometh; and to my servant, Do this, and he doeth it.

9 And when they that followed him, heard this, they marveled. And when Jesus heard this, he said unto them that followed,

10 Verily I say unto you, I have not found so great faith; no, not in Israel.

11 And I say unto you that many shall come from the east, and the west, and shall sit down with Abraham, and Isaac, and Jacob, in the kingdom of heaven.

12 But the children of the wicked one shall be cast out into outer darkness; there shall be weeping and gnashing of teeth.

13 And Jesus said unto the centurion, Go thy way, and as thou hast believed, so be it done unto thee. And his servant was healed in the selfsame hour.

14 And when Jesus was come into

Peter's house, he saw his wife's mother laid, and sick of a fever.

15 And he touched her hand, and the fever left her; and she arose and ministered unto them.

16 Now when the evening was come, they brought unto him many that were possessed with devils; and he cast out the evil spirits with the word, and healed all that were sick.

17 That it might be fulfilled which was spoken by Esaias the prophet, saying, Himself took our infirmities and bare our sicknesses.

18 Now when Jesus saw great multitudes about him, he gave commandment to depart unto the other side of the sea.

19 And a certain scribe came unto him and said, Master, I will follow thee whithersoever thou goest.

20 And Jesus said unto him, The foxes have holes, and the birds of the air have nests; but the Son of man hath not where to lay his head.

21 And another of his disciples said unto him, Lord, suffer me first to go and bury my father.

22 But Jesus said unto him, Follow me, and let the dead bury their dead.

23 And when he was entered into a ship, his disciples came unto him.

24 And, behold, there arose a great tempest in the sea, insomuch that the ship was covered with the waves; but he was asleep.

25 And his disciples came unto him, and awoke him, saying, Lord, save us, else we perish.

26 And he said unto them, Why are ye fearful, O ye of little faith?

27 Then he arose, and rebuked the winds and the sea; and there was a great calm.

28 But the men marveled, saying, What manner of man is this, that even the winds and the sea obey him?

29 And when he was come to the other side, into the country of the Gergesenes, there met him a man possessed with devils, coming out of the tombs, exceeding fierce, so that no man could pass that way.

30 And, behold, he cried out, saying, What have we to do with thee, Jesus, thou Son of God? Art thou come hither to torment us before the time?

31 And there was, a good way off from them, a herd of many swine, feeding.

32 So the devils besought him, saying, If thou cast us out, suffer us to go into the herd of swine.

33 And he said unto them, Go. And when they were come out, they went into the herd of swine; and, behold, the whole herd of swine ran violently down a steep place into the sea, and perished in the waters.

34 And they that kept them fled, and went their way into the city, and told everything which took place, and what was befallen the possessed of the devils.

35 And, behold, the whole city came out to meet Jesus; and when they saw him, they besought him that he would depart out of their coasts.

## CHAPTER 9

*Jesus rejecteth the Jews, with their baptism—Parable of the wine and bottles.*

1 And Jesus entered into a ship, and passed over, and came into his own city.

2 And, behold, they brought to him a man sick of the palsy, lying on a bed; and Jesus, knowing their faith, said unto the sick of the palsy, Son, be of good cheer; thy sins be forgiven thee; go thy way and sin no more.

3 And, behold, certain of the scribes said within themselves, This man blasphemeth.

4 And Jesus, knowing their thoughts, said, Wherefore is it that ye think evil in your hearts?

5 For is it not easier to say, Thy sins be forgiven thee, than to say, Arise and walk?

6 But I said this that ye may know that the Son of man hath power on earth to forgive sins.

7 Then Jesus said unto the sick of the palsy, Arise, take up thy bed, and go unto thy house.

8 And he immediately arose, and departed to his house.

9 But when the multitude saw it, they marveled and glorified God, who had given such power unto men.

10 And as Jesus passed forth from thence, he saw a man named Matthew, sitting at the place where they received tribute, as was customary in those days, and he said unto him, Follow me. And he arose and followed him.

11 And it came to pass, as Jesus sat at meat in the house, behold, many publicans and sinners came and sat down with him, and with his disciples.

12 And when the Pharisees saw them, they said unto his disciples, Why eateth your master with publicans and sinners?

13 But when Jesus heard them, he said unto them, They that be whole need not a physician, but they that are sick.

14 But go ye and learn what this meaneth; I will have mercy and not sacrifice; for I am not come to call the righteous, but sinners to repentance.

15 And while he was thus teaching, there came to him the disciples of John, saying, Why do we and the Pharisees fast oft, but thy disciples fast not?

16 And Jesus said unto them, Can the children of the bridechamber mourn, as long as the bridegroom is with them?

17 But the days will come, when the bridegroom shall be taken from them, and then shall they fast.

18 Then said the Pharisees unto him, Why will ye not receive us with our baptism, seeing we keep the whole law?

19 But Jesus said unto them, Ye keep not the law. If ye had kept the law, ye would have received me, for I am he who gave the law.

20 I receive not you with your baptism, because it profiteth you nothing.

21 For when that which is new is come, the old is ready to be put away.

22 For no man putteth a piece of new cloth on an old garment; for that which is put in to fill it up, taketh from the garment, and the rent is made worse.

23 Neither do men put new wine into old bottles; else the bottles break, and the wine runneth out, and the bottles perish; but they put new wine into new bottles, and both are preserved.

24 While he spake these things unto them, behold, there came a certain ruler and worshiped him, saying, My daughter is even now dying; but come and lay thy hand upon her and she shall live.

25 And Jesus arose and followed him, and also his disciples, and much people thronged him.

26 And, behold, a woman which was diseased with an issue of blood twelve

years, came behind him, and touched the hem of his garment.

27 For she said within herself, If I may but touch his garment, I shall be whole.

28 But Jesus turned him about, and when he saw her, he said, Daughter, be of good comfort; thy faith hath made thee whole. And the woman was made whole from that hour.

29 And when Jesus came into the ruler's house, and saw the minstrels, and the people making a noise,

30 He said unto them, Give place; for the maid is not dead; but sleepeth. And they laughed him to scorn.

31 But when the people were put forth, he went in, and took her by the hand, and the maid arose.

32 And the fame of Jesus went abroad into all that land.

33 And when Jesus departed thence, two blind men followed him, crying, and saying, Jesus, thou Son of David, have mercy on us.

34 And when he was come into the house, the blind men came to him; and Jesus said unto them, Believe ye that I am able to do this? They said unto him, Yea, Lord.

35 Then touched he their eyes, saying, According to your faith, be it unto you.

36 And their eyes were opened; and straitly he charged them, saying, Keep my commandments, and see ye tell no man in this place, that no man know it.

37 But they, when they were departed, spread abroad his fame in all that country.

38 And as they went out, behold, they brought to him a dumb man possessed with a devil.

39 And when the devil was cast out, the dumb man spake. And the multitudes marveled, saying, It was never so seen in Israel.

40 But the Pharisees said, He casteth out the devils, through the prince of the devils.

41 And Jesus went about all the cities and villages, teaching in their synagogues, and preaching the gospel of the kingdom, and healing every sickness and disease among the people.

42 But when he saw the multitudes, he was moved with compassion on them, because they fainted, and were scattered abroad, as sheep having no shepherd.

43 Then said he unto his disciples, The harvest truly is plenteous, but the laborers are few.

44 Pray ye therefore the Lord of the harvest, that he will send forth laborers into his harvest.

## CHAPTER 10

*Christ calleth the Twelve—Giveth them power over unclean spirits—Sendeth them forth—Instructs them.*

1 And when he had called unto him his twelve disciples, he gave them power over unclean spirits, to cast them out, and to heal all manner of sickness and all manner of disease.

2 Now the names of the twelve apostles are these; the first Simon, who is called Peter, and Andrew his brother; James the son of Zebedee, and John his brother; Philip, and Bartholomew; Thomas, and Matthew the publican; James the son of Alpheus; and Lebbeus, whose surname was Thaddeus; Simon the Canaanite; and Judas Iscariot, who also betrayed him.

3 These twelve Jesus sent forth, and commanded them, saying,

4 Go not into the way of the Gentiles, and enter ye not into any city of the Samaritans.

5 But rather go to the lost sheep of the house of Israel.

6 And as ye go, preach, saying, The kingdom of heaven is at hand.

7 Heal the sick; cleanse the lepers; raise the dead; cast out devils; freely ye have received, freely give.

8 Provide neither gold, nor silver, nor brass in your purses.

9 Nor scrip for your journey, neither two coats, neither shoes, nor yet staves; for the workman is worthy of his meat.

10 And into whatsoever town or city ye shall enter, inquire who in it is worthy, and there abide till ye go thence.

11 And when ye come into a house, salute it; and if the house be worthy, let your peace come upon it; but if it be not worthy, let your peace return to you.

12 And whosoever shall not receive you, nor hear your words, when ye depart out of that house, or city, shake off the dust of your feet for a testimony against them.

13 And, verily, I say unto you, It

shall be more tolerable for the land of Sodom and Gomorrah in the day of judgment than for that city.

14 Behold, I send you forth as sheep in the midst of wolves; be ye therefore wise servants, and as harmless as doves.

15 But, beware of men; for they will deliver you up to the councils, and they will scourge you in their synagogues.

16 And ye shall be brought before governors and kings for my sake, for a testimony against them and the Gentiles.

17 But when they deliver you up, take no thought how or what ye shall speak; for it shall be given you in that same hour what ye shall speak; for it is not ye that speak, but the Spirit of your Father which speaketh in you.

18 And the brother shall deliver up the brother to death, and the father the child; and the children shall rise up against their parents and cause them to be put to death.

19 And ye shall be hated of all the world for my name's sake; but he that endureth to the end shall be saved.

20 But when they persecute you in one city, flee ye into another; for verily, I say unto you, Ye shall not have gone over the cities of Israel, till the Son of man be come.

21 Remember, the disciple is not above his master; nor the servant above his lord. It is enough that the disciple be as his master, and the servant as his lord.

22 If they have called the master of the house Beelzebub, how much more shall they call them of his household.

23 Fear them not, therefore; for there is nothing covered, that shall not be revealed; and hid, that shall not be known.

24 What I tell you in darkness, preach ye in light; and what ye hear in the ear, preach ye upon the housetops.

25 And fear not them who are able to kill the body, but are not able to kill the soul; but rather fear him who is able to destroy both soul and body in hell.

26 Are not two sparrows sold for a farthing? And one of them shall not fall on the ground without your Father knoweth it.

27 And the very hairs of your head are all numbered. Fear ye not, there-fore; ye are of more value than many sparrows.

28 Whosoever, therefore, shall confess me before men, him will I confess also before my Father who is in heaven.

29 But whosoever shall deny me before men, him will I also deny before my Father who is in heaven.

30 Think not, that I am come to send peace on earth; I came not to send peace, but a sword.

31 For I am come to set a man at variance against his father, and the daughter against her mother, and the daughter-in-law against her mother-in-law; and a man's foes shall be they of his own household.

32 He who loveth father and mother more than me, is not worthy of me; and he who loveth son or daughter more than me, is not worthy of me.

33 And he who taketh not his cross and followeth after me, is not worthy of me.

34 He who seeketh to save his life shall lose it; and he who loseth his life for my sake shall find it.

35 He who receiveth you, receiveth me; and he who receiveth me, receiveth him who sent me.

36 He that receiveth a prophet, in the name of a prophet, shall receive a prophet's reward.

37 He that receiveth a righteous man, in the name of a righteous man, shall receive a righteous man's reward.

38 And whosoever shall give to drink unto one of these little ones, a cup of cold water only, in the name of a disciple, verily, I say unto you, He shall in no wise lose his reward.

## CHAPTER 11
*John sendeth his disciples to Christ—Testimony of Christ concerning John.*

1 And it came to pass, when Jesus had made an end of commanding his twelve disciples, he departed thence to teach and to preach in their cities.

2 Now when John had heard in the prison the works of Christ, he sent two of his disciples,

3 And said unto him, Art thou he of whom it is written in the prophets that he should come, or do we look for another?

4 Jesus answered and said unto them, Go and tell John again of those things which ye do hear and see;

5 How the blind receive their sight, and the lame walk, and the lepers are cleansed, and the deaf hear, and the dead are raised up, and the poor have the gospel preached unto them.

6 And blessed is John, and whosoever shall not be offended in me.

7 And as they departed, Jesus began to say unto the multitudes concerning John, What went ye out into the wilderness to see? Was it a reed shaken with the wind? And they answered him, No.

8 And he said, But what went ye out for to see? Was it a man clothed in soft raiment? Behold they that wear soft raiment are in king's houses.

9 But what went ye out for to see? A prophet? Yea, I say unto you, and more than a prophet.

10 For this is the one of whom it is written, Behold, I send my messenger before thy face, which shall prepare thy way before thee.

11 Verily, I say unto you, Among them that are born of women, there hath not risen a greater than John the Baptist; notwithstanding, he that is least in the kingdom of heaven, is greater than he.

12 And from the days of John the Baptist until now, the kingdom of heaven suffereth violence, and the violent take it by force.

13 But the days will come, when the violent shall have no power; for all the prophets and the law prophesied that it should be thus until John.

14 Yea, as many as have prophesied have foretold of these days.

15 And if ye will receive it, verily, he was the Elias, who was for to come and prepare all things.

16 He that hath ears to hear, let him hear.

17 But whereunto shall I liken this generation?

18 It is like unto children sitting in the markets, and calling unto their fellows, and saying, We have piped unto you, and ye have not danced; we have mourned for you, and ye have not lamented.

19 For John came neither eating nor drinking, and they say, He hath a devil.

20 The Son of man came eating and drinking, and they say, Behold, a gluttonous man and a wine bibber, a friend of publicans and sinners.

21 But I say unto you, Wisdom is justified of her children.

22 Then began he to upbraid the cities wherein most of his mighty works were done, because they repented not.

23 Woe unto thee, Chorazin! Woe unto thee, Bethsaida! For if the mighty works which were done in you, had been done in Tyre and Sidon, they would have repented long since in sackcloth and ashes.

24 But I say unto you, It shall be more tolerable for Tyre and Sidon at the day of judgment, than for you.

25 And thou, Capernaum, which art exalted unto heaven, shall be brought down to hell; for if the mighty works which have been done in thee, had been done in Sodom, it would have remained until this day.

26 But I say unto you, it shall be more tolerable for the land of Sodom in the day of judgment, than for thee.

27 And at that time, there came a voice out of heaven, and Jesus answered and said, I thank thee, O Father, Lord of heaven and earth, because thou hast hid these things from the wise and prudent, and hast revealed them unto babes. Even so, Father, for so it seemed good in thy sight!

28 All things are delivered unto me of my Father; and no man knoweth the Son, but the Father; neither knoweth any man the Father, save the Son, and they to whom the Son will reveal himself; they shall see the Father also.

29 Then spake Jesus, saying, Come unto me, all ye that labor and are heavy laden, and I will give you rest.

30 Take my yoke upon you, and learn of me; for I am meek and lowly in heart; and ye shall find rest unto your souls; for my yoke is easy, and my burden is light.

## CHAPTER 12

*Jesus teaches the scribes and Pharisees—Restores a withered hand on the Sabbath day.*

1 At that time Jesus went on the Sabbath day through the corn; and his disciples were an hungered, and began to pluck the ears of corn and to eat.

2 But when the Pharisees saw them, they said unto him, Behold, thy disciples do that which is not lawful to do upon the Sabbath day.

3 But he said unto them, Have ye

not read what David did, when he was an hungered, and they that were with him? How he entered into the house of God, and did eat the shewbread, which was not lawful for him to eat, neither for them that were with him; but only for the priests?

4 Or have ye not read in the law, how that on the Sabbath days the priests in the temple profane the Sabbath, and ye say they are blameless?

5 But I say unto you, that in this place is one greater than the temple.

6 But if ye had known what this meaneth, I will have mercy and not sacrifice, ye would not have condemned the guiltless. For the Son of man is Lord even of the Sabbath.

7 And when he was departed thence, he went into their synagogues.

8 And, behold, there was a man which had a withered hand. And they asked him, saying, Is it lawful to heal on the Sabbath days? that they might accuse him.

9 And he said unto them, What man shall there be among you that shall have one sheep, and if it fall into a pit on the Sabbath day, will he not lay hold on it, and lift it out?

10 How much then is a man better than a sheep? Wherefore it is lawful to do well on the Sabbath days.

11 Then said he to the man, Stretch forth thy hand; and he stretched it forth, and it was restored whole, like unto the other.

12 Then the Pharisees went out and held a council against him, how they might destroy him.

13 But Jesus knew when they took counsel, and he withdrew himself from thence; and great multitudes followed him, and he healed their sick, and charged them that they should not make him known;

14 That it might be fulfilled which was spoken by Esaias the prophet, saying, Behold my servant, whom I have chosen; my beloved, in whom my soul is well pleased.

15 I will put my Spirit upon him, and he shall show judgment to the Gentiles. He shall not strive, nor cry; neither shall any man hear his voice in the streets.

16 A bruised reed shall he not break, and smoking flax shall he not quench, till he send forth judgment unto victory.

17 And in his name shall the Gentiles trust.

18 Then was brought unto him one possessed with a devil, blind and dumb; and he healed him; insomuch that the blind and dumb both spake and saw.

19 And all the people were amazed, and said, Is this the Son of David?

20 But when the Pharisees heard that he had cast out the devil, they said, This man doth not cast out devils, but by Beelzebub the prince of devils.

21 And Jesus knew their thoughts, and said unto them, Every kingdom divided against itself is brought to desolation; and every city or house divided against itself, shall not stand. And if Satan cast out Satan, he is divided against himself; how then shall his kingdom stand?

22 And if I by Beelzebub cast out devils, by whom do your children cast out devils? Therefore they shall be your judges.

23 But if I cast out devils by the Spirit of God, then the kingdom of God is come unto you. For they also cast out devils by the Spirit of God, for unto them is given power over devils, that they may cast them out.

24 Or else, how can one enter into a strong man's house, and spoil his goods, except he first bind the strong man, and then he will spoil his house?

25 He that is not with me is against me, and he that gathereth not with me scattereth abroad.

26 Wherefore I say unto you, All manner of sin and blasphemy shall be forgiven unto men who receive me and repent; but the blasphemy against the Holy Ghost, it shall not be forgiven unto men.

27 And whosoever speaketh a word against the Son of man, it shall be forgiven him; but whosoever speaketh against the Holy Ghost, it shall not be forgiven him; neither in this world, nor in the world to come.

28 Either make the tree good and his fruit good; or else make the tree corrupt, and his fruit corrupt; for the tree is known by the fruit.

29 And Jesus said, O ye generation of vipers! how can ye, being evil, speak good things? For out of the abundance of the heart the mouth speaketh.

30 A good man, out of the good trea-

sure of the heart, bringeth forth good things; and an evil man out of the evil treasure, bringeth forth evil things.

31 And again I say unto you, That every idle word that men shall speak, they shall give account thereof in the day of judgment.

32 For by thy words thou shalt be justified, and by thy words thou shalt be condemned.

33 Then certain of the scribes and of the Pharisees answered, saying, Master, we would see a sign from thee. But he answered and said unto them,

34 An evil and adulterous generation seeketh after a sign; and there shall no sign be given to it, but the sign of the prophet Jonas; for as Jonas was three days and three nights in the whale's belly, so shall the Son of man be three days and three nights in the heart of the earth.

35 The men of Nineveh shall rise up in judgment with this generation, and shall condemn it, because they repented at the preaching of Jonas; and, ye behold, a greater than Jonas is here.

36 The queen of the south shall rise up in the day of judgment with this generation, and shall condemn it; for she came from the uttermost parts of the earth to hear the wisdom of Solomon; and, ye behold, a greater than Solomon is here.

37 Then came some of the scribes and said unto him, Master, it is written that, Every sin shall be forgiven; but ye say, Whosoever speaketh against the Holy Ghost shall not be forgiven. And they asked him, saying, How can these things be?

38 And then said unto them, When the unclean spirit is gone out of a man, he walketh through dry places, seeking rest and findeth none; but when a man speaketh against the Holy Ghost, then he saith, I will return into my house from whence I came out; and when he is come, he findeth him empty, swept and garnished; for the good spirit leaveth him unto himself.

39 Then goeth the evil spirit, and taketh with himself seven other spirits more wicked than himself; and they enter in and dwell there; and the last end of that man is worse than the first. Even so shall it be also unto this wicked generation.

40 And while he yet talked to the people, behold, his mother and his brethren stood without, desiring to speak with him.

41 Then one said unto him, Behold, thy mother and thy brethren stand without, desiring to speak with thee.

42 But he answered and said unto the man that told him, Who is my mother? and who are my brethren?

43 And he stretched forth his hand toward his disciples, and said, Behold my mother and my brethren!

44 And he gave them charge concerning her, saying, I go my way, for my Father hath sent me. And whosoever shall do the will of my Father which is in heaven, the same is my brother, and sister, and mother.

## CHAPTER 13

*Jesus teaches the multitude in parables. Parable of the sower—of the tares—grain of mustard seed.*

1 And it came to pass the same day, Jesus went out of the house, and sat by the seaside.

2 And great multitudes were gathered together unto him, so that he went into a ship, and sat; and the whole multitude stood on the shore.

3 And he spake many things unto them in parables, saying, Behold, a sower went forth to sow.

4 And when he sowed, some seeds fell by the wayside, and the fowls came and devoured them up.

5 Some fell upon stony places, where they had not much earth; and forthwith they sprung up; and when the sun was up, they were scorched, because they had no deepness of earth; and because they had no root, they withered away.

6 And some fell among thorns, and thorns sprung up and choked them.

7 But others fell into good ground, and brought forth fruit; some an hundredfold, some sixtyfold, and some thirtyfold. Who hath ears to hear, let him hear.

8 Then the disciples came and said unto him, Why speakest thou unto them in parables?

9 He answered and said unto them, Because it is given unto you to know the mysteries of the kingdom of heaven, but to them it is not given.

10 For whosoever receiveth, to him shall be given, and he shall have more abundance;

11 But whosoever continueth not to

receive, from him shall be taken away even that he hath.

12 Therefore speak I to them in parables; because they, seeing, see not; and hearing, they hear not; neither do they understand.

13 And in them is fulfilled the prophecy of Esaias concerning them, which saith, By hearing, ye shall hear and shall not understand; and seeing, ye shall see and shall not perceive.

14 For this people's heart is waxed gross, and their ears are dull of hearing, and their eyes they have closed, lest at any time they should see with their eyes and hear with their ears, and should understand with their hearts, and should be converted, and I should heal them.

15 But blessed are your eyes, for they see; and your ears, for they hear. And blessed are you because these things are come unto you, that you might understand them.

16 And verily, I say unto you, many righteous prophets have desired to see these days which you see, and have not seen them; and to hear that which you hear, and have not heard.

17 Hear ye therefore the parable of the sower.

18 When any one heareth the word of the kingdom, and understandeth not, then cometh the wicked one, and catcheth away that which was sown in his heart; this is he who received seed by the wayside.

19 But he that received the seed into stony places, the same is he that heareth the word and readily with joy receiveth it, yet hath not root in himself, and endureth but for a while; for when tribulation or persecution ariseth because of the word, by and by he is offended.

20 He also who received seed among the thorns, is he that heareth the word; and the care of this world and the deceitfulness of riches, choke the word, and he becometh unfruitful.

21 But he that received seed into the good ground, is he that heareth the word and understandeth and endureth; which also beareth fruit, and bringeth forth, some an hundredfold, some sixty, and some thirty.

22 Another parable put he forth unto them, saying, The kingdom of heaven is likened unto a man who sowed good seed in his field;

23 But while he slept, his enemy came and sowed tares among the wheat, and went his way.

24 But when the blade sprung up, and brought forth fruit, then appeared the tares also.

25 So the servants of the householder came and said unto him, Sir, didst not thou sow good seed in thy field? whence then hath it tares?

26 He said unto them, An enemy hath done this.

27 And the servants said unto him, Wilt thou then that we go and gather them up?

28 But he said, Nay; lest while ye gather up the tares, ye root up also the wheat with them.

29 Let both grow together until the harvest, and in the time of harvest, I will say to the reapers, Gather ye together first the wheat into my barn; and the tares are bound in bundles to be burned.

30 And another parable put he forth unto them, saying, The kingdom of heaven is like to a grain of mustard seed, which a man took and sowed in his field;

31 Which indeed is the least of all seeds, but when it is grown, it is the greatest among herbs, and becometh a tree, so that the birds of the air come and lodge in the branches thereof.

32 Another parable spake he unto them, The kingdom of heaven is like unto leaven, which a woman took and hid in three measures of meal, till the whole was leavened.

33 All these things spake Jesus unto the multitudes in parables; and without a parable spake he not unto them.

34 That it might be fulfilled which was spoken by the prophets, saying, I will open my mouth in parables; I will utter things which have been kept secret from the foundation of the world.

35 Then Jesus sent the multitude away, and went into the house. And his disciples came unto him, saying, Declare unto us the parable of the tares of the field.

36 He answered and said unto them, He that soweth the good seed is the Son of man.

37 The field is the world; the good seed are the children of the kingdom;

but the tares are the children of the wicked.

38 The enemy that sowed them is the devil.

39 The harvest is the end of the world, or the destruction of the wicked.

40 The reapers are the angels, or the messengers sent of heaven.

41 As, therefore, the tares are gathered and burned in the fire, so shall it be in the end of this world, or the destruction of the wicked.

42 For in that day, before the Son of man shall come, he shall send forth his angels and messengers of heaven.

43 And they shall gather out of his kingdom all things that offend, and them which do iniquity, and shall cast them out among the wicked; and there shall be wailing and gnashing of teeth.

44 For the world shall be burned with fire.

45 Then shall the righteous shine forth as the sun, in the kingdom of their Father. Who hath ears to hear, let him hear.

46 Again, the kingdom of heaven is like unto a treasure hid in a field. And when a man hath found a treasure which is hid, he secureth it, and, straightway, for joy thereof, goeth and selleth all that he hath, and buyeth that field.

47 And again, the kingdom of heaven is like unto a merchantman, seeking goodly pearls, who, when he had found one pearl of great price, he went and sold all that he had and bought it.

48 Again, the kingdom of heaven is like unto a net that was cast into the sea, and gathered of every kind, which, when it was full, they drew to shore, and sat down, and gathered the good into vessels; but cast the bad away.

49 So shall it be at the end of the world.

50 And the world is the children of the wicked.

51 The angels shall come forth, and sever the wicked from among the just, and shall cast them out into the world to be burned. There shall be wailing and gnashing of teeth.

52 Then Jesus said unto them, Have ye understood all these things? They say unto him, Yea, Lord.

53 Then said he unto them, Every scribe well instructed in the things of the kingdom of heaven, is like unto a householder; a man, therefore, which bringeth forth out of his treasure that which is new and old.

54 And it came to pass, when Jesus had finished these parables, he departed thence.

55 And when he was come into his own country, he taught them in their synagogues, insomuch that they were astonished, and said, Whence hath this Jesus this wisdom and these mighty works?

56 Is not this the carpenter's son? Is not his mother called Mary? And his brethren, James, and Joses, and Simon, and Judas? And his sisters, are they not all with us?

57 Whence then hath this man all these things? And they were offended at him.

58 But Jesus said unto them, A prophet is not without honor, save in his own country, and in his own house.

59 And he did not many mighty works there, because of their unbelief.

## CHAPTER 14

*John the Baptist beheaded—A multitude miraculously fed.*

1 At that time, Herod the tetrarch heard of the fame of Jesus, and said unto his servants, This is John the Baptist; he is risen from the dead, and, therefore, mighty works do show forth themselves in him.

2 For Herod had laid hold on John, and bound him, and put him in prison, for Herodias' sake, his brother Philip's wife.

3 For John said unto him, It is not lawful for thee to have her.

4 And when he would have put him to death, he feared the multitude, because they counted him as a prophet.

5 But when Herod's birthday was kept, the daughter of Herodias danced before them and pleased Herod.

6 Whereupon he promised with an oath to give her whatever she would ask.

7 And she, being before instructed of her mother, said, Give me here, John Baptist's head in a charger.

8 And the king was sorry; nevertheless for the oath's sake, and them which sat with him at meat, he commanded it to be given.

9 And he sent and beheaded John in the prison.

10 And his head was brought in a

charger, and given to the damsel; and she brought it to her mother.

11 And his disciples came and took up the body, and buried it; and went and told Jesus.

12 When Jesus heard that John was beheaded, he departed thence by ship into a desert place apart; and when the people had heard of him, they followed him on foot out of the cities.

13 And Jesus went forth, and saw a great multitude, and was moved with compassion towards them, and he healed their sick.

14 And when it was evening, his disciples came to him, saying, This is a desert place, and the time is now past; send the multitude away, that they may go into the villages and buy themselves victuals.

15 But Jesus said unto them, They need not depart; give ye them to eat.

16 And they said unto him, We have here but five loaves and two fishes. He said, Bring them hither to me.

17 And he commanded the multitude to sit down on the grass; and he took the five loaves and the two fishes, and looking up to heaven, he blessed and brake and gave the loaves to the disciples, and the disciples, to the multitude.

18 And they did all eat, and were filled. And they took up of the fragments that remained, twelve baskets full. And they that had eaten were about five thousand men, besides women and children.

19 And straightway Jesus constrained his disciples to get into a ship, and to go before him unto the other side, while he sent the multitudes away. And when he had sent the multitudes away, he went up into a mountain, apart, to pray.

20 And when the evening was come, he was there alone. But the ship was now in the midst of the sea, tossed with the waves; for the wind was contrary.

21 And in the fourth watch of the night, Jesus went unto them, walking on the sea.

22 And when the disciples saw him walking on the sea, they were troubled, saying, It is a spirit; and they cried out for fear.

23 But straightway Jesus spake unto them, saying, Be of good cheer; it is I; be not afraid.

24 And Peter answered him and said, Lord, if it be thou, bid me come unto thee on the water. And he said, Come.

25 And when Peter was come down out of the ship, he walked on the water, to go to Jesus. But when he saw the wind boisterous, he was afraid; and, beginning to sink, he cried, saying, Lord, save me.

26 And immediately Jesus stretched forth his hand, and caught him, and said unto him, O thou of little faith, wherefore didst thou doubt?

27 And when they were come into the ship, the wind ceased.

28 Then they that were in the ship, came and worshiped him, saying, Of a truth, thou art the Son of God.

29 And when they were gone over, they came into the land of Gennesaret.

30 And when the men of that place had knowledge of him, they sent out into all that country round about, and brought unto him all that were diseased; and besought him that they might only touch the hem of his garment; and as many as touched, were made perfectly whole.

## CHAPTER 15

*Christ goeth into the coasts of Tyre and Sidon—Great multitudes come to him— He heals the lame, the blind, and dumb.*

1 Then came to Jesus, scribes and Pharisees, which were of Jerusalem, saying,

2 Why do thy disciples transgress the tradition of the elders? For they wash not their hands when they eat bread.

3 But he answered and said unto them, Why do ye also transgress the commandment of God by your tradition?

4 For God commanded, saying, Honor thy father and mother; and, He that curseth father or mother, let him die the death which Moses shall appoint.

5 But ye say, Whosoever shall say to father or mother, By whatsoever thou mightest be profited by me, it is a gift from me and honor not his father or mother, it is well.

6 Thus have ye made the commandment of God of none effect by your tradition.

7 O ye hypocrites! well did Esaias prophesy of you, saying, This people

draw nigh unto me with their mouth, and honoreth me with their lips; but their heart is far from me.

8 But in vain do they worship me, teaching the doctrines and the commandments of men.

9 And he called the multitude, and said unto them, Hear, and understand.

10 Not that which goeth into the mouth defileth a man; but that which cometh out of the mouth, this defileth the man.

11 Then came his disciples and said unto him, Knowest thou that the Pharisees were offended, after they heard this saying?

12 But he answered and said, Every plant which my heavenly Father hath not planted, shall be rooted up.

13 Let them alone; they be blind leaders of the blind; and if the blind lead the blind, both shall fall into the ditch.

14 Then answered Peter and said unto him, Declare unto us this parable.

15 And Jesus said, Are ye also yet without understanding?

16 Do ye not yet understand, that whatsoever entereth in at the mouth goeth into the belly, and is cast into the draught?

17 But those things which proceed out of the mouth, come forth from the heart; and they defile the man.

18 For out of the heart proceed evil thoughts, murders, adulteries, fornications, thefts, false witness, blasphemies;

19 These are things which defile a man. But to eat with unwashen hands defileth not a man.

20 Then Jesus went thence, and departed into the coasts of Tyre and Sidon.

21 And, behold, a woman of Canaan came out of the same coasts, and cried unto him, saying, Have mercy on me, O Lord, thou Son of David; my daughter is grievously vexed with a devil.

22 But he answered her not a word. And his disciples came and besought him, saying, Send her away; for she crieth after us.

23 He answered, I am not sent but unto the lost sheep of the house of Israel.

24 Then came she and worshiped him, saying, Lord, help me.

25 But he answered and said, It is not meet to take the children's bread, and to cast it to dogs.

26 And she said, Truth, Lord; yet the dogs eat the crumbs that fall from the master's table.

27 Then Jesus answered and said unto her, O woman, great is thy faith; be it unto thee even as thou wilt. And her daughter was made whole from that very hour.

28 And Jesus departed from thence, and came nigh unto the sea of Galilee; and went up into a mountain, and sat down there.

29 And great multitudes came unto him, having with them some lame, blind, dumb, maimed, and many others, and cast them down at Jesus' feet; and he healed them; insomuch that the multitude wondered, when they saw the dumb to speak, the maimed to be whole, the lame to walk, and the blind to see. And they glorified the God of Israel.

30 Then Jesus called his disciples and said, I have compassion on the multitude, because they continue with me now three days, and have nothing to eat; and I will not send them away fasting, lest they faint in the way.

31 And his disciples say unto him, Whence should we have so much bread in the wilderness, as to fill so great a multitude?

32 And Jesus said unto them, How many loaves have ye? And they said, Seven, and a few little fishes.

33 And he commanded the multitude to sit down on the ground.

34 And he took the seven loaves and the fishes, and gave thanks, and brake the bread, and gave to his disciples, and the disciples, to the multitude.

35 And they did all eat, and were filled. And they took up of the broken meat seven baskets full.

36 And they that did eat were four thousand men, besides women and children.

37 And he sent away the multitude, and took ship, and came into the coasts of Magdala.

## CHAPTER 16

*Jesus cometh to the coast of Caesarea Philippi—Asks his disciples who men say he is—Who they say he is—Delivers unto Peter the keys of the kingdom.*

1 The Pharisees also, with the Sad-

ducees, came, and tempting Jesus, desired him that he would show them a sign from heaven.

2 And he answered and said unto them, When it is evening ye say, The weather is fair, for the sky is red; and in the morning ye say, The weather is foul today; for the sky is red and lowering.

3 O hypocrites! ye can discern the face of the sky; but ye cannot tell the signs of the times.

4 A wicked and adulterous generation seeketh after a sign; and there shall no sign be given unto it, but the sign of the prophet Jonas.

5 And he left them and departed.

6 And when his disciples were come to the other side, they had forgotten to take bread.

7 Then Jesus said unto them, Take heed and beware of the leaven of the Pharisees and of the Sadducees.

8 And they reasoned among themselves, saying, He said this because we have taken no bread.

9 And when they reasoned among themselves, Jesus perceived it; and he said unto them, O ye of little faith! why reason ye among yourselves, because ye have brought no bread?

10 Do ye not yet understand, neither remember the five loaves of the five thousand, and how many baskets ye took up?

11 Neither the seven loaves of the four thousand, and how many baskets ye took up?

12 How is it that ye do not understand, that I spake not unto you concerning bread, that ye should beware of the leaven of the Pharisees and of the Sadducees?

13 Then understand they, how that he bade them not beware of the leaven of bread, but of the doctrine of the Pharisees and of the Sadducees.

14 And when Jesus came into the coasts of Caesarea Philippi, he asked his disciples, saying, Whom do men say that I, the Son of man, am?

15 And they said, Some say John the Baptist; some Elias; and others Jeremias; or one of the prophets.

16 He said unto them, But whom say ye that I am?

17 And Simon Peter answered and said, Thou art the Christ, the Son of the living God.

18 And Jesus answered and said

unto him, Blessed art thou, Simon Bar-Jona; for flesh and blood hath not revealed this unto thee, but my Father who is in heaven.

19 And I say also unto thee, That thou art Peter; and upon this rock I will build my church, and the gates of hell shall not prevail against it.

20 And I will give unto thee the keys of the kingdom of heaven; and whatsoever thou shalt bind on earth, shall be bound in heaven; and whatsoever thou shalt loose on earth, shall be loosed in heaven.

21 Then charged he his disciples that they should tell no man that he was Jesus, the Christ.

22 From that time forth began Jesus to show unto his disciples, how that he must go to Jerusalem, and suffer many things of the elders, and chief priests, and scribes, and be killed, and be raised again the third day.

23 Then Peter took him, and began to rebuke him, saying, Be it far from thee, Lord; this shall not be done unto thee.

24 But he turned and said unto Peter, Get thee behind me, Satan; thou art an offense unto me; for thou savorest not the things that be of God, but those that be of men.

25 Then said Jesus unto his disciples, If any man will come after me, let him deny himself, and take up his cross and follow me.

26 And now for a man to take up his cross, is to deny himself of all ungodliness, and every worldly lust, and keep my commandments.

27 Break not my commandments for to save your lives; for whosoever will save his life in this world, shall lose it in the world to come.

28 And whosoever will lose his life in this world, for my sake, shall find it in the world to come.

29 Therefore, forsake the world, and save your souls; for what is a man profited, if he shall gain the whole world, and lose his own soul? Or what shall a man give in exchange for his soul?

30 For the Son of man shall come in the glory of his Father, with his angels; and then he shall reward every man according to his works.

31 Verily, I say unto you, There be some standing here, which shall not

taste of death, till they see the Son of man coming in his kingdom.

## CHAPTER 17

*Christ transfigured upon the mountain.*

1 And after six days, Jesus taketh Peter, James, and John his brother, and bringeth them up into a high mountain, apart, and was transfigured before them; and his face did shine as the sun, and his raiment was white as the light.

2 And, behold, there appeared unto them Moses and Elias, talking with him.

3 Then answered Peter, and said unto Jesus, Lord it is good for us to be here; if thou wilt, let us make here three tabernacles; one for thee, one for Moses, and one for Elias.

4 While he yet spake, behold, a bright cloud overshadowed them; and, behold, a voice out of the cloud, which said, This is my beloved Son, in whom I am well pleased; hear ye him.

5 And when the disciples heard the voice, they fell on their faces, and were sore afraid.

6 And Jesus came and touched them, and said, Arise, and be not afraid.

7 And when they had lifted up their eyes, they saw no man, save Jesus only.

8 And as they came down from the mountain, Jesus charged them, saying, Tell the vision to no man, until the Son of man be risen again from the dead.

9 And his disciples asked him, saying, Why then say the scribes that Elias must first come?

10 And Jesus answered and said unto them, Elias truly shall first come, and restore all things, as the prophets have written.

11 And again I say unto you that Elias has come already, concerning whom it is written, Behold, I will send my messenger, and he shall prepare the way before me; and they knew him not, and have done unto him whatsoever they listed.

12 Likewise shall also the Son of man suffer of them.

13 But I say unto you, Who is Elias? Behold, this is Elias, whom I send to prepare the way before me.

14 Then the disciples understood that he spake unto them of John the Baptist, and also of another who should come and restore all things, as it is written by the prophets.

15 And when they were come to the multitude, there came to him a man kneeling down to him, and saying, Lord, have mercy on my son; for he is lunatic, and sore vexed; for ofttimes he falleth into the fire, and oft into the water.

16 And I brought him to thy disciples, and they could not cure him.

17 Then Jesus answered and said, O faithless and perverse generation! how long shall I be with you? How long shall I suffer you? Bring him hither to me.

18 And Jesus rebuked the devil, and he departed out of him; and the child was cured from that very hour.

19 Then came the disciples to Jesus apart, and said, Why could not we cast him out?

20 And Jesus said unto them, Because of your unbelief; for, verily, I say unto you, If ye have faith as a grain of mustard seed, ye shall say unto this mountain, Remove to yonder place, and it shall remove; and nothing shall be impossible unto you.

21 Howbeit, this kind goeth not out but by prayer and fasting.

22 And while they abode in Galilee, Jesus said unto them, The Son of man shall be betrayed into the hands of men; and they shall kill him; and the third day he shall be raised again. And they were exceeding sorry.

23 And when they were come to Capernaum, they that received tribute came to Peter, and said, Doth not your master pay tribute? He said, Yea.

24 And when he was come into the house, Jesus rebuked him, saying,

25 What thinkest thou, Simon? Of whom do the kings of the earth take custom, or tribute? Of their own children, or of strangers?

26 Peter said unto him, Of strangers. Jesus said unto him, Then are the children free. Notwithstanding, lest we should offend them, go thou to the sea, and cast a hook, and take up the fish, that first cometh up; and when thou hast opened his mouth, thou shalt find a piece of money; that take and give unto them for me and thee.

## CHAPTER 18

*The parable of the lord and his ser-*

*vants—Likened unto the kingdom of heaven.*

1 At the same time came the disciples unto Jesus, saying, Who is the greatest in the kingdom of heaven?

2 And Jesus called a little child unto him, and set him in the midst of them, and said, Verily I say unto you, Except ye be converted, and become as little children, ye shall not enter into the kingdom of heaven.

3 Whosoever, therefore, shall humble himself as this little child, the same is greatest in the kingdom of heaven.

4 And whoso shall receive one such little child in my name, receiveth me.

5 But whoso shall offend one of these little ones which believe in me, it were better for him that a millstone were hanged about his neck and he were drowned in the depth of the sea.

6 Woe unto the world because of offenses! For it must needs be that offenses come; but woe to that man by whom the offense cometh!

7 Wherefore if thy hand or thy foot offend thee, cut it off and cast it from thee; for it is better for thee to enter into life halt or maimed, rather than having two hands or two feet to be cast into everlasting fire.

8 And if thine eye offend thee, pluck it out and cast it from thee; it is better for thee to enter into life with one eye, rather than having two eyes to be cast into hell fire.

9 And a man's hand is his friend, and his foot, also; and a man's eye, are they of his own household.

10 Take heed that ye despise not one of these little ones; for I say unto you, that in heaven their angels do always behold the face of my Father who is in heaven.

11 For the Son of man is come to save that which was lost, and to call sinners to repentance; but these little ones have no need of repentance, and I will save them.

12 How think ye? If a man have a hundred sheep, and one of them be gone astray, doth he not leave the ninety and nine, and goeth into the mountains and seeketh that which is gone astray?

13 And if it so be that he find it, verily, I say unto you, he rejoiceth more over that which was lost, than over the ninety and nine which went not astray.

14 Even so, it is not the will of your Father which is in heaven, that one of these little ones should perish.

15 Moreover, if thy brother shall trespass against thee, go and tell him his fault between thee and him alone; if he shall hear thee, thou hast gained thy brother.

16 But if he will not hear thee, then take with thee one or two more, that in the mouth of two or three witnesses every word may be established.

17 And if he shall neglect to hear them, tell it unto the church; but if he neglect to hear the church, let him be unto thee as a heathen man and a publican.

18 Verily, I say unto you, Whatsoever ye shall bind on earth, shall be bound in heaven; and whatsoever ye shall loose on earth, shall be loosed in heaven.

19 Again, I say unto you, that if two of you shall agree on earth as touching any thing that they shall ask, that they may not ask amiss, it shall be done for them of my Father which is in heaven.

20 For where two or three are gathered together in my name, there am I in the midst of them.

21 Then came Peter to him and said, Lord, how oft shall my brother sin against me, and I forgive him? Till seven times?

22 Jesus said unto him, I say not unto thee, until seven times; but, until seventy times seven.

23 Therefore is the kingdom of heaven likened unto a certain king, who would take account of his servants.

24 And when he had begun to reckon, one was brought unto him who owed him ten thousand talents.

25 But forasmuch as he had not to pay, his lord commanded him to be sold, and his wife, and children, and all that he had, and payment to be made.

26 And the servant besought him, saying, Lord, have patience with me, and I will pay thee all.

27 Then the lord of that servant was moved with compassion, and loosed him, and forgave him the debt. The servant, therefore, fell down and worshiped him.

28 But the same servant went out,

and found one of his fellow servants which owed him a hundred pence; and he laid hands on him, and took him by the throat, saying, Pay me that thou owest.

29 And his fellow servant fell down at his feet, and besought him, saying, Have patience with me, and I will pay thee all.

30 And he would not; but went and cast him into prison, till he should pay the debt.

31 So when his fellow servants saw what was done, they were very sorry, and came and told unto their lord all that was done.

32 Then his lord, after that he had called him, said unto him, O thou wicked servant! I forgave thee all that debt; because thou desiredst me; shouldest not thou also have had compassion on thy fellow servant, even as I had pity on thee?

33 And his lord was wroth, and delivered him to the tormentors, till he should pay all that was due unto him.

34 So likewise shall my heavenly Father do also unto you, if ye from your hearts forgive not every one his brother their trespasses.

## CHAPTER 19

*The Pharisees, tempting Christ, ask if it be lawful to put away one's wife.*

1 And it came to pass, when Jesus had finished these sayings, he departed from Galilee, and came into the coasts of Judea beyond Jordan.

2 And great multitudes followed him; and many believed on him, and he healed them there.

3 The Pharisees came also unto him, tempting him, and saying unto him, Is it lawful for a man to put away his wife for every cause?

4 And he answered and said unto them, Have ye not read, that he who made man at the beginning, made him, male and female,

5 And said, For this cause shall a man leave father and mother, and shall cleave to his wife; and they twain shall be one flesh?

6 Wherefore they are no more twain, but one flesh. What, therefore, God hath joined together, let no man put asunder.

7 They say unto him, Why did Moses then command to give a writing of divorcement, and to put her away?

8 He said unto them, Moses, because of the hardness of your hearts, suffered you to put away your wives; but from the beginning it was not so.

9 And I say unto you, Whosoever shall put away his wife, except for fornication, and shall marry another, committeth adultery; and whoso marrieth her that is put away, doth commit adultery.

10 His disciples say unto him, If the case of the man be so with a wife, it is not good to marry.

11 But he said unto them, All cannot receive this saying; it is not for them save to whom it is given.

12 For there are some eunuchs, which were so born from their mother's womb; and there are some eunuchs which were made eunuchs of men; and there be eunuchs, which have made themselves eunuchs for the kingdom of heaven's sake. He that is able to receive, let him receive my sayings.

13 Then were there brought unto him little children, that he should put his hands on them and pray. And the disciples rebuked them, saying, There is no need, for Jesus hath said, Such shall be saved.

14 But Jesus said, Suffer little children to come unto me, and forbid them not, for of such is the kingdom of heaven.

15 And he laid hands on them, and departed thence.

16 And, behold, one came and said, Good master, what good thing shall I do, that I may have eternal life?

17 And he said unto him, Why callest thou me good? There is none good but one, that is, God; but if thou wilt enter into life, keep the commandments.

18 He saith unto him, Which? Jesus said, Thou shalt not kill. Thou shalt not commit adultery. Thou shalt not steal. Thou shalt not bear false witness.

19 Honor thy father and mother. And, Thou shalt love thy neighbor as thyself.

20 The young man saith unto him, All these things have I kept from my youth up; what lack I yet?

21 Jesus said unto him, If thou wilt be perfect, go, sell that thou hast, and give to the poor, and thou shalt have

treasure in heaven, and come and follow me.

22 But when the young man heard that saying, he went away sorrowful; for he had great possessions.

23 Then said Jesus unto his disciples, Verily, I say unto you, that a rich man shall hardly enter into the kingdom of heaven.

24 And again I say unto you, It is easier for a camel to go through the eye of a needle, than for a rich man to enter the kingdom of God.

25 When his disciples heard this, they were exceedingly amazed, saying, Who then can be saved?

26 But Jesus beheld their thoughts, and said unto them, With men this is impossible; but if they will forsake all things for my sake, with God whatsoever things I speak are possible.

27 Then answered Peter and said unto him, Behold, we have forsaken all, and followed thee; what shall we have therefore?

28 And Jesus said unto them, Verily I say unto you, that ye who have followed me, shall, in the resurrection, when the Son of man shall come sitting on the throne of his glory, ye shall also shall sit upon twelve thrones, judging the twelve tribes of Israel.

29 And everyone that has forsaken houses, or brethren, or sisters, or father, or mother, or wife, or children, or lands, for my name's sake, shall receive a hundredfold, and shall inherit everlasting life.

30 But many of the first shall be last, and the last first.

## CHAPTER 20

*The kingdom of heaven likened unto a man hiring laborers in his vineyard.*

1 For the kingdom of heaven is like unto a man, an householder, who went out early in the morning to hire laborers into his vineyard.

2 And when he had agreed with the laborers for a penny a day, he sent them into his vineyard.

3 And he went out about the third hour, and found others standing idle in the marketplace.

4 And said unto them, Go ye also into the vineyard, and whatsoever is right, I will give you; and they went their way.

5 And again he went out about the sixth and ninth hour and did likewise.

6 And about the eleventh hour he went out, and found others standing idle, and said unto them, Why stand ye here all the day idle?

7 They said unto him, Because no man hath hired us.

8 He said unto them, Go ye also into the vineyard; and whatsoever is right ye shall receive.

9 So when even was come, the lord of the vineyard said unto his steward, Call the laborers and give them their hire, beginning from the last unto the first.

10 And when they came that began about the eleventh hour, they received every man a penny.

11 But when the first came, they supposed that they should have received more; and they likewise received every man a penny. And when they had received a penny, they murmured against the good man of the house, saying, These last have wrought one hour only and thou hast made them equal unto us, who have borne the burden and heat of the day.

12 But he answered one of them, and said, Friend, I do thee no wrong; didst not thou agree with me for a penny?

13 Take thine and go thy way; I will give unto this last even as unto thee. Is it not lawful for me to do what I will with mine own?

14 Is thine eye evil, because I am good?

15 So the last shall be first, and the first last, for many are called, but few chosen.

16 And Jesus, going up to Jerusalem, took the twelve disciples apart in the way, and said unto them,

17 Behold, we go up to Jerusalem, and the Son of man shall be betrayed unto the chief priests, and unto the scribes, and they shall condemn him to death; and shall deliver him to the Gentiles to mock, and to scourge, and to crucify. And the third day he shall rise again.

18 Then came to him the mother of Zebedee's children with her sons, worshiping Jesus, and desiring a certain thing of him.

19 And he said unto her, What wilt thou that I should do?

20 And she said unto him, Grant that these my two sons may sit, the

one on thy right hand, and the other on thy left, in thy kingdom.

21 But Jesus answered and said, Ye know not what ye ask. Are ye able to drink of the cup that I shall drink of, and to be baptized with the baptism that I am baptized with?

22 They say unto him, We are able.

23 And he said unto them, Ye shall drink indeed of my cup, and be baptized with the baptism that I am baptized with; but to sit on my right hand, and on my left, is for whom it is prepared of my Father, but not mine to give.

24 And when the ten heard this, they were moved with indignation against the two brethren.

25 But Jesus called them, and said, Ye know that the princes of the Gentiles exercise dominion over them, and they that are great exercise authority upon them; but it shall not be so among you.

26 But whosoever will be great among you, let him be your minister.

27 And whosoever will be chief among you, let him be your servant;

28 Even as the Son of man came, not to be ministered unto, but to minister; and to give his life a ransom for many.

29 And as they departed from Jericho, a great multitude followed him.

30 And, behold, two blind men sitting by the wayside, when they heard that Jesus passed by, cried out, saying, Have mercy on us, O Lord, Son of David.

31 And the multitude rebuked them, saying, they should hold their peace; but they cried the more, saying, Have mercy on us, O Lord, Son of David.

32 And Jesus stood still, and called them, and said, What will ye that I shall do unto you?

33 They say unto him, Lord, that our eyes may be opened.

34 So Jesus had compassion, and touched their eyes; and immediately their eyes received sight, and they followed him.

## CHAPTER 21

*Christ rideth into Jerusalem on a colt, the foal of an ass.*

1 And when Jesus drew nigh unto Jerusalem, and they were come to Bethphage, unto the mount of Olives, then sent Jesus two disciples,

2 Saying unto them, Go into the village over against you, and straightway ye shall find a colt tied; loose it, and bring it unto me; and if any shall say aught unto you, ye shall say, The Lord hath need of it; and straightway he will send it.

3 All this was done, that it might be fulfilled which was spoken by the prophet, saying,

4 Tell ye the daughter of Zion, Behold, thy king cometh unto thee, and he is meek, and he is sitting upon an ass, and a colt, the foal of an ass.

5 And the disciples went, and did as Jesus commanded them; and brought the colt, and put on it their clothes; and Jesus took the colt and sat thereon; and they followed him.

6 And a very great multitude spread their garments in the way; others cut down branches from the trees, and strewed in the way.

7 And the multitudes that went before, and also that followed after, cried, saying, Hosanna to the Son of David; blessed is he who cometh in the name of the Lord! Hosanna in the highest!

8 And when he was come into Jerusalem, all the city was moved, saying, Who is this?

9 And the multitude said, This is Jesus of Nazareth, the prophet of Galilee.

10 And Jesus went into the temple of God, and cast out all them that sold and bought in the temple, and overthrew the tables of the money changers, and the seats of them that sold doves; and said unto them,

11 It is written, My house shall be called the house of prayer; but ye have made it a den of thieves.

12 And the blind and the lame came to him in the temple; and he healed them.

13 And when the chief priests and scribes saw the wonderful things that he did, and the children of the kingdom crying in the temple, and saying, Hosanna to the Son of David! they were sore displeased, and said unto him, Hearest thou what these say?

14 And Jesus said unto them, Yea; have ye never read the scriptures which saith, Out of the mouth of babes and sucklings, O Lord, thou hast perfected praise?

15 And he left them, and went out of the city unto Bethany, and he lodged there.

16 Now in the morning, as he returned into the city, he hungered.

17 And when he saw a fig tree in the way, he came to it, and there was not any fruit on it, but leaves only. And he said unto it, Let no fruit grow on thee henceforward, for ever. And presently the fig tree withered away.

18 And when the disciples saw this, they marveled, and said, How soon is the fig tree withered away!

19 Jesus answered and said unto them, Verily I say unto you, if ye have faith, and doubt not, ye shall not only do this to the fig tree, but also, if ye shall say unto this mountain, Be thou removed, and be thou cast into the sea, it shall be done.

20 And all things, whatsoever ye shall ask in prayer, in faith believing, ye shall receive.

21 And when he was come into the temple, the chief priests and the elders of the people came unto him as he was teaching, and said, By what authority doest thou these things? And who gave thee this authority?

22 And Jesus answered and said unto them, I also will ask you one thing, which if ye tell me, I, likewise, will tell you by what authority I do these things.

23 The baptism of John, whence was it? From heaven, or of men?

24 And they reasoned with themselves, saying, If we shall say, From heaven; he will say unto us, Why did ye not then believe him? But if we shall say, Of men; we fear the people. For all people held John as a prophet. And they answered Jesus, and said, We cannot tell.

25 And he said, Neither tell I you by what authority I do these things.

26 But what think ye? A man had two sons; and he came to the first, saying, Son, go work today in my vineyard.

27 He answered and said, I will not; but afterward he repented, and went.

28 And he came to the second, and said likewise. And he answered and said, I will serve; and went not.

29 Whether of these twain did the will of their father?

30 They say unto him, The first.

31 Jesus said unto them, Verily I say unto you, That the publicans and the harlots shall go into the kingdom of God before you.

32 For John came unto you in the way of righteousness, and bore record of me, and ye believed him not; but the publicans and the harlots believed him; and ye, afterward, when ye had seen me, repented not, that ye might believe him.

33 For he that believed not John concerning me, cannot believe me, except he first repent.

34 And except ye repent, the preaching of John shall condemn you at the day of judgment. And, again, hear another parable; for unto you that believe not, I speak in parables; that your unrighteousness may be rewarded unto you.

35 Behold, there was a certain householder, who planted a vineyard, and hedged it round about, and digged a winepress in it; and built a tower, and let it out to husbandmen, and went into a far country.

36 And when the time of the fruit drew near, he sent his servants to the husbandmen, that they might receive the fruits of it.

37 And the husbandmen took his servants, and beat one, and killed another, and stoned another.

38 Again, he sent other servants, more than the first; and they did unto them likewise.

39 But last of all, he sent unto them his son, saying, They will reverence my son.

40 But when the husbandmen saw the son, they said among themselves, This is the heir; come, let us kill him, and let us seize on his inheritance.

41 And they caught him, and cast him out of the vineyard, and slew him.

42 And Jesus said unto them, When the lord therefore of the vineyard cometh, what will he do unto those husbandmen?

43 They say unto him, He will destroy those miserable, wicked men, and will let out the vineyard unto other husbandmen, who shall render him the fruits in their seasons.

44 Jesus said unto them, Did ye never read in the scriptures, The stone which the builders rejected, the same is become the head of the corner; this is the Lord's doings, and it is marvelous in our eyes.

45 Therefore say I unto you, The kingdom of God shall be taken from

you, and given to a nation bringing forth the fruits thereof.

46 For whosoever shall fall on this stone, shall be broken; but on whomsoever it shall fall, it will grind him to powder.

47 And when the chief priests and Pharisees had heard his parables, they perceived that he spake of them.

48 And they said among themselves, Shall this man think that he alone can spoil this great kingdom? And they were angry with him.

49 But when they sought to lay hands on him, they feared the multitude, because they learned that the multitude took him for a prophet.

50 And now his disciples came to him, and Jesus said unto them, Marvel ye at the words of the parable which I spake unto them?

51 Verily, I say unto you, I am the stone, and those wicked ones reject me.

52 I am the head of the corner. These Jews shall fall upon me, and shall be broken.

53 And the kingdom of God shall be taken from them, and shall be given to a nation bringing forth the fruits thereof; (meaning the Gentiles.)

54 Wherefore, on whomsoever this stone shall fall, it shall grind him to powder.

55 And when the Lord therefore of the vineyard cometh, he will destroy those miserable, wicked men, and will let again his vineyard unto other husbandmen, even in the last days, who shall render him the fruits in their seasons.

56 And then understood they the parable which he spake unto them, that the Gentiles should be destroyed also, when the Lord should descend out of heaven to reign in his vineyard, which is the earth and the inhabitants thereof.

## CHAPTER 22

*Parable of the marriage supper.*

1 And Jesus answered the people again, and spake unto them in parables, and said,

2 The kingdom of heaven is like unto a certain king, who made a marriage for his son.

3 And when the marriage was ready, he sent forth his servants to call them that were bidden to the wedding; and they would not come.

4 Again he sent forth other servants, saying, Tell them that are bidden, Behold, I have prepared my oxen, and my fatlings have been killed, and my dinner is ready, and all things are prepared; therefore come unto the marriage.

5 But they made light of the servants, and went their ways; one to his farm, another to his merchandise;

6 And the remnant took his servants, and entreated them spitefully, and slew them.

7 But when the king heard that his servants were dead, he was wroth; and he sent forth his armies, and destroyed those murderers, and burned up their city.

8 Then said he to his servants, The wedding is ready; but they who were bidden were not worthy.

9 Go ye therefore into the highways, and as many as ye shall find, bid to the marriage.

10 So those servants went out into the highways, and gathered together all, as many as they found, both bad and good; and the wedding was furnished with guests.

11 But when the king came in to see the guests, he saw there a man who had not a wedding garment.

12 And he said unto him, Friend, how camest thou in hither, not having a wedding garment? And he was speechless.

13 Then said the king unto his servants, Bind him hand and foot, and take and cast him away into outer darkness; there shall be weeping and gnashing of teeth.

14 For many are called, but few chosen; wherefore all do not have on the wedding garment.

15 Then went the Pharisees and took counsel how they might entangle him in his talk.

16 And they sent out unto him their disciples with the Herodians, saying, Master, we know that thou art true, and teachest the way of God in truth, neither carest thou for any; for thou regardest not the person of men.

17 Tell us, therefore, What thinkest thou? Is it lawful to give tribute unto Caesar, or not?

18 But Jesus perceived their wickedness, and said, Ye hypocrites! why

tempt ye me? Show me the tribute money.

19 And they brought unto him a penny.

20 He said unto them, Whose image is this, and superscription?

21 They said unto him, Caesar's. Then said he unto them, Render therefore unto Caesar, the things which are Caesar's; and unto God the things which are God's.

22 And when they had heard him say these words, they marveled, and left him, and went their way.

23 The same day came the Sadducees to him, who say that there is no resurrection, and asked him, saying, Master, Moses said, If a man die, having no children, his brother shall marry his wife, and raise up seed unto his brother.

24 Now there were with us, seven brethren; and the first, when he had married a wife, deceased; and, having no issue, he left his wife unto his brother.

25 Likewise the second also, and the third, and even unto the seventh.

26 And last of all the woman died also.

27 Therefore, in the resurrection, whose wife shall she be of the seven? For they all had her.

28 Jesus answered and said unto them, Ye do err, not knowing the scriptures, nor the power of God.

29 For in the resurrection, they neither marry, nor are given in marriage; but are as the angels of God in heaven.

30 But as touching the resurrection of the dead, have ye not read that which was spoken unto you of God, saying,

31 I am the God of Abraham, and the God of Isaac, and the God of Jacob? God is not the God of the dead, but of the living.

32 And when the multitude heard him, they were astonished at his doctrine.

33 But when the Pharisees heard that he had put the Sadducees to silence, they were gathered together.

34 Then one of them, a lawyer, tempting him, asked, saying,

35 Master, which is the great commandment in the law?

36 Jesus said unto him, Thou shalt love the Lord thy God with all thy

heart, and with all thy soul, and with all thy mind.

37 This is the first and great commandment.

38 And the second is like unto it; Thou shalt love thy neighbor as thyself.

39 On these two commandments hang all the law and the prophets.

40 While the Pharisees were gathered together, Jesus asked them, saying, What think ye of Christ? Whose son is he?

41 They say unto him, The Son of David.

42 He said unto them, How then doth David in spirit call him Lord, saying, The Lord said unto my Lord, Sit thou on my right hand, till I make thine enemies thy footstool?

43 If David then called him Lord, how is he his son?

44 And no man was able to answer him a word, neither durst any man from that day forth ask him any more questions.

## CHAPTER 23

*Christ upbraideth the scribes for their hypocrisy—Weepeth over Jerusalem.*

1 Then spake Jesus to the multitude, and to his disciples, saying, The scribes and the Pharisees sit in Moses' seat.

2 All, therefore, whatsoever they bid you observe, they will make you observe and do; for they are ministers of the law, and they make themselves your judges. But do not ye after their works; for they say, and do not.

3 For they bind heavy burdens and lay on men's shoulders, and they are grievous to be borne; but they will not move them with one of their fingers.

4 And all their works they do to be seen of men. They make broad their phylacteries, and enlarge the borders of their garments, and love the uppermost rooms at feasts, and the chief seats in the synagogues, and greetings in the markets, and to be called of men, Rabbi, Rabbi, (which is master.)

5 But be not ye called Rabbi; for one is your master, which is Christ; and all ye are brethren.

6 And call no one your creator upon the earth, or your heavenly Father; for one is your creator and heavenly Father, even he who is in heaven.

7 Neither be ye called masters; for

one is your master, even he whom your heavenly Father sent, which is Christ; for he hath sent him among you that ye might have life.

8 But he that is greatest among you shall be your servant.

9 And whosoever shall exalt himself shall be abased of him; and he that shall humble himself shall be exalted of him.

10 But woe unto you, scribes and Pharisees, hypocrites! For ye shut up the kingdom of heaven against men; for ye neither go in yourselves, neither suffer ye them that are entering to go in.

11 Woe unto you, scribes and Pharisees! for ye are hypocrites! Ye devour widows' houses, and for a pretense make long prayers; therefore ye shall receive the greater punishment.

12 Woe unto you, scribes and Pharisees, hypocrites! For ye compass sea and land to make one proselyte; and when he is made, ye make him twofold more the child of hell than he was before, like unto yourselves.

13 Woe unto you, blind guides, who say, Whosoever shall swear by the temple, it is nothing; but whosoever shall swear by the gold of the temple, he committeth sin, and is a debtor.

14 You are fools and blind; for which is greater, the gold, or the temple that sanctifieth the gold?

15 And ye say, Whosoever sweareth by the altar, it is nothing; but whosoever sweareth by the gift that is upon it, he is guilty.

16 O fools and blind! For which is the greater, the gift, or the altar that sanctifieth the gift?

17 Verily I say unto you, Whoso, therefore, sweareth by it, sweareth by the altar, and by all things thereon.

18 And whoso shall swear by the temple, sweareth by it, and by him who dwelleth therein.

19 And he that shall swear by heaven, sweareth by the throne of God, and by him who sitteth thereon.

20 Woe unto you, scribes and Pharisees, hypocrites! For ye pay tithe of mint, and anise, and cummin; and have omitted the weightier things of the law; judgment, mercy, and faith; these ought ye to have done, and not to leave the other undone.

21 Ye blind guides, who strain at a gnat, and swallow a camel; who make yourselves appear unto men that ye would not commit the least sin, and yet ye yourselves, transgress the whole law.

22 Woe unto you, scribes and Pharisees, hypocrites! For ye make clean the outside of the cup, and of the platter; but within they are full of extortion and excess.

23 Ye blind Pharisees! Cleanse first the cup and platter within, that the outside of them may be clean also.

24 Woe unto you, scribes and Pharisees, hypocrites! For ye are like unto whited sepulchers, which indeed appear beautiful outwardly, but are within full of the bones of the dead, and of all uncleanness.

25 Even so, ye also outwardly appear righteous unto men, but within ye are full of hypocrisy and iniquity.

26 Woe unto you, scribes and Pharisees, hypocrites! Because ye build the tombs of the prophets, and garnish the sepulchers of the righteous,

27 And say, If we had been in the days of our fathers, we would not have been partakers with them in the blood of the prophets;

28 Wherefore, ye are witnesses unto yourselves of your own wickedness, and ye are the children of them who killed the prophets;

29 And will fill up the measure then of your fathers; for ye, yourselves, kill the prophets like unto your fathers.

30 Ye serpents, and generation of vipers! How can ye escape the damnation of hell?

31 Wherefore, behold, I send unto you prophets, and wise men, and scribes; and of them ye shall kill and crucify; and of them ye shall scourge in your synagogues, and persecute from city to city;

32 That upon you may come all the righteous blood shed upon the earth, from the blood of righteous Abel, unto the blood of Zacharias, son of Barachias, whom ye slew between the temple and the altar.

33 Verily I say unto you, All these things shall come upon this generation.

34 Ye bear testimony against your fathers, when ye, yourselves, are partakers of the same wickedness.

35 Behold your fathers did it through ignorance, but ye do not; wherefore, their sins shall be upon your heads.

36 Then Jesus began to weep over Jerusalem, saying,

37 O Jerusalem! Jerusalem! Ye who will kill the prophets, and will stone them who are sent unto you; how often would I have gathered your children together, even as a hen gathers her chickens under her wings, and ye would not.

38 Behold, your house is left unto you desolate!

39 For I say unto you, that ye shall not see me henceforth, and know that I am he of whom it is written by the prophets, until ye shall say,

40 Blessed is he who cometh in the name of the Lord, in the clouds of heaven, and all the holy angels with him.

41 Then understood his disciples that he should come again on the earth, after that he was glorified and crowned on the right hand of God.

## CHAPTER 24

*Christ foretelleth the destruction of Jerusalem, and the end of the wicked.*

1 And Jesus went out, and departed from the temple; and his disciples came to him for to hear him, saying, Master, show us concerning the buildings of the temple; as thou hast hast said; They shall be thrown down and left unto you desolate.

2 And Jesus said unto them, See ye not all these things? And do ye not understand them? Verily I say unto you, There shall not be left here upon this temple, one stone upon another, that shall not be thrown down.

3 And Jesus left them and went upon the mount of Olives.

4 And as he sat upon the mount of Olives, the disciples came unto him privately, saying, Tell us, when shall these things be which thou hast said concerning the destruction of the temple, and the Jews; and what is the sign of thy coming; and of the end of the world? (or the destruction of the wicked, which is the end of the world.)

5 And Jesus answered and said unto them, Take heed that no man deceive you.

6 For many shall come in my name, saying, I am Christ; and shall deceive many.

7 Then shall they deliver you up to be afflicted, and shall kill you; and ye shall be hated of all nations for my name's sake.

8 And then shall many be offended, and shall betray one another, and shall hate one another.

9 And many false prophets shall arise, and shall deceive many.

10 And because iniquity shall abound, the love of many shall wax cold.

11 But he that remaineth steadfast, and is not overcome, the same shall be saved.

12 When ye therefore, shall see the abomination of desolation, spoken of by Daniel the prophet, concerning the destruction of Jerusalem, then ye shall stand in the holy place. (Whoso readeth let him understand.)

13 Then let them who are in Judea, flee into the mountains.

14 Let him who is on the housetop, flee, and not return to take anything out of his house.

15 Neither let him who is in the field, return back to take his clothes.

16 And woe unto them that are with child, and unto them that give suck in those days!

17 Therefore, pray ye the Lord, that your flight be not in the winter, neither on the Sabbath day.

18 For then, in those days, shall be great tribulations on the Jews, and upon the inhabitants of Jerusalem; such as was not before sent upon Israel, of God, since the beginning of their kingdom until this time; no, nor ever shall be sent again upon Israel.

19 All things which have befallen them, are only the beginning of the sorrows which shall come upon them; and except those days should be shortened, there should none of their flesh be saved.

20 But for the elect's sake, according to the covenant, those days shall be shortened.

21 Behold these things I have spoken unto you concerning the Jews.

22 And again, after the tribulation of those days which shall come upon Jerusalem, if any man shall say unto you, Lo! here is Christ, or there; believe him not.

23 For in those days, there shall also arise false Christs, and false prophets, and shall show great signs and wonders; insomuch that, if possible, they

shall deceive the very elect, who are the elect according to the covenant.

24 Behold, I speak these things unto you for the elect's sake.

25 And ye also shall hear of wars, and rumors of wars; see that ye be not troubled; for all I have told you must come to pass. But the end is not yet.

26 Behold, I have told you before, Wherefore, if they shall say unto you, Behold, he is in the desert; go not forth. Behold, he is in the secret chambers; believe it not.

27 For as the light of the morning cometh out of the east, and shineth even unto the west, and covereth the whole earth; so shall also the coming of the Son of man be.

28 And now I show unto you a parable. Behold, wheresoever the carcass is, there will the eagles be gathered together; so likewise shall mine elect be gathered from the four quarters of the earth.

29 And they shall hear of wars, and rumors of wars. Behold, I speak unto you for mine elect's sake.

30 For nation shall rise against nation, and kingdom against kingdom; there shall be famine and pestilences, and earthquakes in divers places.

31 And again, because iniquity shall abound, the love of men shall wax cold; but he that shall not be overcome, the same shall be saved.

32 And again, this gospel of the kingdom shall be preached in all the world, for a witness unto all nations, and then shall the end come, or the destruction of the wicked.

33 And again shall the abomination of desolation, spoken of by Daniel the prophet, be fulfilled.

34 And immediately after the tribulation of those days, the sun shall be darkened, and the moon shall not give her light, and the stars shall fall from heaven, and the powers of heaven shall be shaken.

35 Verily I say unto you, this generation, in which these things shall be shown forth, shall not pass away until all I have told you shall be fulfilled.

36 Although the days will come that heaven and earth shall pass away, yet my word shall not pass away; but all shall be fulfilled.

37 And as I said before, after the tribulation of those days, and the powers of the heavens shall be shaken,

then shall appear the sign of the Son of man in heaven; and then shall all the tribes of the earth mourn.

38 And they shall see the Son of man coming in the clouds of heaven, with power and great glory.

39 And whoso treasureth up my words, shall not be deceived.

40 For the Son of man shall come, and he shall send his angels before him with the great sound of a trumpet, and they shall gather together the remainder of his elect from the four winds; from one end of heaven to the other.

41 Now learn a parable of the fig tree: When its branches are yet tender, and it begins to put forth leaves, ye know that summer is nigh at hand.

42 So likewise mine elect, when they shall see all these things, they shall know that he is near, even at the doors.

43 But of that day and hour no one knoweth; no, not the angels of God in heaven, but my Father only.

44 But as it was in the days of Noah, so it shall be also at the coming of the Son of man.

45 For it shall be with them as it was in the days which were before the flood; for until the day that Noah entered into the ark, they were eating and drinking, marrying and giving in marriage, and knew not until the flood came and took them all away; so shall also the coming of the Son of man be.

46 Then shall be fulfilled that which is written, that, In the last days,

47 Two shall be in the field; the one shall be taken and the other left.

48 Two shall be grinding at the mill; the one taken and the other left.

49 And what I say unto one, I say unto all men; Watch, therefore, for ye know not at what hour your Lord doth come.

50 But know this, if the good man of the house had known in what watch the thief would come, he would have watched, and would not have suffered his house to have been broken up; but would have been ready.

51 Therefore be ye also ready; for in such an hour as ye think not, the Son of man cometh.

52 Who then is a faithful and wise servant, whom his Lord hath made ruler over his household, to give them meat in due season?

53 Blessed is that servant, whom his Lord when he cometh shall find so doing;

54 And, verily I say unto you, he shall make him ruler over all his goods.

55 But if that evil servant shall say in his heart, My Lord delayeth his coming; and shall begin to smite his fellow servants, and to eat and drink with the drunken; the Lord of that servant shall come in a day when he looketh not for him, and in an hour that he is not aware of, and shall cut him asunder, and shall appoint him his portion with the hypocrites; there shall be weeping and gnashing of teeth.

56 And thus cometh the end of the wicked according to the prophecy of Moses, saying, They should be cut off from among the people. But the end of the earth is not yet; but bye and bye.

## CHAPTER 25

*Parable of the ten virgins—The talents—The judgment.*

1 And then, at that day, before the Son of man comes, the kingdom of heaven shall be likened unto ten virgins, who took their lamps, and went forth to meet the bridegroom.

2 And five of them were wise, and five of them were foolish.

3 They that were foolish took their lamps and took no oil with them; but the wise took oil in their vessels with their lamps.

4 While the bridegroom tarried, they all slumbered and slept.

5 And at midnight there was a cry made, Behold, the bridegroom cometh; go ye out to meet him.

6 Then all those virgins arose, and trimmed their lamps.

7 And the foolish said unto the wise, Give us of your oil; for our lamps are gone out.

8 But the wise answered, saying, Lest there be not enough for us and you, go ye rather to them that sell, and buy for yourselves.

9 And while they went to buy, the bridegroom came; and they that were ready went in with him to the marriage; and the door was shut.

10 Afterward came also the other virgins, saying, Lord, Lord, open unto us.

11 But he answered and said, Verily I say unto you, Ye know me not.

12 Watch therefore; for ye know neither the day nor the hour wherein the Son of man cometh.

13 Now I will liken these things unto a parable.

14 For it is like as a man traveling into a far country, who called his own servants, and delivered unto them his goods.

15 And unto one he gave five talents, to another two, and to another one; to every man according to his several ability; and straightway went on his journey.

16 Then he that had received the five talents, went and traded with the same; and gained other five talents.

17 And likewise he who received two talents, he also gained other two.

18 But he who had received one, went and digged in the earth and hid his lord's money.

19 After a long time the lord of those servants cometh, and reckoneth with them.

20 And so he that had received the five talents came, and brought other five talents, saying, Lord, thou deliveredst unto me five talents; behold, I have gained besides them, five talents more.

21 His lord said unto him, Well done, good and faithful servant; thou hast been faithful over a few things, I will make thee ruler over many things; enter thou into the joy of thy lord.

22 He also that had received two talents came and said, Lord, thou deliveredst unto me two talents; behold, I have gained two talents besides them.

23 His lord said unto him, Well done, good and faithful servant; thou hast been faithful over a few things, I will make thee ruler over many things; enter thou into the joy of thy lord.

24 Then he who had received the one talent came, and said, Lord, I knew thee that thou art a hard man, reaping where thou hast not sown, and gathering where thou hast not scattered.

25 And I was afraid, and went and hid thy talent in the earth; and lo, here is thy talent; take it from me as thou hast from thine other servants, for it is thine.

26 His lord answered and said unto him, O wicked and slothful servant, thou knewest that I reap where I

sowed not, and gather where I have not scattered.

27 Having known this, therefore, thou oughtest to have put my money to the exchangers, and at my coming I should have received mine own with usury.

28 I will take, therefore, the talent from you, and give it unto him who hath ten talents.

29 For unto every one who hath other talents, shall be given, and he shall have in abundance.

30 But from him that hath not obtained other talents, shall be taken away even that which he hath received.

31 And his lord shall say unto his servants, Cast ye the unprofitable servant into outer darkness; there shall be weeping and gnashing of teeth.

32 When the Son of man shall come in his glory, and all the holy angels with him, then he shall sit upon the throne of his glory;

33 And before him shall be gathered all nations; and he shall separate them one from another, as a shepherd divideth sheep from the goats; the sheep on his right hand, but the goats on his left.

34 And he shall sit upon his throne, and the twelve apostles with him.

35 Then shall the King say unto them on his right hand, Come, ye blessed of my Father, inherit the kingdom prepared for you from the foundation of the world.

36 For I was an hungered, and ye gave me meat; I was thirsty, and ye gave me drink; I was a stranger, and ye took me in; naked, and ye clothed me;

37 I was sick, and ye visited me; I was in prison, and ye came unto me.

38 Then shall the righteous answer him, saying, Lord, when saw we thee an hungered, and fed thee; or thirsty, and gave thee drink?

39 When saw we thee a stranger, and took thee in; or naked, and clothed thee?

40 Or when saw we thee sick, or in prison, and came unto thee?

41 And the King shall answer and say unto them, Verily I say unto you, inasmuch as ye have done it unto one of the least of these my brethren, ye have done it unto me.

42 Then shall he say also unto them on the left hand, Depart from me, ye cursed, into everlasting fire, prepared for the devil and his angels.

43 For I was an hungered, and ye gave me no meat; I was thirsty, and ye gave me no drink;

44 I was a stranger, and ye took me not in; naked, and ye clothed me not; sick, and in prison, and ye visited me not.

45 Then shall they also answer him, saying, Lord, when saw we thee an hungered, or athirst, or a stranger, or naked, or sick, or in prison, and did not minister unto thee?

46 Then shall he answer them, saying, Verily I say unto you, Inasmuch as ye did it not to one of the least of these my brethren, ye did it not unto me.

47 And these shall go away into everlasting punishment; but the righteous into life eternal.

## CHAPTER 26

*The Lord's supper—Christ betrayed.*

1 And it came to pass, when Jesus had finished all these sayings, he said unto his disciples,

2 Ye know that after two days is the passover, and then the Son of man is betrayed to be crucified.

3 Then assembled together the chief priests, and the scribes, and the elders of the people, unto the palace of the high priest, who was called Caiaphas, and consulted that they might take Jesus by subtilty and kill him.

4 But they said, Not on the feast day, lest there be an uproar among the people.

5 Now when Jesus was in Bethany, in the house of Simon the leper, there came unto him a woman having an alabaster box of very precious ointment, and poured it on his head as he sat in the house.

6 But when some saw this, they had indignation, saying, Unto what purpose is this waste? For this ointment might have been sold for much, and given to the poor.

7 When they had said thus, Jesus understood them, and he said unto them, Why trouble ye the woman? For she hath wrought a good work upon me.

8 For ye have the poor always with you; but me ye have not always.

9 For she hath poured this ointment on my body, for my burial.

10 And in this thing that she hath done, she shall be blessed; for verily I say unto you, Wheresoever this gospel shall be preached in the whole world, this thing that this woman hath done, shall also be told for a memorial of her.

11 Then one of the twelve, called Judas Iscariot, went unto the chief priests, and said, What will ye give me, and I will deliver him unto you? And they covenanted with him for thirty pieces of silver.

12 And from that time he sought opportunity to betray Jesus.

13 Now on the first day of the feast of unleavened bread, the disciples came unto Jesus, saying unto him, Where wilt thou that we prepare for thee to eat the passover?

14 And he said, Go into the city to such a man, and say unto him, The Master saith, My time is at hand; I will keep the passover at thy house with my disciples.

15 And the disciples did as Jesus appointed them; and they made ready the passover.

16 Now when the evening was come, he sat down with the twelve.

17 And as they did eat, he said, Verily I say unto you, that one of you shall betray me.

18 And they were exceeding sorrowful, and began every one of them to say unto him, Lord, is it I?

19 And he answered and said, He that dippeth his hand with me in the dish, the same shall betray me.

20 But the Son of man goeth as it is written of him; but woe unto that man by whom the Son of man is betrayed! It had been good for that man if he had not been born.

21 Then Judas, who betrayed him, answered and said, Master, is it I? He said unto him, Thou hast said.

22 And as they were eating, Jesus took bread and brake it, and blessed it, and gave to his disciples, and said, Take, eat; this is in remembrance of my body which I give a ransom for you.

23 An he took the cup, and gave thanks, and gave it to them, saying, Drink ye all of it.

24 For this is in remembrance of my blood of the new testament, which is shed for as many as shall believe on my name, for the remission of their sins.

25 And I give unto you a commandment, that ye shall observe to do the things which ye have seen me do, and bear record of me even unto the end.

26 But I say unto you, I will not drink henceforth of this fruit of the vine, until that day when I shall come and drink it new with you in my Father's kingdom.

27 And when they had sung a hymn, they went out into the mount of Olives.

28 Then said Jesus unto them, All ye shall be offended because of me this night; for it is written, I will smite the Shepherd, and the sheep of the flock shall be scattered abroad.

29 But after I am risen again, I will go before you into Galilee.

30 Peter answered and said unto him, Though all men shall be offended because of thee, I will never be offended.

31 Jesus said unto him, Verily I say unto thee, that this night, before the cock crow, thou shalt deny me thrice.

32 Peter said unto him, Though I should die with thee, yet will I not deny thee. Likewise also said all the disciples.

33 Then cometh Jesus with them unto a place called Gethsemane, and said unto the disciples, Sit ye here, while I go yonder and pray.

34 And he took with him Peter and the two sons of Zebedee, and began to be sorrowful and very heavy.

35 Then said he unto them, My soul is exceeding sorrowful, even unto death; tarry ye here and watch with me.

36 And he went a little farther, and fell on his face, and prayed, saying, O my Father, if it be possible, let this cup pass from me; nevertheless, not as I will, but as thou wilt.

37 And he cometh unto the disciples and findeth them asleep, and saith unto Peter, What, could ye not watch with me one hour?

38 Watch and pray that ye enter not into temptation; the spirit indeed is willing; but the flesh is weak.

39 He went away again the second time and prayed, saying, O my Father, if this cup may not pass away from me, except I drink it, thy will be done.

40 And he came and found them

asleep again; for their eyes were heavy.

41 And he left them, and went away again, and prayed the third time, saying the same words.

42 Then cometh he to his disciples, and saith unto them, Sleep on now and take rest. Behold, the hour is at hand, and the Son of man is betrayed into the hands of sinners.

43 And after they had slept, he said unto them, Arise, and let us be going. Behold, he is at hand that doth betray me.

44 And while he yet spake, lo, Judas, one of the twelve, came, and with him a great multitude with swords and staves, from the chief priests and elders of the people.

45 Now he that betrayed him gave them a sign, saying, Whomsoever I shall kiss, that same is he; hold him fast.

46 And forthwith he came to Jesus, and said, Hail, Master! and kissed him.

47 And Jesus said unto him, Judas, wherefore art thou come to betray me with a kiss?

48 Then came they and laid hands on Jesus, and took him.

49 And behold, one of them which were with Jesus, stretched out his hand and drew his sword, and struck a servant of the high priest, and smote off his ear.

50 Then said Jesus unto him, Put up again thy sword into its place; for all they that take the sword shall perish with the sword.

51 Thinkest thou that I cannot now pray to my Father, and he shall presently give me more than twelve legions of angels?

52 But how then shall the scriptures be fulfilled, that thus it must be?

53 In that same hour said Jesus unto the multitudes, Are ye come out as against a thief, with swords and staves, for to take me? I sat daily with you in the temple, teaching, and ye laid no hold on me.

54 But all this was done that the scriptures of the prophets might be fulfilled.

55 Then all the disciples forsook him, and fled.

56 And they that had laid hold on Jesus, led him away to Caiaphas the high priest, where the scribes and the elders were assembled.

57 But Peter followed him afar off unto the high priest's palace, and went in, and sat with the servants to see the end.

58 Now the chief priests, and elders, and all the council, sought false witness against Jesus, to put him to death; but found none.

59 Yea, though many false witnesses came, they found none that could accuse him.

60 At the last came two false witnesses, and said, This man said, I am able to destroy the temple of God, and to build it in three days.

61 And the high priest arose and said unto him, Answerest thou nothing? Knowest thou what these witness against thee?

62 But Jesus held his peace.

63 And the high priest answered and said unto him,

64 I adjure thee by the living God, that thou tell us whether thou be the Christ, the Son of God.

65 Jesus said unto him, Thou hast said. Nevertheless, I say unto you, hereafter shall ye see the Son of man sitting on the right hand of power, and coming in the clouds of heaven.

66 Then the high priest rent his clothes, saying, He hath spoken blasphemy; what further need have we of witnesses? Behold, now, ye have heard his blasphemy. What think ye?

67 They answered and said, He is guilty, and worthy of death.

68 Then did they spit in his face and buffet him; and others smote him with the palms of their hands, saying, Prophesy unto us, thou Christ, who is it that smote thee?

69 Now Peter sat without in the palace; and a damsel came unto him, saying, Thou also wast with Jesus of Galilee.

70 But he denied before them all, saying, I know not what thou sayest.

71 And when he was gone out into the porch, another saw him, and said unto them that were there, This man was also with Jesus of Nazareth.

72 And again he denied with an oath, saying, I do not know the man.

73 And after a while came they that stood by, and said to Peter, Surely thou also art one of them; for thy speech betrayeth thee.

74 Then began he to curse and to swear, saying, I know not the man.

75 And immediately the cock crew.

76 And Peter remembered the words of Jesus, which he said unto him, Before the cock crow, thou shalt deny me thrice. And he went out and wept bitterly.

## CHAPTER 27
*The Crucifixion of Christ.*

1 When the morning was come, all the chief priests and elders of the people took counsel against Jesus, to put him to death.

2 And when they had bound him, they led him away, and delivered him to Pontius Pilate, the governor.

3 Then Judas, who had betrayed him, when he saw that he was condemned, repented himself, and brought again the thirty pieces of silver to the chief priests and elders,

4 Saying, I have sinned in that I have betrayed the innocent blood. And they said unto him, What is that to us? See thou to it; thy sins be upon thee.

5 And they said unto him, What is that to us? See thou to it; thy sins be upon thee.

6 And he cast down the pieces of silver in the temple, and departed, and went, and hanged himself on a tree. And straightway he fell down, and his bowels gushed out, and he died.

7 And the chief priests took the silver pieces, and said, It is not lawful for to put them in the treasury, because it is the price of blood.

8 And they took counsel, and bought with them the potter's field, to bury strangers in. Wherefore that field was called, The field of blood, unto this day.

9 Then was fulfilled that which was spoken by Jeremy, the prophet, saying, And they took the thirty pieces of silver, the price of him that was valued, whom they of the children of Israel did value.

10 And therefore they took the pieces of silver, and gave them for the potter's field, as the Lord appointed by the mouth of Jeremy.

11 And Jesus stood before the governor; and the governor asked him, saying, Art thou the king of the Jews?

12 And Jesus said unto him, Thou sayest truly; for thus it is written of me.

13 And when he was accused of the chief priests and elders, he answered nothing.

14 Then saith Pilate unto him, Hearest thou not how many things they witness against thee?

15 And he answered him not to his questions; yea, never a word, insomuch that the governor marveled greatly.

16 Now at the feast the governor was wont to release unto the people a prisoner, whom they would.

17 And they had then a notable prisoner, called Barabbas.

18 Therefore when they were gathered together, Pilate said unto them, Whom will ye that I release unto you? Barabbas, or Jesus which is called Christ?

19 For he knew that for envy they had delivered him.

20 When he was set down on the judgment seat, his wife sent unto him, saying, Have thou nothing to do with that just man, for I have suffered many things this day in a vision because of him.

21 But the chief priests and elders persuaded the multitude that they should ask Barabbas, and destroy Jesus.

22 And the governor said unto them, Whether of the twain will ye that I release unto you? They said, Barabbas.

23 Pilate said unto them, What shall I do with Jesus, which is called Christ?

24 And all said unto him, Let him be crucified.

25 And the governor said, Why, what evil hath he done? But they cried out the more, saying, Let him be crucified.

26 When Pilate saw that he could prevail nothing, but rather that a tumult was made, he took water, and washed his hands before the multitude, saying, I am innocent of the blood of this just person; see that ye do nothing unto him.

27 Then answered all the people, and said, His blood come upon us and our children.

28 Then released he Barabbas unto them; and when he had scourged Jesus, he delivered him to be crucified.

29 Then the soldiers of the governor took Jesus into the common hall, and gathered unto him the whole band.

30 And they stripped him, and put on him a purple robe.

31 And when they had platted a

crown of thorns, they put it upon his head, and a reed in his right hand; and they bowed the knee before him, and they mocked him, saying, Hail, King of the Jews!

32 And they spit upon him, and took the reed, and smote him on the head.

33 And after that they had mocked him, they took the robe off from him, and put his own raiment on him, and led him away to crucify him.

34 And as they came out, they found a man of Cyrene, Simon by name; him they compelled to bear his cross.

35 And when they were come unto a place called Golgotha, (that is to say, a place of burial,)

36 They gave him vinegar to drink mingled with gall; and when he had tasted the vinegar, he would not drink.

37 And they crucified him, and parted his garments, casting lots; that it might be fulfilled which was spoken by the prophet, They parted my garments among them, and for my vesture they did cast lots.

38 And sitting down they watched him there.

39 And Pilate wrote a title, and put it on the cross, and the writing was,

40 JESUS OF NAZARETH, THE KING OF THE JEWS, in letters of Greek, and Latin, and Hebrew.

41 And the chief priests said unto Pilate, It should be written and set up over his head, his accusation, This is he that said he was Jesus, the King of the Jews.

42 But Pilate answered and said, What I have written, I have written; let it alone.

43 Then were there two thieves crucified with him; one on the right hand, and another on the left.

44 And they that passed by reviled him, wagging their heads, and saying, Thou that destroyest the temple, and buildest it again in three days, save thyself. If thou be the Son of God come down from the cross.

45 Likewise also the chief priests mocking with the scribes and elders, said, He saved others, himself he cannot save. If he be the King of Israel, let him now come down from the cross, and we will believe him.

46 He trusted in God; let him deliver him now; if he will save him, let him save him; for he said, I am the Son of God.

47 One of the thieves also, which were crucified with him, cast the same in his teeth. But the other rebuked him, saying, Dost thou not fear God, seeing thou art under the same condemnation; and this man is just, and hath not sinned; and he cried unto the Lord that he would save him.

48 And the Lord said unto him, This day thou shalt be with me in Paradise.

49 Now from the sixth hour there was darkness over all the land unto the ninth hour.

50 And about the ninth hour, Jesus cried with a loud voice, saying, Eli, Eli, lama sabachthani? (That is to say, My God, my God, why hast thou forsaken me?)

51 Some of them that stood there, when they heard him, said, This man calleth for Elias.

52 And straightway one of them ran, and took a sponge, and filled it with vinegar, and put it on a reed, and gave him to drink.

53 The rest said, Let him be, let us see whether Elias will come to save him.

54 Jesus when he had cried again with a loud voice, saying, Father, it is finished, thy will is done, yielded up the ghost.

55 And behold, the veil of the temple was rent in twain from the top to the bottom; and the earth did quake, and the rocks rent;

56 And the graves were opened; and the bodies of the saints which slept, arose, who were many,

57 And came out of the graves after his resurrection, went into the holy city, and appeared unto many.

58 Now when the centurion, and they that were with him, watching Jesus, heard the earth quake, and saw those things which were done, they feared greatly, saying, Truly this was the Son of God.

59 And many women were there beholding afar off, which followed Jesus from Galilee, ministering unto him for his burial; among whom was Mary Magdalene, and Mary the mother of James and Joses, and the mother of Zebedee's children.

60 When the evening was come, there came a rich man of Arimathea, named Joseph, who also himself was Jesus' disciple; he went to Pilate and begged the body of Jesus.

61 Then Pilate commanded the body to be delivered.

62 And when Joseph had taken the body, he wrapped it in a clean linen cloth, and laid it in his own new tomb, which he had hewn out in the rock; and he rolled a great stone to the door of the sepulcher, and departed.

63 And there was Mary Magdalene, and the other Mary, sitting over against the sepulcher.

64 Now the next day that followed the day of the preparation, the chief priests and Pharisees came together unto Pilate, saying, Sir, we remember that that deceiver said, while he was yet alive, After three days I will rise again.

65 Command therefore, that the sepulcher be made sure until the third day, lest his disciples come by night, and steal him away, and say unto the people, He is risen from the dead; so this last imposture will be worse than the first.

66 Pilate said unto them, Ye have a watch; go your way, make it as sure as ye can.

67 So they went and made the sepulcher sure, sealing the stone and setting a watch.

## CHAPTER 28

*The resurrection of Christ—He sends forth the disciples.*

1 In the end of the Sabbath day, as it began to dawn toward the first day of the week, early in the morning, came Mary Magdalene, and the other Mary to see the sepulcher.

2 And behold, there had been a great earthquake; for two angels of the Lord descended from heaven, and came and rolled back the stone from the door, and sat upon it.

3 And their countenance was like lightning, and their raiment white as snow; and for fear of them the keepers did shake, and became as though they were dead.

4 And the angels answered and said unto the women, Fear not ye; for we know that ye seek Jesus who was crucified.

5 He is not here; for he is risen, as he said. Come, see the place where the Lord lay; and go quickly, and tell his disciples that he is risen from the dead; and, behold, he goeth before you into Galilee; there shall ye see him; lo, I have told you.

6 And they departed quickly from the sepulcher, with fear and great joy; and did run to bring his disciples word.

7 And as they went to tell his disciples, behold Jesus met them, saying, All hail!

8 And they came and held him by the feet, and worshiped him.

9 Then said Jesus unto them, Be not afraid; go tell my brethren that they go into Galilee, and there shall they see me.

10 Now when they were going, behold, some of the watch came into the city, and showed unto the chief priests all the things that were done.

11 And when they were assembled with the elders, and had taken counsel, they gave large money unto the soldiers,

12 Saying, Say ye, His disciples came by night, and stole him while we slept.

13 And if this come to the governor's ears, we will persuade him, and secure you.

14 So they took the money, and did as they were taught; and this saying is commonly reported among the Jews until this day.

15 Then the eleven disciples went away into Galilee, into a mountain where Jesus had appointed them.

16 And when they saw him, they worshiped him; but some doubted.

17 And Jesus came and spake unto them, saying, All power is given unto me in heaven and in earth.

18 Go ye therefore, and teach all nations, baptizing them in the name of the Father, and of the Son, and of the Holy Ghost;

19 Teaching them to observe all things whatsoever I have commanded you; and, lo, I am with you always, unto the end of the world. Amen.

# The Testimony of St. Mark

## CHAPTER 1

1 The beginning of the gospel of Jesus Christ, the Son of God; as it is written in the prophets, Behold, I send my messenger before thy face, which shall prepare thy way before thee.

2 The voice of one crying in the wilderness, Prepare ye the way of the Lord, make his paths straight.

3 John did baptize in the wilderness, and preach the baptism of repentance for the remission of sins.

4 And there went out unto him all the land of Judea, and they of Jerusalem, and many were baptized of him in the river Jordan, confessing their sins.

5 And John was clothed with camels' hair, and with a girdle of skin about his loins; and he did eat locusts and wild honey; and preached, saying, There cometh one mightier than I after me, the latchet of whose shoes I am not worthy to stoop down and unloose.

6 I indeed have baptized you with water; but he shall not only baptize you with water, but with fire, and the Holy Ghost.

7 And it came to pass in those days, that Jesus came from Nazareth of Galilee, and was baptized of John in Jordan.

8 And straightway coming up out of the water, he saw the heavens opened, and the Spirit like a dove descending upon him;

9 And there came a voice from heaven, saying, Thou art my beloved Son, in whom I am well pleased. And John bare record of it.

10 And immediately the Spirit took him into the wilderness.

11 And he was there in the wilderness forty days, Satan seeking to tempt him; and was with the wild beasts; and the angels ministered unto him.

12 Now after that John was put in prison, Jesus came into Galilee, preaching the gospel of the kingdom of God; and saying,

13 The time is fulfilled, and the kingdom of God is at hand; repent ye, and believe the gospel.

14 And now as he walked by the sea of Galilee, he saw Simon and Andrew his brother, casting a net into the sea; for they were fishers.

15 And Jesus said unto them, Come ye after me, and I will make you to become fishers of men.

16 And straightway they forsook their nets, and followed him.

17 And when he had gone a little farther thence, he saw James the son of Zebedee, and John his brother, who also were in the ship mending their nets.

18 And he called them; and straightway they left their father Zebedee in the ship with the hired servants, and went after him.

19 And they went into Capernaum; and straightway on the Sabbath day he entered into the synagogue, and taught.

20 And they were astonished at his doctrine; for he taught them as one that had authority, and not as the scribes.

21 And there was in their synagogue a man with an unclean spirit; and he cried out, saying, Let us alone; what have we to do with thee, thou Jesus of Nazareth? Art thou come to destroy us? I know thee, who thou art, the Holy One of God.

22 And Jesus rebuked him, saying, Hold thy peace, and come out of him.

23 And when the unclean spirit had torn him, and cried with a loud voice, he came out of him.

24 And they were all amazed, insomuch that they questioned among themselves, saying, What thing is this? What new doctrine is this? For with authority commandeth he even the unclean spirits, and they do obey him.

25 And immediately his fame spread abroad throughout all the regions round about Galilee.

26 And forthwith when they were come out of the synagogue, they entered into the house of Simon and Andrew, with James and John.

27 And Simon's wife's mother lay sick of a fever; and they besought him for her.

28 And he came and took her by the hand, and lifted her up; and immediately the fever left her, and she came and ministered unto them.

29 And at evening after sunset, they brought unto him all that were diseased, and them that were possessed with devils; and all the city was gathered together at the door.

30 And he healed many that were sick of divers diseases, and cast out many devils; and suffered not the devils to speak, because they knew him.

31 And in the morning, rising up a great while before day, he went out and departed into a solitary place, and there prayed.

32 And Simon and they that were with him, followed after him.

33 And when they had found him, they said unto him, All men seek for thee.

34 And he said unto them, Let us go into the next towns, that I may preach there also; for therefore came I forth.

35 And he preached in their synagogues throughout all Galilee, and cast out devils.

36 And there came a leper to him, beseeching him, and kneeling down to him, said, If thou wilt, thou canst make me clean.

37 And Jesus, moved with compassion, put forth his hand and touched him, and said unto him, I will; be thou clean.

38 And as soon as he had spoken, immediately the leprosy departed from him, and he was cleansed.

39 And he straitly charged him, and forthwith sent him away; and said unto him, See thou say nothing to any man; but go thy way, show thyself to the priest, and offer for thy cleansing, those things which Moses commanded, for a testimony unto them.

40 But he went out, and began to publish it much, and to blaze abroad the matter, insomuch that Jesus could no more openly enter into the city, but was without in solitary places; and they came to him from every quarter.

## CHAPTER 2

*The preaching of Christ—The word confirmed by signs.*

1 And again, he entered into Capernaum after many days; and it was noised abroad that he was in the house.

2 And straightway many were gathered together, insomuch that there was no room to receive the multitude; no, not so much as about the door; and he preached the word unto them.

3 And they came unto him, bringing one sick of the palsy, which was borne of four persons.

4 And when they could not come nigh unto him, for the press, they uncovered the roof where he was; and when they had broken it up, they let down the bed wherein the sick of the palsy lay.

5 When Jesus saw their faith, he said unto the sick of the palsy, Son, thy sins be forgiven thee.

6 But there were certain of the scribes sitting there, and reasoning in their hearts, why doth this man thus speak blasphemies? Who can forgive sins but God only?

7 And immediately, when Jesus perceived in his spirit, that they so reasoned within themselves, he said unto them, Why reason ye these things in your hearts? Is it not easier to say to the sick of the palsy, Thy sins be forgiven thee; than to say, Arise, and take up thy bed and walk?

8 But that ye may know that the Son of man hath power on earth to forgive sins, (he said to the sick of the palsy,) I say unto thee, Arise, and take up thy bed, and go thy way into thy house.

9 And immediately he arose, took up the bed, and went forth before them all; insomuch that they were all amazed, and many glorified God, saying, We never saw the power of God after this manner.

10 And Jesus went forth again by the seaside; and all the multitude resorted unto him, and he taught them.

11 And as he passed by, he saw Levi the son of Alpheus, sitting at the place where they receive tribute, as was customary in those days, and he said unto him, Follow me; and he arose and followed him.

12 And it came to pass, that, as Jesus sat at meat in his house, many publicans and sinners sat also together with him and his disciples; for there were many, and they followed him.

13 And when the scribes and Pharisees saw him eat with publicans and sinners, they said unto his disciples, How is it that he eateth and drinketh with publicans and sinners?

14 When Jesus heard this, he said unto them, They that are whole have

no need of the physician, but they that are sick.

15 I came not to call the righteous, but sinners to repentance.

16 And they came and said unto him, The disciples of John and of the Pharisees used to fast; and why do the disciples of John and of the Pharisees fast, but thy disciples fast not?

17 And Jesus said unto them, Can the children of the bridechamber fast, while the bridegroom is with them? As long as they have the bridegroom with them, they cannot fast.

18 But the days will come, when the bridegroom shall be taken away from them, and then shall they fast in those days.

19 No man also seweth a piece of new cloth on an old garment; else the new piece that filled it up taketh away from the old, and the rent is made worse.

20 And no man putteth new wine into old bottles; else the new wine doth burst the bottles, and the wine is spilled, and the bottles will be marred; but new wine must be put into new bottles.

21 And it came to pass, that he went through the cornfields on the Sabbath day; and his disciples began, as they went, to pluck the ears of corn.

22 And the Pharisees said unto him, Behold, why do thy disciples on the Sabbath day that which is not lawful?

23 And he said unto them, Have ye never read what David did, when he had need and was an hungered, he, and they who were with him?

24 How he went into the house of God, in the days of Abiathar the high priest, and did eat the shew bread, which is not lawful to eat but for the priests, and gave also to them which were with him?

25 And he said unto them, The Sabbath was made for man, and not man for the Sabbath.

26 Wherefore the Sabbath was given unto man for a day of rest; and also that man should glorify God, and not that man should not eat;

27 For the Son of man made the Sabbath day, therefore the Son of man is Lord also of the Sabbath.

## CHAPTER 3

*The choosing of the Twelve—Their names—The brethren of Christ.*

1 And he entered again into the synagogue; and there was a man there which had a withered hand.

2 And they watched him to see whether he would heal him on the Sabbath day; that they might accuse him.

3 And he said unto the man which had the withered hand, Stand forth.

4 And he said unto them, Is it lawful to do good on the Sabbath days, or to do evil? To save life, or to kill? But they held their peace.

5 And when he had looked round about on them with anger, being grieved for the hardness of their hearts, he said unto the man, Stretch forth thine hand.

6 And he stretched out his hand; and his hand was restored whole as the other.

7 And the Pharisees went forth, and straightway took counsel with the Herodians against him, how they might destroy him.

8 But Jesus withdrew himself, with his disciples, to the sea; and a great multitude from Galilee followed him, and from Judea, and from Jerusalem, and from Idumea and from beyond Jordan; and they about Tyre and Sidon, a great multitude, when they heard what great things he did, came unto him.

9 And he spake unto his disciples, that a small ship should wait on him, because of the multitude, lest they should throng him.

10 For he had healed many; insomuch that they pressed upon him for to touch him. As many as had plagues and unclean spirits, when they saw him, fell down before him, and cried, saying, Thou art the Son of God.

11 And he straitly charged them that they should not make him known.

12 And he goeth up into a mountain, and calleth whom he would; and they came unto him.

13 And he ordained twelve, that they should be with him, and that he might send them forth to preach, and to have power to heal sicknesses, and to cast out devils.

14 And Simon he surnamed Peter; and James the son of Zebedee, and John the brother of James; and he surnamed them Boanerges, which is, The sons of thunder; and Andrew, and Philip, and Bartholomew, and Mat-

thew, and Thomas, and James the son of Alpheus, and Thaddeus, and Simon the Canaanite, and Judas Iscariot, which also betrayed him; and they went into a house.

15 And the multitude cometh together again, so that they could not so much as eat bread.

16 And when his friends heard him speak, they went out to lay hold on him; for they said, He is beside himself.

17 And the scribes which came down from Jerusalem, said, He hath Beelzebub, and by the prince of the devils, he casteth out devils.

18 Now Jesus knew this, and he called them, and said unto them in parables, How can Satan cast out Satan? And if a kingdom be divided against itself, how can that kingdom stand?

19 And if a house be divided against itself, that house cannot stand. And if Satan rise up against himself and be divided, he cannot stand; but speedily hath an end.

20 No man can enter into a strong man's house, and spoil his goods, except he will first bind the strong man, and then he will spoil his house.

21 And then came certain men unto him, accusing him, saying, Why do ye receive sinners, seeing thou makest thyself the Son of God.

22 But he answered them and said, Verily I say unto you, All sins which men have committed, when they repent, shall be forgiven them; for I came to preach repentance unto the sons of men.

23 And blasphemies, wherewith soever they shall blaspheme, shall be forgiven them that come unto me, and do the works which they see me do.

24 But there is a sin which shall not be forgiven. He that shall blaspheme against the Holy Ghost, hath never forgiveness; but is in danger of being cut down out of the world. And they shall inherit eternal damnation.

25 And this he said unto them because they said, He hath an unclean spirit.

26 While he was yet with them, and while he was yet speaking, there came then some of his brethren, and his mother; and standing without, sent unto him, calling unto him.

27 And the multitude sat about him, and they said unto him, Behold thy mother and thy brethren without seek for thee.

28 And he answered them, saying, Who is my mother, or who are my brethren?

29 And he looked round about on them which sat about him, and said, Behold my mother and my brethren!

30 For whosoever shall do the will of God, the same is my brother, and my sister, and mother.

## CHAPTER 4

*The parable of the sower, and of the mustard seed.*

1 And he began again to teach by the seaside; and there was gathered unto him a great multitude; so that he entered into a ship and sat in the sea; and the whole multitude was by the sea on the land.

2 And he taught them many things by parables.

3 And he said unto them in his doctrine, Hearken; Behold, there went out a sower to sow;

4 And it came to pass as he sowed, some fell by the wayside, and the fowls of the air came and devoured it up.

5 And some fell on stony ground, where it had not much earth; and immediately it sprang up, because it had no depth of earth; but when the sun was up, it was scorched; and because it had no root, it withered away.

6 And some fell among thorns, and the thorns grew up and choked it; and it yielded no fruit.

7 And other seed fell on good ground, and did yield fruit, that sprang up and increased, and brought forth, some thirtyfold, and some sixty, and some an hundred.

8 And he said unto them, He that hath ears to hear, let him hear.

9 And when he was alone with the twelve, and they that believed in him, they that were about him with the twelve asked of him the parable.

10 And he said unto them, Unto you it is given to know the mystery of the kingdom of God; but unto them that are without, all these things are done in parables;

11 That seeing, they may see and not perceive; and hearing, they may hear and not understand; lest at any time they should be converted, and their sins should be forgiven them.

12 And he said unto them, Know ye not this parable? And how then will ye know all parables?

13 The sower soweth the word.

14 And these are they by the wayside, where the word is sown; but when they have heard, Satan cometh immediately, and taketh away the word that was sown in their hearts.

15 And these are they likewise which receive the word on stony ground; who, when they have heard the word, immediately receive it with gladness, and have no root in themselves, and so endure but for a time; and afterward, when affliction or persecution ariseth for the word's sake, immediately they are offended.

16 And these are they who receive the word among thorns; such as hear the word, and the cares of this world, and the deceitfulness of riches, and the lusts of other things entering in, choke the word, and it becometh unfruitful.

17 And these are they who receive the word on good ground; such as hear the word, and receive it, and bring forth fruit; some thirtyfold, some sixty and some an hundred.

18 And he said unto them, Is a candle brought to be put under a bushel, or under a bed, and not to be set on a candlestick? I say unto you, Nay;

19 For there is nothing hid which shall not be manifested; neither was anything kept secret, but that it should in due time come abroad. If any man have ears to hear, let him hear.

20 And he said unto them, Take heed what ye hear; for with what measure ye mete, it shall be measured to you; and unto you that continue to receive, shall more be given; for he that receiveth, to him shall be given; but he that continueth not to receive, from him shall be taken even that which he hath.

21 And he said, So is the kingdom of God; as if a man should cast seed into the ground; and should sleep and rise, night and day, and the seed should spring and grow up, he knoweth not how;

22 For the earth bringeth forth fruit of herself, first the blade, then the ear, after that the full corn in the ear.

23 But when the fruit is brought forth, immediately he putteth in the sickle, because the harvest is come.

24 And he said, Whereunto shall I liken the kingdom of God? Or with what comparison shall we compare it?

25 It is like a grain of mustard seed, which, when it is sown in the earth, is less than all the seeds that be in the earth; but, when it is sown, it groweth up, and becometh greater than all herbs, and shooteth out great branches; so that the fowls of the air may lodge under the shadow of it.

26 And with many such parables spake he the word unto them, as they were able to bear; but without a parable spake he not unto them.

27 And when they were alone, he expounded all things unto his disciples.

28 And the same day, when the even was come, he said unto them, Let us pass over unto the other side.

29 And when they had sent away the multitude, they took him, even as he was, in the ship. And there were also with him other little ships.

30 And there arose a great storm of wind, and the waves beat over into the ship; and he was in the hinder part of the ship asleep on a pillow; and they awoke him, and said unto him, Master, carest thou not that we perish?

31 And he arose and rebuked the wind, and said unto the sea, Peace; be still; and the wind ceased, and there was a great calm.

32 And he said unto them, Why are ye so fearful? How is it that ye have no faith?

33 And they feared exceedingly, and said one to another, What manner of man is this, that even the wind and the sea obey him?

## CHAPTER 5

*The unclean spirit at the tombs—Healing of Jairus' daughter.*

1 And they came over unto the other side of the sea, into the country of the Gadarenes.

2 And when he was come out of the ship, immediately there met him out of the tombs, a man with an unclean spirit, who had been dwelling among the tombs.

3 And no man could bind him, no, not with chains; because that he had been often bound with fetters, and chains, and the chains had been plucked asunder by him, and the fetters broken in pieces; neither could any man tame him.

4 And always, night and day, he was

in the mountains, and in the tombs, crying, and cutting himself with stones.

5 But when he saw Jesus afar off, he ran and worshiped him, and cried with a loud voice and said, What have I to do with thee, Jesus, thou Son of the most high God? I adjure thee by God, that thou torment me not. For he said unto him, Come out of the man, unclean spirit.

6 And he commanded him saying, Declare thy name. And he answered, saying, My name is Legion; for we are many.

7 And he besought him much, that he would not send them away out of the country.

8 Now there was there, nigh unto the mountains, a great herd of swine feeding.

9 And all the devils besought him, saying, Send us into the swine, that we may enter into them. And forthwith Jesus gave them leave.

10 And the unclean spirits went out, and entered into the swine; and the herd ran violently down a steep place into the sea, (they were about two thousand,) and were choked in the sea.

11 And they that fed the swine fled, and told the people in the city, and in the country, all that was done unto the swine.

12 And they went out to see what it was that was done. And they came to Jesus, and saw him that was possessed with the devil, and had the Legion, sitting, and clothed, and in his right mind; and they were afraid.

13 And they that saw the miracle, told them that came out, how it befell him that was possessed with the devil, and how the devil was cast out, and concerning the swine.

14 And they began immediately to pray him to depart out of their coasts.

15 And when he was come into the ship, he that had been possessed with the devil, spoke to Jesus, and prayed him that he might be with him.

16 Howbeit, Jesus suffered him not, but said unto him, Go home to thy friends and tell them how great things the Lord hath done for thee, and hath had compassion on thee.

17 And he departed, and began to publish in Decapolis, how great things Jesus had done for him; and all that heard him did marvel.

18 And when Jesus had passed over again by ship unto the other side, much people gathered unto him; and he was nigh unto the sea.

19 And behold there cometh one of the rulers of the synagogue, Jairus by name; and when he saw him he fell at his feet, and besought him greatly, saying, My little daughter lieth at the point of death; come and lay thy hands on her that she may be healed; and she shall live.

20 And he went with him; and much people followed him and thronged him.

21 And a certain woman, which had an issue of blood twelve years, and had suffered many things of many physicians, and had spent all that she had, and was nothing bettered but rather grew worse; when she had heard of Jesus, she came in the press behind, and touched his garment; for she said, If I may touch but his clothes, I shall be whole.

22 And straightway the fountain of her blood was dried up; and she felt in her body that she was healed of that plague.

23 And Jesus, immediately knowing in himself that virtue had gone out of him, turned him about in the press and said, Who touched my clothes?

24 And his disciples said unto him, Thou seest the multitude thronging thee, and sayest thou, Who touched me?

25 And he looked round about to see her that had done this thing; but the woman, fearing and trembling, knowing what was done in her, came and fell down before him, and told him all the truth.

26 And he said unto her, Daughter, thy faith hath made thee whole; go in peace, and be whole of thy plague.

27 While he yet spake, there came from the ruler of the synagogue's house, a man who said, Thy daughter is dead; why troublest thou the Master any further?

28 As soon as he spake, Jesus heard the word that was spoken, and said unto the ruler of the synagogue, Be not afraid, only believe.

29 And he suffered no man to follow him, save Peter, and James, and John the brother of James.

30 And he cometh to the house of the ruler of the synagogue, and seeth the

tumult, and them that wept and wailed greatly.

31 And when he was come in he said unto them, Why make ye this ado, and weep? The damsel is not dead, but sleepeth. And they laughed him to scorn.

32 But when he had put them all out, he taketh the father and the mother of the damsel, and them that were with him, and entereth in where the damsel was lying;

33 And he took the damsel by the hand, and said unto her, Talitha cumi; which is, being interpreted, Damsel, I say unto thee, Arise.

34 And straightway the damsel arose and walked; for she was twelve years old. And they were astonished with a great astonishment.

35 And he charged them straitly that no man should know it; and commanded that something should be given her to eat.

## CHAPTER 6
*The twelve called and sent out—The five loaves and two fishes.*

1 And he went out from thence, and came into his own country; and his disciples followed him.

2 And when the Sabbath day was come, he began to teach in the synagogue; and many hearing, were astonished at his words, saying, From whence hath this man these things?

3 And what wisdom is this that is given unto him, that even such mighty works are wrought by his hands?

4 Is not this the carpenter, the son of Mary, the brother of James, and Joses, and of Judah and Simon?

5 And are not his sisters here with us? And they were offended at him.

6 But Jesus said unto them, A prophet is not without honor, save in his own country, and among his own kin, and in his own house.

7 And he could do no mighty work there, save that he laid his hands upon a few sick folk and they were healed.

8 And he marveled because of their unbelief. And he went round about the villages, teaching.

9 And he called the twelve, and began to send them forth by two and two; and gave them power over unclean spirits; and commanded them that they should take nothing for their journey, save a staff only; no scrip, nor bread, nor money in their purse; but should be shod with sandals, and not take two coats.

10 And he said unto them, In whatsoever place ye enter into a house, there abide till ye depart from that place.

11 And whosoever shall not receive you, nor hear you; when ye depart thence shake off the dust of your feet for a testimony against them.

12 Verily I say unto you, it shall be more tolerable for Sodom and Gomorrah in the day of judgment, than for that city.

13 And they went out, and preached that men should repent.

14 And they cast out many devils, and anointed with oil many that were sick, and they were healed.

15 And King Herod heard of Jesus; for his name was spread abroad; and he said, That John the Baptist was risen from the dead, and therefore, mighty works do show forth themselves in him.

16 Others said, That it is Elias; and others said, That it is a prophet, or as one of the prophets.

17 But when Herod heard of him, he said, It is John whom I beheaded; he is risen from the dead.

18 For Herod himself had sent forth and laid hold upon John, and bound him in prison for Herodias' sake, his brother Philip's wife; for he had married her.

19 For John had said unto Herod, It is not lawful for thee to have thy brother's wife.

20 Therefore Herodias had a quarrel against him, and would have killed him; but she could not.

21 For Herod feared John, knowing that he was a just man, and a holy man, and one who feared God and observed to worship him; and when he heard him he did many things for him, and heard him gladly.

22 But when Herod's birthday was come, he made a supper for his lords, high captains, and the chief priests of Galilee.

23 And when the daughter of Herodias came in, and danced, and pleased Herod and them that sat with him, the king said unto the damsel, Ask of me whatsoever thou wilt, and I will give it thee.

24 And he sware unto her, Whatso-

ever thou shalt ask of me, I will give it thee, unto the half of my kingdom.

25 And she went forth, and said unto her mother, What shall I ask? and she said, The head of John the Baptist.

26 And she came in straightway with haste unto the king, and asked, saying, I will that thou give me, by and by, in a charger, the head of John the Baptist.

27 And the king was exceeding sorry; but for his oath's sake, and for their sakes which sat with him, he would not reject her.

28 And immediately the king sent an executioner, and commanded his head to be brought; and he went and beheaded him in the prison.

29 And brought his head in a charger, and gave it to the damsel; and the damsel gave it to her mother.

30 And when John's disciples heard of it, they came and took up his corpse and laid it in a tomb.

31 Now the apostles gathered themselves together unto Jesus, and told him all things; both what they had done, and what they had taught.

32 And he said unto them, Come ye yourselves apart into a solitary place, and rest a while; for there were many coming and going, and they had no leisure, not so much as to eat.

33 And they departed into a solitary place by ship, privately.

34 And the people saw them departing; and many knew Jesus, and ran afoot thither out of all cities, and outran them, and came together unto him.

35 And Jesus when he came out, saw much people, and was moved with compassion towards them, because they were as sheep not having a shepherd; and he began to teach them many things.

36 And when the day was now far spent, his disciples came unto him and said, This is a solitary place, and now the time for departure is come, send them away, that they may go into the country round about, and into the villages, and buy themselves bread; for they have nothing to eat.

37 And he answered and said unto them, Give ye them to eat.

38 And they said unto him, Shall we go and buy two hundred pennyworth of bread, and give them to eat?

39 He said unto them, How many loaves have ye? Go and see.

40 And when they knew, they say, Five, and two fishes.

41 And he commanded them to make all sit down by companies, upon the green grass.

42 And they sat down in ranks, by hundreds, and by fifties.

43 And when he had taken the five loaves and two fishes, he looked up to heaven, and blessed, and broke the loaves, and gave to his disciples to set before the multitude; and the two fishes divided he among them all.

44 And they did all eat and were filled.

45 And they took up twelve baskets full of the fragments, and of the fishes.

46 And they that did eat of the loaves, were about five thousand men.

47 And straightway he constrained his disciples to get into the ship, and to go to the other side before him, unto Bethsaida, while he sent away the people.

48 And when he had sent them away, he departed into a mountain to pray.

49 And when even was come, the ship was in the midst of the sea, and he alone on the land, and he saw them toiling in rowing; for the wind was contrary unto them.

50 And about the fourth watch of the night he cometh unto them, walking upon the sea, as if he would have passed by them.

51 And when they saw him walking upon the sea, they supposed it had been a spirit, and cried out;

52 For they all saw him, and were troubled.

53 And immediately he talked with them, and said unto them, Be of good cheer; it is I; be not afraid.

54 And he went up unto them into the ship; and the wind ceased; and they were sore amazed in themselves beyond measure, and wondered.

55 For they considered not of the loaves; for their hearts were hardened.

56 And when they had passed over, they came into the land of Gennesaret, and drew to the shore.

57 And when they were come out of the ship, straightway the people knew him, and ran through the whole region round about, and began to carry about

in beds, those that were sick, where they heard he was.

58 And whithersoever he entered, into villages, or cities, or country, they laid the sick in the streets, and besought him that they might touch if it were but the border of his garment; and as many as touched him were made whole.

## CHAPTER 7

*What defileth a man—The Syrophoeni-cian woman's child healed.*

1 Then came together unto him, the Pharisees, and certain of the scribes, which came from Jerusalem.

2 And when they saw some of his disciples eat bread with defiled (that is to say, with unwashen) hands, they found fault.

3 For the Pharisees, and all the Jews, except they wash hands oft, eat not; holding the tradition of the elders.

4 And when they come from the market, except they wash their bodies, they eat not.

5 And many other things there be, which they have received to hold, as the washing of cups, and pots, brazen vessels, and of tables.

6 And the Pharisees and scribes asked him, Why walk not thy disciples according to the traditions of the elders, but eat bread with unwashen hands?

7 He answered and said unto them, Well hath Isaiah prophesied of you hypocrites, as it is written, This people honoreth me with their lips, but their heart is far from me. Howbeit, in vain do they worship me, teaching the doctrines and commandments of men.

8 For laying aside the commandment of God, ye hold the tradition of men; the washing of pots and of cups; and many other such like things ye do.

9 And he said unto them, Yea, altogether ye reject the commandment of God, that ye may keep your own tradition.

10 Full well is it written of you, by the prophets whom ye have rejected.

11 They testified these things of a truth, and their blood shall be upon you.

12 Ye have kept not the ordinances of God; for Moses said, Honor thy father and thy mother; and whoso curseth father or mother, let him die the death of the transgressor, as it is written in your law; but ye keep not the law.

13 Ye say, If a man shall say to his father or mother, Corban, that is to say, a gift, by whatsoever thou mightest be profited by me, he is of age. And ye suffer him no more to do aught for his father or his mother; making the word of God of none effect through your tradition, which ye have delivered; and many such like things do ye.

14 And when he had called all the people, he said unto them, Hearken unto me every one, and understand;

15 There is nothing from without, that entering into a man, can defile him, which is food; but the things which come out of him; those are they that defile the man, that proceedeth forth out of the heart.

16 If any man have ears to hear, let him hear.

17 And when he was entered into the house from among the people, his disciples asked him concerning the parable.

18 And he said unto them, Are ye without understanding also? Do ye not perceive, that whatsoever thing from without entereth into the man, cannot defile him; because it entereth not into his heart, but into the belly, and goeth out into the draught, purging all meats?

19 And he said, That which cometh out of a man, defileth the man.

20 For from within, out of the hearts of men, proceed evil thoughts, adulteries, fornications, murders, thefts, covetousness, wickedness, deceit, lasciviousness, an evil eye, blasphemy, pride, foolishness;

21 All these evil things come from within, and defile the man.

22 And from thence he arose, and went into the borders of Tyre and Sidon, and entered into a house, and would that no man should come unto him.

23 But he could not deny them; for he had compassion upon all men.

24 For a woman, whose young daughter had an unclean spirit, heard of him and came and fell at his feet.

25 The woman was a Greek, a Syrophoenician by nation; and she besought him that he would cast forth the devil out of her daughter.

26 But Jesus said unto her, Let the children of the kingdom first be filled;

for it is not meet to take the children's bread, and to cast it unto the dogs.

27 And she answered and said unto him, Yes, Lord; thou sayest truly, yet the dogs under the table eat of the children's crumbs.

28 And he said unto her, For this saying, go thy way; the devil is gone out of thy daughter.

29 And when she was come to her house, she found that the devil had gone out, and her daughter was laid upon the bed.

30 And again, departing from the coasts of Tyre and Sidon, he came unto the sea of Galilee, through the midst of the coasts of Decapolis.

31 And they brought unto him one that was deaf, and had an impediment in his speech; and they besought him to put his hand upon him.

32 And he took him aside from the multitude, and put his fingers into his ears, and he spit and touched his tongue;

33 And looking up to heaven, he sighed, and said unto him, Ephphatha, that is, Be opened.

34 And straightway his ears were opened, and the string of his tongue was loosed; and he spake plain.

35 And he charged them that they should tell no man; but the more he charged them, so much the more a great deal they published him;

36 And were beyond measure astonished, saying, He hath done all things well; he maketh both the deaf to hear, and the dumb to speak.

## CHAPTER 8

*Feeding the multitude—Healing the blind man—Self-denial taught.*

1 In those days, the multitude being very great, and having nothing to eat, Jesus called his disciples, and said unto them,

2 I have compassion on the multitude, because they have now been with me three days, and have nothing to eat; and if I send them away fasting to their own houses, they will faint by the way; for divers of them came from afar.

3 And his disciples answered him, From whence can a man satisfy these, so great a multitude, with bread, here in the wilderness?

4 And he asked them, How many loaves have ye? and they said, Seven.

5 And he commanded the people to sit down on the ground; and he took the seven loaves, and gave thanks, and brake, and gave to his disciples to set before the people; and they did set them before the people.

6 And they had a few small fishes; and he blessed them, and commanded to set them also before the people, that they should eat.

7 So they did eat, and were filled, and they took up of the broken bread that was left, seven baskets.

8 And they that had eaten were about four thousand; and he sent them away.

9 And straightway he entered into a ship with his disciples, and came into the parts of Dalmanutha.

10 And the Pharisees came forth, and began to question with him, seeking of him a sign from heaven, tempting him.

11 And he sighed deeply in his spirit, and said, Why doth this generation seek after a sign?

12 Verily I say unto you, There shall no sign be given unto this generation, save the sign of the prophet Jonah; for as Jonah was three days and three nights in the whale's belly, so likewise shall the Son of man be buried in the bowels of the earth.

13 And he left them, and entering into the ship again, he departed to the other side.

14 Now the multitude had forgotten to take bread; neither had they, in the ship with them, more than one loaf.

15 And he charged them, saying, Take heed, and beware of the leaven of the Pharisees, and the leaven of Herod.

16 And they reasoned among themselves, saying, He hath said this, because we have no bread.

17 And when they said this among themselves, Jesus knew it, and he said unto them,

18 Why reason ye because ye have no bread? Perceive ye not yet, neither understand ye? Are your hearts yet hardened?

19 Having eyes, see ye not? And having ears, hear ye not? And do ye not remember?

20 When I brake the five loaves among the five thousand, how many baskets full of fragments took ye up? They say unto him, Twelve.

21 And when the seven among the four thousand, how many baskets full of fragments took ye up? And they said, Seven.

22 And he said unto them, How is it that ye do not understand?

23 And he cometh to Bethsaida; and they bring a blind man unto him, and besought him to touch him.

24 And he took the blind man by the hand, and led him out of the town; and when he had spit upon his eyes, and put his hands upon him, he asked him if he saw aught.

25 And he looked up and said, I see men as trees walking.

26 After that he put his hands again upon his eyes, and made him look up; and he was restored and saw every man clearly.

27 And he sent him away to his house, saying, Neither go into the town, nor tell what is done, to any in the town.

28 And Jesus went out, and his disciples, into the towns of Caesarea Philippi; and by the way he asked his disciples, saying unto them, Whom do men say that I am?

29 And they answered, John the Baptist; but some say, Elias; and others, One of the prophets.

30 And he said unto them, But whom say ye that I am?

31 And Peter answered and said unto him, Thou art the Christ, the Son of the living God.

32 And he charged them that they should tell no man of him.

33 And he began to teach them, that the Son of man must suffer many things, and be rejected of the elders, and the chief priests, and scribes, and be killed, and after three days rise again.

34 And he spake that saying openly. And Peter took him, and began to rebuke him.

35 But when he had turned about and looked on his disciples, he rebuked Peter, saying, Get thee behind me, Satan; for thou savorest not the things that be of God, but the things that be of men.

36 And when he had called the people, with his disciples also, he said unto them, Whosoever will come after me, let him deny himself, and take up his cross, and follow me.

37 For whosoever will save his life, shall lose it; or whosoever will save his life, shall be willing to lay it down for my sake; and if he is not willing to lay it down for my sake, he shall lose it.

38 But whosoever shall be willing to lose his life for my sake, and the gospel, the same shall save it.

39 For what shall it profit a man if he shall gain the whole world, and lose his own soul? Or what shall a man give in exchange for his soul?

40 Therefore deny yourselves of these, and be not ashamed of me.

41 Whosoever shall be ashamed of me, and of my words, in this adulterous and sinful generation, of him also shall the Son of man be ashamed, when he cometh in the glory of his Father with the holy angels.

42 And they shall not have part in that resurrection when he cometh.

43 For verily I say unto you, That he shall come; and he that layeth down his life for my sake and the gospel's, shall come with him, and shall be clothed with his glory in the cloud, on the right hand of the Son of man.

44 And he said unto them again, Verily I say unto you, That there be some of them that stand here, which shall not taste of death, till they have seen the kingdom of God come with power.

## CHAPTER 9

*Transfiguration–Elias–Offending members to be cut off.*

1 And after six days Jesus taketh Peter, and James, and John, who asked him many questions concerning his sayings; and Jesus leadeth them up into a high mountain apart by themselves. And he was transfigured before them.

2 And his raiment became shining, exceeding white, as snow; so white as no fuller on earth could whiten them.

3 And there appeared unto them Elias with Moses, or in other words, John the Baptist and Moses; and they were talking with Jesus.

4 And Peter answered and said to Jesus, Master, it is good for us to be here; and let us make three tabernacles; one for thee, and one for Moses, and one for Elias; for he knew not what to say; for they were sore afraid.

5 And there was a cloud that overshadowed them; and a voice came out

of the cloud, saying, This is my beloved Son; hear him.

6 And suddenly, when they had looked round about with great astonishment, they saw no man any more, save Jesus only, with themselves. And immediately they departed.

7 And as they came down from the mountain, he charged them that they should tell no man what things they had seen till the Son of man was risen from the dead.

8 And they kept that saying with themselves, questioning one with another what the rising from the dead should mean.

9 And they asked him, saying, Why say the scribes that Elias must first come?

10 And he answered and told them saying, Elias verily cometh first, and prepareth all things; and teacheth you of the prophets; how it is written of the Son of man, that he must suffer many things, and be set at naught.

11 Again I say unto you, That Elias is indeed come, but they have done unto him whatsoever they listed; and even as it is written of him; and he bore record of me, and they received him not. Verily this was Elias.

12 And when he came to the disciples, he saw a great multitude about them, and the scribes questioning with them.

13 And straightway all the people, when they beheld him, were greatly amazed, and running to him, saluted him.

14 And Jesus asked the scribes, What questioned ye with them?

15 And one of the multitude answered, and said, Master, I have brought unto thee my son, who hath a dumb spirit that is a devil; and when he seizeth him, he teareth him; and he foameth and gnasheth with his teeth, and pineth away; and I spake to thy disciples that they might cast him out, and they could not.

16 Jesus spake unto him and said, O faithless generation! how long shall I be with you? How long shall I suffer you? Bring him unto me. And they brought him unto Jesus.

17 And when the man saw him, immediately he was torn by the spirit; and he fell on the ground and wallowed, foaming.

18 And Jesus asked his father, How long a time is it since this came unto him? and his father said, When a child;

19 And ofttimes it hath cast him into the fire and into the waters, to destroy him, but if thou canst, I ask thee to have compassion on us, and help us.

20 Jesus said unto him, If thou wilt believe all things I shall say unto you, this is possible to him that believeth.

21 And immediately the father of the child cried out, and said, with tears, Lord, I believe; help thou mine unbelief.

22 When Jesus saw that the people came running together, he rebuked the foul spirit, saying unto him, I charge thee to come out of him, and enter no more into him.

23 Now the dumb and deaf spirit cried, and rent him sore, and came out of him; and he was as one dead, insomuch that many said, He is dead.

24 But Jesus took him by the hand, and lifted him up; and he arose.

25 When Jesus was come into the house, his disciples asked him privately, Why could not we cast him out?

26 And he said unto them, This kind can come forth by nothing but by prayer and fasting.

27 And they departed thence, and passed through Galilee privately; for he would not that any man should know it.

28 And he taught his disciples, and said unto them, The Son of man is delivered into the hands of men, and they shall kill him; and after that he is killed, he shall rise the third day.

29 But they understood not that saying, and were afraid to ask him.

30 And he came to Capernaum; and being in the house, he asked them, Why was it that ye disputed among yourselves by the way?

31 But they held their peace, being afraid, for by the way they had disputed among themselves, who was the greatest among them.

32 Now Jesus sat down and called the twelve, and said unto them, If any man desire to be first, he shall be last of all, and servant of all.

33 And he took a child, and sat in the midst of them; and when he had taken the child in his arms, he said unto them,

34 Whosoever shall humble himself

like one of these children, and receiveth me, ye shall receive in my name.

35 And whosoever shall receive me, receiveth not me only, but him that sent me, even the Father.

36 And John spake unto him, saying, Master, we saw one casting out devils in thy name, and he followed not us; and we forbade him, because he followed not us.

37 But Jesus said, Forbid him not; for there is no man which shall do a miracle in my name, that can speak evil of me. For he that is not against us is on our part.

38 And whosoever shall give you a cup of water to drink, in my name, because ye belong to Christ, verily I say unto you, He shall not lose his reward.

39 And whosoever shall offend one of these little ones that believe in me, it is better for him that a millstone were hanged about his neck, and he were cast into the sea.

40 Therefore, if thy hand offend thee, cut it off; or if thy brother offend thee and confess not and forsake not, he shall be cut off. It is better for thee to enter into life maimed, than having two hands, to go into hell.

41 For it is better for thee to enter into life without thy brother, than for thee and thy brother to be cast into hell; into the fire that never shall be quenched, where their worm dieth not, and the fire is not quenched.

42 And again, if thy foot offend thee, cut it off; for he that is thy standard, by whom thou walkest, if he become a transgressor, he shall be cut off.

43 It is better for thee, to enter halt into life, than having two feet to be cast into hell; into the fire that never shall be quenched.

44 Therefore, let every man stand or fall, by himself, and not for another; or not trusting another.

45 Seek unto my Father, and it shall be done in that very moment what ye shall ask, if ye ask in faith, believing that ye shall receive.

46 And if thine eye which seeth for thee, him that is appointed to watch over thee to show thee light, become a transgressor and offend thee, pluck him out.

47 It is better for thee to enter into the kingdom of God, with one eye, than having two eyes to be cast into hell fire.

48 For it is better that thyself should be saved, than to be cast into hell with thy brother, where their worm dieth not, and where the fire is not quenched.

49 For every one shall be salted with fire; and every sacrifice shall be salted with salt; but the salt must be good.

50 For if the salt have lost his saltness, wherewith will ye season it? (the sacrifice;) therefore it must needs be that ye have salt in yourselves, and have peace one with another.

## CHAPTER 10

*Of divorcement—Blessing of children—Deceitfulness of riches—Reward of the saints—Self-denial—Self-exaltation—Blind Bartimeus.*

1 And he arose from thence and cometh into the coasts of Judea by the farther side of Jordan; and the people resort unto him again; and as he was accustomed to teach, he also taught them again.

2 And the Pharisees came to him and asked him, Is it lawful for a man to put away his wife? This they said, thinking to tempt him.

3 And he answered and said unto them, What did Moses command you?

4 And they said, Moses suffered to write a bill of divorcement, and to put her away.

5 Jesus answered and said unto them, For the hardness of your hearts he wrote you this precept;

6 But from the beginning of the creation, God made them male and female.

7 For this cause shall a man leave his father, and mother, and cleave to his wife; and they twain shall be one flesh; so then they are no more twain but one flesh; what therefore God hath joined together, let not man put asunder.

8 And in the house his disciples asked him again of the same matter.

9 And he said unto them, Whosoever shall put away his wife, and marry another, committeth adultery against her.

10 And if a woman shall put away her husband, and be married to another, she committeth adultery.

11 And they brought young children to him, that he should touch them; and the disciples rebuked those that brought them.

12 But when Jesus saw and heard them, he was much displeased, and

said unto them, Suffer the little children to come unto me, and forbid them not; for of such is the kingdom of God.

13 Verily I say unto you, Whosoever shall not receive the kingdom of God as a little child, he shall not enter therein.

14 And he took them up in his arms, and put his hands upon them, and blessed them.

15 And when he was gone forth into the way, there came one running, and kneeled to him, and asked him, Good Master, what shall I do that I may inherit eternal life?

16 And Jesus said unto him, Why callest thou me good? None is good but one, that is God.

17 Thou knowest the commandments, Do not commit adultery; Do not kill; Do not steal; Do not bear false witness; Defraud not; Honor thy father and mother.

18 And the man answered and said unto him, Master, all these have I observed from my youth.

19 Then Jesus beholding him, loved him, and said unto him, One thing thou lackest;

20 Go thy way, sell whatsoever thou hast, and give to the poor, and thou shalt have treasure in heaven; and come, take up the cross, and follow me.

21 And the man was sad at that saying, and went away grieved; for he had great possessions.

22 And Jesus looked round about, and said unto his disciples, How hardly shall they that have riches enter into the kingdom of my Father!

23 And the disciples were astonished at his words. But Jesus spake again, and said unto them, Children, how hard is it for them who trust in riches to enter into the kingdom of God!

24 It is easier for a camel to go through the eye of a needle, than for a rich man to enter into the kingdom of God.

25 And they were astonished out of measure, saying among themselves, Who then can be saved?

26 And Jesus, looking upon them, said, With men that trust in riches, it is impossible; but not impossible with men who trust in God and leave all for my sake, for with such all these things are possible.

27 Then Peter began to say unto him, Lo, we have left all, and have followed thee.

28 And Jesus answered and said, Verily I say unto you, There is no man that hath left house, or brethren, or sisters, or father, or mother, or wife, or children, or lands, for my sake and the gospel's,

29 But he shall receive a hundredfold now in this time, houses, and brethren, and sisters, and mothers, and children, and lands, with persecutions; and in the world to come, eternal life.

30 But there are many who make themselves first, that shall be last, and the last first.

31 This he said, rebuking Peter; and they were in the way going up to Jerusalem; and Jesus went before, and they were amazed; and as they followed, they were afraid.

32 And he took again the twelve, and began to tell them what things should happen unto him.

33 And Jesus said, Behold, we go up to Jerusalem; and the Son of man shall be delivered unto the chief priests, and unto the scribes; and they shall condemn him to death; and shall deliver him to the Gentiles.

34 And they shall mock him, and shall scourge him, and shall spit upon him, and shall kill him; and the third day he shall rise again.

35 And James, and John, the sons of Zebedee, came unto him, saying, Master, we would that thou shouldest do for us whatsoever we shall desire.

36 And he said unto them, What will ye that I should do unto you?

37 They said unto him, Grant unto us that we may sit, one on thy right hand, and the other on thy left hand, in thy glory.

38 But Jesus said unto them, Ye know not what ye ask. Can ye drink of the cup that I drink of? And be baptized with the baptism that I am baptized with?

39 And they said unto him, We can.

40 And Jesus said unto them, Ye shall indeed drink of the cup that I drink of; and be baptized with the baptism that I am baptized with; but to sit on my right hand, and on my left hand, is not mine to give; but they shall receive it for whom it is prepared.

41 And when the ten heard, they

began to be much displeased with James and John.

42 But Jesus called them, and said unto them, Ye know that they who are appointed to rule over the Gentiles exercise lordship over them; and their great ones exercise authority upon them.

43 But it shall not be so among you; but whosoever will be great among you, shall be your minister.

44 And whosoever of you will be the chiefest, shall be servant of all.

45 For even the Son of man came, not to be ministered unto, but to minister, and to give his life a ransom for many.

46 And they came to Jericho; and as he went out of Jericho with his disciples and a great number of people, blind Bartimeus, the son of Timeus, sat by the highway side begging.

47 And when he heard that it was Jesus of Nazareth, he began to cry out, and say, Jesus, Son of David, have mercy on me.

48 And many charged him that he should hold his peace; but he cried the more exceedingly, saying, Son of David, have mercy on me.

49 And Jesus stood still, and commanded him to be called. And they called the blind man, saying unto him, Be of good comfort; arise, he calleth thee.

50 And he, casting away his garment, arose and came to Jesus.

51 And Jesus said unto him, What wilt thou that I should do unto thee?

52 And the blind man said unto him, Lord, that I might receive my sight.

53 And Jesus said unto him, Go thy way; thy faith hath made thee whole.

54 And immediately he received his sight, and followed Jesus in the way.

## CHAPTER 11

*Christ's entry into Jerusalem—He driveth out the money changers and teaches in the Temple—He teacheth forgiveness.*

1 And when they came nigh to Jerusalem, unto Bethphage and Bethany, at the mount of Olives, he sendeth forth two of his disciples, and said unto them,

2 Go your way into the village over against you; and as soon as ye have entered into it, ye shall find a colt tied, whereon no man ever sat; loose him and bring him to me.

3 And if any man say unto you, Why do ye this? say ye that the Lord hath need of him; and straightway he will send him hither.

4 And they went their way, and found the colt tied by the door without, in a place where two ways met; and they loosed him.

5 And certain of them who stood by, said unto the disciples, Why loose ye the colt?

6 And they said unto them even as Jesus had commanded; and they let them go.

7 And they brought the colt to Jesus, and cast their garments on it; and Jesus sat upon it.

8 And many spread their garments in the way; and others cut down branches of trees, and strewed them in the way.

9 And they that went before him, and they that followed after, cried, saying,

10 Hosanna! Blessed is he that cometh in the name of the Lord;

11 That bringeth the kingdom of our father David;

12 Blessed is he that cometh in the name of the Lord; Hosanna in the highest.

13 And Jesus entered into Jerusalem, and into the temple. And when he had looked round about upon all things, and blessed the disciples, the eventide was come; and he went out unto Bethany with the twelve.

14 And on the morrow, when they came from Bethany he was hungry; and seeing a fig tree afar off having leaves, he came to it with his disciples; and as they supposed, he came to it to see if he might find anything thereon.

15 And when he came to it, there was nothing but leaves; for as yet the figs were not ripe.

16 And Jesus spake and said unto it, No man eat fruit of thee hereafter, forever. And the disciples heard him.

17 And they came to Jerusalem. And Jesus went into the temple, and began to cast out them that sold and bought in the temple, and overthrew the tables of the money changers, and the seats of them who sold doves;

18 And would not suffer that any man should carry a vessel through the temple.

19 And he taught, saying unto them, Is it not written, My house shall be

called of all nations the house of prayer? But ye have made it a den of thieves.

20 And the scribes and chief priests heard him, and sought how they might destroy him; for they feared him because all the people were astonished at his doctrine.

21 And when even was come he went out of the city.

22 And in the morning as they passed by, they saw the fig tree dried up from the roots.

23 And Peter calling to remembrance, said unto him, Master, behold the fig tree which thou cursedst is withered away.

24 And Jesus spake and said unto him, Have faith in God.

25 For verily I say unto you, That whosoever shall say unto this mountain, Be thou removed, and be thou cast into the sea; and shall not doubt in his heart, but shall believe that those things which he saith shall come to pass; he shall have whatsoever he saith fulfilled.

26 Therefore I say unto you, Whatsoever things ye desire, when ye pray, believe that ye receive, and ye shall have whatsoever ye ask.

27 And when ye stand praying, forgive if ye have aught against any; that your Father also who is in heaven, may forgive you your trespasses.

28 But if you do not forgive, neither will your Father who is in heaven forgive your trespasses.

29 And they came again to Jerusalem; and as he was walking in the temple, there came to him the chief priests, and the scribes, and the elders, and said unto him,

30 By what authority doest thou these things, and who gave thee this authority to do these things?

31 And Jesus answered and said unto them, I will also ask of you one question, answer me, and then I will tell you by what authority I do these things.

32 Was the baptism of John from heaven, or of man? Answer me.

33 And they reasoned with themselves, saying, If we shall say, From heaven; he will say, Why then did ye not believe him?

34 But if we shall say, Of men; we shall offend the people. Therefore they feared the people; for all people believed John, that he was a prophet indeed.

35 And they answered and said unto Jesus, We cannot tell.

36 And Jesus answering said unto them, Neither do I tell you by what authority I do these things.

## CHAPTER 12

*Parable of the vineyard—Tribute money—Neither marrying nor giving in marriage in the resurrection—The great commandment—Widow's mite.*

1 And Jesus began to speak unto them by parables, saying,

2 A man planted a vineyard, and set a hedge about it, and digged the wine vat, and built a tower, and let it out to husbandmen, and went into a far country.

3 And at the season he sent to the husbandmen a servant, that he might receive from the husbandmen of the fruit of the vineyard.

4 And they caught the servant, and beat him, and sent him away empty.

5 And again he sent unto them another servant; and at him they cast stones, and wounded him in the head, and sent him away shamefully handled.

6 And again he sent another; and him they killed, and many others; beating some, and killing some.

7 Having yet therefore one son, his well beloved, he sent him also last unto them, saying, They will reverence my son.

8 But those husbandmen said among themselves, This is the heir; come, let us kill him, and the inheritance shall be ours.

9 And they took him and cast him out of the vineyard, and killed him.

10 What shall therefore the lord of the vineyard do? Lo, he will come and destroy the husbandmen, and will give the vineyard unto others.

11 Again, have ye not read this scripture; The stone which the builders rejected, is become the head of the corner; this was the Lord's doing, and it is marvelous in our eyes.

12 And now they were angry when they heard these words; and they sought to lay hold on him, but feared the people.

13 For they knew that he had spoken the parable against them; and they left him and went their way.

14 And they sent unto him certain of the Pharisees and of the Herodians, to catch him in his words.

15 And when they were come, they said unto him, Master, we know that thou art true and carest for no man; for thou regardest not the person of men, but teachest the way of God in truth.

16 Is it lawful to give tribute to Caesar, or not? Shall we give, or shall we not give?

17 But he knowing their hypocrisy, said unto them, Why tempt ye me? Bring me a penny that I may see it.

18 And they brought the penny; and he said unto them; Whose image and superscription is this?

19 And they said unto him, Caesar's.

20 And Jesus answering said unto them, Render to Caesar the things which are Caesar's; and to God the things that are God's.

21 And they marveled at it.

22 Then came unto him the Sadducees, who say there is no resurrection; and they asked him, saying,

23 Master, Moses wrote unto us in his law, If a man's brother die, and leave a wife, and leave no children, that his brother should take his wife, and raise up seed unto his brother.

24 Now there were seven brethren; and the first took a wife, and dying left no seed.

25 And the second took her, and died, neither left he any seed; and the third likewise.

26 And the seven had her, and left no seed; last of all the woman died also.

27 In the resurrection therefore, when they shall rise, whose wife shall she be of them, for the seven had her to wife?

28 And Jesus answering said unto them, Ye do err therefore, because ye know not, and understand not the scriptures, neither the power of God.

29 For when they shall rise from the dead, they neither marry, nor are given in marriage; but are as the angels of God who are in heaven.

30 And as touching the dead, that they rise; have ye not read in the book of Moses, how in the bush, God spake unto him, saying,

31 I am the God of Abraham, and the God of Isaac, and the God of Jacob?

32 He is not therefore the God of the dead, but the God of the living; for he raiseth them up out of their graves. Ye therefore do greatly err.

33 And one of the scribes came, and having heard them reasoning together, and perceiving that he had answered them well, asked him, Which is the first commandment of all?

34 And Jesus answered him, The first of all the commandments is: Hearken, and hear, O Israel; The Lord our God is one Lord;

35 And thou shalt love the Lord thy God with all thy heart, and with all thy soul, and with all thy mind, and with all thy strength.

36 This is the first commandment. And the second is like this, Thou shalt love thy neighbor as thyself. There is none other commandment greater than these.

37 And the scribe said unto him, Well, Master, thou hast said the truth; for there is one God, and there is none other but him.

38 And to love him with all the heart, and with all the understanding, and with all the soul, and with all the strength; and to love his neighbor as himself, is more than all whole burnt offerings and sacrifices.

39 And when Jesus saw that he answered discreetly, he said unto him, Thou art not far from the kingdom of God.

40 And no man after that durst ask him, saying, Who art thou?

41 And Jesus spake and said, while he taught in the temple, How say the scribes that Christ is the Son of David?

42 For David himself said by the Holy Ghost, The Lord said unto my Lord, Sit thou on my right hand, until I make thine enemies thy footstool.

43 David therefore himself calleth him Lord; and whence is he his son?

44 And the common people heard him gladly; but the high priest and the elders were offended at him.

45 And he said unto them in his doctrine, Beware of the scribes which love to go in long clothing, and have salutations in the marketplaces, and the chief seats in the synagogues, and the uppermost rooms at feasts;

46 Who devour widows' houses, and for a pretense make long prayers; these shall receive greater damnation.

47 And after this, Jesus sat over against the treasury, and beheld how

the people cast money into the treasury; and many that were rich cast in much.

48 And there came a certain poor widow, and she cast in two mites, which make a farthing.

49 And Jesus called his disciples, and said unto them, Verily I say unto you, that this poor widow hath cast more in, than all they who have cast into the treasury;

50 For all the rich did cast in of their abundance; but she, notwithstanding her want, did cast in all that she had; yea, even all her living.

## CHAPTER 13
*The destruction of Jerusalem—Christ's second coming.*

1 And as Jesus went out of the temple, his disciples came to him for to hear him, saying, Master, show us concerning the buildings of the temple.

2 And he said unto them, Behold ye these stones of the temple, and all this great work, and buildings of the temple?

3 Verily I say unto you, they shall be thrown down and left unto the Jews desolate.

4 And Jesus said unto them, See ye not all these things, and do ye not understand them?

5 Verily I say unto you, There shall not be left here upon this temple, one stone upon another, that shall not be thrown down.

6 And Jesus left them and went upon the mount of Olives.

7 And as he sat upon the mount of Olives, the disciples came unto him privately, saying,

8 Tell us, when shall these things be which thou hast said, concerning the destruction of the temple, and the Jews?

9 And what is the sign of thy coming, and of the end of the world, (or the destruction of the wicked, which is the end of the world?)

10 And Jesus answered and said unto them, Take heed that no man deceive you, for many shall come in my name, saying, I am Christ, and shall deceive many.

11 Then shall they deliver you up to be afflicted, and shall kill you, and ye shall be hated of all nations for my name's sake.

12 And then shall many be offended, and shall betray one another; and many false prophets shall arise, and shall deceive many;

13 And because iniquity shall abound, the love of many shall wax cold; but he that shall endure unto the end, the same shall be saved.

14 When ye therefore shall see the abomination of desolation, spoken of by Daniel the prophet concerning the destruction of Jerusalem, then ye shall stand in the holy place. (Whoso readeth let him understand.)

15 Then let them who be in Judea flee into the mountains;

16 And let him who is on the housetop flee, and not return to take anything out of his house;

17 Neither let him who is in the field, return back to take his clothes.

18 And woe unto them that are with child, and unto them that give suck in those days.

19 Therefore pray ye the Lord, that your flight be not in the winter, neither on the Sabbath day.

20 For then, in those days, shall be great tribulation on the Jews, and upon the inhabitants of Jerusalem; such as was not before sent upon Israel, of God, since the beginning of their kingdom, (for it is written their enemies shall scatter them,) until this time; no, nor ever shall be sent again upon Israel.

21 All these things are the beginnings of sorrows.

22 And except those days should be shortened, there should no flesh be saved; but for the elect's sake, according to the covenant, those days shall be shortened.

23 Behold these things I have spoken unto you concerning the Jews.

24 And then immediately after the tribulation of those days which shall come upon Jerusalem, if any man shall say unto you, Lo, here is Christ; or there; believe him not.

25 For in those days there shall also arise false Christs, and false prophets, and shall show great signs and wonders; insomuch, that if possible, they shall deceive the very elect, who are the elect according to the covenant.

26 Behold, I speak these things unto you, for the elect's sake;

27 And ye also shall hear of wars, and rumors of wars; see that ye be not

troubled; for all I have told you must come to pass, but the end is not yet.

28 Behold, I have told you before, wherefore if they shall say unto you, Behold, he is in the desert; go not forth; Behold, he is in the secret chambers; believe it not.

29 For as the light of the morning cometh out of the east, and shineth even unto the west, and covereth the whole earth, so shall also the coming of the Son of man be.

30 And now I show unto you a parable. Behold, wheresoever the carcass is, there will the eagles be gathered together;

31 So likewise, shall mine elect be gathered from the four quarters of the earth.

32 And they shall hear of wars and rumors of wars. Behold, I speak unto you for mine elect's sake.

33 For nation shall rise against nation, and kingdom against kingdom;

34 There shall be famines, and pestilences, and earthquakes in divers places.

35 And again, because iniquity shall abound, the love of men shall wax cold; but he who shall not be overcome, the same shall be saved.

36 And again this gospel of the kingdom shall be preached in all the world, for a witness unto all nations, and then shall the end come, or the destruction of the wicked.

37 And again shall the abomination of desolation, spoken of by Daniel the prophet, be fulfilled.

38 And immediately after the tribulation of those days, the sun shall be darkened, and the moon shall not give her light, and the stars shall fall from heaven, and the powers of heaven shall be shaken.

39 Verily I say unto you, This generation in which these things shall be shown forth, shall not pass away till all I have told you shall be fulfilled.

40 Although the days will come that heaven and earth shall pass away, yet my words shall not pass away, but all shall be fulfilled.

41 And as I said before, After the tribulation of those days, and the powers of the heavens shall be shaken, then shall appear the sign of the Son of man in heaven; and then shall all the tribes of the earth mourn;

42 And they shall see the Son of man coming in the clouds of heaven, with power and great glory.

43 And whoso treasureth up my words shall not be deceived.

44 For the Son of man shall come; and he shall send his angels before him with the great sound of a trumpet, and they shall gather together his elect from the four winds, from one end of heaven to the other.

45 Now learn a parable of the fig tree. When his branches are yet tender, and putteth forth leaves, ye know that summer is nigh at hand.

46 So likewise, mine elect when they shall see all these things, they shall know that he is near, even at the doors.

47 But of that day and hour no one knoweth; no, not the angels of God in heaven, but my Father only.

48 But as it was in the days of Noah, so it shall be also at the coming of the Son of man; for it shall be with them as it was in the days which were before the flood.

49 Until the day that Noah entered into the ark, they were eating and drinking, marrying and giving in marriage, and knew not until the flood came and took them all away; so shall also the coming of the Son of man be.

50 Then shall be fulfilled that which is written, That in the last days, two shall be in the field, one shall be taken and the other left.

51 Two shall be grinding at the mill; the one taken, and the other left.

52 And what I say unto one, I say unto all men.

53 Watch therefore, for ye know not at what hour your Lord doth come.

54 But know this, if the good man of the house had known in what watch the thief would come, he would have watched, and would not have suffered his house to have been broken up; but would have been ready.

55 Therefore, be ye also ready, for in such an hour as ye think not, the Son of man cometh.

56 Who then is a faithful and wise servant, whom his lord hath made ruler over his household, to give them meat in due season?

57 Blessed is that servant whom his lord, when he cometh, shall find so doing.

58 And verily I say unto you, he

shall make him ruler over all his goods.

59 But if that evil servant shall say in his heart, My lord delayeth his coming; and shall begin to smite his fellow servants, and to eat and drink with the drunken;

60 The lord of that servant shall come in a day when he looketh not for him, and in an hour that he is not aware of, and shall cut him asunder, and shall appoint his portion with the hypocrites.

61 There shall be weeping and gnashing of teeth; and thus cometh the end.

## CHAPTER 14

*Christ anointed by the woman—The Passover eaten—Christ's betrayal.*

1 After two days was the passover, and the feast of unleavened bread.

2 And the chief priests, and the scribes, sought how they might take Jesus by craft, and put him to death.

3 But they said among themselves, Let us not take him on the feast day, lest there be an uproar among the people.

4 And Jesus being in Bethany, in the house of Simon the leper, as he sat at meat, there came a woman having an alabaster box of ointment of spikenard, very precious, and she brake the box, and poured the ointment on his head.

5 And there were some among the disciples who had indignation within themselves, and said, Why was this waste of the ointment made? for it might have been sold for more than three hundred pence, and have been given to the poor. And they murmured against her.

6 And Jesus said unto them, Let her alone; why trouble ye her? For she hath wrought a good work on me.

7 Ye have the poor with you always, and whensoever ye will, ye may do them good; but me ye have not always.

8 She has done what she could, and this which she has done unto me, shall be had in remembrance in generations to come, wheresoever my gospel shall be preached; for verily she has come beforehand to anoint my body to the burying.

9 Verily I say unto you, Wheresoever this gospel shall be preached throughout the whole world, what she hath done shall be spoken of also for a memorial of her.

10 And now the first day of unleavened bread, when they killed the passover, his disciples said unto him, Where wilt thou that we go and prepare, that thou mayest eat the passover?

11 And he sendeth forth two of his disciples, and said unto them, Go ye into the city, and there shall meet you a man bearing a pitcher of water; follow him;

12 And wheresoever he shall go in, say ye to the good man of the house, The Master saith, Where is the guest chamber, where I shall eat the passover with my disciples?

13 And he will show you a large upper room, furnished and prepared; there make ready for us.

14 And his disciples went forth and came into the city, and found as he had said unto them; and they made ready the passover.

15 And in the evening he cometh with the twelve.

16 And as they sat and did eat, Jesus said, Verily I say unto you, One of you who eateth with me shall betray me.

17 And they all began to be very sorrowful, and began to say unto him one by one, Is it I? and another said, Is it I?

18 And he answered and said unto them, It is one of the twelve who dippeth with me in the dish.

19 The Son of man indeed goeth as it is written of him; but woe to that man by whom the Son of man is betrayed! Good were it for that man if he had never been born.

20 And as they did eat, Jesus took bread and blessed it, and brake, and gave to them, and said, Take it, and eat.

21 Behold, this is for you to do in remembrance of my body; for as oft as ye do this ye will remember this hour that I was with you.

22 And he took the cup, and when he had given thanks, he gave it to them; and they all drank of it.

23 And he said unto them, This is in remembrance of my blood which is shed for many, and the new testament which I give unto you; for of me ye shall bear record unto all the world.

24 And as oft as ye do this ordi-

nance, ye will remember me in this hour that I was with you and drank with you of this cup, even the last time in my ministry.

25 Verily I say unto you, Of this ye shall bear record; for I will no more drink of the fruit of the vine with you, until that day that I drink it new in the kingdom of God.

26 And now they were grieved, and wept over him.

27 And when they had sung a hymn, they went out into the mount of Olives.

28 And Jesus said unto them, All ye shall be offended because of me this night; for it is written, I will smite the shepherd and the sheep shall be scattered.

29 But after that I am risen, I will go before you into Galilee.

30 And he said unto Judas Iscariot, What thou doest, do quickly; but beware of innocent blood.

31 Nevertheless, Judas Iscariot, even one of the twelve, went unto the chief priests to betray Jesus unto them; for he turned away from him, and was offended because of his words.

32 And when the chief priests heard of him they were glad, and promised to give him money; and he sought how he might conveniently betray Jesus.

33 But Peter said unto Jesus, Although all men shall be offended with thee, yet I will never be offended.

34 And Jesus said unto him, Verily I say unto thee, That this day, even in this night, before the cock crow twice, thou shalt deny me thrice.

35 But he spake the more vehemently. If I should die with thee, yet will I not deny thee in any wise. Likewise also said they all.

36 And they came to a place which was named Gethsemane, which was a garden; and the disciples began to be sore amazed, and to be very heavy, and to complain in their hearts, wondering if this be the Messiah.

37 And Jesus knowing their hearts, said to his disciples, Sit ye here, while I shall pray.

38 And he taketh with him, Peter, and James, and John, and rebuked them, and said unto them, My soul is exceeding sorrowful, even unto death; tarry ye here and watch.

39 And he went forward a little, and fell on the ground, and prayed, that if it were possible the hour might pass from him.

40 And he said, Abba, Father, all things are possible unto thee; take away this cup from me; nevertheless, not my will, but thine be done.

41 And he cometh and findeth them sleeping, and said unto Peter, Simon, sleepest thou? Couldest not thou watch one hour?

42 Watch ye and pray, lest ye enter into temptation.

43 And they said unto him, The spirit truly is ready, but the flesh is weak.

44 And again he went away and prayed, and spake the same words.

45 And when he returned, he found them asleep again, for their eyes were heavy; neither knew they what to answer him.

46 And he cometh to them the third time, and said unto them, Sleep on now and take rest; it is enough, the hour is come; behold, the Son of man is betrayed into the hands of sinners.

47 And after they had finished their sleep, he said, Rise up, let us go; lo, he who betrayeth me is at hand.

48 And immediately while he yet spake, cometh Judas, one of the twelve, and with him a great multitude, with swords and staves, from the chief priests, and the scribes and the elders.

49 And he who betrayed him had given them a token, saying, Whomsoever I shall kiss, that same is he; take him, and lead him away safely.

50 And as soon as he was come, he goeth straightway to him, and said, Master, Master, and kissed him.

51 And they laid their hands on him, and took him.

52 And one of them, who stood by, drew his sword, and smote a servant of the high priest, and cut off his ear.

53 But Jesus commanded him to return his sword, saying, He who taketh the sword shall perish with the sword. And he put forth his finger and healed the servant of the high priest.

54 And Jesus answered and said unto them, Are ye come out as against a thief, with swords and staves to take me?

55 I was daily with you in the temple teaching, and ye took me not; but the scriptures must be fulfilled.

56 And the disciples, when they

heard this saying, all forsook him and fled.

57 And there followed him a certain young man, a disciple, having a linen cloth cast about his naked body; and the young man laid hold on him, and he left the linen cloth and fled from them naked, and saved himself out of their hands.

58 And they led Jesus away to the high priest, and with him were assembled all the chief priests, and the elders and the scribes.

59 And Peter followed him afar off, even unto the palace of the high priest; and he sat with the servants, and warmed himself at the fire.

60 And the chief priests and all the council sought for witness against Jesus, to put him to death, but found none;

61 Though many bare false witness against him, yet their witness agreed not together.

62 And there arose certain men and bare false witness against him, saying, We heard him say, I will destroy this temple that is made with hands, and within three days I will build another made without hands;

63 But neither did their witness agree together.

64 And the high priest stood up in the midst, and asked Jesus, saying,

65 Answerest thou nothing? Knowest thou not what these witness against thee?

66 But he held his peace, and answered nothing.

67 Again the high priest asked him and said unto him, Art thou the Christ, the Son of the Blessed?

68 And Jesus said, I am; and ye shall see the Son of man sitting on the right hand of power, and coming in the clouds of heaven.

69 Then the high priest rent his clothes and said, What need we any further witnesses? Ye have heard the blasphemy; what think ye?

70 And they all condemned him to be guilty of death.

71 And some began to spit on him, and to cover his face, and to buffet him, and to say unto him, Prophesy;

72 And the servants did strike him with the palms of their hands.

73 And as Peter was beneath in the palace, there cometh one of the maids of the high priest,

74 And when she saw Peter warming himself, she looked upon him and said, Thou also wast with Jesus of Nazareth.

75 But he denied, saying, I know not, neither understand I what thou sayest.

76 And he went out into the porch; and the cock crew.

77 And a maid saw him again, and began to say to them who stood by, This is one of them.

78 And he denied it again.

79 And a little after, they who stood by, said again to Peter, Surely thou art one of them; for thou art a Galilean, thy speech agreeth thereto. But he began to curse and to swear, saying, I know not this man of whom ye speak.

80 And the second time the cock crew;

81 And Peter called to mind the words that Jesus said unto him, Before the cock crow twice, thou shalt deny me thrice.

82 And he went out, and fell upon his face, and wept bitterly.

## CHAPTER 15

*Christ's trial, crucifixion, and burial.*

1 And straightway in the morning, the chief priests held a consultation with the elders and scribes;

2 And the whole council condemned him, and bound him, and carried him away, and delivered him to Pilate.

3 And Pilate asked him, Art thou the King of the Jews?

4 And Jesus answering, said unto him, I am, even as thou sayest.

5 And the chief priests accused him of many things; but he answered nothing.

6 And Pilate asked him again, saying, Answerest thou nothing? Behold how many things they witness against thee.

7 But Jesus yet answered nothing; so that Pilate marveled.

8 Now it was common at the feast, for Pilate to release unto them one prisoner, whomsoever they desired.

9 And there was a man named Barabbas, bound with them who had made insurrection with him, who had committed murder in the insurrection.

10 And the multitude, crying aloud began to desire him to deliver Jesus unto them.

11 But Pilate answered unto them,

saying, Will ye that I release unto you the King of the Jews?

12 For he knew that the chief priests had delivered him for envy.

13 But the chief priests moved the people that he should rather release Barabbas unto them, as he had before done unto them.

14 And Pilate spake again and said unto them, What will ye then that I shall do with him whom ye call the King of the Jews?

15 And they cried out again, Deliver him unto us to be crucified. Away with him. Crucify him.

16 Then Pilate said unto them, Why, what evil hath he done?

17 But they cried out the more exceedingly, Crucify him.

18 And now Pilate, willing to content the people, released Barabbas unto them, and delivered Jesus, when he had scourged him, to be crucified.

19 And, the soldiers led him away into the hall called Praetorium; and they called together the whole band;

20 And they clothed him with purple, and platted a crown of thorns and put it upon his head;

21 And began to salute him, Saying, Hail, King of the Jews.

22 And they smote him on the head with a reed, and did spit upon him, and bowing their knees worshiped him.

23 And when they had mocked him, they took off the purple from him, and put his own clothes on him, and led him out to crucify him.

24 And they compelled one Simon, a Cyrenian, who passed by, coming out of the country, the father of Alexander and Rufus, to bear his cross.

25 And they bring him unto the place Golgotha, which is, (being interpreted,) The place of a burial.

26 And they gave him to drink, vinegar mingled with gall; and when he had tasted the vinegar, he would not drink.

27 And when they had crucified him, they parted his garments, casting lots upon them, what every man should take.

28 And it was the third hour, when they crucified him.

29 And Pilate wrote his accusation and put it upon the cross, THE KING OF THE JEWS.

30 There were certain of the chief priests who stood by, and said unto Pilate, Write, that he said, I am the King of the Jews.

31 But Pilate said unto them, What I have written, I have written.

32 And with him they crucified two thieves, the one on his right hand, and the other on his left.

33 And the scripture was fulfilled, which said, And he was numbered with the transgressors.

34 And they who passed by railed on him, wagging their heads, and saying, Ah, thou who destroyest the temple and buildest it in three days, save thyself, and come down from the cross.

35 Likewise also, the chief priests mocking, said among themselves with the scribes, He saved others; himself he cannot save.

36 Let Christ, the King of Israel, descend now from the cross, that we may see and believe.

37 And one of them who was crucified with him, reviled him also, saying, If thou art the Christ, save thyself and us.

38 And when the sixth hour was come, there was darkness over the whole land, until the ninth hour.

39 And at the ninth hour, Jesus cried with a loud voice, saying, Eloi, Eloi, lama sabachthani? which is, being interpreted, My God, my God, why hast thou forsaken me?

40 And some of them who stood by, when they heard him, said, Behold, he calleth Elias.

41 And one ran and filled a sponge full of vinegar, and put it on a reed and gave him to drink; others spake, saying, Let him alone; let us see whether Elias will come to take him down.

42 And Jesus cried with a loud voice, and gave up the ghost.

43 And the veil of the temple was rent in twain, from the top to the bottom.

44 And when the centurion who stood over against him, saw that he so cried out and gave up the ghost, he said, Truly, this man is the Son of God.

45 There were also women looking on afar off, among whom was Mary Magdalene, and Mary the mother of James the younger, and of Joses, and Salome; who also when he was in Galilee, followed him and ministered unto him; and many other women who came with him unto Jerusalem.

46 And now, when the even was come; because it was the preparation day, that is the day before the Sabbath,

47 Joseph of Arimathea, an honorable counselor, who also waited for the kingdom of God, came and went in boldly unto Pilate, and craved the body of Jesus. And Pilate marveled, and asked if he were already dead.

48 And calling the centurion, he asked him if he had been any while dead.

49 And when he knew it of the centurion, he gave the body to Joseph.

50 And Joseph bought fine linen, and took him down, and wrapped him in the linen, and laid him in a sepulcher which was hewn out of a rock, and rolled a stone unto the door of the sepulcher.

51 And Mary Magdalene, and Mary the mother of Joses, beheld where he was laid.

## CHAPTER 16

*Christ's resurrection—The great commission given.*

1 And when the Sabbath was passed, Mary Magdalene, and Mary the mother of James and Salome, bought sweet spices, that they might come and anoint him.

2 And very early in the morning, the first day of the week, they came unto the sepulcher at the rising of the sun; and they said among themselves, Who shall roll us away the stone from the door of the sepulcher?

3 But when they looked, they saw that the stone was rolled away, (for it was very great,) and two angels sitting thereon, clothed in long white garments; and they were affrighted.

4 But the angels said unto them, Be not affrighted; ye seek Jesus of Nazareth, who was crucified; he is risen; he is not here; behold the place where they laid him;

5 And go your way, tell his disciples and Peter, that he goeth before you into Galilee; there shall ye see him as he said unto you.

6 And they, entering into the sepulcher, saw the place where they laid Jesus.

7 And they went out quickly, and fled from the sepulcher; for they trembled and were amazed; neither said they anything to any man, for they were afraid.

8 Now when Jesus was risen, early on the first day of the week, he appeared first to Mary Magdalene, out of whom he had cast seven devils;

9 And she went and told them who had been with him, as they mourned and wept.

10 And they, when they heard that he was alive, and had been seen of her, believed not.

11 After that, he appeared in another form unto two of them, as they walked and went into the country;

12 And they went and told it unto the residue; neither believed they them.

13 Afterward he appeared unto the eleven as they sat at meat, and upbraided them with their unbelief and hardness of heart, because they believed not them which had seen him after he was risen.

14 And he said unto them, Go ye into all the world, and preach the gospel to every creature.

15 He that believeth and is baptized, shall be saved; but he that believeth not, shall be damned.

16 And these signs shall follow them that believe;

17 In my name shall they cast out devils; they shall speak with new tongues;

18 They shall take up serpents; and if they drink any deadly thing, it shall not hurt them;

19 They shall lay hands on the sick, and they shall recover.

20 So then, after the Lord had spoken unto them, he was received up into heaven, and sat on the right hand of God.

21 And they went forth and preached everywhere, the Lord working with them, and confirming the word with signs following. Amen.

# The Testimony of St. Luke

## CHAPTER 1

*The birth of John—His mission—The Annunciation of the Savior.*

1 As I am a messenger of Jesus Christ, and knowing that many have taken in hand to set forth in order a declaration of those things which are most surely believed among us;

2 Even as they delivered them unto us, who from the beginning were eye-witnesses and ministers of the word;

3 It seemed good to me also, having had perfect understanding of all things from the very first, to write unto thee, in order, most excellent Theophilus,

4 That thou mightest know the certainty of those things wherein thou hast been instructed.

5 There was in the days of Herod, the king of Judea, a certain priest named Zacharias, of the course of Abia; and his wife being of the daughters of Aaron, and her name Elizabeth,

6 Were both righteous before God, walking in all the commandments and ordinances of the Lord blameless;

7 And they had no child. Elizabeth was barren, and they were both well stricken in years.

8 And while he executed the priest's office before God, in the order of his priesthood,

9 According to the law, (his lot was to burn incense when he went into the temple of the Lord,)

10 The whole multitude of the people were praying without at the time of incense.

11 And there appeared unto him an angel of the Lord, standing on the right side of the altar of incense.

12 And when Zacharias saw the angel, he was troubled and fear fell upon him.

13 But the angel said unto him, Fear not, Zacharias, for thy prayer is heard, and thy wife Elizabeth shall bear thee a son, and thou shalt call his name John.

14 Thou shalt have joy and gladness, and many shall rejoice at his birth;

15 For he shall be great in the sight of the Lord, and shall drink neither wine nor strong drink; and he shall be filled with the Holy Ghost, even from his mother's womb.

16 And many of the children of Israel shall he turn to the Lord their God;

17 And he shall go before the Lord in the spirit and power of Elias, to turn the hearts of the fathers to the children, and the disobedient to the wisdom of the just, to make ready a people prepared for the Lord.

18 And Zacharias said unto the angel, Whereby shall I know this? for I am an old man, and my wife is well stricken in years.

19 And the angel answering, said unto him, I am Gabriel, who stand in the presence of God, and am sent to speak unto thee, and to show thee these glad tidings.

20 And behold, thou shalt be dumb, and not able to speak until the day that these things shall be performed, because thou believest not my words which shall be fulfilled in their season.

21 And the people waited for Zacharias, and marveled that he tarried so long in the temple.

22 And when he came out, he could not speak unto them; and they perceived that he had seen a vision in the temple; for he beckoned unto them, and remained speechless.

23 And as soon as the days of his ministration were accomplished, he departed to his own house.

24 And after those days, his wife Elizabeth conceived, and hid herself five months, saying,

25 Thus hath the Lord dealt with me in the days wherein he looked on me, to take away my reproach from among men.

26 And in the sixth month the angel Gabriel was sent from God, unto a city of Galilee, named Nazareth,

27 To a virgin, espoused to a man whose name was Joseph, of the house of David; and the virgin's name was Mary.

28 And the angel came in unto her and said, Hail, thou virgin, who art highly favored of the Lord. The Lord is with thee, for thou art chosen and blessed among women.

29 And when she saw the angel, she was troubled at his saying, and pondered in her mind what manner of salutation this should be.

30 And the angel said unto her, Fear not, Mary, for thou hast found favor with God.

31 And behold, thou shalt conceive, and bring forth a son, and shall call his name Jesus.

32 He shall be great, and shall be called the Son of the Highest; and the Lord God shall give unto him the throne of his father David;

33 And he shall reign over the house of Jacob for ever; and of his kingdom there shall be no end.

34 Then said Mary unto the angel; How can this be?

35 And the angel answered and said unto her, Of the Holy Ghost, and the power of the Highest. Therefore also, that holy child that shall be born of thee shall be called the Son of God.

36 And behold, thy cousin Elizabeth, she hath also conceived a son, in her old age; and this is the sixth month with her who is called barren.

37 For with God nothing can be impossible.

38 And Mary said, Behold the handmaid of the Lord; be it unto me according to thy word. And the angel departed from her.

39 And in those days, Mary went into the hill country with haste, into a city of Juda,

40 And entered into the house of Zacharias, and saluted Elizabeth.

41 And it came to pass, that when Elizabeth heard the salutation of Mary, the babe leaped in her womb.

42 And Elizabeth was filled with the Holy Ghost, and she spake out with a loud voice and said, Blessed art thou among women, and blessed is the fruit of thy womb.

43 And why is it, that this blessing is upon me, that the mother of my Lord should come to me? For lo, as soon as the voice of thy salutation sounded in mine ears, the babe leaped in my womb for joy.

44 And blessed art thou who believed, for those things which were told thee by the angel of the Lord, shall be fulfilled.

45 And Mary said, My soul doth magnify the Lord,

46 And my spirit rejoiceth in God my Savior.

47 For he hath regarded the low estate of his handmaiden; for behold, from henceforth all generations shall call me blessed.

48 For he who is mighty hath done to me great things; and I will magnify his holy name,

49 For his mercy on those who fear him from generation to generation.

50 He hath showed strength with his arm; he hath scattered the proud in the imagination of their hearts.

51 He hath put down the mighty from their high seats; and exalted them of low degree.

52 He hath filled the hungry with good things; but the rich he hath sent empty away.

53 He hath helped his servant Israel in remembrance of mercy,

54 As he spake to our fathers, to Abraham, and to his seed forever.

55 And Mary abode with Elizabeth about three months, and returned to her own house.

56 And now Elizabeth's full time came that she should be delivered; and she brought forth a son.

57 And her neighbors, and her cousins heard how the Lord had showed great mercy upon her; and they rejoiced with her.

58 And it came to pass, that on the eighth day they came to circumcise the child; and they called him Zacharias, after the name of his father.

59 And his mother answered and said, Not so; but he shall be called John.

60 And they said unto her, There is none of thy kindred that is called by this name.

61 And they made signs to his father, and asked him how he would have him called.

62 And he asked for a writing table, and wrote, saying, His name is John, and they all marveled.

63 And his mouth was opened immediately, and he spake with his tongue, and praised God.

64 And fear came on all who dwelt round about them. And all these sayings were noised abroad throughout all the hill country of Judea.

65 And all they that heard them laid them up in their hearts, saying, What manner of child shall this be? And the hand of the Lord was with him.

66 And his father Zacharias was filled with the Holy Ghost, and prophesied, saying,

67 Blessed be the Lord God of Israel; for he hath visited and redeemed his people,

68 And hath raised up an horn of salvation for us, in the house of his servant David,

69 As he spake by the mouth of his holy prophets, ever since the world began,

70 That we should be saved from our enemies, and from the hand of all those who hate us;

71 To perform the mercy promised to our fathers, and to remember his holy covenant;

72 The oath which he sware to our father Abraham,

73 That he would grant unto us, that we, being delivered out of the hand of our enemies, might serve him without fear,

74 In holiness and righteousness before him, all the days of our lives.

75 And thou, child, shalt be called the prophet of the Highest, for thou shalt go before the face of the Lord to prepare his ways,

76 To give knowledge of salvation unto his people, by baptism for the remission of their sins,

77 Through the tender mercy of our God; whereby the dayspring from on high hath visited us,

78 To give light to them who sit in darkness and the shadow of death; to guide our feet into the way of peace.

79 And the child grew, and waxed strong in spirit, and was in the deserts until the day of his showing unto Israel.

## CHAPTER 2

*Birth of Christ—The Shepherds' vision—Simeon and Anna prophesy.*

1 And it came to pass in those days, that there went out a decree from Caesar Augustus, that all his empire should be taxed.

2 This same taxing was when Cyrenius was governor of Syria.

3 And all went to be taxed, every one in his own city.

4 And Joseph also went up from Galilee, out of the city of Nazareth, into Judea, unto the city of David, which is called Bethlehem; (because he was of the house and lineage of David,)

5 To be taxed, with Mary his espoused wife, she being great with child.

6 And so it was, that while they were there, the days were accomplished that she should be delivered.

7 And she brought forth her first-born son, and wrapped him in swaddling clothes, and laid him in a manger, because there was none to give room for them in the inns.

8 And there were in the same country, shepherds abiding in the field, keeping watch over their flocks by night.

9 And lo, an angel of the Lord appeared unto them, and the glory of the Lord shone round about them; and they were sore afraid.

10 But the angel said unto them, Fear not, for behold, I bring you good tidings of great joy, which shall be to all people.

11 For unto you is born this day, in the city of David, a Savior, who is Christ the Lord.

12 And this is the way you shall find the babe, he is wrapped in swaddling clothes, and is lying in a manger.

13 And suddenly there was with the angel, a multitude of the heavenly host, praising God, and saying,

14 Glory to God in the highest; and on earth, peace; goodwill to men.

15 And it came to pass, when the angels were gone away from them into heaven, the shepherds said one to another, Let us now go, even unto Bethlehem, and see this thing which is come to pass, which the Lord has made known unto us.

16 And they came with haste, and found Mary and Joseph, and the babe lying in a manger.

17 And when they had seen, they made known abroad the saying which was told them concerning this child.

18 All they who heard it, wondered at those things which were told them by the shepherds;

19 But Mary kept all these things and pondered them in her heart.

20 And the shepherds returned, glorifying and praising God for all the things which they had heard and seen, as they were manifested unto them.

21 And when eight days were accomplished for the circumcising of the child, his name was called Jesus; which was so named of the angel, before he was conceived.

22 And when the days of her purification, according to the law of Moses,

were accomplished; they brought him to Jerusalem, to present him to the Lord;

23 As it is written in the law of the Lord, Every male which openeth the womb shall be called holy to the Lord;

24 And to offer a sacrifice according to that which is written in the law of the Lord, A pair of turtledoves, or two young pigeons.

25 And behold, there was a man at Jerusalem, whose name was Simeon; and the same man was just and devout, waiting for the consolation of Israel; and the Holy Ghost was upon him.

26 And it was revealed unto him by the Holy Ghost, that he should not see death before he had seen the Lord's Christ.

27 And he came by the Spirit into the temple; and when the parents brought in the child, even Jesus, to do for him after the custom of the law,

28 Then took he him up in his arms, and blessed God, and said,

29 Lord, now lettest thy servant depart in peace, according to thy word;

30 For mine eyes have seen thy salvation,

31 Which thou hast prepared before the face of all people;

32 A light to lighten the Gentiles, and the glory of thy people Israel.

33 And Joseph, and Mary, marveled at those things which were spoken of the child.

34 And Simeon blessed them, and said unto Mary, Behold, this child is set for the fall and rising again of many in Israel; and for a sign which shall be spoken against;

35 Yea, a spear shall pierce through him to the wounding of thine own soul also; that the thoughts of many hearts may be revealed.

36 And there was one Anna, a prophetess, the daughter of Phanuel, of the tribe of Asher. She was of great age, and had lived with a husband only seven years, whom she married in her youth,

37 And she lived a widow of about fourscore and four years, who departed not from the temple, but served God with fastings and prayers, night and day.

38 And she, coming in that instant, gave thanks likewise unto the Lord, and spake of him, to all those who looked for redemption in Jerusalem.

39 And when they had performed all things according to the law of the Lord, they returned into Galilee to their own city, Nazareth.

40 And the child grew, and waxed strong in spirit, being filled with wisdom, and the grace of God was upon him.

41 Now his parents went to Jerusalem every year at the feast of the passover.

42 And when he was twelve years old, they went up to Jerusalem, after the custom, to the feast.

43 And when they had fulfilled the days, as they returned, the child Jesus tarried behind, in Jerusalem; and Joseph and his mother knew not that he tarried;

44 But they, supposing him to have been in the company, went a day's journey; and they sought him among his kindred and acquaintance.

45 And when they found him not, they turned back again to Jerusalem, seeking him.

46 And it came to pass, that after three days they found him in the temple, sitting in the midst of the doctors, and they were hearing him, and asking him questions.

47 And all who heard him were astonished at his understanding, and answers.

48 And when his parents saw him, they were amazed; and his mother said unto him, Son, why hast thou thus dealt with us? Behold, thy father and I have sought thee sorrowing.

49 And he said unto them, Why is it that ye sought me? Knew ye not that I must be about my Father's business?

50 And they understood not the saying which he spake unto them.

51 And he went down with them, and came to Nazareth, and was subject unto them. And his mother kept all these sayings in her heart.

52 And Jesus increased in wisdom and stature, and in favor with God and man.

## CHAPTER 3

*Preaching of John concerning Christ—John preaching to the multitude—Baptism of Christ—Genealogy of Christ.*

1 Now in the fifteenth year of the reign of Tiberius Caesar, Pontius Pi-

late being governor of Judea, and Herod being tetrarch of Galilee, and his brother Philip tetrarch of Iturea and of the region of Trachonitis, and Lysanias the tetrarch of Abilene; Annas and Caiaphas being the high priests.

2 Now in this same year, the word of God came unto John, the son of Zacharias, in the wilderness.

3 And he came into all the country about Jordan, preaching the baptism of repentance for the remission of sins.

4 As it is written in the book of the prophet Esaias; and these are the words, saying, The voice of one crying in the wilderness, Prepare ye the way of the Lord, and make his paths straight.

5 For behold, and lo, he shall come, as it is written in the book of the prophets, to take away the sins of the world, and to bring salvation unto the heathen nations, to gather together those who are lost, who are of the sheepfold of Israel;

6 Yea, even the dispersed and afflicted; and also to prepare the way, and make possible the preaching of the gospel unto the Gentiles;

7 And to be a light unto all who sit in darkness, unto the uttermost parts of the earth; to bring to pass the resurrection from the dead, and to ascend up on high, to dwell on the right hand of the Father,

8 Until the fullness of time, and the law and the testimony shall be sealed, and the keys of the kingdom shall be delivered up again unto the Father;

9 To administer justice unto all; to come down in judgment upon all, and to convince all the ungodly of their ungodly deeds, which they have committed; and all this in the day that he shall come;

10 For it is a day of power; yea, every valley shall be filled, and every mountain and hill shall be brought low; the crooked shall be made straight, and the rough ways made smooth;

11 And all flesh shall see the salvation of God.

12 Then said John to the multitude that came forth to be baptized of him, crying against them with a loud voice, saying, O generation of vipers, who hath warned you to flee from the wrath to come?

13 Bring forth therefore fruits worthy of repentance, and begin not to say within yourselves, Abraham is our father; we have kept the commandments of God, and none can inherit the promises but the children of Abraham; for I say unto you, That God is able of these stones to raise up children unto Abraham.

14 And now also, the axe is laid unto the root of the trees; every tree therefore which bringeth not forth good fruit, shall be hewn down, and cast into the fire.

15 And the people asked him, saying, What shall we do then?

16 He answered and said unto them, He that hath two coats, let him impart to him that hath none; and he that hath meat, let him do likewise.

17 Then came also publicans to be baptized, and said unto him, Master, what shall we do?

18 And he said unto them, Exact no more than that which is appointed unto you.

19 For it is well known unto you, Theophilus, that after the manner of the Jews, and according to the custom of their law in receiving money into the treasury, that out of the abundance which was received, was appointed unto the poor, every man his portion;

20 And after this manner did the publicans also, wherefore John said unto them, Exact no more than that which is appointed you.

21 And the soldiers likewise demanded of him, saying, And what shall we do? And he said unto them, Do violence to no man, neither accuse any falsely; and be content with your wages.

22 And as the people were in expectation, and all men mused in their hearts of John, whether he were the Christ, or not;

23 John answered, saying unto all, I indeed baptize you with water, but there cometh one mightier than I, the latchet of whose shoes I am not worthy to unloose, he shall baptize you with the Holy Ghost, and with fire;

24 Whose fan is in his hand, and he will thoroughly purge his floor, and will gather the wheat into his garner; but the chaff he will burn with fire unquenchable.

25 And many other things, in his ex-

hortation, preached he unto the people.

26 But Herod, the tetrarch, being reproved of him for Herodias, his brother Philip's wife, and for all the evils which Herod had done;

27 Added yet this above all, that he shut up John in prison.

28 Now when all the people were baptized, it came to pass that Jesus also came unto John; and being baptized of him, and praying, the heaven was opened;

29 And the Holy Ghost descended, in bodily shape like a dove, upon him; and a voice came from heaven, which said, Thou art my beloved Son, in thee I am well pleased.

30 And Jesus himself began to be about thirty years of age, having lived with his father, being, as was supposed of the world, the son of Joseph, who was from the loins of Heli,

31 Who was from the loins of Matthat, who was the son of Levi, who was a descendant of Melchi, and of Janna, and of Joseph,

32 And of Mattathias, and of Amos, and of Naum, and of Esli, and of Nagge,

33 And of Maath and of Mattathias, and of Semei, and of Joseph, and of Juda,

34 And of Joanna, and of Resa, and of Zorobabel, and of Salathiel, who was the son of Neri,

35 Who was a descendant of Melchi, and of Addi, and of Cosam, and of Elmodam, and of Er,

36 And of Jose, and of Eliezer, and of Joram, and of Matthat, and of Levi,

37 And of Simeon, and of Juda, and of Joseph, and of Jonan, and of Eliakim,

38 And of Melea, and of Menan, and of Mattatha, and of Nathan, and of David,

39 And of Jesse, and of Obed, and of Booz, and of Salmon, and of Naasson,

40 And of Aminadab, and of Aram, and of Esrom, and of Phares, and of Juda,

41 And of Jacob, and of Isaac, and of Abraham, and of Thara, and of Nachor,

42 And of Saruch, and of Ragau, and of Phalec, and of Heber, and of Sala,

43 And of Cainan, and of Arphaxad, and of Shem, and of Noah, and of Lamech,

44 And of Mathusala, and of Enoch,

and of Jared, and of Maleleel, and of Cainan,

45 And of Enos, and of Seth, and of Adam, who was formed of God, and the first man upon the earth.

## CHAPTER 4

*Christ led by the Spirit into the wilderness—Tempted of Satan—Preaches in Nazareth and Galilee.*

1 And Jesus, being full of the Holy Ghost, returned from Jordan, and was led by the Spirit into the wilderness.

2 And after forty days, the devil came unto him, to tempt him. And in those days, he did eat nothing; and when they were ended, he afterwards hungered.

3 And the devil said unto him, If thou be the Son of God, command this stone that it be made bread.

4 And Jesus answered him, saying, It is written, that man shall not live by bread alone, but by every word of God.

5 And the Spirit taketh him up into a high mountain, and he beheld all the kingdoms of the world, in a moment of time.

6 And the devil came unto him, and said unto him, All this power will I give unto thee, and the glory of them; for they are delivered unto me, and to whomsoever I will, I give them.

7 If thou therefore, wilt worship me, all shall be thine.

8 Jesus answered and said unto him, Get thee behind me, Satan; for it is written, Thou shalt worship the Lord thy God, and him only shalt thou serve.

9 And the Spirit brought him to Jerusalem, and set him on a pinnacle of the temple. And the devil came unto him, and said unto him, If thou be the Son of God, cast thyself down from hence;

10 For it is written, He shall give his angels charge over thee, to keep thee; and in his hands they shall bear thee up, lest at any time thou dash thy foot against a stone.

11 And Jesus answering, said unto him, It is written, Thou shalt not tempt the Lord thy God.

12 And when the devil had ended all the temptation, he departed from him for a season.

13 And Jesus returned in the power of the Spirit, into Galilee.

14 And there went out a fame of him through all the region round about;

15 And he taught in their synagogues, being glorified of all who believed on his name.

16 And he came to Nazareth, where he had been brought up; and as his custom was he went into the synagogue on the Sabbath day, and stood up to read.

17 And there was delivered unto him, the book of the prophet Esaias. And when he had opened the book, he found the place where it was written,

18 The Spirit of the Lord is upon me, because he hath anointed me to preach the gospel to the poor, he hath sent me to heal the brokenhearted, to preach deliverance to the captives, and the recovering of sight to the blind; to set at liberty them that are bruised;

19 To preach the acceptable year of the Lord.

20 And he closed the book, and he gave it again to the minister, and he sat down.

21 And the eyes of all those who were in the synagogue, were fastened on him. And he began to say unto them, This day is this scripture fulfilled in your ears.

22 And all bare him witness, and wondered at the gracious words which proceeded out of his mouth. And they said, Is not this Joseph's son?

23 And he said unto them, Ye will surely say unto me this proverb, Physician, heal thyself. Whatsoever we have heard was done in Capernaum, do also here in thy country.

24 And he said, Verily I say unto you, No prophet is accepted in his own country.

25 But I tell you the truth, many widows were in Israel in the days of Elias, when the heaven was shut up three years and six months, and great famine was throughout all the land;

26 But unto none of them was Elias sent, save unto Sarepta, of Sidon, unto a woman who was a widow.

27 And many lepers were in Israel, in the time of Eliseus the prophet; and none of them were cleansed, save Naaman the Syrian.

28 And all they in the synagogue, when they heard these things, were filled with wrath,

29 And rose up, and thrust him out of the city, and led him unto the brow of the hill, whereon their city was built, that they might cast him down headlong.

30 But he, passing through the midst of them, went his way,

31 And came down to Capernaum, a city of Galilee, and taught them on the Sabbath days.

32 And they were astonished at his doctrine; for his words were with power.

33 And in the synagogue there was a man which had a spirit of an unclean devil, and he cried out with a loud voice,

34 Saying, Let us alone; what have we to do with thee, Jesus of Nazareth? Art thou come to destroy us? I know thee, who thou art, The Holy One of God.

35 Jesus rebuked him, saying, Hold thy peace, and come out of him. And when the devil had thrown him in the midst, he came out of him, and hurt him not.

36 And they were all amazed, and spake among themselves, saying, What a word is this! for with authority and power he commandeth the unclean spirits, and they come out.

37 And the fame of him went out in every place round about.

38 And he arose, and went out of the synagogue, and entered into Simon's house. And Simon's wife's mother was taken with a great fever; and they besought him for to heal her.

39 And he stood over her, and rebuked the fever, and it left her; and immediately she arose, and ministered unto them.

40 Now, when the sun was setting, all they who had any sick, with divers diseases, brought them unto him, and he laid his hands on every one of them, and healed them.

41 And devils also came out of many, crying out, and saying, Thou art Christ, the Son of God. And he, rebuking them, suffered them not to speak; for they knew that he was Christ.

42 And when it was day, he departed and went into a solitary place; and the people sought him, and came unto him, and desired him that he should not depart from them.

43 But he said unto them, I must preach the kingdom of God to other cities also, for therefore am I sent.

44 And he preached in the synagogues of Galilee.

## CHAPTER 5

*Great draught of fishes—Calling of Peter, James, John, and Levi—Christ healeth the palsy—Parable of new wine, and old bottles.*

1 And it came to pass, as the people pressed upon him, to hear the word of God, he stood by the lake of Gennesaret,

2 And saw two ships standing on the lake; but the fishermen were gone out of them, and were wetting their nets.

3 And he entered into one of the ships, which was Simon's, and prayed him that he would thrust out a little from the land. And he sat down, and taught the people out of the ship.

4 Now, when he had done speaking, he said to Simon, Launch out into the deep, and let down your net for a draught.

5 And Simon answering, said unto him, Master, we have toiled all the night, and have taken nothing; nevertheless, at thy word I will let down the net.

6 And when they had done this, they enclosed a great multitude of fishes; and their net brake.

7 And they beckoned unto their partners, who were in the other ship, that they should come and help them. And they came and filled both the ships, so that they began to sink.

8 When Simon Peter saw the multitude of fishes, he fell down at Jesus' knees, saying, Depart from me; for I am a sinful man, O Lord.

9 For he was astonished, and all who were with him, at the draught of the fishes which they had taken.

10 And so were also James, and John, the sons of Zebedee, who were partners with Simon. And Jesus said unto Simon, Fear not from henceforth, for thou shalt catch men.

11 And when they had brought their ships to land, they forsook all, and followed him.

12 And it came to pass, when he was in a certain city, behold, a man, full of leprosy, who, seeing Jesus, fell on his face, and besought him, saying, Lord, if thou wilt, thou canst make me clean.

13 And he put forth his hand and touched him, saying, I will; be thou clean. And immediately the leprosy departed from him.

14 And he charged him to tell no man; but said unto him, Go and show thyself to the priests, and offer for thy cleansing, according as Moses commanded, for a testimony unto them.

15 But so much the more went there a fame abroad of him; and great multitudes came together to hear, and to be healed by him of their infirmities.

16 And he withdrew himself into the wilderness, and prayed.

17 And it came to pass on a certain day, as he was teaching, that there were Pharisees and doctors of the law sitting by, who were come out of every town of Galilee, and Judea, and Jerusalem. And the power of the Lord was present to heal them.

18 And behold, men brought in a bed, a man who was taken with a palsy; and they sought to bring him in, and to lay him before Jesus.

19 And when they found that they could not bring him in for the multitude, they went upon the housetop, and let him down through the tiling, with his couch, into the midst, before Jesus.

20 Now he saw their faith, and said unto the man, Thy sins are forgiven thee.

21 And the Scribes and Pharisees began to reason, saying, Who is this that speaketh blasphemies? Who can forgive sins but God alone?

22 But Jesus perceived their thoughts, and he said unto them, What reason ye in your hearts?

23 Does it require more power to forgive sins than to make the sick rise up and walk?

24 But, that ye may know that the Son of man hath power upon earth to forgive sins, I said it. And he said unto the sick of the palsy, I say unto thee, Arise, and take up thy couch, and go unto thy house.

25 And immediately he rose up before them, and took up that whereon he lay, and departed to his own house, glorifying God.

26 And they were all amazed, and they glorified God, and were filled with fear, saying, We have seen strange things today.

27 And after these things he went forth, and saw a publican, named Levi, sitting at the the place where they re-

ceived custom; and he said unto him, Follow me.

28 And he left all, rose up, and followed him.

29 And Levi made him a great feast, in his own house; and there was a great company of publicans, and of others, that sat down with them.

30 But the scribes and Pharisees murmured against his disciples, saying, Why do ye eat and drink with publicans and sinners?

31 Jesus answering, said unto them, They that are whole need not a physician; but they that are sick.

32 I came not to call the righteous, but sinners to repentance.

33 And they said unto him, Why do the disciples of John fast often, and make prayers, and likewise the disciples of the Pharisees; but thine eat and drink?

34 And he said unto them, Can ye make the children of the bridechamber fast while the bridegroom is with them?

35 But the days will come when the bridegroom shall be taken away from them; and then shall they fast in those days.

36 And he spake also a parable unto them, saying, No man putteth a piece of new cloth upon an old garment; if so, then the new maketh a rent, and agreeth not with the old.

37 And no man putteth new wine into old bottles; else the new wine will burst the bottles and be spilled, and the bottles shall perish.

38 But new wine must be put into new bottles, and both are preserved.

39 No man also, having drunk old wine, desireth new; for he saith, The old is better.

## CHAPTER 6

*The Sabbath made for man—Calling of the twelve—Sundry instructions on duty—Parable of the house founded on a rock.*

1 And it came to pass on the second Sabbath after this, that he went through the cornfields; and his disciples plucked the ears of corn, and did eat, rubbing them in their hands.

2 And certain of the Pharisees said unto them, Why do ye that which is not lawful to do on the Sabbath days?

3 Jesus answering them, said, Have ye not read so much as this, what David did, when he himself was an hungered, and they who were with him;

4 How he went into the house of God, and did take and eat the shewbread, and gave also to them who were with him, which it is not lawful to eat, but for the priests alone?

5 And he said unto them, That the Son of man is Lord also of the Sabbath.

6 And it came to pass also on another Sabbath, that he entered into the synagogue, and taught. And there was a man whose right hand was withered;

7 And the scribes and Pharisees watched him, whether he would heal on the Sabbath day; that they might find an accusation against him.

8 But he knew their thoughts, and said to the man who had the withered hand, Rise up, and stand forth in the midst. And he arose and stood forth.

9 Then said Jesus unto them, I will ask you one thing; Is it lawful on the Sabbath days to do good, or to do evil? To save life, or to destroy?

10 And looking round about upon them all, he said unto the man, Stretch forth thy hand. And he did so; and his hand was restored whole as the other.

11 And they were filled with madness; and communed one with another what they might do to Jesus.

12 And it came to pass in those days, that he went out into a mountain to pray, and continued all night in prayer to God.

13 And when it was day, he called his disciples; and of them he chose twelve, whom also he named apostles.

14 Simon, whom he also named Peter, and Andrew his brother, James and John, Philip and Bartholomew,

15 Matthew and Thomas, James the son of Alpheus, and Simon called Zelotes,

16 And Judas the brother of James, and Judas Iscariot, who also was the traitor.

17 And he came down with them and stood in the plain, and the company of his disciples, and a great multitude of people out of all Judea and Jerusalem, and from the seacoasts of Tyre and Sidon, who came to hear him, and to be healed of their diseases;

18 And they who were vexed with unclean spirits; and they were healed.

19 And the whole multitude sought to touch him; for there went virtue out of him and healed them all.

20 And he lifted up his eyes on his disciples, and said, Blessed are the poor; for theirs is the kingdom of God.

21 Blessed are they who hunger now; for they shall be filled. Blessed are they who weep now; for they shall laugh.

22 Blessed are ye when men shall hate you, and when they shall separate you from among them, and shall reproach you, and cast out your name as evil, for the Son of man's sake.

23 Rejoice ye in that day, and leap for joy; for behold your reward shall be great in heaven; for in the like manner did their fathers unto the prophets.

24 But woe unto you that are rich! For ye have received your consolation.

25 Woe unto you who are full! For ye shall hunger. Woe unto you who laugh now! For ye shall mourn and weep.

26 Woe unto you, when all men shall speak well of you! For so did their fathers to the false prophets.

27 But I say unto you who hear my words, Love your enemies, do good to them who hate you.

28 Bless them who curse you, and pray for them who despitefully use you and persecute you.

29 And unto him who smiteth thee on the cheek, offer also the other; or, in other words, it is better to offer the other, than to revile again. And him who taketh away thy cloak, forbid not to take thy coat also.

30 For it is better that thou suffer thine enemy to take these things, than to contend with him. Verily I say unto you, Your heavenly Father who seeth in secret, shall bring that wicked one into judgment.

31 Therefore give to every man who asketh of thee; and of him who taketh away thy goods, ask them not again.

32 And as ye would that men should do to you, do ye also to them likewise.

33 For if ye love them only who love you, what reward have you? For sinners also do even the same.

34 And if ye lend to them of whom ye hope to receive, what reward have you? for sinners also lend to sinners, to receive as much again.

35 But love ye your enemies, and do good, and lend, hoping for nothing again; and your reward shall be great;

and ye shall be the children of the Highest; for he is kind unto the unthankful, and to the evil.

36 Be ye therefore merciful, as your Father also is merciful.

37 Judge not, and ye shall not be judged; condemn not, and ye shall not be condemned; forgive, and ye shall be forgiven.

38 Give, and it shall be given unto you; good measure, pressed down, and shaken together, and running over, shall men give into your bosom. For with the same measure that ye mete withal, it shall be measured to you again.

39 And he spake a parable unto them, Can the blind lead the blind? Shall they not both fall into the ditch?

40 A disciple is not above his master; but every one that is perfect shall be as his master.

41 And why beholdest thou the mote which is in thy brother's eye, but perceivest not the beam which is in thine own eye?

42 Again, how canst thou say to thy brother, Let me pull out the mote that is in thine eye, when thou thyself beholdest not the beam which is in thine own eye? Thou hypocrite, cast out first the beam out of thine own eye, and then shalt thou see clearly to pull out the mote which is in thy brother's eye.

43 For a good tree bringeth not forth corrupt fruit; neither doth a corrupt tree bring forth good fruit;

44 For every tree is known by his own fruit. For of thorns men do not gather figs, nor of a bramble bush gather they grapes.

45 A good man out of the good treasure of his heart, bringeth forth that which is good. And an evil man out of the evil treasure of his heart, bringeth forth that which is evil; for of the abundance of the heart his mouth speaketh.

46 And why call ye me, Lord, Lord, and do not the things which I say?

47 Whosoever cometh to me, and heareth my sayings and doeth them, I will show you to whom he is like.

48 He is like a man which built a house, and digged deep, and laid the foundation on a rock, and when the flood arose, the stream beat vehemently upon that house, and could not

shake it; for it was founded upon a rock.

49 But he that heareth and doeth not, is like a man that without a foundation built a house upon the earth; against which the stream did beat vehemently, and immediately it fell; and the ruin of that house was great.

## CHAPTER 7

*The centurion's servant—Widow's son raised—Christ's testimony of John—Jesus anointed by the woman—He commmendeth the act.*

1 Now when he had ended all these sayings in the audience of the people, he entered into Capernaum.

2 And a certain centurion's servant, who was dear unto him, was sick and ready to die.

3 And when he heard of Jesus, he sent unto him the elders of the Jews, beseeching him that he would come and heal his servant.

4 And when they came to Jesus they besought him instantly, saying, That he was worthy for whom he should do this;

5 For he loveth our nation, and he hath built us a synagogue.

6 Then Jesus went with them, and when he was now not far from the house, the centurion sent friends to him, saying unto him, Lord, trouble not thyself; for I am not worthy that thou shouldest enter under my roof.

7 Wherefore, neither thought I myself worthy to come unto thee; but say the word, and my servant shall be healed.

8 For I also am a man set under authority, having under me soldiers, and I say unto one, Go, and he goeth; and to another, Come, and he cometh; and to my servant, Do this, and he doeth it.

9 When Jesus heard these things, he marveled at him, and turned him about, and said unto the people who followed him, I say unto you, I have not found so great faith, no, not in Israel.

10 And they who were sent, returning to the house, found the servant whole who had been sick.

11 And it came to pass the day after, that he went into a city called Nain; and many of his disciples went with him, and much people.

12 Now, when he came nigh to the gate of the city, behold, there was a dead man carried out, the only son of his mother, and she was a widow; and many people of the city were with her.

13 And now the Lord saw her, and had compassion on her, and he said unto her, Weep not.

14 And he came and touched the bier; and they that bare it stood still, and he said, Young man, I say unto thee, Arise.

15 And he who was dead, sat up, and began to speak; and he delivered him to his mother.

16 And there came a fear on all; and they glorified God, saying, That a great prophet is risen up among us; and, That God hath visited his people.

17 And this rumor of him went forth throughout all Judea, and throughout all the region round about.

18 And the disciples of John showed him of all these things.

19 And John calling two of his disciples, sent them to Jesus, saying, Art thou he that should come, or look we for another?

20 When the men were come unto him, they said, John Baptist hath sent us unto thee, saying, Art thou he who should come, or look we for another?

21 And in the same hour he cured many of infirmities, and plagues, and of evil spirits, and unto many blind he gave sight.

22 Then Jesus, answering, said unto them, Go your way, and tell John what things ye have seen and heard; how that the blind see, the lame walk, the lepers are cleansed, the deaf hear, the dead are raised, and to the poor the gospel is preached;

23 And blessed are they who shall not be offended in me.

24 And when the messengers of John were departed, he began to speak unto the people concerning John; What went ye out into the wilderness to see? A reed shaken with the wind? Or a man clothed in soft raiment?

25 Behold, they who are gorgeously apparelled, and live delicately, are in king's courts.

26 But what went ye out for to see? A prophet? Yea, I say unto you, and much more than a prophet.

27 This is the one of whom it is written, Behold I send my messenger before thy face, who shall prepare thy way before thee.

28 For I say unto you, Among those

who are born of women, there is not a greater prophet than John the Baptist; but he who is least in the kingdom of God is greater than he.

29 And all the people who heard him, and the publicans, justified God, being baptized with the baptism of John.

30 But the Pharisees, and lawyers, rejected the counsel of God against themselves, not being baptized of him.

31 And the Lord said, Whereunto then shall I liken the men of this generation? And to what are they like?

32 They are like unto children sitting in the marketplace, and calling one to another, and saying, We have piped for you, and ye have not danced; we have mourned for you, and ye have not wept.

33 For John the Baptist came neither eating bread, nor drinking wine; and ye say he hath a devil.

34 The Son of man is come, eating and drinking; and ye say, Behold a gluttonous man, and a wine bibber; a friend of publicans and sinners!

35 But wisdom is justified of all her children.

36 And one of the Pharisees desired him that he would eat with him. And he went into the Pharisee's house, and sat down to meat.

37 And behold, a woman in the city, who was a sinner, when she knew that Jesus sat at meat in the Pharisee's house, brought an alabaster box of ointment.

38 And stood at his feet weeping, and began to wash his feet with tears, and did wipe them with the hairs of her head, and kissed his feet, and anointed them with ointment.

39 Now when the Pharisee who had bidden him saw this, he spake within himself, saying, This man, if he were a prophet, would have known who, or what manner of woman this is who toucheth him; for she is a sinner.

40 And Jesus answering, said unto him, Simon, I have somewhat to say unto thee. And he said, Master, say on.

41 And Jesus said, There was a certain creditor, who had two debtors; the one owed five hundred pence, and the other fifty.

42 And when he found they had nothing to pay, he frankly forgave them both. Tell me therefore, which of them will love him most?

43 Simon answered and said, I suppose the man to whom he forgave most. And he said unto him, Thou hast rightly judged.

44 And he turned to the woman, and said unto Simon, Seest thou this woman? I entered into thy house, thou gavest me no water for my feet; but she hath washed my feet with tears, and wiped them with the hairs of her head.

45 Thou gavest me no kiss; but this woman since the time I came in, hath not ceased to kiss my feet.

46 My head with oil thou didst not anoint; but this woman hath anointed my feet with ointment.

47 Wherefore I say unto thee, Her sins which are many, are forgiven; for she loved much. But to whom little is forgiven, the same loveth little.

48 And he said unto her, Thy sins are forgiven.

49 And they who sat at meat with him, began to say within themselves, Who is this that forgiveth sins also?

50 And he said to the woman, Thy faith hath saved thee; go in peace.

## CHAPTER 8

*Parable of the sower—Who are brethren of Christ—Christ stilleth the tempest—Jairus' daughter raised—Swine drowned.*

1 And it came to pass afterward, that he went throughout every city and village, preaching and showing the glad tidings of the kingdom of God; and the twelve who were ordained of him, were with him,

2 And certain women who had been healed of evil spirits and infirmities, Mary called Magdalene, out of whom went seven devils;

3 And Joanna the wife of Chuza, Herod's steward, and Susanna, and many others, who ministered unto him with their substance.

4 And when much people were gathered together, and were come to him out of every city, he spake by a parable, saying,

5 A sower went out to sow his seed; and as he sowed, some fell by the wayside; and it was trodden down, and the fowls of the air devoured it.

6 And some fell upon a rock; and as soon as it was sprung up, it withered away, because it lacked moisture.

7 And some fell among thorns; and

the thorns sprang up with it, and choked it.

8 And others fell on good ground, and sprang up, and bare fruit an hundredfold.

9 And when he had said these things, he cried, He who hath ears to hear, let him hear. And his disciples asked him, saying, What might this parable be?

10 And he said, Unto you it is given to know the mysteries of the kingdom of God; but to others in parables; that seeing they might not see, and hearing they might not understand.

11 Now the parable is this; The seed is the word of God.

12 That which fell by the wayside are they who hear; and the devil cometh and taketh away the word out of their hearts, lest they should believe and be saved.

13 That which fell on the rock are they, who, when they hear, receive the word with joy; and they have no root, but for a while believe, and in a time of temptation fall away.

14 And that which fell among thorns are they, who, when they have heard, go forth and are choked with cares, and riches, and pleasures of life, and bring no fruit to perfection.

15 But that which fell on the good ground are they, who receive the word in an honest and good heart, having heard the word, keep what they hear, and bring forth fruit with patience.

16 For no man, when he hath lighted a candle, covereth it with a vessel, or putteth it under a bed; but setteth it on a candlestick, that they who enter in may see the light.

17 For nothing is secret, which shall not be made manifest; neither hid, which shall not be made known, and go abroad.

18 Take heed therefore how ye hear; for whosoever receiveth, to him shall be given; and whosoever receiveth not, from him shall be taken even that which he seemeth to have.

19 Then came to him his mother and his brethren, and could not speak to him for the multitude.

20 And some who stood by, said unto him, Thy mother and thy brethren stand without, desiring to see thee.

21 And he answered and said unto them, My mother and my brethren are those which hear the word of God, and do it.

22 Now it came to pass on a certain day, that he went into a ship with his disciples; and he said unto them, Let us go over unto the other side of the lake. And they launched forth.

23 But as they sailed he fell asleep; and there came down a storm of wind on the lake; and they were filled with fear, and were in danger.

24 And they came to him and awoke him, saying, Master, Master, we perish. Then he arose, and rebuked the wind and the raging of the waters, and they ceased; and there was a calm.

25 And he said unto them, Where is your faith? and they being afraid, wondered, saying one to another, What manner of man is this? For he commandeth even the winds and waters, and they obey him.

26 And they arrived at the country of the Gadarenes, which is over against Galilee.

27 And when he went forth to land, there met him out of the city a certain man, who had devils for a long time, and he would wear no clothes, neither abode in a house, but in the tombs.

28 When he saw Jesus, he cried out and fell down before him, and with a loud voice said, What have I to do with thee, Jesus, thou Son of God most high? I beseech thee torment me not.

29 (For he had commanded the unclean spirit to come out of the man.) For ofttimes it had caught him; and he was kept bound with chains, and in fetters; and he brake the bands, and was driven of the devil into the wilderness.

30 Jesus asked him, saying, What is thy name? And he said, Legion; because many devils were entered into him.

31 And there was there a herd of many swine, feeding on the mountain.

32 And they besought him that he would suffer them to enter into the swine, and he suffered them.

33 And they besought him also, that he would not command them to go out into the deep. And he said unto them, Come out of the man.

34 Then went the devils out of the man, and entered into the swine; and the herd ran violently down a steep place into the lake, and were choked.

35 When they who fed the swine saw

what was done, they fled, and went and told the people in the city and in the country.

36 Then they went out to see what was done; and came to Jesus, and found the man out of whom the devils were departed, sitting at the feet of Jesus, clothed, and in his right mind; and they were afraid.

37 They also who saw the miracle, told them by what means he who was possessed of the devils was healed.

38 Then the whole multitude of the country of the Gadarenes round about, besought Jesus to depart from them; for they were taken with great fear. And Jesus went up into the ship, and returned back again.

39 Now, the man out of whom the devils were departed, besought him that he might be with him. But Jesus sent him away, saying,

40 Return to thine own house, and show how great things God hath done unto thee. And he went his way, and published throughout the whole city, how great things Jesus had done unto him.

41 And it came to pass, that, when Jesus was returned, the people received him; for they were all waiting for him.

42 And behold, there came a man named Jairus, and he was a ruler of the synagogue; and he fell down at Jesus' feet, and besought him that he would come into his house;

43 For he had an only daughter, about twelve years of age, and she lay a-dying. But as he went, the people thronged him.

44 And a woman, having an issue of blood twelve years, who had spent all her living upon physicians, neither could be healed of any,

45 Came behind Jesus, and touched the border of his garment: and immediately her issue of blood staunched.

46 And Jesus said, Who touched me? When all denied, Peter and they that were with him, said, Master, the multitude throng thee, and press upon thee, and sayest thou, Who touched me?

47 And Jesus said, Some one hath touched me; for I perceive that virtue is gone out of me.

48 And when the woman found that she was not hid, she came trembling, and falling down before him, she declared unto him before all the people for what cause she had touched him, and how she was healed immediately.

49 And he said unto her, Daughter, be of good comfort; thy faith hath made thee whole; go in peace.

50 While he yet spake, there cometh one from the ruler of the synagogue's house, saying to him, Thy daughter is dead; trouble not the Master.

51 But Jesus heard him, and he said unto the ruler of the synagogue, Fear not; believe only, and she shall be made whole. And when he came into the house, he suffered no man to go in, save Peter, and James, and John, and the father and the mother of the maiden.

52 And all wept and bewailed her; but he said, Weep not; she is not dead, but sleepeth. And they laughed him to scorn, knowing that she was dead.

53 And he put them all out, and took her by the hand, and he called, saying, Maid, arise.

54 And her spirit came again, and she arose straightway; and he commanded to give her meat.

55 And her parents were astonished; but he charged them that they should tell no man what was done.

## CHAPTER 9

*Christ instructs his Apostles—Sends them forth—Miracle of five loaves and two fishes—The transfiguration—Moses and Elias appear—Jesus, homeless.*

1 Then he called his twelve disciples together, and he gave them power and authority over all devils, and to cure diseases.

2 And he sent them to preach the kingdom of God, and to heal the sick.

3 And he said unto them, Take nothing for your journey, neither staves, nor scrip, neither bread, neither money; neither have two coats apiece.

4 And into whatsoever house ye enter, there abide until ye depart thence.

5 And whosoever will not receive you, when ye go out of that city, shake off the very dust from your feet for a testimony against them.

6 And they departed, and went through the towns, preaching the gospel, and healing everywhere.

7 Now Herod the tetrarch heard of all that was done by Jesus; and he was perplexed, because that it was said of

some, That John was risen from the dead;

8 And of some, That Elias had appeared; and of others, That one of the old prophets was risen again.

9 And Herod said, John have I beheaded; but who is this, of whom I hear such things? And he desired to see him.

10 And the apostles, when they returned, told Jesus all that they had done. And he took them, and went aside privately into a solitary place belonging to the city called Bethsaida.

11 And the people, when they knew it, followed him; and he received them, and spake unto them of the kingdom of God, and healed them who had need of healing.

12 And when the day began to wear away, then came the twelve, and said unto him, Send the multitude away, that they may go into the towns and country round about, and lodge, and get victuals; for we are here in a solitary place.

13 But he said unto them, Give ye them to eat. And they said, We have but five loaves and two fishes; and except we should go and buy meat, we can provide no more food for all this multitude.

14 For they were in number about five thousand men. And Jesus said unto his disciples, Make them sit down by fifties in a company.

15 And they did so, and made them all sit down.

16 Then he took the five loaves, and the two fishes, and looking up to heaven, he blessed them, and brake, and gave to the disciples to set before the multitude.

17 And they did eat, and were all filled. And there was taken up of the fragments which remained, twelve baskets.

18 And it came to pass, as he went alone with his disciples to pray, he asked them, saying, Who say the people that I am?

19 They answering said, Some say, John the Baptist; but others say, Elias; and others, That one of the old prophets is risen again.

20 He said unto them, But who say ye that I am? Peter answering said, The Christ, the Son of God.

21 And he straitly charged them,

and commanded them to tell no man of him,

22 Saying, the Son of man must suffer many things, and be rejected of the elders, and chief priests, and scribes; and be slain, and be raised the third day.

23 And he said unto them all, If any man will come after me, let him deny himself, and take up his cross daily, and follow me.

24 For whosoever will save his life, must be willing to lose it for my sake; and whosoever will be willing to lose his life for my sake, the same shall save it.

25 For what doth it profit a man if he gain the whole world, and yet he receive him not whom God hath ordained, and he lose his own soul, and he himself be a castaway?

26 For whosoever shall be ashamed of me, and of my words, of him shall the Son of man be ashamed, when he shall come in his own kingdom, clothed in the glory of his Father, with the holy angels.

27 Verily, I tell you of a truth, there are some standing here who shall not taste of death, until they see the kingdom of God coming in power.

28 And it came to pass, eight days after these sayings, that he took Peter and John and James, and went up into a mountain to pray.

29 And as he prayed, the fashion of his countenance was changed, and his raiment was white and glittering.

30 And behold, there came and talked with him two men, even Moses and Elias,

31 Who appeared in glory, and spake of his death, and also his resurrection, which he should accomplish at Jerusalem.

32 But Peter and they who were with him were heavy with sleep, and when they were awake they saw his glory, and the two men who stood with him.

33 And after the two men departed from him, Peter said unto Jesus, Master, it is good for us to be here; let us make three tabernacles; one for thee, and one for Moses, and one for Elias; not knowing what he said.

34 While he thus spake, there came a cloud, and overshadowed them all; and they feared as they entered into the cloud.

35 And there came a voice out of the cloud, saying, This is my beloved Son; hear him.

36 And when the voice was past, Jesus was found alone. And these things they kept close, and they told no man, in those days, any of the things which they had seen.

37 And it came to pass that on the next day, when they were come down from the hill, much people met him.

38 And behold, a man of the company cried out, saying, Master, I beseech thee, look upon my son; for he is mine only child.

39 And, lo, a spirit taketh him, and he suddenly crieth out; and it teareth him, that he foameth, and bruising him hardly, departeth from him.

40 And I besought thy disciples to cast him out, and they could not.

41 And Jesus answering, said, O faithless and perverse generation, how long shall I be with you, and suffer you? Bring thy son hither.

42 And as he was coming, the devil threw him down, and tare him again. And Jesus rebuked the unclean spirit, and healed the child, and delivered him again to his father.

43 And they were all amazed at the mighty power of God. But while they wondered every one, at all the things which Jesus did, he said unto his disciples,

44 Let these sayings sink down into your hearts; for the Son of man shall be delivered into the hands of men.

45 But they understood not this saying, and it was hid from them that they perceived it not; and they feared to ask him of that saying.

46 Then there arose a reasoning among them, who of them should be greatest.

47 And Jesus perceiving the thoughts of their hearts, took a child and set him in the midst;

48 And said unto them, Whosoever shall receive this child in my name, receiveth me; and whosoever shall receive me, receiveth him who sent me; for he who is least among you all, the same shall be great.

49 And John spake and said, Master, we saw one casting out devils in thy name; and we forbade him, because he followeth not with us.

50 And Jesus said unto him, Forbid not any; for he who is not against us is for us.

51 And it came to pass, when the time was come that he should be received up, he steadfastly set his face to go to Jerusalem;

52 And sent messengers before his face; and they went and entered into a village of the Samaritans to make ready for him.

53 And the Samaritans would not receive him, because his face was turned as though he would go to Jerusalem.

54 And when his disciples, James and John, saw that they would not receive him, they said, Lord, wilt thou that we command fire to come down from heaven and consume them, even as Elias did?

55 But he turned and rebuked them, and said, Ye know not what manner of spirit ye are of.

56 For the Son of man is not come to destroy men's lives, but to save them. And they went to another village.

57 And it came to pass, as they went in the way, a certain man said unto him, Lord, I will follow thee whithersoever thou goest.

58 And Jesus said unto him, The foxes have holes, and the birds of the air have nests; but the Son of man hath not where to lay his head.

59 And he said unto another, Follow me. But he said, Lord, suffer me first to go and bury my father.

60 Jesus said unto him, Let the dead bury their dead; but go thou and preach the kingdom of God.

61 And another also said, Lord, I will follow thee; but let me first go and bid them farewell who are at my house.

62 And Jesus said unto him, No man having put his hand to the plough, and looking back, is fit for the kingdom of God.

## CHAPTER 10

*Seventy appointed—Their instructions—Their return—The good Samaritan—Mary's choice.*

1 After these things the Lord appointed other seventy also, and sent them two and two before his face, into every city and place where he himself would come.

2 And he said unto them, The harvest truly is great, but the laborers

few; pray ye therefore the Lord of the harvest, that he would send forth laborers into his harvest.

3 Go your ways; behold I send you forth as lambs among wolves.

4 Carry neither purse, nor scrip, nor shoes; nor salute any man by the way.

5 And into whatsoever house ye enter, first say, Peace to this house.

6 And if the son of peace be there, your peace shall rest upon it; if not, it shall turn to you again.

7 And into whatsoever house they receive you, remain, eating and drinking such things as they give; for the laborer is worthy of his hire. Go not from house to house.

8 And into whatsoever city ye enter, and they receive you, eat such things as are set before you;

9 And heal the sick that are therein, and say, The kingdom of God is come nigh unto you.

10 But into whatsoever city ye enter, and they receive you not, go your ways out into the streets of the same, and say,

11 Even the very dust of your city which cleaveth on us, we do wipe off against you; notwithstanding, be sure of this, that the kingdom of God is come nigh unto you.

12 But I say unto you, That it shall be more tolerable in the day of judgment for Sodom, than for that city.

13 Then began he to upbraid the people in every city wherein his mighty works were done, who received him not, saying,

14 Woe unto thee, Chorazin! Woe unto thee, Bethsaida! For if the mighty works had been done in Tyre and Sidon, which have been done in you, they would have repented, sitting in sackcloth and ashes.

15 But it shall be more tolerable for Tyre and Sidon in the day of judgment, than for you.

16 And thou, Capernaum, which art exalted to heaven, shalt be cast down to hell.

17 And he said unto his disciples, He that heareth you, heareth me; and he that despiseth you, despiseth me; and he that despiseth me, despiseth him who sent me.

18 And the seventy returned again with joy, saying, Lord, even the devils are subject to us through thy name.

19 And he said unto them, As light-ning falleth from heaven, I beheld Satan also falling.

20 Behold, I will give unto you power over serpents and scorpions, and over all the power of the enemy; and nothing shall by any means hurt you.

21 Notwithstanding, in this rejoice not, that the spirits are subject unto you; but rather rejoice, because your names are written in heaven.

22 In that hour Jesus rejoiced in spirit, and said, I thank thee, O Father, Lord of heaven and earth, that thou hast hid these things from them who think they are wise and prudent, and hast revealed them unto babes; even so, Father; for so it seemed good in thy sight.

23 All things are delivered to me of my Father; and no man knoweth that the Son is the Father, and the Father is the Son, but him to whom the Son will reveal it.

24 And he turned him unto the disciples, and said privately, Blessed are the eyes which see the things that ye see.

25 For I tell you, That many prophets and kings have desired to see those things which ye see, and have not seen them; and to hear those things which ye hear, and have not heard them.

26 And, behold, a certain lawyer stood up, and tempted him, saying, Master, what shall I do to inherit eternal life?

27 He said unto him, What is written in the law? How readest thou?

28 And he answering, said, Thou shalt love the Lord thy God with all thy heart, and with all thy soul, and with all thy strength, and with all thy mind; and thy neighbor as thyself.

29 And he said unto him, Thou hast answered right; this do, and thou shalt live.

30 But he, willing to justify himself, said unto Jesus, And who is my neighbor?

31 And Jesus answering, said, A certain man went down from Jerusalem to Jericho, and fell among thieves, which stripped him of his raiment and wounded him, and departed, leaving him half dead.

32 And by chance, there came down a certain priest that way; and when he saw him, he passed by on the other side of the way.

33 And likewise a Levite, when he was at the place, came and looked on him, and passed by on the other side of the way; for they desired in their hearts that it might not be known that they had seen him.

34 But a certain Samaritan, as he journeyed, came where he was; and when he saw him, he had compassion on him.

35 And went to him, and bound up his wounds, pouring in oil and wine, and set him on his own beast, and brought him to an inn, and took care of him.

36 And on the morrow, when he departed, he took money, and gave to the host, and said unto him, Take care of him, and whatsoever thou spendest more, when I come again, I will repay thee.

37 Who now of these three, thinkest thou, was neighbor unto him that fell among the thieves?

38 And he said, He who showed mercy on him. Then said Jesus unto him, Go, and do likewise.

39 Now it came to pass, as they went, they entered into a certain village; and a certain woman named Martha received him into her house.

40 And she had a sister, called Mary, who also sat at Jesus' feet, and heard his words.

41 But Martha was cumbered about much serving, and came to him, and said, Lord, dost thou not care that my sister hath left me to serve alone? Bid her therefore that she help me.

42 And Jesus answered and said unto her, Martha, Martha, thou art careful and troubled about many things;

43 But one thing is needful; and Mary hath chosen that good part, which shall not be taken away from her.

## CHAPTER 11

*The Lord's prayer—The state of one to whom an evil spirit returns—The key of knowledge.*

1 And it came to pass, as Jesus was praying in a certain place, when he ceased, one of his disciples said unto him, Lord, teach us to pray, as John also taught his disciples.

2 And he said unto them, When ye pray, say, Our Father who art in heaven, hallowed be thy name. Thy kingdom come. Thy will be done as in heaven, so in earth.

3 Give us day by day our daily bread.

4 And forgive us our sins; for we also forgive every one who is indebted to us. And let us not be led unto temptation; but deliver us from evil; for thine is the kingdom and power. Amen.

5 And he said unto them, Your heavenly Father will not fail to give unto you whatsoever ye ask of him. And he spake a parable, saying,

6 Which of you shall have a friend, and shall go unto him at midnight, and say unto him, Friend, lend me three loaves;

7 For a friend of mine has come to me in his journey, and I have nothing to set before him;

8 And he from within shall answer and say, Trouble me not; the door is now shut, and my children are with me in bed; I cannot rise and give thee.

9 I say unto you, Though he will not rise and give him because he is his friend, yet because of his importunity, he will rise and give him as many as he needeth.

10 And I say unto you, Ask, and it shall be given you; seek, and ye shall find; knock, and it shall be opened unto you.

11 For every one who asketh, receiveth; and he that seeketh, findeth; and to him that knocketh, it shall be opened.

12 If a son shall ask bread of any of you who is a father, will he give him a stone? or, if a fish, will he for a fish give him a serpent?

13 Or if he shall ask an egg, will he offer him a scorpion?

14 If ye then, being evil, know how to give good gifts unto your children, how much more shall your heavenly Father give good gifts, through the Holy Spirit, to them who ask him.

15 And he was casting a devil out of a man, and he was dumb. And it came to pass, when the devil was gone out, the dumb spake; and the people wondered.

16 But some of them said, He casteth out devils through Beelzebub, the chief of the devils.

17 And others tempting, sought of him a sign from heaven.

18 But he, knowing their thoughts, said unto them, Every kingdom di-

vided against itself is brought to desolation; and a house divided cannot stand, but falleth.

19 If Satan also be divided against himself, how can his kingdom stand? I say this, because you say I cast out devils through Beelzebub.

20 And if I, by Beelzebub, cast out devils, by whom do your sons cast out devils? Therefore shall they be your judges.

21 But if I, with the finger of God cast out devils, no doubt the kingdom of God has come upon you.

22 When a strong man armed keepeth his palace, his goods are in peace;

23 But when a stronger than he shall come upon him, and overcome him, he taketh from him all his armor wherein he trusted and divideth his goods.

24 He that is not with me, is against me; and he that gathereth not with me, scattereth.

25 When the unclean spirit is gone out of a man, it walketh through dry places, seeking rest; and finding none, it saith, I will return unto my house whence I came out.

26 And when it cometh, it findeth the house swept and garnished.

27 Then goeth the evil spirit, and taketh seven other spirits more wicked than himself, and they enter in, and dwell there; and the last end of that man is worse than the first.

28 And it came to pass, as he spake these things, a certain woman of the company, lifted up her voice, and said unto him, Blessed is the womb which bare thee, and the paps which thou hast sucked.

29 And he said, Yea, and blessed are all they who hear the word of God, and keep it.

30 When the people were gathered thick together, he began to say, This is an evil generation; they seek a sign, and there shall no sign be given them, but the sign of Jonas the prophet.

31 For as Jonas was a sign unto the Ninevites, so also shall the Son of man be to this generation.

32 The queen of the south shall rise up in the day of judgment with the men of this generation, and condemn them; for she came from the utmost parts of the earth, to hear the wisdom of Solomon; and, behold, a greater than Solomon is here.

33 The men of Nineveh shall rise up in the day of judgment with this generation; and shall condemn it; for they repented at the preaching of Jonas; and, behold, a greater than Jonas is here.

34 No man when he hath lighted a candle, putteth it in a secret place, neither under a bushel, but on a candlestick, that they who come in may see the light.

35 The light of the body is the eye; therefore when thine eye is single, thy whole body also is full of light; but when thine eye is evil, thy body also is full of darkness.

36 Take heed therefore, that the light which is in thee be not darkness.

37 If thy whole body therefore is full of light, having no part dark, the whole shall be full of light, as when the bright shining of a candle lighteneth a room and doth give the light in all the room.

38 And as he spake, a certain Pharisee besought him to dine with him; and he went in, and sat down to meat.

39 And when the Pharisee saw him, he marveled that he had not first washed before dinner.

40 And the Lord said unto him; Now do you Pharisees make clean the outside of the cup and the platter: but your inward part is full of ravening and wickedness.

41 O fools, did not he who made that which is without, make that which is within also?

42 But if ye would rather give alms of such things as ye have; and observe to do all things which I have commanded you, then would your inward parts be clean also.

43 But I say unto you, Woe be unto you, Pharisees! For ye tithe mint, and rue, and all manner of herbs, and pass over judgment, and the love of God; these ought ye to have done, and not to leave the other undone.

44 Woe unto you, Pharisees! for you love the uppermost seats in the synagogues, and greetings in the markets.

45 Woe unto you, scribes and Pharisees, hypocrites! For ye are as graves which appear not, and the men who walk over are not aware of them.

46 Then answered one of the law-

yers, and said unto him, Master, thus saying, thou reproachest us also.

47 And he said, Woe unto you, lawyers, also! For ye lade men with burdens grievous to be borne, and ye yourselves touch not the burdens with one of your fingers.

48 Woe unto you! For you build the sepulchers of the prophets, and your fathers killed them.

49 Truly ye bear witness that ye allow the deeds of your fathers; for they indeed killed them, and ye build their sepulchers.

50 Therefore also said the wisdom of God, I will send them prophets, and apostles, and some of them they shall slay and persecute;

51 That the blood of all the prophets, which was shed from the foundation of the world, may be required of this generation; from the blood of Abel unto the blood of Zacharias, who perished between the altar and the temple.

52 Verily I say unto you, It shall be required of this generation.

53 Woe unto you, lawyers! For ye have taken away the key of knowledge, the fullness of the scriptures; ye enter not in yourselves into the kingdom; and those who were entering in, ye hindered.

54 And as he said these things unto them, the scribes and Pharisees began to be angry, and to urge vehemently, endeavoring to provoke him to speak of many things;

55 Laying wait for him, and seeking to catch something out of his mouth, that they might accuse him.

## CHAPTER 12

*Sundry instructions to the disciples—Sin against the Holy Ghost—The foolish rich man—Christ's different appearings.*

1 In the meantime, when there were gathered together an innumerable multitude of people, insomuch that they trode one upon another, he began to say unto his disciples first of all, Beware ye of the leaven of the Pharisees, which is hypocrisy.

2 For there is nothing covered which shall not be revealed; neither hid which shall not be known.

3 Therefore, whatsoever ye have spoken in darkness, shall be heard in the light; and that which ye have spoken in the ear in closets, shall be proclaimed upon the housetops.

4 And I say unto you my friends, Be not afraid of them who kill the body, and after that have no more that they can do;

5 But I will forewarn you whom ye shall fear; fear him, who after he hath killed, hath power to cast into hell; yea, I say unto you, Fear him.

6 Are not five sparrows sold for two farthings, and not one of them is forgotten before God?

7 But even the very hairs of your head are all numbered. Fear not therefore; ye are of more value than many sparrows.

8 Also I say unto you, Whosoever shall confess me before men, him shall the Son of man also confess before the angels of God.

9 But he who denieth me before men, shall be denied before the angels of God.

10 Now his disciples knew that he said this, because they had spoken evil against him before the people; for they were afraid to confess him before men.

11 And they reasoned among themselves, saying, He knoweth our hearts, and he speaketh to our condemnation, and we shall not be forgiven. But he answered them, and said unto them,

12 Whosoever shall speak a word against the Son of man, and repenteth, it shall be forgiven him; but unto him who blasphemeth against the Holy Ghost, it shall not be forgiven him.

13 And again I say unto you, They shall bring you unto the synagogues, and before magistrates, and powers. When they do this, take ye no thought how, or what thing ye shall answer, or what ye shall say;

14 For the Holy Ghost shall teach you in the same hour what ye ought to say.

15 And one of the company said unto him, Master, speak to my brother, that he divide the inheritance with me.

16 And he said unto him, Man, who made me a judge, or a divider over you?

17 And he said unto them, Take heed, and beware of covetousness; for a man's life consisteth not in the abundance of the things which he possesseth.

18 And he spake a parable unto them, saying, The ground of a certain rich man brought forth plentifully;

19 And he thought within himself,

saying, What shall I do, because I have no room where to bestow my fruits?

20 And he said, This will I do; I will pull down my barns and build greater; and there will I bestow all my fruits, and my goods.

21 And I will say to my soul, Soul, thou hast much goods laid up for many years; take thine ease, eat, drink, and be merry.

22 But God said unto him, Thou fool! This night thy soul shall be required of thee; then whose shall those things be which thou hast provided?

23 So shall it be with him who layeth up treasure for himself, and is not rich toward God.

24 And he said unto his disciples, Therefore I say unto you, Take no thought for your life, what ye shall eat; neither for the body, what ye shall put on.

25 For the life is more than meat, and the body than raiment.

26 Consider the ravens; for they neither sow nor reap; which neither have storehouse nor barn; nevertheless God feedeth them. Are ye not better than the fowls?

27 And who of you by taking thought, can add to his stature one cubit?

28 If ye then be not able to do that which is least, why take ye thought for the rest?

29 Consider the lilies, how they grow; they toil not, they spin not; and yet I say unto you, that Solomon in all his glory was not arrayed like one of these.

30 If then God so clothe the grass, which is today in the field, and tomorrow is cast in the oven; how much more will he provide for you, if ye are not of little faith?

31 Therefore, seek not what ye shall eat, or what ye shall drink, neither be ye of doubtful mind;

32 For all these things do the nations of the world seek after; and your Father who is in heaven, knoweth that ye have need of these things.

33 And ye are sent unto them to be their ministers, and the laborer is worthy of his hire; for the law saith, That a man shall not muzzle the ox that treadeth out the corn.

34 Therefore seek ye to bring forth the kingdom of God, and all these things shall be added unto you.

35 Fear not, little flock; for it is your Father's good pleasure to give you the kingdom.

36 This he spake unto his disciples, saying, Sell that ye have and give alms; provide not for yourselves bags which wax old, but rather provide a treasure in the heavens, that faileth not; where no thief approacheth, neither moth corrupteth.

37 For where your treasure is, there will your heart be also.

38 Let your loins be girded about and have your lights burning;

39 That ye yourselves may be like unto men who wait for their Lord, when he will return from the wedding; that, when he cometh and knocketh, they may open unto him immediately.

40 Verily I say unto you, Blessed are those servants, whom the Lord when he cometh shall find watching; for he shall gird himself, and make them to sit down to meat, and will come forth and serve them.

41 For, behold, he cometh in the first watch of the night, and he shall also come in the second watch, and again he shall come in the third watch.

42 And verily I say unto you, He hath already come, as it is written of him; and again when he shall come in the second watch, or come in the third watch, blessed are those servants when he cometh, that he shall find so doing;

43 For the Lord of those servants shall gird himself, and make them to sit down to meat, and will come forth and serve them.

44 And now, verily I say these things unto you, that ye may know this, that the coming of the Lord is as a thief in the night.

45 And it is like unto a man who is an householder, who, if he watcheth not his goods, the thief cometh in an hour of which he is not aware, and taketh his goods, and divideth them among his fellows.

46 And they said among themselves, If the good man of the house had known what hour the thief would come, he would have watched, and not have suffered his house to be broken through and the loss of his goods.

47 And he said unto them, Verily I say unto you, be ye therefore ready also; for the Son of man cometh at an hour when ye think not.

48 Then Peter said unto him, Lord,

speakest thou this parable unto us, or unto all?

49 And the Lord said, I speak unto those whom the Lord shall make rulers over his household, to give his children their portion of meat in due season.

50 And they said, Who then is that faithful and wise servant?

51 And the Lord said unto them, It is that servant who watcheth, to impart his portion of meat in due season.

52 Blessed be that servant whom his Lord shall find, when he cometh, so doing.

53 Of a truth I say unto you, that he will make him ruler over all that he hath.

54 But the evil servant is he who is not found watching. And if that servant is not found watching, he will say in his heart, My Lord delayeth his coming; and shall begin to beat the menservants, and the maidens, and to eat, and drink, and to be drunken.

55 The Lord of that servant will come in a day he looketh not for, and at an hour when he is not aware, and will cut him down, and will appoint him his portion with the unbelievers.

56 And that servant who knew his Lord's will, and prepared not for his Lord's coming, neither did according to his will, shall be beaten with many stripes.

57 But he that knew not his Lord's will, and did commit things worthy of stripes, shall be beaten with few. For unto whomsoever much is given, of him shall much be required; and to whom the Lord has committed much, of him will men ask the more.

58 For they are not well pleased with the Lord's doings; therefore I am come to send fire on the earth; and what is it to you, if I will that it be already kindled?

59 But I have a baptism to be baptized with; and how am I straightened until it be accomplished!

60 Suppose ye that I am come to give peace on earth? I tell you, nay; but rather division.

61 For from henceforth there shall be five in one house, divided, three against two, and two against three.

62 The father shall be divided against the son, and the son against the father; the mother against the daughter, and the daughter against

the mother; the mother-in-law against her daughter-in-law, and the daughter-in-law against her mother-in-law.

63 And he said also unto the people, When ye see a cloud rise out of the west, ye say straightway, There cometh a shower; and so it is.

64 And when the south wind blows, ye say, There will be heat; and it cometh to pass.

65 O hypocrites! Ye can discern the face of the sky, and of the earth; but how is it that ye do not discern this time?

66 Yea, and why even of yourselves judge ye not what is right?

67 Why goest thou to thine adversary for a magistrate, when thou art in the way with thine enemy? Why not give diligence that thou mayest be delivered from him; lest he hale thee to the judge, and the judge deliver thee to the officer, and the officer cast thee into prison?

68 I tell thee, thou shalt not depart thence, till thou hast paid the very last mite.

## CHAPTER 13

*Parable of the fig tree—Woman cured of infirmity—Kingdom of God like a grain of mustard, and leaven.*

1 And there were present at that time, some who spake unto him of the Galileans, whose blood Pilate had mingled with their sacrifices.

2 And Jesus said unto them, Suppose ye that these Galileans were sinners above all the Galileans, because they suffered such things?

3 I tell you, Nay; but except ye repent, ye shall all likewise perish.

4 Or those eighteen, on whom the tower in Siloam fell, and slew them; think ye that they were sinners above all men who dwelt in Jerusalem?

5 I tell you, Nay; but except ye repent, ye shall all likewise perish.

6 He spake also this parable, A certain husbandman had a fig tree planted in the vineyard. He came and sought fruit thereon and found none.

7 Then said he unto the dresser of his vineyard, Behold, these three years I come seeking fruit on this fig tree, and find none. Cut it down, why cumbereth it the ground?

8 And he, answering, said unto him, Lord, let it alone this year also, till I shall dig about and dung it.

9 And if it bear fruit, the tree is saved, and if not, after that thou shalt cut it down. And many other parables spake he unto the people.

10 And after this, as he was teaching in one of the synagogues on the Sabbath;

11 Behold, there was a woman who had a spirit of infirmity eighteen years, and was bowed together, and could in no wise straighten up.

12 And when Jesus saw her, he called and said unto her, Woman, thou art loosed from thine infirmities.

13 And he laid hands on her; and immediately she was made straight, and glorified God.

14 And the ruler of the synagogue was filled with indignation, because that Jesus had healed on the Sabbath day, and said unto the people, There are six days in which men ought to work; in them therefore come and be healed, and not on the Sabbath day.

15 The Lord then said unto him, O hypocrite! Doth not each one of you on the Sabbath loose his ox or his ass from the stall, and lead him away to watering?

16 And ought not this woman, being a daughter of Abraham, whom Satan hath bound, lo, these eighteen years, be loosed from this bond on the Sabbath day?

17 And when he had said these things, all his adversaries were ashamed; and all his disciples rejoiced for all the glorious things which were done by him.

18 Then said he, Unto what is the kingdom of God like? and whereunto shall I resemble it?

19 It is like a grain of mustard, which a man took, and cast into his garden; and it grew, and waxed a great tree; and the fowls of the air lodged in the branches of it.

20 And again he said, Whereunto shall I liken the kingdom of God?

21 It is like leaven, which a woman took and hid in three measures of meal, till the whole was leavened.

22 And he went through the cities and villages, teaching, and journeying toward Jerusalem.

23 And there said one unto him, Lord, are there few only that be saved? and he answered him, and said,

24 Strive to enter in at the strait gate; for I say unto you, Many shall seek to enter in, and shall not be able; for the Lord shall not always strive with man.

25 Therefore, when once the Lord of the kingdom is risen up, and hath shut the door of the kingdom, then ye shall stand without, and knock at the door, saying, Lord, Lord, open unto us. But the Lord shall answer and say unto you, I will not receive you, for ye know not from whence ye are.

26 Then shall ye begin to say, We have eaten and drunk in thy presence, and thou hast taught in our streets.

27 But he shall say, I tell you, ye know not from whence ye are; depart from me, all workers of iniquity.

28 There shall be weeping and gnashing of teeth among you, when ye shall see Abraham, and Isaac, and Jacob, and all the prophets, in the kingdom of God, and you are thrust out.

29 And verily I say unto you, They shall come from the east, and the west; and from the north, and the south, and shall sit down in the kingdom of God;

30 And, behold, there are last which shall be first, and there are first which shall be last, and shall be saved therein.

31 And as he was thus teaching, there came to him certain of the Pharisees, saying unto him, Get thee out, and depart hence; for Herod will kill thee.

32 And he said unto them, Go ye and tell Herod, Behold, I cast out devils, and do cures today and tomorrow, and the third day I shall be perfected.

33 Nevertheless, I must walk today and tomorrow, and the third day; for it cannot be that a prophet perish out of Jerusalem.

34 This he spake, signifying of his death. And in this very hour he began to weep over Jerusalem.

35 Saying, O Jerusalem, Jerusalem, thou who killest the prophets, and stonest them who are sent unto thee; how often would I have gathered thy children together, as a hen her brood under her wings, and ye would not.

36 Behold, your house is left unto you desolate. And verily I say unto you, Ye shall not know me, until ye have received from the hand of the Lord a just recompense for all your sins; until the time come when ye shall say, Blessed

is he that cometh in the name of the Lord.

## CHAPTER 14

*Jesus healeth the dropsy on the Sabbath—Parable of the wedding; Parable of the great supper—Men are to forsake all for Christ.*

1 And it came to pass, as he went into the house of one of the chief Pharisees to eat bread on the Sabbath day, that they watched him.

2 And, behold, there was a certain man before him, who had the dropsy.

3 And Jesus spake unto the lawyers, and Pharisees, saying, Is it lawful to heal on the Sabbath day?

4 And they held their peace. And he took the man, and healed him, and let him go;

5 And spake unto them again, saying, Which of you shall have an ass or an ox fallen into a pit and will not straightway pull him out on the Sabbath day?

6 And they could not answer him to these things.

7 And he put forth a parable unto them concerning those who were bidden to a wedding; for he knew how they chose out the chief rooms, and exalted themselves one above another; wherefore he spake unto them, saying,

8 When thou art bidden of any man to a wedding, sit not down in the highest room, lest a more honorable man than thou be bidden of him;

9 And he who bade thee, with him who is more honorable, come, and say to thee, Give this man place; and thou begin with shame to take the lowest room.

10 But when thou art bidden, go and sit down in the lowest room; that when he who bade thee, cometh, he may say unto thee, Friend, go up higher; then shalt thou have honor of God, in the presence of them who sit at meat with thee.

11 For whosoever exalteth himself shall be abased; and he who humbleth himself shall be exalted.

12 Then said he also concerning him who bade to the wedding, When thou makest a dinner, or a supper, call not thy friends, nor thy brethren, neither thy kinsmen, nor rich neighbors; lest they also bid thee again, and a recompense be made thee.

13 But when thou makest a feast, call the poor, the maimed, the lame, the blind,

14 And thou shalt be blessed; for they cannot recompense thee; for thou shalt be recompensed at the resurrection of the just.

15 And when one of them who sat at meat with him, heard these things, he said unto him, Blessed is he who shall eat bread in the kingdom of God.

16 Then said he unto him, A certain man made a great supper and bade many;

17 And sent his servants at supper time, to say to them who were bidden, Come, for all things are now ready.

18 And they all, with one consent, began to make excuse. The first said unto him, I have bought a piece of ground, and I must needs go and see it; I pray thee have me excused.

19 And another said, I have bought five yoke of oxen, and I go to prove them; I pray thee have me excused.

20 And another said, I have married a wife, therefore I cannot come.

21 So that servant came and showed his lord these things. Then the master of the house, being angry, said to his servants, Go out quickly into the streets and lanes of the city, and bring hither the poor, and the maimed, the halt and the blind.

22 And the servant said, Lord, it is done as thou hast commanded, and yet there is room.

23 The lord said unto his servant, Go out into the highways, and hedges, and compel men to come in, that my house may be filled;

24 For I say unto you, That none of those men who were bidden, shall taste of my supper.

25 And when he had finished these sayings, he departed thence, and there went great multitudes with him, and he turned and said unto them,

26 If any man come to me, and hate not his father, and mother, and wife, and children, and brethren, and sisters, or husband, yea and his own life also; or in other words, is afraid to lay down his life for my sake, he cannot be my disciple.

27 And whosoever doth not bear his cross, and come after me, cannot be my disciple.

28 Wherefore, settle this in your hearts, that ye will do the things which I shall teach, and command you.

29 For which of you intending to build a tower, sitteth not down first, and counteth the cost, whether he have money to finish his work?

30 Lest, unhappily, after he has laid the foundation and is not able to finish his work, all who behold, begin to mock him,

31 Saying, This man began to build, and was not able to finish. And this he said, signifying there should not any man follow him, unless he was able to continue; saying,

32 Or what king, going to make war against another king, sitteth not down first, and consulteth whether he be able with ten thousand, to meet him who cometh against him with twenty thousand.

33 Or else, while the other is yet a great way off, he sendeth an embassage, and desireth conditions of peace.

34 So likewise, whosoever of you forsaketh not all that he hath he cannot be my disciple.

35 Then certain of them came to him, saying, Good Master, we have Moses and the prophets, and whosoever shall live by them, shall he not have life?

36 And Jesus answered, saying, Ye know not Moses, neither the prophets; for if ye had known them, ye would have believed on me; for to this intent they were written. For I am sent that ye might have life. Therefore I will liken it unto salt which is good;

37 But if the salt has lost its savor, wherewith shall it be seasoned?

38 It is neither fit for the land, nor yet for the dunghill; men cast it out. He who hath ears to hear, let him hear. These things he said, signifying that which was written, verily must all be fulfilled.

## CHAPTER 15

*Parable of the lost sheep, and also the ten pieces of silver—Parable of the prodigal son.*

1 Then drew near unto him, many of the publicans, and sinners, to hear him.

2 And the Pharisees and scribes murmured, saying, This man receiveth sinners and eateth with them.

3 And he spake this parable unto them, saying,

4 What man of you having a hundred sheep, if he lose one of them, doth not leave the ninety and nine, and go into the wilderness after that which is lost, until he find it?

5 And when he hath found it, he layeth it on his shoulders, rejoicing.

6 And when he cometh home, he calleth together his friends and neighbors, and saith unto them, Rejoice with me; for I found my sheep which was lost.

7 I say unto you, that likewise joy shall be in heaven over one sinner that repenteth, more than over ninety and nine just persons, who need no repentance.

8 Either, what woman having ten pieces of silver, if she lose one piece, doth not light a candle, and sweep the house, and seek diligently till she find it?

9 And when she hath found it, she calleth her friends and her neighbors together, saying, Rejoice with me, for I have found the piece which I had lost.

10 Likewise I say unto you, there is joy in the presence of the angels of God over one sinner who repenteth.

11 And he said, A certain man had two sons;

12 And the younger of them said to his father, Father, give me the portion of goods which falleth to me. And he divided unto them his living.

13 And not many days after, the younger son gathered all together, and took his journey into a far country, and there wasted his substance with riotous living.

14 And when he had spent all, there arose a mighty famine in that land and he began to be in want.

15 And he went and joined himself to a citizen of that country; and he sent him into his fields to feed swine.

16 And he would fain have filled his belly with the husks which the swine did eat; and no man gave unto him.

17 And when he came to himself he said, How many hired servants of my father's have bread enough and to spare, and I perish with hunger!

18 I will arise and go to my father, and will say unto him, Father, I have sinned against heaven, and before thee;

19 And am no more worthy to be called thy son; make me as one of thy hired servants.

20 And he arose and came to his father. But when he was yet a great way

off, his father saw him, and had compassion, and ran, and fell on his neck, and kissed him.

21 And the son said unto him, Father, I have sinned against heaven, and in thy sight, and am no more worthy to be called thy son.

22 But the father said unto his servants, Bring forth the best robe, and put it on him; and put a ring on his finger, and shoes on his feet;

23 And bring hither the fatted calf, and kill it; and let us eat and be merry;

24 For this my son was dead, and is alive again; he was lost, and is found. And they began to be merry.

25 Now his elder son was in the field; and as he came, and drew nigh to the house, he heard music and dancing.

26 And he called one of the servants, and asked what these things meant.

27 And he said unto him, Thy brother is come; and thy father hath killed the fatted calf, because he hath received him safe and sound.

28 And he was angry, and would not go in; therefore came his father out and entreated him.

29 And he answering, said to his father, Lo, these many years do I serve thee, neither transgressed I at any time thy commandment; and thou never gavest me a kid, that I might make merry with my friends;

30 But as soon as this thy son was come, who hath devoured thy living with harlots, thou hast killed for him the fatted calf.

31 And he said unto him, Son, thou art ever with me, and all that I have is thine.

32 It was meet that we should make merry, and be glad; for this thy brother was dead, and is alive again; was lost, and is found.

## CHAPTER 16

*Parable of the wise steward—Concerning putting away—History of the rich man and Lazarus.*

1 And he said also unto his disciples, There was a certain rich man who had a steward; and the same was accused unto him, that he had wasted his goods.

2 And he called him, and said unto him, How is it that I hear this of thee? Give an account of thy stewardship; for thou mayest be no longer steward.

3 Then the steward said within himself, What shall I do? For my lord taketh away from me the stewardship. I cannot dig; to beg I am ashamed.

4 I am resolved what to do, that, when I am put out of the stewardship, they may receive me into their houses.

5 So he called every one of his lord's debtors, and said unto the first, How much owest thou unto my lord?

6 And he said, A hundred measures of oil. And he said unto him, Take thy bill, and sit down quickly, and write fifty.

7 Then said he to another, And how much owest thou? And he said, A hundred measures of wheat. And he said unto him, Take thy bill, and write fourscore.

8 And the lord commended the unjust steward, because he had done wisely; for the children of this world are wiser in their generation, than the children of light.

9 And I say unto you, Make to yourselves friends, of the mammon of unrighteousness; that when ye fail, they may receive you into everlasting habitations.

10 He who is faithful in that which is least, is faithful also in much; and he who is unjust in the least, is also unjust in much.

11 If therefore ye have not been faithful in the unrighteous mammon, who will commit to your trust the true riches?

12 And if ye have not been faithful in that which is another man's, who shall give unto you that which is your own?

13 No servant can serve two masters; for either he will hate the one, and love the other; or else he will hold to the one, and despise the other. Ye cannot serve God and mammon.

14 And the Pharisees also who were covetous, heard all these things; and they derided him.

15 And he said unto them, Ye are they who justify yourselves before men; but God knoweth your hearts; for that which is highly esteemed among men, is an abomination in the sight of God.

16 And they said unto him, We have the law, and the prophets; but as for this man we will not receive him to be our ruler; for he maketh himself to be a judge over us.

17 Then said Jesus unto them, The law and the prophets testify of me; yea, and all the prophets who have written, even until John, have foretold of these days.

18 Since that time, the kingdom of God is preached, and every man who seeketh truth presseth into it.

19 And it is easier for heaven and earth to pass, than for one tittle of the law to fail.

20 And why teach ye the law, and deny that which is written; and condemn him whom the Father hath sent to fulfill the law, that ye might all be redeemed?

21 O fools! for you have said in your hearts, There is no God. And you pervert the right way; and the kingdom of heaven suffereth violence of you; and you persecute the meek; and in your violence you seek to destroy the kingdom; and ye take the children of the kingdom by force. Woe unto you, ye adulterers!

22 And they reviled him again, being angry for the saying, that they were adulterers.

23 But he continued, saying, Whosoever putteth away his wife, and marrieth another, committeth adultery; and whosoever marrieth her who is put away from her husband, committeth adultery. Verily I say unto you, I will liken you unto the rich man.

24 For there was a certain rich man, who was clothed in purple, and fine linen, and fared sumptuously every day.

25 And there was a certain beggar named Lazarus, who was laid at his gate, full of sores,

26 And desiring to be fed with the crumbs which fell from the rich man's table; moreover the dogs came and licked his sores.

27 And it came to pass, that the beggar died, and was carried of the angels into Abraham's bosom. The rich man also died, and was buried.

28 And in hell he lifted up his eyes, being in torments, and saw Abraham afar off, and Lazarus in his bosom.

29 And he cried, and said, Father Abraham, have mercy on me, and send Lazarus that he may dip the tip of his finger in water, and cool my tongue; for I am tormented in this flame.

30 But Abraham said, Son, remember that thou in thy lifetime receivedst thy good things, and likewise Lazarus, evil things; but now he is comforted, and thou art tormented.

31 And besides all this, between us and you, there is a great gulf fixed; so that they who would pass from hence to you, cannot; neither can they pass to us that would come from thence.

32 Then he said, I pray thee therefore, father, that thou wouldest send him to my father's house,

33 For I have five brethren, that he may testify unto them, lest they also come into this place of torment.

34 Abraham said unto him, They have Moses and the prophets; let them hear them.

35 And he said, Nay, father Abraham; but if one went unto them from the dead, they will repent.

36 And he said unto him, If they hear not Moses and the prophets, neither will they be persuaded, though one should rise from the dead.

## CHAPTER 17

*Woe for offenses—The ten lepers—The coming of Christ as a thief in the night—The gathering of the saints.*

1 Then said he unto the disciples, It is impossible but that offenses will come; but woe to him through whom they come.

2 It were better for him that a millstone were hanged about his neck, and he cast into the sea, than that he should offend one of these little ones.

3 Take heed to yourselves. If your brother trespass against you, rebuke him; and if he repent, forgive him.

4 And if he trespass against you seven times in a day, and seven times in a day turn to you again, saying, I repent; you shall forgive him.

5 And the apostles said unto him, Lord, increase our faith.

6 And the Lord said, If you had faith as a grain of mustard seed, you might say unto this sycamore tree, Be thou plucked up by the roots, and be thou planted in the sea; and it should obey you.

7 But who of you, having a servant plowing, or feeding cattle, will say unto him when he is come from the field, Go and sit down to meat?

8 Will he not rather say unto him, Make ready wherewith I may sup, and gird yourself and serve me till I have

eaten and drunken; and afterward, by and by, you shalt eat and drink?

9 Doth he thank that servant because he doeth the things which were commanded him? I say unto you, Nay.

10 So likewise ye, when ye shall have done all those things which are commanded you, say, We are unprofitable servants. We have done that which was no more than our duty to do.

11 It came to pass, as he went to Jerusalem, that he passed through the midst of Galilee and Samaria.

12 And as he entered into a certain village, there met him ten men who were lepers, who stood afar off;

13 And they lifted up their voices, and said, Jesus, Master, have mercy on us.

14 And he said unto them, Go show yourselves unto the priests. And it came to pass, as they went, they were cleansed.

15 One of them, when he saw he was healed, turned back, and with a loud voice glorified God,

16 And fell down on his face at Jesus' feet, giving him thanks; and he was a Samaritan.

17 And Jesus answering, said, Were there not ten cleansed? But where are the nine?

18 There are not found that returned to give glory to God, save this stranger.

19 And he said unto him, Arise, go thy way; thy faith hath made thee whole.

20 And when he was demanded of the Pharisees, when the kingdom of God should come, he answered them, and said, The kingdom of God cometh not with observation;

21 Neither shall they say, Lo, here! or, Lo, there! For, behold, the kingdom of God has already come unto you.

22 And he said unto his disciples, The days will come, when they will desire to see one of the days of the Son of man, and they shall not see it.

23 And if they shall say to you, See here! or, See there! Go not after them, nor follow them.

24 For as the light of the morning, that shineth out of the one part under heaven, and lighteneth to the other part under heaven; so shall also the Son of man be in his day.

25 But first he must suffer many things, and be rejected of this generation.

26 And as it was in the days of Noe; so shall it be also in the days of the Son of man.

27 They did eat, they drank, they married wives, they were given in marriage, until the day that Noe entered into the ark, and the flood came, and destroyed them all.

28 Likewise also as it was in the days of Lot; they did eat, they drank, they bought, they sold, they planted, they builded;

29 But the same day that Lot went out of Sodom, it rained fire and brimstone from heaven, and destroyed them all.

30 Even thus shall it be in the day when the Son of man is revealed.

31 In that day, the disciple who shall be on the housetop, and his stuff in the house, let him not come down to take it away; and he who is in the field, let him likewise not return back.

32 Remember Lot's wife.

33 Whosoever shall seek to save his life, shall lose it; and whosoever shall lose his life, shall preserve it.

34 I tell you, in that night there shall be two in one bed; the one shall be taken, and the other shall be left. Two shall be grinding together; the one shall be taken, the other left.

35 Two shall be in the field; the one shall be taken, and the other left.

36 And they answered and said unto him, Where, Lord, shall they be taken?

37 And he said unto them, Wheresoever the body is gathered; or, in other words, whithersoever the saints are gathered; thither will the eagles be gathered together; or, thither will the remainder be gathered together.

38 This he spake, signifying the gathering of his saints; and of angels descending and gathering the remainder unto them; the one from the bed, the other from the grinding, and the other from the field, whithersoever he listeth.

39 For verily there shall be new heavens, and a new earth, wherein dwelleth righteousness.

40 And there shall be no unclean thing; for the earth becoming old, even as a garment, having waxed in corruption, wherefore it vanisheth away, and

the footstool remaineth sanctified, cleansed from all sin.

## CHAPTER 18

*Unjust judge—Pharisee and publican— The commandments—No security in riches—Christ blesses children.*

1 And he spake a parable unto them, saying, that men ought always to pray and not faint.

2 Saying, There was in a city a judge, who feared not God, nor regarded man.

3 And there was a widow in that city; and she came unto him, saying, Avenge me of mine adversary.

4 And he would not for a while; but afterward, he said within himself, Though I fear not God, nor regard man;

5 Yet because this widow troubleth me, I will avenge her; lest by her continual coming she weary me.

6 And the Lord said, Hear what the unjust judge saith.

7 And shall not God avenge his own elect, who cry day and night unto him, though he bear long with men?

8 I tell you that he will come, and when he does come, he will avenge his saints speedily. Nevertheless, when the Son of man cometh, shall he find faith on the earth?

9 He spake this parable unto certain men, who trusted in themselves that they were righteous, and despised others.

10 Two men went up into the temple to pray; the one a Pharisee, and the other a publican.

11 The Pharisee stood and prayed thus with himself; God, I thank thee that I am not as other men, extortioners, unjust, adulterers; or even as this publican.

12 I fast twice in the week; I give tithes of all that I possess.

13 But the publican, standing afar off, would not lift up so much as his eyes unto heaven, but smote upon his breast, saying, God be merciful to me a sinner.

14 I tell you, this man went down to his house justified, rather than the other; for every one who exalteth himself, shall be abased; and he who humbleth himself, shall be exalted.

15 And they brought unto him also, infants, that he might touch them; but when his disciples saw it, they rebuked them.

16 But Jesus called them, and said, Suffer little children to come unto me, and forbid them not; for of such is the kingdom of God.

17 Verily I say unto you, Whosoever will not receive the kingdom of God as a little child, shall in no wise enter therein.

18 And a certain ruler asked him, saying, Good Master, what shall I do to inherit eternal life?

19 And Jesus said unto him, Why callest thou me good? None is good, save one, that is, God.

20 Thou knowest the commandments; Do not commit adultery. Do not kill. Do not steal. Do not bear false witness. Honor thy father and thy mother.

21 And he said, All these have I kept from my youth up.

22 Now when Jesus heard these things, he said unto him, Yet thou lackest one thing; sell all that thou hast, and distribute unto the poor, and thou shalt have treasure in heaven, and come, follow me.

23 And when he heard this, he was very sorrowful; for he was very rich.

24 And when Jesus saw that he was very sorrowful, he said, How hardly shall they who have riches enter into the kingdom of God!

25 For it is easier for a camel to go through a needle's eye, than for a rich man to enter into the kingdom of God.

26 And they that heard said unto him, Who then can be saved?

27 And he said unto them, It is impossible for them who trust in riches, to enter into the kingdom of God; but he who forsaketh the things which are of this world, it is possible with God, that he should enter in.

28 Then Peter said, Lo, we have left all, and followed thee.

29 And he said unto them, Verily I say unto you, There is no man who has left house, or parents, or brethren, or wife, or children, for the kingdom of God's sake,

30 Who shall not receive manifold more in this present time; and in the world to come, life everlasting.

31 Then he took the twelve, and said unto them, Behold, we go up to Jerusalem, and all things which are written

by the prophets concerning the Son of man, shall be accomplished.

32 For he shall be delivered unto the Gentiles, and shall be mocked, and spitefully entreated, and spitted on.

33 And they shall scourge and put him to death; and the third day he shall rise again.

34 And they understood none of these things; and this saying was hid from them; neither remembered they the things which were spoken.

35 And it came to pass, as he was come nigh unto Jericho, a certain blind man sat by the wayside begging.

36 And hearing the multitude pass by, he asked what it meant.

37 And they told him that Jesus of Nazareth passed by.

38 And he cried, saying, Jesus, son of David, have mercy on me.

39 And they who went before, rebuked him, telling him that he should hold his peace; but he cried so much the more, saying, Son of David, have mercy on me.

40 And Jesus stood, and commanded him to be brought unto him; and when he was come near, he asked him,

41 Saying, What wilt thou that I shall do unto thee? and he said, Lord, that I may receive my sight.

42 And Jesus said unto him, Receive thy sight; thy faith hath saved thee.

43 And immediately he received his sight; and he followed him, glorifying God. And all the disciples when they saw this, gave praise unto God.

## CHAPTER 19

*Zaccheus—Parable of the ten servants—Christ's entry into Jerusalem.*

1 And Jesus entered, and passed through Jericho.

2 And behold, there was a man named Zaccheus, who was the chief among the publicans; and he was rich.

3 And he sought to see Jesus, who he was; and could not for the press, because he was little of stature.

4 And he ran before, and climbed up into a sycamore tree to see him; for he was to pass that way.

5 And when Jesus came to the place, he looked up, and saw him, and said unto him, Zaccheus, make haste, and come down; for today I must abide at thy house.

6 And he made haste, and came down, and received him joyfully.

7 And when the disciples saw it, they all murmured, saying, That he was gone to be a guest with a man who is a sinner.

8 And Zaccheus stood, and said unto the Lord, Behold, Lord, the half of my goods I give to the poor; and if I have taken any thing from any man by unjust means, I restore fourfold.

9 And Jesus said unto him, This day is salvation come to this house, forasmuch as he also is a son of Abraham;

10 For the Son of man is come to seek and to save that which was lost.

11 And as they heard these things, he added and spake a parable, because he was nigh to Jerusalem, and because the Jews taught that the kingdom of God should immediately appear.

12 He said therefore, A certain nobleman went into a far country to receive for himself a kingdom, and to return.

13 And he called his ten servants, and delivered them ten pounds, and said unto them, Occupy till I come.

14 But his citizens hated him, and sent a messenger after him, saying, We will not have this man to reign over us.

15 And it came to pass, that when he was returned, having received the kingdom, then he commanded these servants to be called unto him, to whom he had given the money, that he might know how much every man had gained by trading.

16 Then came the first, saying, Lord, thy pound hath gained ten pounds.

17 And he said unto him, Well done, thou good servant; because thou hast been faithful in a very little, have thou authority over ten cities.

18 And the second came, saying, Lord, thy pound hath gained five pounds.

19 And he said likewise to him, Be thou also over five cities.

20 And another came, saying, Lord, behold thy pound which I have kept laid up in a napkin;

21 For I feared thee, because thou art an austere man; thou takest up that thou layedst not down, and reapest that which thou didst not sow.

22 And he said unto him, Out of thine own mouth will I judge thee, O wicked servant. Thou knewest that I was an austere man, taking up that I

laid not down, and reaping that I did not sow.

23 Wherefore then, gavest not thou my money into the bank, that at my coming I might have received mine own with usury?

24 And he said unto them who stood by, Take from him the pound, and give it to him who hath ten pounds.

25 For I say unto you, That unto every one who occupieth, shall be given; and from him who occupieth not, even that he hath received shall be taken away from him.

26 But those mine enemies, who would not that I should reign over them, bring them hither, and slay them before me.

27 And when he had thus spoken, he went before, ascending up to Jerusalem.

28 And it came to pass, when he was come nigh to Bethphage and Bethany, at the mount called the mount of Olives, he sent two of his disciples;

29 Saying, Go ye into the village over against you, in the which at your entering ye shall find a colt tied, whereon yet never man sat; loose him, and bring him to me.

30 And if any man ask you, Why do ye loose the colt? Thus shall ye say unto him, Because the Lord hath need of him.

31 And they who were sent, went their way, and found even as he had said unto them.

32 And as they were loosing the colt, the owners thereof said unto them, Why loose ye the colt?

33 And they said, The Lord hath need of him.

34 And they brought him to Jesus; and they cast their garments upon the colt, and they set Jesus thereon.

35 And as he went, they spread their clothes in the way.

36 And when he was come nigh, even now at the descent of the mount of Olives, the whole multitude of the disciples began to rejoice, and praise God with a loud voice, for all the mighty works that they had seen;

37 Saying, Blessed is the King that cometh in the name of the Lord, peace in heaven, and glory in the highest!

38 And some of the Pharisees from among the multitude, said unto him, Master, rebuke thy disciples.

39 And he answered and said unto them, If these should hold their peace, the stones would immediately cry out.

40 And when he was come near, he beheld the city, and wept over it;

41 Saying, If thou hadst known, even thou, at least in this thy day, the things which belong unto thy peace! But now they are hid from thine eyes.

42 For the days shall come upon thee, that thine enemies shall cast a trench about thee, and compass thee round, and keep thee in on every side;

43 And shall lay thee even with the ground, and thy children within thee, and they shall not leave in thee, one stone upon another; because thou knewest not the time of thy visitation.

44 And he went into the temple, and began to cast out them that sold therein, and them who bought,

45 Saying unto them, It is written, My house is a house of prayer; but ye have made it a den of thieves.

46 And he taught daily in the temple. But the chief priests, and the scribes, and the chief of the people sought to destroy him,

47 And could not find what they might do; for all the people were very attentive to hear him.

## CHAPTER 20

*The baptism of John—Parable of the vineyard—Christ asked concerning the tribute—Of divorcement, and marriage in the resurrection.*

1 And it came to pass, that on one of those days, as he taught the people in the temple, and preached the gospel, the chief priests, and the scribes, came upon him with the elders,

2 And spake unto him, saying, Tell us, by what authority doest thou these things? Or, who is he who gave thee this authority?

3 And he answered, and said unto them, I will also ask you one thing; answer me.

4 The baptism of John; was it from heaven, or of men?

5 And they reasoned with themselves, saying, If we shall say, From heaven; he will say, Why then believed ye him not?

6 And if we say, Of men, all the people will stone us; for they are persuaded that John was a prophet.

7 And they answered that they could not tell whence it was.

8 Jesus said unto them, Neither tell

I you, by what authority I do these things.

9 Then began he to speak to the people, this parable. A certain man planted a vineyard, and let it out to husbandmen, and went into a far country for a long time.

10 And at the season of the harvest, he sent his servant to the husbandmen, that they should give him of the fruit of the vineyard; but the husbandmen beat him, and sent him away empty.

11 And again he sent another servant; and they beat him also, and entreated him shamefully, and sent him away empty.

12 And again he sent a third, and they wounded him also, and cast him out.

13 Then said the lord of the vineyard, What shall I do? I will send my beloved son; it may be, they will reverence him, when they see him.

14 But when the husbandmen saw him, they reasoned among themselves, saying, This is the heir; come, let us kill him, that the inheritance may be ours.

15 So they cast him out of the vineyard, and killed him. What therefore shall the lord of the vineyard do unto them?

16 He shall come and destroy these husbandmen, and shall give the vineyard to others. And when they heard this, they said, God forbid!

17 And he beheld them, and said, What is this then which is written, The stone which the builders rejected, the same is become the head of the corner?

18 Whosoever shall fall upon that stone, shall be broken; but on whomsoever it shall fall, it shall grind him to powder.

19 And the chief priests, and the scribes, the same hour, sought to lay hands on him; but they feared the people; for they perceived that he had spoken this parable against them.

20 And they watched him, and sent forth spies, who should feign themselves just men, that they might take hold of his words, that so doing, they might deliver him unto the power and authority of the governor.

21 And they asked him, saying, Master, we know that thou sayest and teachest rightly; neither regardest thou the person of any, but teachest the way of God truly.

22 Is it lawful for us to give tribute unto Caesar, or no?

23 But he perceived their craftiness, and said unto them, Why tempt ye me?

24 Show me a penny. Whose image and superscription hath it? They answered, and said, Caesar's.

25 And he said unto them, Render therefore unto Caesar, the things which be Caesar's; and unto God, the things which be God's.

26 And they could not take hold of his words before the people, and they marveled at his answer, and held their peace.

27 Then came to him certain of the Sadducees, who deny there is any resurrection; and they asked him,

28 Saying, Master, Moses wrote unto us, saying, If any man's brother die, having a wife, and he die without children, that his brother should take his wife, and raise up seed unto his brother.

29 There were therefore seven brethren; the first took a wife, and died without children.

30 And the second took her to wife, and he died childless.

31 And the third took her in like manner; and the seven also; and they left no children, and died.

32 And last of all, the woman died also.

33 Therefore in the resurrection whose wife of them is she? for seven had her to wife?

34 And Jesus answering, said unto them, The children of this world marry and are given in marriage;

35 But they who shall be accounted worthy to obtain that world, through resurrection from the dead, neither marry nor are given in marriage.

36 Neither can they die any more; for they are equal unto the angels; and are the children of God, being the children of the resurrection.

37 Now that the dead are raised, even Moses showed at the bush, when he calleth the Lord, the God of Abraham, and the God of Isaac, and the God of Jacob.

38 For he is not a God of the dead, but of the living; for all live unto him.

39 Then certain of the scribes an-

swering, said, Master, thou hast well said.

40 And after that they durst not ask him any question at all.

41 And he said unto them, How say they that Christ is David's son?

42 And David himself said in the book of Psalms, The Lord said unto my Lord, Sit thou on my right hand,

43 Till I make thine enemies thy footstool.

44 David therefore calleth him Lord; how is he then his son?

45 Then in the audience of all the people, he said unto his disciples,

46 Beware of the scribes, who desire to walk in long robes, and love greetings in the markets, and the highest seats in the synagogues, and the chief rooms at feasts;

47 Who devour widows' houses, and for a show, make long prayers; the same shall receive greater damnation.

## CHAPTER 21

*The widow's mite—Destruction of Jerusalem—Signs of Christ's coming—Tribulation of the Jews—Parable of the fig tree—Undue cares of the world forbidden.*

1 And he looked up, and saw the rich men casting in their gifts into the treasury;

2 And saw also, a certain poor widow casting in thither two mites.

3 And he said, Of a truth I say unto you, that this poor widow hath cast in more than they all.

4 For all these have of their abundance cast in unto the offerings of God; but she of her penury hath cast in all the living that she had.

5 And as some spake of the temple, how it was adorned with goodly stones, and gifts, he said,

6 These things which ye behold, the days will come, in the which there shall not be left one stone upon another, which shall not be thrown down.

7 And the disciples asked him, saying, Master, when shall these things be? And what sign wilt thou show, when these things shall come to pass?

8 And he said, The time draweth near, and therefore take heed that ye be not deceived; for many shall come in my name, saying, I am Christ; go ye not therefore after them.

9 And when ye shall hear of wars and commotions, be not terrified; for these things must first come to pass; but this is not the end.

10 Then said he unto them, Nation shall rise against nation, and kingdom against kingdom; and great earthquakes shall be in divers places, and famines, and pestilences; and fearful sights, and great signs shall there be from heaven.

11 But before all these things shall come, they shall lay their hands on you, and persecute you; delivering you up to the synagogues, and into prisons; being brought before kings and rulers for my name's sake.

12 Settle this therefore in your hearts, not to meditate before what ye shall answer;

13 For I will give you a mouth and wisdom, which all your adversaries shall not be able to gainsay nor resist.

14 And it shall turn to you for a testimony.

15 And ye shall be betrayed both by parents, and brethren, and kinsfolk, and friends; and some of you shall they cause to be put to death.

16 And ye shall be hated of all the world for my name's sake.

17 But there shall not a hair of your head perish.

18 In your patience possess ye your souls.

19 And when ye shall see Jerusalem compassed with armies, then know that the desolation thereof is nigh.

20 Then let them who are in Judea flee to the mountains; and let them who are in the midst of it, depart out; and let not them who are in the countries, return to enter into the city.

21 For these be the days of vengeance, that all things which are written may be fulfilled.

22 But woe unto them who are with child, and to them who give suck, in those days! For there shall be great distress in the land, and wrath upon this people.

23 And they shall fall by the edge of the sword, and shall be led away captive into all nations; and Jerusalem shall be trodden down of the Gentiles, until the times of the Gentiles be fulfilled.

24 Now these things he spake unto them, concerning the destruction of Jerusalem. And then his disciples asked him, saying, Master, tell us concerning thy coming?

25 And he answered them, and said, In the generation in which the times of the Gentiles shall be fulfilled, there shall be signs in the sun, and in the moon, and in the stars; and upon the earth distress of nations with perplexity, like the sea and the waves roaring. The earth also shall be troubled, and the waters of the great deep;

26 Men's hearts failing them for fear, and for looking after those things which are coming on the earth. For the powers of heaven shall be shaken.

27 And when these things begin to come to pass, then look up and lift up your heads, for the day of your redemption draweth nigh.

28 And then shall they see the Son of man coming in a cloud, with power and great glory.

29 And he spake to them a parable, saying, Behold the fig tree, and all the trees.

30 When they now shoot forth, ye see and know of your own selves that summer is now nigh at hand.

31 So likewise ye, when ye see these things come to pass, know ye that the kingdom of God is nigh at hand.

32 Verily I say unto you, this generation, the generation when the times of the Gentiles be fulfilled, shall not pass away till all be fulfilled.

33 Heaven and earth shall pass away, but my words shall not pass away.

34 Let my disciples therefore take heed to themselves, lest at any time their hearts be overcharged with surfeiting, and drunkenness, and cares of this life, and that day come upon them unawares.

35 For as a snare shall it come on all them who dwell on the face of the whole earth.

36 And what I say unto one, I say unto all, Watch ye therefore, and pray always, and keep my commandments, that ye may be counted worthy to escape all these things which shall come to pass, and to stand before the Son of man when he shall come clothed in the glory of his Father.

37 And in the day time, he was teaching in the temple; and at night, he went out and abode in the mount that is called Olives.

38 And the people came early in the morning to him in the temple, to hear him.

## CHAPTER 22

*Judas betrayeth Christ—Institution of the Lord's supper—Christ's agony—His arrest—Peter denies him.*

1 Now the feast of unleavened bread drew nigh, which is called the passover.

2 And the chief priests, and the scribes, sought how they might kill him; but they feared the people.

3 Then entered Satan into Judas, surnamed Iscariot, being of the number of the twelve.

4 And he went his way, and communed with the chief priests and captains, how he might betray him unto them.

5 And they were glad, and covenanted to give him money.

6 And he promised them, and sought opportunity to betray him unto them in the absence of the multitude.

7 Then came the day of unleavened bread, when the passover must be killed.

8 And he sent Peter and John, saying, Go, and prepare us the passover, that we may eat.

9 And they said unto him, Where wilt thou that we prepare?

10 And he said unto them, Behold, when ye have entered into the city, there shall a man meet you bearing a pitcher of water; follow him into the house where he entereth in.

11 And ye shall say unto the good man of the house, The Master saith unto you, Where is the guestchamber, where I shall eat the passover with my disciples?

12 And he shall show you a large upper room furnished; there make ready.

13 And they went, and found as he had said unto them; and they made ready the passover.

14 And when the hour was come, he sat down, and the twelve apostles with him.

15 And he said unto them, With desire I have desired to eat this passover with you before I suffer;

16 For I say unto you, I will not any more eat thereof, until it be fulfilled which is written in the prophets concerning me. Then I will partake with you, in the kingdom of God.

17 And he took the cup, and gave thanks, and said, Take this and divide among yourselves;

18 For I say unto you, That I will not drink of the fruit of the vine, until the kingdom of God shall come.

19 And he took bread, and gave thanks, and brake, and gave unto them, saying, This is my body which is given for you; this do in remembrance of me.

20 Likewise also the cup, after supper, saying, This cup is the new testament in my blood which is shed for you.

21 But behold, the hand of him who betrayeth me is with me on the table.

22 And truly the Son of man goeth as it was determined; but woe unto that man by whom he is betrayed.

23 And they began to inquire among themselves, who of them it was who should do this thing.

24 There was also a strife among them, who of them should be accounted the greatest.

25 And he said unto them, The kings of the Gentiles exercise lordship over them, and they who exercise authority upon them, are called benefactors.

26 But it ought not to be so with you; but he who is greatest among you, let him be as the younger; and he who is chief, as he who doth serve.

27 For whether is he greater, who sitteth at meat, or he who serveth? I am not as he who sitteth at meat, but I am among you as he who serveth.

28 Ye are they who have continued with me in my temptations;

29 And I appoint unto you a kingdom, as my Father hath appointed unto me;

30 That ye may eat and drink at my table in my kingdom; and sit on twelve thrones, judging the twelve tribes of Israel.

31 And the Lord said, Simon, Simon, behold Satan hath desired you, that he may sift the children of the kingdom as wheat.

32 But I have prayed for you, that your faith fail not; and when you are converted strengthen your brethren.

33 And he said unto him, being aggrieved, Lord, I am ready to go with you, both into prison, and unto death.

34 And the Lord said, I tell you, Peter, that the cock shall not crow this day, before that you will thrice deny that you know me.

35 And he said unto them, When I sent you without purse and scrip, or shoes, lacked ye any thing? And they said, Nothing.

36 Then said he unto them, I say unto you again, He who hath a purse, let him take it, and likewise his scrip; and he who hath no sword, let him sell his garment and buy one.

37 For I say unto you, This that is written must yet be accomplished in me, And he was reckoned among the transgressors; for the things concerning me have an end.

38 And they said, Lord, behold here are two swords. And he said unto them, It is enough.

39 And he came out, and went, as he was accustomed, to the mount of Olives; and his disciples followed him.

40 And when he was at the place, he said unto them, Pray that ye enter not into temptation.

41 And he was withdrawn from them about a stone's cast, and kneeled down, and prayed,

42 Saying, Father, if thou be willing, remove this cup from me; nevertheless, not my will, but thine, be done.

43 And there appeared an angel unto him from heaven, strengthening him.

44 And being in an agony, he prayed more earnestly; and he sweat as it were great drops of blood falling down to the ground.

45 And when he rose up from prayer, and was come to his disciples, he found them sleeping; for they were filled with sorrow;

46 And he said unto them, Why sleep ye? rise and pray, lest ye enter into temptation.

47 And while he yet spake, behold, a multitude, and he who was called Judas, one of the twelve, went before them, and drew near unto Jesus to kiss him.

48 But Jesus said unto him, Judas, betrayest thou the Son of man with a kiss?

49 When they who were about him, saw what would follow, they said unto him, Lord, shall we smite with a sword?

50 And one of them smote the servant of the high priest, and cut off his right ear.

51 And Jesus answered and said, Suffer ye thus far. And he touched his ear and healed him.

52 Then Jesus said unto the chief priests, and captains of the temple, and the elders, who were come to him, Are ye come out as against a thief, with swords and staves?

53 When I was daily with you in the temple, ye stretched forth no hands against me; but this is your hour, and the power of darkness.

54 Then took they him, and led him, and brought him into the high priest's house. And Peter followed afar off.

55 And when they had kindled a fire in the midst of the hall, and were set down together, Peter sat down among them.

56 But a certain maid beheld him, as he sat by the fire, and earnestly looked upon him, and said, This man was also with him.

57 And he denied him, saying, Woman I know him not.

58 And after a little while another saw him, and said, Thou art also of them. And Peter said, Man, I am not.

59 And about the space of one hour, another confidently affirmed, saying, Of a truth, this man was also with him; for he is a Galilean.

60 And Peter said, Man, I know not what thou sayest. And immediately, while he yet spake, the cock crew.

61 And the Lord turned, and looked upon Peter. And Peter remembered the word of the Lord, how he had said unto him, Before the cock crow, thou shalt deny me thrice.

62 And Peter went out, and wept bitterly.

63 And the men who held Jesus, mocked him, and smote him.

64 And when they had blindfolded him, they struck him on the face, and asked him, saying, Prophesy, who is it who smote thee?

65 And many other things blasphemously spake they against him.

66 And as soon as it was day, the elders of the people and the chief priests, and the scribes, came together, and led him into their council,

67 Saying, Art thou the Christ? Tell us. And he said unto them, If I tell you, ye will not believe.

68 And if I also ask you, ye will not answer me, nor let me go.

69 Hereafter shall the Son of man sit on the right hand of the power of God.

70 Then said they all, Art thou then the Son of God? And he said unto them, Ye say that I am.

71 And they said, What need we of any further witness? For we ourselves have heard of his own mouth.

## CHAPTER 23

*Pilate sends Jesus to Herod—He is scourged and sent back—Scattering of Israel foretold—Christ crucified—Penitent thief—Jesus buried by Joseph of Arimathea.*

1 And the whole multitude of them arose, and led him unto Pilate.

2 And they began to accuse him, saying, We found this man perverting the nation, and forbidding to give tribute to Caesar, saying, that he himself is Christ, a king.

3 And Pilate asked him, saying, Art thou the King of the Jews? And he answered him, and said, Yea, thou sayest it.

4 Then said Pilate to the chief priests and the people, I find no fault in this man.

5 And they were the more fierce, saying, He stirreth up the people, teaching throughout all Jewry, beginning from Galilee, to this place.

6 When Pilate heard of Galilee, he asked whether the man were a Galilean.

7 And as soon as he knew that he belonged unto Herod's jurisdiction, he sent him to Herod, who himself also was at Jerusalem at that time.

8 And when Herod saw Jesus, he was exceeding glad; for he was desirous to see him, of a long time, because he had heard many things of him; and hoped to have seen some miracle done by him.

9 Then he questioned with him in many words; but he answered him nothing.

10 And the chief priests and scribes stood and vehemently accused him.

11 And Herod with his men of war set him at naught, and mocked him, and arrayed him in a gorgeous robe, and sent him again to Pilate.

12 And the same day Pilate and Herod were made friends together; for before this they were at enmity between themselves.

13 And Pilate, when he had called

together the chief priests and the rulers, and the people,

14 Said unto them, You have brought this man unto me, as one who perverteth the people; and behold, I, having examined him before you, have found no fault in this man, touching those things whereof ye accuse him.

15 No, nor yet Herod; for I sent you to him; and lo, nothing worthy of death is done unto him;

16 I will therefore chastise him, and release him.

17 For of necessity he must release one unto them at the feast.

18 But they cried out all at once, saying, Away with this man, and release unto us Barabbas;

19 Who for a certain sedition made in the city, and for murder, was cast into prison.

20 Pilate therefore, willing to release Jesus, spake again to them.

21 But they cried, saying, Crucify him, crucify him.

22 And he said unto them the third time, Why, what evil hath he done? I have found no cause of death in him; I will therefore chastise him, and let him go.

23 And they were instant in loud voices, requiring that he might be crucified; and the voices of them, and of the chief priests, prevailed.

24 And Pilate gave sentence that it should be as they required.

25 And he released unto them him who for sedition and murder was cast into prison, whom they had desired; and delivered Jesus to their will.

26 And as they led him away, they laid hold upon one Simon, a Cyrenian, coming out of the country, and on him they laid the cross, that he might bear it after Jesus.

27 And there followed him a great company of people, and of women, who also bewailed and lamented him.

28 But Jesus turned unto them and said, Daughters of Jerusalem, weep not for me, but weep for yourselves, and for your children.

29 For behold, the days are coming, in the which they shall say, Blessed are the barren, and the wombs which never bare, and the paps which never gave suck.

30 Then shall they begin to say to the mountains, Fall on us; and to the hills, Cover us.

31 And if things are done in the green tree, what shall be done in the dry tree?

32 This he spake, signifying the scattering of Israel, and the desolation of the heathen, or in other words, the Gentiles.

33 And there were also two others, malefactors, led with him to be put to death.

34 And when they were come to the place, which is called Calvary, there they crucified him, and the malefactors; one on the right hand, and the other on the left.

35 Then said Jesus, Father, forgive them; for they know not what they do. (Meaning the soldiers who crucified him,) and they parted his raiment and cast lots.

36 And the people stood, beholding, and the rulers also with them, derided, saying, He saved others; let him save himself, if he be the Christ, the chosen of God.

37 And the soldiers also mocked him, coming to him, and offering him vinegar,

38 And saying, If thou be the King of the Jews, save thyself.

39 And a superscription also was written over him, in letters of Greek, and Latin, and Hebrew, THIS IS THE KING OF THE JEWS.

40 And one of the malefactors who was crucified with him, railed on him, saying, If thou be the Christ, save thyself and us.

41 But the other answering, rebuked him, saying, Dost thou not fear God, seeing thou art in the same condemnation?

42 And we indeed justly; for we receive the due reward of our deeds; but this man hath done nothing amiss.

43 And he said to Jesus, Lord, remember me when thou comest into thy kingdom.

44 And Jesus said unto him, Verily I say unto thee; Today shalt thou be with me in Paradise.

45 And it was about the sixth hour, and there was darkness over all the earth until the ninth hour.

46 And the sun was darkened, and the veil of the temple was rent in the midst.

47 And when Jesus had cried with a loud voice, he said, Father, into thy

hands I commend my spirit. And having said thus, he gave up the ghost.

48 Now when the centurion saw what was done, he glorified God, saying, Certainly this was a righteous man.

49 And all the people who came together to that sight, beholding the things which were done, smote their breasts, and returned.

50 And all his acquaintance, and women who followed him from Galilee, stood afar off, beholding these things.

51 And, behold, a man named Joseph, a counselor; a good man and a just one;

52 The same day had not consented to the counsel and deed of them; a man of Arimathea, a city of the Jews; who also himself waited for the kingdom of God.

53 He went unto Pilate, and begged the body of Jesus.

54 And he took it down and wrapped it in linen, and laid it in a sepulcher, which was hewed in a stone, wherein never man before was laid.

55 And that day was the preparation, and the Sabbath drew on.

56 And the women also, who came with him from Galilee, followed after, and beheld the sepulcher, and how his body was laid.

57 And they returned, and prepared spices and ointments; and rested the Sabbath day according to the commandment.

## CHAPTER 24

*The women come to the sepulcher—Jesus talketh to two of his disciples—He appears to the apostles—Promises them the Holy Spirit—Ascends up into heaven.*

1 Now upon the first day of the week, very early in the morning, the women came unto the sepulcher, bringing the spices which they had prepared, and certain others with them.

2 And they found the stone rolled away from the sepulcher, and two angels standing by it in shining garments.

3 And they entered into the sepulcher, and not finding the body of the Lord Jesus, they were much perplexed thereabout;

4 And were affrighted, and bowed down their faces to the earth. But behold the angels said unto them, Why seek ye the living among the dead?

5 He is not here, but is risen. Remember how he spake unto you when he was yet in Galilee,

6 Saying, The Son of man must be delivered into the hands of sinful men, and be crucified, and the third day rise again?

7 And they remembered his words,

8 And returned from the sepulcher, and told all these things unto the eleven, and to all the rest.

9 It was Mary Magdalene, and Joanna, and Mary the mother of James, and other women who were with them, who told these things unto the apostles.

10 And their words seemed to them as idle tales, and they believed them not.

11 Then arose Peter, and ran unto the sepulcher and went in, and he beheld the linen clothes laid by themselves; and he departed, wondering in himself at that which was come to pass.

12 And behold, two of them went that same day to a village called Emmaus, which was from Jerusalem threescore furlongs.

13 And they talked together of all these things which had happened.

14 And it came to pass, that while they communed together, and reasoned, Jesus himself drew near, and went with them.

15 But their eyes were holden, or covered, that they could not know him.

16 And he said unto them, What manner of communications are these which ye have one with another, as ye walk and are sad?

17 And the one of them, whose name was Cleopas, answering, said unto him, Art thou a stranger in Jerusalem, and hast not known the things which are come to pass there in these days?

18 And he said unto them, What things? And they said unto him, Concerning Jesus of Nazareth, who was a prophet mighty in deed and word before God and all the people;

19 And how the chief priests and our rulers delivered him to be condemned to death, and have crucified him.

20 But we trusted that it had been he who should have redeemed Israel. And besides all this, today is the third day since these things were done;

21 Yea, and certain women also of our company made us astonished, who were early at the sepulcher;

22 And when they found not his body, they came, saying, that they had also seen a vision of angels, who said that he was alive.

23 And certain of them who were with us, went to the sepulcher, and found it even so as the women had said; but him they saw not.

24 Then he said unto them, O fools, and slow of heart to believe all that the prophets have spoken!

25 Ought not Christ to have suffered these things, and to enter into his glory?

26 And beginning at Moses and all the prophets, he expounded unto them in all the scriptures the things concerning himself.

27 And they drew nigh unto the village whither they went; and he made as though he would have gone farther.

28 But they constrained him, saying, Abide with us; for it is toward evening, and the day is far spent. And he went in to tarry with them.

29 And it came to pass, as he sat at meat with them, he took bread, and blessed, and brake, and gave to them.

30 And their eyes were opened, and they knew him; and he was taken up out of their sight.

31 And they said one to another, Did not our hearts burn within us, while he talked with us by the way, and while he opened to us the scriptures?

32 And they rose up the same hour and returned to Jerusalem, and found the eleven gathered together, and those who were with them,

33 Saying, The Lord is risen indeed, and hath appeared to Simon.

34 And they told what things they saw and heard in the way, and how he was known to them, in breaking of bread.

35 And as they thus spake, Jesus himself stood in the midst of them, and said unto them, Peace be unto you.

36 But they were terrified and affrighted, and supposed that they had seen a spirit.

37 And he said unto them, Why are you troubled, and why do thoughts arise in your hearts?

38 Behold my hands and my feet, that it is I, myself. Handle me, and see; for a spirit hath not flesh and bones, as ye see me have.

39 When he had thus spoken, he showed them his hands and his feet.

40 And while they yet wondered and believed not for joy, he said unto them, Have ye here any meat?

41 And they gave him a piece of a broiled fish, and a honeycomb.

42 And he took it and did eat before them.

43 And he said unto them, These are the words which I spake unto you while I was yet with you, that all things must be fulfilled which were written in the law of Moses, and in the prophets, and in the Psalms, concerning me.

44 Then opened he their understanding, that they might understand the scriptures,

45 And said unto them, Thus it is written, and thus it behooved Christ to suffer, and to rise from the dead the third day;

46 And that repentance and remission of sins should be preached in his name among all nations, beginning at Jerusalem.

47 And ye are witnesses of these things.

48 And, behold, I send the promise of my Father upon you; but tarry ye in the city of Jerusalem, until ye be endued with power from on high.

49 And he led them out as far as to Bethany, and he lifted up his hands and blessed them.

50 And it came to pass, while he blessed them, he was taken from them, and carried up into heaven.

51 And they worshiped him, and returned to Jerusalem with great joy;

52 And were continually in the temple, praising and blessing God. Amen.

# The Testimony of St. John

CHAPTER 1

*The gospel preached in the beginning—
John beareth record of the gospel, and of
Christ—Is Elias—Andrew, Philip, and
Peter called.*

1 In the beginning was the gospel
preached through the Son. And the
gospel was the word, and the word was
with the Son, and the Son was with
God, and the Son was of God.

2 The same was in the beginning
with God.

3 All things were made by him; and
without him was not anything made
which was made.

4 In him was the gospel, and the
gospel was the life, and the life was
the light of men;

5 And the light shineth in the world,
and the world perceiveth it not.

6 There was a man sent from God,
whose name was John.

7 The same came into the world for
a witness, to bear witness of the light,
to bear record of the gospel through
the Son, unto all, that through him
men might believe.

8 He was not that light, but came to
bear witness of that light,

9 Which was the true light, which
lighteth every man that cometh into
the world;

10 Even the Son of God. He who was
in the world, and the world was made
by him, and the world knew him not.

11 He came unto his own, and his
own received him not.

12 But as many as received him, to
them gave he power to become the
sons of God; only to them who believe
on his name.

13 He was born, not of blood, nor of
the will of the flesh, nor of the will of
man, but of God.

14 And the same word was made
flesh, and dwelt among us, and we beheld his glory, the glory as of the Only
Begotten of the Father, full of grace
and truth.

15 John bear witness of him, and
cried, saying, This was he of whom I
spake; He who cometh after me, is preferred before me; for he was before me.

16 For in the beginning was the
Word, even the Son, who is made flesh,
and sent unto us by the will of the Fa-

ther. And as many as believe on his
name shall receive of his fullness. And
of his fullness have all we received,
even immortality and eternal life,
through his grace.

17 For the law was given through
Moses, but life and truth came through
Jesus Christ.

18 For the law was after a carnal
commandment, to the administration
of death; but the gospel was after the
power of an endless life, through Jesus
Christ, the Only Begotten Son, who is
in the bosom of the Father.

19 And no man hath seen God at
any time, except he hath borne record
of the Son; for except it is through him
no man can be saved.

20 And this is the record of John,
when the Jews sent priests and Levites from Jerusalem, to ask him; Who
art thou?

21 And he confessed, and denied not
that he was Elias; but confessed, saying; I am not the Christ.

22 And they asked him, saying; How
then art thou Elias? And he said, I am
not that Elias who was to restore all
things. And they asked him, saying,
Art thou that prophet? And he answered, No.

23 Then said they unto him, Who art
thou? that we may give an answer to
them that sent us. What sayest thou of
thyself?

24 He said, I am the voice of one crying in the wilderness, Make straight
the way of the Lord, as saith the
prophet Esaias.

25 And they who were sent were of
the Pharisees.

26 And they asked him, and said
unto him, Why baptizest thou then, if
thou be not the Christ, nor Elias who
was to restore all things, neither that
prophet?

27 John answered them, saying, I
baptize with water, but there standeth
one among you, whom ye know not;

28 He it is of whom I bear record. He
is that prophet, even Elias, who, coming after me, is preferred before me,
whose shoe's latchet I am not worthy
to unloose, or whose place I am not
able to fill; for he shall baptize, not
only with water, but with fire, and
with the Holy Ghost.

29 The next day John seeth Jesus coming unto him, and said; Behold the Lamb of God, who taketh away the sin of the world!

30 And John bare record of him unto the people, saying, This is he of whom I said; After me cometh a man who is preferred before me; for he was before me, and I knew him, and that he should be made manifest to Israel; therefore am I come baptizing with water.

31 And John bare record, saying; When he was baptized of me, I saw the Spirit descending from heaven like a dove, and it abode upon him.

32 And I knew him; for he who sent me to baptize with water, the same said unto me; Upon whom thou shalt see the Spirit descending, and remaining on him, the same is he who baptizeth with the Holy Ghost.

33 And I saw, and bare record that this is the Son of God.

34 These things were done in Bethabara, beyond Jordan, where John was baptizing.

35 Again, the next day after, John stood, and two of his disciples,

36 And looking upon Jesus as he walked, he said, Behold the Lamb of God!

37 And the two disciples heard him speak, and they followed Jesus.

38 Then Jesus turned, and saw them following him, and said unto them, What seek ye? They say unto him, Rabbi, (which is to say, being interpreted, Master;) Where dwellest thou?

39 He said unto them, Come and see. And they came and saw where he dwelt, and abode with him that day; for it was about the tenth hour.

40 One of the two who heard John, and followed Jesus, was Andrew, Simon Peter's brother.

41 He first findeth his own brother Simon, and saith unto him, We have found the Messias, which is, being interpreted, the Christ.

42 And he brought him to Jesus. And when Jesus beheld him, he said, Thou art Simon, the son of Jona, thou shalt be called Cephas, which is, by interpretation, a seer, or a stone. And they were fishermen. And they straightway left all, and followed Jesus.

43 The day following, Jesus would go forth into Galilee, and findeth Philip, and saith unto him, Follow me.

44 Now Philip was at Bethsaida, the city of Andrew and Peter.

45 Philip findeth Nathanael, and saith unto him, We have found him, of whom Moses in the law, and the prophets, did write, Jesus of Nazareth, the son of Joseph.

46 And Nathanael said unto him, Can there any good thing come out of Nazareth? Philip said unto him, Come and see.

47 Jesus saw Nathanael coming unto him, and said of him, Behold an Israelite indeed, in whom is no guile!

48 Nathanael said unto him, Whence knowest thou me? Jesus answering said unto him, Before Philip called thee, when thou wast under the fig tree, I saw thee.

49 Nathanael answered and said unto him, Rabbi, thou art the Son of God; thou art the King of Israel.

50 Jesus answered and said unto him, Because I said unto thee, I saw thee under the fig tree, believest thou? Thou shalt see greater things than these.

51 And he said unto him, Verily, verily, I say unto you, Hereafter ye shall see heaven open, and the angels of God ascending and descending upon the Son of man.

## CHAPTER 2

*Marriage at Cana—Jesus driveth the traffickers out of the temple.*

1 And on the third day of the week, there was a marriage in Cana of Galilee; and the mother of Jesus was there.

2 And Jesus was called, and his disciples, to the marriage.

3 And when they wanted wine, his mother said unto him, They have no wine.

4 Jesus said unto her, Woman, what wilt thou have me to do for thee? that will I do; for mine hour is not yet come.

5 His mother said unto the servants, Whatsoever he saith unto you, see that ye do it.

6 There were set there six waterpots of stone, after the manner of the purifying of the Jews, containing two or three firkins apiece.

7 Jesus said unto them, Fill the waterpots with water. And they filled them up to the brim.

8 And he said, Draw out now, and

bear unto the governor of the feast. And they bare unto him.

9 When the governor of the feast had tasted the water which was made wine, (he knew not whence it was, but the servants who drew the water knew,) the governor of the feast called the bridegroom,

10 And said unto him, Every man at the beginning doth set forth good wine; and when men have well drunk, then that which is worse; but thou hast kept the good wine until now.

11 This beginning of miracles did Jesus in Cana of Galilee, and manifested forth his glory; and the faith of his disciples was strengthened in him.

12 After this he went down to Capernaum, he, and his mother, and his brethren, and his disciples; and they continued there not many days.

13 And the Jews' passover was at hand, and Jesus went up to Jerusalem,

14 And found in the temple those who sold oxen, and sheep, and doves, and the changers of money sitting.

15 And when he had made a scourge of small cords, he drove them all out of the temple, and the sheep, and the oxen; and poured out the changers' money, and overthrew the tables;

16 And said unto them who sold doves, Take these things hence; make not my Father's house a house of merchandise.

17 And his disciples remembered that it was written, The zeal of thy house hath eaten me up.

18 Then spake the Jews and said unto him, What sign showest thou unto us, seeing thou doest these things?

19 Jesus answered and said unto them, Destroy this temple, and in three days I will raise it up.

20 Then said the Jews, Forty and six years was this temple in building, and wilt thou rear it up, in three days?

21 But he spake of the temple of his body.

22 When therefore he was risen from the dead, his disciples remembered that he had said this unto them, and they remembered the scripture, and the word which Jesus had said unto them.

23 Now when he was in Jerusalem, at the passover, on the feast day, many believed on his name, when they saw the miracles which he did.

24 But Jesus did not commit himself unto them, because he knew all things,

25 And needed not that any should testify of man; for he knew what was in man.

## CHAPTER 3

*The new birth of water and spirit—Love of God declared—John baptizeth—Christ baptizeth.*

1 There was a man of the Pharisees named Nicodemus, a ruler of the Jews;

2 The same came to Jesus by night, and said unto him, Rabbi, we know that thou art a teacher come from God; for no man can do these miracles which thou doest, except God be with him.

3 Jesus answered and said unto him, Verily, verily, I say unto thee, Except a man be born again, he cannot see the kingdom of God.

4 Nicodemus said unto him, How can a man be born when he is old? Can he enter the second time into his mother's womb and be born?

5 Jesus answered, Verily, verily, I say unto thee, Except a man be born of water, and the Spirit, he cannot enter into the kingdom of God.

6 That which is born of the flesh, is flesh; and that which is born of the Spirit, is spirit.

7 Marvel not that I said unto thee, Ye must be born again.

8 The wind bloweth where it listeth, and thou hearest the sound thereof, but canst not tell whence it cometh, and whither it goeth; so is every one who is born of the Spirit.

9 Nicodemus answered and said unto him, How can these things be?

10 Jesus answered and said, Art thou a master of Israel, and knowest not these things?

11 Verily, verily, I say unto thee, We speak that we do know, and testify that we have seen; and ye receive not our witness.

12 If I have told you earthly things, and ye believe not, how shall ye believe if I tell you heavenly things?

13 I tell you, No man hath ascended up to heaven, but he who came down from heaven, the Son of man who is in heaven.

14 And as Moses lifted up the serpent in the wilderness, even so must the Son of man be lifted up;

15 That whosoever believeth on him

should not perish, but have eternal life.

16 For God so loved the world, that he gave his Only Begotten Son, that whosoever believeth on him should not perish; but have everlasting life.

17 For God sent not his Son into the world to condemn the world; but that the world through him might be saved.

18 He who believeth on him is not condemned; but he who believeth not is condemned already, because he hath not believed on the name of the Only Begotten Son of God, which before was preached by the mouth of the holy prophets; for they testified of me.

19 And this is the condemnation, that light is come into the world, and men love darkness rather than light, because their deeds are evil.

20 For every one who doeth evil hateth the light, neither cometh to the light, lest his deeds should be reproved.

21 But he who loveth truth, cometh to the light, that his deeds may be made manifest.

22 And he who obeyeth the truth, the works which he doeth they are of God.

23 After these things came Jesus and his disciples into the land of Judea; and there he tarried with them, and baptized;

24 And John also was baptizing in Aenon, near to Salim, because there was much water there; and they came and were baptized;

25 For John was not yet cast into prison.

26 Then there arose a question between some of John's disciples, and the Jews, about purifying.

27 And they came unto John, and said unto him, Rabbi, he who was with thee beyond Jordan, to whom thou bearest witness, behold, the same baptizeth, and he receiveth of all people who come unto him.

28 John answered and said, A man can receive nothing, except it be given him from heaven.

29 Ye yourselves bear me witness that I said, I am not the Christ, but that I am sent before him.

30 He who hath the bride, is the bridegroom; but the friend of the bridegroom, who standeth and heareth him, rejoiceth greatly because of the bridegroom's voice; this my joy therefore is fulfilled.

31 He must increase, but I must decrease.

32 He who cometh from above is above all; he who is of the earth is earthly, and speaketh of the earth; he who cometh from heaven is above all. And what he hath seen and heard, that he testifieth; and but few men receive his testimony.

33 He who hath received his testimony, hath set to his seal that God is true.

34 For he whom God hath sent, speaketh the words of God; for God giveth him not the Spirit by measure, for he dwelleth in him, even the fullness.

35 The Father loveth the Son, and hath given all things into his hands.

36 And he who believeth on the Son hath everlasting life; and shall receive of his fullness. But he who believeth not the Son, shall not receive of his fullness; for the wrath of God is upon him.

## CHAPTER 4

*The Pharisees seek to destroy Jesus—The woman and the well—The water of life eternal—The nobleman's son healed.*

1 When therefore the Pharisees had heard that Jesus made and baptized more disciples than John,

2 They sought more diligently some means that they might put him to death; for many received John as a prophet, but they believed not on Jesus.

3 Now the Lord knew this, though he himself baptized not so many as his disciples;

4 For he suffered them for an example, preferring one another.

5 And he left Judea, and departed again into Galilee,

6 And said unto his disciples, I must needs go through Samaria.

7 Then he cometh to the city of Samaria which is called Sychar, near to the parcel of ground which Jacob gave to his son Joseph; the place where Jacob's well was.

8 Now Jesus being weary with his journey, it being about the sixth hour, sat down on the well;

9 And there came a woman of Samaria to draw water; Jesus said unto her, Give me to drink.

10 Now his disciples were gone away into the city to buy meat.

11 Wherefore he being alone, the woman of Samaria said unto him, How is it that thou being a Jew, askest drink of me, who am a woman of Samaria? The Jews have no dealings with the Samaritans.

12 Jesus answered and said unto her, If thou knewest the gift of God, and who it is that saith to thee, Give me to drink, thou wouldest have asked of him, and he would have given thee living water?

13 The woman said unto him, Sir, thou hast nothing to draw with, and the well is deep; from whence then hast thou that living water?

14 Art thou greater than our father Jacob, who gave us the well, and drank thereof himself, and his children, and his cattle?

15 Jesus answered and said unto her, Whosoever shall drink of this well, shall thirst again;

16 But whosoever drinketh of the water which I shall give him shall never thirst; but the water that I shall give him shall be in him a well of water springing up into everlasting life.

17 The woman said unto him, Sir, give me of this water that I thirst not, neither come hither to draw.

18 Jesus said unto her, Go, call thy husband and come hither.

19 The woman answered and said, I have no husband. Jesus said unto her, Thou hast well said, I have no husband.

20 For thou hast had five husbands, and he whom thou now hast, is not thy husband; in that saidst thou truly.

21 The woman said unto him, Sir, I perceive that thou art a prophet.

22 Our fathers worshiped in this mountain; and ye say that in Jerusalem is the place where men ought to worship.

23 Jesus said unto her, Woman, believe me, the hour cometh, when ye shall neither in this mountain, nor yet at Jerusalem, worship the Father.

24 Ye worship ye know not what; we know what we worship; and salvation is of the Jews.

25 And the hour cometh, and now is, when the true worshipers shall worship the Father in spirit and in truth;

for the Father seeketh such to worship him.

26 For unto such hath God promised his Spirit. And they who worship him, must worship in spirit and in truth.

27 The woman said unto him, I know that Messias cometh, who is called Christ; when he is come, he will tell us all things.

28 Jesus said unto her, I who speak unto thee am the Messias.

29 And upon this came his disciples, and marveled that he talked with the woman; yet no man said, What seekest thou? or, Why talkest thou with her?

30 The woman then left her waterpot, and went her way into the city, and said to the men,

31 Come see a man who told me all things that I have ever done. Is not this the Christ?

32 Then they went out of the city, and came unto him.

33 In the meantime his disciples prayed him, saying, Master, eat.

34 But he said unto them, I have meat to eat that ye know not of.

35 Therefore said the disciples one to another, Hath any man brought him meat to eat?

36 Jesus said unto them, My meat is to do the will of him who sent me, and to finish his work.

37 Say not ye there are yet four months, then cometh harvest? Behold, I say unto you, Lift up your eyes, and look on the fields; for they are white already to harvest.

38 And he who reapeth, receiveth wages, and gathereth fruit unto life eternal; that both he who soweth, and he who reapeth, may rejoice together.

39 And herein is that saying true, One soweth and another reapeth.

40 I have sent you to reap that whereon ye bestowed no labor; the prophets have labored, and ye have entered into their labors.

41 And many of the Samaritans of that city believed on him for the saying of the woman, who testified, saying, He told me all that I have ever done.

42 So when the Samaritans were come unto him, they besought him that he would tarry with them; and he abode there two days.

43 And many more believed because of his own word;

44 And said unto the woman, Now we believe, not because of thy saying;

we have heard for ourselves, and know that this is indeed the Christ, the Savior of the world.

45 Now after two days he departed thence, and went into Galilee.

46 For Jesus himself testified, that a prophet hath no honor in his own country.

47 Then when he had come into Galilee, the Galileans received him, having seen all the things which he did at Jerusalem at the feast; for they also went unto the feast.

48 So Jesus came again into Cana of Galilee, where he made the water wine. And there was a certain nobleman, whose son was sick at Capernaum.

49 When he heard that Jesus was come out of Judea into Galilee, he went unto him, and besought him that he would come down, and heal his son; for he was at the point of death.

50 Then said Jesus unto him, Except ye see signs and wonders, ye will not believe.

51 The nobleman said unto him, Sir, come down before my child die.

52 Jesus said unto him, Go thy way, thy son liveth. And the man believed the word which Jesus had spoken unto him, and he went his way.

53 And as he was going down to his house, his servants met him, and spake, saying, Thy son liveth.

54 Then inquired he of them the hour when he began to mend. And they said unto him, Yesterday at the seventh hour the fever left him.

55 So the father knew that this son was healed in the same hour in the which Jesus said unto him, Thy son liveth; and himself believed, and his whole house;

56 This being the second miracle which Jesus had done when he had come out of Judea into Galilee.

## CHAPTER 5

*Impotent man healed—The resurrection—Testimony of Christ.*

1 After this there was a feast of the Jews; and Jesus went up to Jerusalem.

2 Now there is at Jerusalem by the sheep market, a pool which is called in the Hebrew tongue, Bethesda, having five porches.

3 In these porches lay a great many impotent folk, of blind, halt, withered, waiting for the moving of the water.

4 For an angel went down at a certain season into the pool, and troubled the water, whosoever then first after the troubling of the water stepped in, was made whole of whatsoever disease he had.

5 And a certain man was there, who had an infirmity thirty and eight years.

6 And Jesus saw him lie, and knew that he had been now a long time afflicted; and he said unto him, Wilt thou be made whole?

7 The impotent man answered him, Sir, I have no man when the water is troubled, to put me into the pool; but while I am coming, another steppeth down before me.

8 Jesus saith unto him, Rise, take up thy bed and walk.

9 And immediately the man was made whole, and took up his bed, and walked; and it was on the Sabbath day.

10 The Jews therefore said unto him who was cured, It is the Sabbath day; it is not lawful for thee to carry thy bed.

11 He answered them, He who made me whole, said unto me, Take up thy bed and walk.

12 Then answered they him, saying, What man is he who said unto thee, Take up thy bed and walk?

13 And he that was healed knew not who it was; for Jesus had conveyed himself away, a multitude being in the place.

14 Afterward Jesus findeth him in the temple, and said unto him, Behold, thou art made whole; sin no more, lest a worse thing come unto thee.

15 The man departed, and told the Jews that it was Jesus who had made him whole;

16 And therefore did the Jews persecute Jesus, and sought to slay him, because he had done these things on the Sabbath day.

17 But Jesus answered them, My Father worketh hitherto, and I work.

18 Therefore the Jews sought the more to kill him, because he had not only broken the Sabbath, but said also that God was his father, making himself equal with God.

19 Then answered Jesus and said unto them, Verily, verily, I say unto you, The Son can do nothing of himself, but what he seeth the Father do;

for what things soever he doeth, these also doeth the Son likewise.

20 For the Father loveth the Son, and showeth him all things that himself doeth; and he will show him greater works than these, that ye may marvel.

21 For as the Father raiseth up the dead and quickeneth them; even so the Son quickeneth whom he will.

22 For the Father judgeth no man; but hath committed all judgment unto the Son;

23 That all should honor the Son, even as they honor the Father. He who honoreth not the Son, honoreth not the Father who hath sent him.

24 Verily, verily, I say unto you, He who heareth my word, and believeth on him who sent me, hath everlasting life, and shall not come into condemnation; but is passed from death into life.

25 Verily, verily, I say unto you, The hour is coming, and now is, when the dead shall hear the voice of the Son of God; and they who hear shall live.

26 For as the Father hath life in himself, so hath he given to the Son to have life in himself;

27 And hath given him authority to execute judgment also, because he is the Son of man.

28 Marvel not at this; for the hour is coming, in the which all who are in their graves shall hear his voice,

29 And shall come forth; they who have done good, in the resurrection of the just; and they who have done evil, in the resurrection of the unjust.

30 And shall all be judged of the Son of man. For as I hear, I judge, and my judgment is just;

31 For I can of mine own self do nothing; because I seek not mine own will, but the will of the Father who hath sent me.

32 Therefore if I bear witness of myself, yet my witness is true.

33 For I am not alone, there is another who beareth witness of me, and I know that the testimony which he giveth of me is true.

34 Ye sent unto John, and he bare witness also unto the truth.

35 And he received not his testimony of man, but of God, and ye yourselves say that he is a prophet, therefore ye ought to receive his testimony. These things I say that ye might be saved.

36 He was a burning and a shining light; and ye were willing for a season to rejoice in his light.

37 But I have a greater witness than the testimony of John; for the works which the Father hath given me to finish, the same works that I do, bear witness of me, that the Father hath sent me.

38 And the Father himself who hath sent me, hath borne witness of me. And verily I testify unto you, that ye have never heard his voice at any time, nor seen his shape;

39 For ye have not his word abiding in you; and him whom he hath sent, ye believe not.

40 Search the scriptures; for in them ye think ye have eternal life; and they are they which testify of me.

41 And ye will not come to me that ye might have life, lest ye should honor me.

42 I receive not honor from men.

43 But I know you, that ye have not the love of God in you.

44 I am come in my Father's name, and ye receive me not; if another shall come in his own name, him ye will receive.

45 How can ye believe, who seek honor one of another, and seek not the honor which cometh from God only?

46 Do not think that I will accuse you to the Father; there is Moses who accuseth you, in whom ye trust.

47 For had ye believed Moses, ye would have believed me; for he wrote of me.

48 But if ye believe not his writings, how shall ye believe my words?

## CHAPTER 6

*Christ feedeth five thousand—The people would make him king—He walketh on the sea—Himself the bread of life—Many leave him.*

1 After these things Jesus went over the sea of Galilee, which is the sea of Tiberias.

2 And a great multitude followed him, because they saw his miracles which he did on them that were diseased.

3 And Jesus went up into a mountain, and there he sat with his disciples.

4 And the passover, a feast of the Jews, was nigh.

5 When Jesus then lifted up his eyes, and saw a great company come unto him, he saith unto Philip, Whence

shall we buy bread, that these may eat?

6 And this he said to prove him; for he himself knew what he would do.

7 Philip answered him, Two hundred pennyworth of bread is not sufficient for them, that every one of them may take a little.

8 One of his disciples, Andrew, Simon Peter's brother, saith unto him,

9 There is a lad here, which hath five barley loaves, and two small fishes; but what are they among so many?

10 And Jesus said, Make the men sit down. Now there was much grass in the place. So the men sat down, in number about five thousand.

11 And Jesus took the loaves; and when he had given thanks, he distributed to the disciples, and the disciples to them that were set down; and likewise of the fishes as much as they would.

12 When they had eaten and were satisfied, he said unto his disciples, Gather up the fragments that remain, that nothing be lost.

13 Therefore they gathered them together, and filled twelve baskets with the fragments of the five barley loaves, which remained over and above unto them that had eaten.

14 Then those men, when they had seen the miracle that Jesus did, said, This is of a truth that prophet that should come into the world.

15 When Jesus therefore perceived that they would come and take him by force, to make him a king, he departed again into a mountain himself alone.

16 And when even was come, his disciples went down unto the sea,

17 And entered into a ship, and went over the sea toward Capernaum. And it was now dark, and Jesus had not come to them.

18 And the sea arose by reason of a great wind that blew.

19 So when they had rowed about five and twenty or thirty furlongs, they saw Jesus walking on the sea, and drawing nigh unto the ship; and they were afraid.

20 But he saith unto them, It is I; be not afraid.

21 Then they willingly received him into the ship; and immediately the ship was at the land whither they went.

22 The day following, when the people, which stood on the other side of the sea, saw that there was none other boat there, save that one whereinto his disciples were entered, and that Jesus went not with his disciples into the boat, but that his disciples were gone away alone;

23 (Howbeit there came other boats from Tiberias nigh unto the place where they did eat bread, after that the Lord had given thanks:)

24 When the people therefore saw that Jesus was not there, neither his disciples, they also took shipping, and came to Capernaum, seeking for Jesus.

25 And when they had found him on the other side of the sea, they said unto him, Rabbi, how camest thou hither?

26 Jesus answered them and said, Verily, verily, I say unto you, Ye seek me, not because ye desire to keep my sayings, neither because ye saw the miracles, but because ye did eat of the loaves and were filled.

27 Labor not for the meat which perisheth, but for that meat which endureth unto everlasting life, which the Son of man hath power to give unto you; for him hath God the Father sealed.

28 Then said they unto him, What shall we do, that we might work the works of God?

29 Jesus answered and said unto them, This is the work of God, that ye believe on him whom he hath sent.

30 They said therefore unto him, What sign shewest thou then, that we may see, and believe thee? What dost thou work?

31 Our fathers did eat manna in the desert; as it is written, He gave them bread from heaven to eat.

32 Then Jesus said unto them, Verily, verily, I say unto you, Moses gave you not that bread from heaven; but my Father giveth you the true bread from heaven.

33 For the bread of God is he which cometh down from heaven, and giveth life unto the world.

34 Then said they unto him, Lord, evermore give us this bread.

35 And Jesus said unto them, I am the bread of life; he that cometh to me shall never hunger; and he that believeth on me shall never thirst.

36 But I said unto you, That ye also have seen me, and believe not.

37 All that the Father giveth me shall come to me; and him that cometh to me I will in no wise cast out.

38 For I came down from heaven, not to do mine own will, but the will of him that sent me.

39 And this is the Father's will which hath sent me, that of all which he hath given me I should lose nothing, but should raise it up again at the last day.

40 And this is the will of him that sent me, that every one which seeth the Son, and believeth on him, may have everlasting life; and I will raise him up in the resurrection of the just at the last day.

41 The Jews then murmured at him, because he said, I am the bread which came down from heaven.

42 And they said, Is not this Jesus, the son of Joseph, whose father and mother we know? how is it then that he saith, I came down from heaven?

43 Jesus therefore answered and said unto them, Murmur not among yourselves.

44 No man can come to me, except he doeth the will of my Father who hath sent me. And this is the will of him who hath sent me, that ye receive the Son; for the Father beareth record of him; and he who receiveth the testimony, and doeth the will of him who sent me, I will raise up in the resurrection of the just.

45 For it is written in the prophets, And these shall all be taught of God. Every man therefore that hath heard, and hath learned of the Father, cometh unto me.

46 Not that any man hath seen the Father, save he which is of God, he hath seen the Father.

47 Verily, verily, I say unto you, He that believeth on me hath everlasting life.

48 I am that bread of life.

49 This is the bread which cometh down from heaven, that a man may eat thereof, and not die.

50 Your fathers did eat manna in the wilderness, and are dead.

51 But I am the living bread which came down from heaven; if any man eat of this bread, he shall live for ever; and the bread that I will give is my flesh, which I will give for the life of the world.

52 The Jews therefore strove among themselves, saying, How can this man give us his flesh to eat?

53 Then Jesus said unto them, Verily, verily, I say unto you, Except ye eat the flesh of the Son of man, and drink his blood, ye have no life in you.

54 Whoso eateth my flesh, and drinketh my blood, hath eternal life; and I will raise him up in the resurrection of the just at the last day.

55 For my flesh is meat indeed, and my blood is drink indeed.

56 He that eateth my flesh, and drinketh my blood, dwelleth in me, and I in him.

57 As the living Father hath sent me, and I live by the Father; so he that eateth me, even he shall live by me.

58 This is that bread which came down from heaven; not as your fathers did eat manna, and are dead; he that eateth of this bread shall live for ever.

59 These things said he in the synagogue, as he taught in Capernaum.

60 Many therefore of his disciples, when they had heard this, said, This is a hard saying; who can hear it?

61 When Jesus knew in himself that his disciples murmured at it, he said unto them, Doth this offend you?

62 What and if ye shall see the Son of man ascend up where he was before?

63 It is the Spirit that quickeneth; the flesh profiteth nothing; the words that I speak unto you, they are spirit, and they are life.

64 But there are some of you that believe not. For Jesus knew from the beginning who they were that believed not, and who should betray him.

65 And he said, Therefore said I unto you, that no man can come unto me, except he doeth the will of my Father who hath sent me.

66 From that time many of his disciples went back, and walked no more with him.

67 Then said Jesus unto the twelve, Will ye also go away?

68 Then Simon Peter answered him, Lord, to whom shall we go? thou hast the words of eternal life.

69 And we believe and are sure that thou art that Christ, the Son of the living God.

70 Jesus answered them, Have not I

chosen you twelve, and one of you is a devil?

71 He spake of Judas Iscariot the son of Simon; for he it was that should betray him, being one of the twelve.

## CHAPTER 7

*Jesus reproveth his kinsmen—Goeth up to the feast of tabernacles—Teacheth in the temple.*

1 After these things Jesus walked in Galilee; for he would not walk in Jewry, because the Jews sought to kill him.

2 Now the Jews' feast of tabernacles was at hand.

3 His brethren therefore said unto him, Depart hence, and go into Judea, that thy disciples there also may see the works that thou doest.

4 For there is no man that doeth any thing in secret, but he himself seeketh to be known openly. If thou do these things, show thyself to the world.

5 For neither did his brethren believe in him.

6 Then Jesus said unto them, My time is not yet come; but your time is always ready.

7 The world cannot hate you; but me it hateth, because I testify of it, that the works thereof are evil.

8 Go ye up unto this feast; I go not up yet unto this feast; for my time is not yet full come.

9 When he had said these words unto them, he continued still in Galilee.

10 But after his brethren were gone up, then went he also up unto the feast, not openly, but as it were in secret.

11 Then the Jews sought him at the feast, and said, Where is he?

12 And there was much murmuring among the people concerning him; for some said, He is a good man; others said, Nay; but he deceiveth the people.

13 Howbeit no man spake openly of him for fear of the Jews.

14 Now about the midst of the feast Jesus went up into the temple, and taught.

15 And the Jews marveled, saying, How knoweth this man letters, having never learned?

16 Jesus answered them, and said, My doctrine is not mine, but his that sent me.

17 If any man will do his will, he shall know of the doctrine, whether it be of God, or whether I speak of myself.

18 He that speaketh of himself seeketh his own glory; but he that seeketh his glory that sent him, the same is true, and no unrighteousness is in him.

19 Did not Moses give you the law, and yet none of you keepeth the law? Why go ye about to kill me?

20 The people answered and said, Thou hast a devil; who goeth about to kill thee?

21 Jesus answered and said unto them, I have done one work, and ye all marvel.

22 Moses therefore gave unto you circumcision; (not because it is of Moses, but of the fathers;) and ye on the Sabbath day circumcise a man.

23 If a man on the Sabbath day receive circumcision, that the law of Moses should not be broken; are ye angry at me, because I have made a man every whit whole on the Sabbath day?

24 Judge not according to your traditions, but judge righteous judgment.

25 Then said some of them of Jerusalem, Is not this he, whom they seek to kill?

26 But, lo, he speaketh boldly, and they say nothing unto him. Do the rulers know indeed that this is the very Christ?

27 Howbeit we know this man whence he is; but when Christ cometh, no man knoweth whence he is.

28 Then cried Jesus in the temple as he taught, saying, Ye both know me, and ye know whence I am; and I am not come of myself, but he that sent me is true, whom ye know not.

29 But I know him; for I am from him, and he hath sent me.

30 Then they sought to take him; but no man laid hands on him, because his hour was not yet come.

31 And many of the people believed on him, and said, When Christ cometh, will he do more miracles than these which this man hath done?

32 The Pharisees heard that the people murmured such things concerning him; and the Pharisees and the chief priests sent officers to take him.

33 Then said Jesus unto them, Yet a little while I am with you, and then I go unto him that sent me.

34 Ye shall seek me, and shall not find me; and where I am, thither ye cannot come.

35 Then said the Jews among themselves, Whither will he go, that we shall not find him? will he go unto the dispersed among the Gentiles, and teach the Gentiles?

36 What manner of saying is this that he said, Ye shall seek me, and shall not find me; and where I am thither ye cannot come?

37 In the last day, that great day of the feast, Jesus stood and cried, saying, If any man thirst, let him come unto me, and drink.

38 He that believeth on me, as the scripture hath said, out of his belly shall flow rivers of living water.

39 (But this spake he of the Spirit, which they that believe on him should receive; for the Holy Ghost was promised unto them who believe, after that Jesus was glorified.)

40 Many of the people therefore, when they heard this saying, said, Of a truth this is the Prophet.

41 Others said, This is the Christ. But some said, Shall Christ come out of Galilee?

42 Hath not the scripture said, That Christ cometh of the seed of David, and out of the town of Bethlehem, where David was?

43 So there was a division among the people because of him.

44 And some of them would have taken him; but no man laid hands on him.

45 Then came the officers to the chief priests and Pharisees; and they said unto them, Why have ye not brought him?

46 The officers answered, Never man spake like this man.

47 Then answered them the Pharisees, Are ye also deceived?

48 Have any of the rulers or of the Pharisees believed on him?

49 But this people who knoweth not the law are cursed.

50 Nicodemus saith unto them, (he that came to Jesus by night being one of them,)

51 Doth our law judge any man, before it hear him, and know what he doeth?

52 They answered and said unto him, Art thou also of Galilee? Search, and look; for out of Galilee ariseth no prophet.

53 And every man went unto his own house.

## CHAPTER 8

*The woman taken in adultery—Christ the light of the world.*

1 And Jesus went unto the mount of Olives.

2 Early in the morning he came again into the temple, and all the people came unto him; and he sat down, and taught them.

3 And the scribes and Pharisees brought unto him a woman taken in adultery; and when they had set her in the midst of the people,

4 They say unto him, Master, this woman was taken in adultery, in the very act.

5 Now Moses in the law commanded us, that such should be stoned; but what sayest thou?

6 This they said, tempting him, that they might have to accuse him. But Jesus stooped down, and with his finger wrote on the ground, as though he heard them not.

7 So when they continued asking him, he lifted up himself, and said unto them, He that is without sin among you, let him first cast a stone at her.

8 And again he stooped down, and wrote on the ground.

9 And they which heard it, being convicted by their own conscience, went out one by one, beginning at the eldest, even unto the last; and Jesus was left alone, and the woman standing in the midst of the temple.

10 When Jesus had raised up himself, and saw none of her accusers, and the woman standing, he said unto her, Woman, where are those thine accusers? hath no man condemned thee?

11 She said, No man, Lord. And Jesus said unto her, Neither do I condemn thee; go, and sin no more. And the woman glorified God from that hour, and believed on his name.

12 Then spake Jesus again unto them, saying, I am the light of the world; he that followeth me shall not walk in darkness, but shall have the light of life.

13 The Pharisees therefore said unto him, Thou bearest record of thyself; thy record is not true.

14 Jesus answered and said unto them, Though I bear record of myself, yet my record is true; for I know whence I came, and whither I go; but ye cannot tell whence I come, and whither I go.

15 Ye judge after the flesh; I judge no man.

16 And yet if I judge, my judgment is true; for I am not alone, but I and the Father that sent me.

17 It is also written in your law, that the testimony of two men is true.

18 I am one that bear witness of myself, and the Father that sent me beareth witness of me.

19 Then said they unto him, Where is thy Father? Jesus answered, Ye neither know me, nor my Father; if ye had known me, ye should have known my Father also.

20 These words spake Jesus in the treasury, as he taught in the temple; and no man laid hands on him; for his hour was not yet come.

21 Then said Jesus again unto them, I go my way, and ye shall seek me, and shall die in your sins; whither I go, ye cannot come.

22 Then said the Jews, Will he kill himself? because he saith, Whither I go, ye cannot come.

23 And he said unto them, Ye are from beneath; I am from above; ye are of this world; I am not of this world.

24 I said therefore unto you, that ye shall die in your sins; for if ye believe not that I am he, ye shall die in your sins.

25 Then said they unto him, Who art thou? And Jesus saith unto them, Even the same that I said unto you from the beginning.

26 I have many things to say and to judge of you; but he that sent me is true; and I speak to the world those things which I have heard of him.

27 They understood not that he spake to them of the Father.

28 Then said Jesus unto them, When ye have lifted up the Son of man, then shall ye know that I am he, and that I do nothing of myself; but as my Father hath taught me, I speak these things.

29 And he that sent me is with me; the Father hath not left me alone; for I do always those things that please him.

30 As he spake these words, many believed on him.

31 Then said Jesus to those Jews which believed on him, If ye continue in my word, then are ye my disciples indeed;

32 And ye shall know the truth, and the truth shall make you free.

33 They answered him, We be Abraham's seed, and were never in bondage to any man; how sayest thou, Ye shall be made free?

34 Jesus answered them, Verily, verily, I say unto you, Whosoever committeth sin is the servant of sin.

35 And the servant abideth not in the house for ever, but the Son abideth ever.

36 If the Son therefore shall make you free, ye shall be free indeed.

37 I know that ye are Abraham's seed; but ye seek to kill me because my word hath no place in you.

38 I speak that which I have seen with my Father; and ye do that which ye have seen with your father.

39 They answered and said unto him, Abraham is our father. Jesus saith unto them, If ye were Abraham's children, ye would do the works of Abraham.

40 But now ye seek to kill me, a man that hath told you the truth, which I have heard of God; this did not Abraham.

41 Ye do the deeds of your father. Then said they to him, We be not born of fornication; we have one Father, even God.

42 Jesus said unto them, If God were your Father, ye would love me; for I proceeded forth and came from God; neither came I of myself, but he sent me.

43 Why do ye not understand my speech? even because ye cannot bear my word.

44 Ye are of your father the devil, and the lusts of your father ye will do; he was a murderer from the beginning, and abode not in the truth, because there is no truth in him. When he speaketh a lie, he speaketh of his own; for he is a liar, and the father of it.

45 And because I tell you the truth, ye believe me not.

46 Which of you convinceth me of sin? And if I say the truth, why do ye not believe me?

47 He that is of God receiveth God's words; ye therefore receive them not, because ye are not of God.

48 Then answered the Jews, and said unto him, Say we not well that thou art a Samaritan, and hast a devil?

49 Jesus answered, I have not a devil; but I honor my Father, and ye do dishonor me.

50 And I seek not mine own glory; there is one that seeketh and judgeth.

51 Verily, verily, I say unto you, If a man keep my saying, he shall never see death.

52 Then said the Jews unto him, Now we know that thou hast a devil. Abraham is dead, and the prophets; and thou sayest, If a man keep my saying, he shall never taste of death.

53 Art thou greater than our father Abraham, which is dead? and the prophets are dead; whom makest thou thyself?

54 Jesus answered, If I honor myself, my honor is nothing; it is my Father that honoreth me; of whom ye say, that he is your God;

55 Yet ye have not known him; but I know him; and if I should say, I know him not, I shall be a liar like unto you; but I know him, and keep his saying.

56 Your father Abraham rejoiced to see my day; and he saw it, and was glad.

57 Then said the Jews unto him, Thou art not yet fifty years old, and hast thou seen Abraham?

58 Jesus said unto them, Verily, verily, I say unto you, Before Abraham was, I am.

59 Then took they up stones to cast at him; but Jesus hid himself, and went out of the temple, going through the midst of them, and so passed by.

## CHAPTER 9

*Sight restored to blind man.*

1 And as Jesus passed by, he saw a man which was blind from his birth.

2 And his disciples asked him saying, Master, who did sin, this man, or his parents, that he was born blind?

3 Jesus answered, Neither hath this man sinned, nor his parents; but that the works of God should be made manifest in him.

4 I must work the works of him that sent me, while I am with you; the time cometh when I shall have finished my work, then I go unto the Father.

5 As long as I am in the world, I am the light of the world.

6 When he had thus spoken, he spat on the ground, and made clay of the spittle, and he anointed the eyes of the blind man with the clay,

7 And said unto him, Go, wash in the pool of Siloam, (which is by interpretation, Sent.) He went his way therefore, and washed, and came seeing.

8 The neighbors therefore, and they which before had seen him that he was blind, said, Is not this he that sat and begged?

9 Some said, This is he; others said, He is like him; but he said, I am he.

10 Therefore said they unto him, How were thine eyes opened?

11 He answered and said, A man that is called Jesus made clay, and anointed mine eyes, and said unto me, Go to the pool of Siloam, and wash; and I went and washed, and I received sight.

12 Then said they unto him, Where is he? He said, I know not.

13 And they brought him who had been blind to the Pharisees.

14 And it was the Sabbath day when Jesus made the clay, and opened his eyes.

15 Then again the Pharisees also asked him how he had received his sight. He said unto them, He put clay upon mine eyes, and I washed, and do see.

16 Therefore said some of the Pharisees, This man is not of God, because he keepeth not the Sabbath day. Others said, How can a man that is a sinner do such miracles? And there was a division among them.

17 They say unto the blind man again, What sayest thou of him who hath opened thine eyes? He said, He is a prophet.

18 But the Jews did not believe concerning him, that he had been blind, and received his sight, until they called the parents of him that had received his sight.

19 And they asked them, saying, Is this your son, who ye say was born blind? how then doth he now see?

20 His parents answered them and said, We know that this is our son, and that he was born blind.

21 But by what means he now seeth, we know not; or who hath opened his eyes, we know not; he is of age; ask him; he shall speak for himself.

22 These words spake his parents, because they feared the Jews; for the Jews had agreed already, that if any man did confess that he was Christ, he should be put out of the synagogue.

23 Therefore said his parents, He is of age; ask him.

24 Then again called they the man that was blind, and said unto him, Give God the praise; we know that this man is a sinner.

25 He answered and said, Whether he be a sinner or no, I know not; one thing I know, that, whereas I was blind, now I see.

26 Then said they to him again, What did he to thee? how opened he thine eyes?

27 He answered them, I have told you already, and ye did not believe; wherefore would you believe if I should tell you again? and would you be his disciples?

28 Then they reviled him, and said, Thou art his disciple; but we are Moses' disciples.

29 We know that God spake unto Moses; as for this man we know not from whence he is.

30 The man answered and said unto them, Why herein is a marvelous thing, that ye know not from whence he is, and yet he hath opened mine eyes.

31 Now we know that God heareth not sinners; but if any man be a worshiper of God, and doeth his will, him he heareth.

32 Since the world began was it not heard that any man opened the eyes of one that was born blind, except he be of God.

33 If this man were not of God, he could do nothing.

34 They answered and said unto him, Thou wast altogether born in sins, and dost thou teach us? And they cast him out.

35 Jesus heard that they had cast him out; and when he had found him, he said unto him, Dost thou believe on the Son of God?

36 He answered and said, Who is he, Lord, that I might believe on him?

37 And Jesus said unto him, Thou hast both seen him, and it is he that talketh with thee.

38 And he said, Lord, I believe. And he worshiped him.

39 And Jesus said, For judgment I am come into this world, that they which see not might see; and that they which see might be made blind.

40 And some of the Pharisees which were with him heard these words, and said unto him, Are we blind also?

41 Jesus said unto them, If ye were blind, ye should have no sin; but now ye say, We see; therefore your sin remaineth.

## CHAPTER 10

*Christ is the door, and the good shepherd—Divers opinions of him—Many believed on him.*

1 Verily, verily, I say unto you, He that entereth not by the door into the sheepfold, but climbeth up some other way, the same is a thief and a robber.

2 But he that entereth in by the door is the shepherd of the sheep.

3 To him the porter openeth; and the sheep hear his voice; and he calleth his own sheep by name, and leadeth them out.

4 And when he putteth forth his own sheep, he goeth before them, and the sheep follow him; for they know his voice.

5 And a stranger will they not follow, but will flee from him; for they know not the voice of strangers.

6 This parable spake Jesus unto them; but they understood not what things they were which he spake unto them.

7 Then said Jesus unto them again, Verily, verily, I say unto you, I am the door of the sheepfold.

8 All that ever came before me who testified not of me are thieves and robbers; but the sheep did not hear them.

9 I am the door; by me if any man enter in, he shall be saved, and shall go in and out, and find pasture.

10 The thief cometh not, but for to steal, and to kill, and to destroy; I am come that they might have life, and that they might have it more abundantly.

11 I am the good shepherd; the good shepherd giveth his life for his sheep.

12 And the shepherd is not as a hireling, whose own the sheep are not, who seeth the wolf coming, and leaveth the sheep, and fleeth; and the wolf catcheth the sheep and scattereth them.

13 For I am the good shepherd, and know my sheep, and am known of mine.

14 But he who is a hireling fleeth, because he is a hireling, and careth not for the sheep.

15 As the Father knoweth me, even so know I the Father; and I lay down my life for the sheep.

16 And other sheep I have, which are not of this fold; them also I must bring, and they shall hear my voice; and there shall be one fold, and one shepherd.

17 Therefore doth my Father love me, because I lay down my life, that I might take it again.

18 No man taketh it from me, but I lay it down of myself. I have power to lay it down, and I have power to take it again. This commandment have I received of my Father.

19 There was a division therefore again among the Jews for these sayings.

20 And many of them said, He hath a devil, and is mad; why hear ye him?

21 Others said, These are not the words of him that hath a devil. Can a devil open the eyes of the blind?

22 And it was at Jerusalem the feast of the dedication, and it was winter.

23 And Jesus walked in the temple in Solomon's porch.

24 Then came the Jews round about him, and said unto him, How long dost thou make us to doubt? If thou be the Christ, tell us plainly.

25 Jesus answered them, I told you, and ye believed not; the works that I do in my Father's name, they bear witness of me.

26 But ye believe not, because ye are not of my sheep, as I said unto you.

27 My sheep hear my voice, and I know them, and they follow me;

28 And I give unto them eternal life; and they shall never perish, neither shall any man pluck them out of my hand.

29 My Father, which gave them me, is greater than all; and no man is able to pluck them out of my Father's hand.

30 I and my Father are one.

31 Then the Jews took up stones again to stone him.

32 Jesus answered them, Many good works have I showed you from my Father; for which of those works do ye stone me?

33 The Jews answered him, saying, For a good work we stone thee not; but for blasphemy; and because that thou, being a man, makest thyself God.

34 Jesus answered them, Is it not written in your law, I said, Ye are gods?

35 If he called them gods, unto whom the word of God came, and the scripture cannot be broken;

36 Say ye of him, whom the Father hath sanctified, and sent into the world, Thou blasphemest; because I said, I am the Son of God?

37 If I do not the works of my Father, believe me not.

38 But if I do, though ye believe not me, believe the works; that ye may know, and believe, that the Father is in me, and I in him.

39 Therefore they sought again to take him; but he escaped out of their hand,

40 And went away again beyond Jordan into the place where John at first baptized; and there he abode.

41 And many resorted unto him, and said, John did no miracle; but all things that John spake of this man were true.

42 And many believed on him there.

## CHAPTER 11

*Christ raiseth Lazarus—Many Jews believe—Caiaphas prophesieth.*

1 Now a certain man was sick, whose name was Lazarus, of the town of Bethany;

2 And Mary, his sister, who anointed the Lord with ointment and wiped his feet with her hair, lived with her sister Martha, in whose house her brother Lazarus was sick.

3 Therefore his sisters sent unto him, saying, Lord, behold, he whom thou lovest is sick.

4 And when Jesus heard he was sick, he said, This sickness is not unto death, but for the glory of God, that the Son of God might be glorified thereby.

5 Now Jesus loved Martha, and her sister, and Lazarus.

6 And Jesus tarried two days, after he heard that Lazarus was sick, in the same place where he was.

7 After that he said unto his disciples, Let us go into Judea again.

8 But his disciples said unto him, Master, the Jews of late sought to stone thee; and goest thou thither again?

9 Jesus answered, Are there not twelve hours in the day? If any man walk in the day, he stumbleth not, because he seeth the light of this world.

10 But if a man walk in the night, he

stumbleth, because there is no light in him.

11 These things said he; and after that he saith unto them, Our friend Lazarus sleepeth; but I go, that I may awake him out of sleep.

12 Then said his disciples, Lord, if he sleep, he shall do well.

13 Howbeit Jesus spake of his death; but they thought that he had spoken of taking of rest in sleep.

14 Then said Jesus unto them plainly, Lazarus is dead.

15 And I am glad for your sakes that I was not there, to the intent ye may believe; nevertheless let us go unto him.

16 Then said Thomas, which is called Didymus, unto his fellow disciples, Let us also go, that we may die with him; for they feared lest the Jews should take Jesus and put him to death, for as yet they did not understand the power of God.

17 And when Jesus came to Bethany, to Martha's house, Lazarus had already been in the grave four days.

18 Now Bethany was nigh unto Jerusalem, about fifteen furlongs off.

19 And many of the Jews came to Martha and Mary, to comfort them concerning their brother.

20 Then Martha, as soon as she heard that Jesus was coming, went and met him; but Mary sat still in the house.

21 Then said Martha unto Jesus, Lord, if thou hadst been here, my brother had not died.

22 But I know, that even now, whatsoever thou wilt ask of God, God will give it thee.

23 Jesus saith unto her, Thy brother shall rise again.

24 Martha saith unto him, I know that he shall rise again in the resurrection at the last day.

25 Jesus said unto her, I am the resurrection, and the life; he that believeth in me, though he were dead, yet shall he live;

26 And whosoever liveth and believeth in me shall never die. Believest thou this?

27 She saith unto him, Yea, Lord; I believe that thou art the Christ, the Son of God, which should come into the world.

28 And when she had so said, she went her way, and called Mary her sister secretly, saying, The Master is come, and calleth for thee.

29 As soon as Mary heard that Jesus was come, she arose quickly, and came unto him.

30 Now Jesus was not yet come into the town, but was in the place where Martha met him.

31 The Jews then which were with her in the house, and comforted her, when they saw Mary, that she rose up hastily and went out, followed her, saying, She goeth unto the grave to weep there.

32 Then when Mary was come where Jesus was, and saw him, she fell down at his feet, saying unto him, Lord, if thou hadst been here, my brother had not died.

33 When Jesus therefore saw her weeping, and the Jews also weeping which came with her, he groaned in the spirit, and was troubled,

34 And said, Where have ye laid him? They say unto him, Lord, come and see.

35 Jesus wept.

36 Then said the Jews, Behold how he loved him!

37 And some of them said, Could not this man, which opened the eyes of the blind, have caused that even this man should not have died?

38 Jesus therefore again groaning in himself cometh to the grave. It was a cave, and a stone lay upon it.

39 Jesus said, Take ye away the stone. Martha, the sister of him that was dead, saith unto him, Lord, by this time he stinketh; for he hath been dead four days.

40 Jesus saith unto her, Said I not unto thee, that, if thou wouldest believe, thou shouldest see the glory of God?

41 Then they took away the stone from the place where the dead was laid. And Jesus lifted up his eyes, and said, Father, I thank thee that thou hast heard me.

42 And I knew that thou hearest me always; but because of the people which stand by I said it, that they may believe that thou hast sent me.

43 And when he thus had spoken, he cried with a loud voice, Lazarus, come forth.

44 And he that was dead came forth, bound hand and foot with graveclothes; and his face was bound about

with a napkin. Jesus saith unto them, Loose him, and let him go.

45 Then many of the Jews which came to Mary, and had seen the things which Jesus did, believed on him.

46 But some of them went their ways to the Pharisees, and told them what things Jesus had done.

47 Then gathered the chief priests and the Pharisees a council, and said, What shall we do? for this man doeth many miracles.

48 If we let him thus alone, all men will believe on him; and the Romans shall come and take away both our place and nation.

49 And one of them, named Caiaphas, being the high priest that same year, said unto them, Ye know nothing at all,

50 Nor consider that it is expedient for us, that one man should die for the people, and that the whole nation perish not.

51 And this spake he not of himself; but being high priest that year, he prophesied that Jesus should die for that nation;

52 And not for that nation only, but that also he should gather together in one the children of God that were scattered abroad.

53 Then from that day forth they took counsel together for to put him to death.

54 Jesus therefore walked no more openly among the Jews; but went thence unto a country near to the wilderness, into a city called Ephraim, and there continued with his disciples.

55 And the Jews' passover was nigh at hand; and many went out of the country up to Jerusalem before the passover, to purify themselves.

56 Then sought they for Jesus, and spake among themselves, as they stood in the temple, What think ye of Jesus? Will he not come to the feast?

57 Now both the chief priests and the Pharisees had given a commandment, that, if any man knew where he was, he should show them, that they might take him.

## CHAPTER 12

*Mary anointing Jesus' feet—Christ rideth into Jerusalem—He foretelleth his death—Many chief rulers believe, but do not confess him.*

1 Then Jesus six days before the passover came to Bethany, where Lazarus was which had been dead, whom he raised from the dead.

2 There they made him a supper; and Martha served; but Lazarus was one of them that sat at the table with him.

3 Then took Mary a pound of ointment of spikenard, very costly, and anointed the feet of Jesus, and wiped his feet with her hair; and the house was filled with the odor of the ointment.

4 Then saith one of his disciples, Judas Iscariot, Simon's son, which should betray him,

5 Why was not this ointment sold for three hundred pence, and given to the poor?

6 This he said, not that he cared for the poor; but because he was a thief, and had the bag, and bare what was put therein.

7 Then said Jesus, Let her alone; for she hath preserved this ointment until now, that she might anoint me in token of my burial.

8 For the poor always ye have with you; but me ye have not always.

9 Much people of the Jews therefore knew that he was there; and they came not for Jesus' sake only, but that they might see Lazarus also, whom he had raised from the dead.

10 But the chief priests consulted that they might put Lazarus also to death;

11 Because that by reason of him many of the Jews went away, and believed on Jesus.

12 On the next day much people that were come to the feast, when they heard that Jesus was coming to Jerusalem,

13 Took branches of palm trees, and went forth to meet him, and cried, Hosanna; Blessed is the King of Israel that cometh in the name of the Lord.

14 And Jesus, when he had sent two of his disciples and got a young ass, sat thereon; as it is written,

15 Fear not, daughter of Sion; behold, thy King cometh, sitting on an ass's colt.

16 These things understood not his disciples at the first; but when Jesus was glorified, then remembered they that these things were written of him,

and that they had done these things unto him.

17 The people therefore that was with him when he called Lazarus out of his grave, and raised him from the dead, bare record.

18 For this cause the people also met him, for that they heard that he had done this miracle.

19 The Pharisees therefore said among themselves, Perceive ye how ye prevail nothing? behold, the world is gone after him.

20 And there were certain Greeks among them that came up to worship at the feast;

21 The same came therefore to Philip, which was of Bethsaida of Galilee, and desired him, saying, Sir, we would see Jesus.

22 Philip cometh and telleth Andrew; and again Andrew and Philip tell Jesus.

23 And Jesus answered them, saying, The hour is come, that the Son of man should be glorified.

24 Verily, verily, I say unto you, Except a corn of wheat fall into the ground and die, it abideth alone; but if it die, it bringeth forth much fruit.

25 He that loveth his life shall lose it; and he that hateth his life in this world shall keep it unto life eternal.

26 If any man serve me, let him follow me; and where I am, there shall also my servant be; if any man serve me, him will my Father honor.

27 Now is my soul troubled; and what shall I say? Father, save me from this hour; but for this cause came I unto this hour.

28 Father, glorify thy name. Then came there a voice from heaven, saying, I have both glorified it, and will glorify it again.

29 The people therefore that stood by, and heard it, said that it thundered; others said, An angel spake to him.

30 Jesus answered and said, This voice came not because of me, but for your sakes.

31 Now is the judgment of this world; now shall the prince of this world be cast out.

32 And I, if I be lifted up from the earth, will draw all men unto me.

33 This he said, signifying what death he should die.

34 The people answered him, We have heard out of the law that Christ abideth for ever; and how sayest thou, The Son of man must be lifted up? who is this Son of man?

35 Then Jesus said unto them, Yet a little while is the light with you. Walk while ye have the light, lest darkness come upon you; for he that walketh in darkness knoweth not whither he goeth.

36 While ye have light, believe in the light, that ye may be the children of light. These things spake Jesus, and departed, and did hide himself from them.

37 But though he had done so many miracles before them, yet they believed not on him;

38 That the saying of Esaias the prophet might be fulfilled, which he spake, Lord, who hath believed our report? and to whom hath the arm of the Lord been revealed?

39 Therefore they could not believe, because that Esaias said again,

40 He hath blinded their eyes, and hardened their heart; that they should not see with their eyes, nor understand with their heart, and be converted, and I should heal them.

41 These things said Esaias, when he saw his glory, and spake of him.

42 Nevertheless among the chief rulers also many believed on him; but because of the Pharisees they did not confess him, lest they should be put out of the synagogue;

43 For they loved the praise of men more than the praise of God.

44 Jesus cried and said, He that believeth on me, believeth not on me, but on him that sent me.

45 And he that seeth me seeth him that sent me.

46 I am come a light into the world, that whosoever believeth on me should not abide in darkness.

47 And if any man hear my words, and believe not, I judge him not; for I came not to judge the world, but to save the world.

48 He that rejecteth me, and receiveth not my words, hath one that judgeth him; the word that I have spoken, the same shall judge him in the last day.

49 For I have not spoken of myself; but the Father which sent me, he gave me a commandment, what I should say, and what I should speak.

50 And I know that his commandment is life everlasting; whatsoever I speak therefore, even as the Father said unto me, so I speak.

## CHAPTER 13

*Jesus washeth the disciples' feet—Commandeth them to love one another.*

1 Now before the feast of the passover, when Jesus knew that his hour was come that he should depart out of this world unto the Father, having loved his own which were in the world, he loved them unto the end.

2 And supper being ended, the devil having now put into the heart of Judas Iscariot, Simon's son, to betray him;

3 Jesus knowing that the Father had given all things into his hands, and that he was come from God, and went to God;

4 He riseth from supper, and laid aside his garments; and took a towel, and girded himself.

5 After that he poureth water into a basin, and he began to wash the disciples' feet, and to wipe them with the towel wherewith he was girded.

6 Then cometh he to Simon Peter; and Peter saith unto him, Lord, dost thou wash my feet?

7 Jesus answered and said unto him, What I do thou knowest not now; but thou shalt know hereafter.

8 Peter saith unto him, Thou needest not to wash my feet. Jesus answered him, If I wash thee not, thou hast no part with me.

9 Simon Peter saith unto him, Lord, not my feet only, but also my hands and my head.

10 Jesus saith to him, He that has washed his hands and his head, needeth not save to wash his feet, but is clean every whit; and ye are clean, but not all. Now this was the custom of the Jews under their law; wherefore, Jesus did this that the law might be fulfilled.

11 For he knew who should betray him; therefore said he, Ye are not all clean.

12 So after he had washed their feet, and had taken his garments, and was set down again, he said unto them, Know ye what I have done to you?

13 Ye call me Master and Lord; and ye say well; for so I am.

14 If I then, your Lord and Master, have washed your feet; ye also ought to wash one another's feet.

15 For I have given you an example, that ye should do as I have done to you.

16 Verily, verily, I say unto you, The servant is not greater than his lord; neither he that is sent greater than he that sent him.

17 If ye know these things, happy are ye if ye do them.

18 I speak not of you all; I know whom I have chosen; but that the Scripture may be fulfilled, He that eateth bread with me hath lifted up his heel against me.

19 Now I tell you before it come, that, when it is come to pass, ye may believe that I am the Christ.

20 Verily, verily, I say unto you, He that receiveth whomsoever I send receiveth me; and he that receiveth me receiveth him that sent me.

21 When Jesus had thus said, he was troubled in spirit, and testified, and said, Verily, verily, I say unto you, that one of you shall betray me.

22 Then the disciples looked one on another, doubting of whom he spake.

23 Now there was leaning on Jesus' bosom one of his disciples, whom Jesus loved.

24 Simon Peter therefore beckoned to him, that he should ask who it should be of whom he spake.

25 He then lying on Jesus' breast saith unto him, Lord, who is it?

26 Jesus answered, He it is, to whom I shall give a sop, when I have dipped it. And when he had dipped the sop, he gave it to Judas Iscariot, the son of Simon.

27 And after the sop Satan entered into him. Then said Jesus unto him, That thou doest, do quickly.

28 Now no man at the table knew for what intent he spake this unto him.

29 For some of them thought, because Judas had the bag, that Jesus had said unto him, Buy those things that we have need of against the feast; or, that he should give something to the poor.

30 He then, having received the sop, went immediately out; and it was night.

31 Therefore, when he was gone out, Jesus said, Now is the Son of man glorified, and God is glorified in him.

32 If God be glorified in him, God shall also glorify him in himself, and shall straightway glorify him.

33 Little children, yet a little while I am with you. Ye shall seek me; and as I said unto the Jews, Whither I go, ye cannot come; so now I say to you.

34 A new commandment I give unto you, That ye love one another; as I have loved you, that ye also love one another.

35 By this shall all men know that ye are my disciples, if ye have love one to another.

36 Simon Peter said unto him, Lord, whither goest thou? Jesus answered him, Whither I go, thou canst not follow me now; but thou shalt follow me afterwards.

37 Peter said unto him, Lord, why cannot I follow thee now? I will lay down my life for thy sake.

38 Jesus answered him, Wilt thou lay down thy life for my sake? Verily, verily, I say unto thee, The cock shall not crow, till thou hast denied me thrice.

## CHAPTER 14

*Christ the way, the truth, and the life, and one with the Father—Their prayers in his name effectual—Requesteth love and obedience—Promiseth the Holy Ghost, the Comforter.*

1 Let not your heart be troubled; ye believe in God, believe also in me.

2 In my Father's house are many mansions; if it were not so, I would have told you. I go to prepare a place for you.

3 And when I go, I will prepare a place for you, and come again, and receive you unto myself; that where I am, ye may be also.

4 And whither I go ye know, and the way ye know.

5 Thomas saith unto him, Lord, we know not whither thou goest; and how can we know the way?

6 Jesus saith unto him, I am the way, the truth, and the life; no man cometh unto the Father, but by me.

7 If ye had known me, ye should have known my Father also; and from henceforth ye know him, and have seen him.

8 Philip saith unto him, Lord, show us the Father, and it sufficeth us.

9 Jesus saith unto him, Have I been so long time with you, and yet hast thou not known me, Philip? he that hath seen me hath seen the Father; and how sayest thou then, Show us the Father?

10 Believest thou not that I am in the Father, and the Father in me? the words that I speak unto you I speak not of myself; but the Father that dwelleth in me, he doeth the works.

11 Believe me that I am in the Father, and the Father in me; or else believe me for the very works' sake.

12 Verily, verily, I say unto you, He that believeth on me, the works that I do shall he do also; and greater works than these shall he do; because I go unto my Father.

13 And whatsoever ye shall ask in my name, that will I do, that the Father may be glorified in the Son.

14 If ye shall ask any thing in my name, I will do it.

15 If ye love me, keep my commandments.

16 And I will pray the Father, and he shall give you another Comforter, that he may abide with you for ever;

17 Even the Spirit of truth; whom the world cannot receive, because it seeth him not, neither knoweth him; but ye know him; for he dwelleth with you, and shall be in you.

18 I will not leave you comfortless; I will come to you.

19 Yet a little while, and the world seeth me no more; but ye see me; because I live, ye shall live also.

20 At that day ye shall know that I am in my Father, and ye in me, and I in you.

21 He that hath my commandments, and keepeth them, he it is that loveth me; and he that loveth me shall be loved of my Father, and I will love him, and will manifest myself to him.

22 Judas saith unto him, (not Iscariot,) Lord, how is it thou wilt manifest thyself unto us, and not unto the world?

23 Jesus answered and said unto him, If a man love me, he will keep my words; and my Father will love him, and we will come unto him, and make our abode with him.

24 He that loveth me not keepeth not my sayings; and the word which ye hear is not mine, but the Father's which sent me.

25 These things have I spoken unto you, being yet present with you.

26 But the Comforter, which is the Holy Ghost, whom the Father will send in my name, he shall teach you all things, and bring all things to your remembrance, whatsoever I have said unto you.

27 Peace I leave with you, my peace I give unto you; not as the world giveth, give I unto you. Let not your heart be troubled, neither let it be afraid.

28 Ye have heard how I said unto you, I go away, and come again unto you. If ye loved me, ye would rejoice, because I said, I go unto the Father; for my Father is greater than I.

29 And now I have told you before it come to pass, that, when it is come to pass, ye might believe.

30 Hereafter I will not talk much with you; for the prince of darkness, who is of this world, cometh, but hath no power over me, but he hath power over you.

31 And I tell you these things, that ye may know that I love the Father; and as the Father gave me commandment, even so I do. Arise, let us go hence.

## CHAPTER 15

*The parable of the vine—The hatred and persecution of the world—The office of the Holy Ghost, and of the apostles.*

1 I am the true vine, and my Father is the husbandman.

2 Every branch in me that beareth not fruit he taketh away; and every branch that beareth fruit, he purgeth it, that it may bring forth more fruit.

3 Now ye are clean through the word which I have spoken unto you.

4 Abide in me, and I in you. As the branch cannot bear fruit of itself, except it abide in the vine; no more can ye, except ye abide in me.

5 I am the vine, ye are the branches. He that abideth in me, and I in him, the same bringeth forth much fruit; for without me ye can do nothing.

6 If a man abide not in me, he is cast forth as a branch, and is withered; and men gather them, and cast them into the fire, and they are burned.

7 If ye abide in me, and my words abide in you, ye shall ask what ye will, and it shall be done unto you.

8 Herein is my Father glorified, that ye bear much fruit; so shall ye be my disciples.

9 As the Father hath loved me, so have I loved you; continue ye in my love.

10 If ye keep my commandments, ye shall abide in my love; even as I have kept my Father's commandments, and abide in his love.

11 These things have I spoken unto you, that my joy might remain in you, and that your joy might be full.

12 This is my commandment, That ye love one another, as I have loved you.

13 Greater love hath no man than this, that a man lay down his life for his friends.

14 Ye are my friends, if ye do whatsoever I command you.

15 Henceforth I call you not servants; for the servant knoweth not what his lord doeth; but I have called you friends; for all things that I have heard of my Father I have made known unto you.

16 Ye have not chosen me, but I have chosen you, and ordained you, that ye should go and bring forth fruit; and that your fruit should remain; that whatsoever ye shall ask of the Father in my name, he may give it you.

17 These things I command you, that ye love one another.

18 If the world hate you, ye know that it hated me before it hated you.

19 If ye were of the world, the world would love his own; but because ye are not of the world, but I have chosen you out of the world, therefore the world hateth you.

20 Remember the word that I said unto you, The servant is not greater than his lord. If they have persecuted me, they will also persecute you; if they have kept my saying, they will keep yours also.

21 But all these things will they do unto you for my name's sake, because they know not him that sent me.

22 If I had not come and spoken unto them, they had not had sin; but now they have no cloak for their sin.

23 He that hateth me hateth my Father also.

24 If I had not done among them the works which none other man did, they had not had sin; but now have they both seen and hateth both me and my Father.

25 But this cometh to pass, that the word might be fulfilled that is written

in their law, They hated me without a cause.

26 But when the Comforter is come, whom I will send unto you from the Father, even the Spirit of truth, which proceedeth from the Father, he shall testify of me;

27 And ye also shall bear witness, because ye have been with me from the beginning.

## CHAPTER 16

*Christ forewarneth of persecution—The promise of the Holy Ghost—Resurrection and ascension—Their prayers in his name acceptable to his Father—Peace in Christ, and in the world affliction.*

1 These things have I spoken unto you, that ye should not be offended.

2 They shall put you out of the synagogues; yea, the time cometh, that whosoever killeth you will think that he doeth God service.

3 And these things will they do unto you, because they have not known the Father, nor me.

4 But these things have I told you, that when the time shall come, ye may remember that I told you of them. And these things I said not unto you at the beginning because I was with you.

5 But now I go my way to him that sent me; and none of you asketh me, Whither goest thou?

6 But because I have said these things unto you, sorrow hath filled your heart.

7 Nevertheless I tell you the truth; It is expedient for you that I go away; for if I go not away, the Comforter will not come unto you; but if I depart, I will send him unto you.

8 And when he is come, he will reprove the world of sin, and of righteousness, and of judgment;

9 Of sin, because they believe not on me;

10 Of righteousness, because I go to my Father, and they see me no more;

11 Of judgment, because the prince of this world is judged.

12 I have yet many things to say unto you, but ye cannot bear them now.

13 Howbeit when he, the Spirit of truth, is come, he will guide you into all truth; for he shall not speak of himself; but whatsoever he shall hear, that shall he speak; and he will show you things to come.

14 He shall glorify me; for he shall receive of mine, and shall show it unto you.

15 All things that the Father hath are mine; therefore said I, that he shall take of mine, and shall show it unto you.

16 A little while, and ye shall not see me; and again, a little while, and ye shall see me, because I go to the Father.

17 Then said some of his disciples among themselves, What is this that he saith unto us, A little while, and ye shall not see me; and again, a little while, and ye shall see me; and, Because I go to the Father?

18 They said therefore, What is this that he saith, A little while? we cannot tell what he saith.

19 Now Jesus knew that they were desirous to ask him, and said unto them, Do ye inquire among yourselves of that I said, A little while, and ye shall not see me; and again, a little while, and ye shall see me?

20 Verily, Verily, I say unto you, That ye shall weep and lament, but the world shall rejoice; and ye shall be sorrowful, but your sorrow shall be turned into joy.

21 A woman when she is in travail hath sorrow, because her hour is come; but as soon as she is delivered of the child, she remembereth no more the anguish, for joy that a man is born into the world.

22 And ye now therefore have sorrow; but I will see you again, and your heart shall rejoice, and your joy no man taketh from you.

23 And in that day ye shall ask me nothing but it shall be done unto you. Verily, verily, I say unto you, Whatsoever ye shall ask the Father in my name, he will give it you.

24 Hitherto have ye asked nothing in my name; ask, and ye shall receive, that your joy may be full.

25 These things have I spoken unto you in proverbs; but the time cometh, when I shall no more speak unto you in proverbs, but I shall show you plainly of the Father.

26 At that day ye shall ask in my name; and I say not unto you, that I will pray the Father for you;

27 For the Father himself loveth you, because ye have loved me, and have believed that I came out from God.

28 I came forth from the Father, and am come into the world; again, I leave the world, and go to the Father.

29 His disciples said unto him, Lo, now speakest thou plainly, and speakest no proverb.

30 Now are we sure that thou knowest all things, and needest not that any man should ask thee; by this we believe that thou camest forth from God.

31 Jesus answered them, Do ye now believe?

32 Behold, the hour cometh, yea, is now come, that ye shall be scattered, every man to his own, and shall leave me alone; and yet I am not alone, because the Father is with me.

33 These things I have spoken unto you, that in me ye might have peace. In the world ye shall have tribulation; but be of good cheer; I have overcome the world.

## CHAPTER 17

*Christ prayeth to his Father to glorify him—To keep his apostles in unity and truth, and all other believers, with him.*

1 These words spake Jesus, and lifted up his eyes to heaven, and said, Father, the hour is come; glorify thy Son, that thy Son also may glorify thee;

2 As thou hast given him power over all flesh, that he should give eternal life to as many as thou hast given him.

3 And this is life eternal, that they might know thee the only true God, and Jesus Christ, whom thou hast sent.

4 I have glorified thee on the earth; I have finished the work which thou gavest me to do.

5 And now, O Father, glorify thou me with thine own self with the glory which I had with thee before the world was.

6 I have manifested thy name unto the men which thou gavest me out of the world; thine they were, and thou gavest them me; and they have kept thy word.

7 Now they have known that all things whatsoever thou hast given me are of thee.

8 For I have given unto them the words which thou gavest me; and they have received them, and have known surely that I came out from thee, and they have believed that thou didst send me.

9 I pray for them; I pray not for the world, but for them which thou hast given me; for they are thine.

10 And all mine are thine, and thine are mine; and I am glorified in them.

11 And now I am no more in the world, but these are in the world, and I come to thee. Holy Father, keep through thine own name those whom thou hast given me, that they may be one, as we are.

12 While I was with them in the world, I kept them in thy name; those that thou gavest me I have kept, and none of them is lost, but the son of perdition; that the scripture might be fulfilled.

13 And now come I to thee; and these things I speak in the world, that they might have my joy fulfilled in themselves.

14 I have given them thy word; and the world hath hated them, because they are not of the world, even as I am not of the world.

15 I pray not that thou shouldest take them out of the world, but that thou shouldest keep them from the evil.

16 They are not of the world, even as I am not of the world.

17 Sanctify them through thy truth; thy word is truth.

18 As thou hast sent me into the world, even so have I also sent them into the world.

19 And for their sakes I sanctify myself, that they also might be sanctified through the truth.

20 Neither pray I for these alone, but for them also which shall believe on me through their word;

21 That they all may be one; as thou, Father, art in me, and I in thee, that they also may be one in us; that the world may believe that thou hast sent me.

22 And the glory which thou gavest me I have given them; that they may be one, even as we are one;

23 I in them, and thou in me, that they may be made perfect in one; and that the world may know that thou hast sent me, and hast loved them, as thou hast loved me.

24 Father, I will that they also, whom thou hast given me, be with me where I am; that they may behold my glory, which thou hast given me; for

thou lovedst me before the foundation of the world.

25 O righteous Father, the world hath not known thee; but I have known thee, and these have known that thou hast sent me.

26 And I have declared unto them thy name, and will declare it; that the love wherewith thou hast loved me may be in them, and I in them.

## CHAPTER 18

*Judas betrayeth Jesus—The officers fall to the ground—Peter smiteth off Malchus' ear—Peter's denial—Jesus examined before Caiaphas—Before Pilate—The Jews ask Barabbas.*

1 When Jesus had spoken these words, he went forth with his disciples over the brook Cedron, where was a garden, into the which he entered, and his disciples.

2 And Judas also, which betrayed him, knew the place; for Jesus ofttimes resorted thither with his disciples.

3 Judas then, having received a band of men and officers from the chief priests and Pharisees, cometh thither with lanterns and torches and weapons.

4 Jesus therefore, knowing all things that should come upon him, went forth, and said unto them, Whom seek ye?

5 They answered him, Jesus of Nazareth. Jesus saith unto them, I am he. And Judas also, which betrayed him, stood with them.

6 As soon then as he had said unto them, I am he, they went backward, and fell to the ground.

7 Then asked he them again, Whom seek ye? And they said, Jesus of Nazareth.

8 Jesus answered, I have told you that I am he; if therefore ye seek me, let these go their way;

9 That the saying might be fulfilled, which he spake, Of them which thou gavest me have I lost none.

10 Then Simon Peter having a sword drew it, and smote the high priest's servant, and cut off his right ear. The servant's name was Malchus.

11 Then said Jesus unto Peter, Put up thy sword into the sheath; the cup which my Father hath given me, shall I not drink it?

12 Then the band and the captain and officers of the Jews took Jesus, and bound him,

13 And led him away to Annas first; for he was father-in-law to Caiaphas, which was the high priest that same year.

14 Now Caiaphas was he, which gave counsel to the Jews, that it was expedient that one man should die for the people.

15 And Simon Peter followed Jesus, and so did another disciple; that disciple was known unto the high priest, and went in with Jesus into the palace of the high priest.

16 But Peter stood at the door without. Then went out that other disciple, which was known unto the high priest, and spake unto her that kept the door, and brought in Peter.

17 Then saith the damsel that kept the door unto Peter, Art not thou also one of this man's disciples? He saith, I am not.

18 And the servants and officers stood there, who had made a fire of coals, for it was cold; and they warmed themselves; and Peter stood with them, and warmed himself.

19 The high priest then asked Jesus of his disciples, and of his doctrine.

20 Jesus answered him, I spake openly to the world; I ever taught in the synagogue, and in the temple, whither the Jews always resort; and in secret have I said nothing.

21 Why askest thou me? ask them which heard me, what I have said unto them; behold, they know what I said.

22 And when he had thus spoken, one of the officers which stood by struck Jesus with the palm of his hand, saying, Answerest thou the high priest so?

23 Jesus answered him, If I have spoken evil, bear witness of the evil; but if well, why smitest thou me?

24 Now Annas had sent him bound unto Caiaphas the high priest.

25 And Simon Peter stood and warmed himself. They said therefore unto him, Art not thou also one of his disciples? He denied it, and said, I am not.

26 One of the servants of the high priest, being his kinsman whose ear Peter cut off, saith, Did I not see thee in the garden with him?

27 Peter then denied again; and immediately the cock crew.

28 Then led they Jesus from Caiaphas unto the hall of judgment; and it was early; and they themselves went not into the judgment hall, lest they should be defiled; but that they might eat the passover.

29 Pilate then went out unto them, and said, What accusation bring ye against this man?

30 They answered and said unto him, If he were not a malefactor, we would not have delivered him up unto thee.

31 Then said Pilate unto them, Take ye him, and judge him according to your law. The Jews therefore said unto him, It is not lawful for us to put any man to death;

32 That the saying of Jesus might be fulfilled, which he spake signifying what death he should die.

33 Then Pilate entered into the judgment hall again, and called Jesus, and said unto him, Art thou the King of the Jews?

34 Jesus answered him, Sayest thou this thing of thyself, or did others tell it thee of me?

35 Pilate answered, Am I a Jew? Thine own nation and the chief priests have delivered thee unto me; what hast thou done?

36 Jesus answered, My kingdom is not of this world; if my kingdom were of this world, then would my servants fight, that I should not be delivered to the Jews; but now is my kingdom not from hence.

37 Pilate therefore said unto him, Art thou a king then? Jesus answered, Thou sayest that I am a king. To this end was I born, and for this cause came I into the world, that I should bear witness unto the truth. Every one that is of the truth heareth my voice.

38 Pilate saith unto him, What is truth? And when he had said this, he went out again unto the Jews, and saith unto them, I find in him no fault.

39 But ye have a custom, that I should release unto you one at the passover; will ye therefore that I release unto you the King of the Jews?

40 Then cried they all again, saying, Not this man, but Barabbas. Now Barabbas was a robber.

## CHAPTER 19

*Christ is scourged, crowned with thorns, and beaten—Pilate delivereth him to be crucified—They cast lots for his garments—He dieth—His side is pierced—He is buried by Joseph and Nicodemus.*

1 Then Pilate therefore took Jesus, and scourged him.

2 And the soldiers platted a crown of thorns, and put it on his head, and they put on him a purple robe,

3 And said, Hail, King of the Jews! and they smote him with their hands.

4 Pilate therefore went forth again, and saith unto them, Behold, I bring him forth to you, that ye may know that I find no fault in him.

5 Then came Jesus forth, wearing the crown of thorns, and the purple robe. And Pilate saith unto them, Behold the man!

6 When the chief priests therefore and officers saw him, they cried out, saying, Crucify him, crucify him. Pilate saith unto them, Take ye him, and crucify him; for I find no fault in him.

7 The Jews answered him, We have a law, and by our law he ought to die, because he made himself the Son of God.

8 When Pilate therefore heard that saying, he was the more afraid;

9 And went again into the judgment hall, and saith unto Jesus, Whence art thou? But Jesus gave him no answer.

10 Then saith Pilate unto him, Speakest thou not unto me? knowest thou not that I have power to crucify thee, and have power to release thee?

11 Jesus answered, Thou couldest have no power against me, except it were given thee from above; therefore he that delivered me unto thee hath the greater sin.

12 And from thenceforth Pilate sought to release him; but the Jews cried out, saying, If thou let this man go, thou art not Caesar's friend; whosoever maketh himself a king speaketh against Caesar.

13 When Pilate therefore heard that saying, he brought Jesus forth, and sat down in the judgment seat in a place called the Pavement, but in the Hebrew, Gabbatha.

14 And it was the preparation of the passover, and about the sixth hour; and he saith unto the Jews, Behold your King!

15 But they cried out, Away with him, away with him, crucify him. Pilate saith unto them, Shall I crucify your

King? The chief priests answered, We have no king but Caesar.

16 Then delivered he him therefore unto them to be crucified. And they took Jesus, and led him away.

17 And he bearing his cross went forth into a place called the place of a burial; which is called in the Hebrew Golgotha;

18 Where they crucified him, and two others with him, on either side one, and Jesus in the midst.

19 And Pilate wrote a title, and put it on the cross. And the writing was JESUS OF NAZARETH THE KING OF THE JEWS.

20 This title then read many of the Jews; for the place where Jesus was crucified was nigh to the city; and it was written in Hebrew, and Greek, and Latin.

21 Then said the chief priests of the Jews to Pilate, Write not, The King of the Jews; but that he said, I am King of the Jews.

22 Pilate answered, What I have written I have written.

23 Then the soldiers, when they had crucified Jesus, took his garments, and made four parts, to every soldier a part; and also his coat; now the coat was without seam, woven from the top throughout.

24 They said therefore among themselves, Let us not rend it, but cast lots for it, whose it shall be; that the scripture might be fulfilled, which saith, They parted my raiment among them, and for my vesture they did cast lots. These things therefore the soldiers did.

25 Now there stood by the cross of Jesus his mother, and his mother's sister, Mary the wife of Cleophas, and Mary Magdalene.

26 When Jesus therefore saw his mother, and the disciple standing by, whom he loved, he saith unto his mother, Woman, behold thy son!

27 Then saith he to the disciple, Behold thy mother! And from that hour that disciple took her unto his own home.

28 After this, Jesus knowing that all things were now accomplished, that the scripture might be fulfilled, saith, I thirst.

29 Now there was a vessel full of vinegar, mingled with gall, and they filled a sponge with it, and put upon hyssop, and put to his mouth.

30 When Jesus therefore had received the vinegar, he said, It is finished; and he bowed his head, and gave up the ghost.

31 The Jews therefore, because it was the preparation, that the bodies should not remain upon the cross on the Sabbath day, (for that Sabbath day was a high day,) besought Pilate that their legs might be broken, and that they might be taken away.

32 Then came the soldiers, and brake the legs of the first, and of the other which was crucified with him.

33 But when they came to Jesus, and saw that he was dead already, they brake not his legs;

34 But one of the soldiers with a spear pierced his side, and forthwith came there out blood and water.

35 And he that saw it bare record, and his record is true; and he knoweth that he saith true, that ye might believe.

36 For these things were done, that the scripture should be fulfilled, A bone of him shall not be broken.

37 And again another scripture saith, They shall look on him whom they pierced.

38 And after this Joseph of Arimathea, being a disciple of Jesus, but secretly for fear of the Jews, besought Pilate that he might take away the body of Jesus; and Pilate gave him leave. He came therefore, and took the body of Jesus.

39 And there came also Nicodemus, (which at the first came to Jesus by night,) and brought a mixture of myrrh and aloes, about a hundred pound weight.

40 Then took they the body of Jesus, and wound it in linen clothes with the spices, as the manner of the Jews is to bury.

41 Now in the place where he was crucified there was a garden; and in the garden a new sepulcher, wherein was never man yet laid.

42 There laid they Jesus therefore because of the Jews' preparation day; for the sepulcher was nigh at hand.

## CHAPTER 20

*Mary cometh to the sepulcher—So do Peter and John—Jesus appeareth to Mary Magdalene, and to his disciples.*

1 The first day of the week cometh Mary Magdalene early, when it was

yet dark, unto the sepulcher, and seeth the stone taken away from the sepulcher, and two angels sitting thereon.

2 Then she runneth, and cometh to Simon Peter, and to the other disciple, whom Jesus loved, and saith unto them, They have taken away the Lord out of the sepulcher, and we know not where they have laid him.

3 Peter therefore went forth, and that other disciple, and came to the sepulcher.

4 So they ran both together; and the other disciple did outrun Peter, and came first to the sepulcher.

5 And he stooping down, and looking in, saw the linen clothes lying; yet went he not in.

6 Then cometh Simon Peter following him, and went into the sepulcher, and seeth the linen clothes lie,

7 And the napkin, that was about his head, not lying with the linen clothes, but wrapped together in a place by itself.

8 Then went in also that other disciple, which came first to the sepulcher, and he saw, and believed.

9 For as yet they knew not the scripture, that he must rise again from the dead.

10 Then the disciples went away again unto their own homes.

11 But Mary stood without at the sepulcher weeping; and as she wept, she stooped down, and looked into the sepulcher,

12 And seeth two angels in white sitting, the one at the head, and the other at the feet, where the body of Jesus had lain.

13 And they say unto her, Woman, why weepest thou? She saith unto them, Because they have taken away my Lord, and I know not where they have laid him.

14 And when she had thus said, she turned herself back, and saw Jesus standing, and knew not that it was Jesus.

15 Jesus saith unto her, Woman, why weepest thou? whom seekest thou? She, supposing him to be the gardener, saith unto him, Sir, if thou have borne him hence, tell me where thou hast laid him, and I will take him away.

16 Jesus saith unto her, Mary. She turned herself, and saith unto him, Rabboni; which is to say, Master.

17 Jesus saith unto her, Hold me not; for I am not yet ascended to my Father; but go to my brethren, and say unto them, I ascend unto my Father, and your Father; and to my God, and your God.

18 Mary Magdalene came and told the disciples that she had seen the Lord, and that he had spoken these things unto her.

19 Then the same day at evening, being the first day of the week, when the doors were shut where the disciples were assembled for fear of the Jews, came Jesus and stood in the midst, and saith unto them, Peace be unto you.

20 And when he had so said, he showed unto them his hands and his side. Then were the disciples glad, when they saw the Lord.

21 Then said Jesus to them again, Peace be unto you; as my Father hath sent me, even so send I you.

22 And when he had said this, he breathed on them, and saith unto them, Receive ye the Holy Ghost;

23 Whosesoever sins ye remit, they are remitted unto them; and whosesoever sins ye retain, they are retained.

24 But Thomas, one of the twelve, called Didymus, was not with them when Jesus came.

25 The other disciples therefore said unto him, We have seen the Lord. But he said unto them, Except I shall see in his hands the print of the nails, and put my finger into the print of the nails, and thrust my hand into his side, I will not believe.

26 And after eight days again his disciples were within, and Thomas with them; then came Jesus, the doors being shut, and stood in the midst, and said, Peace be unto you.

27 Then saith he to Thomas, Reach hither thy finger, and behold my hands; and reach hither thy hand, and thrust it into my side; and be not faithless, but believing.

28 And Thomas answered and said unto him, My Lord and my God.

29 Jesus saith unto him, Thomas, because thou hast seen me, thou hast believed; blessed are they that have not seen, and yet have believed.

30 And many other signs truly did Jesus in the presence of his disciples, which are not written in this book;

31 But these are written, that ye might believe that Jesus is the Christ, the Son of God; and that believing ye might have life through his name.

## CHAPTER 21

*Christ appearing again to his disciples— He dineth with them.*

1 After these things Jesus showed himself again to the disciples at the sea of Tiberias; and on this wise showed he himself.

2 There were together Simon Peter, and Thomas called Didymus, and Nathanael of Cana in Galilee, and the sons of Zebedee, and two other of his disciples.

3 Simon Peter saith unto them, I go a fishing. They say unto him, we also go with thee. They went forth, and entered into a ship immediately; and that night they caught nothing.

4 But when the morning was now come, Jesus stood on the shore; but the disciples knew not that it was Jesus.

5 Then Jesus saith unto them, Children, have ye any meat? They answered him, No.

6 And he said unto them, Cast the net on the right side of the ship, and ye shall find. They cast therefore, and now they were not able to draw it for the multitude of fishes.

7 Therefore that disciple whom Jesus loved saith unto Peter, It is the Lord. Now when Simon Peter heard that it was the Lord, he girt his fisher's coat unto him, (for he was naked,) and did cast himself into the sea.

8 And the other disciples came in a little ship, (for they were not far from land, but as it were two hundred cubits,) dragging the net with fishes.

9 As soon then as they were come to land, they saw a fire of coals there, and fish laid thereon, and bread.

10 Jesus saith unto them, Bring of the fish which ye have now caught.

11 Simon Peter went up, and drew the net to land full of great fishes, a hundred and fifty and three; and for all there were so many, yet was not the net broken.

12 Jesus saith unto them, Come and dine. And none of the disciples durst ask him, Who art thou? knowing that it was the Lord.

13 Jesus then cometh, and taketh bread, and giveth them, and fish likewise.

14 This is now the third time that Jesus showed himself to his disciples, after that he was risen from the dead.

15 So when they had dined, Jesus saith to Simon Peter, Simon, son of Jonas, lovest thou me more than these? He saith unto him, Yea, Lord; thou knowest that I love thee. He saith unto him, Feed my lambs.

16 He saith to him again the second time, Simon, son of Jonas, lovest thou me? He saith unto him, Yea, Lord; thou knowest that I love thee. He saith unto him, Feed my sheep.

17 He saith unto him the third time, Simon, son of Jonas, lovest thou me? Peter was grieved because he said unto him the third time, Lovest thou me? And he said unto him, Lord, thou knowest all things; thou knowest that I love thee. Jesus said unto him, Feed my sheep.

18 Verily, verily, I say unto thee, When thou wast young, thou girdedst thyself, and walkedst whither thou wouldest; but when thou shalt be old, thou shalt stretch forth thy hands, and another shall gird thee, and carry thee whither thou wouldest not.

19 This spake he, signifying by what death he should glorify God. And when he had spoken this, he saith unto him, Follow me.

20 Then Peter, turning about, seeth the disciple whom Jesus loved following; which also leaned on his breast at supper, and said, Lord, which is he that betrayeth thee?

21 Peter seeing him saith to Jesus, Lord, and what shall this man do?

22 Jesus saith unto him, If I will that he tarry till I come, what is that to thee? follow thou me.

23 Then went this saying abroad among the brethren that that disciple should not die; yet Jesus said not unto him, He shall not die; but if I will that he tarry till I come, what is that to thee?

24 This is the disciple which testifieth of these things, and wrote these things; and we know that his testimony is true.

25 And there are also many other things which Jesus did, the which, if they should be written every one, I suppose that even the world itself could not contain the books that should be written. Amen.

# The Acts of the Apostles

## CHAPTER 1

*The Holy Ghost promised, by virtue whereof the apostles should be Christ's witnesses, even to the utmost parts of the earth—Two angels speak of Christ's second coming—Matthias chosen in place of Judas.*

1 The former treatise have I made, O Theophilus, of all that Jesus began both to do and teach,

2 Until the day in which he was taken up, after that he through the Holy Ghost had given commandments unto the apostles whom he had chosen;

3 To whom also he showed himself alive after his sufferings by many infallible proofs, being seen of them forty days, and speaking of the things pertaining to the kingdom of God;

4 And, being with them when they were assembled together, commanded them that they should not depart from Jerusalem, but wait for the promise of the Father, which, saith he, ye have heard of me.

5 For John truly baptized with water; but ye shall be baptized with the Holy Ghost not many days hence.

6 When they therefore were come together, they asked of him, saying, Lord, wilt thou at this time restore again the kingdom to Israel?

7 And he said unto them, It is not for you to know the times or the seasons, which the Father hath put in his own power.

8 But ye shall receive power, after that the Holy Ghost is come upon you; and ye shall be witnesses unto me both in Jerusalem, and in all Judea, and Samaria, and unto the uttermost part of the earth.

9 And when he had spoken these things, while they beheld, he was taken up; and a cloud received him out of their sight.

10 And while they looked steadfastly toward heaven as he went up, behold, two men stood by them in white apparel;

11 Which also said, Ye men of Galilee, why stand ye gazing up into heaven? this same Jesus, which is taken up from you into heaven, shall so come in like manner as ye have seen him go into heaven.

12 Then returned they unto Jerusalem from the mount called Olivet, which is from Jerusalem a Sabbath day's journey.

13 And when they were come in, they went up into an upper room, where abode both Peter, and James, and John, and Andrew, Philip, and Thomas, Bartholomew, and Matthew, James the son of Alpheus, and Simon Zelotes, and Judas the brother of James.

14 These all continued with one accord in prayer and supplication, with the women, and Mary the mother of Jesus, and with his brethren.

15 And in those days Peter stood up in the midst of the disciples, and said, (the number of names together were about a hundred and twenty,)

16 Men and brethren, this scripture must needs have been fulfilled, which the Holy Ghost by the mouth of David spake before concerning Judas, which was guide to them that took Jesus.

17 For he was numbered with us, and had obtained part of this ministry.

18 Now this man purchased a field with the reward of iniquity; and falling headlong, he burst asunder in the midst, and all his bowels gushed out.

19 And it was known unto all the dwellers at Jerusalem; insomuch as that field is called, in their proper tongue, Aceldama, that is to say, The field of blood.

20 For it is written in the book of Psalms, Let his habitation be desolate, and let no man dwell therein; and, His bishopric let another take.

21 Wherefore of these men which have companied with us all the time that the Lord Jesus went in and out among us,

22 Beginning from the baptism of John, unto that same day that he was taken up from us, must one be ordained to be a witness with us of his resurrection.

23 And they appointed two, Joseph called Barsabas, who was surnamed Justus, and Matthias.

24 And they prayed, and said, Thou, Lord, which knowest the hearts of all men, show whether of these two thou hast chosen,

25 That he may take part of this min-

istry and apostleship, from which Judas by transgression fell, that he might go to his own place.

26 And they gave forth their lots; and the lot fell upon Matthias; and he was numbered with the eleven apostles.

## CHAPTER 2

*The apostles, filled with the Holy Ghost, and speaking divers languages, are admired by some, and derided by others— Peter's testimony—A great number that were converted were baptized—The apostles work many miracles—God daily increasing his church.*

1 And when the day of Pentecost was fully come, they were all with one accord in one place.

2 And suddenly there came a sound from heaven as of a rushing mighty wind, and it filled all the house where they were sitting.

3 And there appeared unto them cloven tongues like as of fire, and it rested upon each of them.

4 And they were all filled with the Holy Ghost, and began to speak with other tongues, as the Spirit gave them utterance.

5 And there were dwelling at Jerusalem Jews, devout men, out of every nation under heaven.

6 Now when this was noised abroad, the multitude came together, and were confounded, because that every man heard them speak in his own language.

7 And they were all amazed and marveled, saying one to another, Behold, are not all these which speak Galileans?

8 And how hear we every man in our own tongue, wherein we were born?

9 Parthians, and Medes, and Elamites, and the dwellers in Mesopotamia, and in Judea, and Cappadocia, in Pontus, and Asia,

10 Phrygia, and Pamphylia, in Egypt, and in the parts of Libya about Cyrene, and strangers of Rome, Jews and proselytes,

11 Cretes and Arabians, we do hear them speak in our tongues the wonderful works of God.

12 And they were all amazed, and were in doubt, saying one to another, What meaneth this?

13 Others mocking said, These men are full of new wine.

14 But Peter, standing up with the eleven, lifted up his voice, and said unto them, Ye men of Judea, and all ye that dwell at Jerusalem, be this known unto you, and hearken to my words;

15 For these are not drunken, as ye suppose, seeing it is but the third hour of the day.

16 But this is that which was spoken by the prophet Joel;

17 And it shall come to pass in the last days, saith God, I will pour out of my Spirit upon all flesh; and your sons and your daughters shall prophesy, and your young men shall see visions, and your old men shall dream dreams;

18 And on my servants and on my handmaidens I will pour out in those days of my Spirit; and they shall prophesy;

19 And I will show wonders in heaven above, and signs in the earth beneath; blood, and fire, and vapor of smoke;

20 The sun shall be turned into darkness, and the moon into blood, before the great and notable day of the Lord come;

21 And it shall come to pass, that whosoever shall call on the name of the Lord shall be saved.

22 Ye men of Israel, hear these words; Jesus of Nazareth, a man approved of God among you by miracles and wonders and signs, which God did by him in the midst of you, as ye yourselves also know;

23 Him, being delivered by the determinate counsel and foreknowledge of God, ye have taken, and by wicked hands have crucified and slain;

24 Whom God hath raised up, having loosed the pains of death; because it was not possible that he should be holden of it.

25 For David speaketh concerning him, I foresaw the Lord always before my face; for he is on my right hand, that I should not be moved;

26 Therefore did my heart rejoice, and my tongue was glad; moreover also my flesh shall rest in hope;

27 Because thou wilt not leave my soul in prison, neither wilt thou suffer thine Holy One to see corruption.

28 Thou hast made known to me the ways of life; thou shalt make me full of joy with thy countenance.

29 Men and brethren, let me freely speak unto you of the patriarch David,

that he is both dead and buried, and his sepulcher is with us unto this day.

30 Therefore being a prophet, and knowing that God had sworn with an oath to him, that of the fruit of his loins, according to the flesh, he would raise up Christ to sit on his throne;

31 He, seeing this before, spake of the resurrection of Christ, that his soul was not left in hell, neither his flesh did see corruption.

32 This Jesus hath God raised up, whereof we all are witnesses.

33 Therefore being by the right hand of God exalted, and having received of the Father the promise of the Holy Ghost, he hath shed forth this, which ye now see and hear.

34 For David is not ascended into the heavens; but he saith himself, The Lord said unto my Lord, Sit thou on my right hand,

35 Until I make thy foes thy footstool.

36 Therefore let all the house of Israel know assuredly, that God hath made that same Jesus whom ye have crucified, both Lord and Christ.

37 Now when they heard this, they were pricked in their heart, and said unto Peter and to the rest of the apostles, Men and brethren, what shall we do?

38 Then Peter said unto them, Repent, and be baptized every one of you in the name of Jesus Christ for the remission of sins, and ye shall receive the gift of the Holy Ghost.

39 For the promise is unto you, and to your children, and to all that are afar off, even as many as the Lord our God shall call.

40 And with many other words did he testify and exhort, saying, Save yourselves from this untoward generation.

41 Then they that gladly received his word were baptized; and the same day there were added unto them about three thousand souls.

42 And they continued steadfastly in the apostles' doctrine and fellowship, and in breaking of bread, and in prayers.

43 And fear came upon every soul; and many wonders and signs were done by the apostles.

44 And all that believed were together, and had all things common;

45 And sold their possessions and goods, and parted them to all men, as every man had need.

46 And they, continuing daily with one accord in the temple, and breaking bread from house to house, did eat their meat with gladness and singleness of heart,

47 Praising God, and having favor with all the people. And the Lord added to the church daily such as should be saved.

## CHAPTER 3

*A lame man restored—Peter exhorteth them by repentance and faith to seek remission of their sins, and salvation in Jesus.*

1 Now Peter and John went up together into the temple at the ninth hour, for prayer.

2 And a certain man lame from his mother's womb was carried, whom they laid daily at the gate of the temple which is called Beautiful, to ask alms of them that entered into the temple;

3 Who, seeing Peter and John about to go into the temple, asked an alms.

4 And Peter and John, fastening their eyes upon him, said, Look on us.

5 And he gave heed unto them, expecting to receive something of them.

6 Then Peter said, Silver and gold have I none; but such as I have give I thee; In the name of Jesus Christ of Nazareth rise up and walk.

7 And he took him by the right hand, and lifted him up; and immediately his feet and ankle bones received strength.

8 And he leaping up stood, and walked, and entered with them into the temple, walking, and leaping, and praising God.

9 And all the people saw him walking and praising God;

10 And they knew that it was he which sat for alms at the Beautiful gate of the temple; and they were filled with wonder and amazement at that which had happened unto him.

11 And as the lame man which was healed held Peter and John, all the people ran together unto them in the porch that is called Solomon's, greatly wondering.

12 And when Peter saw this, he answered and said unto the people, Ye men of Israel, why marvel ye at this? or why look ye so earnestly on us, as

though by our own power or holiness we had made this man to walk?

13 The God of Abraham, and of Isaac, and of Jacob, the God of our fathers, hath glorified his Son Jesus; whom ye delivered up, and denied him in the presence of Pilate, when he was determined to let him go.

14 But ye denied the Holy One and the Just, and desired a murderer to be granted unto you;

15 And killed the Prince of life, whom God hath raised from the dead; whereof we are witnesses.

16 And this man, through faith in his name, hath been made strong, whom ye see and know; yea, the faith which is in him hath given him this perfect soundness in the presence of you all.

17 And now, brethren, I know that through ignorance ye have done this, as also your rulers.

18 But those things, which God before had showed by the mouth of all his prophets, that Christ should suffer, he hath so fulfilled.

19 Repent ye therefore, and be converted, that your sins may be blotted out, when the times of refreshing shall come from the presence of the Lord;

20 And he shall send Jesus Christ, which before was preached unto you, whom ye have crucified;

21 Whom the heavens must receive until the times of restitution of all things which God hath spoken by the mouth of all his holy prophets since the world began.

22 For Moses truly said unto the fathers, A Prophet shall the Lord your God raise up unto you of your brethren, like unto me; him shall ye hear in all things whatsoever he shall say unto you.

23 And it shall come to pass, that every soul, which will not hear that prophet, shall be destroyed from among the people.

24 Yea, and all the prophets from Samuel and those that follow after, as many as have spoken, have likewise foretold of these days.

25 Ye are the children of the prophets, and of the covenant which God made with our fathers, saying unto Abraham, And in thy seed shall all the kindreds of the earth be blessed.

26 Unto you first God, having raised up his Son Jesus, sent him to bless you, in turning away every one of you from his iniquities.

## CHAPTER 4

*Rulers offended—Peter and John imprisoned—Salvation by Jesus only—All things common.*

1 And as they spake unto the people, the priests, and the captain of the temple, and the Sadducees, came upon them,

2 Being grieved that they taught the people, and preached through Jesus the resurrection from the dead.

3 And they laid hands on them, and put them in hold unto the next day; for it was now eventide.

4 Howbeit many of them which heard the word believed; and the number of the men was about five thousand.

5 And it came to pass on the morrow, that their rulers, and elders, and scribes,

6 And Annas the high priest, and Caiaphas, and John, and Alexander, and as many as were of the kindred of the high priest, were gathered together at Jerusalem.

7 And when they had set them in the midst, they asked, By what power, or by what name, have ye done this?

8 Then Peter, filled with the Holy Ghost, said unto them, Ye rulers of the people, and elders of Israel,

9 If we this day be examined of the good deed done to the impotent man, by what means he is made whole;

10 Be it known unto you all, and to all the people of Israel, that by the name of Jesus Christ of Nazareth, whom ye crucified, whom God raised from the dead, even by him doth this man stand here before you whole.

11 This is the stone which was set at naught of you builders, which is become the head of the corner.

12 Neither is there salvation in any other; for there is none other name under heaven given among men, whereby we must be saved.

13 Now when they saw the boldness of Peter and John, and perceived that they were unlearned and ignorant men, they marveled; and they took knowledge of them, that they had been with Jesus.

14 And beholding the man which was healed standing with them, they could say nothing against it.

15 But when they had commanded them to go aside out of the council, they conferred among themselves,

16 Saying, What shall we do to these men? for that indeed a notable miracle hath been done by them is manifest to all them that dwell in Jerusalem; and we cannot deny it.

17 But that it spread no further among the people, let us straitly threaten them, that they speak henceforth to no man in this name.

18 And they called them, and commanded them not to speak at all nor teach in the name of Jesus.

19 But Peter and John answered and said unto them, Whether it be right in the sight of God to hearken unto you more than unto God, judge ye.

20 For we cannot but speak the things which we have seen and heard.

21 So when they had further threatened them, they let them go, finding nothing how they might punish them, because of the people; for many glorified God for that which was done.

22 For the man was above forty years old, on whom this miracle of healing was showed.

23 And being let go, they went to their own company, and reported all that the chief priests and elders had said unto them.

24 And when they heard that, they lifted up their voice to God with one accord, and said, Lord, thou art God, which hast made heaven, and earth, and the sea, and all that in them is;

25 Who by the mouth of thy servant David hast said, Why did the heathen rage, and the people imagine vain things?

26 The kings of the earth stood up, and the rulers were gathered together against the Lord, and against his Christ.

27 For of a truth against thy holy child Jesus, whom thou hast anointed, both Herod, and Pontius Pilate, with the Gentiles, and the people of Israel, were gathered together,

28 For to do whatsoever thy hand and thy counsel determined before to be done.

29 And now, Lord, behold their threatenings; and grant unto thy servants, that with all boldness they may speak thy word,

30 By stretching forth thine hand to heal; and that signs and wonders may be done by the name of thy holy child Jesus.

31 And when they had prayed, the place was shaken where they were assembled together; and they were all filled with the Holy Ghost, and they spake the word of God with boldness.

32 And the multitude of them that believed were of one heart and of one soul; neither said any of them that aught of the things which he possessed was his own; but they had all things common.

33 And with great power gave the apostles witness of the resurrection of the Lord Jesus; and great grace was upon them all.

34 Neither was there any among them that lacked; for as many as were possessors of lands or houses sold them, and brought the prices of the things that were sold,

35 And laid them down at the apostles' feet; and distribution was made unto every man according as he had need.

36 And Joses, who by the apostles was surnamed Barnabas, (which is, being interpreted, The son of consolation,) a Levite, and of the country of Cyprus,

37 Having land, sold it, and brought the money, and laid it at the apostles' feet.

## CHAPTER 5

*Death of Ananias and Sapphira—Many miracles wrought—The apostles again imprisoned and beaten.*

1 But a certain man named Ananias, with Sapphira his wife, sold a possession,

2 And kept back part of the price, his wife also being privy to it, and brought a certain part, and laid it at the apostles' feet.

3 But Peter said, Ananias, why hath Satan filled thine heart to lie to the Holy Ghost, and to keep back part of the price of the land?

4 While it remained, was it not thine own? and after it was sold, was it not in thine own power? why hast thou conceived this thing in thine heart? thou hast not lied unto men, but unto God.

5 And Ananias hearing these words fell down, and gave up the ghost; and

great fear came on all them that heard these things.

6 And the young men arose, wound him up, and carried him out, and buried him.

7 And it was about the space of three hours after, when his wife, not knowing what was done, came in.

8 And Peter answered unto her, Tell me whether ye sold the land for so much? And she said, Yea, for so much.

9 Then Peter said unto her, How is it that ye have agreed together to tempt the Spirit of the Lord? behold, the feet of them which have buried thy husband are at the door, and shall carry thee out.

10 Then fell she down straightway at his feet, and yielded up the ghost; and the young men came in, and found her dead, and carrying her forth, buried her by her husband.

11 And great fear came upon all the church, and upon as many as heard these things.

12 And by the hands of the apostles were many signs and wonders wrought among the people; (and they were all with one accord in Solomon's porch.

13 And of the rulers durst no man join himself to them; but the people magnified them.

14 And believers were the more added to the Lord, multitudes both of men and women;)

15 Insomuch that they brought forth the sick into the streets, and laid them on beds and couches, that at the least the shadow of Peter passing by might overshadow some of them.

16 There came also a multitude out of the cities round about unto Jerusalem, bringing sick folks, and them which were vexed with unclean spirits; and they were healed every one.

17 Then the high priest rose up, and all they that were with him, (which is the sect of the Sadducees,) and were filled with indignation.

18 And laid their hands on the apostles, and put them in the common prison.

19 But the angel of the Lord by night opened the prison doors, and brought them forth, and said,

20 Go, stand and speak in the temple to the people all the words of this life.

21 And when they heard that, they entered into the temple early in the morning, and taught. But the high priest came, and they that were with him, and called the council together, and all the senate of the children of Israel, and sent to the prison to have them brought.

22 But when the officers came, and found them not in the prison, they returned, and told,

23 Saying, The prison truly found we shut with all safety, and the keepers standing without before the doors; but when we had opened, we found no man within.

24 Now when the high priest and the captain of the temple and the chief priests heard these things, they doubted of them whereunto this would grow.

25 Then came one and told them, saying, Behold, the men whom ye put in prison are standing in the temple, and teaching the people.

26 Then went the captain with the officers, and brought them without violence; for they feared the people, lest they should have been stoned.

27 And when they had brought them, they set them before the council; and the high priest asked them,

28 Saying, Did not we straitly command you that ye should not teach in this name? and, behold, ye have filled Jerusalem with your doctrine, and intend to bring this man's blood upon us.

29 Then Peter and the other apostles answered and said, We ought to obey God rather than men.

30 The God of our fathers raised up Jesus, whom ye slew and hanged on a tree.

31 Him hath God exalted with his right hand to be a Prince and a Savior, for to give repentance to Israel, and forgiveness of sins.

32 And we are his witnesses of these things; and so is also the Holy Ghost, whom God hath given to them that obey him.

33 When they heard that, they were cut to the heart, and took counsel to slay them.

34 Then stood there up one in the council, a Pharisee, named Gamaliel, a doctor of the law, had in reputation among all the people, and commanded to put the apostles forth a little space;

35 And said unto them, Ye men of Israel, take heed to yourselves what ye intend to do as touching these men.

36 For before these days rose up

Theudas, boasting himself to be somebody; to whom a number of men, about four hundred, joined themselves; who was slain; and all, as many as obeyed him, were scattered, and brought to naught.

37 After this man rose up Judas of Galilee in the days of the taxing, and drew away much people after him; he also perished; and all, even as many as obeyed him, were dispersed.

38 And now I say unto you, Refrain from these men, and let them alone; for if this counsel or this work be of men, it will come to naught;

39 But if it be of God, ye cannot overthrow it; be careful, therefore, lest ye be found even to fight against God.

40 And to him they agreed; and when they had called the apostles, and beaten them, they commanded that they should not speak in the name of Jesus, and let them go.

41 And they departed from the presence of the council, rejoicing that they were counted worthy to suffer shame for his name.

42 And daily in the temple, and in every house, they ceased not to teach and preach Jesus Christ.

## CHAPTER 6

*Seven men chosen—Stephen accused of blasphemy.*

1 And in those days, when the number of the disciples was multiplied, there arose a murmuring of the Grecians against the Hebrews, because their widows were neglected in the daily ministration.

2 Then the twelve called the multitude of the disciples unto them, and said, It is not reason that we should leave the word of God, and serve tables.

3 Wherefore, brethren, look ye out among you seven men of honest report, full of the Holy Ghost and wisdom, whom we may appoint over this business.

4 But we will give ourselves continually to prayer, and to the ministry of the word.

5 And the saying pleased the whole multitude; and they chose Stephen, a man full of faith and of the Holy Ghost, and Philip, and Prochorus, and Nicanor, and Timon, and Parmenas, and Nicolas a proselyte of Antioch;

6 Whom they set before the apostles;

and when they had prayed, they laid their hands on them.

7 And the word of God increased; and the number of the disciples multiplied in Jerusalem greatly; and a great company of the priests were obedient to the faith.

8 And Stephen, full of faith and power, did great wonders and miracles among the people.

9 And there arose certain of the synagogue, who are called Libertines, and also Cyrenians, and Alexandrians, and of them of Cilicia, and of Asia, disputing with Stephen.

10 And they were not able to resist the wisdom and the spirit by which he spake.

11 Then they suborned men, which said, We have heard him speak blasphemous words against Moses, and against God.

12 And they stirred up the people, and the elders, and the scribes, and came upon him, and caught him, and brought him to the council,

13 And set up false witnesses, which said, This man ceaseth not to speak blasphemous words against this holy place, and the law;

14 For we have heard him say, that this Jesus of Nazareth shall destroy this place, and shall change the customs which Moses delivered us.

15 And all that sat in the council, looking steadfastly on him, saw his face as it had been the face of an angel.

## CHAPTER 7

*Stephen's answer—Stephen is stoned by the Jews, Saul standing by.*

1 Then said the high priest, Are these things so?

2 And he said, Men, brethren, and fathers, hearken; The God of glory appeared unto our father Abraham, when he was in Mesopotamia, before he dwelt in Charran,

3 And said unto him, Get thee out of thy country, and from thy kindred, and come into the land which I shall show thee.

4 Then came he out of the land of the Chaldeans, and dwelt in Charran; and from thence, when his father was dead, he removed him into this land, wherein ye now dwell.

5 And he gave him none inheritance in it, no, not so much as to set his foot on; yet he promised that he would give

it to him for a possession, and to his seed after him, when as yet he had no child.

6 And God spake on this wise, That his seed should sojourn in a strange land; and that they should bring them into bondage, and entreat them evil four hundred years.

7 And the nation to whom they shall be in bondage will I judge, said God; and after that shall they come forth, and serve me in this place.

8 And he gave him the covenant of circumcision; and so Abraham begat Isaac, and circumcised him the eighth day; and Isaac begat Jacob; and Jacob begat the twelve patriarchs.

9 And the patriarchs, moved with envy, sold Joseph into Egypt; but God was with him,

10 And delivered him out of all his afflictions, and gave him favor and wisdom in the sight of Pharaoh king of Egypt; and he made him governor over Egypt and all his house.

11 Now there came a dearth over all the land of Egypt and Chanaan, and great affliction; and our fathers found no sustenance.

12 But when Jacob heard that there was corn in Egypt, he sent out our fathers first.

13 And at the second time Joseph was made known to his brethren; and Joseph's kindred was made known unto Pharaoh.

14 Then sent Joseph, and called his father Jacob to him, and all his kindred, threescore and fifteen souls.

15 So Jacob went down into Egypt, and died, he, and our fathers.

16 And were carried over into Sychem, and laid in the sepulcher that Abraham bought for a sum of money of the sons of Emmor, the father of Sychem.

17 But when the time of the promise drew nigh, which God had sworn to Abraham, the people grew and multiplied in Egypt,

18 Till another king arose, which knew not Joseph.

19 The same dealt subtilely with our kindred, and evil entreated our fathers, so that they cast out their young children, to the end they might not live.

20 In which time Moses was born, and was exceeding fair, and nourished up in his father's house three months;

21 And when he was cast out, Pharaoh's daughter took him up, and nourished him for her own son.

22 And Moses was learned in all the wisdom of the Egyptians, and was mighty in words and in deeds.

23 And when he was full forty years old, it came into his heart to visit his brethren the children of Israel.

24 And seeing one of them suffer wrong, he defended him, and avenged him that was oppressed, and smote the Egyptian;

25 For he supposed his brethren would have understood how that God by his hand would deliver them; but they understood not.

26 And the next day he showed himself unto them as they strove, and would have set them at one again, saying, Sirs, ye are brethren; why do ye wrong one to another?

27 But he that did his neighbor wrong thrust him away, saying, Who made thee a ruler and a judge over us?

28 Wilt thou kill me, as thou didst the Egyptian yesterday?

29 Then fled Moses at this saying, and was a stranger in the land of Midian, where he begat two sons.

30 And when forty years were expired, there appeared to him in the wilderness of mount Sinai an angel of the Lord in a flame of fire in a bush.

31 When Moses saw it, he wondered at the sight; and as he drew near to behold it, the voice of the Lord came unto him,

32 Saying, I am the God of thy fathers, the God of Abraham, and the God of Isaac, and the God of Jacob. Then Moses trembled, and durst not behold.

33 Then said the Lord to him, Put off thy shoes from thy feet; for the place where thou standest is holy ground.

34 I have seen, I have seen the affliction of my people which is in Egypt, and I have heard their groaning, and am come down to deliver them. And now come, I will send thee into Egypt.

35 This Moses whom they refused, saying, Who made thee a ruler and a judge? the same did God send to be a ruler and a deliverer by the hand of the angel which appeared to him in the bush.

36 He brought them out, after that he had showed wonders and signs in

the land of Egypt, and in the Red sea, and in the wilderness forty years.

37 This is that Moses, which said unto the children of Israel, A prophet shall the Lord your God raise up unto you of your brethren, like unto me; him shall ye hear.

38 This is he, that was in the church in the wilderness with the angel which spake to him in the mount Sinai, and with our fathers; who received the lively oracles to give unto us.

39 Whom our fathers would not obey, but thrust him from them, and in their hearts turned back again into Egypt,

40 Saying unto Aaron, Make us gods to go before us; for as for this Moses, which brought us out of the land of Egypt, we know not what is become of him.

41 And they made a calf in those days, and offered sacrifice unto the idol, and rejoiced in the works of their own hands.

42 Then God turned, and gave them up to worship the host of heaven; as it is written in the book of the prophets, O ye house of Israel, have ye offered to me slain beasts and sacrifices by the space of forty years in the wilderness?

43 Yea, ye took up the tabernacle of Moloch, and the star of your god Remphan, figures which ye made to worship them; and I will carry you away beyond Babylon.

44 Our fathers had the tabernacle of witness in the wilderness, as he had appointed, speaking unto Moses, that he should make it according to the pattern that he had seen.

45 Which also our fathers that came after brought in with Jesus into the possession of the Gentiles, whom God drave out before the face of our fathers, unto the days of David;

46 Who found favor before God, and desired to find a tabernacle for the God of Jacob.

47 But Solomon built him a house.

48 Howbeit the most High dwelleth not in temples made with hands; as saith the prophet,

49 Heaven is my throne, and earth is my footstool; what house will ye build me? saith the Lord; or what is the place of my rest?

50 Hath not my hand made all these things?

51 Ye stiff-necked and uncircumcised in heart and ears, ye do always resist the Holy Ghost; as your fathers did, so do ye.

52 Which of the prophets have not your fathers persecuted? and they have slain them which showed before the coming of the Just One; of whom ye have been now the betrayers and murderers.

53 Who have received the law by the disposition of angels, and have not kept it.

54 When they heard these things, they were cut to the heart, and they gnashed on him with their teeth.

55 But he, being full of the Holy Ghost, looked up steadfastly into heaven, and saw the glory of God, and Jesus standing on the right hand of God.

56 And said, Behold, I see the heavens opened, and the Son of man standing on the right hand of God.

57 Then they cried out with a loud voice, and stopped their ears, and ran upon him with one accord,

58 And cast him out of the city, and stoned him; and the witnesses laid down their clothes at a young man's feet, whose name was Saul.

59 And they stoned Stephen; and he, calling upon God, said, Lord Jesus, receive my spirit.

60 And he kneeled down, and cried with a loud voice, Lord, lay not this sin to their charge. And when he had said this, he fell asleep.

## CHAPTER 8

*Persecution in Jerusalem—Philip preaches in Samaria—By prayer and imposition of hands the Holy Ghost is given—Simon the sorcerer—Philip baptizes the Ethiopian eunuch.*

1 And Saul was consenting unto his death. And at that time there was a great persecution against the church which was at Jerusalem; and they were all scattered abroad throughout the regions of Judea and Samaria, except the apostles.

2 And devout men carried Stephen to his burial, and made great lamentation over him.

3 As for Saul, he made havoc of the church, entering into every house, and haling men and women committed them to prison.

4 Therefore they that were scattered

abroad went everywhere preaching the word.

5 Then Philip went down to the city of Samaria, and preached Christ unto them.

6 And the people with one accord gave heed unto those things which Philip spake, hearing and seeing the miracles which he did.

7 For unclean spirits, crying with loud voice, came out of many that were possessed with them; and many taken with palsies, and that were lame, were healed.

8 And there was great joy in that city.

9 But there was a certain man, called Simon, which beforetime in the same city used sorcery, and bewitched the people of Samaria, giving out that himself was some great one;

10 To whom they all gave heed, from the least to the greatest, saying, This man is the great power of God.

11 And to him they had regard, because that of long time he had bewitched them with sorceries.

12 But when they believed Philip preaching the things concerning the kingdom of God, and the name of Jesus Christ, they were baptized, both men and women.

13 Then Simon himself believed also; and when he was baptized, he continued with Philip, and wondered, beholding the miracles and signs which were done.

14 Now when the apostles which were at Jerusalem heard that Samaria had received the word of God, they sent unto them Peter and John;

15 Who, when they were come down, prayed for them, that they might receive the Holy Ghost.

16 (For as yet he was fallen upon none of them: only they were baptized in the name of the Lord Jesus.)

17 Then laid they their hands on them, and they received the Holy Ghost.

18 And when Simon saw that through laying on of the apostles' hands the Holy Ghost was given, he offered them money,

19 Saying, Give me also this power, that on whomsoever I lay hands, he may receive the Holy Ghost.

20 But Peter said unto him, Thy money perish with thee, because thou

hast thought that the gift of God may be purchased with money.

21 Thou hast neither part nor lot in this matter: for thy heart is not right in the sight of God.

22 Repent therefore of this thy wickedness, and pray God, if perhaps the thought of thine heart may be forgiven thee.

23 For I perceive that thou art in the gall of bitterness, and in the bond of iniquity.

24 Then answered Simon, and said, Pray ye to the Lord for me, that none of these things which ye have spoken come upon me.

25 And they, when they had testified and preached the word of the Lord, returned to Jerusalem, and preached the gospel in many villages of the Samaritans.

26 And the angel of the Lord spake unto Philip, saying, Arise, and go toward the south, unto the way that goeth down from Jerusalem unto Gaza, which is desert.

27 And he arose and went: and, behold, a man of Ethiopia, a eunuch of great authority under Candace queen of the Ethiopians, who had the charge of all her treasure, and had come to Jerusalem for to worship,

28 Was returning, and sitting in his chariot read Esaias the prophet.

29 Then the Spirit said unto Philip, Go near, and join thyself to this chariot.

30 And Philip ran thither to him, and heard him read the prophet Esaias, and said, Understandest thou what thou readest?

31 And he said, How can I, except some man should guide me? And he desired Philip that he would come up and sit with him.

32 The place of the scripture which he read was this, He was led as a sheep to the slaughter; and like a lamb dumb before his shearer, so opened he not his mouth:

33 In his humiliation his judgment was taken away: and who shall declare his generation? for his life is taken from the earth.

34 And the eunuch answered Philip, and said, I pray thee, of whom speaketh the prophet this? of himself, or of some other man?

35 Then Philip opened his mouth, and

began at the same scripture, and preached unto him Jesus.

36 And as they went on their way, they came unto a certain water; and the eunuch said, See, here is water; what doth hinder me to be baptized?

37 And Philip said, If thou believest with all thine heart, thou mayest. And he answered and said, I believe that Jesus Christ is the Son of God.

38 And he commanded the chariot to stand still; and they went down both into the water, both Philip and the eunuch; and he baptized him.

39 And when they were come up out of the water, the Spirit of the Lord caught away Philip, that the eunuch saw him no more; and he went on his way rejoicing.

40 But Philip was found at Azotus; and passing through he preached in all the cities, till he came to Caesarea.

## CHAPTER 9

*Saul's conversion—He is baptized by Ananias—He preacheth Christ—The Jews lay wait to kill him—Peter healeth Aeneas of the palsy.*

1 And Saul, yet breathing out threatenings and slaughter against the disciples of the Lord, went unto the high priest,

2 And desired of him letters to Damascus to the synagogues, that if he found any of this way, whether they were men or women, he might bring them bound unto Jerusalem.

3 And as he journeyed, he came near Damascus, and suddenly there shined round about him a light from heaven;

4 And he fell to the earth, and heard a voice saying unto him, Saul, Saul, why persecutest thou me?

5 And he said, Who art thou, Lord? And the Lord said, I am Jesus whom thou persecutest; it is hard for thee to kick against the pricks.

6 And he trembling and astonished said, Lord, what wilt thou have me to do? And the Lord said unto him, Arise, and go into the city, and it shall be told thee what thou must do.

7 And they who were journeying with him saw indeed the light, and were afraid; but they heard not the voice of him who spake to him.

8 And Saul arose from the earth; and when his eyes were opened, he saw no man; but they led him by the hand, and brought him into Damascus.

9 And he was three days without sight, and neither did eat nor drink.

10 And there was a certain disciple at Damascus, named Ananias; and to him said the Lord in a vision, Ananias. And he said, Behold, I am here, Lord.

11 And the Lord said unto him, Arise, and go into the street which is called Straight, and inquire in the house of Judas for one called Saul, of Tarsus; for, behold, he prayeth,

12 And hath seen in a vision a man named Ananias coming in, and putting his hand on him, that he might receive his sight.

13 Then Ananias answered, Lord, I have heard by many of this man, how much evil he hath done to thy saints at Jerusalem;

14 And here he hath authority from the chief priests to bind all that call on thy name.

15 But the Lord said unto him, Go thy way; for he is a chosen vessel unto me, to bear my name before the Gentiles, and kings, and the children of Israel;

16 For I will show him how great things he must suffer for my name's sake.

17 And Ananias went his way, and entered into the house; and putting his hands on him said, Brother Saul, the Lord, even Jesus, that appeared unto thee in the way as thou camest, hath sent me, that thou mightest receive thy sight, and be filled with the Holy Ghost.

18 And immediately there fell from his eyes as it had been scales; and he received sight forthwith, and arose, and was baptized.

19 And when he had received meat, he was strengthened. Then was Saul certain days with the disciples which were at Damascus.

20 And straightway he preached Christ in the synagogues, that he is the Son of God.

21 But all that heard him were amazed, and said; Is not this he that destroyed them which called on this name in Jerusalem, and came hither for that intent, that he might bring them bound unto the chief priests?

22 But Saul increased the more in strength, and confounded the Jews which dwelt at Damascus, proving that this is very Christ.

23 And after that many days were

fulfilled, the Jews took counsel to kill him;

24 But their lying in wait was known of Saul. And they watched the gates day and night to kill him.

25 Then the disciples took him by night, and let him down by the wall in a basket.

26 And when Saul was come to Jerusalem, he assayed to join himself to the disciples; but they were all afraid of him, and believed not that he was a disciple.

27 But Barnabas took him, and brought him to the apostles, and declared unto them how he had seen the Lord in the way, and that he had spoken to him, and how he had preached boldly at Damascus in the name of Jesus.

28 And he was with them coming in and going out at Jerusalem.

29 And he spake boldly in the name of the Lord Jesus, and disputed against the Grecians; but they went about to slay him.

30 When the brethren knew this, they brought him down to Caesarea, and sent him forth to Tarsus.

31 Then had the churches rest throughout all Judea and Galilee and Samaria, and were edified; and walking in the fear of the Lord, and in the comfort of the Holy Ghost, were multiplied.

32 And it came to pass, as Peter passed throughout all these regions, he came down also to the saints which dwelt at Lydda.

33 And there he found a certain man named Aeneas, which had kept his bed eight years, and was sick of the palsy.

34 And Peter said unto him, Aeneas, Jesus Christ maketh thee whole; arise, and make thy bed. And he arose immediately.

35 And all that dwelt at Lydda and Saron saw him, and turned to the Lord.

36 Now there was at Joppa a certain disciple named Tabitha, which by interpretation is called Dorcas; this woman was full of good works and almsdeeds which she did.

37 And it came to pass in those days, that she was sick, and died; whom when they had washed, they laid her in an upper chamber.

38 And forasmuch as Lydda was nigh to Joppa, and the disciples had heard that Peter was there, they sent

unto him two men, desiring that he would not delay to come to them.

39 Then Peter arose and went with them. When he was come, they brought him into the upper chamber; and all the widows stood by him weeping, and showing the coats and garments which Dorcas made, while she was with them.

40 But Peter put them all forth, and kneeled down, and prayed; and turning to the body said, Tabitha, arise. And she opened her eyes; and when she saw Peter, she sat up.

41 And he gave her his hand, and lifted her up; and when he had called the saints and widows; he presented her alive.

42 And it was known throughout all Joppa; and many believed in the Lord.

43 And it came to pass, that he tarried many days in Joppa with one Simon a tanner.

## CHAPTER 10

*Peter preacheth Christ to Cornelius and his company—The Holy Ghost falleth on them.*

1 There was a certain man in Caesarea called Cornelius, a centurion of the band called the Italian band,

2 A devout man, and one that feared God with all his house, which gave much alms to the people, and prayed to God always.

3 He saw in a vision evidently, about the ninth hour of the day, an angel of God coming in to him, and saying unto him, Cornelius.

4 And when he looked on him, he was afraid, and said, What is it, Lord? And he said unto him, Thy prayers and thine alms are come up for a memorial before God.

5 And now send men to Joppa, and call for one Simon, whose surname is Peter;

6 He lodgeth with one Simon a tanner, whose house is by the seaside; he shall tell thee what thou oughtest to do.

7 And when the angel which spake unto Cornelius was departed, he called two of his household servants, and a devout soldier of them that waited on him continually;

8 And when he had declared all these things unto them, he sent them to Joppa.

9 On the morrow, as they went on

their journey, and drew nigh unto the city, Peter went up upon the housetop to pray about the sixth hour;

10 And he became very hungry, and would have eaten; but while they made ready, he fell into a trance,

11 And saw heaven opened, and a certain vessel descending unto him, as it had been a great sheet knit at the four corners, and let down to the earth;

12 Wherein were all manner of four-footed beasts of the earth, and wild beasts, and creeping things, and fowls of the air.

13 And there came a voice to him, Rise, Peter; kill, and eat.

14 But Peter said, Not so, Lord; for I have never eaten any thing that is common or unclean.

15 And the voice spake unto him again the second time, What God hath cleansed, that call not thou common.

16 This was done thrice; and the vessel was received up again into heaven.

17 Now while Peter doubted in himself what this vision which he had seen should mean, behold, the men which were sent from Cornelius had made inquiry for Simon's house, and stood before the gate,

18 And called, and asked whether Simon, which was surnamed Peter, were lodged there.

19 While Peter thought on the vision, the Spirit said unto him, Behold, three men seek thee.

20 Arise therefore, and get thee down, and go with them, doubting nothing; for I have sent them.

21 Then Peter went down to the men which were sent unto him from Cornelius; and said, Behold, I am he whom ye seek; what is the cause wherefore ye are come?

22 And they said, Cornelius the centurion, a just man, and one that feareth God, and of good report among all the nation of the Jews, was warned from God by a holy angel to send for thee into his house, and to hear words of thee.

23 Then called he them in, and lodged them. And on the morrow Peter went away with them, and certain brethren from Joppa accompanied him.

24 And the morrow after they entered into Caesarea. And Cornelius waited for them, and had called together his kinsmen and near friends.

25 And as Peter was coming in, Cornelius met him, and fell down at his feet, and worshiped him.

26 But Peter took him up, saying, Stand up; I myself also am a man.

27 And as he talked with him, he went in, and found many that were come together.

28 And he said unto them, Ye know how that it is an unlawful thing for a man that is a Jew to keep company, or come unto one of another nation; but God hath showed me that I should not call any man common or unclean.

29 Therefore came I unto you without gainsaying, as soon as I was sent for; I ask therefore for what intent ye have sent for me?

30 And Cornelius said, Four days ago I was fasting until this hour; and at the ninth hour I prayed in my house, and, behold, a man stood before me in bright clothing,

31 And said, Cornelius, thy prayer is heard, and thine alms are had in remembrance in the sight of God.

32 Send therefore to Joppa, and call hither Simon, whose surname is Peter; he is lodged in the house of one Simon a tanner by the seaside; who, when he cometh, shall speak unto thee.

33 Immediately therefore I sent to thee; and thou hast well done that thou art come. Now therefore are we all here present before God, to hear all things that are commanded thee of God.

34 Then Peter opened his mouth, and said, Of a truth I perceive that God is no respecter of persons;

35 But in every nation he that feareth him, and worketh righteousness, is accepted with him.

36 The word which God sent unto the children of Israel, preaching peace by Jesus Christ; (he is Lord of all;)

37 That word, I say, ye know, which was published throughout all Judea, and began from Galilee, after the baptism which John preached;

38 How God anointed Jesus of Nazareth with the Holy Ghost and with power; who went about doing good, and healing all that were oppressed of the devil; for God was with him.

39 And we are witnesses of all things which he did both in the land of the

Jews, and in Jerusalem; whom they slew and hanged on a tree;

40 Him God raised up the third day, and showed him openly;

41 Not to all the people, but unto witnesses chosen before of God, even to us, who did eat and drink with him after he rose from the dead.

42 And he commanded us to preach unto the people, and to testify that it is he which was ordained of God to be the Judge of quick and dead.

43 To him give all the prophets witness, that through his name whosoever believeth in him shall receive remission of sins.

44 While Peter yet spake these words, the Holy Ghost fell on all them which heard the word.

45 And they of the circumcision which believed were astonished, as many as came with Peter, because that on the Gentiles also was poured out the gift of the Holy Ghost.

46 For they heard them speak with tongues, and magnify God. Then answered Peter,

47 Can any man forbid water, that these should not be baptized, which have received the Holy Ghost as well as we?

48 And he commanded them to be baptized in the name of the Lord. Then prayed they him to tarry certain days.

## CHAPTER 11

*Peter's defense—The gospel preached in Phenice, Cyprus, and Antioch—The disciples called Christians—They send relief to the brethren in Judea.*

1 And the apostles and brethren that were in Judea heard that the Gentiles had also received the word of God.

2 And when Peter was come up to Jerusalem, they that were of the circumcision contended with him,

3 Saying, Thou wentest in to men uncircumcised, and didst eat with them.

4 But Peter rehearsed the matter from the beginning, and expounded it by order unto them, saying,

5 I was in the city of Joppa praying; and in a trance I saw a vision, A certain vessel descend, as it had been a great sheet, let down from heaven by four corners; and it came even to me;

6 Upon the which when I had fastened mine eyes, I considered, and saw fourfooted beasts of the earth, and wild beasts, and creeping things, and fowls of the air.

7 And I heard a voice saying unto me, Arise, Peter; slay and eat.

8 But I said, Not so, Lord; for nothing common or unclean hath at any time entered into my mouth.

9 But the voice answered me again from heaven, What God hath cleansed, that call not thou common.

10 And this was done three times; and all were drawn up again into heaven.

11 And, behold, immediately there were three men already come unto the house where I was, sent from Caesarea unto me.

12 And the Spirit bade me go with them, nothing doubting. Moreover these six brethren accompanied me, and we entered into the man's house;

13 And he showed us how he had seen an angel in his house, which stood and said unto him, Send men to Joppa, and call for Simon, whose surname is Peter;

14 Who shall tell thee words, whereby thou and all thy house shall be saved.

15 And as I began to speak, the Holy Ghost fell on them, as on us at the beginning.

16 Then remembered I the word of the Lord, how that he said, John indeed baptized with water; but ye shall be baptized with the Holy Ghost.

17 Forasmuch then as God gave them the like gift as he did unto us, who believed on the Lord Jesus Christ, what was I, that I could withstand God?

18 When they heard these things, they held their peace and glorified God, saying, Then hath God also to the Gentiles granted repentance unto life.

19 Now they which were scattered abroad upon the persecution that arose about Stephen traveled as far as Phenice, and Cyprus, and Antioch, preaching the word to none but unto the Jews only.

20 And some of them were men of Cyprus and Cyrene, which, when they were come to Antioch, spake unto the Grecians, preaching the Lord Jesus.

21 And the hand of the Lord was with them; and a great number believed, and turned unto the Lord.

22 Then tidings of these things came

unto the ears of the church which was in Jerusalem; and they sent forth Barnabas, that he should go as far as Antioch.

23 Who, when he came, and had seen the grace of God, was glad, and exhorted them all, that with purpose of heart they would cleave unto the Lord.

24 For he was a good man, and full of the Holy Ghost and of faith; and much people was added unto the Lord.

25 Then departed Barnabas to Tarsus, for to seek Saul;

26 And when he had found him, he brought him unto Antioch. And it came to pass, that a whole year they assembled themselves with the church, and taught much people. And the disciples were called Christians first in Antioch.

27 And in these days came prophets from Jerusalem unto Antioch.

28 And there stood up one of them named Agabus, and signified by the Spirit that there should be great dearth throughout all the world; which came to pass in the days of Claudius Caesar.

29 Then the disciples, every man according to his ability, determined to send relief unto the brethren which dwelt in Judea;

30 Which also they did, and sent it to the elders by the hands of Barnabas and Saul.

## CHAPTER 12

*King Herod persecuteth the saints, killeth James, and imprisoneth Peter; whom an angel delivereth upon the prayers of the church—Herod is stricken by an angel and dieth—The word of God prospereth.*

1 Now about that time Herod the king stretched forth his hands to vex certain of the church.

2 And he killed James the brother of John with the sword.

3 And because he saw it pleased the Jews, he proceeded further to take Peter also. (Then were the days of unleavened bread.)

4 And when he had apprehended him, he put him in prison, and delivered him to four quaternions of soldiers to keep him; intending after Easter to bring him forth to the people.

5 Peter therefore was kept in prison: but prayer was made without ceasing of the church unto God for him.

6 And when Herod would have brought him forth, the same night Peter was sleeping between two soldiers, bound with two chains; and the keepers before the door kept the prison.

7 And, behold, the angel of the Lord came unto him, and a light shined in the prison; and he smote Peter on the side, and raised him up, saying, Arise up quickly. And his chains fell off from his hands.

8 And the angel said unto him, Gird thyself, and bind on thy sandals; and so he did. And he saith unto him, Cast thy garment about thee, and follow me.

9 And he went out, and followed him; and wist not that it was true which was done by the angel; but thought he saw a vision.

10 When they were past the first and the second ward, they came unto the iron gate that leadeth unto the city; which opened to them of his own accord; and they went out, and passed on through one street; and forthwith the angel departed from him.

11 And when Peter was come to himself, he said, Now I know of a surety, that the Lord hath sent his angel, and hath delivered me out of the hand of Herod, and from all the expectation of the people of the Jews.

12 And when he had considered the thing, he came to the house of Mary the mother of John, whose surname was Mark; where many were gathered together praying.

13 And as Peter knocked at the door of the gate, a damsel came to hearken, named Rhoda.

14 And when she knew Peter's voice, she opened not the gate for gladness, but ran in, and told how Peter stood before the gate.

15 And they said unto her, Thou art mad. But she constantly affirmed that it was even so. Then said they, It is his angel.

16 But Peter continued knocking; and when they had opened the door, and saw him, they were astonished.

17 But he, beckoning unto them with the hand to hold their peace, declared unto them how the Lord had brought him out of the prison. And he said, Go show these things unto James, and to the brethren. And he departed, and went into another place.

18 Now as soon as it was day, there

was no small stir among the soldiers, what was become of Peter.

19 And when Herod had sought for him, and found him not, he examined the keepers, and commanded that they should be put to death. And he went down from Judea to Caesarea, and there abode.

20 And Herod was highly displeased with them of Tyre and Sidon; but they came with one accord to him, and, having made Blastus the king's chamberlain their friend, desired peace; because their country was nourished by the king's country.

21 And upon a set day Herod, arrayed in royal apparel, sat upon his throne, and made an oration unto them.

22 And the people gave a shout, saying, It is the voice of a god, and not of a man.

23 And immediately the angel of the Lord smote him, because he gave not God the glory; and he was eaten of worms, and gave up the ghost.

24 But the word of God grew and multiplied.

25 And Barnabas and Saul returned from Jerusalem, when they had fulfilled their ministry, and took with them John, whose surname was Mark.

## CHAPTER 13

*Paul and Barnabas are called by the Holy Ghost—Elymas the sorcerer—Paul preacheth at Antioch.*

1 Now there were in the church that was at Antioch certain prophets and teachers; as Barnabas, and Simeon that was called Niger, and Lucius of Cyrene, and Manaen, which had been brought up with Herod the tetrarch, and Saul.

2 As they ministered to the Lord, and fasted, the Holy Ghost said, Separate me Barnabas and Saul for the work whereunto I have called them.

3 And when they had fasted and prayed, and laid their hands on them, they sent them away.

4 So they, being sent forth by the Holy Ghost, departed unto Seleucia; and from thence they sailed to Cyprus.

5 And when they were at Salamis, they preached the word of God in the synagogues of the Jews; and they had also John to their minister.

6 And when they had gone through the isle unto Paphos, they found a certain sorcerer, a false prophet, a Jew, whose name was Bar-jesus;

7 Which was with the deputy of the country, Sergius Paulus, a prudent man; who called for Barnabas and Saul, and desired to hear the word of God.

8 But Elymas the sorcerer (for so is his name by interpretation) withstood them, seeking to turn away the deputy from the faith.

9 Then Saul, (who also is called Paul,) filled with the Holy Ghost, set his eyes on him,

10 And said, O full of all subtilty and all mischief, thou child of the devil, thou enemy of all righteousness, wilt thou not cease to pervert the right ways of the Lord?

11 And now, behold, the hand of the Lord is upon thee, and thou shalt be blind, not seeing the sun for a season. And immediately there fell on him a mist and a darkness; and he went about seeking some to lead him by the hand.

12 Then the deputy, when he saw what was done, believed, being astonished at the doctrine of the Lord.

13 Now when Paul and his company loosed from Paphos, they came to Perga in Pamphylia; and John departing from them returned to Jerusalem.

14 But when they departed from Perga, they came to Antioch in Pisidia, and went into the synagogue on the Sabbath day, and sat down.

15 And after the reading of the law and the prophets, the rulers of the synagogue sent unto them, saying, Ye men and brethren, if ye have any word of exhortation for the people, say on.

16 Then Paul stood up, and beckoning with his hand said, Men of Israel, and ye that fear God, give audience.

17 The God of this people of Israel chose our fathers, and exalted the people when they dwelt as strangers in the land of Egypt, and with a high arm brought he them out of it.

18 And about the time for forty years suffered he their manners in the wilderness.

19 And when he had destroyed seven nations in the land of Chanaan, he divided their land to them by lot.

20 And after that he gave unto them judges about the space of four hundred and fifty years, until Samuel the prophet.

21 And afterward they desired a king; and God gave unto them Saul the son of Cis, a man of the tribe of Benjamin, by the space of forty years.

22 And when he had removed him, he raised up unto them David to be their king; to whom also he gave testimony, and said, I have found David the son of Jesse, a man after mine own heart, which shall fulfill all my will.

23 Of this man's seed hath God, according to his promise, raised unto Israel a Savior, Jesus;

24 When John had first preached before his coming the baptism of repentance to all the people of Israel.

25 And as John fulfilled his course, he said, Whom think ye that I am? I am not he. But, behold, there cometh one after me, whose shoes of his feet I am not worthy to loose.

26 Men and brethren, children of the stock of Abraham, and whosoever among you feareth God, to you is the word of this salvation sent.

27 For they that dwell at Jerusalem, and their rulers, because they knew him not, nor yet the voices of the prophets which are read every Sabbath day, they have fulfilled them in condemning him.

28 And though they found no cause of death in him, yet desired they Pilate that he should be slain.

29 And when they had fulfilled all that was written of him, they took him down from the tree, and laid him in a sepulcher.

30 But God raised him from the dead;

31 And he was seen many days of them which came up with him from Galilee to Jerusalem, who are his witnesses unto the people.

32 And we declare unto you glad tidings, how that the promise which was made unto the fathers,

33 God hath fulfilled the same unto us their children, in that he hath raised up Jesus again; as it is also written in the second psalm, Thou art my Son, this day have I begotten thee.

34 And as concerning that he raised him up from the dead, now no more to return to corruption, he said on this wise, I will give you the sure mercies of David.

35 Wherefore he saith also in another psalm, Thou shalt not suffer thine Holy One to see corruption.

36 For David, after he had served his own generation by the will of God, fell asleep, and was laid unto his fathers, and saw corruption;

37 But he, whom God raised again, saw no corruption.

38 Be it known unto you therefore, men and brethren, that through this man is preached unto you the forgiveness of sins;

39 And by him all that believe are justified from all things, from which ye could not be justified by the law of Moses.

40 Beware therefore, lest that come upon you, which is spoken of in the prophets;

41 Behold, ye despisers, and wonder, and perish; for I work a work in your days, a work which ye shall in no wise believe, though a man declare it unto you.

42 And when the Jews were gone out of the synagogue, the Gentiles besought that these words might be preached to them the next Sabbath.

43 Now when the congregation was broken up, many of the Jews and religious proselytes followed Paul and Barnabas; who, speaking to them, persuaded them to continue in the grace of God.

44 And the next Sabbath day came almost the whole city together to hear the word of God.

45 But when the Jews saw the multitudes, they were filled with envy, and spake against those things which were spoken by Paul, contradicting and blaspheming.

46 Then Paul and Barnabas waxed bold, and said, It was necessary that the word of God should first have been spoken to you; but seeing ye put it from you, and judge yourselves unworthy of everlasting life, lo, we turn to the Gentiles.

47 For so hath the Lord commanded us, saying, I have set thee to be a light of the Gentiles, that thou shouldest be for salvation unto the ends of the earth.

48 And when the Gentiles heard this, they were glad, and glorified the word of the Lord; and as many as believed were ordained unto eternal life.

49 And the word of the Lord was published throughout all the region.

50 But the Jews stirred up the devout and honorable women, and the

chief men of the city, and raised persecution against Paul and Barnabas, and expelled them out of their coasts.

51 But they shook off the dust of their feet against them, and came unto Iconium.

52 And the disciples were filled with joy, and with the Holy Ghost.

## CHAPTER 14

*A cripple healed—Paul is stoned—They confirm the disciples.*

1 And it came to pass in Iconium, that they went both together into the synagogue of the Jews, and so spake, that a great multitude both of the Jews and also of the Greeks believed.

2 But the unbelieving Jews stirred up the Gentiles, and made their minds evil affected against the brethren.

3 Long time therefore abode they speaking boldly in the Lord, which gave testimony unto the word of his grace, and granted signs and wonders to be done by their hands.

4 But the multitude of the city was divided; and part held with the Jews, and part with the apostles.

5 And when there was an assault made both of the Gentiles, and also of the Jews with their rulers, to use them despitefully, and to stone them,

6 They were ware of it, and fled unto Lystra and Derbe, cities of Lycaonia, and unto the region that lieth round about;

7 And there they preached the gospel.

8 And there sat a certain man at Lystra, impotent in his feet, being a cripple from his mother's womb, who never had walked;

9 The same heard Paul speak; who steadfastly beholding him, and perceiving that he had faith to be healed,

10 Said with a loud voice, Stand upright on thy feet. And he leaped and walked.

11 And when the people saw what Paul had done, they lifted up their voices, saying in the speech of Lycaonia, The gods are come down to us in the likeness of men.

12 And they called Barnabas, Jupiter; and Paul, Mercurius, because he was the chief speaker.

13 Then the priest of Jupiter, which was before their city, brought oxen and garlands unto the gates, and would have done sacrifice with the people.

14 When the apostles, Barnabas and Paul, heard this, they rent their clothes, and ran in among the people, crying out,

15 And saying, Sirs, why do ye these things? We also are men of like passions with you, and preach unto you that ye should turn from these vanities unto the living God, which made heaven, and earth, and the sea, and all things that are therein;

16 Who in times past suffered all nations to walk in their own ways.

17 Nevertheless he left not himself without witness, in that he did good, and gave us rain from heaven, and fruitful seasons, filling our hearts with food and gladness.

18 And with these sayings scarce restrained they the people, that they had not done sacrifice unto them.

19 And there came thither certain Jews from Antioch and Iconium, who persuaded the people, and, having stoned Paul, drew him out of the city, supposing he had been dead.

20 Howbeit, as the disciples stood round about him, he rose up, and came into the city; and the next day he departed with Barnabas to Derbe.

21 And when they had preached the gospel to that city, and had taught many, they returned again to Lystra, and to Iconium, and Antioch,

22 Confirming the souls of the disciples, and exhorting them to continue in the faith, and that we must through much tribulation enter into the kingdom of God.

23 And when they had ordained them elders in every church, and had prayed with fasting, they commended them to the Lord, on whom they believed.

24 And after they had passed throughout Pisidia, they came to Pamphylia.

25 And when they had preached the word in Perga, they went down into Attalia;

26 And thence sailed to Antioch, from whence they had been recommended to the grace of God for the work which they fulfilled.

27 And when they were come, and had gathered the church together, they rehearsed all that God had done with them, and how he had opened the door of faith unto the Gentiles.

28 And there they abode long time with the disciples.

## CHAPTER 15

*Dissension touching circumcision—The decision of James—Separation of Paul and Barnabas.*

1 And certain men which came down from Judea taught the brethren, and said, Except ye be circumcised after the manner of Moses, ye cannot be saved.

2 When therefore Paul and Barnabas had no small dissension and disputation with them, they determined that Paul and Barnabas, and certain other of them, should go up to Jerusalem unto the apostles and elders about this question.

3 And being brought on their way by the church, they passed through Phenice and Samaria, declaring the conversion of the Gentiles; and they caused great joy unto all the brethren.

4 And when they were come to Jerusalem, they were received of the church, and of the apostles and elders, and they declared all things that God had done with them.

5 But there rose up certain of the sect of the Pharisees which believed, saying, That it was needful to circumcise them, and to command them to keep the law of Moses.

6 And the apostles and elders came together for to consider of this matter.

7 And when there had been much disputing, Peter rose up, and said unto them, Men and brethren, ye know how that a good while ago God made choice among us, that the Gentiles by my mouth should hear the word of the gospel, and believe.

8 And God, which knoweth the hearts, bare them witness, giving them the Holy Ghost, even as he did unto us;

9 And put no difference between us and them, purifying their hearts by faith.

10 Now therefore why tempt ye God, to put a yoke upon the neck of the disciples, which neither our fathers nor we were able to bear?

11 But we believe that through the grace of the Lord Jesus Christ we shall be saved, even as they.

12 Then all the multitude kept silence, and gave audience to Barnabas and Paul, declaring what miracles and wonders God had wrought among the Gentiles by them.

13 And after they had held their peace, James answered, saying, Men and brethren, hearken unto me;

14 Simeon hath declared how God at the first did visit the Gentiles, to take out of them a people for his name.

15 And to this agree the words of the prophets; as it is written,

16 After this I will return, and will build again the tabernacle of David, which is fallen down; and I will build again the ruins thereof, and I will set it up;

17 That the residue of men might seek after the Lord, and all the Gentiles, upon whom my name is called, saith the Lord, who doeth all these things.

18 Known unto God are all his works from the beginning of the world.

19 Wherefore my sentence is, that we trouble not them, which from among the Gentiles are turned to God;

20 But that we write unto them, that they abstain from pollutions of idols, and from fornication, and from things strangled, and from blood.

21 For Moses of old time hath in every city them that preach him, being read in the synagogues every Sabbath day.

22 Then pleased it the apostles and elders, with the whole church, to send chosen men of their own company to Antioch with Paul and Barnabas; namely, Judas surnamed Barsabas, and Silas, chief men among the brethren;

23 And they wrote letters by them after this manner; The apostles and elders and brethren send greeting unto the brethren which are of the Gentiles in Antioch and Syria and Cilicia;

24 Forasmuch as we have heard, that certain men which went out from us have troubled you with words, subverting your souls, saying, Ye must be circumcised, and keep the law; to whom we gave no such commandment;

25 It seemed good unto us, being assembled with one accord, to send chosen men unto you with our beloved Barnabas and Paul,

26 Men that have hazarded their lives for the name of our Lord Jesus Christ.

27 We have sent therefore Judas and

Silas, who shall also tell you the same things by mouth.

28 For it seemed good to the Holy Ghost, and to us, to lay upon you no greater burden than these necessary things;

29 That ye abstain from meats offered to idols, and from blood, and from things strangled, and from fornication; from which if ye keep yourselves, ye shall do well. Fare ye well.

30 So when they were dismissed, they came to Antioch; and when they had gathered the multitude together, they delivered the epistle;

31 Which when they had read, they rejoiced for the consolation.

32 And Judas and Silas, being prophets also themselves, exhorted the brethren with many words, and confirmed them.

33 And after they had tarried there a space, they were let go in peace from the brethren unto the apostles.

34 Notwithstanding it pleased Silas to abide there still.

35 Paul also and Barnabas continued in Antioch, teaching and preaching the word of the Lord, with many others also.

36 And some days after, Paul said unto Barnabas, Let us go again and visit our brethren in every city where we have preached the word of the Lord, and see how they do.

37 And Barnabas determined to take with them John, whose surname was Mark.

38 But Paul thought not good to take him with them, who departed from them from Pamphylia, and went not with them to the work.

39 And the contention was so sharp between them, that they departed asunder one from the other; and so Barnabas took Mark and sailed unto Cyprus;

40 And Paul chose Silas, and departed, being recommended by the brethren unto the grace of God.

41 And he went through Syria and Cilicia, confirming the churches.

## CHAPTER 16

*Paul circumciseth Timothy—Converteth Lydia—Casteth out a spirit of divination—Paul and Silas are whipped and imprisoned—The jailer is converted, and they are delivered.*

1 Then came he to Derbe and Lystra; and, behold, a certain disciple was there, named Timotheus, the son of a certain woman, which was a Jewess, and believed; but his father was a Greek;

2 Which was well reported of by the brethren that were at Lystra and Iconium.

3 Him would Paul have to go forth with him; and took and circumcised him because of the Jews which were in those quarters; for they knew all that his father was a Greek.

4 And as they went through the cities, they delivered them the decrees for to keep, that were ordained of the apostles and elders which were at Jerusalem.

5 And so were the churches established in the faith, and increased in number daily.

6 Now when they had gone throughout Phrygia and the region of Galatia, and were forbidden of the Holy Ghost to preach the word in Asia,

7 After they were come to Mysia, they assayed to go into Bithynia; but the Spirit suffered them not.

8 And they passing by Mysia came down to Troas.

9 And a vision appeared to Paul in the night; There stood a man of Macedonia, and prayed him, saying, Come over into Macedonia, and help us.

10 And after he had seen the vision, immediately we endeavored to go into Macedonia, assuredly gathering that the Lord had called us for to preach the gospel unto them.

11 Therefore loosing from Troas, we came with a straight course to Samothracia, and the next day to Neapolis;

12 And from thence to Philippi, which is the chief city of that part of Macedonia, and a colony; and we were in that city abiding certain days.

13 And on the Sabbath we went out of the city by a river side, where the people resorted for prayer to be made; and we sat down, and spake unto the women which resorted thither.

14 And a certain woman named Lydia, a seller of purple, of the city of Thyatira, which worshiped God, heard us; whose heart the Lord opened, that she attended unto the things which were spoken of Paul.

15 And when she was baptized, and her household, she besought us, saying,

If ye have judged me to be faithful to the Lord, come into my house, and abide there. And she constrained us.

16 And it came to pass, as we went to prayer, a certain damsel possessed with a spirit of divination met us, which brought her masters much gain by soothsaying;

17 The same followed Paul and us, and cried, saying, These men are the servants of the most high God, which show unto us the way of salvation.

18 And this did she many days. But Paul, being grieved, turned and said to the spirit, I command thee in the name of Jesus Christ to come out of her. And he came out the same hour.

19 And when her masters saw that the hope of their gains was gone, they caught Paul and Silas, and drew them into the marketplace unto the rulers,

20 And brought them to the magistrates, saying, These men, being Jews, do exceedingly trouble our city,

21 And teach customs, which are not lawful for us to receive, neither to observe, being Romans.

22 And the multitude rose up together against them; and the magistrates rent off their clothes, and commanded to beat them.

23 And when they had laid many stripes upon them, they cast them into prison, charging the jailer to keep them safely;

24 Who, having received such a charge, thrust them into the inner prison, and made their feet fast in the stocks.

25 And at midnight Paul and Silas prayed, and sang praises unto God; and the prisoners heard them.

26 And suddenly there was a great earthquake, so that the foundations of the prison were shaken; and immediately all the doors were opened, and every one's bands were loosed.

27 And the keeper of the prison awaking out of his sleep, and seeing the prison doors open, he drew out his sword, and would have killed himself, supposing that the prisoners had been fled.

28 But Paul cried with a loud voice, saying, Do thyself no harm; for we are all here.

29 Then he called for a light, and sprang in, and came trembling, and fell down before Paul and Silas,

30 And brought them out, and said, Sirs, what must I do to be saved?

31 And they said, Believe on the Lord Jesus Christ, and thou shalt be saved and thy house.

32 And they spake unto him the word of the Lord, and to all that were in his house.

33 And he took them the same hour of the night, and washed their stripes; and was baptized, he and all his, straightway.

34 And when he had brought them into his house, he set meat before them, and rejoiced, believing in God with all his house.

35 And when it was day, the magistrates sent the serjeants, saying, Let those men go.

36 And the keeper of the prison told this saying to Paul, The magistrates have sent to let you go; now therefore depart, and go in peace.

37 But Paul said unto them, They have beaten us openly uncondemned, being Romans, and have cast us into prison; and now do they thrust us out privily? nay verily; but let them come themselves and fetch us out.

38 And the serjeants told these words unto the magistrates; and they feared, when they heard that they were Romans.

39 And they came and besought them, and brought them out, and desired them to depart out of the city.

40 And they went out of the prison, and entered into the house of Lydia; and when they had seen the brethren, they comforted them, and departed.

## CHAPTER 17

*Paul preacheth at Thessalonica, Berea, and Athens.*

1 Now when they had passed through Amphipolis and Apollonia, they came to Thessalonica, where was a synagogue of the Jews;

2 And Paul, as his manner was, went in unto them, and three Sabbath days reasoned with them out of the scriptures,

3 Opening and alleging, that Christ must needs have suffered, and risen again from the dead; and that this Jesus, whom I preach unto you, is Christ.

4 And some of them believed, and consorted with Paul and Silas; and of

the devout Greeks a great multitude, and of the chief women not a few.

5 But the Jews which believed not, moved with envy, took unto them certain lewd fellows of the baser sort, and gathered a company, and set all the city on an uproar, and assaulted the house of Jason, and sought to bring them out to the people.

6 And when they found them not, they drew Jason and certain brethren unto the rulers of the city, crying, These that have turned the world upside down are come hither also;

7 Whom Jason hath received; and these all do contrary to the decrees of Caesar, saying that there is another king, one Jesus.

8 And they troubled the people and the rulers of the city, when they heard these things.

9 And when they had taken security of Jason, and of the others, they let him go.

10 And the brethren immediately sent away Paul and Silas by night unto Berea; who coming thither went into the synagogue of the Jews.

11 These were more noble than those in Thessalonica, in that they received the word with all readiness of mind, and searched the scriptures daily, whether those things were so.

12 Therefore many of them believed; also of honorable women which were Greeks, and of men, not a few.

13 But when the Jews of Thessalonica had knowledge that the word of God was preached of Paul at Berea, they came thither also, and stirred up the people.

14 And then immediately the brethren sent away Paul to go as it were to the sea; but Silas and Timotheus abode there still.

15 And they that conducted Paul brought him unto Athens; and receiving a commandment unto Silas and Timotheus for to come to him with all speed, they departed.

16 Now while Paul waited for them at Athens, his spirit was stirred in him, when he saw the city wholly given to idolatry.

17 Therefore disputed he in the synagogue with the Jews, and with the devout persons, and in the market daily with them that met with him.

18 Then certain philosophers of the Epicureans, and of the Stoics, encoun-

tered him. And some said, What will this babbler say? other some, He seemeth to be a setter forth of strange gods; because he preached unto them Jesus, and the resurrection.

19 And they took him and brought him unto the Areopagus, saying, May we know what this new doctrine is, whereof thou speakest?

20 For thou bringest certain strange things to our ears; we would know therefore what these things mean.

21 (For all the Athenians and strangers which were there, spent their time in nothing else, but either to tell or hear some new thing.)

22 Then Paul stood in the midst of Mars' hill, and said, Ye men of Athens, I perceive that in all things ye are too superstitious.

23 For as I passed by, and beheld your devotions, I found an altar with this inscription, TO THE UNKNOWN GOD. Whom therefore ye ignorantly worship, him declare I unto you.

24 God that made the world and all things therein, seeing that he is Lord of heaven and earth, dwelleth not in temples made with hands;

25 Neither is worshiped with men's hands, as though he needed any thing, seeing he giveth to all life, and breath, and all things;

26 And hath made of one blood all nations of men for to dwell on all the face of the earth, and hath determined the times before appointed, and the bounds of their habitation;

27 That they should seek the Lord, if they are willing to find him, for he is not far from every one of us;

28 For in him we live, and move, and have our being; as certain also of your own poets have said, For we are also his offspring.

29 Forasmuch then as we are the offspring of God, we ought not to think that the Godhead is like unto gold, or silver, or stone, graven by art and man's device.

30 And the times of this ignorance God winked at; but now commandeth all men every where to repent;

31 Because he hath appointed a day, in the which he will judge the world in righteousness by him whom he hath ordained; and he hath given assurance of this unto all men, in that he hath raised him from the dead.

32 And when they heard of the res-

urrection of the dead, some mocked, and others said, We will hear thee again of this matter.

33 So Paul departed from among them.

34 Howbeit certain men clave unto him, and believed; among the which was Dionysius the Areopagite, and a woman named Damaris, and others with them.

## CHAPTER 18

*Paul laboreth with his hands, and preacheth at Corinth—A vision—He is accused before Gallio—Apollos preacheth Christ.*

1 After these things Paul departed from Athens, and came to Corinth.

2 And found a certain Jew named Aquila, born in Pontus, lately come from Italy, with his wife Priscilla, (because that Claudius had commanded all Jews to depart from Rome,) and came unto them.

3 And because he was of the same craft, he abode with them, and wrought; (for by their occupation they were tentmakers.)

4 And he reasoned in the synagogue every Sabbath, and persuaded the Jews and the Greeks.

5 And when Silas and Timotheus were come from Macedonia, Paul was pressed in the spirit, and testified to the Jews that Jesus was Christ.

6 And when they opposed themselves, and blasphemed, he shook his raiment, and said unto them, Your blood be upon your own heads; I am clean; from henceforth I will go unto the Gentiles.

7 And he departed thence, and entered into a certain man's house, named Justus, one that worshiped God, whose house joined hard to the synagogue.

8 And Crispus, the chief ruler of the synagogue, believed on the Lord with all his house; and many of the Corinthians hearing believed, and were baptized.

9 Then spake the Lord to Paul in the night by a vision, Be not afraid, but speak, and hold not thy peace;

10 For I am with thee, and no man shall set on thee to hurt thee; for I have much people in this city.

11 And he continued there a year and six months, teaching the word of God among them.

12 And when Gallio was the deputy of Achaia, the Jews made insurrection with one accord against Paul, and brought him to the judgment seat,

13 Saying, This fellow persuadeth men to worship God contrary to the law.

14 And when Paul was now about to open his mouth, Gallio said unto the Jews, If it were a matter of wrong or wicked lewdness, O ye Jews, reason would that I should bear with you;

15 But if it be a question of words and names, and of your law, look ye to it; for I will be no judge of such matters.

16 And he drave them from the judgment seat.

17 Then all the Greeks took Sosthenes, the chief ruler of the synagogue, and beat him before the judgment seat. And Gallio cared for none of those things.

18 And Paul after this tarried there yet a good while, and then took his leave of the brethren, and sailed thence into Syria, and with him Priscilla and Aquila; having shorn his head in Cenchrea; for he had a vow.

19 And he came to Ephesus, and left them there; but he himself entered into the synagogue, and reasoned with the Jews.

20 When they desired him to tarry longer time with them, he consented not;

21 But bade them farewell, saying, I must by all means keep this feast that cometh in Jerusalem; but I will return again unto you, if God will. And he sailed from Ephesus.

22 And when he had landed at Caesarea, and gone up, and saluted the church, he went down to Antioch.

23 And after he had spent some time there, he departed, and went over all the country of Galatia and Phrygia in order, strengthening all the disciples.

24 And a certain Jew named Apollos, born at Alexandria, an eloquent man, and mighty in the scriptures, came to Ephesus.

25 This man was instructed in the way of the Lord; and being fervent in the spirit, he spake and taught diligently the things of the Lord, knowing only the baptism of John.

26 And he began to speak boldly in the synagogue; whom when Aquila and Priscilla had heard, they took him

unto them, and expounded unto him the way of God more perfectly.

27 And when he was disposed to pass into Achaia, the brethren wrote, exhorting the disciples to receive him; who, when he was come, helped them much which had believed through grace;

28 For he mightily convinced the Jews, and that publicly, showing by the scriptures that Jesus was Christ.

## CHAPTER 19

*The Holy Ghost is given—The word confirmed by miracles—Demetrius raiseth an uproar against Paul.*

1 And it came to pass, that, while Apollos was at Corinth, Paul having passed through the upper coasts came to Ephesus; and finding certain disciples,

2 He said unto them, Have ye received the Holy Ghost since ye believed? And they said unto him, We have not so much as heard whether there be any Holy Ghost.

3 And he said unto them, Unto what then were ye baptized? And they said, Unto John's baptism.

4 Then said Paul, John verily baptized with the baptism of repentance, saying unto the people, that they should believe on him which should come after him, that is, on Christ Jesus.

5 When they heard this, they were baptized in the name of the Lord Jesus.

6 And when Paul had laid his hands upon them, the Holy Ghost came on them; and they spake with tongues, and prophesied.

7 And all the men were about twelve.

8 And he went into the synagogue, and spake boldly for the space of three months, disputing and persuading the things concerning the kingdom of God.

9 But when divers were hardened, and believed not, but spake evil of that way before the multitude, he departed from them, and separated the disciples, disputing daily in the school of one Tyrannus.

10 And this continued by the space of two years; so that all they which dwelt in Asia heard the word of the Lord Jesus, both Jews and Greeks.

11 And God wrought special miracles by the hands of Paul;

12 So that from his body were brought unto the sick handkerchiefs or aprons, and the diseases departed from them, and the evil spirits went out of them.

13 Then certain of the vagabond Jews, exorcists, took upon them to call over them which had evil spirits the name of the Lord Jesus, saying, We adjure you by Jesus whom Paul preacheth.

14 And there were seven sons of one Sceva, a Jew, and chief of the priests, which did so.

15 And the evil spirit answered and said, Jesus I know, and Paul I know; but who are ye?

16 And the man in whom the evil spirit was leaped on them, and overcame them, and prevailed against them, so that they fled out of that house naked and wounded.

17 And this was known to all the Jews and Greeks also dwelling at Ephesus; and fear fell on them all, and the name of the Lord Jesus was magnified.

18 And many that believed came, and confessed, and showed their deeds.

19 Many of them also which used curious arts brought their books together, and burned them before all men; and they counted the price of them, and found it fifty thousand pieces of silver.

20 So mightily grew the word of God and prevailed.

21 After these things were ended, Paul purposed in the spirit, when he had passed through Macedonia and Achaia, to go to Jerusalem, saying, After I have been there, I must also see Rome.

22 So he sent into Macedonia two of them that ministered unto him, Timotheus and Erastus; but he himself stayed in Asia for a season.

23 And the same time there arose no small stir about that way.

24 For a certain man named Demetrius, a silversmith, which made silver shrines for Diana, brought no small gain unto the craftsmen;

25 Whom he called together with the workmen of like occupation, and said, Sirs, ye know that by this craft we have our wealth.

26 Moreover ye see and hear, that not alone at Ephesus, but almost through-

out all Asia, this Paul hath persuaded and turned away much people, saying that they be no gods, which are made with hands;

27 So that not only this our craft is in danger to be set at naught; but also that the temple of the great goddess Diana should be despised and her magnificence should be destroyed, whom all Asia and the world worshipeth.

28 And when they heard these sayings, they were full of wrath, and cried out, saying, Great is Diana of the Ephesians.

29 And the whole city was filled with confusion; and having caught Gaius and Aristarchus, men of Macedonia, Paul's companions in travel, they rushed with one accord into the theatre.

30 And when Paul would have entered in unto the people, the disciples suffered him not.

31 And certain of the chief of Asia, which were his friends, sent unto him, desiring him that he would not adventure himself into the theatre.

32 Some therefore cried one thing, and some another; for the assembly was confused; and the more part knew not wherefore they were come together.

33 And they drew Alexander out of the multitude, the Jews putting him forward. And Alexander beckoned with the hand, and would have made his defense unto the people.

34 But when they knew that he was a Jew, all with one voice about the space of two hours cried out, Great is Diana of the Ephesians.

35 And when the town clerk had appeased the people, he said, Ye men of Ephesus, what man is there that knoweth not how that the city of the Ephesians is a worshiper of the great goddess Diana, and of the image which fell down from Jupiter?

36 Seeing then that these things cannot be spoken against, ye ought to be quiet, and to do nothing rashly.

37 For ye have brought hither these men, which are neither robbers of churches, nor yet blasphemers of your goddess.

38 Wherefore if Demetrius, and the craftsmen which are with him, have a matter against any man, the law is open, and there are deputies; let them implead one another.

39 But if ye inquire any thing concerning other matters, it shall be determined in a lawful assembly.

40 For we are in danger to be called in question for this day's uproar, there being no cause whereby we may give an account of this concourse.

41 And when he had thus spoken, he dismissed the assembly.

## CHAPTER 20

*Paul goeth to Macedonia—The Lord's supper—Eutychus raised to life—Paul warneth them of false teachers.*

1 And after the uproar was ceased, Paul called unto him the disciples, and embraced them, and departed for to go into Macedonia.

2 And when he had gone over those parts, and had given them much exhortation, he came into Greece,

3 And there abode three months. And when the Jews laid wait for him, as he was about to sail into Syria, he purposed to return through Macedonia.

4 And there accompanied him into Asia Sopater of Berea; and of the Thessalonians, Aristarchus and Secundus; and Gaius of Derbe, and Timotheus; and of Asia, Tychicus and Trophimus.

5 These going before tarried for us at Troas.

6 And we sailed away from Philippi after the days of unleavened bread, and came unto them to Troas in five days; where we abode seven days.

7 And upon the first day of the week, when the disciples came together to break bread, Paul preached unto them, ready to depart on the morrow; and continued his speech until midnight.

8 And there were many lights in the upper chamber, where they were gathered together.

9 And there sat in a window a certain young man named Eutychus, being fallen into a deep sleep; and as Paul was long preaching, he sunk down with sleep, and fell down from the third loft, and was taken up dead.

10 And Paul went down, and fell on him, and embracing him said, Trouble not yourselves, for his life is in him.

11 When he therefore was come up again, and had broken bread, and eaten, and talked a long while, even till break of day, so he departed.

12 And they brought the young man alive, and were not a little comforted.

13 And he went before to ship, and sailed unto Assos, there intending to take in Paul; for so had he appointed, minding himself to go afoot.

14 And when he met with us at Assos, we took him in, and came to Mitylene.

15 And we sailed thence, and came the next day over against Chios; and the next day we arrived at Samos, and tarried at Trogyllium; and the next day we came to Miletus.

16 For Paul had determined to sail by Ephesus, because he would not spend the time in Asia; for he hasted, if it were possible for him, to be at Jerusalem the day of Pentecost.

17 And from Miletus he sent to Ephesus, and called the elders of the church.

18 And when they were come to him, he said unto them, Ye know, from the first day that I came into Asia, after what manner I have been with you at all seasons,

19 Serving the Lord with all humility of mind, and with many tears, and temptations, which befell me by the lying in wait of the Jews;

20 And how I kept back nothing that was profitable unto you, but have showed you, and have taught you publicly, and from house to house,

21 Testifying both to the Jews, and also to the Greeks, repentance toward God, and faith on the name of our Lord Jesus Christ.

22 And now, behold, I go bound in the spirit unto Jerusalem, not knowing the things that shall befall me there;

23 Save that the Holy Ghost witnesseth in every city, saying that bonds and afflictions abide me.

24 But none of these things move me, neither count I my life dear unto myself, so that I might finish my course with joy, and the ministry, which I have received of the Lord Jesus, to testify the gospel of the grace of God.

25 And now, behold, I know that ye all, among whom I have gone preaching the kingdom of God, shall see my face no more.

26 Wherefore I take you to record this day, that I am pure from the blood of all men.

27 For I have not shunned to declare unto you all the counsel of God.

28 Take heed therefore unto yourselves, and to all the flock, over the which the Holy Ghost hath made you overseers, to feed the church of God, which he hath purchased with his own blood.

29 For I know this, that after my departing shall grievous wolves enter in among you, not sparing the flock.

30 Also of your own selves shall men arise, speaking perverse things, to draw away disciples after them.

31 Therefore watch, and remember, that by the space of three years I ceased not to warn every one night and day with tears.

32 And now, brethren, I commend you to God, and to the word of his grace, which is able to build you up, and to give you an inheritance among all them which are sanctified.

33 I have coveted no man's silver, or gold, or apparel.

34 Yea, ye yourselves know, that these hands have ministered unto my necessities, and to them that were with me.

35 I have showed you all things, how that so laboring ye ought to support the weak, and to remember the words of the Lord Jesus, how he said, It is more blessed to give than to receive.

36 And when he had thus spoken, he kneeled down, and prayed with them all.

37 And they all wept sore, and fell on Paul's neck, and kissed him,

38 Sorrowing most of all for the words which he spake, that they should see his face no more. And they accompanied him unto the ship.

## CHAPTER 21

*Paul cometh to Jerusalem.*

1 And it came to pass, that after we were gotten from them, and had launched, we came with a straight course unto Coos, and the day following unto Rhodes, and from thence unto Patara;

2 And finding a ship sailing over unto Phoenicia, we went aboard, and set forth.

3 Now when we had discovered Cyprus, we left it on the left hand, and sailed into Syria, and landed at Tyre; for there the ship was to unlade her burden.

4 And finding disciples, we tarried there seven days; who said to Paul through the Spirit, that he should not go up to Jerusalem.

5 And when we had accomplished those days, we departed and went our way; and they all brought us on our way, with wives and children, till we were out of the city; and we kneeled down on the shore, and prayed.

6 And when we had taken our leave one of another, we took ship; and they returned home again.

7 And when we had finished our course from Tyre, we came to Ptolemais, and saluted the brethren, and abode with them one day.

8 And the next day we that were of Paul's company departed, and came unto Caesarea; and we entered into the house of Philip the evangelist, which was one of the seven; and abode with him.

9 And the same man had four daughters, virgins, which did prophesy.

10 And as we tarried there many days, there came down from Judea a certain prophet, named Agabus.

11 And when he was come unto us, he took Paul's girdle, and bound his own hands and feet, and said, Thus saith the Holy Ghost, So shall the Jews at Jerusalem bind the man that owneth this girdle, and shall deliver him into the hands of the Gentiles.

12 And when we heard these things, both we, and they of that place, besought him not to go up to Jerusalem.

13 Then Paul answered, What mean ye to weep and to break mine heart? for I am ready not to be bound only, but also to die at Jerusalem for the name of the Lord Jesus.

14 And when he would not be persuaded, we ceased, saying, The will of the Lord be done.

15 And after those days we took up our carriages, and went up to Jerusalem.

16 There went with us also certain of the disciples of Caesarea, and brought with them one Mnason of Cyprus, an old disciple, with whom we should lodge.

17 And when we were come to Jerusalem, the brethren received us gladly.

18 And the day following Paul went in with us unto James; and all the elders were present.

19 And when he had saluted them, he declared particularly what things God had wrought among the Gentiles by his ministry.

20 And when they heard it, they glorified the Lord, and said unto him, Thou seest, brother, how many thousands of Jews there are which believe; and they are all zealous of the law;

21 And they are informed of thee, that thou teachest all the Jews which are among the Gentiles to forsake Moses, saying that they ought not to circumcise their children, neither to walk after the customs.

22 What is it therefore? the multitude must needs come together; for they will hear that thou art come.

23 Do therefore this that we say to thee; we have four men which have a vow on them;

24 Them take, and purify thyself with them, and be at charges with them, that they may shave their heads; and all may know that those things, whereof they were informed concerning thee, are nothing; but that thou thyself also walkest orderly, and keepest the law.

25 As touching the Gentiles which believe, we have written and concluded that they observe no such thing, save only that they keep themselves from things offered to idols, and from blood, and from things strangled, and from fornication.

26 Then Paul took the men, and the next day purifying himself with them entered into the temple, to signify the accomplishment of the days of purification, until that an offering should be offered for every one of them.

27 And when the seven days were almost ended, the Jews which were of Asia, when they saw him in the temple, stirred up all the people, and laid hands on him,

28 Crying out, Men of Israel, help; this is the man, that teacheth all men every where against the people, and the law, and this place; and further brought Greeks also into the temple, and hath polluted this holy place.

29 (For they had seen before with him in the city Trophimus an Ephesian, whom they supposed that Paul had brought into the temple.)

30 And all the city was moved, and the people ran together; and they took, and drew him out of the temple; and forthwith the doors were shut.

31 And as they went about to kill him, tidings came unto the chief captain of the band, that all Jerusalem was in an uproar;

32 Who immediately took soldiers and centurions, and ran down unto them; and when they saw the chief captain and the soldiers, they left beating of Paul.

33 Then the chief captain came near, and took him, and commanded him to be bound with two chains; and demanded who he was, and what he had done.

34 And some cried one thing, some another, among the multitude; and when he could not know the certainty for the tumult, he commanded him to be carried into the castle.

35 And when he came upon the stairs, so it was, that he was borne of the soldiers for the violence of the people.

36 For the multitude of the people followed after, crying, Away with him.

37 And as Paul was to be led into the castle, he said unto the chief captain, May I speak unto thee? Who said, Canst thou speak Greek?

38 Art not thou that Egyptian, which before these days madest an uproar, and leddest out into the wilderness four thousand men that were murderers?

39 But Paul said, I am a man which am a Jew of Tarsus, a city in Cilicia, a citizen of no mean city; and, I beseech thee, suffer me to speak unto the people.

40 And when he had given him license, Paul stood on the stairs, and beckoned with the hand unto the people. And when there was made a great silence, he spake unto them in the Hebrew tongue, saying,

## CHAPTER 22

*Paul declareth his conversion.*

1 Men, brethren, and fathers, hear ye my defense which I make now unto you.

2 (And when they heard that he spake in the Hebrew tongue to them, they kept the more silence; and he saith,)

3 I am verily a man which am a Jew, born in Tarsus, a city in Cilicia, yet brought up in this city at the feet of Gamaliel, and taught according to the perfect manner of the law of the fathers, and was zealous toward God, as ye all are this day.

4 And I persecuted this way unto the death, binding and delivering into prisons both men and women.

5 As also the high priest doth bear me witness, and all the estate of the elders; from whom also I received letters unto the brethren, and went to Damascus, to bring them which were there bound unto Jerusalem, for to be punished.

6 And it came to pass, that, as I made my journey, and was come nigh unto Damascus about noon, suddenly there shone from heaven a great light round about me.

7 And I fell unto the ground, and heard a voice saying unto me, Saul, Saul, why persecutest thou me?

8 And I answered, Who art thou, Lord? And he said unto me, I am Jesus of Nazareth, whom thou persecutest.

9 And they that were with me saw indeed the light, and were afraid; but they heard not the voice of him that spake to me.

10 And I said, What shall I do, Lord? And the Lord said unto me, Arise, and go into Damascus; and there it shall be told thee of all things which are appointed of thee to do.

11 And when I could not see for the glory of that light, being led by the hand of them that were with me, I came into Damascus.

12 And one Ananias, a devout man according to the law, having a good report of all the Jews which dwelt there,

13 Came unto me, and stood, and said unto me, Brother Saul, receive thy sight. And the same hour I looked up upon him.

14 And he said, The God of our fathers hath chosen thee, that thou shouldest know his will, and see that Just One, and shouldest hear the voice of his mouth.

15 For thou shalt be his witness unto all men of what thou hast seen and heard.

16 And now why tarriest thou? arise, and be baptized, and wash away thy sins, calling on the name of the Lord.

17 And it came to pass, that, when I was come again to Jerusalem, even while I prayed in the temple, I was in a trance;

18 And saw him saying unto me, Make haste, and get thee quickly out of

Jerusalem; for they will not receive thy testimony concerning me.

19 And I said, Lord, they know that I imprisoned and beat in every synagogue them that believed on thee;

20 And when the blood of thy martyr Stephen was shed, I also was standing by, and consenting unto his death, and kept the raiment of them that slew him.

21 And he said unto me, Depart; for I will send thee far hence unto the Gentiles.

22 And they gave him audience unto this word, and then lifted up their voices, and said, Away with such a fellow from the earth; for it is not fit that he should live.

23 And as they cried out, and cast off their clothes, and threw dust into the air,

24 The chief captain commanded him to be brought into the castle, and bade that he should be examined by scourging; that he might know wherefore they cried so against him.

25 And as they bound him with thongs, Paul said unto the centurion that stood by, Is it lawful for you to scourge a man that is a Roman, and uncondemned?

26 When the centurion heard that, he went and told the chief captain, saying, Take heed what thou doest; for this man is a Roman.

27 Then the chief captain came, and said unto him, Tell me, art thou a Roman? He said, Yea.

28 And the chief captain answered, With a great sum obtained I this freedom. And Paul said, But I was freeborn.

29 Then straightway they departed from him which should have examined him, and the chief captain also was afraid after he knew that he was a Roman, because he had bound him, and he loosed him from his bands.

30 On the morrow, because he would have known the certainty wherefore he was accused of the Jews, he commanded the chief priests and all their council to appear, and brought Paul down, and set him before them.

## CHAPTER 23

*Paul pleadeth his cause—Dissension among his accusers—The Jews lay wait for Paul.*

1 And Paul, earnestly beholding the council, said, Men and brethren, I have lived in all good conscience before God until this day.

2 And the high priest Ananias commanded them that stood by him to smite him on the mouth.

3 Then said Paul unto him, God shall smite thee, thou whited wall; for sittest thou to judge me after the law, and commandest me to be smitten contrary to the law?

4 And they that stood by said, Revilest thou God's high priest?

5 Then said Paul, I did not know, brethren, that he was the high priest; for it is written, Thou shalt not speak evil of the ruler of thy people.

6 But when Paul perceived that the one part were Sadducees, and the other Pharisees, he cried out in the council, Men and brethren, I am a Pharisee, the son of a Pharisee; of the hope and resurrection of the dead I am called in question.

7 And when he had so said, there arose a dissension between the Pharisees and the Sadducees; and the multitude was divided.

8 For the Sadducees say that there is no resurrection, neither angel, nor spirit; but the Pharisees confess both.

9 And there arose a great cry; and the scribes that were of the Pharisees' part arose, and strove, saying, We find no evil in this man; but if a spirit or an angel hath spoken to him, let us not fight against God.

10 And when there arose a great dissension, the chief captain, fearing lest Paul should have been pulled in pieces of them, commanded the soldiers to go down, and to take him by force from among them, and to bring him into the castle.

11 And the night following the Lord stood by him, and said, Be of good cheer, Paul; for as thou hast testified of me in Jerusalem, so must thou bear witness also at Rome.

12 And when it was day, certain of the Jews banded together, and bound themselves under a curse, saying that they would neither eat nor drink till they had killed Paul.

13 And they were more than forty which had made this conspiracy.

14 And they came to the chief priests and elders, and said, We have bound ourselves under a great curse, that we

will eat nothing until we have slain Paul.

15 Now therefore ye with the council signify to the chief captain that he bring him down unto you tomorrow, as though you would inquire something more perfectly concerning him; and we, before he come near, are ready to kill him.

16 And when Paul's sister's son heard of their lying in wait, he went and entered into the castle, and told Paul.

17 Then Paul called one of the centurions unto him, and said, Bring this young man unto the chief captain; for he hath a certain thing to tell him.

18 So he took him, and brought him to the chief captain, and said, Paul the prisoner called me unto him, and prayed me to bring this young man unto thee, who hath something to say unto thee.

19 Then the chief captain took him by the hand, and went with him aside privately, and asked him, What is that thou hast to tell me?

20 And he said, The Jews have agreed to desire thee that thou wouldest bring down Paul tomorrow into the council, as though they would inquire somewhat of him more perfectly.

21 But do not thou yield unto them; for there lie in wait for him of them more than forty men, which have bound themselves with an oath, that they will neither eat nor drink till they have killed him; and now are they ready, looking for a promise from thee.

22 So the chief captain then let the young man depart, and charged him, See thou tell no man that thou hast showed these things to me.

23 And he called unto him two centurions, saying, Make ready two hundred soldiers to go to Caesarea, and horsemen threescore and ten, and spearmen two hundred, at the third hour of the night;

24 And provide them beasts, that they may set Paul on, and bring him safe unto Felix the governor.

25 And he wrote a letter after this manner:

26 Claudius Lysias unto the most excellent governor Felix sendeth greeting.

27 This man was taken of the Jews, and would have been killed of them; then came I with an army, and rescued him, having understood that he was a Roman.

28 And when I would have known the cause wherefore they accused him, I brought him forth into their council;

29 Whom I perceived to be accused of questions of their law, but to have nothing laid to his charge worthy of death or of bonds.

30 And when it was told me how that the Jews laid wait for the man, I sent straightway to thee, and gave commandment to his accusers also to say before thee what they had against him. Farewell.

31 Then the soldiers, as it was commanded them, took Paul, and brought him by night to Antipatris.

32 On the morrow they left the horsemen to go with him, and returned to the castle;

33 Who, when they came to Caesarea, and delivered the epistle to the governor, presented Paul also before him.

34 And when the governor had read the letter, he asked of what province he was. And when he understood that he was of Cilicia;

35 I will hear thee, said he, when thine accusers are also come. And he commanded him to be kept in Herod's judgment hall.

## CHAPTER 24

*Paul preacheth Christ to the governor and his wife—Paul in prison.*

1 And after five days Ananias the high priest descended with the elders, and with a certain orator named Tertullus, who informed the governor against Paul.

2 And when he was called forth, Tertullus began to accuse him, saying, Seeing that by thee we enjoy great quietness, and that very worthy deeds are done unto this nation by thy providence,

3 We accept it always, and in all places, most noble Felix, with all thankfulness.

4 Notwithstanding, that I be not further tedious unto thee, I pray thee that thou wouldst hear us of thy clemency a few words.

5 For we have found this man a pestilent fellow, and a mover of sedition among all the Jews throughout the world, and a ringleader of the sect of the Nazarenes;

6 Who also hath gone about to pro-

fane the temple; whom we took, and would have judged according to our law,

7 But the chief captain Lysias came upon us, and with great violence took him away out of our hands,

8 Commanding his accusers to come unto thee; by examining of whom thyself mayest take knowledge of all these things, whereof we accuse him.

9 And the Jews also assented, saying that these things were so.

10 Then Paul, after that the governor had beckoned unto him to speak, answered, Forasmuch as I know that thou hast been of many years a judge unto this nation, I do the more cheerfully answer for myself;

11 Because that thou mayest understand, that there are yet but twelve days since I went up to Jerusalem for to worship.

12 And they neither found me in the temple disputing with any man, neither raising up the people, neither in the synagogues, nor in the city;

13 Neither can they prove the things whereof they now accuse me.

14 But this I confess unto thee, that after the way which they call heresy, so worship I the God of my fathers, believing all things which are written in the law and in the prophets;

15 And have hope toward God, which they themselves also allow, that there shall be a resurrection of the dead, both of the just and unjust.

16 And herein do I exercise myself, to have always a conscience void of offense toward God, and toward men.

17 Now after many years I came to bring alms to my nation, and offerings.

18 Whereupon certain Jews from Asia found me purified in the temple, neither with multitude, nor with tumult.

19 Who ought to have been here before thee, and object, if they had aught against me.

20 Or else let these same here say, if they have found any evildoing in me while I stood before the council,

21 Except it be for this one voice, that I cried standing among them, Touching the resurrection of the dead I am called in question by you this day.

22 And when Felix heard these things, having more perfect knowledge of that way, he deferred them, and said, When Lysias the chief captain

shall come down, I will know the uttermost of your matter.

23 And he commanded a centurion to keep Paul, and to let him have liberty, and that he should forbid none of his acquaintance to minister or come unto him.

24 And after certain days, when Felix came with his wife Drusilla, which was a Jewess, he sent for Paul, and heard him concerning the faith in Christ.

25 And as he reasoned of righteousness, temperance, and judgment to come, Felix trembled, and answered, Go thy way for this time; when I have a convenient season, I will call for thee.

26 He hoped also that money should have been given him of Paul, that he might loose him; wherefore he sent for him the oftener, and communed with him.

27 But after two years Porcius Festus came into Felix' room; and Felix, willing to show the Jews a pleasure, left Paul bound.

## CHAPTER 25

*Paul answereth before Festus and King Agrippa.*

1 Now when Festus was come into the province, after three days he ascended from Caesarea to Jerusalem.

2 Then the high priest and the chief of the Jews informed him against Paul, and besought him,

3 And desired favor against him, that he would send for him to Jerusalem, laying wait in the way to kill him.

4 But Festus answered, that Paul should be kept at Caesarea, and that he himself would depart shortly thither.

5 Let them therefore, said he, which among you are able, go down with me, and accuse this man, if there be any wickedness in him.

6 And when he had tarried among them more than ten days, he went down unto Caesarea; and the next day sitting on the judgment seat commanded Paul to be brought.

7 And when he was come, the Jews which came down from Jerusalem stood round about, and laid many and grievous complaints against Paul, which they could not prove.

8 While he answered for himself, Neither against the law of the Jews,

neither against the temple, nor yet against Caesar, have I offended any thing at all.

9 But Festus, willing to do the Jews a pleasure, answered Paul, and said, Wilt thou go up to Jerusalem, and there be judged of these things before me?

10 Then said Paul, I stand at Caesar's judgment seat, where I ought to be judged; to the Jews have I done no wrong, as thou very well knowest.

11 For if I be an offender, or have committed any thing worthy of death, I refuse not to die; but if there be none of these things whereof these accuse me, no man may deliver me unto them. I appeal unto Caesar.

12 Then Festus, when he had conferred with the council, answered, Hast thou appealed unto Caesar? unto Caesar shalt thou go.

13 And after certain days king Agrippa and Bernice came unto Caesarea to salute Festus.

14 And when they had been there many days, Festus declared Paul's cause unto the king, saying, There is a certain man left in bonds by Felix;

15 About whom, when I was at Jerusalem, the chief priests and the elders of the Jews informed me, desiring to have judgment against him.

16 To whom I answered, It is not the manner of the Romans to deliver any man to die, before that he which is accused have the accusers face to face, and have license to answer for himself concerning the crime laid against him.

17 Therefore, when they were come hither, without any delay on the day following I sat on the judgment seat, and commanded the man to be brought forth.

18 Against whom when the accusers stood up, they brought none accusation of such things as I supposed;

19 But had certain questions against him of their own superstition, and of one Jesus, which was dead, whom Paul affirmed to be alive.

20 And because I doubted of such manner of questions, I asked him whether he would go to Jerusalem, and there be judged of these matters.

21 But when Paul had appealed to be reserved unto the hearing of Augustus, I commanded him to be kept till I might send him to Caesar.

22 Then Agrippa said unto Festus, I would also hear the man myself. Tomorrow, said he, thou shalt hear him.

23 And on the morrow, when Agrippa was come, and Bernice, with great pomp, and was entered into the place of hearing, with the chief captains, and principal men of the city, at Festus' commandment Paul was brought forth.

24 And Festus said, King Agrippa, and all men which are here present with us, ye see this man, about whom all the multitude of the Jews have dealt with me, both at Jerusalem, and also here, crying that he ought not to live any longer.

25 But when I found that he had committed nothing worthy of death, and that he himself hath appealed to Augustus, I have determined to send him.

26 Of whom I have no certain thing to write unto my lord. Wherefore I have brought him forth before you, and specially before thee, O king Agrippa, that, after examination had, I might have somewhat to write.

27 For it seemeth to me unreasonable to send a prisoner, and not withal to signify the crimes laid against him.

## CHAPTER 26

*Paul, in the presence of Agrippa—Festus chargeth him to be mad—Agrippa almost persuaded to be a Christian.*

1 Then Agrippa said unto Paul, Thou art permitted to speak for thyself. Then Paul stretched forth the hand, and answered for himself;

2 I think myself happy, king Agrippa, because I shall answer for myself this day before thee touching all the things whereof I am accused of the Jews;

3 Especially because I know thee to be expert in all customs and questions which are among the Jews; wherefore I beseech thee to hear me patiently.

4 My manner of life from my youth, which was at the first among mine own nation at Jerusalem, know all the Jews;

5 Which knew me from the beginning, if they would testify, that after the most straitest sect of our religion I lived a Pharisee.

6 And now I stand and am judged for the hope of the promise made of God unto our fathers;

7 Unto which promise our twelve

tribes, instantly serving God day and night, hope to come. For which hope's sake, king Agrippa, I am accused of the Jews.

8 Why should it be thought a thing incredible with you, that God should raise the dead?

9 I verily thought with myself, that I ought to do many things contrary to the name of Jesus of Nazareth.

10 Which thing I also did in Jerusalem; and many of the saints did I shut up in prison, having received authority from the chief priests; and when they were put to death, I gave my voice against them.

11 And I punished them oft in every synagogue, and compelled them to blaspheme; and being exceedingly mad against them, I persecuted them even unto strange cities.

12 Whereupon as I went to Damascus with authority and commission from the chief priests,

13 At midday, O king, I saw in the way a light from heaven, above the brightness of the sun, shining round about me and them which journeyed with me.

14 And when we were all fallen to the earth, I heard a voice speaking unto me, and saying in the Hebrew tongue, Saul, Saul, why persecutest thou me? it is hard for thee to kick against the pricks.

15 And I said, Who art thou, Lord? And he said, I am Jesus whom thou persecutest.

16 But rise, and stand upon thy feet; for I have appeared unto thee for this purpose, to make thee a minister and a witness both of these things which thou hast seen, and of those things in the which I will appear unto thee;

17 Delivering thee from the people, and from the Gentiles, unto whom now I send thee,

18 To open their eyes, and to turn them from darkness to light, and from the power of Satan unto God, that they may receive forgiveness of sins, and inheritance among them which are sanctified by faith that is in me.

19 Whereupon, O king Agrippa, I was not disobedient unto the heavenly vision:

20 But showed first unto them of Damascus, and at Jerusalem, and throughout all the coasts of Judea, and then to the Gentiles, that they should repent and turn to God, and do works meet for repentance.

21 For these causes the Jews caught me in the temple, and went about to kill me.

22 Having therefore obtained help of God, I continue unto this day, witnessing both to small and great, saying none other things than those which the prophets and Moses did say should come;

23 That Christ should suffer, and that he should be the first that should rise from the dead, and show light unto the people, and to the Gentiles.

24 And as he thus spake for himself, Festus said with a loud voice, Paul, thou art beside thyself; much learning doth make thee mad.

25 But he said, I am not mad, most noble Festus; but speak forth the words of truth and soberness.

26 For the king knoweth of these things, before whom also I speak freely; for I am persuaded that none of these things are hidden from him; for this thing was not done in a corner.

27 King Agrippa, believest thou the prophets? I know that thou believest.

28 Then Agrippa said unto Paul, Almost thou persuadest me to be a Christian.

29 And Paul said, I would to God, that not only thou, but also all that hear me this day, were both almost, and altogether such as I am, except these bonds.

30 And when he had thus spoken, the king rose up, and the governor, and Bernice, and they that sat with them;

31 And when they were gone aside, they talked between themselves, saying, This man doeth nothing worthy of death or of bonds.

32 Then said Agrippa unto Festus, This man might have been set at liberty, if he had not appealed unto Caesar.

## CHAPTER 27

*Paul shipping toward Rome, foretelleth of the danger of the voyage—They suffer shipwreck, yet all come safe to land.*

1 And when it was determined that we should sail into Italy, they delivered Paul and certain other prisoners unto one named Julius, a centurion of Augustus' band.

2 And entering into a ship of Adra-

myttium, we launched, meaning to sail by the coasts of Asia; one Aristarchus, a Macedonian of Thessalonica, being with us.

3 And the next day we touched at Sidon. And Julius courteously entreated Paul, and gave him liberty to go unto his friends to refresh himself.

4 And when we had launched from thence, we sailed under Cyprus, because the winds were contrary.

5 And when we had sailed over the sea of Cilicia and Pamphylia, we came to Myra, a city of Lycia.

6 And there the centurion found a ship of Alexandria, sailing into Italy; and he put us therein.

7 And when we had sailed slowly many days, and scarce were come over against Cnidus, the wind not suffering us, we sailed under Crete, over against Salmone;

8 And, hardly passing it, came unto a place which is called the Fair Havens; nigh whereunto was the city of Lasea.

9 Now when much time was spent, and when sailing was now dangerous, because the fast was now already past, Paul admonished them,

10 And said unto them, Sirs, I perceive that this voyage will be with hurt and much damage, not only of the lading and ship, but also of our lives.

11 Nevertheless the centurion believed the master and the owner of the ship, more than those things which were spoken by Paul.

12 And because the haven was not commodious to winter in, the more part advised to depart thence also, if by any means they might attain to Phenice, and there to winter; which is a haven of Crete, and lieth toward the southwest and northwest.

13 And when the south wind blew softly, supposing that they had obtained their purpose, loosing thence, they sailed close by Crete.

14 But not long after there arose against it a tempestuous wind, called Euroclydon.

15 And when the ship was caught, and could not bear up into the wind, we let her drive.

16 And running under a certain island which is called Clauda, we had much work to come by the boat;

17 Which when they had taken up, they used helps, undergirding the ship; and, fearing lest they should fall into the quicksands, strake sail, and so were driven.

18 And we being exceedingly tossed with a tempest, the next day they lightened the ship;

19 And the third day we cast out with our own hands the tackling of the ship.

20 And when neither sun nor stars in many days appeared, and no small tempest lay on us, all hope that we should be saved was then taken away.

21 But after long abstinence, Paul stood forth in the midst of them, and said, Sirs, ye should have hearkened unto me, and not have loosed from Crete, and to have gained this harm and loss.

22 And now I exhort you to be of good cheer; for there shall be no loss of any man's life among you, but of the ship.

23 For there stood by me this night the angel of God, whose I am, and whom I serve,

24 Saying, Fear not, Paul; thou must be brought before Caesar; and lo, God hath given thee all them that sail with thee.

25 Wherefore, sirs, be of good cheer; for I believe God, that it shall be even as it was told me.

26 Howbeit we must be cast upon a certain island.

27 But when the fourteenth night was come, as we were driven up and down in Adria, about midnight the shipmen deemed that they drew near to some country;

28 And sounded, and found it twenty fathoms; and when they had gone a little further, they sounded again, and found it fifteen fathoms.

29 Then fearing lest we should have fallen upon rocks, they cast four anchors out of the stern, and wished for the day.

30 And as the shipmen were about to flee out of the ship, when they had let down the boat into the sea, under color as though they would have cast anchors out of the foreship,

31 Paul said to the centurion and to the soldiers, Except these abide in the ship, ye cannot be saved.

32 Then the soldiers cut off the ropes of the boat, and let her fall off.

33 And while the day was coming on, Paul besought them all to take

meat, saying, This day is the four-teenth day ye have tarried and contin-ued fasting, having taken nothing.

34 Wherefore I pray you to take some meat; for this is for your health; for there shall not a hair fall from the head of any of you.

35 And when he had thus spoken, he took bread, and gave thanks to God in the presence of them all; and when he had broken it, he began to eat.

36 Then were they all of good cheer, and they also took some meat.

37 And we were in all in the ship two hundred threescore and sixteen souls.

38 And when they had eaten enough, they lightened the ship, and cast out the wheat into the sea.

39 And when it was day, they knew not the land; but they discovered a cer-tain creek with a shore, into the which they were minded, if it were possible, to thrust in the ship.

40 And when they had taken up the anchors, they committed themselves un-to the sea, and loosed the rudder bands, and hoised up the mainsail to the wind, and made toward shore.

41 And falling into a place where two seas met, they ran the ship aground; and the forepart stuck fast, and remained unmovable, but the hin-der part was broken with the violence of the waves.

42 And the soldiers' counsel was to kill the prisoners, lest any of them should swim out, and escape.

43 But the centurion, willing to save Paul, kept them from their purpose; and commanded that they which could swim should cast themselves first into the sea, and get to land;

44 And the rest, some on boards, and some on broken pieces of the ship. And so it came to pass, that they es-caped all safe to land.

## CHAPTER 28

*Paul entertained by the barbarians—The viper on his hand—He healeth many dis-eases—They depart to Rome—Paul preacheth there two years.*

1 And when they were escaped, then they knew that the island was called Melita.

2 And the barbarous people showed us no little kindness; for they kindled a fire, and received us every one, be-cause of the present rain, and because of the cold.

3 And when Paul had gathered a bundle of sticks, and laid them on the fire, there came a viper out of the heat, and fastened on his hand.

4 And when the barbarians saw the venomous beast hang on his hand, they said among themselves, No doubt this man is a murderer, whom, though he hath escaped the sea, yet vengeance suffereth not to live.

5 And he shook off the beast into the fire, and felt no harm.

6 Howbeit they looked when he should have swollen, or fallen down dead suddenly; but after they had looked a great while, and saw no harm come to him, they changed their minds, and said that he was a god.

7 In the same quarters were posses-sions of the chief man of the island, whose name was Publius; who re-ceived us, and lodged us three days courteously.

8 And it came to pass, that the fa-ther of Publius lay sick of a fever and of a bloody flux; to whom Paul entered in, and prayed, and laid his hands on him, and healed him.

9 So when this was done, others also, which had diseases in the island, came, and were healed;

10 Who also honored us with many honors; and when we departed, they laded us with such things as were nec-essary.

11 And after three months we de-parted in a ship of Alexandria, which had wintered in the isle, whose sign was Castor and Pollux.

12 And landing at Syracuse, we tar-ried there three days.

13 And from thence we fetched a compass, and came to Rhegium; and after one day the south wind blew, and we came the next day to Puteoli;

14 Where we found brethren, and were desired to tarry with them seven days; and so we went toward Rome.

15 And from thence, when the breth-ren heard of us, they came to meet us as far as Appii Forum, and the Three Taverns; whom when Paul saw, he thanked God, and took courage.

16 And when we came to Rome, the centurion delivered the prisoners to the captain of the guard; but Paul was suffered to dwell by himself with a sol-dier that kept him.

17 And it came to pass, that after three days Paul called the chief of the Jews together; and when they were come together, he said unto them, Men and brethren, though I have committed nothing against the people, or customs of our fathers, yet was I delivered prisoner from Jerusalem into the hands of the Romans;

18 Who, when they had examined me, would have let me go, because there was no cause of death in me.

19 But when the Jews spake against it, I was constrained to appeal unto Caesar; not that I had aught to accuse my nation of.

20 For this cause therefore have I called for you, to see you, and to speak with you; because that for the hope of Israel I am bound with this chain.

21 And they said unto him, We neither received letters out of Judea concerning thee, neither any of the brethren that came showed or spake any harm of thee.

22 But, we desire to hear of thee what thou thinkest; for as concerning this sect, we know that every where it is spoken against.

23 And when they had appointed him a day, there came many to him into his lodging; to whom he expounded and testified the kingdom of God, persuading them concerning Jesus, both out of the law of Moses, and out of the prophets, from morning till evening.

24 And some believed the things which were spoken, and some believed not.

25 And when they agreed not among themselves, they departed, after that Paul had spoken one word, Well spake the Holy Ghost by Esaias the prophet unto our fathers,

26 Saying, Go unto this people, and say, Hearing ye shall hear, and shall not understand; and seeing ye shall see, and not perceive.

27 For the heart of this people is waxed gross, and their ears are dull of hearing, and their eyes have they closed; lest they should see with their eyes, and hear with their ears, and understand with their heart, and should be converted, and I should heal them.

28 Be it known therefore unto you, that the salvation of God is sent unto the Gentiles, and that they will hear it.

29 And when he had said these words, the Jews departed, and had great reasoning among themselves.

30 And Paul dwelt two whole years in his own hired house, and received all that came in unto him,

31 Preaching the kingdom of God and teaching those things which concern the Lord Jesus Christ, with all confidence, no man forbidding him.

## The Epistle of Paul the Apostle to the
# Romans

### CHAPTER 1

*Paul declareth the gospel to the Romans.*

1 Paul, an apostle, a servant of God, called of Jesus Christ, and separated to preach the gospel,

2 (Which he had promised before by his prophets in the holy scriptures,)

3 Concerning his Son Jesus Christ our Lord, which was made of the seed of David according to the flesh;

4 And declared the Son of God with power, by the Spirit according to the truth through the resurrection from the dead;

5 By whom we have received grace and apostleship, through obedience, and faith in his name, to preach the gospel among all nations;

6 Among whom ye also are called of Jesus Christ;

7 Wherefore I write to all who are in Rome, beloved of God, called saints; Grace to you, and peace, from God our Father, and the Lord Jesus Christ.

8 First, I thank my God through Jesus Christ, that you all are steadfast, and your faith is spoken of throughout the whole world.

9 For God is my witness, whom I serve, that without ceasing I make mention of you always in my prayers, that you may be kept through the Spirit, in the gospel of his Son,

10 Making request of you, to remember me in your prayers, I now write unto you, that you will ask him in faith, that if by any means, at length, I

may serve you with my labors, and may have a prosperous journey by the will of God, to come unto you.

11 For I long to see you, that I may impart unto you some spiritual gift, that it may be established in you to the end;

12 That I may be comforted together with you by the mutual faith both of you and me.

13 Now I would not have you ignorant, brethren, that oftentimes I purposed to come unto you, (but was hindered hitherto,) that I might have some fruit among you also, even as among other Gentiles.

14 I am debtor both to the Greeks, and to the Barbarians; both to the wise, and to the unwise.

15 And, as much as in me is, I am ready to preach the gospel to you that are at Rome also.

16 For I am not ashamed of the gospel of Christ; for it is the power of God unto salvation to every one that believeth; to the Jew first, and also to the Greek.

17 For therein is the righteousness of God revealed through faith on his name; as it is written, The just shall live by faith.

18 For the wrath of God is revealed from heaven against all ungodliness and unrighteousness of men; who love not the truth, but remain in unrighteousness,

19 After that which may be known of God is manifest to them.

20 For God hath revealed unto them the invisible things of him, from the creation of the world, which are clearly seen; things which are not seen being understood by the things that are made, through his eternal power and Godhead; so that they are without excuse;

21 Because that, when they knew God, they glorified him not as God, neither were they thankful, but became vain in their imaginations, and their foolish hearts were darkened.

22 Professing themselves to be wise, they became fools.

23 And changed the glory of the uncorruptible God into an image made like to corruptible man, and to birds, and fourfooted beasts, and creeping things.

24 Wherefore God also gave them up to uncleanness, through the lusts of their own hearts; to dishonor their own bodies between themselves:

25 Who changed the truth of God into a lie, and worshiped and served the creature more than the Creator, who is blessed for ever. Amen.

26 For this cause God gave them up unto vile affections; for even their women did change the natural use into that which is against nature:

27 And likewise also the men, leaving the natural use of the woman, burned in their lust one toward another; men with men working that which is unseemly, and receiving in themselves that recompense of their error which was meet.

28 And even as they did not like to retain God according to some knowledge, God gave them over to a reprobate mind, to do those things which are not convenient;

29 Being filled with all unrighteousness, fornication, wickedness, covetousness, maliciousness; full of envy, murder, debate, deceit, malignity; whisperers,

30 Backbiters, haters of God, despiteful, proud, boasters, inventors of evil things, disobedient to parents,

31 Without understanding, covenantbreakers, without natural affection, implacable, unmerciful:

32 And some who, knowing the judgment of God, that they which commit such things are worthy of death, are inexcusable, not only do the same, but have pleasure in them that do them.

## CHAPTER 2

*They that sin cannot escape the judgment of God.*

1 Therefore thou art inexcusable, O man, whosoever thou art that thus judgest; for wherein thou judgest another, thou condemnest thyself; for thou that judgest doest the same things.

2 But we are sure that the judgment of God is according to truth against them which commit such things.

3 And thinkest thou this, O man, that judgest them which do such things, and doest the same, that thou shalt escape the judgment of God?

4 Or despisest thou the riches of his goodness and forbearance and longsuffering; not knowing that the goodness of God leadeth thee to repentance?

5 But, after thy hardness and im-

penitent heart, treasurest up unto thyself wrath against the day of wrath and revelation of the righteous judgment of God;

6 Who will render to every man according to his deeds;

7 To them who by patient continuance in well doing seek for glory and honor and immortality, eternal life;

8 But unto them that are contentious, and do not obey the truth, but obey unrighteousness, indignation and wrath,

9 Tribulation and anguish, upon every soul of man that doeth evil; of the Jew first, and also of the Gentile;

10 But glory, honor, and peace, to every man that worketh good; to the Jew first, and also to the Gentile;

11 For there is no respect of persons with God.

12 For as many as have sinned without the law shall also perish without law; and as many as have sinned in the law shall be judged by the law;

13 (For not the hearers of the law are just before God, but the doers of the law shall be justified.

14 For when the Gentiles, which have not the law, do by nature the things contained in the law, these, having not the law, are a law unto themselves;

15 Which show the work of the law written in their hearts, their conscience also bearing witness, and their thoughts the meanwhile accusing or else excusing one another;)

16 In the day when God shall judge the secrets of men by Jesus Christ according to the gospel.

17 Behold, thou art called a Jew, and restest in the law, and makest thy boast of God,

18 And knowest his will, and approvest the things that are more excellent, being instructed out of the law;

19 And art confident that thou thyself art a guide of the blind, a light of them which are in darkness,

20 An instructor of the foolish, a teacher of babes, which hast the form of knowledge and of the truth in the law.

21 Thou therefore which teachest another, teachest thou not thyself? thou that preachest a man should not steal, dost thou steal?

22 Thou that sayest a man should not commit adultery, dost thou commit adultery? thou that abhorrest idols, dost thou commit sacrilege?

23 Thou that makest thy boast of the law, through breaking the law dishonorest thou God?

24 For the name of God is blasphemed among the Gentiles through you, as it is written.

25 For circumcision verily profiteth, if thou keep the law; but if thou be a breaker of the law, thy circumcision is made uncircumcision.

26 Therefore, if the uncircumcision keep the righteousness of the law, shall not his uncircumcision be counted for circumcision?

27 And shall not uncircumcision which is by nature, if it fulfill the law, judge thee, who by the letter and circumcision dost transgress the law?

28 For he is not a Jew, which is one outwardly; neither is that circumcision, which is outward in the flesh;

29 But he is a Jew, which is one inwardly; and circumcision is that of the heart, in the spirit, and not in the letter; whose praise is not of men, but of God.

## CHAPTER 3

*The Jews' advantage—No flesh is justified by the law.*

1 What advantage then hath the Jew over the Gentile? or what profit of circumcision, who is not a Jew from the heart?

2 But he who is a Jew from the heart, I say hath much every way; chiefly because that unto them were committed the oracles of God.

3 For what if some did not believe? shall their unbelief make the faith of God without effect?

4 God forbid; yea, let God be true, but every man a liar; as it is written, That thou mightest be justified in thy sayings, and mightest overcome when thou art judged.

5 But if we remain in our unrighteousness and commend the righteousness of God, how dare we say, God is unrighteous who taketh vengeance? (I speak as a man who fears God,)

6 God forbid; for then how shall God judge the world?

7 For if the truth of God hath more abounded through my lie, (as it is called of the Jews,) unto his glory; why yet am I also judged as a sinner? and

not received? Because we are slanderously reported;

8 And some affirm that we say, (whose damnation is just,) Let us do evil that good may come. But this is false.

9 If not so; what then are we better than they? No, in no wise; for we have proved before, that Jews and Gentiles are all under sin.

10 As it is written, there is none righteous, no, not one;

11 There is none that understandeth, there is none that seeketh after God.

12 They are all gone out of the way, they are together become unprofitable; there is none that doeth good, no, not one.

13 Their throat is an open sepulcher; with their tongues they have used deceit; the poison of asps is under their lips;

14 Whose mouth is full of cursing and bitterness;

15 Their feet are swift to shed blood;

16 Destruction and misery are in their ways;

17 And the way of peace have they not known;

18 There is no fear of God before their eyes.

19 Now we know that what things soever the law saith, it saith to them who are under the law; that every mouth may be stopped, and all the world may become guilty before God.

20 For by the law is the knowledge of sin; therefore by the deeds of the law shall no flesh be justified in his sight.

21 But now the righteousness of God without the law is manifested, being witnessed by the law and the prophets;

22 Even the righteousness of God which is by faith of Jesus Christ unto all and upon all them that believe; for there is no difference;

23 For all have sinned, and come short of the glory of God;

24 Therefore being justified only by his grace through the redemption that is in Christ Jesus;

25 Whom God has set forth to be a propitiation through faith in his blood, to declare his righteousness for the remission of sins that are past, through the forbearance of God;

26 To declare, I say, at this time his righteousness; that he might be just, and the justifier of him which believeth in Jesus.

27 Where is boasting then? It is excluded. By what law? of works? Nay; but by the law of faith.

28 Therefore we conclude that a man is justified by faith alone without the deeds of the law.

29 Is he the God of the Jews only? is he not also of the Gentiles? Yes, of the Gentiles also;

30 Seeing that God will justify the circumcision by faith, and uncircumcision through faith.

31 Do we then make void the law through faith? God forbid; yea, we establish the law.

## CHAPTER 4

*Abraham's faith—Abraham is the father of all that believe—The righteousness of faith.*

1 What shall we say then that Abraham our father, as pertaining to the flesh, hath found?

2 For if Abraham were justified by the law of works, he hath to glory in himself; but not of God.

3 For what saith the scripture? Abraham believed God, and it was counted unto him for righteousness.

4 Now to him who is justified by the law of works, is the reward reckoned, not of grace, but of debt.

5 But to him that seeketh not to be justified by the law of works, but believeth on him who justifieth not the ungodly, his faith is counted for righteousness.

6 Even as David also describeth the blessedness of the man, unto whom God imputeth righteousness without the law of works,

7 Saying, Blessed are they through faith whose iniquities are forgiven, and whose sins are covered.

8 Blessed is the man to whom the Lord will not impute sin.

9 Cometh this blessedness then upon the circumcision only, or upon the uncircumcision also? for we say that faith was reckoned to Abraham, for righteousness.

10 How was it then reckoned? when he was in circumcision, or in uncircumcision? Not in circumcision, but in uncircumcision.

11 And he received the sign of circumcision, a seal of the righteousness

of the faith which he had yet being uncircumcised; that he might be the father of all them that believe, though they be not circumcised; that righteousness might be imputed unto them also;

12 And the father of circumcision to them who are not of the circumcision only, but who also walk in the steps of that faith of our father Abraham, which he had being yet uncircumcised.

13 For the promise, that he should be the heir of the world, was not to Abraham, or to his seed, through the law, but through the righteousness of faith.

14 For if they which are of the law be heirs, faith is made void, and the promise made of none effect;

15 Because the law worketh wrath; for where no law is, there is no transgression.

16 Therefore ye are justified of faith and works, through grace, to the end the promise might be sure to all the seed; not to them only who are of the law, but to them also who are of the faith of Abraham; who is the father of us all,

17 (As it is written, I have made thee a father of many nations,) before him whom he believed, even God, who quickeneth the dead, and calleth those things which be not as though they were;

18 Who against hope believed in hope, that he might become the father of many nations, according to that which was spoken, So shall thy seed be.

19 And being not weak in faith, he considered not his own body now dead, when he was about a hundred years old, neither yet the deadness of Sarah's womb;

20 He staggered not at the promise of God through unbelief; but was strong in faith, giving glory to God;

21 And being fully persuaded, that what he had promised, he was able also to perform.

22 And therefore it was imputed to him for righteousness.

23 Now it was not written for his sake alone, that it was imputed to him;

24 But for us also, to whom it shall be imputed, if we believe on him that raised up Jesus our Lord from the dead;

25 Who was delivered for our offenses, and was raised again for our justification.

## CHAPTER 5

*Christ died for us, by whom we are reconciled to God—As sin and death came by Adam, so righteousness and life by Jesus Christ.*

1 Therefore being justified by faith, we have peace with God through our Lord Jesus Christ;

2 By whom also we have access by faith into this grace wherein we stand, and rejoice in hope of the glory of God.

3 And not only this, but we glory in tribulations also; knowing that tribulation worketh patience;

4 And patience, experience; and experience, hope;

5 And hope maketh not ashamed; because the love of God is shed abroad in our hearts by the Holy Ghost which is given unto us.

6 For when we were yet without strength, in due time Christ died for the ungodly.

7 For scarcely for a righteous man will one die; yet peradventure for a good man some would even dare to die.

8 But God commendeth his love toward us, in that, while we were yet sinners, Christ died for us.

9 Much more then, being now justified by his blood, we shall be saved from wrath through him.

10 For if, when we were enemies, we were reconciled to God by the death of his Son; much more, being reconciled, we shall be saved by his life.

11 And not only so, but we also joy in God through our Lord Jesus Christ, by whom we have now received the atonement.

12 Wherefore, as by one man sin entered into the world, and death by sin; and so death passed upon all men, for that all have sinned;

13 (For, before the law, sin was in the world; yet sin is not imputed to those who have no law.

14 Nevertheless, death reigned from Adam to Moses, even over them that had not sinned after the similitude of Adam's transgression, who is the figure of him that was to come. For I say, that through the offense, death reigned over all.

15 But the offense is not as the free gift, for the gift aboundeth. For, if through the offense of one, many be

dead; much more the grace of God, and the gift by grace, hath abounded by one man, Jesus Christ, unto many.

16 And not as, by one that sinned, is the gift; for the judgment is by one to condemnation, but the free gift is of many offenses unto justification.

17 For if by one man's offense death reigned by one; much more they which receive abundance of grace and of the gift of righteousness shall reign in life by one, Jesus Christ.)

18 Therefore, as by the offense of one judgment came upon all men to condemnation; even so by the righteousness of one the free gift came upon all men unto justification of life.

19 For as by one man's disobedience many were made sinners, so by the obedience of one shall many be made righteous.

20 Moreover the law entered, that the offense might abound. But where sin abounded, grace did much more abound;

21 That as sin hath reigned unto death, even so might grace reign through righteousness unto eternal life by Jesus Christ our Lord.

## CHAPTER 6

*Dead unto sin—Manner of baptism into Christ.*

1 What shall we say then? Shall we continue in sin that grace may abound?

2 God forbid. How shall we, that are dead to sin, live any longer therein?

3 Know ye not, that so many of us as were baptized into Jesus Christ were baptized into his death?

4 Therefore we are buried with him by baptism into death; that like as Christ was raised up from the dead by the glory of the Father, even so we also should walk in newness of life.

5 For if we have been planted together in the likeness of his death, we shall be also in the likeness of his resurrection;

6 Knowing this, that our old man is crucified with him, that the body of sin might be destroyed, that henceforth we should not serve sin.

7 For he that is dead to sin is freed from sin.

8 Now if we be dead with Christ, we believe that we shall also live with him;

9 Knowing that Christ being raised from the dead dieth no more; death hath no more dominion over him.

10 For in that he died, he died unto sin once; but in that he liveth, he liveth unto God.

11 Likewise reckon ye also yourselves to be dead indeed unto sin, but alive unto God through Jesus Christ our Lord.

12 Let not sin therefore reign in your mortal body, that ye should obey it in the lusts thereof.

13 Neither yield ye your members as instruments of unrighteousness unto sin; but yield yourselves unto God, as those that are alive from the dead, and your members as instruments of righteousness unto God.

14 For in so doing sin shall not have dominion over you; for ye are not under the law, but under grace.

15 What then? shall we sin, because we are not under the law, but under grace? God forbid.

16 Know ye not, that to whom ye yield yourselves servants to obey, his servants ye are to whom ye obey; whether of sin unto death, or of obedience unto righteousness?

17 But God be thanked, that ye are not the servants of sin, for ye have obeyed from the heart that form of doctrine which was delivered you.

18 Being then made free from sin, ye became the servants of righteousness.

19 I speak after the manner of men because of the infirmity of your flesh; for as ye have in times past yielded your members servants to uncleanness and to iniquity unto iniquity; even so now yield your members servants to righteousness unto holiness.

20 For when ye were the servants of sin, ye were free from righteousness.

21 What fruit had ye then in those things whereof ye are now ashamed? for the end of those things is death.

22 But now being made free from sin, and become servants to God, ye have your fruit unto holiness, and the end everlasting life.

23 For the wages of sin is death; but the gift of God is eternal life through Jesus Christ our Lord.

## CHAPTER 7

*The object and operation of the law.*

1 Know ye not, brethren, (for I speak to them that know the law,) how that

the law hath dominion over a man only as long as he liveth?

2 For the woman which hath a husband is bound by the law to her husband only as long as he liveth; for if the husband be dead, she is loosed from the law of her husband.

3 So then if, while her husband liveth, she be married to another man, she shall be called an adulteress; but if her husband be dead, she is free from that law; so that she is no adulteress, though she be married to another man.

4 Wherefore, my brethren, ye also are become dead to the law by the body of Christ; that ye should be married to another, even to him who is raised from the dead, that we should bring forth fruit unto God.

5 For when we were in the flesh, the motions of sins, which were not according to the law, did work in our members to bring forth fruit unto death.

6 But now we are delivered from the law wherein we were held, being dead to the law, that we should serve in newness of spirit, and not in the oldness of the letter.

7 What shall we say then? Is the law sin? God forbid. Nay, I had not known sin, but by the law; for I had not known lust, except the law had said, Thou shalt not covet.

8 But sin, taking occasion by the commandment, wrought in me all manner of concupiscence. For without the law sin was dead.

9 For once I was alive without transgression of the law, but when the commandment of Christ came, sin revived, and I died.

10 And when I believed not the commandment of Christ which came, which was ordained to life, I found it condemned me unto death.

11 For sin, taking occasion, denied the commandment, and deceived me; and by it I was slain.

12 Nevertheless, I found the law to be holy, and the commandment to be holy, and just, and good.

13 Was then that which is good made death unto me? God forbid. But sin, that it might appear sin by that which is good working death in me; that sin, by the commandment, might become exceeding sinful.

14 For we know that the commandment is spiritual; but when I was under law, I was yet carnal, sold under sin.

15 But now I am spiritual; for that which I am commanded to do, I do; and that which I am commanded not to allow, I allow not.

16 For what I know is not right, I would not do; for that which is sin, I hate.

17 If then I do not that which I would not allow, I consent unto the law, that it is good; and I am not condemned.

18 Now then, it is no more I that do sin; but I seek to subdue that sin which dwelleth in me.

19 For I know that in me, that is, in my flesh, dwelleth no good thing; for to will is present with me, but to perform that which is good I find not, only in Christ.

20 For the good that I would have done when under the law, I find not to be good; therefore, I do it not.

21 But the evil which I would not do under the law, I find to be good; that, I do.

22 Now if I do that, through the assistance of Christ, I would not do under the law, I am not under the law; and it is no more that I seek to do wrong, but to subdue sin that dwelleth in me.

23 I find then that under the law, that when I would do good evil was present with me; for I delight in the law of God after the inward man.

24 And now I see another law, even the commandment of Christ, and it is imprinted in my mind.

25 But my members are warring against the law of my mind, and bringing me into captivity to the law of sin which is in my members.

26 And if I subdue not the sin which is in me, but with the flesh serve the law of sin; O wretched man that I am! who shall deliver me from the body of this death?

27 I thank God through Jesus Christ our Lord, then, that so with the mind I myself serve the law of God.

## CHAPTER 8

*They that live in the Spirit, are free from condemnation, and are sure of the deliverance decreed of God—All creation to participate in the redemption of Christ.*

1 There is therefore now no condemnation to them which are in Christ

Jesus, who walk not after the flesh, but after the Spirit.

2 For the law of the Spirit of life in Christ Jesus hath made me free from the law of sin and death.

3 For what the law could not do, in that it was weak through the flesh, God sending his own Son in the likeness of sinful flesh, and for sin, condemned sin in the flesh;

4 That the righteousness of the law might be fulfilled in us, who walk not after the flesh, but after the Spirit.

5 For they that are after the flesh do mind the things of the flesh; but they that are after the Spirit, the things of the Spirit.

6 For to be carnally minded is death; but to be spiritually minded is life and peace.

7 Because the carnal mind is enmity against God; for it is not subject to the law of God, neither indeed can be.

8 So then they that are after the flesh cannot please God.

9 But ye are not after the flesh, but after the Spirit, if so be that the Spirit of God dwell in you. Now if any man have not the Spirit of Christ, he is none of his.

10 And if Christ be in you, though the body shall die because of sin, yet the Spirit is life, because of righteousness.

11 And if the Spirit of him that raised up Jesus from the dead, dwell in you, he that raised up Christ from the dead shall also quicken your mortal bodies by his Spirit that dwelleth in you.

12 Therefore, brethren, we are debtors, not to the flesh, to live after the flesh.

13 For if ye live after the flesh, unto sin, ye shall die; but if ye through the Spirit do mortify the deeds of the body, ye shall live unto Christ.

14 For as many as are led by the Spirit of God, they are the sons of God.

15 For ye have not received the spirit of bondage again to fear; but ye have received the Spirit of adoption; whereby we cry, Abba, Father.

16 The Spirit itself beareth witness with our spirit, that we are the children of God;

17 And if children, then heirs; heirs of God, and joint heirs with Christ; if so be that we suffer with him, that we may be also glorified together.

18 For I reckon that the sufferings of this present time are not worthy to be named with the glory which shall be revealed in us.

19 For the earnest expectation of the creature waiteth for the manifestation of the sons of God.

20 For the creature was made subject to tribulation not willingly, but by reason of him who hath subjected it in hope;

21 Because the creature itself also shall be delivered from the bondage of corruption into the glorious liberty of the children of God.

22 For we know that the whole creation groaneth and travaileth in pain together until now.

23 And not only they, but ourselves also, which have the firstfruits of the Spirit, even we ourselves groan within ourselves, waiting for the adoption, to wit, the redemption of our body.

24 For we are saved by hope; but hope that is seen is not hope; for what a man seeth, why doth he yet hope for?

25 But if we hope for that we see not, then with patience we do wait for it.

26 Likewise the Spirit also helpeth our infirmities; for we know not what we should pray for as we ought; but the Spirit itself maketh intercession for us with groanings which cannot be uttered.

27 And he that searcheth the hearts knoweth what is the mind of the Spirit, because he maketh intercession for the saints according to the will of God.

28 And we know that all things work together for good to them that love God, to them who are the called according to his purpose.

29 For him whom he did foreknow, he did also predestinate to be conformed to his own image, that he might be the firstborn among many brethren.

30 Moreover, him whom he did predestinate, him he also called; and him whom he called, him he also sanctified; and him whom he sanctified, him he also glorified.

31 What shall we then say to these things? If God be for us, who can prevail against us?

32 He that spared not his own Son, but delivered him up for us all, how

174

shall he not with him also freely give us all things?

33 Who shall lay any thing to the charge of God's elect? It is God that justifieth.

34 Who is he that condemneth? It is Christ that died, yea rather, that is risen again, who is even at the right hand of God, who also maketh intercession for us.

35 Who shall separate us from the love of Christ? shall tribulation, or distress, or persecution, or famine, or nakedness, or peril, or sword?

36 As it is written, For thy sake we are killed all the day long; we are accounted as sheep for the slaughter.

37 Nay, in all these things we are more than conquerors through him that loved us.

38 For I am persuaded, that neither death, nor life, nor angels, nor principalities, nor powers, nor things present, nor things to come,

39 Nor height, nor depth, nor any other creature, shall be able to separate us from the love of God, which is in Christ Jesus our Lord.

## CHAPTER 9

*Paul's sorrow for the Jews—Reasons therefore—The calling of the Gentiles.*

1 I say the truth in Christ, I lie not, my conscience also bearing me witness in the Holy Ghost,

2 That I have great heaviness and continual sorrow in my heart,

3 (For once I could have wished that myself were accursed from Christ,) for my brethren, my kinsmen according to the flesh;

4 Who are Israelites; of whom are the adoption, and the glory, and the covenants, and the giving of the law, and the service of God,

5 And the promises which are made unto the fathers; and of whom, as concerning the flesh, Christ was, who is God over all, blessed for ever. Amen.

6 Not as though the word of God hath taken none effect. For they are not all Israel, which are of Israel.

7 Neither, because they are all children of Abraham, are they the seed; but, In Isaac shall thy seed be called.

8 That is, They which are the children of the flesh, these are not the children of God; but the children of the promise are counted for the seed.

9 For this is the word of promise. At this time will I come, and Sarah shall have a son.

10 And not only Sarah; but when Rebecca also had conceived by one, our father Isaac,

11 (For the children being not yet born, neither having done any good or evil, that the purpose of God according to election might stand, not of works, but of him that calleth;)

12 It was said unto her, The elder shall serve the younger.

13 As it is written, Jacob have I loved, but Esau have I hated.

14 What shall we say then? Is there unrighteousness with God? God forbid.

15 For he saith to Moses, I will have mercy on whom I will have mercy, and I will have compassion on whom I will have compassion.

16 So then it is not of him that willeth, nor of him that runneth, but of God that showeth mercy.

17 For the scripture saith unto Pharaoh, Even for this same purpose have I raised thee up, that I might show my power in thee, and that my name might be declared throughout all the earth.

18 Therefore hath he mercy on whom he will have mercy, and whom he will he hardeneth.

19 Thou wilt say then unto me, Why doth he yet find fault? For who hath resisted his will?

20 Nay but, O man, who art thou that repliest against God? Shall the thing formed say to him that formed it, Why hast thou made me thus?

21 Hath not the potter power over the clay, of the same lump to make one vessel unto honor, and another unto dishonor?

22 What if God, willing to show his wrath, and to make his power known, endured with much longsuffering the vessels of wrath fitted to destruction;

23 And that he might make known the riches of his glory on the vessels of mercy, which he had before prepared unto glory,

24 Even us, whom he hath called, not of the Jews only, but also of the Gentiles?

25 As he saith also in Hosea, I will call them my people, which were not my people; and her beloved, which was not beloved.

26 And it shall come to pass, that in the place where it was said unto them,

Ye are not my people; there shall they be called the children of the living God.

27 Esaias also crieth concerning Israel, Though the number of the children of Israel be as the sand of the sea, a remnant shall be saved;

28 For he will finish the work, and cut it short in righteousness; because a short work will the Lord make upon the earth.

29 And as Esaias said before, Except the Lord of Sabaoth had left us a seed, we had been as Sodoma, and been made like unto Gomorrha.

30 What shall we say then? That the Gentiles, which followed not after righteousness, have attained to righteousness, even the righteousness which is of faith.

31 But Israel, which followed after the law of righteousness, hath not attained to the law of righteousness.

32 Wherefore they stumbled at that stumbling stone, not by faith, but as it were by the works of the law;

33 As it is written, Behold, I lay in Sion a stumbling stone and rock of offense; and whosoever believeth on him shall not be ashamed.

## CHAPTER 10

*The righteousness of the law, and of faith contrasted.*

1 Brethren, my heart's desire and prayer to God for Israel is, that they might be saved.

2 For I bear them record that they have a zeal of God, but not according to knowledge.

3 For they, being ignorant of God's righteousness, and going about to establish their own righteousness, have not submitted themselves unto the righteousness of God.

4 For Christ is the end of the law for righteousness to every one that believeth.

5 For Moses describeth the righteousness which is of the law, That the man which doeth those things shall live by them.

6 But the righteousness which is of faith speaketh on this wise, Say not in thine heart, Who shall ascend into heaven? (that is, to bring Christ down from above;)

7 Or, Who shall descend into the deep? (that is, to bring up Christ again from the dead.)

8 But what saith it? The word is nigh thee, even in thy mouth, and in thy heart; that is, the word of faith, which we preach;

9 That if thou shalt confess with thy mouth the Lord Jesus, and shalt believe in thine heart that God hath raised him from the dead, thou shalt be saved.

10 For with the heart man believeth unto righteousness; and with the mouth confession is made unto salvation.

11 For the scripture saith, Whosoever believeth on him shall not be ashamed.

12 For there is no difference between the Jew and the Greek; for the same Lord over all is rich unto all that call upon him.

13 For whosoever shall call upon the name of the Lord shall be saved.

14 How then shall they call on him in whom they have not believed? and how shall they believe in him of whom they have not heard? and how shall they hear without a preacher?

15 And how shall they preach, except they be sent? as it is written, How beautiful are the feet of them that preach the gospel of peace, and bring glad tidings of good things!

16 So then faith cometh by hearing, and hearing by the word of God.

17 But I say, Have they not heard? Yes verily, their sound went into all the earth, and their words unto the ends of the world.

18 But they have not all obeyed the gospel. For Esaias saith, Lord, who hath believed our report?

19 But I say, Did not Israel know? Now Moses saith, I will provoke you to jealousy by them that are no people, and by a foolish nation I will anger you.

20 But Esaias is very bold, and saith, I was found of them that sought me not; I was made manifest unto them that asked not after me.

21 But to Israel he saith, All day long I have stretched forth my hands unto a disobedient and gainsaying people.

## CHAPTER 11

*God hath not cast off all Israel—Promise of their salvation.*

1 I say then, Hath God cast away his people? God forbid. For I also am an

176

Israelite, of the seed of Abraham, of the tribe of Benjamin.

2 God hath not cast away his people which he foreknew. Know ye not what the scripture saith of Elias? how he maketh complaint to God against Israel, saying,

3 Lord, they have killed thy prophets, and digged down thine altars; and I am left alone, and they seek my life.

4 But what saith the answer of God unto him? I have reserved to myself seven thousand men, who have not bowed the knee to the image of Baal.

5 Even so then at this present time also there is a remnant according to the election of grace.

6 And if by grace, then it is no more of works: otherwise grace is no more grace. But if it be of works, then it is no more grace; otherwise work is no more work.

7 What then? Israel hath not obtained that which they seek for; but the election hath obtained it, and the rest were blinded.

8 (According as it is written, God hath given them the spirit of slumber, eyes that they should not see, and ears that they should not hear;) unto this day.

9 And David saith, Let their table be made a snare, and a trap, and a stumbling block, and a recompense unto them;

10 Let their eyes be darkened, that they may not see, and bow down their back alway.

11 I say then, have they stumbled that they should fall? God forbid: but rather through their fall salvation is come unto the Gentiles, for to provoke them to jealousy.

12 Now if the fall of them is the riches of the world, and the diminishing of them the riches of the Gentiles; how much more their fullness?

13 For I speak to you Gentiles, inasmuch as I am the apostle of the Gentiles, I magnify mine office.

14 If by any means I may provoke to emulation them which are my flesh, and might save some of them.

15 For if the casting away of them is the reconciling of the world, what shall the restoring of them be, but life from the dead?

16 For if the firstfruit is holy, the lump is also holy; and if the root is holy, so are the branches.

17 And if some of the branches be broken off, and thou, being a wild olive tree, wast grafted in among them, and with them partakest of the root and fatness of the olive tree;

18 Boast not against the branches. But if thou boast, thou bearest not the root, but the root thee.

19 For if thou boast, thou wilt say, The branches were broken off, that we might be grafted in.

20 Well; because of unbelief they were broken off, and thou standest by faith. Be not highminded, but fear:

21 For if God spared not the natural branches, take heed lest he also spare not thee.

22 Behold therefore the goodness and severity of God: on them which fell, severity; but toward thee, goodness, if thou continue in his goodness: otherwise thou also shalt be cut off.

23 And they also, if they abide not still in unbelief, shall be grafted in: for God is able to graft them in again.

24 For if thou wast cut out of the olive tree which is wild by nature, and wast grafted contrary to nature into a good olive tree: how much more shall these, which be the natural branches, be grafted into their own olive tree?

25 For I would not, brethren, that ye should be ignorant of this mystery, lest ye should be wise in your own conceits; that blindness in part is happened to Israel, until the fullness of the Gentiles be come in.

26 And then all Israel shall be saved: as it is written, There shall come out of Sion the Deliverer, and shall turn away ungodliness from Jacob:

27 For this is my covenant unto them, when I shall take away their sins.

28 As concerning the gospel, they are enemies for your sakes: but as touching the election, they are beloved for the fathers' sakes.

29 For the gifts and calling of God are without repentance.

30 For as ye in times past have not believed God, yet have now obtained mercy through their unbelief;

31 Even so have these also now not believed, that through your mercy they also may obtain mercy.

32 For God hath concluded them all in unbelief, that he might have mercy upon all.

33 O the depth of the riches both of

the wisdom and knowledge of God!
how unsearchable are his judgments,
and his ways past finding out!

34 For who hath known the mind of
the Lord? or who hath been his counselor?

35 Or who hath first given to him,
and it shall be recompensed unto him
again?

36 For of him, and through him, and
to him, are all things; to whom be
glory for ever. Amen.

## CHAPTER 12

*God's mercies move us to serve him—
Unity of the church—Christian duties
enjoined.*

1 I beseech you therefore, brethren,
by the mercies of God, that ye present
your bodies a living sacrifice, holy, acceptable unto God, which is your rea-
sonable service.

2 And be not conformed to this
world; but be ye transformed by the renewing of your mind, that ye may
prove what that good, and acceptable,
and perfect will of God is.

3 For I say, through the grace given
unto me, to every man that is among
you, not to think of himself more
highly than he ought to think, but to
think soberly, according as God hath
dealt to every man the measure of
faith.

4 For as we have many members in
one body, and all members have not
the same office;

5 So we, being many, are one body in
Christ, and every one members one of
another.

6 Having then gifts differing according to the grace that is given to us,
whether prophecy, let us prophesy according to the proportion of faith;

7 Or ministry, let us wait on our
ministering; or he that teacheth, on
teaching;

8 Or he that exhorteth, on exhortation; he that giveth, let him do it with
simplicity; he that ruleth, with diligence; he that showeth mercy, with
cheerfulness.

9 Let love be without dissimulation.
Abhor that which is evil and cleave to
that which is good.

10 Be kindly affectioned one to another with brotherly love; in honor preferring one another;

11 Not slothful in business; fervent
in spirit; serving the Lord;

12 Rejoicing in hope; patient in tribulation; continuing instant in prayer;

13 Distributing to the necessity of
saints; given to hospitality.

14 Bless them which persecute you;
bless, and curse not.

15 Rejoice with them that do rejoice,
and weep with them that weep.

16 Be of the same mind one toward
another. Mind not high things, but
condescend to men of low estate. Be
not wise in your own conceits.

17 Recompense to no man evil for
evil. Provide things honest in the sight
of all men.

18 If it be possible, as much as lieth
in you, live peaceably with all men.

19 Dearly beloved, avenge not yourselves, but rather give place unto
wrath; for it is written, Vengeance is
mine; I will repay, saith the Lord.

20 Therefore if thine enemy hunger,
feed him; if he thirst, give him drink;
for in so doing thou shalt heap coals of
fire on his head.

21 Be not overcome of evil, but overcome evil with good.

## CHAPTER 13

*Subjection to rulers—Love is the fulfill-
ing of the law—Gluttony and drunkenness reproved.*

1 Let every soul be subject unto the
higher powers. For there is no power
in the church but of God; the powers
that be are ordained of God.

2 Whosoever therefore resisteth the
power, resisteth the ordinance of God;
and they that resist shall receive to
themselves punishment.

3 For rulers are not a terror to good
works, but to the evil. Wilt thou then
not be afraid of the power? do that
which is good, and thou shalt have
praise of the same;

4 For he is the minister of God to thee
for good. But if thou do that which is
evil, be afraid; for he beareth not the
rod in vain; for he is the minister of
God, a revenger to execute wrath upon
him that doeth evil.

5 Wherefore ye must needs be subject, not only for wrath, but also for
conscience' sake.

6 For, for this cause pay ye your consecrations also unto them; for they are
God's ministers, attending continually
upon this very thing.

7 But first, render to all their dues,
according to custom, tribute to whom

tribute, custom to whom custom, that your consecrations may be done in fear of him to whom fear belongs, and in honor of him to whom honor belongs.

8 Therefore owe no man any thing, but to love one another; for he that loveth another hath fulfilled the law.

9 For this, Thou shalt not commit adultery, Thou shalt not kill, Thou shalt not steal, Thou shalt not bear false witness, Thou shalt not covet; and if there be any other commandment, it is briefly comprehended in this saying, namely, Thou shalt love thy neighbor as thyself.

10 Love worketh no ill to his neighbor; therefore love is the fulfilling of the law.

11 And that, knowing the time, that now it is high time to awake out of sleep; for now is our salvation nearer than when we believed.

12 The night is far spent, the day is at hand; let us therefore cast off the works of darkness, and let us put on the armor of light.

13 Let us walk honestly, as in the day; not in rioting and drunkenness, not in chambering and wantonness, not in strife and envying.

14 But put ye on the Lord Jesus Christ, and make not provision for the flesh, to gratify the lusts thereof.

## CHAPTER 14

*Self-righteousness forbidden—Charity enjoined.*

1 Him that is weak in the faith receive ye, but not to doubtful disputations.

2 For one believeth that he may eat all things; another, who is weak, eateth herbs.

3 Let not him that eateth despise him that eateth not; and let not him which eateth not judge him that eateth; for God hath received him.

4 Who art thou that judgest another man's servant? to his own master he standeth or falleth; yea, he shall be holden up; for God is able to make him stand.

5 One man esteemeth one day above another; another esteemeth every day alike. Let every man be fully persuaded in his own mind.

6 He that regardeth the day, regardeth it unto the Lord; and he that regardeth not the day, to the Lord he doth not regard it. He that eateth,

eateth to the Lord, for he giveth God thanks; and he that eateth not, to the Lord he eateth not, and giveth God thanks.

7 For none of us liveth to himself, and no man dieth to himself.

8 For whether we live, we live unto the Lord; and whether we die, we die unto the Lord; whether we live therefore, or die, we are the Lord's.

9 For to this end Christ both died, and rose, and revived, that he might be Lord both of the dead and living.

10 But why dost thou judge thy brother? or why dost thou set at naught thy brother? for we shall all stand before the judgment seat of Christ.

11 For I live, saith the Lord, as it is written. And every knee shall bow to me, and every tongue shall swear to God.

12 So then every one of us shall give account of himself to God.

13 Let us not therefore judge one another any more; but judge this rather, that no man put a stumbling block or an occasion to fall in his brother's way.

14 I know, and am persuaded by the Lord Jesus, that there is nothing unclean of itself; but to him that esteemeth any thing to be unclean, to him it is unclean.

15 But if thy brother be grieved with thy meat, thou walkest not charitably if thou eatest. Therefore destroy not him with thy meat, for whom Christ died.

16 Let not then your good be evil spoken of;

17 For the kingdom of God is not meat and drink; but righteousness, and peace, and joy in the Holy Ghost.

18 For he that in these things serveth Christ is acceptable to God, and approved of men.

19 Let us therefore follow after the things which make for peace, and things wherewith one may edify another.

20 For meat destroy not the work of God. All things indeed are pure; but it is evil for that man who eateth with offense.

21 It is good neither to eat flesh, nor to drink wine, nor any thing whereby thy brother stumbleth, or is offended, or is made weak.

22 Hast thou faith? have it to thyself before God. Happy is he that condemneth not himself in that thing which he alloweth.

23 And he that doubteth is condemned if he eat, because it is not of faith; for whatsoever is not of faith is sin.

## CHAPTER 15

*The strong must bear with the weak— Christ our example.*

1 We then that are strong ought to bear the infirmities of the weak, and not to please ourselves.

2 Let every one of us please his neighbor for his good to edification.

3 For even Christ pleased not himself; but, as it is written, The reproaches of them that reproached thee fell on me.

4 For whatsoever things were written aforetime were written for our learning, that we through patience and comfort of the scriptures might have hope.

5 Now the God of patience and consolation grant you to be likeminded one toward another according as was Christ Jesus;

6 That ye may with one mind and one mouth glorify God, even the Father of our Lord Jesus Christ.

7 Wherefore receive ye one another, as Christ also received us, to the glory of God.

8 Now I say that Jesus Christ was a minister of the circumcision for the truth of God, to confirm the promises made unto the fathers;

9 And that the Gentiles might glorify God for his mercy; as it is written, For this cause I will confess to thee among the Gentiles, and sing unto thy name.

10 And again he saith, Rejoice, ye Gentiles, with his people.

11 And again, Praise the Lord, all ye Gentiles; and laud him, all ye people.

12 And again, Esaias saith, There shall be a root of Jesse, and he that shall rise to reign over the Gentiles; in him shall the Gentiles trust.

13 Now the God of hope fill you with all joy and peace in believing, that ye may abound in hope, through the power of the Holy Ghost.

14 And I myself also am persuaded of you, my brethren, that ye also are full of goodness, filled with all knowledge, able also to admonish one another.

15 Nevertheless, brethren, I have written the more boldly unto you in some sort, as putting you in mind, because of the grace that is given to me of God.

16 That I should be the minister of Jesus Christ to the Gentiles, ministering the gospel of God, that the offering up of the Gentiles might be acceptable, being sanctified by the Holy Ghost.

17 I have therefore whereof I may glory through Jesus Christ in those things which pertain to God.

18 For I will not dare to speak of any of those things which Christ hath not wrought by me, to make the Gentiles obedient, by word and deed.

19 Through mighty signs and wonders, by the power of the Spirit of God; so that from Jerusalem, and round about unto Illyricum, I have fully preached the gospel of Christ.

20 Yea, so have I strived to preach the gospel, not where Christ was named, lest I should build upon another man's foundation;

21 But as it is written, To whom he was not spoken of, they shall see; and they that have not heard shall understand.

22 For which cause also I have been much hindered from coming to you.

23 But now having no more place in these parts, and having a great desire these many years to come unto you;

24 When I take my journey into Spain, I will come to you; for I trust to see you in my journey, and to be brought on my way thitherward by you, if first I be somewhat filled through your prayers.

25 But now I go unto Jerusalem to minister unto the saints.

26 For it hath pleased them of Macedonia and Achaia to make a certain contribution for the poor saints which are at Jerusalem.

27 It hath pleased them verily; and their debtors they are. For if the Gentiles have been made partakers of their spiritual things, their duty is also to minister unto them in carnal things.

28 When therefore I have performed this, and have sealed to them this fruit, I will come by you into Spain.

29 And I am sure that, when I come unto you, I shall come in the fullness of the blessing of the gospel of Christ.

30 Now I beseech you, brethren, for the Lord Jesus Christ's sake, and for the love of the Spirit, that ye strive together with me in your prayers to God for me;

31 That I may be delivered from them

that do not believe in Judea; and that my service which I have for Jerusalem may be accepted of the saints;

32 That I may come unto you with joy by the will of God, and may with you be refreshed.

33 Now the God of peace be with you all. Amen.

## CHAPTER 16

*Paul adviseth them to take heed of those which cause dissension, and avoid them.*

1 I commend unto you Phoebe our sister, which is a servant of the church which is at Cenchrea;

2 That ye receive her in the Lord, as becometh saints, and that ye assist her in whatsoever business she hath need of you; for she hath been a succorer of many, and of myself also.

3 Greet Priscilla and Aquila, my helpers in Christ Jesus;

4 Who have for my life laid down their own necks; unto whom not only I give thanks, but also all the churches of the Gentiles.

5 Likewise greet the church that is in their house. Salute my well-beloved Epenetus, who is the firstfruits of Achaia unto Christ.

6 Greet Mary, who bestowed much labor on us.

7 Salute Andronicus and Junia, my kinsmen, and my fellow prisoners, who are of note among the apostles, who also were in Christ before me.

8 Greet Amplias, my beloved in the Lord.

9 Salute Urbane, our helper in Christ, and Stachys my beloved.

10 Salute Apelles approved in Christ. Salute them which are of Aristobulus' church.

11 Salute Herodian my kinsman. Greet them that be of the church of Narcissus, which are in the Lord.

12 Salute Tryphena and Tryphosa, who labour in the Lord. Salute the beloved Persis, which laboured much in the Lord.

13 Salute Rufus chosen in the Lord, and his mother and mine.

14 Salute Asyncritus, Phlegon, Hermas, Patrobas, Hermes, and the brethren which are with them.

15 Salute Philologus, and Julia, Nereus, and his sister, and Olympas, and all the saints which are with them.

16 Salute one another with a holy salutation. The churches of Christ salute you.

17 Now I beseech you, brethren, mark them which cause divisions and offenses contrary to the doctrine which ye have learned; and avoid them.

18 For they that are such serve not our Lord Jesus Christ, but their own belly; and by good words and fair speeches deceive the hearts of the simple.

19 For your obedience is come abroad to all men. I am glad therefore on your behalf; but yet I would have you wise unto that which is good, and simple concerning evil.

20 And the God of peace shall bruise Satan under your feet shortly. The grace of our Lord Jesus Christ be with you. Amen.

21 Timotheus my workfellow, and Lucius, and Jason, and Sosipater, my kinsmen, salute you.

22 I Tertius, who wrote this epistle, salute you in the Lord.

23 Gaius mine host, and of the whole church, saluteth you. Erastus the chamberlain of the city saluteth you, and Quartus a brother.

24 The grace of our Lord Jesus Christ be with you all. Amen.

25 Now to him that is of power to stablish you according to the gospel, and the preaching of Jesus Christ, according to the revelation of the mystery, which was kept secret since the world began,

26 But now is made manifest, and by the scriptures of the prophets, according to the commandment of the everlasting God, made known to all nations for the obedience of faith;

27 To God only wise, be glory through Jesus Christ forever. Amen.

Written to the Romans from Corinthus, and sent by Phoebe, servant of the church at Cenchrea.

## The First Epistle of Paul the Apostle to the
# Corinthians

### CHAPTER 1

*Paul exhorteth to unity—The low estate of those who are called.*

1 Paul, an apostle, called of Jesus Christ through the will of God; and Sosthenes our brother,

2 Unto the church of God which is at Corinth, to them that are sanctified in Christ Jesus, called to be saints, with all that in every place call upon the name of Jesus Christ our Lord, both theirs and ours;

3 Grace be unto you, and peace, from God our Father, and from the Lord Jesus Christ.

4 I thank my God always on your behalf, for the grace of God which is given you of Jesus Christ;

5 That in every thing ye are enriched of him, in all utterance, and in all knowledge;

6 Even as the testimony of Christ was confirmed in you;

7 So that ye come behind in no gift; waiting for the coming of our Lord Jesus Christ;

8 Who shall also confirm you unto the end, that ye may be blameless in the day of our Lord Jesus Christ.

9 God is faithful, by whom ye were called unto the fellowship of his Son Jesus Christ our Lord.

10 Now I beseech you, brethren, in the name of our Lord Jesus Christ, that ye all speak the same thing, and that there be no divisions among you; but that ye be perfectly joined together in the same mind and in the same judgment.

11 For it hath been declared unto me of you, my brethren, by them which are of the house of Chloe, that there are contentions among you.

12 Now this I say, that many of you saith, I am of Paul; and I of Apollos; and I of Cephas; and I of Christ.

13 Is Christ divided? was Paul crucified for you? or were ye baptized in the name of Paul?

14 I thank God that I baptized none of you, but Crispus and Gaius;

15 Lest any should say that I had baptized in mine own name.

16 And I baptized also the household of Stephanas; besides, I know not whether I baptized any other.

17 For Christ sent me not to baptize, but to preach the gospel; not with wisdom of words, lest the cross of Christ should be made of none effect.

18 For the preaching of the cross is to them that perish, foolishness; but unto us which are saved, it is the power of God.

19 For it is written, I will destroy the wisdom of the wise, and will bring to nothing the understanding of the prudent.

20 Where is the wise? where is the scribe? where is the disputer of this world? hath not God made foolish the wisdom of this world?

21 For after that in the wisdom of God the world by wisdom knew not God, it pleased God by the foolishness of preaching to save them that believe.

22 For the Jews require a sign, and the Greeks seek after wisdom;

23 But we preach Christ crucified, unto the Jews a stumbling block, and unto the Greeks foolishness;

24 But unto them who believe, both Jews and Greeks, Christ the power of God, and the wisdom of God.

25 Because the foolishness of God is wiser than men; and the weakness of God is stronger than men.

26 For ye see your calling, brethren, how that not many wise men after the flesh, not many mighty, not many noble, are chosen;

27 For God hath chosen the foolish things of the world to confound the wise; and God hath chosen the weak things of the world to confound the things which are mighty;

28 And base things of the world, and things which are despised, hath God chosen, yea, and things which are not, to bring to naught things that are mighty;

29 That no flesh should glory in his presence.

30 But of him are ye in Christ Jesus, who of God is made unto us wisdom, and righteousness, and sanctification, and redemption;

31 That, according as it is written,

He that glorieth, let him glory in the Lord.

## CHAPTER 2

*He declareth that his preaching consisteth in the power of God—The spiritual man receiveth the things of God.*

1 And I, brethren, when I came to you, came not with excellency of speech or of wisdom, declaring unto you the testimony of God.

2 For I determined not to know any thing among you, save Jesus Christ, and him crucified.

3 And I was with you in weakness, and in fear, and in much trembling.

4 And my speech and my preaching was not with enticing words of man's wisdom, but in demonstration of the Spirit and of power;

5 That your faith should not stand in the wisdom of men, but in the power of God.

6 Howbeit we speak wisdom among them that are perfect; yet not the wisdom of this world, nor of the princes of this world, that come to naught;

7 But we speak the wisdom of God in a mystery, even the hidden wisdom, which God ordained before the world unto our glory;

8 Which none of the princes of this world knew; for had they known it, they would not have crucified the Lord of glory.

9 But as it is written, Eye hath not seen, nor ear heard, neither have entered into the heart of man, the things which God hath prepared for them that love him.

10 But God hath revealed them unto us by his Spirit; for the Spirit searcheth all things, yea, the deep things of God.

11 For what man knoweth the things of a man, save the spirit of man which is in him? even so the things of God knoweth no man, except he has the Spirit of God.

12 Now we have received, not the spirit of the world, but the Spirit which is of God; that we might know the things that are freely given to us of God.

13 Which things also we speak, not in the words which man's wisdom teacheth, but which the Holy Ghost teacheth; comparing spiritual things with spiritual.

14 But the natural man receiveth not the things of the Spirit of God; for they are foolishness unto him; neither can he know them, because they are spiritually discerned.

15 But he that is spiritual judgeth all things, yet he himself is judged of no man.

16 For who hath known the mind of the Lord, that he may instruct him? But we have the mind of Christ.

## CHAPTER 3

*Strife and division reproved—Ministers are God's fellow laborers—Christ the only foundation—The temples of God.*

1 And I, brethren, could not speak unto you as unto spiritual, but as unto carnal, even as unto babes in Christ.

2 I have fed you with milk, and not with meat; for hitherto ye were not able to receive it, neither yet now are ye able.

3 For ye are yet carnal; for whereas there is among you envying, and strife, and divisions, are ye not carnal, and walk as men?

4 For while one saith, I am of Paul, and another, I am of Apollos; are ye not carnal?

5 Who then is Paul, and who is Apollos, but ministers by whom ye believed, even as the Lord gave to every man?

6 I have planted, Apollos watered; but God gave the increase.

7 So then neither is he that planteth any thing, neither he that watereth; but God that giveth the increase.

8 Now he that planteth and he that watereth are one; and every man shall receive his own reward according to his own labour.

9 For we are labourers together with God; ye are God's husbandry, ye are God's building.

10 According to the grace of God which is given unto me, as a wise master builder, I have laid the foundation, and another buildeth thereon. But let every man take heed how he buildeth thereupon.

11 For other foundation can no man lay than that is laid, which is Jesus Christ.

12 Now if any man build upon this foundation gold, silver, precious stones, wood, hay, stubble;

13 Every man's work shall be made manifest; for the day shall declare it, because it shall be revealed by fire;

and the fire shall try every man's work of what sort it is.

14 If any man's work abide which he hath built thereupon, he shall receive a reward.

15 If any man's work shall be burned, he shall suffer loss; but he himself may be saved; yet so as by fire.

16 Know ye not that ye are the temple of God, and that the Spirit of God dwelleth in you?

17 If any man defile the temple of God, him shall God destroy; for the temple of God is holy, which temple ye are.

18 Let no man deceive himself. If any man among you seemeth to be wise in this world, let him become a fool, that he may be wise.

19 For the wisdom of this world is foolishness with God; for it is written, He taketh the wise in their own craftiness.

20 And again, The Lord knoweth the thoughts of the wise, that they are vain.

21 Therefore let no man glory in men; for all things are yours;

22 Whether Paul, or Apollos, or Cephas, or the world, or life, or death, or things present, or things to come; all are yours;

23 And ye are Christ's; and Christ is God's.

## CHAPTER 4

*In what manner ministers ought to be accounted of—The saints, though reproached, should be examples to the world.*

1 Let a man so account of us, as of the ministers of Christ, and stewards of the mysteries of God.

2 Moreover it is required of stewards, that a man be found faithful.

3 But with me it is a very small thing that I should be judged of you, or of man's judgment; yea, I judge not mine own self.

4 For though I know nothing against myself; yet I am not hereby justified; but he who judgeth me is the Lord.

5 Therefore I judge nothing before the time, until the Lord come, who both will bring to light the hidden things of darkness, and will make manifest the counsels of the hearts; and then shall every man have praise of God.

6 And these things, brethren, I have in a figure transferred to myself and to Apollos for your sakes; that ye might learn in us not to think of men above that which is written, that no one of you be puffed up for one against another.

7 For who maketh thee to differ from another? and what hast thou that thou didst not receive? now if thou didst receive it, why dost thou glory, as if thou hadst not received it?

8 Now ye are full, now ye are rich, ye have reigned as kings without us; and I would to God ye did reign, that we also might reign with you.

9 For I think that God hath set forth us the apostles last, as it were appointed to death; for we are made a spectacle unto the world, and to angels, and to men.

10 We are fools for Christ's sake, but ye are wise in Christ; we are weak, but ye are strong; ye are honorable, but we are despised.

11 Even unto this present hour we both hunger, and thirst, and are naked, and are buffeted, and have no certain dwelling place;

12 And labour, working with our own hands; being reviled, we bless; being persecuted, we suffer it;

13 Being defamed, we entreat; we are made as the filth of the world, and are the offscouring of all things unto this day.

14 I write not these things to shame you, but as my beloved sons I warn you.

15 For though ye have ten thousand instructors in Christ, yet have ye not many fathers, for in Christ Jesus I have begotten you through the gospel.

16 Wherefore I beseech you, be ye followers of me.

17 For this cause have I sent unto you Timotheus, who is my beloved son, and faithful in the Lord, who shall bring you into remembrance of my ways which be in Christ, as I teach everywhere in every church.

18 Now some are puffed up, as though I would not come to you.

19 But I will come to you shortly, if the Lord will, and will know, not the speech of them which are puffed up, but the power.

20 For the kingdom of God is not in word, but in power.

21 What will ye? shall I come unto

you with a rod, or in love, and in the spirit of meekness?

## CHAPTER 5

*The adulterer to be cast out—Saints must shun bad company.*

1 It is reported commonly that there is fornication among you, and such fornication as is not so much as named among the Gentiles, that one should have his father's wife.

2 And ye are puffed up, and have not rather mourned, that he that hath done this deed might be taken away from among you.

3 For verily, as absent in body but present in spirit, I have judged already him who hath so done this deed, as though I were present,

4 In the name of our Lord Jesus Christ, when ye are gathered together, and have the Spirit, with the power of our Lord Jesus Christ,

5 To deliver such a one unto Satan for the destruction of the flesh, that the spirit may be saved in the day of the Lord Jesus.

6 Your glorying is not good. Know ye not that a little leaven leaveneth the whole lump?

7 Purge out therefore the old leaven, that ye may be a new lump, as ye are unleavened. For even Christ our passover is sacrificed for us;

8 Therefore let us keep the feast, not with old leaven, neither with the leaven of malice and wickedness; but with the unleavened bread of sincerity and truth.

9 I wrote unto you in an epistle not to company with fornicators;

10 Yet not altogether with the fornicators of this world, or with the covetous, or extortioners, or with idolaters; for then must ye needs go out of the world.

11 But now I have written unto you not to keep company, if any man that is called a brother be a fornicator, or covetous, or an idolator, or a railer, or a drunkard, or an extortioner; with such a one, no, not to eat.

12 For what have I to do to judge them also that are without? do not they judge them that are within?

13 But them that are without, God judgeth. Therefore put away from among yourselves that wicked person.

## CHAPTER 6

*Saints should not go to law—The unrighteous shall not inherit the kingdom of God—Our bodies are the members of Christ, and temples of the Holy Ghost— They must not be defiled.*

1 Dare any of you, having a matter against another, go to law before the unjust, and not before the saints?

2 Do ye not know that the saints shall judge the world? and if the world shall be judged by you, are ye unworthy to judge the smallest matters?

3 Know ye not that we shall judge angels? how much more things that pertain to this life?

4 If then ye have judgments of things pertaining to this life, set them to judge who are least esteemed in the church.

5 I speak to your shame. Is it so, that there is not a wise man among you? no, not one that shall be able to judge between his brethren?

6 But brother goeth to law with brother, and that before the unbelievers.

7 Now therefore there is utterly a fault among you, because ye go to law one with another. Why do you not rather take wrong? Why do ye not rather suffer yourselves to be defrauded?

8 Nay, ye do wrong, and defraud, and that your brethren.

9 Know ye not that the unrighteous shall not inherit the kingdom of God? Be not deceived; neither fornicators, nor idolaters, nor adulterers, nor effeminate, nor abusers of themselves with mankind,

10 Nor thieves, nor covetous, nor drunkards, nor revilers, nor extortioners, shall inherit the kingdom of God.

11 And such were some of you; but ye are washed, but ye are sanctified, but ye are justified in the name of the Lord Jesus, and by the Spirit of our God.

12 All these things are not lawful unto me, and all these things are not expedient. All things are not lawful for me, therefore I will not be brought under the power of any.

13 Meats for the belly, and the belly for meats; but God shall destroy both it and them. Now the body is not for fornication, but for the Lord; and the Lord for the body.

14 And God hath both raised up the

Lord, and will also raise up us by his own power.

15 Know ye not that your bodies are the members of Christ? shall I then take the members of Christ, and make them the members of a harlot? God forbid.

16 What! know ye not that he which is joined to a harlot is one body? for two, saith he, shall be one flesh.

17 But he that is joined unto the Lord is one spirit.

18 Flee fornication. Every sin that a man committeth is against the body of Christ, and he who committeth fornication sinneth against his own body.

19 What! know ye not that your body is the temple of the Holy Ghost which is in you, which ye have of God, and ye are not your own?

20 For ye are bought with a price; therefore glorify God in your body, and in your spirit, which are God's.

## CHAPTER 7

*Paul treateth of virgins and widows.*

1 Now concerning the things whereof ye wrote unto me, saying, It is good for a man not to touch a woman.

2 Nevertheless, I say, to avoid fornication, let every man have his own wife, and let every woman have her own husband.

3 Let the husband render unto the wife due benevolence; and likewise also the wife unto the husband.

4 The wife hath not power of her own body, but the husband; and likewise also the husband hath not power of his own body, but the wife.

5 Depart ye not one from the other, except it be with consent for a time, that ye may give yourselves to fasting and prayer; and come together again, that Satan tempt you not for your incontinency.

6 And now what I speak is by permission, and not by commandment.

7 For I would that all men were even as myself. But every man hath his proper gift of God, one after this manner, and another after that.

8 I say therefore to the unmarried and widows, It is good for them if they abide even as I.

9 But if they cannot abide, let them marry; for it is better to marry than that any should commit sin.

10 And unto the married I command,

yet not I, but the Lord, Let not the wife depart from her husband;

11 But if she depart, let her remain unmarried, or be reconciled to her husband; but let not the husband put away his wife.

12 But to the rest speak I, not the Lord; If any brother hath a wife that believeth not, and she be pleased to dwell with him, let him not put her away.

13 And the woman which hath a husband that believeth not, and if he be pleased to dwell with her, let her not leave him.

14 For the unbelieving husband is sanctified by the wife, and the unbelieving wife is sanctified by the husband; else were your children unclean; but now are they holy.

15 But if the unbelieving depart, let him depart. A brother or a sister is not under bondage in such cases; but God hath called us to peace.

16 For what knowest thou, O wife, whether thou shalt save thy husband? or how knowest thou, O man, whether thou shalt save thy wife?

17 But as God hath distributed to every man, as the Lord hath called every one, so let him walk. And so ordain I in all churches.

18 Is any man called being circumcised? let him not become uncircumcised. Is any called in uncircumcision? let him not be circumcised.

19 Circumcision is nothing, and uncircumcision is nothing, but the keeping of the commandments of God.

20 Let every man abide in the same calling wherein he was called.

21 Art thou called being a servant? care not for it; but if thou mayest be made free, use it rather.

22 For he that is called in the Lord, being a servant, is the Lord's freeman; likewise also he that is called, being free, is Christ's servant.

23 Ye are bought with a price; be not ye the servants of men.

24 Brethren, let every man, wherein he is called, therein abide with God.

25 Now concerning virgins I have no commandment of the Lord; yet I give my judgment, as one that hath obtained mercy of the Lord to be faithful.

26 I suppose therefore that this is good for the present distress, for a man so to remain that he may do greater good.

27 Art thou bound unto a wife? seek not to be loosed. Art thou loosed from a wife? seek not a wife.

28 But if thou marry, thou hast not sinned; and if a virgin marry, she hath not sinned. Nevertheless, such shall have trouble in the flesh. For I spare you not.

29 But I speak unto you who are called unto the ministry. For this I say, brethren, the time that remaineth is but short, that ye shall be sent forth unto the ministry. Even they who have wives, shall be as though they had none; for ye are called and chosen to do the Lord's work.

30 And it shall be with them who weep, as though they wept not; and them who rejoice, as though they rejoiced not, and them who buy, as though they possessed not;

31 And them who use this world, as not using it; for the fashion of this world passeth away.

32 But I would, brethren, that ye magnify your calling. I would have you without carefulness. For he who is unmarried, careth for the things that belong to the Lord, how he may please the Lord; therefore he prevaileth.

33 But he who is married, careth for the things that are of the world, how he may please his wife; therefore there is a difference, for he is hindered.

34 There is a difference also, between a wife and a virgin. The unmarried woman careth for the things of the Lord, that she may be holy both in body and in spirit; but she that is married careth for the things of the world, how she may please her husband.

35 And this I speak for your own profit; not that I may cast a snare upon you, but for that which is comely, and that ye may attend upon the Lord without distraction.

36 But if any man think that he behaveth himself uncomely toward his virgin whom he hath espoused, if she pass the flower of age, and need so require, let him do what he hath promised, he sinneth not; let them marry.

37 Nevertheless he that standeth steadfast in his heart, having no necessity, but hath power over his own will, and hath so decreed in his heart that he will keep his virgin, doeth well.

38 So then he that giveth himself in marriage doeth well; but he that giveth himself not in marriage doeth better.

39 The wife is bound by the law as long as her husband liveth; but if her husband be dead, she is at liberty to be married to whom she will; only in the Lord.

40 But she is happier if she so abide, after my judgment; and I think also that I have the Spirit of God.

## CHAPTER 8

*To abstain from meats offered to idols—Charity enjoined.*

1 Now as touching things offered unto idols, we know that we all have knowledge. Knowledge puffeth up, but charity edifieth.

2 And if any man think that he knoweth any thing, he knoweth nothing yet as he ought to know.

3 But if any man love God, the same is known of him.

4 As concerning therefore the eating of those things which are in the world offered in sacrifice unto idols, we know that an idol is nothing, and that there is none other God but one.

5 For though there be that are called gods, whether in heaven or in earth, (as there be gods many, and lords many,)

6 But to us there is but one God, the Father, of whom are all things, and we in him; and one Lord Jesus Christ, by whom are all things, and we by him.

7 Howbeit there is not in every man that knowledge; for some with conscience of the idol unto this hour eat it as a thing offered unto an idol, and their conscience being weak is defiled.

8 But meat commendeth us not to God; for neither, if we eat, are we the better; neither, if we eat not, are we the worse.

9 But take heed lest by any means this liberty of yours become a stumbling block to them that are weak.

10 For if any man see thee which hast knowledge sit at meat in the idol's temple, shall not the conscience of him which is weak be emboldened to eat those things which are offered to idols;

11 And through thy knowledge shall the weak brother perish, for whom Christ died?

12 But when ye sin so against the brethren, and wound their weak conscience, ye sin against Christ.

13 Wherefore, if meat make my brother to offend, I will eat no flesh while the world standeth, lest I make my brother to offend.

## CHAPTER 9

*The minister to live by the gospel—The Christian race.*

1 Am I not an apostle? am I not free? have I not seen Jesus Christ our Lord? are not ye my work in the Lord?

2 If I be not an apostle unto others, yet doubtless I am to you; for the seal of mine apostleship are ye in the Lord.

3 Mine answer to them that do examine me is this;

4 Have we not power to eat and to drink?

5 Have we not power to lead about a sister, a wife, as well as other apostles, and as the brethren of the Lord, and Cephas?

6 Or I only and Barnabas, have not we power to forbear working?

7 Who goeth a warfare any time at his own charges? who planteth a vineyard, and eateth not of the fruit thereof? or who feedeth a flock, and eateth not of the milk of the flock?

8 Say I these things as a man? or saith not the law the same also?

9 For it is written in the law of Moses, Thou shalt not muzzle the mouth of the ox that treadeth out the corn. Doth God take care for oxen?

10 Or saith he it altogether for our sakes? For our sakes, no doubt, this is written; that he that plougheth should plough in hope; and that he that thresheth in hope should be partaker of his hope.

11 If we have sown unto you spiritual things, is it a great thing if we shall reap your carnal things?

12 If others be partakers of this power over you, are not we rather? Nevertheless we have not used this power; but suffer all things, lest we should hinder the gospel of Christ.

13 Do ye not know that they which minister about holy things live of the things of the temple? and they which wait at the altar are partakers with the altar?

14 Even so hath the Lord ordained that they which preach the gospel shall live of the gospel.

15 But I have used none of these things; neither have I written these things, that it should be so done unto me; for it were better for me to die, than that any man should make my glorying void.

16 For though I preach the gospel, I have nothing to glory of; for necessity is laid upon me; yea, woe is unto me, if I preach not the gospel!

17 For if I do this thing willingly, I have a reward; but if against my will, a dispensation of the gospel is committed unto me.

18 What is my reward then? Verily that, when I preach the gospel, I may make the gospel of Christ without charge, that I abuse not my power in the gospel.

19 For though I be free from all men, yet have I made myself servant unto all, that I might gain the more.

20 And unto the Jews I became as a Jew, that I might gain the Jews; to them that are under the law, as under the law, that I might gain them that are under the law;

21 To them that are without law, as without law, (being not without law to God, but under law to Christ,) that I might gain them that are without law.

22 To the weak became I as weak, that I might gain the weak; I am made all things to all men, that I might by all means save some.

23 And this I do for the gospel's sake, that I might be partaker thereof with you.

24 Know ye not that they which run in a race all run, but only one receiveth the prize? So run, that ye may obtain.

25 And every man that striveth for the mastery is temperate in all things. Now they do it to obtain a corruptible crown; but we an incorruptible.

26 I therefore so run, not as uncertainly; so fight I, not as one that beateth the air;

27 But I keep under my body, and bring it into subjection; lest that by any means, when I have preached to others, I myself should be a castaway.

## CHAPTER 10

*The cloud, the sea, the manna and the spiritual Rock—Israel's punishment our warnings.*

1 Moreover, brethren, I would not that ye should be ignorant, how that all our fathers were under the cloud, and all passed through the sea;

2 And were all baptized unto Moses in the cloud and in the sea;

3 And did all eat the same spiritual meat;

4 And did all drink the same spiritual drink; for they drank of that spiritual Rock that followed them; and that Rock was Christ.

5 But with many of them God was not well pleased; for they were overthrown in the wilderness.

6 Now these things were our examples, to the intent we should not lust after evil things, as they also lusted.

7 Neither be ye idolaters, as were some of them; as it is written, The people sat down to eat and drink, and rose up to play.

8 Neither let us commit fornication, as some of them committed, and fell in one day three and twenty thousand.

9 Neither let us tempt Christ, as some of them also tempted, and were destroyed of serpents.

10 Neither murmur ye, as some of them also murmured, and were destroyed of the destroyer.

11 Now, all these things happened unto them for ensamples; and they were written for our admonition also, and for an admonition for those upon whom the end of the world shall come.

12 Wherefore let him that thinketh he standeth take heed lest he fall.

13 There hath no temptation taken you but such as is common to man; but God is faithful, who will not suffer you to be tempted above that ye are able; but will with the temptation also make a way to escape, that ye may be able to bear it.

14 Wherefore, my dearly beloved, flee from idolatry.

15 I speak as to wise men; judge ye what I say.

16 The cup of blessing which we bless, is it not the communion of the blood of Christ? The bread which we break, is it not the communion of the body of Christ?

17 For we being many are one bread, and one body; for we are all partakers of that one bread.

18 Behold Israel after the flesh; are not they which eat of the sacrifices partakers of the altar?

19 What say I then? that the idol is anything, or that which is offered in sacrifice to idols is anything?

20 But I say, that the things which the Gentiles sacrifice, they sacrifice to devils, and not to God; and I would not that ye should have fellowship with devils.

21 Ye cannot drink the cup of the Lord, and the cup of devils; ye cannot be partakers of the Lord's table, and of the table of devils.

22 Do we provoke the Lord to jealousy? are we stronger than he?

23 All things are not lawful for me, for all things are not expedient; all things are not lawful, for all things edify not.

24 Let no man seek therefore his own, but every man another's good.

25 Whatsoever is sold in the shambles, that eat, asking no questions for conscience' sake;

26 For the earth is the Lord's, and the fullness thereof.

27 If any of them that believe not bid you to a feast, and ye be disposed to eat; whatsoever is set before you, eat, asking no questions for conscience' sake.

28 But if any man say unto you, This is offered in sacrifice unto idols, eat not for his sake that showed it, and for conscience' sake; for the earth is the Lord's, and the fullness thereof;

29 Conscience, I say, not thine own, but of the other; for why is my liberty judged of another man's conscience?

30 For if I by grace be a partaker, why am I evil spoken of for that for which I give thanks?

31 Whether therefore ye eat, or drink, or whatsoever ye do, do all to the glory of God.

32 Give none offense, neither to the Jews, nor to the Gentiles, nor to the church of God;

33 Even as I please all men in all things, not seeking mine own profit, but of the many, that they may be saved.

## CHAPTER 11

*The woman subject to man; man subject to Christ; Christ subject to God—The sacrament treated of.*

1 Be ye followers of me, even as I also am of Christ.

2 Now I praise you, brethren, that ye remember me in all things, and keep the ordinances, as I delivered them to you.

3 But I would have you know, that the head of every man is Christ; and

the head of the woman is the man; and the head of Christ is God.

4 Every man praying or prophesying, having his head covered, dishonoreth his head.

5 But every woman that prayeth or prophesieth with her head uncovered dishonoreth her head; for that is even all one as if she were shaven.

6 For if the woman be not covered, let her also be shorn; but if it be a shame for a woman to be shorn or shaven, let her be covered.

7 For a man indeed ought not to cover his head, forasmuch as he is the image and glory of God; but the woman is the glory of the man.

8 For the man is not of the woman; but the woman of the man.

9 Neither was the man created for the woman; but the woman for the man.

10 For this cause ought the woman to have a covering on her head because of the angels.

11 Nevertheless neither is the man without the woman, neither the woman without the man, in the Lord.

12 For as the woman is of the man, even so is the man also by the woman; but all things of God.

13 Judge in yourselves; is it comely that a woman pray unto God uncovered?

14 Doth not even nature itself teach you, that, if a man have long hair, it is a shame unto him?

15 But if a woman have long hair, it is a glory to her; for her hair is given her for a covering.

16 But if any man seem to be contentious, we have no such custom, neither the churches of God.

17 Now in this that I declare unto you I praise you not, that ye come together not for the better, but for the worse.

18 For first of all, when ye come together in the church, I hear that there be divisions among you; and I partly believe it.

19 For there must be also divisions among you, that they which are approved may be made manifest among you.

20 When ye come together into one place, is it not to eat the Lord's supper?

21 But in eating every one taketh before his own supper; and one is hungry, and another is drunken.

22 What! have ye not houses to eat and to drink in? or despise ye the church of God, and shame them that have not? What shall I say to you? shall I praise you in this? I praise you not.

23 For I have received of the Lord that which also I delivered unto you, That the Lord Jesus, the same night in which he was betrayed, took bread;

24 And when he had given thanks, he brake it, and said, Take, eat; this is my body, which is broken for you; this do in remembrance of me.

25 After the same manner also he took the cup, when he had supped, saying, This cup is the new testament in my blood; this do ye, as oft as ye drink it, in remembrance of me.

26 For as often as ye eat this bread, and drink this cup, ye do show the Lord's death till he come.

27 Wherefore whosoever shall eat this bread, and drink this cup of the Lord, unworthily, shall be guilty of the body and blood of the Lord.

28 But let a man examine himself, and so let him eat of that bread, and drink of that cup.

29 For he that eateth and drinketh unworthily, eateth and drinketh condemnation to himself, not discerning the Lord's body.

30 For this cause many are weak and sickly among you, and many sleep.

31 For if we would judge ourselves, we should not be judged.

32 But when we are judged, we are chastened of the Lord, that we should not be condemned with the world.

33 Wherefore, my brethren, when ye come together to eat, tarry one for another.

34 And if any man hunger, let him eat at home; that ye come not together unto condemnation. And the rest will I set in order when I come.

## CHAPTER 12

*Spiritual gifts—Their object—The unity of the body of Christ, and the officers of the church.*

1 Now concerning spiritual things, brethren, I would not have you ignorant.

2 Ye know that ye were Gentiles, carried away unto these dumb idols, even as ye were led.

3 Wherefore I give you to understand, that no man speaking by the Spirit of God calleth Jesus accursed; and that no man can know that Jesus is the Lord, but by the Holy Ghost.

4 Now there are diversities of gifts, but the same Spirit.

5 And there are differences of administrations, but the same Lord.

6 And there are diversities of operations, but it is the same God which worketh all in all.

7 But the manifestation of the Spirit is given to every man to profit withal.

8 For to one is given by the Spirit the word of wisdom; to another the word of knowledge by the same Spirit;

9 To another faith by the same Spirit; to another the gifts of healing by the same Spirit;

10 To another the working of miracles; to another prophecy; to another discerning of spirits; to another divers kinds of tongues; to another the interpretation of tongues;

11 But all these worketh that one and the selfsame Spirit, dividing to every man severally as he will.

12 For as the body is one, and hath many members, and all the members of that one body, being many, are one body; so also is Christ.

13 For by one Spirit are we all baptized into one body, whether we be Jews or Gentiles, whether we be bond or free; and have been all made to drink into one Spirit.

14 For the body is not one member, but many.

15 If the foot shall say, Because I am not the hand, I am not of the body; is it therefore not of the body?

16 And if the ear shall say, Because I am not the eye, I am not of the body; is it therefore not of the body?

17 If the whole body were an eye, where were the hearing? If the whole were hearing, where were the smelling?

18 But now hath God set the members every one of them in the body, as it hath pleased him.

19 And if they were all one member, where were the body?

20 But now are they many members, yet but one body.

21 And the eye cannot say unto the hand, I have no need of thee; nor again the head to the feet, I have no need of you.

22 Nay, much more those members of the body, which seem to be more feeble, are necessary;

23 And those members of the body, which we think to be less honorable, upon these we bestow more abundant honor; and our uncomely parts have more abundant comeliness.

24 For our comely parts have no need; but God hath tempered the body together, having given more abundant honor to that part which lacked;

25 That there should be no schism in the body; but that the members should have the same care one for another.

26 And whether one member suffer, all the members suffer with it; or one member be honored, all the members rejoice with it.

27 Now ye are the body of Christ, and members in particular.

28 And God hath set some in the church, first apostles, secondarily prophets, thirdly teachers, after that miracles, then gifts of healings, helps, governments, diversities of tongues.

29 Are all apostles? are all prophets? are all teachers? are all workers of miracles?

30 Have all the gifts of healing? do all speak with tongues? do all interpret?

31 I say unto you, Nay; for I have shown unto you a more excellent way, therefore covet earnestly the best gifts.

## CHAPTER 13

*Of faith, hope, perfection, and charity.*

1 Though I speak with the tongues of men and of angels, and have not charity, I am become as sounding brass, or a tinkling cymbal.

2 And though I have the gift of prophecy, and understand all mysteries, and all knowledge; and though I have all faith, so that I could remove mountains, and have not charity, I am nothing.

3 And though I bestow all my goods to feed the poor, and though I give my body to be burned, and have not charity, it profiteth me nothing.

4 Charity suffereth long, and is kind; charity envieth not; charity vaunteth not itself, is not puffed up,

5 Doth not behave itself unseemly, seeketh not her own, is not easily provoked, thinketh no evil;

6 Rejoiceth not in iniquity, but rejoiceth in the truth;

7 Beareth all things, believeth all

things, hopeth all things, endureth all things.

8 Charity never faileth; but whether there be prophecies, they shall fail; whether there be tongues, they shall cease; whether there be knowledge, it shall vanish away.

9 For we know in part, and we prophesy in part.

10 But when that which is perfect is come, then that which is in part shall be done away.

11 When I was a child, I spake as a child, I understood as a child, I thought as a child; but when I became a man, I put away childish things.

12 For now we see through a glass, darkly; but then face to face; now I know in part; but then shall I know even as also I am known.

13 And now abideth faith, hope, charity, these three; but the greatest of these is charity.

## CHAPTER 14

*Edification, the object of spiritual gifts— Women are forbidden to rule in the church.*

1 Follow after charity, and desire spiritual gifts, but rather that ye may prophesy.

2 For he that speaketh in another tongue speaketh not unto men, but unto God; for no man understandeth him; howbeit in the spirit he speaketh mysteries.

3 But he that prophesieth speaketh unto men to edification, and exhortation, and comfort.

4 He that speaketh in another tongue edifieth himself; but he that prophesieth edifieth the church.

5 I would that ye all spake with tongues, but rather that ye prophesied; for greater is he that prophesieth than he that speaketh with tongues, except he interpret, that the church may receive edifying.

6 Now, brethren, if I come unto you speaking with tongues, what shall I profit you, except I shall speak to you either by revelation, or by knowledge, or by prophesying, or by doctrine?

7 And even things without lifegiving sound, whether pipe or harp, except they give a distinction in the sounds, how shall it be known what is piped or harped?

8 For if the trumpet give an uncer-tain sound, who shall prepare himself to the battle?

9 So likewise ye, except ye utter by the tongue words easy to be under-stood, how shall it be known what is spoken? for ye shall speak into the air.

10 There are, it may be, so many kinds of voices in the world, and none of them is without signification.

11 Therefore if I know not the meaning of the voice, I shall be unto him that speaketh a barbarian, and he that speaketh shall be a barbarian unto me.

12 Even so ye, forasmuch as ye are zealous of spiritual gifts, seek that ye may excel to the edifying of the church.

13 Wherefore let him that speaketh in another tongue pray that he may interpret.

14 For if I pray in another tongue, my spirit prayeth, but my understanding is unfruitful.

15 What is it then? I will pray with the spirit, and I will pray with the understanding also; I will sing with the spirit, and I will sing with the understanding also.

16 Else, when thou shalt bless with the spirit, how shall he that occupieth the room of the unlearned say Amen at thy giving of thanks, seeing he understandeth not what thou sayest?

17 For thou verily givest thanks well, but the other is not edified.

18 I thank my God, I speak with tongues more than ye all;

19 Yet in the church I had rather speak five words with my understanding, that by my voice I might teach others also, than ten thousand words in another tongue.

20 Brethren, be not children in understanding; howbeit in malice be ye children, but in understanding be men.

21 In the law, it is written, With men of other tongues and other lips will I speak unto this people: and yet for all that will they not hear me, saith the Lord.

22 Wherefore tongues are for a sign, not to them that believe, but to them that believe not; but prophesying serveth not for them that believe not, but for them which believe.

23 If therefore the whole church be come together into one place, and all speak with tongues, and there come in those that are unlearned, or unbelievers, will they not say that ye are mad?

24 But if all prophesy, and there

come in one that believeth not, or one unlearned, he is convinced of all, he is judged of all;

25 And thus are the secrets of his heart made manifest; and so falling down on his face he will worship God, and report that God is in you of a truth.

26 How is it then, brethren? when ye come together, every one of you hath a psalm, hath a doctrine, hath a tongue, hath a revelation, hath an interpretation. Let all things be done unto edifying.

27 If any man speak in another tongue, let it be by two, or at the most by three, and that by course; and let one interpret.

28 But if there be no interpreter, let him keep silence in the church; and let him speak to himself, and to God.

29 Let the prophets speak two or three, and let the other judge.

30 If any thing be revealed to another that sitteth by, let the first hold his peace.

31 For ye may all prophesy one by one, that all may learn, and all may be comforted.

32 And the spirits of the prophets are subject to the prophets.

33 For God is not the author of confusion, but of peace, as in all churches of the saints.

34 Let your women keep silence in the churches; for it is not permitted unto them to rule; but to be under obedience, as also saith the law.

35 And if they will learn any thing, let them ask their husbands at home; for it is a shame for women to rule in the church.

36 What! came the word of God out from you? or came it unto you only?

37 If any man think himself to be a prophet, or spiritual, let him acknowledge that the things that I write unto you are the commandments of the Lord.

38 But if any man be ignorant, let him be ignorant.

39 Wherefore, brethren, covet to prophesy, and forbid not to speak with tongues.

40 Let all things be done decently and in order.

## CHAPTER 15

*The resurrection.*

1 Moreover, brethren, I declare unto you the gospel which I preached unto you, which also ye have received, and wherein ye stand;

2 By which also ye are saved, if ye keep in memory what I preached unto you, unless ye have believed in vain.

3 For I delivered unto you first of all that which I also received, how that Christ died for our sins according to the scriptures;

4 And that he was buried, and that he rose again the third day according to the scriptures;

5 And that he was seen of Cephas, then of the twelve;

6 After that, he was seen of about five hundred brethren at once; of whom the greater part remain unto this present, but some are fallen asleep.

7 After that, he was seen of James, then of all the apostles.

8 And last of all he was seen of me also, as of one born out of due time.

9 For I am the least of the apostles, that am not meet to be called an apostle, because I persecuted the church of God.

10 But by the grace of God I am what I am; and his grace which was bestowed upon me was not in vain; for I labored more abundantly than they all; yet not I, but the grace of God which was with me.

11 Therefore whether it were I or they, so we preach, and so ye believed.

12 Now if Christ be preached that he rose from the dead, how say some among you that there is no resurrection of the dead?

13 But if there be no resurrection of the dead, then is Christ not risen;

14 And if Christ be not risen, then is our preaching vain, and your faith is also vain.

15 Yea, and we are found false witnesses of God; because we have testified of God that he raised up Christ; whom he raised not up, if so be that the dead rise not.

16 For if the dead rise not, then is not Christ raised;

17 And if Christ be not raised, your faith is vain; ye are yet in your sins.

18 Then they also which are fallen asleep in Christ are perished.

19 If in this life only we have hope in Christ, we are of all men most miserable.

20 But now is Christ risen from the

dead, and become the firstfruits of them that slept.

21 For since by man came death, by man came also the resurrection of the dead.

22 For as in Adam all die, even so in Christ shall all be made alive.

23 But every man in his own order; Christ the firstfruits; afterward they that are Christ's at his coming.

24 Afterward cometh the end, when he shall have delivered up the kingdom to God, even the Father; when he shall have put down all rule, and all authority and power.

25 For he must reign, till he hath put all enemies under his feet.

26 The last enemy, death, shall be destroyed.

27 For he saith, When it is manifest that he hath put all things under his feet, and that all things are put under, he is excepted of the Father who did put all things under him.

28 And when all things shall be subdued unto him, then shall the Son also himself be subject unto him that put all things under him, that God may be all in all.

29 Else what shall they do which are baptized for the dead, if the dead rise not at all? Why are they then baptized for the dead?

30 And why stand we in jeopardy every hour?

31 I protest unto you the resurrection of the dead; and this is my rejoicing which I have in Christ Jesus our Lord daily, though I die.

32 If after the manner of men I have fought with beasts at Ephesus, what advantageth it me, if the dead rise not? let us eat and drink; for tomorrow we die.

33 Be not deceived; evil communications corrupt good manners.

34 Awake to righteousness, and sin not; for some have not the knowledge of God; I speak this to your shame.

35 But some man will say, How are the dead raised up? and with what body do they come?

36 Thou fool, that which thou sowest is not quickened, except it die;

37 And that which thou sowest, thou sowest not that body which shall be, but grain, it may be of wheat, or some other;

38 But God giveth it a body as it hath pleased him, and to every seed his own body.

39 All flesh is not the same flesh; but there is one kind of flesh of men, another flesh of beasts, another of fishes, and another of birds.

40 Also celestial bodies, and bodies terrestial, and bodies telestial; but the glory of the celestial, one; and the terrestial, another; and the telestial, another.

41 There is one glory of the sun, and another glory of the moon, and another glory of the stars; for one star differeth from another star in glory.

42 So also is the resurrection of the dead. It is sown in corruption, it is raised in incorruption;

43 It is sown in dishonor, it is raised in glory; it is sown in weakness, it is raised in power;

44 It is sown a natural body, it is raised a spiritual body. There is a natural body, and there is a spiritual body.

45 And so it is written, The first man Adam was made a living soul; the last Adam was made a quickening spirit.

46 Howbeit, that which is natural first, and not that which is spiritual; but afterwards, that which is spiritual;

47 The first man is of the earth, earthy; the second man is the Lord from heaven.

48 As is the earthy, such are they also that are earthy; and as is the heavenly, such are they also that are heavenly.

49 And as we have borne the image of the earthy, we shall also bear the image of the heavenly.

50 Now this I say, brethren, that flesh and blood cannot inherit the kingdom of God; neither doth corruption inherit incorruption.

51 Behold, I show you a mystery; We shall not all sleep, but we shall all be changed,

52 In a moment, in the twinkling of an eye, at the sound of the last trump; for the trumpet shall sound, and the dead shall be raised incorruptible, and we shall be changed.

53 For this corruptible must put on incorruption, and this mortal must put on immortality.

54 So when this corruptible shall have put on incorruption, and this mortal shall have put on immortality,

then shall be brought to pass the saying that is written, Death is swallowed up in victory.

55 O death, where is thy sting? O grave, where is thy victory?

56 The sting of death is sin; and the strength of sin is the law.

57 But thanks be to God, which giveth us the victory through our Lord Jesus Christ.

58 Therefore, my beloved brethren, be ye steadfast, unmovable, always abounding in the work of the Lord, forasmuch as ye know that your labor is not in vain in the Lord.

## CHAPTER 16

*Offerings solicited—Commendeth Timothy—Friendly admonitions.*

1 Now concerning the collection for the saints, as I have given order to the churches at Galatia, even so do ye.

2 Upon the first day of the week let every one of you lay by him in store, as God hath prospered him, that there be no gatherings when I come.

3 And when I come, whomsoever ye shall approve by your letters, them will I send to bring your liberality unto Jerusalem.

4 And if it be meet that I go also, they shall go with me.

5 Now I will come unto you, when I shall pass through Macedonia; for I do pass through Macedonia.

6 And it may be that I will abide, yea, and winter with you, that ye may bring me on my journey whithersoever I go.

7 For I will not see you now by the way; but I trust to tarry a while with you, if the Lord permit.

8 But I will tarry at Ephesus until Pentecost.

9 For a great door and effectual is opened unto me, but there are many adversaries.

10 Now if Timotheus come, see that he may be with you without fear; for he worketh the work of the Lord, as I also do.

11 Let no man therefore despise him; but conduct him forth in peace, that he may come unto me; for I look for him with the brethren.

12 As touching our brother Apollos, I greatly desired him to come unto you with the brethren; but his will was not at all to come at this time; but he will come when he shall have convenient time.

13 Watch ye, stand fast in the faith, quit you like men, be strong.

14 Let all your things be done with charity.

15 I beseech you, brethren, (ye know the house of Stephanas, that it is the firstfruits of Achaia, and that they have addicted themselves to the ministry of the saints,)

16 That ye submit yourselves unto such, and to every one that helpeth with us, and laboreth.

17 I am glad of the coming of Stephanas and Fortunatus and Achaicus; for that which was lacking on your part they have supplied.

18 For they have refreshed my spirit and yours; therefore acknowledge ye them that are such.

19 The churches of Asia salute you. Aquila and Priscilla salute you much in the Lord, with the church that is in their house.

20 All the brethren greet you. Greet ye one another with a holy salutation.

21 The salutation of me Paul with mine own hand.

22 If any man love not the Lord Jesus Christ, let him be Anathema, Maranatha.

23 The grace of our Lord Jesus Christ be with you.

24 My love be with you all in Christ Jesus. Amen.

The first epistle to the Corinthians was written from Philippi by Stephanas, and Fortunatus, and Achaicus, and Timotheus.

---

## The Second Epistle of Paul the Apostle to the
# Corinthians

## CHAPTER 1

*The apostle encourageth them against troubles—His sincere manner of preaching the gospel—The earnest of the Spirit.*

1 Paul, an apostle of Jesus Christ by

the will of God, and Timothy our brother, unto the church of God which is at Corinth, with all the saints which are in all Achaia;

2 Grace be to you, and peace, from God our Father, and from the Lord Jesus Christ.

3 Blessed be God, even the Father of our Lord Jesus Christ, the Father of mercies, and the God of all comfort;

4 Who comforteth us in all our tribulation, that we may be able to comfort them which are in any trouble, by the comfort wherewith we ourselves are comforted of God.

5 For as the sufferings of Christ abound in us, so our consolation also aboundeth by Christ.

6 And whether we be afflicted, it is for your consolation and salvation, which is effectual in the enduring of the same sufferings which we also suffer; or whether we be comforted, it is for your consolation and salvation.

7 And our hope of you is steadfast, knowing, that as ye are partakers of the sufferings, so shall ye be also of the consolation.

8 For we would not, brethren, have you ignorant of our trouble which came to us in Asia, that we were pressed out of measure, above strength, insomuch that we despaired even of life;

9 But we had the sentence of death in ourselves, that we should not trust in ourselves, but in God which raiseth the dead;

10 Who delivered us from so great a death, and doth deliver; in whom we trust that he will yet deliver us;

11 Ye also helping together by prayer for us, that for the gift bestowed upon us by the means of many persons thanks may be given by many on our behalf.

12 For our rejoicing is this, the testimony of our conscience, that in simplicity and godly sincerity, not with fleshly wisdom, but by the grace of God, we have had our conversation in the world, and more abundantly to you-ward.

13 For we write none other things unto you, than what ye read or acknowledge; and I trust ye shall acknowledge even to the end;

14 As also ye have acknowledged us in part, that we are your rejoicing, even as ye also are ours in the day of the Lord Jesus.

15 And in this confidence I was minded to come unto you before, that ye might have a second benefit;

16 And to pass by you into Macedonia, and to come again out of Macedonia unto you, and of you to be brought on my way toward Judea.

17 When I therefore was thus minded, did I use lightness? or the things that I purpose, do I purpose according to the flesh, that with me there shall be yea, yea, and nay, nay?

18 But as God is true, our word toward you was not yea and nay.

19 For the Son of God, Jesus Christ, who was preached among you by us, even by me and Silvanus and Timotheus, was not yea and nay, but in him was yea.

20 For all the promises of God in him are yea, and in him Amen, unto the glory of God by us.

21 Now he which stablisheth us with you in Christ, and hath anointed us, is God.

22 Who hath also sealed us, and given the earnest of the Spirit in our hearts.

23 Moreover I call God for a record upon my soul, that to spare you I came not as yet unto Corinth.

24 Not for that we have dominion over your faith, but are helpers of your joy; for by faith ye stand.

## CHAPTER 2

*Of forgiveness—The minister the savor of Christ.*

1 But I determined this with myself, that I would not come again to you in heaviness.

2 For if I make you sorry, who is he then that maketh me glad, but the same which is made sorry by me?

3 And I wrote this same unto you, lest, when I came, I should have sorrow from them of whom I ought to rejoice; having confidence in you all, that my joy is the joy of you all.

4 For out of much affliction and anguish of heart I wrote unto you with many tears; not that ye should be grieved, but that ye might know the love which I have more abundantly unto you.

5 But if any have caused grief, he hath not grieved me, but in part; that I may not overcharge you all.

6 Sufficient to such a man is this punishment, which was inflicted of many.

7 So that contrariwise ye ought rather to forgive him, and comfort him, lest perhaps such a one should be swallowed up with overmuch sorrow.

8 Wherefore I beseech you that ye would confirm your love toward him.

9 For to this end also did I write, that I might know the proof of you, whether ye be obedient in all things.

10 To whom ye forgive any thing, I forgive also; for if I forgave any thing, to whom I forgave it, for your sakes forgave I it in the person of Christ;

11 Lest Satan should get an advantage of us; for we are not ignorant of his devices.

12 Furthermore, when I came to Troas to preach Christ's gospel, and a door was opened unto me of the Lord,

13 I had no rest in my spirit, because I found not Titus my brother; but taking my leave of them, I went from thence into Macedonia.

14 Now thanks be unto God, which always causeth us to triumph in Christ, and makest manifest the savor of his knowledge by us in every place.

15 For we are unto God a sweet savor of Christ, in them that are saved, and in them that perish;

16 To the one we are the savor of death unto death; and to the other the savor of life unto life. And who is sufficient for these things?

17 For we are not as many, which corrupt the word of God; but as of sincerity, but as of God, in the sight of God speak we in Christ.

## CHAPTER 3

*Office work of the Spirit—The Spirit, liberty.*

1 Do we begin again to commend ourselves? or need we, as some others, epistles of commendation to you, or letters of commendation from you?

2 Ye are our epistle written in our hearts, known and read of all men;

3 Forasmuch as ye are manifestly declared to be the epistle of Christ ministered by us, written not with ink, but with the Spirit of the living God; not in tables of stone, but in fleshly tables of the heart.

4 And such trust have we through Christ toward God.

5 Not that we are sufficient of ourselves to think any thing as of ourselves; but our sufficiency is of God;

6 Who also hath made us able ministers of the new testament; not of the letter, but of the Spirit; for the letter killeth, but the Spirit giveth life.

7 But if the ministration of death, written and engraven in stones, was glorious, so that the children of Israel could not steadfastly behold the face of Moses for the glory of his countenance; which glory was to be done away;

8 How shall not the ministration of the Spirit be rather glorious?

9 For if the ministration of condemnation be glory, much more doth the ministration of righteousness exceed in glory.

10 For even that which was made glorious had no glory in this respect, by reason of the glory that excelleth.

11 For if that which is done away was glorious, much more that which remaineth is glorious.

12 Seeing then that we have such hope, we use great plainness of speech;

13 And not as Moses, which put a veil over his face, that the children of Israel could not steadfastly look to the end of that which is abolished;

14 But their minds were blinded; for until this day remaineth the same veil untaken away in the reading of the old testament; which veil is done away in Christ.

15 But even unto this day, when Moses is read, the veil is upon their heart.

16 Nevertheless, when their heart shall turn to the Lord, the veil shall be taken away.

17 Now the Lord is that Spirit; and where the Spirit of the Lord is, there is liberty.

18 But we all, with open face beholding as in a glass the glory of the Lord, are changed into the same image from glory to glory, even as by the Spirit of the Lord.

## CHAPTER 4

*Paul's manner of preaching the gospel— His faithfulness in tribulation.*

1 Therefore, seeing we have this ministry, as we have received mercy, we faint not;

2 But have renounced the hidden things of dishonesty, not walking in craftiness, nor handling the word of God deceitfully; but, by manifestation

of the truth, commending ourselves to every man's conscience in the sight of God.

3 But if our gospel be hid, it is hid to them that are lost;

4 In whom the god of this world hath blinded the minds of them which believe not, lest the light of the glorious gospel of Christ, who is the image of God, should shine unto them.

5 For we preach not ourselves, but Christ Jesus the Lord; and ourselves your servants for Jesus' sake.

6 For God, who commanded the light to shine out of darkness, hath shined in our hearts, to give the light of the knowledge of the glory of God in the face of Jesus Christ.

7 But we have this treasure in earthen vessels, that the excellency of the power may be of God, and not of us.

8 We are troubled on every side, yet not distressed; we are perplexed, but not in despair;

9 Persecuted, but not forsaken; cast down, but not destroyed;

10 Always bearing about in the body the dying of the Lord Jesus, that the life also of Jesus might be made manifest in our body.

11 For we which live are alway delivered unto death for Jesus' sake, that the life also of Jesus might be made manifest in our mortal flesh.

12 So then it worketh death unto us, but life unto you.

13 We having the same spirit of faith, according as it is written, I believed, and therefore have I spoken; we also believe, and therefore speak;

14 Knowing that he which raised up the Lord Jesus shall raise up us also by Jesus, and shall present us with you.

15 For we bear all things for your sakes, that the abundant grace might, through the thanksgiving of many, redound to the glory of God.

16 For which cause we faint not; but though our outward man perish, yet the inward man is renewed day by day.

17 For our light affliction, which is but for a moment, worketh for us a far more exceeding and eternal weight of glory;

18 While we look not at the things which are seen, but at the things which are not seen; for the things which are seen are temporal; but the things which are not seen are eternal.

## CHAPTER 5

*Paul's hope in the resurrection—The judgment seat of Christ—The new creature.*

1 For we know that, if our earthly house of this tabernacle were dissolved, we have a building of God, a house not made with hands, eternal in the heavens.

2 For in this we groan, earnestly desiring to be clothed upon with our house which is from heaven;

3 If so be that being clothed we shall not be found naked.

4 For we that are in this tabernacle do groan, being burdened: not for that we would be unclothed, but clothed upon, that mortality might be swallowed up of life.

5 Now he that hath wrought us for the selfsame thing is God, who also hath given unto us the earnest of the Spirit.

6 Therefore we are always confident, knowing that, whilst we are at home in the body, we are absent from the Lord:

7 (For we walk by faith, not by sight;)

8 We are confident, I say, and willing rather to be absent from the body, and to be present with the Lord.

9 Wherefore we labour, that, whether present or absent, we may be accepted of him.

10 For we must all appear before the judgment seat of Christ, that every one may receive a reward of the deeds done in the body; things according to what he hath done, whether good or bad.

11 Knowing therefore the terror of the Lord, we persuade men; but we are made manifest unto God; and I trust also are made manifest in your consciences.

12 For we commend not ourselves again unto you, but give you occasion to glory on our behalf, that ye may have somewhat to answer them which glory in appearance, and not in heart.

13 For we bear record that we are not beside ourselves; for whether we glory, it is to God, or whether we be sober, it is for your sakes.

14 For the love of Christ constraineth us; because we thus judge,

that if one died for all, then are all dead;

15 And he died for all, that they which live should not henceforth live unto themselves, but unto him which died for them, and rose again.

16 Wherefore, henceforth live we no more after the flesh; yea, though we once lived after the flesh, yet since we have known Christ, now henceforth live we no more after the flesh.

17 Therefore if any man live in Christ, he is a new creature; old things are passed away; behold, all things are become new,

18 And receiveth all the things of God, who hath reconciled us to himself by Jesus Christ, and hath given to us the ministry of reconciliation:

19 To wit, that God is in Christ, reconciling the world unto himself, not imputing their trespasses unto them; and hath committed unto us the word of reconciliation.

20 Now then we are ambassadors for Christ, as though God did beseech you by us; we pray you in Christ's stead, be ye reconciled to God.

21 For he hath made him to be sin for us, who knew no sin; that we might be made the righteousness of God in him.

## CHAPTER 6

*Paul's manner of life and preaching.*

1 We then, as workers together with Christ, beseech you also that ye receive not the grace of God in vain.

2 (For he saith, I have heard thee in a time accepted, and in the day of salvation have I succored thee; behold, now is the day of salvation.)

3 Giving no offense in anything, that the ministry be not blamed;

4 But in all things approving ourselves as the ministers of God, in much patience, in afflictions, in necessities, in distresses,

5 In stripes, in imprisonments, in tumults, in labours, in watchings, in fastings;

6 By pureness, by knowledge, by longsuffering, by kindness, by the Holy Ghost, by love unfeigned,

7 By the word of truth, by the power of God, by the armor of righteousness on the right hand and on the left,

8 By honor and dishonor, by evil report and good report; as deceivers, and yet true;

9 As unknown, and yet well known; as dying, and, behold, we live; as chastened, and not killed;

10 As sorrowful, yet always rejoicing; as poor, yet making many rich; as having nothing, yet possessing all things.

11 O ye Corinthians, our mouth is open unto you, our heart is enlarged.

12 Ye are not straitened in us, but ye are straitened in your own bowels.

13 Now for a recompense in the same, (I speak as unto my children,) be ye also enlarged.

14 Be ye not unequally yoked together with unbelievers; for what fellowship hath righteousness with unrighteousness? and what communion hath light with darkness?

15 And what concord hath Christ with Belial? or what part hath he that believeth with an infidel?

16 And what agreement hath the temple of God with idols? for ye are the temple of the living God; as God hath said, I will dwell in them, and walk in them; and I will be their God, and they shall be my people.

17 Wherefore come out from among them, and be ye the separate, saith the Lord, and touch not the unclean thing; and I will receive you,

18 And will be a Father unto you, and ye shall be my sons and daughters, saith the Lord Almighty.

## CHAPTER 7

*Purity of flesh and spirit enjoined.*

1 Having therefore these promises, dearly beloved, let us cleanse ourselves from all filthiness of the flesh and spirit, perfecting holiness in the fear of God.

2 Receive us; we have wronged no man, we have corrupted no man, we have defrauded no man.

3 I speak not this to condemn you; for I have said before, that ye are in our hearts to die and live with you.

4 Great is my boldness of speech toward you, great is my glorying of you; I am filled with comfort, I am exceeding joyful in all our tribulation.

5 For when we were come into Macedonia, our flesh had no rest, but we were troubled on every side; without were fightings, within were fears.

6 Nevertheless God, that comforteth those that are cast down, comforted us by the coming of Titus;

7 And not by his coming only, but by the consolation wherewith he was comforted in you, when he told us your earnest desire, your mourning, your fervent mind toward me; so that I rejoiced the more.

8 For though I made you sorry with a letter, I do not repent, though I did repent; for I perceive that the same epistle hath made you sorry, though it were but for a season.

9 Now I rejoice, not that ye were made sorry, but that ye sorrowed to repentance; for ye were made sorry after a godly manner, that ye might receive damage by us in nothing;

10 For godly sorrow worketh repentance to salvation not to be repented of; but the sorrow of the world worketh death.

11 For behold this selfsame thing that ye sorrowed after a godly sort, what carefulness it wrought in you, yea, what clearing of yourselves, yea, what indignation, yea, what fear, yea, what vehement desire, yea, what zeal, yea, what revenge! In all things ye have approved yourselves to be clear in this matter.

12 Wherefore, though I wrote unto you, I did it not for his cause that had done the wrong, nor for his cause that suffered wrong, but that our care for you in the sight of God might appear unto you.

13 Therefore we were comforted in your comfort; yea, and exceedingly the more joyed we for the joy of Titus, because his spirit was refreshed by you all.

14 For if I have boasted anything to him of you, I am not ashamed; but as we spake all things to you in truth, even so our boasting, which I made before Titus, is found a truth.

15 And his inward affection is more abundant toward you, whilst he remembereth the obedience of you all, how with fear and trembling ye received him.

16 I rejoice therefore that I have confidence in you in all things.

## CHAPTER 8

*Liberality enjoined.*

1 Moreover, brethren, we would have you to know of the grace of God bestowed on the churches of Macedonia;

2 How that in a great trial of affliction, the abundance of their joy and their deep poverty abounded unto the riches of their liberality.

3 For to their power, I bear record, yea, and beyond their power they were willing of themselves;

4 Praying us with much entreaty that we would receive the gift, and take upon us the fellowship of the ministering to the saints.

5 And this they did, not as we required, but first gave their own selves to the Lord, and unto us by the will of God.

6 Insomuch that we desired Titus that as he had begun, so he would also finish in you the same grace also.

7 Therefore, as ye abound in every thing, in faith, and utterance, and knowledge, and in all diligence, and in your love to us, see that ye abound in this grace also.

8 I speak not by commandment, but by occasion of the forwardness of others, and to prove the sincerity of your love.

9 For ye know the grace of our Lord Jesus Christ, that, though he was rich, yet for your sakes he became poor, that ye through his poverty might be rich.

10 And herein I give my advice; for this is expedient for you, who have begun before, not only to do, but also to be forward a year ago.

11 Now therefore perform the doing of it; that as there was a readiness to will, so there may be a performance also out of that which ye have.

12 For if there be first a willing mind, it is accepted according to that a man hath, and not according to that he hath not.

13 For I mean not that other men be eased, and ye be burdened;

14 But by an equality, that now at this time your abundance may be a supply for their want, that their abundance also may be a supply for your want; that there may be equality;

15 As it is written, He that had gathered much had nothing over; and he that had gathered little had no lack.

16 But thanks be to God, which put the same earnest care into the heart of Titus for you.

17 For indeed he accepted the exhortation; but being more forward, of his own accord he went unto you.

18 And we have sent with him the

brother, whose praise is in the gospel throughout all the churches;

19 And not that only, but who was also chosen of the churches to travel with us with this grace, which is administered by us to the glory of the same Lord, and declaration of your ready mind;

20 Avoiding this, that no man should blame us in this abundance which is administered by us;

21 Providing for honest things, not only in the sight of the Lord, but also in the sight of men.

22 And we have sent with them our brother, whom we have proved diligent in many things, but now much more diligent.

23 Therefore we send him unto you, in consequence of the great confidence which we have in you, that you will receive the things concerning you, to the glory of Christ; whether we send by the hand of Titus, my partner and fellow laborer, or our brethren, the messengers of the churches.

24 Wherefore show ye to them, and before the churches, the proof of your love, and of our boasting on your behalf.

## CHAPTER 9

*Reasons for liberality.*

1 For as touching the ministering to the saints, it is superfluous for me to write to you;

2 For I know the forwardness of your mind, for which I boast of you to them of Macedonia, that Achaia was ready a year ago; and your zeal hath provoked very many.

3 Yet have I sent the brethren, lest our boasting of you should be in vain in this behalf; that, as I said, ye may be ready;

4 Lest haply if they of Macedonia come with me, and find you unprepared, we (that we say not, ye) should be ashamed in this same confident boasting.

5 Therefore I thought it necessary to exhort the brethren, that they would go before unto you, and make up beforehand your bounty, whereof ye had notice before, that the same might be ready, as a matter of bounty, and not as of covetousness.

6 But this I say, He which soweth sparingly shall reap also sparingly;

and he which soweth bountifully shall reap also bountifully.

7 Every man according as he purposeth in his heart, so let him give; not grudgingly, or of necessity; for God loveth a cheerful giver.

8 And God is able to make all grace abound toward you; that ye, always having all sufficiency in all things, may abound to every good work;

9 (As it is written, He hath dispersed abroad; he hath given to the poor; his righteousness remaineth for ever.

10 Now he that ministereth seed to the sower both minister bread for your food, and multiply your seed sown, and increase the fruits of your righteousness;)

11 Being enriched in everything to all bountifulness, which causeth through us thanksgiving to God.

12 For the administration of this service not only supplieth the want of the saints, but is abundant also by many thanksgivings unto God;

13 While by the experiment of this ministration they glorify God for your professed subjection into the gospel of Christ, and for your liberal distribution unto them, and unto all men;

14 And by their prayer for you, which long after you for the exceeding grace of God in you.

15 Thanks be unto God for his unspeakable gift.

## CHAPTER 10

*Paul's commendation as a minister.*

1 Now I Paul myself beseech you by the meekness and gentleness of Christ, who in presence am base among you, but being absent am bold toward you;

2 But I beseech you, that I may not be bold when I am present with that confidence, wherewith I think to be bold against some, which think of us as if we walked according to the flesh.

3 For though we walk in the flesh, we do not war after the flesh;

4 (For the weapons of our warfare are not carnal, but mighty through God to the pulling down of strongholds;)

5 Casting down imaginations, and every high thing that exalteth itself against the knowledge of God, and bringing into captivity every thought to the obedience of Christ;

6 And having in a readiness to re-

venge all disobedience, when your obedience is fulfilled.

7 Do ye look on things after the outward appearance? If any man trust to himself that he is Christ's, let him of himself think this again, that, as he is Christ's, even so are we Christ's.

8 For though I should boast somewhat more of our authority, which the Lord hath given us for edification, and not for your destruction, I should not be ashamed;

9 That I may not seem as if I would terrify you by letters.

10 For his letters, say they, are weighty and powerful; but his bodily presence is weak, and his speech contemptible.

11 Let such a one think this, that, such as we are in word by letters when we are absent, such will we be also in deed when we are present.

12 For we dare not make ourselves of the number, or compare ourselves with some that commend themselves; but they, measuring themselves by themselves, and comparing themselves among themselves, are not wise.

13 But we will not boast of things without our measure, but according to the measure of the rule which God hath distributed to us, a measure to reach even unto you.

14 For we stretch not ourselves beyond our measure, as though we reached not unto you; for we are come as far as to you also in preaching the gospel of Christ;

15 Not boasting of things without our measure, that is, of other men's labours; but having hope, when your faith is increased, that we shall be enlarged by you according to our rule abundantly,

16 To preach the gospel in the regions beyond you, and not to boast in another man's line of things made ready to our hand.

17 But he that glorieth, let him glory in the Lord.

18 For not he that commendeth, himself is approved, but whom the Lord commendeth.

## CHAPTER 11

*Superiority of Paul's ministry—Satan transformed—Paul's sufferings.*

1 Would to God ye could bear with me a little in my folly; and indeed bear with me.

2 For I am jealous over you with godly jealousy; for I have espoused you to one husband, that I may present you as a chaste virgin to Christ.

3 But I fear, lest by any means, as the serpent beguiled Eve through his subtilty, so your minds should be corrupted from the simplicity that is in Christ.

4 For if he that cometh preacheth another Jesus, whom we have not preached, or if ye receive another spirit, which ye have not received, or another gospel, which ye have not accepted, ye might well bear with me.

5 For I suppose I was not a whit behind the very chiefest apostles.

6 But though I be rude in speech, yet not in knowledge; but we have been thoroughly made manifest among you in all things.

7 Have I committed an offense in abasing myself that ye might be exalted, because I have preached to you the gospel of God freely?

8 I robbed other churches, taking wages of them, to do you service.

9 And when I was present with you, and wanted, I was chargeable to no man; for that which was lacking to me the brethren which came from Macedonia supplied; and in all things I have kept myself from being burdensome unto you, and so will I keep myself.

10 As the truth of Christ is in me, no man shall stop me of this boasting in the regions of Achaia.

11 Wherefore? because I love you not? God knoweth.

12 But what I do, that I will do, that I may cut off occasion from them which desire occasion; that wherein they glory, they may be found even as we.

13 For such are false apostles, deceitful workers, transforming themselves into the apostles of Christ.

14 And no marvel; for Satan himself is transformed into an angel of light.

15 Therefore it is no great thing if his ministers also be transformed as the ministers of righteousness; whose end shall be according to their works.

16 I say again, Let no man think me a fool; if otherwise, yet as a fool receive me, that I may boast myself a little.

17 That which I speak, I speak it not after the Lord, but as it were foolishly, in this confidence of boasting.

18 Seeing that many glory after the flesh, I will glory also.

19 For ye suffer fools gladly, seeing ye yourselves are wise.

20 For ye suffer, if a man bring you into bondage, if a man devour you, if a man take of you, if a man exalt himself, if a man smite you on the face.

21 I speak as concerning reproach, as though we had been weak. Howbeit, whereinsoever any is bold, (I speak foolishly,) I am bold also.

22 Are they Hebrews? so am I. Are they Israelites? so am I. Are they the seed of Abraham? so am I.

23 Are they ministers of Christ? (I speak as a fool.) so am I; in labors more abundant, in stripes above measure, in prisons more frequent, in deaths oft.

24 Of the Jews five times received I forty stripes save one.

25 Thrice was I beaten with rods, once was I stoned, thrice I suffered shipwreck, a night and a day I have been in the deep;

26 In journeyings often, in perils of waters, in perils of robbers, in perils by mine own countrymen, in perils by the heathen, in perils in the city, in perils in the wilderness, in perils in the sea, in perils among false brethren;

27 In weariness and painfulness, in watchings often, in hunger and thirst, in fastings often, in cold and nakedness.

28 Beside those things that are without, that which cometh upon me daily, the care of all the churches.

29 Who is weak, and I am not weak? who is offended, and I anger not?

30 If I must needs glory, I will glory of the things which concern mine infirmities.

31 The God and Father of our Lord Jesus Christ, which is blessed for evermore, knoweth that I lie not.

32 In Damascus the governor under Aretus the king kept the city of the Damascenes with a garrison, desirous to apprehend me;

33 And through a window in a basket was I let down by the wall, and escaped his hands.

## CHAPTER 12

*Of one caught up into Paradise—The signs of an apostle.*

1 It is not expedient for me doubtless to glory, I will come to visions and revelations of the Lord.

2 I knew a man in Christ above fourteen years ago, (whether in the body, I cannot tell; or whether out of the body, I cannot tell; God knoweth;) such a one caught up to the third heaven.

3 And I knew such a man, (whether in the body, or out of the body, I cannot tell; God knoweth;)

4 How that he was caught up into paradise, and heard unspeakable words, which it is not lawful for a man to utter.

5 Of such a one will I glory; yet of myself I will not glory, but in mine infirmities.

6 For though I would desire to glory, I shall not be a fool; for I will say the truth; but now I forbear, lest any man should think of me above that which he seeth of me, or that he heareth of me.

7 And lest I should be exalted above measure through the abundance of the revelations, there was given to me a thorn in the flesh, the messenger of Satan to buffet me, lest I should be exalted above measure.

8 For this thing I besought the Lord thrice, that it might depart from me.

9 And he said unto me, My grace is sufficient for thee; for my strength is made perfect in weakness. Most gladly therefore will I rather glory in my infirmities, that the power of Christ may rest upon me.

10 Therefore I take pleasure in infirmities, in reproaches, in necessities, in persecutions, in distresses for Christ's sake; for when I am weak, then am I strong.

11 I am become a fool in glorying; ye have compelled me; for I ought to have been commended of you; for in nothing am I behind the very chiefest apostles, though I be nothing.

12 Truly the signs of an apostle were wrought among you in all patience, in signs, and wonders, and mighty deeds.

13 For what is it wherein ye were inferior to other churches, except it be that I myself was not burdensome to you? forgive me this wrong.

14 Behold, the third time I am ready to come to you; and I will not be burdensome to you; for I seek not yours, but you; for the children ought not to lay up for the parents, but the parents for the children.

15 And I will very gladly spend and be spent for you; though the more

abundantly I love you, the less I be loved.

16 But be it so, I did not burden you; nevertheless, being crafty, I caught you with guile.

17 Did I make a gain of you by any of them whom I sent unto you?

18 I desired Titus, and with him I sent a brother. Did Titus make a gain of you? walked we not in the same spirit? walked we not in the same steps?

19 Again, think ye that we excuse ourselves unto you? we speak before God in Christ; but we do all things, dearly beloved, for your edifying.

20 For I fear, lest, when I come, I shall not find you such as I would, and that I shall be found unto you such as ye would not; lest there be debates, envyings, wraths, strifes, backbitings, whisperings, swellings, tumults;

21 And lest, when I come again, my God will humble me among you, and that I shall bewail many which have sinned already, and have not repented of the uncleanness and fornication and lasciviousness which they have committed.

## CHAPTER 13

*Paul threateneth offenders—Exhorteth to unity and peace.*

1 This is the third time I am coming to you. In the mouth of two or three witnesses shall every word be established.

2 I told you before, and foretell you, as if I were present, the second time; and being absent now I write to them which heretofore have sinned, and to all other, that, if I come again, I will not spare;

3 Since ye seek a proof of Christ speaking in me, which to you-ward is not weak, but is mighty in you.

4 For though he was crucified through weakness, yet he lived by the power of God. For we also are weak in him, but we shall live with him by the power of God toward you.

5 Examine yourselves, whether ye be in the faith; prove your own selves. Know ye not your own selves, how that Jesus Christ is in you, except ye be reprobates?

6 But I trust that ye shall know that we are not reprobates.

7 Now I pray to God that ye do no evil; not that we should appear approved, but that ye should do that which is honest, though we be as reprobates.

8 For we can do nothing against the truth, but for the truth.

9 For we are glad, when we are weak, and ye are strong; and this also we wish, even your perfection.

10 Therefore I write these things being absent, lest being present I should use sharpness, according to the power which the Lord hath given me to edification, and not to destruction.

11 Finally, brethren, farewell. Be perfect, be of good comfort, be of one mind, live in peace; and the God of love and peace shall be with you.

12 Greet one another with a holy salutation.

13 All the saints salute you.

14 The grace of the Lord Jesus Christ, and the love of God, and the communion of the Holy Ghost, be with you all. Amen.

The second epistle to the Corinthians was written from Philippi, a city of Macedonia, by Titus and Lucas.

---

## The Epistle of Paul the Apostle to the
# Galatians

## CHAPTER 1

*The gospel unchangeable—Paul received it by revelation.*

1 Paul, an apostle, (not of men, neither by man, but by Jesus Christ, and God the Father, who raised him from the dead;)

2 And all the brethren which are with me, unto the churches of Galatia;

3 Grace be to you, and peace, from God the Father, and from our Lord Jesus Christ,

4 Who gave himself for our sins, that he might deliver us from this present evil world, according to the will of God and our Father;

5 To whom be glory for ever and ever. Amen.

6 I marvel that ye are so soon removed from him that called you into the grace of Christ unto another gospel;

7 Which is not another; but there be some that trouble you, and would pervert the gospel of Christ.

8 But though we, or an angel from heaven, preach any other gospel unto you than that which we have preached unto you, let him be accursed.

9 As we said before, so say I now again, If any man preach any other gospel unto you than that ye have received, let him be accursed.

10 For do I now please men, or God? or do I seek to please men? for if I yet pleased men, I should not be the servant of Christ.

11 But I certify you, brethren, that the gospel which was preached of me is not after man.

12 For I neither received it of man, neither was I taught it, but by the revelation of Jesus Christ.

13 For ye have heard of my conversation in time past in the Jews' religion, how that beyond measure I persecuted the church of God, and wasted it;

14 And profited in the Jews' religion above many my equals in mine own nation, being more exceedingly zealous of the traditions of my fathers.

15 But when it pleased God, who separated me from my mother's womb, and called me by his grace,

16 To reveal his Son in me, that I might preach him among the heathen; immediately I conferred not with flesh and blood;

17 Neither went I up to Jerusalem to them which were apostles before me; but I went into Arabia, and returned again unto Damascus.

18 Then after three years I went up to Jerusalem to see Peter, and abode with him fifteen days.

19 But of the other apostles saw I none, save James the Lord's brother.

20 Now the things which I write unto you, behold, before God, I lie not.

21 Afterwards I came into the regions of Syria and Cilicia;

22 And was unknown by face unto the churches of Judea which were in Christ;

23 But they had heard only, That he which persecutest us in times past now preacheth the faith which once he destroyed.

24 And they glorified God on account of me.

## CHAPTER 2

*False brethren—Justification by faith—Peter dissembling.*

1 Then fourteen years after I went up again to Jerusalem with Barnabas, and took Titus with me also.

2 And I went up by revelation, and communicated unto them that gospel which I preach among the Gentiles, but privately to them which were of reputation, lest by any means I should run, or had run, in vain.

3 But neither Titus, who was with me, being a Greek, was compelled to be circumcised.

4 Notwithstanding, there were some brought in by false brethren unawares, who came in privily to spy out our liberty which we have in Christ Jesus, that they might bring us into bondage;

5 To whom we gave place by subjection, no, not for an hour; that the truth of the gospel might continue with you.

6 But of those who seemed to be somewhat, whatsoever they were, it maketh no matter to me; God accepteth no man's person; for they who seemed to be somewhat in conference added nothing to me;

7 But contrariwise, when they saw that the gospel of the uncircumcision was committed unto me, as the gospel of the circumcision was unto Peter;

8 (For he that wrought effectually in Peter to the apostleship of the circumcision, the same was mighty in me toward the Gentiles;)

9 And when James, Cephas, and John, who seemed to be pillars, perceived the grace that was given unto me, they gave to me and Barnabas the right hands of fellowship; that we should go unto the heathen, and they unto the circumcision.

10 Only they would that we should remember the poor; the same which I was also forward to do.

11 But when Peter was come to Antioch, I withstood him to the face, because he was to be blamed.

12 For before that certain came from James, he did eat with Gentiles; but when they were come, he withdrew and separated himself, fearing them which were of the circumcision.

13 And the other Jews dissembled likewise with him; insomuch that Barnabas also was carried away with their dissimulation.

14 But when I saw that they walked not uprightly according to the truth of the gospel, I said unto Peter before them all, If thou, being a Jew, livest after the manner of the Gentiles, and not as do the Jews, why compellest thou the Gentiles to live as do the Jews?

15 We who are Jews by nature, and not sinners of the Gentiles,

16 Knowing that a man is not justified by the works of the law, but by the faith of Jesus Christ, even we have believed in Jesus Christ, that we might be justified by the faith of Christ, and not by the works of the law; for by the works of the law shall no flesh be justified.

17 But if, while we seek to be justified by Christ, we ourselves also are found sinners, is therefore Christ the minister of sin? God forbid.

18 For if I build again the things which I destroyed, I make myself a transgressor.

19 For I through the law am dead to the law, that I might live unto God.

20 I am crucified with Christ; nevertheless I live; yet not I, but Christ liveth in me; and the life which I now live in the flesh I live by the faith of the Son of God, who loved me, and gave himself for me.

21 I do not frustrate the grace of God; for if righteousness come by the law, then Christ is dead in vain.

## CHAPTER 3

*The unfaithful reproved—The faithful blessed with Abraham—Baptism into Christ.*

1 O foolish Galatians, who hath bewitched you, that ye should not obey the truth, before whose eyes Jesus Christ hath been evidently set forth, crucified among you?

2 This only would I learn of you, Received ye the Spirit by the works of the law, or by the hearing of faith?

3 Are ye so foolish? having begun in the Spirit, are ye now made perfect by the flesh?

4 Have ye suffered so many things in vain? if it be yet in vain.

5 He therefore that ministereth to you the Spirit, and worketh miracles among you, doeth he it by the works of the law, or by the hearing of faith?

6 Even as Abraham believed God, and it was accounted to him for righteousness.

7 Know ye therefore that they which are of faith, the same are the children of Abraham.

8 And the scripture, foreseeing that God would justify the heathen through faith, preached before the gospel unto Abraham, saying, In thee shall all nations be blessed.

9 So then they which be of faith are blessed with faithful Abraham.

10 For as many as are of the works of the law are under the curse; for it is written, Cursed is every one that continueth not in all things which are written in the book of the law to do them.

11 But that no man is justified by the law in the sight of God, it is evident; for, The just shall live by faith.

12 And the law is not of faith; but, The man that doeth them shall live in them.

13 Christ hath redeemed us from the curse of the law, being made a curse for us; for it is written, Cursed is every one that hangeth on a tree:

14 That the blessing of Abraham might come on the Gentiles through Jesus Christ; that they might receive the promise of the Spirit through faith.

15 Brethren, I speak after the manner of men; Though it be but a man's covenant, yet when it be confirmed, no man disannulleth, or addeth thereto.

16 Now to Abraham and his seed were the promises made. He saith not, And to seeds, as of many; but as of one, And to thy seed, which is Christ.

17 And this I say, that the covenant, that was confirmed before of God in Christ, the law, which was four hundred and thirty years after, cannot disannul, that it should make the promise of none effect.

18 For if the inheritance is of the law, then it is no more of promise; but God gave it to Abraham by promise.

19 Wherefore then, the law was added because of transgressions, till the seed should come to whom the promise was made in the law given to Moses, who was ordained by the hand of angels to be a mediator of this first covenant, (the law.)

20 Now this mediator was not a me-

diator of the new covenant; but there is one mediator of the new covenant, who is Christ, as it is written in the law concerning the promises made to Abraham and his seed. Now Christ is the mediator of life; for this is the promise which God made unto Abraham.

21 Is the law then against the promises of God? God forbid; for if there had been a law given which could have given life, verily righteousness should have been by the law.

22 But the scripture hath concluded all under sin, that the promise by faith of Jesus Christ might be given to them that believe.

23 But before faith came, we were kept under the law, shut up unto the faith which should afterwards be revealed.

24 Wherefore the law was our schoolmaster until Christ, that we might be justified by faith.

25 But after that faith is come, we are no longer under a schoolmaster.

26 For ye are all the children of God by faith in Jesus Christ.

27 For as many of you as have been baptized into Christ have put on Christ.

28 There is neither Jew nor Greek, there is neither bond nor free, there is neither male nor female; for ye are all one in Christ Jesus.

29 And if ye are Christ's then are ye Abraham's seed, and heirs according to the promise.

## CHAPTER 4

*Redemption through Christ—Sons of God.*

1 Now I say, That the heir, as long as he is a child, differeth nothing from a servant, though he be lord of all;

2 But is under tutors and governors until the time appointed of the father.

3 Even so we, when we were children, were in bondage under the elements of the world;

4 But when the fullness of the time was come, God sent forth his Son, made of a woman, made under the law,

5 To redeem them that were under the law, that we might receive the adoption of sons.

6 And because ye are sons, God hath sent forth the Spirit of his Son into your hearts, crying, Abba, Father.

7 Wherefore thou art no more a ser-

vant, but a son; and if a son, then an heir of God through Christ.

8 Howbeit then, when ye knew not God, ye did service unto them which by nature are no gods.

9 But now, after that ye have known God, or rather are known of God, how turn ye again to the weak and beggarly elements, whereunto ye desire again to be in bondage?

10 Ye observe days, and months, and times, and years.

11 I am afraid of you, lest I have bestowed upon you labour in vain.

12 Brethren, I beseech you to be perfect as I am perfect; for I am persuaded as ye have a knowledge of me, ye have not injured me at all by your sayings.

13 Ye know how through infirmity of the flesh I preached the gospel unto you at the first.

14 And my temptation which was in my flesh ye despised not, nor rejected; but received me as an angel of God, even as Christ Jesus.

15 Where is then the blessedness ye spake of? for I bear you record, that, if it had been possible, ye would have plucked out your own eyes, and have given them to me.

16 Am I therefore become your enemy, because I tell you the truth?

17 They zealously affect you, but not well; yea, they would exclude you, that ye might affect them.

18 But it is good to be zealously affected always in a good thing, and not only when I am present with you.

19 My little children, of whom I travail in birth again until Christ be formed in you,

20 I desire to be present with you now, and to change my voice; for I stand in doubt of you.

21 Tell me, ye that desire to be under the law, do ye not hear the law?

22 For it is written, that Abraham had two sons, the one by a bondmaid, the other by a free woman.

23 But he who was of the bondwoman was born after the flesh; but he of the free woman was by promise.

24 Which things are an allegory; for these are the two covenants; the one from the mount Sinai, which gendereth to bondage, which is Agar.

25 For this Agar is mount Sinai in Arabia, and answereth to Jerusalem

which now is, and is in bondage with her children.

26 But Jerusalem which is above is free, which is the mother of us all.

27 For it is written, Rejoice, thou barren that bearest not; break forth and cry, thou that travailest not; for the desolate hath many more children than she which hath a husband.

28 Now we, brethren, as Isaac was, are the children of promise.

29 But as then he that was born after the flesh persecuted him that was born after the Spirit, even so it is now.

30 Nevertheless what saith the scripture? Cast out the bondwoman and her son; for the son of the bondwoman shall not be heir with the son of the free woman.

31 So then, brethren, we are not children of the bondwoman, but of the free.

## CHAPTER 5

*The liberty of the gospel—The works of the flesh—The fruits of the Spirit.*

1 Stand fast therefore in the liberty wherewith Christ hath made us free, and be not entangled again with the yoke of bondage.

2 Behold, I Paul say unto you, that if ye be circumcised, Christ shall profit you nothing.

3 For I testify again to every man that is circumcised, that he is a debtor to do the whole law.

4 Christ is become of no effect unto you, whosoever of you are justified by the law; ye are fallen from grace.

5 For we through the Spirit wait for the hope of righteousness by faith.

6 For in Jesus Christ neither circumcision availeth any thing, nor uncircumcision; but faith which worketh by love.

7 Ye did run well; who did hinder you that ye should not obey the truth?

8 This persuasion cometh not of him that calleth you.

9 A little leaven leaveneth the whole lump.

10 I have confidence in you through the Lord, that ye will be none otherwise minded; but he that troubleth you shall bear his judgment, whosoever he be.

11 And I, brethren, if I yet preach circumcision, why do I yet suffer persecution? then is the offense of the cross ceased.

12 I would they were even cut off which trouble you.

13 For, brethren, ye have been called unto liberty; only use not liberty for an occasion to the flesh, but by love serve one another.

14 For all the law is fulfilled in one word, even in this; Thou shalt love thy neighbor as thyself.

15 But if ye bite and devour one another, take heed that ye be not consumed one of another.

16 This I say then, Walk in the Spirit, and ye shall not fulfill the lust of the flesh.

17 For the flesh lusteth against the Spirit, and the Spirit against the flesh; and these are contrary the one to the other; so that ye cannot do the things that ye would.

18 But if ye be led of the Spirit, ye are not under the law.

19 Now the works of the flesh are manifest, which are these, Adultery, fornication, uncleanness, lasciviousness,

20 Idolatry, witchcraft, hatred, variance, emulations, wrath, strife, seditions, heresies,

21 Envyings, murders, drunkenness, revellings, and such like; of the which I tell you before, as I have also told you in time past, that they which do such things shall not inherit the kingdom of God.

22 But the fruit of the Spirit is love, joy, peace, long-suffering, gentleness, goodness, faith,

23 Meekness, temperance; against such there is no law.

24 And they that are Christ's have crucified the flesh with the affections and lusts.

25 If we live in the Spirit, let us also walk in the Spirit.

26 Let us not be desirous of vainglory, provoking one another, envying one another.

## CHAPTER 6

*Deal kindly with the erring—Do good to all men.*

1 Brethren, if a man be overtaken in a fault, ye which are spiritual, restore such a one in the spirit of meekness; considering thyself, lest thou also be tempted.

2 Bear ye one another's burdens, and so fulfill the law of Christ.

3 For if a man think himself to be

something, when he is nothing, he deceiveth himself.

4 But let every man prove his own work, and then shall he have rejoicing in himself alone, and not in another.

5 For every man shall bear his own burden.

6 Let him that is taught in the word communicate unto him that teacheth in all good things.

7 Be not deceived; God is not mocked; for whatsoever a man soweth, that shall he also reap.

8 For he that soweth to his flesh shall of the flesh reap corruption; but he that soweth to the Spirit shall of the Spirit reap life everlasting.

9 And let us not be weary in well doing; for in due season we shall reap, if we faint not.

10 As we have therefore opportunity, let us do good unto all men, especially unto them who are of the household of faith.

11 Ye see how large a letter I have written unto you with mine own hand.

12 As many as desire to make a fair show in the flesh, they constrain you to be circumcised; only lest they should suffer persecution for the cross of Christ.

13 For neither they themselves who are circumcised keep the law; but desire to have you circumcised, that they may glory in your flesh.

14 But God forbid that I should glory, save in the cross of our Lord Jesus Christ, by whom the world is crucified unto me, and I unto the world.

15 For in Christ Jesus neither circumcision availeth any thing, nor uncircumcision, but a new creature.

16 And as many as walk according to this rule, peace be on them, and mercy, and upon the Israel of God.

17 From henceforth let no man trouble me; for I bear in my body the marks of the Lord Jesus.

18 Brethren, the grace of our Lord Jesus Christ be with your spirit. Amen.

Unto the Galatians, written from Rome.

## The Epistle of Paul the Apostle to the
# Ephesians

### CHAPTER 1

*Redemption through Christ—The dispensation of the fullness of times—Sealing of the Spirit.*

1 Paul, an apostle of Jesus Christ by the will of God, to the saints which are at Ephesus, and to the faithful in Christ Jesus;

2 Grace be to you, and peace, from God our Father, and from the Lord Jesus Christ.

3 Blessed be the God and Father of our Lord Jesus Christ, who hath blessed us with all spiritual blessings in heavenly places in Christ;

4 According as he hath chosen us in him before the foundation of the world, that we should be holy and without blame before him in love;

5 Having predestinated us unto the adoption of children by Jesus Christ to himself, according to the good pleasure of his will,

6 To the praise of the glory of his grace, wherein he hath made us accepted in the beloved;

7 In whom we have redemption through his blood, the forgiveness of sins, according to the riches of his grace;

8 Wherein he hath abounded toward us in all wisdom and prudence;

9 Having made known unto us the mystery of his will, according to his good pleasure which he hath purposed in himself;

10 That in the dispensation of the fullness of times he might gather together in one all things in Christ, both which are in heaven, and which are on earth; even in him;

11 In whom also we have obtained an inheritance, being predestinated according to the purpose of him who worketh all things after the counsel of his own will;

12 That we should be to the praise of his glory, who first trusted in Christ.

13 In whom ye also trusted, after that ye heard the word of truth, the gospel of your salvation; in whom also, after that ye believed, ye were sealed with that Holy Spirit of promise,

14 Which is the earnest of our inheritance until the redemption of the purchased possession, unto the praise of his glory.

15 Wherefore I also, after I heard of your faith in the Lord Jesus, and love unto all the saints,

16 Cease not to give thanks for you, making mention of you in my prayers;

17 That the God of our Lord Jesus Christ, the Father of glory, may give unto you the spirit of wisdom and revelation in the knowledge of him;

18 The eyes of your understanding being enlightened; that ye may know what is the hope of his calling, and what the riches of the glory of his inheritance in the saints,

19 And what is the exceeding greatness of his power to us-ward who believe, according to the working of his mighty power,

20 Which he wrought in Christ, when he raised him from the dead, and set him at his own right hand in the heavenly places,

21 Far above all principality, and power, and might, and dominion, and every name that is named, not only in this world, but also in that which is to come;

22 And hath put all things under his feet, and gave him to be the head over all things to the church,

23 Which is his body, the fullness of him that filleth all in all.

## CHAPTER 2

*The prince of the power of the air—Salvation by grace, and adoption through Christ—Foundation of the church.*

1 And you hath he quickened, who were dead in trespasses and sins;

2 Wherein in time past ye walked according to the course of this world, according to the prince of the power of the air, the spirit that now worketh in the children of disobedience;

3 Among whom also we all had our conversation in times past in the lusts of our flesh, fulfilling the desires of the flesh, and of the mind; and were by nature the children of wrath, even as others.

4 But God, who is rich in mercy, for his great love wherewith he loved us,

5 Even when we were dead in sins, hath quickened us together with Christ, (by grace ye are saved;)

6 And hath raised us up together, and made us to sit together in heavenly places in Christ Jesus;

7 That in the ages to come he might show the exceeding riches of his grace, in his kindness toward us, through Christ Jesus.

8 For by grace are ye saved through faith; and that not of yourselves; but it is the gift of God;

9 Not of works, lest any man should boast.

10 For we are his workmanship, created in Christ Jesus unto good works, which God hath before ordained that we should walk in them.

11 Wherefore remember, that ye were in time past Gentiles in the flesh, who are called Uncircumcision by that which is called the Circumcision in the flesh made by hands;

12 That at that time ye were without Christ, being aliens from the commonwealth of Israel, and strangers from the covenants of promise, having no hope, and without God in the world;

13 But now, in Christ Jesus, ye who sometimes were far off are made nigh by the blood of Christ.

14 For he is our peace, who hath made both one, and hath broken down the middle wall of partition between us;

15 Having abolished in his flesh the enmity, even the law of commandments contained in ordinances; for to make in himself of twain one new man, so making peace;

16 And that he might reconcile both unto God in one body by the cross, having slain the enmity thereby;

17 And came and preached peace to you which were afar off, and to them that were nigh.

18 For through him we both have access by one Spirit unto the Father.

19 Now therefore ye are no more strangers and foreigners, but fellow citizens with the saints, and of the household of God;

20 And are built upon the foundation of the apostles and prophets, Jesus Christ himself being the chief cornerstone;

21 In whom all the building fitly framed together groweth unto an holy temple in the Lord;

22 In whom ye also are builded together for an habitation of God through the Spirit.

## CHAPTER 3

*Mystery of the gospel—The family [kingdom] in heaven and on earth—The love of Christ.*

1 For this cause, I, Paul, am the prisoner of Jesus Christ among you Gentiles.

2 For the dispensation of the grace of God which is given me to you-ward;

3 As ye have heard that by revelation he made known unto me the mystery of Christ; as I wrote before in few words;

4 Whereby, when ye read, ye may understand my knowledge in the mystery of Christ,

5 Which in other ages was not made known unto the sons of men, as it is now revealed unto his holy apostles and prophets by the Spirit;

6 That the Gentiles should be fellow heirs, and of the same body, and partakers of his promise in Christ by the gospel;

7 Whereof I was made a minister, according to the gift of the grace of God given unto me by the effectual working of his power.

8 Unto me, who am less than the least of all saints, is this grace given, that I should preach among the Gentiles the unsearchable riches of Christ;

9 And to make all men see what is the fellowship of the mystery, which from the beginning of the world hath been hid in God, who created all things by Jesus Christ;

10 To the intent that now unto the principalities and powers in heavenly places might be known by the church the manifold wisdom of God,

11 According to the eternal purpose which he purposed in Christ Jesus our Lord;

12 In whom we have boldness and access with confidence by the faith of him.

13 Wherefore I desire that ye faint not at my tribulations for you, which is your glory.

14 For this cause I bow my knees unto the Father of our Lord Jesus Christ,

15 Of whom the whole family in heaven and earth is named,

16 That he would grant you, according to the riches of his glory, to be strengthened with might by his Spirit in the inner man;

17 That Christ may dwell in your hearts by faith; that ye, being rooted and grounded in love,

18 May be able to comprehend with all saints what is the breadth, and length, and depth, and height;

19 And to know the love of Christ, which passeth knowledge, that ye might be filled with all the fullness of God.

20 Now unto him that is able to do exceeding abundantly above all that we ask or think, according to the power that worketh in us,

21 Unto him be glory in the church by Christ Jesus throughout all ages, world without end. Amen.

## CHAPTER 4

*One body; one spirit; one hope; one Lord; one faith; one baptism—Officers of the church, Christ the head—Seal of the Spirit.*

1 I therefore, the prisoner of the Lord, beseech you that ye walk worthy of the vocation wherewith ye are called,

2 With all lowliness and meekness, with long-suffering, forbearing one another in love;

3 Endeavoring to keep the unity of the Spirit in the bond of peace,

4 In one body, and one Spirit, even as ye are called in one hope of your calling;

5 One Lord, one faith, one baptism,

6 One God and Father of all, who is above all, and through all, and in you all.

7 But unto every one of us is given grace according to the measure of the gift of Christ.

8 Wherefore he saith, When he ascended up on high, he led captivity captive, and gave gifts unto men.

9 (Now that he ascended, what is it but that he also descended first into the lower parts of the earth?

10 He who descended, is the same also who ascended up into heaven, to glorify him who reigneth over all heavens, that he might fill all things.)

11 And he gave some, apostles; and some, prophets; and some, evangelists; and some, pastors and teachers;

12 For the perfecting of the saints, for the work of the ministry, for the edifying of the body of Christ;

13 Till we, in the unity of the faith, all come to the knowledge of the Son of God, unto a perfect man, unto the mea-

sure of the stature of the fullness of Christ;

14 That we henceforth be no more children, tossed to and fro, and carried about with every wind of doctrine, by the sleight of men, and cunning craftiness, whereby they lie in wait to deceive;

15 But speaking the truth in love, may grow up into him in all things, which is the head, even Christ;

16 From whom the whole body fitly joined together and compacted by that which every joint supplieth, according to the effectual working in the measure of every part, maketh increase of the body unto the edifying of itself in love.

17 This I say therefore, and testify in the Lord, that ye henceforth walk not as other Gentiles walk, in the vanity of their mind,

18 Having the understanding darkened, being alienated from the life of God through the ignorance that is in them, because of the blindness of their heart;

19 Who being past feeling have given themselves over unto lasciviousness, to work all uncleanness with greediness.

20 But ye have not so learned Christ;

21 If so be that ye have learned him, and have been taught by him, as the truth is in Jesus;

22 And now I speak unto you concerning the former conversation, by exhortation, that ye put off the old man, which is corrupt according to the deceitful lusts;

23 And be renewed in the mind of the Spirit;

24 And that ye put on the new man, which after God is created in righteousness and true holiness.

25 Wherefore putting away lying, speak every man truth with his neighbor; for we are members one of another.

26 Can ye be angry, and not sin? let not the sun go down upon your wrath;

27 Neither give place to the devil.

28 Let him that stole steal no more; but rather let him labor, working with his hands for the things which are good, that he may have to give to him that needeth.

29 Let no corrupt communication proceed out of your mouth, but that which is good to the use of edifying, that it may minister grace unto the hearers.

30 And grieve not the Holy Spirit of God, whereby ye are sealed unto the day of redemption.

31 Let all bitterness, and wrath, and anger, and clamor, and evil speaking, be put away from you, with all malice;

32 And be ye kind one to another, tenderhearted, forgiving one another, even as God for Christ's sake hath forgiven you.

## CHAPTER 5

*Fruits of the Spirit—The husband the head of the wife—Christ the head of the church.*

1 Be ye therefore followers of God, as dear children;

2 And walk in love, as Christ also hath loved us, and hath given himself for us an offering and a sacrifice to God for a sweet smelling savor.

3 But fornication, and all uncleanness, or covetousness, let it not be once named among you, as becometh saints;

4 Neither filthiness, nor foolish talking, nor jesting, which are not convenient; but rather giving of thanks.

5 For this ye know, that no whoremonger, nor unclean person, nor covetous man, who is an idolater, hath any inheritance in the kingdom of Christ and of God.

6 Let no man deceive you with vain words; for because of these things cometh the wrath of God upon the children of disobedience,

7 Be not ye therefore partakers with them.

8 For ye were sometime darkness, but now are ye light in the Lord; walk as children of light;

9 (For the fruit of the Spirit is in all goodness and righteousness and truth;)

10 Proving what is acceptable unto the Lord.

11 And have no fellowship with the unfruitful works of darkness, but rather reprove them.

12 For it is a shame even to speak of those things which are done of them in secret.

13 But all things that are reproved are made manifest by the light; for whatsoever doth make manifest is light.

14 Wherefore he saith, Awake thou that sleepest, and arise from the dead, and Christ shall give thee light.

15 See then that ye walk circumspectly, not as fools, but as wise,

16 Redeeming the time, because the days are evil.

17 Wherefore be ye not unwise, but understanding what is the will of the Lord.

18 And be not drunk with wine, wherein is excess; but be filled with the Spirit;

19 Speaking to yourselves in psalms and hymns and spiritual songs, singing and making melody in your heart to the Lord;

20 Giving thanks always for all things unto God and the Father in the name of our Lord Jesus Christ;

21 Submitting yourselves one to another in the fear of God.

22 Wives, submit yourselves unto your own husbands, as unto the Lord.

23 For the husband is the head of the wife, even as Christ is the head of the church; and he is the Savior of the body.

24 Therefore as the church is subject unto Christ, so let the wives be to their own husbands in every thing.

25 Husbands, love your wives, even as Christ also loved the church, and gave himself for it;

26 That he might sanctify and cleanse it with the washing of water by the word,

27 That he might present it to himself a glorious church, not having spot, or wrinkle, or any such thing; but that it should be holy and without blemish.

28 So ought men to love their wives as their own bodies. He that loveth his wife loveth himself.

29 For no man ever yet hated his own flesh; but nourisheth and cherisheth it, even as the Lord the church;

30 For we are members of his body, of his flesh, and of his bones.

31 For this cause shall a man leave his father and mother, and shall be joined unto his wife, and they two shall be one flesh.

32 This is a great mystery; but I speak concerning Christ and the church.

33 Nevertheless, let every one of you in particular so love his wife even as himself; and the wife see that she reverence her husband.

## CHAPTER 6

*The duty of children, and servants—Our life a warfare—The armor of a Christian.*

1 Children, obey your parents in the Lord; for this is right.

2 Honor thy father and mother; which is the first commandment with promise;

3 That it may be well with thee, and thou mayest live long on the earth.

4 And ye fathers provoke not your children to wrath; but bring them up in the nurture and admonition of the Lord.

5 Servants, be obedient to them that are your masters according to the flesh, with fear and trembling, in singleness of your heart, as unto Christ;

6 Not with eye-service, as men pleasers; but as the servants of Christ, doing the will of God from the heart;

7 With goodwill doing service, as to the Lord, and not to men;

8 Knowing that whatsoever good thing any man doeth, the same shall he receive of the Lord, whether he be bond or free.

9 And, ye masters, do the same things unto them, forbearing threatening; knowing that your Master also is in heaven; neither is there respect of persons with him.

10 Finally, my brethren, be strong in the Lord, and in the power of his might.

11 Put on the whole armor of God, that ye may be able to stand against the wiles of the devil.

12 For we wrestle not against flesh and blood, but against principalities, against powers, against the rulers of the darkness of this world, against spiritual wickedness in high places.

13 Wherefore take unto you the whole armor of God, that ye may be able to withstand in the evil day, and having done all to stand.

14 Stand therefore, having your loins girt about with truth, and having on the breastplate of righteousness;

15 And your feet shod with the preparation of the gospel of peace;

16 Above all, taking the shield of faith, wherewith ye shall be able to quench all the fiery darts of the wicked.

17 And take the helmet of salvation, and the sword of the Spirit, which is the word of God;

18 Praying always with all prayer and supplication in the Spirit, and watching thereunto with all perseverance and supplication for all saints;

19 And for me, that utterance may

be given unto me, that I may open my mouth boldly, to make known the mystery of the gospel,

20 For which I am an ambassador in bonds; that therein I may speak boldly, as I ought to speak.

21 But that ye also may know my affairs, and how I do, Tychicus, a beloved brother and faithful minister in the Lord, shall make known to you all things;

22 Whom I have sent unto you for the same purpose, that ye might know our affairs, and that he might comfort your hearts.

23 Peace be to the brethren, and love with faith, from God the Father and the Lord Jesus Christ.

24 Grace be with all them that love our Lord Jesus Christ in sincerity. Amen.

Written from Rome unto the Ephesians by Tychicus.

## The Epistle of Paul the Apostle to the
# Philippians

### CHAPTER 1

*Exhortation to righteousness—Paul's devotedness to Christ—Desire to be with Christ—Duty to suffer for Christ.*

1 Paul and Timotheus, the servants of Jesus Christ, to all the saints in Christ Jesus which are at Philippi, with the bishops and deacons:

2 Grace be unto you, and peace, from God our Father and from the Lord Jesus Christ.

3 I thank my God upon every remembrance of you,

4 Always in every prayer of mine, for the steadfastness of you all, making request with joy,

5 For your fellowship in the gospel from the first day until now;

6 Being confident of this very thing, that he which hath begun a good work in you will perform it until the day of Jesus Christ;

7 Even as it is meet for me to think this of you all, because I have you in my heart; inasmuch as both in my bonds, and in the defense and confirmation of the gospel, ye all are partakers of my grace.

8 For God is my record, how greatly I long after you all in the bowels of Jesus Christ.

9 And this I pray, that your love may abound yet more and more in knowledge and in all judgment;

10 That ye may approve things that are excellent; that ye may be sincere and without offense till the day of Christ;

11 Being filled with the fruits of righteousness, which are by Jesus Christ, unto the glory and praise of God.

12 But I would ye should understand, brethren, that the things which happened unto me have fallen out rather unto the furtherance of the gospel;

13 So that my bonds in Christ are manifest in all the palace, and in all other places;

14 And many of the brethren in the Lord, waxing confident by my bonds, are much more bold to speak the word without fear.

15 Some indeed preach Christ even of envy and strife; and some also of goodwill;

16 The one preach Christ of contention, not sincerely, supposing to add affliction to my bonds;

17 But the other of love, knowing that I am set for the defense of the gospel.

18 What then? notwithstanding, every way, whether in pretense, or in truth, Christ is preached; and I therein do rejoice, yea, and will rejoice.

19 For I know that this shall turn to my salvation through your prayer, and the supply of the Spirit of Jesus Christ,

20 According to my earnest expectation and my hope, that in nothing I shall be ashamed, but that with all boldness, as always, so now also Christ shall be magnified in my body, whether it be by life, or by death.

21 But if I live in the flesh, ye are the fruit of my labor. Yet what I shall choose I know not.

22 For me to live, is to do the will of Christ; and to die, is my gain.

23 Now I am in a strait betwixt two, having a desire to depart, and to be with Christ; which is far better;

24 Nevertheless to abide in the flesh is more needful for you.

25 And having this confidence, I know that I shall abide and continue with you all for your furtherance and joy of faith;

26 That your rejoicing with me may be more abundant in Jesus Christ, for my coming to you again.

27 Therefore let your conversation be as it becometh the gospel of Christ; that whether I come and see you, or else be absent, I may hear of your affairs, that ye stand fast in one spirit, with one mind striving together for the faith of the gospel;

28 And in nothing terrified by your adversaries, who reject the gospel, which bringeth on them destruction; but you who receive the gospel, salvation; and that of God.

29 For unto you it is given in the behalf of Christ, not only to believe on him, but also to suffer for his sake;

30 Having the same conflict which ye saw in me, and now know to be in me.

## CHAPTER 2

*Paul exhorteth to unity, Christ's humility and exaltation—The saints to be lights to the world.*

1 If there be therefore any consolation in Christ, if any comfort of love, if any fellowship of the Spirit, if any bowels and mercies,

2 Fulfill ye my joy, that ye be likeminded, having the same love, being of one accord, of one mind.

3 Let nothing be done through strife or vainglory; but in lowliness of mind let each esteem other better than themselves.

4 Look not every man on his own things, but every man also on the things of others.

5 Let this mind be in you, which was also in Christ Jesus;

6 Who, being in the form of God, thought it not robbery to be equal with God;

7 But made himself of no reputation, and took upon him the form of a servant, and was made in the likeness of men;

8 And being found in fashion as a man, he humbled himself, and became obedient unto death, even the death of the cross.

9 Wherefore God also hath highly exalted him, and given him a name which is above every name;

10 That at the name of Jesus every knee should bow, of things in heaven, and things in earth, and things under the earth;

11 And that every tongue should confess that Jesus Christ is Lord, to the glory of God the Father.

12 Wherefore, my beloved, as ye have always obeyed, not as in my presence only, but now much more in my absence, work out your own salvation with fear and trembling;

13 For it is God which worketh in you both to will and to do of his good pleasure.

14 Do all things without murmurings and disputings;

15 That ye may be blameless and harmless, the sons of God, without rebuke, in the midst of a crooked and perverse nation, among whom ye shine as lights in the world;

16 Holding forth the word of life; that I may rejoice in the day of Christ, that I have not run in vain, neither laboured in vain.

17 Yea, and if I be offered a sacrifice upon the service of your faith, I joy, and rejoice with you all.

18 For the same cause also do ye joy, and rejoice with me.

19 But I trust in the Lord Jesus to send Timotheus shortly unto you, that I also may be of good comfort, when I know your state.

20 For I have no man like-minded, who will naturally care for your state.

21 For all seek their own, not the things which are Jesus Christ's.

22 But ye know the proof of him, that, as a son with the father, he hath served with me in the gospel.

23 Him therefore I hope to send presently, so soon as I shall see how it will go with me.

24 But I trust in the Lord that I also myself shall come shortly.

25 Yet I supposed it necessary to send to you Epaphroditus, my brother, and companion in labour, and fellow soldier, but your messenger, and he that ministered to my wants.

26 For he longed after you all, and was full of heaviness, because that ye had heard he had been sick.

27 For indeed he was sick nigh unto death; but God had mercy on him; and not on him only, but on me also, lest I should have sorrow upon sorrow.

28 I sent him therefore the more carefully, that, when ye see him again, ye may rejoice, and that I may be the less sorrowful.

29 Receive him therefore in the Lord with all gladness; and hold such in reputation;

30 Because for the work of Christ he was nigh unto death, not regarding his life, to supply your lack of service toward me.

## CHAPTER 3

*Paul warneth to beware of false teachers—The superiority of the righteousness of Christ—Second coming of Christ.*

1 Finally, my brethren, rejoice in the Lord. To write the same things to you, to me indeed is not grievous, and for you it is safe.

2 Beware of dogs, beware of evil workers, beware of the concision.

3 For we are the circumcision, which worship God in the spirit, and rejoice in Christ Jesus, and have no confidence in the flesh.

4 Though I might also have confidence in the flesh. If any other man thinketh that he hath whereof he might trust in the flesh, I more;

5 Circumcised the eighth day, of the stock of Israel, of the tribe of Benjamin, a Hebrew of the Hebrews; as touching the law, a Pharisee;

6 Concerning zeal, persecuting the church; touching the righteousness which is in the law, blameless.

7 But what things were gain to me, those I counted loss for Christ.

8 Yea doubtless, and I count all things but loss for the excellency of the knowledge of Christ Jesus my Lord; for whom I have suffered the loss of all things, and do count them but dung, that I may win Christ,

9 And be found in him, not having mine own righteousness, which is of the law, but that which is through the faith of Christ, the righteousness which is of God by faith;

10 That I may know him, and the power of his resurrection, and the fellowship of his sufferings, being made conformable unto his death;

11 If by any means I might attain unto the resurrection of the just.

12 Not as though I had already attained, either were already perfect; but I follow after, if that I may apprehend that for which also I am apprehended of Christ Jesus.

13 Brethren, I count not myself to have apprehended; but this one thing I do, forgetting those things which are behind, and reaching forth unto those things which are before,

14 I press toward the mark for the prize of the high calling of God in Christ Jesus.

15 Let us therefore, as many as be perfect, be thus minded; and if in any thing ye be otherwise minded, God shall reveal even this unto you.

16 Nevertheless, whereto we have already attained, let us walk by the same rule, let us mind the same thing.

17 Brethren, be followers together of me, and mark them which walk so as ye have us for an ensample.

18 (For many walk, of whom I have told you often, and now tell you even weeping, as the enemies of the cross of Christ;

19 Whose end is destruction, whose God is their belly, and who glory in their shame, who mind earthly things.)

20 For our conversation is in heaven; from whence also we look for the Savior, the Lord Jesus Christ;

21 Who shall change our vile body, that it may be fashioned like unto his glorious body, according to the working whereby he is able even to subdue all things unto himself.

## CHAPTER 4

*The book of life—Exhortations and admonitions—Christ the strength of the Christian.*

1 Therefore, my brethren dearly beloved and longed for, my joy and crown, so stand fast in the Lord, my dearly beloved.

2 I beseech Euodias, and beseech Syntyche, that they be of the same mind in the Lord.

3 And I entreat thee also, true yokefellow, help those women which laboured with me in the gospel, with Clement also, and with other my fellow labourers, whose names are in the book of life.

4 Rejoice in the Lord always; and again I say, Rejoice.

5 Let your moderation be known unto all men. The Lord is at hand.

6 Be afflicted for nothing; but in everything by prayer and supplication with thanksgiving let your requests be made known unto God.

7 And the peace of God, which passeth all understanding, shall keep your hearts and minds through Christ Jesus.

8 Finally, brethren, whatsoever things are true, whatsoever things are honest, whatsoever things are just; whatsoever things are pure, whatsoever things are lovely, whatsoever things are of good report; if there be any virtue, and if there be any praise, think on these things.

9 Those things, which ye have both learned, and received, and heard, and seen in me, do; and the God of peace shall be with you.

10 But I rejoiced in the Lord greatly, that now at the last your care of me hath flourished again; wherein ye were also careful, but ye lacked opportunity.

11 Not that I speak in respect of want; for I have learned, in whatsoever state I am, therewith to be content.

12 I know both how to be abased, and I know how to abound; every where and in all things I am instructed both to be full and to be hungry, both to abound and to suffer need.

13 I can do all things through Christ which strengtheneth me.

14 Notwithstanding, ye have well done, that ye did communicate with my affliction.

15 Now ye Philippians know also, that in the beginning of the gospel, when I departed from Macedonia, no church communicated with me as concerning giving and receiving, but ye only.

16 For even in Thessalonica ye sent once and again unto my necessity.

17 Not because I desire a gift; but I desire fruit that may abound to your account.

18 But I have all, and abound; I am full, having received of Epaphroditus the things which were sent from you, an odor of a sweet smell, a sacrifice acceptable, well pleasing to God.

19 But my God shall supply all your need according to his riches in glory by Christ Jesus.

20 Now unto God and our Father be glory for ever and ever. Amen.

21 Salute every saint in Christ Jesus. The brethren which are with me greet you.

22 All the saints salute you, chiefly they that are of Caesar's household.

23 The grace of our Lord Jesus Christ be with you all. Amen.

It was written to the Philippians from Rome by Epaphroditus.

## The Epistle of Paul the Apostle to the
# Colossians

### CHAPTER 1

*The unity of the gospel—The personality of God—Christ the head of the church— The mystery of the gospel.*

1 Paul, an apostle of Jesus Christ, by the will of God, and Timotheus our brother,

2 To the saints and faithful brethren in Christ which are at Colosse; Grace be unto you, and peace, from God our Father and the Lord Jesus Christ.

3 We give thanks to God and the Father of our Lord Jesus Christ, praying always for you,

4 Since we heard of your faith in Christ Jesus, and of your love to all the saints,

5 For the hope which is laid up for you in heaven, whereof ye heard before in the word of the truth of the gospel;

6 Which is come unto you, as in all generations of the world; and bringeth forth fruit, as it doth also in you, since the day ye heard of it, and knew the grace of God in truth;

7 As ye also learned of Epaphras our dear fellow servant, who is for you a faithful minister of Christ;

8 Who also declared unto us your love in the Spirit.

9 For this cause we also, since the day we heard it, do not cease to pray for you, and to desire that ye might be filled with the knowledge of his will in

all wisdom and spiritual understanding;

10 That ye might walk worthy of the Lord unto all pleasing, being fruitful in every good work, and increasing in the knowledge of God;

11 Strengthened with all might, according to his glorious power, unto all patience and long-suffering with joyfulness;

12 Giving thanks unto the Father, which hath made us meet to be partakers of the inheritance of the saints in light;

13 Who hath delivered us from the power of darkness, and hath translated us into the kingdom of his dear Son;

14 In whom we have redemption through his blood, even the forgiveness of sins;

15 Who is the image of the invisible God, the firstborn of every creature.

16 For by him were all things created, that are in heaven, and that are in earth, visible and invisible, whether they be thrones, or dominions, or principalities, or powers; all things were created by him, and for him;

17 And he is before all things, and by him all things consist.

18 And he is the head of the body, the church; who is the beginning, the firstborn from the dead; that in all things he might have the preeminence.

19 For it pleased the Father that in him should all fullness dwell;

20 And, having made peace through the blood of his cross, by him to reconcile all things unto himself; by him, I say, whether they be things in earth, or things in heaven.

21 And you, that were sometime alienated and enemies in your mind by wicked works, yet now hath he reconciled,

22 In the body of his flesh through death, to present you holy and unblamable and unreprovable in his sight;

23 If ye continue in the faith grounded and settled, and be not moved away from the hope of the gospel, which ye have heard, and which was preached to every creature which is under heaven; whereof I Paul am made a minister;

24 Who now rejoice in my sufferings for you, and fill up that which is behind of the afflictions of Christ in my

flesh for his body's sake, which is the church;

25 Whereof I am made a minister, according to the dispensation of God which is given to me for you, to fulfill the word of God;

26 Even the mystery which hath been hid from ages and from generations but now is made manifest to his saints;

27 To whom God would make known what is the riches of the glory of this mystery among the Gentiles; which is Christ in you, the hope of glory;

28 Whom we preach, warning every man, and teaching every man in all wisdom; that we may present every man perfect in Christ Jesus;

29 Whereunto I also labour, striving according to his working, which worketh in me mightily.

## CHAPTER 2

*Necessity of abiding in Christ—The personality of God—Baptism a burial—Shadows of things to come.*

1 For I would that ye knew what great conflict I have for you, and for them at Laodicea, and for as many as have not seen my face in the flesh;

2 That their hearts might be comforted, being knit together in love, and unto all riches of the full assurance of understanding, to the acknowledgment of the mystery of God and of Christ, who is of God, even the Father;

3 In whom are hid all the treasures of wisdom and knowledge.

4 And this I say, lest any man should beguile you with enticing words.

5 For though I be absent in the flesh, yet am I with you in the spirit, joying and beholding your order, and the steadfastness of your faith in Christ.

6 As ye have therefore received Christ Jesus the Lord, so walk ye in him;

7 Rooted and built up in him, and established in the faith, as ye have been taught, abounding therein with thanksgiving.

8 Beware lest any man spoil you through philosophy and vain deceit, after the tradition of men, after the rudiments of the world, and not after Christ.

9 For in him dwelleth all the fullness of the Godhead bodily.

10 And ye are complete in him, which

is the head of all principality and power;

11 In whom also ye are circumcised with the circumcision made without hands, in putting off the body of the sins of the flesh by the circumcision of Christ;

12 Buried with him in baptism, wherein also ye are risen with him through the faith of the operation of God, who hath raised him from the dead.

13 And you, being dead in your sins and the uncircumcision of your flesh, hath he quickened together with him, having forgiven you all trespasses;

14 Blotting out the handwriting of ordinances that was against us, which was contrary to us, and took it out of the way, nailing it to his cross;

15 And having spoiled principalities and powers, he made a show of them openly, triumphing over them in it.

16 Let no man therefore judge you in meat, or in drink, or in respect of a holyday, or of the new moon, or of the sabbath days;

17 Which are a shadow of things to come; but the body is of Christ.

18 Let no man beguile you of your reward in a voluntary humility and worshiping of angels, intruding into those things which he hath not seen, vainly puffed up by his fleshly mind,

19 And not holding the Head, from which all the body by joints and bands having nourishment ministered, and knit together, increaseth with the increase of God.

20 Wherefore if ye be dead with Christ from the rudiments of the world, why, as though living in the world, are ye subject to ordinances,

21 Which are after the doctrines and commandments of men, who teach you to touch not, taste not, handle not; all those things which are to perish with the using?

22 Which things have indeed a show of wisdom in will-worship, and humility, and neglecting the body as to the satisfying the flesh, not in any honor to God.

## CHAPTER 3

*We should seek the things of God—Exhortation to mortification, to put off the old man, and to put on Christ. Charity, humility, and other duties.*

1 If ye then be risen with Christ, seek those things which are above, where Christ sitteth on the right hand of God.

2 Set your affection on things above, not on things on the earth.

3 For ye are dead, and your life is hid with Christ in God.

4 When Christ, who is our life, shall appear, then shall ye also appear with him in glory.

5 Mortify therefore your members which are upon the earth; fornication, uncleanness, inordinate affection, evil concupiscence, and covetousness, which is idolatry;

6 For which things' sake the wrath of God cometh on the children of disobedience;

7 In the which ye also walked sometime, when ye lived in them.

8 But now ye also put off all these; anger, wrath, malice, blasphemy, filthy communication out of your mouth.

9 Lie not one to another, seeing that ye have put off the old man with his deeds;

10 And have put on the new man, which is renewed in knowledge after the image of him that created him;

11 Where there is neither Greek nor Jew, circumcision nor uncircumcision, Barbarian, Scythian, bond nor free; but Christ is all, and in all.

12 Put on therefore, as the elect of God, holy and beloved, bowels of mercies, kindness, humbleness of mind, meekness, long-suffering;

13 Forbearing one another, and forgiving one another, if any man have a quarrel against any; even as Christ forgave you, so also do ye.

14 And above all these things put on charity, which is the bond of perfectness.

15 And let the peace of God rule in your hearts, to the which also ye are called in one body; and be ye thankful.

16 Let the word of Christ dwell in you richly in all wisdom; teaching and admonishing one another in psalms and hymns and spiritual songs, singing with grace in your hearts to the Lord.

17 And whatsoever ye do in word or deed, do all in the name of the Lord Jesus, giving thanks to God and the Father by him.

18 Wives, submit yourselves unto your own husbands, as it is fit in the Lord.

19 Husbands, love your wives, and be not bitter against them.

20 Children, obey your parents in all things; for this is well pleasing unto the Lord.

21 Fathers, provoke not your children to anger, lest they be discouraged.

22 Servants, obey in all things your masters according to the flesh; not with eye-service, as men-pleasers; but in singleness of heart, fearing God;

23 And whatsoever ye do, do it heartily, as to the Lord, and not unto men;

24 Knowing that of the Lord ye shall receive the reward of the inheritance; for ye serve the Lord Christ.

25 But he that doeth wrong shall receive for the wrong which he hath done; and there is no respect of persons.

## CHAPTER 4

*Fervency in prayer—Walk wisely toward them that are without.*

1 Masters, give unto your servants that which is just and equal; knowing that ye also have a Master in heaven.

2 Continue in prayer, and watch in the same with thanksgiving;

3 Withal praying also for us, that God would open unto us a door of utterance, to speak the mystery of Christ, for which I am also in bonds;

4 That I may make it manifest, as I ought to speak.

5 Walk in wisdom toward them that are without, redeeming the time.

6 Let your speech be always with grace, seasoned with salt, that ye may know how ye ought to answer every man.

7 All my state shall Tychicus declare unto you, who is a beloved brother, and a faithful minister and fellow servant in the Lord;

8 Whom I sent unto you for the same purpose, that he might know your estate, and comfort your hearts;

9 With Onesimus, a faithful and beloved brother, who is one of you. They shall make known unto you all things which are done here.

10 Aristarchus my fellow prisoner saluteth you, and Marcus, sister's son to Barnabas, (touching whom ye received commandments; if he come unto you, receive him;)

11 And Jesus, which is called Justus, who are of the circumcision. These only are my fellow workers in the kingdom of God, which have been a comfort unto me.

12 Epaphras, who is one of you, a servant of Christ, saluteth you, always labouring fervently for you in prayers, that ye may stand perfect and complete in all the will of God.

13 For I bear him record, that he hath a great zeal for you, and them that are in Laodicea, and them in Hierapolis.

14 Luke the beloved physician, and Demas, greet you.

15 Salute the brethren which are in Laodicea, and Nymphas, and the church which is in his house.

16 And when this epistle is read among you, cause that it be read also in the church of the Laodiceans; and that ye likewise read the epistle from Laodicea.

17 And say to Archippus, Take heed to the ministry which thou hast received in the Lord, that thou fulfill it.

18 The salutation by the hand of me Paul. Remember my bonds. Grace be with you. Amen.

Written from Rome to the Colossians by Tychicus and Onesimus.

## The First Epistle of Paul the Apostle to the
# Thessalonians

## CHAPTER 1

*The gospel in power—Second coming of Christ.*

1 Paul, and Silvanus, and Timotheus, servants of God the Father and the Lord Jesus Christ, unto the church of the Thessalonians; grace unto you, and peace from God our Father, and the Lord Jesus Christ.

2 We give thanks always, making mention of you all, in our prayers to God for you;

3 Remembering without ceasing your work of faith, and labour of love, and

patience of hope in our Lord Jesus Christ, in the sight of God and our Father;

4 Knowing, brethren beloved, your election of God.

5 For our gospel came not unto you in word only, but also in power, and in the Holy Ghost, and in much assurance; as ye know what manner of men we were among you for your sake.

6 And ye became followers of us, and of the Lord, having received the word in much affliction, with joy of the Holy Ghost;

7 So that ye were ensamples to all that believe in Macedonia and Achaia.

8 For from you sounded out the word of the Lord not only in Macedonia and Achaia, but also in every place your faith toward God is spread abroad; so that we need not to speak any thing.

9 For they themselves show of us what manner of entering in we had unto you, and how ye turned to God from idols to serve the living and true God;

10 And to wait for his Son from heaven, whom he raised from the dead, even Jesus, which delivered us from the wrath to come.

## CHAPTER 2

*The manner of Paul's ministrations— The coming of Christ.*

1 For yourselves, brethren, know our entrance in unto you, that it was not in vain;

2 But even after that we had suffered before, and were shamefully entreated, as ye know, at Philippi, we were bold in our God to speak unto you the gospel of God with much contention.

3 For our exhortation was not of deceit, nor of uncleanness, nor in guile;

4 But as we were allowed of God to be put in trust with the gospel, even so we speak; not as pleasing men, but God, which trieth our hearts.

5 For neither at any time used we flattering words, as ye know, nor a cloak of covetousness; God is witness;

6 Nor of men sought we glory, neither of you, nor yet of others, when we might have been burdensome, as the apostles of Christ.

7 But we were gentle among you, even as a nurse cherisheth her children;

8 So being affectionately desirous of you, we were willing to have imparted unto you, not the gospel of God only, but also our own souls, because you were dear unto us.

9 For ye remember, brethren, our labour and travail; for labouring night and day, because we would not be chargeable unto any of you, we preached unto you the gospel of God.

10 Ye are witnesses, and God also, how holily and justly and unblamably we behaved ourselves among you that believe;

11 As ye know how we exhorted and comforted and charged every one of you, as a father doth his children,

12 That ye would walk worthy of God, who hath called you unto his kingdom and glory.

13 For this cause also thank we God without ceasing, because, when ye received the word of God which ye heard of us, ye received it not as the word of men, but, as it is in truth, the word of God, which effectually worketh also in you that believe.

14 For ye, brethren, became followers of the churches of God which in Judea are in Christ Jesus; for ye also have suffered like things of your own countrymen, even as they have of the Jews;

15 Who both killed the Lord Jesus, and their own prophets, and have persecuted us; and they please not God, and are contrary to all men;

16 Forbidding us to speak to the Gentiles that they might be saved, to fill up their sins always; for the wrath is coming upon them to the uttermost.

17 But we, brethren, being taken from you for a short time in presence, not in heart, endeavored the more abundantly to see your face with great desire.

18 Wherefore we would have come unto you, even I Paul, once and again; but Satan hindered us.

19 For what is our hope, or joy, or crown of rejoicing? Are not even ye in the presence of our Lord Jesus Christ at his coming?

20 For ye are our glory and joy.

## CHAPTER 3

*Paul testifieth his love.*

1 Wherefore when we could no longer forbear, we thought it good to be left at Athens alone;

2 And sent Timotheus, our brother, and minister of God, and our fellow-labourer in the gospel of Christ, to es-

tablish you, and to comfort you concerning your faith;

3 That no man should be moved by these afflictions; for yourselves know that we are appointed thereunto.

4 For verily, when we were with you, we told you before that we should suffer tribulation; even as it came to pass, and ye know.

5 For this cause, when I could no longer forbear, I sent to know your faith, lest by some means the tempter have tempted you, and our labour be in vain.

6 But now when Timotheus came from you unto us, and brought us good tidings of your faith and charity, and that ye have good remembrance of us always, desiring greatly to see us, as we also to see you;

7 Therefore, brethren, we were comforted over you in all our affliction and distress by your faith;

8 For now we live, if ye stand fast in the Lord.

9 For what thanks can we render to God again for you, for all the joy wherewith we joy for your sakes before our God;

10 Night and day praying exceedingly that we might see your face, and might perfect that which is lacking in your faith?

11 Now God himself and our Father, and our Lord Jesus Christ, direct our way unto you.

12 And the Lord make you to increase and abound in love one toward another, and toward all men, even as we do toward you;

13 To the end he may establish your hearts unblamable in holiness before God, even our Father, at the coming of our Lord Jesus Christ with all his saints.

## CHAPTER 4

*The second coming of Christ.*

1 Furthermore then we beseech you, brethren, and exhort you by the Lord Jesus, that as ye have received of us how ye ought to walk and to please God, so ye would abound more and more.

2 For ye know what commandments we gave you by the Lord Jesus.

3 For this is the will of God, even your sanctification, that ye should abstain from fornication;

4 That every one of you should know how to possess his vessel in sanctification and honor;

5 Not in the lust of concupiscence, even as the Gentiles which know not God;

6 That no man go beyond and defraud his brother in any matter; because that the Lord is the avenger of all such, as we also have forewarned you and testified.

7 For God hath not called us unto uncleanness, but unto holiness.

8 He therefore that despiseth, despiseth not man, but God, who hath also given unto us his Holy Spirit.

9 But as touching brotherly love ye need not that I write unto you; for ye yourselves are taught of God to love one another.

10 And indeed ye do it toward all the brethren which are in all Macedonia; but we beseech you, brethren, that ye increase more and more;

11 And that ye study to be quiet, and to do your own business, and to work with your own hands, as we commanded you;

12 That ye may walk honestly toward them that are without, and that ye may have lack of nothing.

13 But I would not have you to be ignorant, brethren, concerning them which are asleep, that ye sorrow not, even as others which have no hope.

14 For if we believe that Jesus died and rose again, even so them also which sleep in Jesus will God bring with him.

15 For this we say unto you by the word of the Lord, that they who are alive at the coming of the Lord, shall not prevent them who remain unto the coming of the Lord, who are asleep.

16 For the Lord himself shall descend from heaven with a shout, with the voice of the archangel, and with the trump of God; and the dead in Christ shall rise first;

17 Then they who are alive, shall be caught up together into the clouds with them who remain, to meet the Lord in the air; and so shall we be ever with the Lord.

18 Wherefore comfort one another with these words.

## CHAPTER 5

*Christ's second coming.*

1 But of the times and the seasons, brethren, ye have no need that I write unto you.

2 For yourselves know perfectly that

the day of the Lord so cometh as a thief in the night.

3 For when they shall say, Peace and safety; then sudden destruction cometh upon them, as travail upon a woman with child; and they shall not escape.

4 But ye, brethren, are not in darkness, that that day should overtake you as a thief.

5 Ye are all the children of light, and the children of the day; we are not of the night, nor of darkness.

6 Therefore let us not sleep, as do others; but let us watch and be sober.

7 For they that sleep sleep in the night; and they that be drunken are drunken in the night.

8 But let us, who are of the day, be sober, putting on the breastplate of faith and love; and for a helmet, the hope of salvation.

9 For God hath not appointed us to wrath, but to obtain salvation by our Lord Jesus Christ,

10 Who died for us, that, whether we wake or sleep, we should live together with him.

11 Wherefore comfort yourselves together, and edify one another, even as also ye do.

12 And we beseech you, brethren, to know them which labour among you, and are over you in the Lord, and admonish you;

13 And to esteem them very highly in love for their work's sake. And be at peace among yourselves.

14 Now we exhort you, brethren, warn them that are unruly, comfort the feebleminded, support the weak, be patient toward all men.

15 See that none render evil for evil unto any man; but ever follow that which is good, both among yourselves, and to all men.

16 Rejoice evermore.

17 Pray without ceasing.

18 In every thing give thanks; for this is the will of God in Christ Jesus concerning you.

19 Quench not the Spirit.

20 Despise not prophesyings.

21 Prove all things; hold fast that which is good.

22 Abstain from all appearance of evil.

23 And the very God of peace sanctify you wholly; and I pray God your whole spirit and soul and body be preserved blameless unto the coming of our Lord Jesus Christ.

24 Faithful is he that calleth you who also will do it.

25 Brethren, pray for us.

26 Greet all the brethren with a holy salutation.

27 I charge you by the Lord, that this epistle be read unto all the holy brethren.

28 The grace of our Lord Jesus Christ be with you. Amen.

The first epistle unto the Thessalonians was written from Athens.

## The Second Epistle of Paul the Apostle to the
# Thessalonians

### CHAPTER 1
*Destruction of the wicked.*

1 Paul, and Sylvanus, and Timotheus, the servants of God the Father and our Lord Jesus Christ, unto the church of the Thessalonians;

2 Grace unto you, and peace, from God our Father and our Lord Jesus Christ.

3 We are bound to thank God always for you, brethren, as it is meet, because that your faith groweth exceedingly, and the charity of every one of you all toward each other aboundeth;

4 So that we ourselves glory in you in the churches of God, for your patience and faith in all your persecutions and tribulations that ye endure;

5 Which is a manifest token of the righteous judgment of God, that ye may be counted worthy of the kingdom of God, for which ye also suffer;

6 Seeing it is a righteous thing with God to recompense tribulation to them that trouble you;

7 And to you who are troubled rest with us, when the Lord Jesus shall be revealed from heaven with his mighty angels,

8 In flaming fire taking vengeance on them that know not God, and that

obey not the gospel of our Lord Jesus Christ;

9 Who shall be punished with destruction from the presence of the Lord, and from the glory of his everlasting power;

10 When he shall come to be glorified in his saints, and to be admired in all them that believe (because our testimony among you was believed) in that day.

11 Wherefore also we pray always for you, that our God would count you worthy of this calling, and fulfill all the good pleasure of his goodness, and the work of faith with power;

12 That the name of our Lord Jesus Christ may be glorified in you, and ye in him, according to the grace of our God and the Lord Jesus Christ.

## CHAPTER 2

*The apostasy, and the man of sin.*

1 Now we beseech you, brethren, by the coming of our Lord Jesus Christ, and by our gathering together unto him,

2 That ye be not soon shaken in mind, or be troubled by letter, except ye receive it from us; neither by spirit, nor by word, as that the day of Christ is at hand.

3 Let no man deceive you by any means; for there shall come a falling away first, and that man of sin be revealed, the son of perdition;

4 Who opposeth and exalteth himself above all that is called God, or that is worshiped; so that he as God sitteth in the temple of God, showing himself that he is God.

5 Remember ye not, that, when I was yet with you, I told you these things?

6 And now ye know what withholdeth that he might be revealed in his time.

7 For the mystery of iniquity doth already work, and he it is who now worketh, and Christ suffereth him to work, until the time is fulfilled that he shall be taken out of the way.

8 And then shall that wicked one be revealed, whom the Lord shall consume with the spirit of his mouth, and shall destroy with the brightness of his coming.

9 Yea, the Lord, even Jesus, whose coming is not until after there cometh a falling away, by the working of Satan with all power, and signs and lying wonders,

10 And with all deceivableness of unrighteousness in them that perish; because they received not the love of the truth, that they may be saved.

11 And for this cause God shall send them strong delusion, that they should believe a lie;

12 That they all might be damned who believed not the truth, but had pleasure in unrighteousness.

13 But we are bound to give thanks always to God for you, brethren beloved of the Lord, because God hath from the beginning chosen you to salvation through sanctification of the Spirit and belief of the truth;

14 Whereunto he called you by our gospel, to the obtaining of the glory of our Lord Jesus Christ.

15 Therefore, brethren, stand fast, and hold the traditions which ye have been taught, whether by word, or our epistle.

16 Now our Lord Jesus Christ himself, and God, even our Father, which hath loved us, and hath given us everlasting consolation and good hope through grace,

17 Comfort your hearts, and stablish you in every good word and work.

## CHAPTER 3

*Evil company to be avoided.*

1 Finally, brethren, pray for us, that the word of the Lord may have free course, and be glorified, even as it is with you;

2 And that we may be delivered from unreasonable and wicked men; for all men have not faith.

3 But the Lord is faithful, who shall stablish you, and keep you from evil.

4 And we have confidence in the Lord touching you, that ye both do and will do the things which we command you.

5 And the Lord direct your hearts into the love of God, and into the patient waiting for Christ.

6 Now we command you, brethren, in the name of the Lord Jesus Christ, that ye withdraw yourselves from every brother that walketh disorderly, and not after the tradition which he received of us.

7 For yourselves know how ye ought to follow us; for we behaved not ourselves disorderly among you;

8 Neither did we eat any man's bread for naught; but wrought with labour and travail night and day, that

we might not be chargeable to any of you;

9 Not because we have not power, but to make ourselves an ensample unto you to follow us.

10 For even when we were with you, this we commanded you, that if any would not work, neither should he eat.

11 For we hear that there are some which walk among you disorderly, working not at all, but are busybodies.

12 Now them that are such we command and exhort by our Lord Jesus Christ, that with quietness they work, and eat their own bread.

13 But ye, brethren, be not weary in well doing.

14 And if any man obey not our word by this epistle, note that man, and have no company with him, that he may be ashamed.

15 Yet count him not as an enemy, but admonish him as a brother.

16 Now the Lord of peace himself give you peace always by all means. The Lord be with you all.

17 The salutation of Paul with mine own hand, which is the token in every epistle; so I write.

18 The grace of our Lord Jesus Christ be with you all. Amen.

The second epistle to the Thessalonians was written from Athens.

---

The First Epistle of Paul the Apostle to

# Timothy

## CHAPTER 1

*Paul's charge to Timothy—The object of the law.*

1 Paul, an apostle of Jesus Christ by the commandment of God and the Lord Jesus Christ, our Savior and our hope;

2 Unto Timothy, my own son in the faith; Grace, mercy, and peace, from God our Father, and Jesus Christ our Lord.

3 As I besought thee to abide still at Ephesus, when I went into Macedonia, that thou mightest charge some that they teach no other doctrine,

4 Neither give heed to fables and endless genealogies, which minister questions, rather than godly edifying which is in faith; so do.

5 Now the end of the commandment is charity out of a pure heart, and of a good conscience, and of faith unfeigned;

6 From which some having swerved have turned aside unto vain jangling;

7 Desiring to be teachers of the law; understanding neither what they say, nor whereof they affirm.

8 But we know that the law is good, if a man use it lawfully;

9 Knowing this, that the law is not made for a righteous man, but for the lawless and disobedient, for the ungodly and for sinners, for unholy and

profane, for murderers of fathers and murderers of mothers, for manslayers,

10 For whoremongers, for them that defile themselves with mankind, for men-stealers, for liars, for perjured persons, and if there be any other thing that is contrary to sound doctrine:

11 According to the glorious gospel of the blessed God, which was committed to my trust.

12 And I thank Christ Jesus our Lord, who hath enabled me, for that he counted me faithful, putting me into the ministry;

13 Who was before a blasphemer, and a persecutor, and injurious; but I obtained mercy, because I did it ignorantly in unbelief.

14 And the grace of our Lord was exceeding abundant with faith and love which is in Christ Jesus.

15 This is a faithful saying, and worthy of all acceptation, that Christ Jesus came into the world to save sinners; of whom I am chief.

16 Howbeit for this cause I obtained mercy, that in me first Jesus Christ might show forth all long-suffering, for a pattern to them which should hereafter believe on him to life everlasting.

17 Now unto the King eternal, immortal, invisible, the only wise God, be honor and glory for ever and ever. Amen.

18 This charge I commit unto thee,

son Timothy, according to the prophecies which went before on thee, that thou by them mightest war a good warfare;

19 Holding faith, and a good conscience; which some having put away, concerning faith have made shipwreck;

20 Of whom is Hymeneus and Alexander; whom I have delivered unto Satan, that they may learn not to blaspheme.

## CHAPTER 2
*Pray for all men—Women are not permitted to teach.*

1 I exhort therefore, that, first of all, supplications, prayers, intercessions, and giving thanks, be made for all men;

2 For kings, and for all that are in authority; that we may lead a quiet and peaceful life in all godliness and honesty.

3 For this is good and acceptable in the sight of God our Savior;

4 Who is willing to have all men to be saved, and to come unto the knowledge of the truth which is in Christ Jesus, who is the Only Begotten Son of God, and ordained to be a Mediator between God and man; who is one God, and hath power over all men.

5 For there is one God, and one mediator between God and men, the man Christ Jesus;

6 Who gave himself a ransom for all, to be testified in due time.

7 Whereunto I am ordained a preacher, and an apostle, (I speak the truth in Christ, and lie not,) a teacher of the Gentiles in faith and verity.

8 I will therefore that men pray every where, lifting up holy hands, without wrath and doubting.

9 In like manner also, that women adorn themselves in modest apparel, with shamefacedness and sobriety; not with braided hair, or gold, or pearls, or costly array;

10 But (which becometh women professing godliness) with good works.

11 Let the women learn in silence with all subjection.

12 For I suffer not a woman to teach, nor to usurp authority over the man, but to be in silence.

13 For Adam was first formed, then Eve.

14 And Adam was not deceived, but the woman being deceived was in the transgression.

15 Notwithstanding they shall be saved in childbearing, if they continue in faith and charity and holiness with sobriety.

## CHAPTER 3
*Of bishops, and deacons, and their wives—The pillar and ground of the truth.*

1 This is a true saying, If a man desire the office of a bishop, he desireth a good work.

2 A bishop then must be blameless, the husband of one wife, vigilant, sober, of good behavior, given to hospitality, apt to teach;

3 Not given to wine, no striker, not greedy of filthy lucre; but patient, not a brawler, not covetous;

4 One that ruleth well his own house, having his children in subjection with all gravity;

5 (For if a man know not how to rule his own house, how shall he take care of the church of God?)

6 Not a novice, lest being lifted up with pride he fall into the condemnation of the devil.

7 Moreover he must have a good report of them which are without; lest he fall into reproach and the snare of the devil.

8 Likewise the deacons must be grave, not double-tongued, not given to much wine, not greedy of filthy lucre;

9 Holding the mystery of the faith in a pure conscience.

10 And let these also first be proved; then let them use the office of a deacon, being found blameless.

11 Even so must their wives be grave, not slanderers, sober, faithful in all things.

12 Let the deacons be the husbands of one wife, ruling their children and their own houses well.

13 For they that have used the office of deacon well purchase to themselves a good degree, and great boldness in the faith which is in Christ Jesus.

14 These things I write unto thee, hoping to come unto thee shortly;

15 But if I tarry long, that thou mayest know how thou oughtest to behave thyself in the house of God, which is the church of the living God.

16 The pillar and ground of the truth is, (and without controversy, great is the mystery of godliness,) God was manifest in the flesh, justified in

the Spirit, seen of angels, preached unto the Gentiles, believed on in the world, received up into glory.

## CHAPTER 4
*Paul foretelleth the apostasy.*

1 Now the Spirit speaketh expressly, that in the latter times some shall depart from the faith, giving heed to seducing spirits, and the doctrines of devils;

2 Speaking lies in hypocrisy; having their conscience seared as with a hot iron;

3 Forbidding to marry, and commanding to abstain from meats, which God hath created to be received with thanksgiving of them which believe and know the truth.

4 For every creature of God is good, and nothing to be refused, if it be received with thanksgiving;

5 For it is sanctified by the word of God and prayer.

6 It thou put the brethren in remembrance of these things, thou shalt be a good minister of Jesus Christ, nourished up in the words of faith and of good doctrine, whereunto thou hast attained.

7 But refuse profane and old wives' fables, and excercise thyself rather unto godliness.

8 For bodily excercise profiteth little; but godliness is profitable unto all things, having promise of the life that now is, and of that which is to come.

9 This is a faithful saying, and worthy of all acceptation.

10 For therefore we both labour and suffer reproach, because we trust in the living God, who is the Savior of all men, specially of those that believe.

11 These things command and teach.

12 Let no man despise thy youth; but be thou an example of the believers, in word, in conversation, in charity, in spirit, in faith, in purity.

13 Till I come, give attendance to reading, to exhortation, to doctrine.'

14 Neglect not the gift that is in thee, which was given thee by prophecy, with the laying on of the hands of the presbytery.

15 Meditate upon these things; give thyself wholly to them; that thy profiting may appear to all.

16 Take heed unto thyself, and unto the doctrine; continue in them; for in doing this thou shalt both save thyself, and them that hear thee.

## CHAPTER 5
*Rules to be observed in reproving—Of widows—Of elders—Carefulness in ordinations.*

1 Rebuke not an elder, but entreat him as a father; and the younger men as brethren;

2 The elder women as mothers; the younger as sisters, with all purity.

3 Honor widows that are widows indeed.

4 But if any widow have children or nephews, let them learn first to show piety at home, and to requite their parents; for that is good and acceptable before God.

5 Now she that is a widow indeed, and desolate, trusteth in God, and continueth in supplications and prayers night and day.

6 But she that liveth in pleasure is dead while she liveth.

7 And these things give in charge, that they may be blameless.

8 But if any provide not for his own, and specially for those of his own house, he hath denieth the faith, and is worse than an infidel.

9 Let not a widow be taken into the number under threescore years old, having been the wife of one man,

10 Well reported of for good works; if she have brought up children, if she have lodged strangers, if she have washed the saints' clothes, if she have relieved the afflicted, if she have diligently followed every good work.

11 But the younger widows refuse: for when they have begun to wax wanton against Christ, they will marry;

12 Having damnation, because they have cast off their first faith.

13 And withal they learn to be idle, wandering about from house to house; and not only idle, but tattlers also and busybodies, speaking things which they ought not.

14 I will therefore that the younger women marry, bear children, guide the house, give none occasion to the adversary to speak reproachfully.

15 For some are already turned aside after Satan.

16 If any man or woman that believeth have widows, let them relieve them, and let not the church be charged; that it may relieve them that are widows indeed.

17 Let the elders that rule well be counted worthy of double honor, espe-

cially they who labour in the word and doctrine.

18 For the scripture saith, Thou shalt not muzzle the ox that treadeth out the corn. And, the labourer is worthy of his reward.

19 Against an elder receive not an accusation, but before two or three witnesses.

20 Them that sin rebuke before all, that others also may fear.

21 I charge thee before God, and the Lord Jesus Christ, and the elect angels, that thou observe these things without preferring one before another, doing nothing by partiality.

22 Lay hands suddenly on no man, neither be partaker of other men's sins; keep thyself pure.

23 Some men's sins are open beforehand, going before to judgment; and some men they follow after.

24 Likewise also the good works of some are manifest beforehand; and they that are otherwise cannot be hid.

25 Drink no longer water, but use a little wine for thy stomach's sake and thine often infirmities.

## CHAPTER 6

*Duty of servants—Avoid unwise teachers—Godliness is gain—Love of money—What to flee, and what to follow, and whereof to admonish the rich.*

1 Let as many servants as are under the yoke count their own masters worthy of all honor, that the name of God and his doctrine be not blasphemed.

2 And they that have believing masters, let them not despise them, because they are brethren; but rather do them service, because they are faithful and beloved, partakers of the benefit. These things teach and exhort.

3 If any man teach otherwise, and consent not to wholesome words, even the words of our Lord Jesus Christ, and to the doctrine which is according to godliness;

4 He is proud, knowing nothing, but doting about questions and strifes of words, whereof cometh envy, strife, railings, evil surmisings,

5 Perverse disputings of men of corrupt minds, and destitute of the truth, supposing that gain is godliness; from such withdraw thyself.

6 But godliness with contentment is great gain.

7 For we brought nothing into this world, and it is certain we can carry nothing out.

8 And having food and raiment, let us be therewith content.

9 But they that will be rich fall into temptation and a snare, and into many foolish and hurtful lusts, which drown men in destruction and perdition.

10 For the love of money is the root of all evil; which while some coveted after, they have erred from the faith, and pierced themselves through with many sorrows.

11 But thou, O man of God, flee these things; and follow after righteousness, godliness, faith, love, patience, meekness.

12 Fight the good fight of faith, lay hold on eternal life, whereunto thou art also called, and hast professed a good profession before many witnesses.

13 I give thee charge in the sight of God, who quickeneth all things, and before Christ Jesus, who before Pontius Pilate witnessed a good confession;

14 That thou keep this commandment without spot, unrebukable, until the appearing of our Lord Jesus Christ;

15 Which in his times he shall show, who is the blessed and only Potentate, the King of kings, and Lord of lords, to whom be honor and power everlasting;

16 Whom no man hath seen, nor can see, unto whom no man can approach, only he who hath the light and the hope of immortality dwelling in him.

17 Charge them that are rich in this world, that they be not high-minded, nor trust in uncertain riches, but in the living God, who giveth us richly all things to enjoy;

18 That they do good, that they be rich in good works, ready to distribute, willing to communicate;

19 Laying up in store for themselves a good foundation against the time to come, that they may lay hold on eternal life.

20 O Timothy, keep that which is committed to thy trust, avoiding profane and vain babblings, and oppositions of science falsely so called;

21 Which some professing have erred concerning the faith. Grace be with thee. Amen.

The first to Timothy was written from Laodicea, which is the chiefest city of Phrygia Pacatiana.

# Timothy

## CHAPTER 1

*Paul's love to Timothy—He is exhorted to persist in the form and truth of that doctrine which he had learned.*

1 Paul, an apostle of Jesus Christ by the will of God, according to the promise of life which is in Christ Jesus,

2 To Timothy, my dearly beloved son; Grace, mercy, and peace, from God the Father and Christ Jesus our Lord.

3 I thank God, whom I serve from my forefathers with pure conscience, that without ceasing I have remembrance of thee in my prayers night and day;

4 Greatly desiring to see thee, being mindful of thy tears, that I may be filled with joy;

5 When I call to remembrance the unfeigned faith that is in thee, which dwelt first in thy grandmother Lois, and thy mother Eunice; and I am persuaded that in thee also.

6 Wherefore I put thee in remembrance, that thou stir up the gift of God, which is in thee by the putting on of my hands.

7 For God hath not given us the spirit of fear; but of power and of love, and of a sound mind.

8 Be not thou therefore ashamed of the testimony of our Lord, nor of me his prisoner; but be thou partaker of the afflictions of the gospel according to the power of God;

9 Who hath saved us, and called us with a holy calling, not according to our works, but according to his own purpose and grace, which was given us in Christ Jesus before the world began;

10 But is now made manifest by the appearing of our Savior Jesus Christ, who hath abolished death, and hath brought life and immortality to light through the gospel;

11 Whereunto I am appointed a preacher, and an apostle, and a teacher of the Gentiles.

12 For the which cause I also suffer these things; nevertheless I am not ashamed; for I know whom I have believed, and am persuaded that he is able to keep that which I have committed unto him against that day.

13 Hold fast the form of sound words, which thou hast heard of me, in faith and love which is in Christ Jesus.

14 That good thing which was committed unto thee keep by the Holy Ghost which dwelleth in us.

15 This thou knowest, that all they which are in Asia be turned away from me; of whom are Phygellus and Hermogenes.

16 The Lord give mercy unto the house of Onesiphorus; for he oft refreshed me, and was not ashamed of my chain;

17 But when he was in Rome, he sought me out very diligently, and found me.

18 The Lord grant unto him that he may find mercy of the Lord in that day; and in how many things he ministered unto me at Ephesus, thou knowest very well.

## CHAPTER 2

*He is exhorted to constancy, perseverance, and to divide the word of God aright—The foundation of the Lord is sure.*

1 Thou therefore, my son, be strong in the grace that is in Christ Jesus.

2 And the things that thou hast heard of me among many witnesses, the same commit thou to faithful men, who shall be able to teach others also.

3 Thou therefore endure hardness, as a good soldier of Jesus Christ.

4 No man that warreth entangleth himself with the affairs of this life; that he may please him who hath chosen him to be a soldier.

5 And if a man also strive for masteries, he is not crowned, except he strive lawfully.

6 The husbandman that laboureth must be first partaker of the fruits.

7 Consider what I say, that the Lord give thee understanding in all things.

8 Remember that Jesus Christ of the seed of David was raised from the dead, according to the gospel;

9 Wherein I suffer trouble, as an evildoer, even unto bonds; but the word of God is not bound.

10 Therefore I endure all things for the elect's sake, that they may also ob-

tain the salvation which is in Christ Jesus with eternal glory.

11 For this is a faithful saying, If we be dead with him, we shall also live with him;

12 If we suffer, we shall also reign with him; if we deny him, he also will deny us;

13 If we believe not, yet he abideth faithful; he cannot deny himself.

14 Of these things put them in remembrance, charging them before the Lord that they strive not about words to no profit, but to the subverting of the hearers.

15 Study to show thyself approved unto God, a workman that needeth not to be ashamed, rightly dividing the word of truth.

16 But shun profane and vain babblings; for they will increase unto more ungodliness.

17 And their word will eat as doth a canker; of whom is Hymeneus and Philetus;

18 Who concerning the truth have erred, saying that the resurrection is past already; and overthrow the faith of some.

19 Nevertheless the foundation of God standeth sure, having this seal, The Lord knoweth them that are his. And, Let every one that nameth the name of Christ depart from iniquity.

20 But in a great house there are not only vessels of gold and of silver, but also of wood and of earth; and some to honor, and some to dishonor.

21 If a man therefore purge himself from these, he shall be a vessel unto honor, sanctified, and meet for the master's use, and prepared unto every good work.

22 Flee also youthful lusts; but follow righteousness, faith, charity, peace, with them that call on the Lord out of a pure heart.

23 But foolish and unlearned questions avoid, knowing that they do gender strifes.

24 And the servant of the Lord must not strive; but be gentle unto all men, apt to teach, patient;

25 In meekness instructing those that oppose themselves; if God peradventure will give them repentance to the acknowledging of the truth;

26 And that they may recover themselves out of the snare of the devil,

who are taken captive by him at his will.

## CHAPTER 3

*Perils of the last days—Apostasy—Use of scripture.*

1 This know also, that in the last days perilous times shall come.

2 For men shall be lovers of their own selves, covetous, boasters, proud, blasphemers, disobedient to parents, unthankful, unholy,

3 Without natural affection, trucebreakers, false accusers, incontinent, fierce, despisers of those that are good,

4 Traitors, heady, high-minded, lovers of pleasures more than lovers of God;

5 Having a form of godliness, but denying the power thereof; from such turn away.

6 For of this sort are they which creep into houses, and lead captive silly women laden with sins, led away with divers lusts,

7 Ever learning, and never able to come to a knowledge of the truth.

8 Now as Jannes and Jambres withstood Moses, so do these also resist the truth; men of corrupt minds, reprobate concerning the faith.

9 But they shall proceed no further; for their folly shall be manifest unto all men, as theirs also was.

10 But thou hast fully known my doctrine, manner of life, purpose, faith, long-suffering, charity, patience,

11 Persecutions, afflictions, which came unto me at Antioch, at Iconium, at Lystra; what persecutions I endured; but out of them all the Lord delivered me.

12 Yea, and all that will live godly in Christ Jesus shall suffer persecution.

13 For evil men and seducers shall wax worse and worse, deceiving, and being deceived.

14 But continue thou in the things which thou hast learned and hast been assured of, knowing of whom thou hast learned them;

15 And that from a child thou hast known the holy scriptures, which are able to make thee wise unto salvation through faith which is in Christ Jesus.

16 And all scripture given by inspiration of God, is profitable for doctrine, for reproof, for correction, for instruction in righteousness;

17 That the man of God may be per-

fect, thoroughly furnished unto all good works.

## CHAPTER 4

*Explanations of duty—The apostasy—Assurance of a crown—Trust in God.*

1 I charge thee therefore before God, and the Lord Jesus Christ, who shall judge the quick and the dead at his appearing in his kingdom;

2 Preach the word; be instant in season, those who are out of season; reprove, rebuke, exhort with all long-suffering and doctrine.

3 For the time will come when they will not endure sound doctrine; but after their own lusts shall they heap to themselves teachers, having itching ears;

4 And they shall turn away their ears from the truth, and shall be turned unto fables.

5 But watch thou in all things, endure afflictions, do the work of an evangelist, make full proof of thy ministry.

6 For I am now ready to be offered, and the time of my departure is at hand.

7 I have fought a good fight, I have finished my course, I have kept the faith;

8 Henceforth there is laid up for me a crown of righteousness, which the Lord, the righteous judge, shall give me at that day; and not to me only, but unto all them also that love his appearing.

9 Do thy diligence to come shortly unto me;

10 For Demas hath forsaken me, having loved this present world, and is departed unto Thessalonica; Crescens to Galatia, Titus unto Dalmatia.

11 Only Luke is with me. Take Mark, and bring him with thee; for he is profitable to me for the ministry.

12 And Tychicus have I sent to Ephesus.

13 The cloak that I left at Troas with Carpus, when thou comest, bring with thee, and the books, but especially the parchments.

14 Alexander the coppersmith did me much evil; the Lord reward him according to his works;

15 Of whom be thou ware; for he hath greatly withstood our words.

16 At my first answer no man stood with me, but all men forsook me; I pray God that it may not be laid to their charge.

17 Notwithstanding the Lord stood with me, and strengthened me; that by me the preaching might be fully known, and that all the Gentiles might hear; and I was delivered out of the mouth of the lion.

18 And the Lord shall deliver me from every evil work, and will preserve me unto his heavenly kingdom; to whom be glory for ever and ever. Amen.

19 Salute Prisca and Aquila, and the household of Onesiphorus.

20 Erastus abode at Corinth; but Trophimus have I left at Miletum sick.

21 Do thy diligence to come before winter. Eubulus greeteth thee, and Pudens, and Linus, and Claudia, and all the brethren.

22 The Lord Jesus Christ be with you, and grace be with you all. Amen.

The second epistle unto Timotheus, ordained the first bishop of the church of the Ephesians, was written from Rome, when Paul was brought before Nero the second time.

## The Epistle of Paul to
# Titus

## CHAPTER 1

*Promise of eternal life—Ordination of elders, qualification of bishops.*

1 Paul, a servant of God, and an apostle of Jesus Christ, according to the faith of God's elect, and the acknowledging of the truth which is after godliness;

2 In hope of eternal life, which God, that cannot lie, promised before the world began;

3 But hath in due times manifested his word through preaching, which is committed unto me according to the commandment of God our Savior;

4 To Titus, mine own son after the

common faith; Grace, mercy, and peace, from God the Father and the Lord Jesus Christ our Savior.

5 For this cause left I thee in Crete, that thou shouldest set in order the things that are wanting, and ordain elders in every city, as I had appointed thee;

6 If any be blameless, the husband of one wife, having faithful children not accused of riot or unruly.

7 For a bishop must be blameless, as the steward of God; not self-willed, not soon angry, not given to wine, no striker, not given to filthy lucre;

8 But a lover of hospitality, a lover of good men, sober, just, holy, temperate;

9 Holding fast the faithful word as he hath been taught, that he may be able by sound doctrine both to exhort and to convince the gainsayers.

10 For there are many unruly and vain talkers and deceivers, specially they of the circumcision;

11 Whose mouths must be stopped, who subvert whole houses, teaching things which they ought not, for filthy lucre's sake.

12 One of themselves, even a prophet of their own, said, The Cretians are always liars, evil beasts, slow bellies.

13 This witness is true. Wherefore rebuke them sharply, that they may be sound in the faith;

14 Not giving heed to Jewish fables, and commandments of men, that turn from the truth.

15 Unto the pure, let all things be pure; but unto them who are defiled and unbelieving, nothing is pure; but even their mind and conscience is defiled.

16 They profess that they know God; but in works they deny him, being abominable, and disobedient, and unto every good work reprobate.

## CHAPTER 2

*Directions for doctrine and life—The duty of saints—Second coming of Christ.*

1 But speak thou the things which become sound doctrine;

2 That the aged men be sober, grave, temperate, sound in faith, in charity, in patience.

3 The aged women, likewise, that they may be in behavior as becometh holiness, not false accusers, not given to much wine, teachers of good things;

4 That they may teach the young

women to be sober, to love their husbands, to love their children,

5 To be discreet, chaste, keepers at home, good, obedient to their own husbands, that the word of God be not blasphemed.

6 Young men likewise exhort to be sober-minded.

7 In all things showing thyself a pattern of good works; in doctrine showing uncorruptness, gravity, sincerity,

8 Sound speech, that cannot be condemned; that he that is of the contrary part may be ashamed, having no evil thing to say of you.

9 Exhort servants to be obedient unto their own masters, and to please them well in all things; not answering again;

10 Nor purloining, but showing all good fidelity; that they may adorn the doctrine of God our Savior in all things.

11 For the grace of God which bringeth salvation to all men, hath appeared;

12 Teaching us that, denying ungodliness and worldly lusts, we should live soberly, righteously, and godly, in this present world;

13 Looking for that blessed hope, and the glorious appearing of the great God and our Savior Jesus Christ;

14 Who gave himself for us, that he might redeem us from all iniquity, and purify unto himself a peculiar people, zealous of good works.

15 These things speak, and exhort, and rebuke with all authority. Let no man despise thee.

## CHAPTER 3

*Civil rulers to be honored as such—Of regeneration—Duties of saints—Of heretics.*

1 Put them in mind to be subject to principalities and powers, to obey magistrates, to be ready to every good work,

2 To speak evil of no man, to be no brawlers, but gentle, showing all meekness unto all men.

3 For we ourselves also were sometime foolish, disobedient, deceived, serving divers lusts and pleasures, living in malice and envy, hateful, and hating one another.

4 But after that the kindness and love of God our Savior toward man appeared,

5 Not by works of righteousness which we have done, but according to his

mercy he saved us, by the washing of regeneration, and renewing of the Holy Ghost;

6 Which he shed on us abundantly through Jesus Christ our Savior;

7 That being justified by his grace, we should be made heirs according to the hope of eternal life.

8 This is a faithful saying, and these things I will that thou affirm constantly, that they which have believed in God might be careful to maintain good works. These things are good and profitable unto men.

9 But avoid foolish questions, and genealogies, and contentions, and strivings about the law; for they are unprofitable and vain.

10 A man that is a heretic, after the first and second admonition, reject;

11 Knowing that he that is such is subverted, and sinneth, being condemned of himself.

12 When I shall send Artemas unto thee, or Tychicus, be diligent to come unto me to Nicopolis; for I have determined there to winter.

13 Bring Zenas the lawyer and Apollos on their journey diligently, that nothing be wanting unto them.

14 And let ours also learn to maintain good works for necessary uses, that they be not unfruitful.

15 All that are with me salute thee. Greet them that love us in the faith. Grace be with you all. Amen.

It was written to Titus, ordained the first bishop of the church of the Cretians, from Nicopolis of Macedonia.

<br>

## The Epistle of Paul to
# Philemon

*Master and servant one in Christ.*

1 Paul, a prisoner of Jesus Christ, and Timothy our brother, unto Philemon our dearly beloved, and fellow labourer,

2 And to our beloved Apphia, and Archippus our fellow soldier, and to the church in thy house;

3 Grace to you, and peace from God our Father and the Lord Jesus Christ.

4 I thank my God, making mention of thee always in my prayers,

5 Hearing of thy love and faith, which thou hast toward the Lord Jesus, and toward all saints;

6 That the communication of thy faith may become effectual by the acknowledging of every good thing which is in you in Christ Jesus.

7 For we have great joy and consolation in thy love, because the bowels of the saints are refreshed by thee, brother.

8 Wherefore, though I might be much bold in Christ to enjoin thee that which is convenient,

9 Yet for love's sake I rather beseech thee, being such a one as Paul the aged, and now also a prisoner of Jesus Christ.

10 I beseech thee for my son Onesimus, whom I have begotten in my bonds;

11 Which in time past was to thee unprofitable, but now profitable to thee and to me;

12 Whom I have sent again; thou therefore receive him, that is, mine own bowels;

13 Whom I would have retained with me, that in thy stead he might have ministered unto me in the bonds of the gospel;

14 But without thy mind would I do nothing; that thy benefit should not be as it were of necessity, but willingly.

15 For perhaps he therefore departed for a season, that thou shouldest receive him for ever;

16 Not now as a servant, but above a servant, a brother beloved, specially to me, but how much more unto thee, both in the flesh, and in the Lord?

17 If thou count me therefore a partner, receive him as myself.

18 If he hath wronged thee, or oweth thee aught, put that on mine account;

19 I Paul have written it with mine own hand, I will repay it; albeit I do not say to thee how thou owest unto me even thine own self besides.

20 Yea, brother, let me have joy of thee in the Lord; refresh my bowels in the Lord.

21 Having confidence in thy obedience I wrote unto thee, knowing that thou wilt also do more than I say.

22 But withal prepare me also a lodging; for I trust that through your prayers I shall be given unto you.

23 There salute thee Epaphras, my fellow prisoner in Christ Jesus;

24 Marcus, Aristarchus, Demas, Lucas, my fellow labourers.

25 The grace of our Lord Jesus Christ be with you. Amen.

Written from Rome to Philemon, by Onesimus, a servant.

## The Epistle to the
# Hebrews

### CHAPTER 1

*The personality of God—Christ preferred above the angels—The heaven and earth to be changed.*

1 God, who at sundry times and in divers manners spake in time past unto the fathers by the prophets,

2 Hath in these last days spoken unto us by his Son, whom he hath appointed heir of all things, by whom also he made the worlds;

3 Who being the brightness of his glory, and the express image of his person, and upholding all things by the word of his power, when he had by himself purged our sins, sat down on the right hand of the Majesty on high;

4 Being made so much better than the angels, as he hath by inheritance obtained a more excellent name than they.

5 For unto which of the angels said he at any time, Thou art my Son, this day have I begotten thee? And again, I will be to him a Father, and he shall be to me a Son?

6 And again, when he bringeth in the first begotten into the world, he saith, And let all the angels of God worship him, who maketh his ministers as a flame of fire.

7 And of the angels he saith, Angels are ministering spirits.

8 But unto the Son he saith, Thy throne, O God, is for ever and ever; a scepter of righteousness is the scepter of thy kingdom.

9 Thou hast loved righteousness, and hated iniquity; therefore God, even thy God, hath anointed thee with the oil of gladness above thy fellows.

10 And, Thou, Lord, in the beginning hast laid the foundation of the earth; and the heavens are the works of thine hands.

11 They shall perish, but thou remainest; and they all shall wax old as doth a garment;

12 And as a vesture shalt thou fold them up, and they shall be changed; but thou art the same, and thy years shall not fail.

13 But to which of the angels said he at any time, Sit on my right hand, until I make thine enemies thy footstool?

14 Are they not all ministering spirits, sent forth to minister for them who shall be heirs of salvation?

### CHAPTER 2

*The world to come—Man's inheritance— Perfection attained through suffering— Obedience to Christ enforced from his example.*

1 Therefore we ought to give the more earnest heed to the things which we have heard, lest at any time we should let them slip.

2 For if the word spoken by angels was steadfast, and every transgression and disobedience received a just recompense of reward;

3 How shall we escape, if we neglect so great salvation; which at the first began to be spoken by the Lord, and was confirmed unto us by them that heard him;

4 God also bearing them witness, both with signs and wonders, and with divers miracles, and gifts of the Holy Ghost, according to his own will?

5 For unto the angels hath he not put in subjection the world to come, whereof we speak.

6 But one in a certain place, testified, saying, What is man, that thou art mindful of him? or the son of man, that thou visitest him?

7 Thou madest him a little lower than the angels; thou crownedst him with glory and honor, and didst set him over the works of thy hands;

8 Thou hast put all things in subjection under his feet. For in that he put all in subjection under him, he left nothing that is not put under him. But

now we see not yet all things put under him.

9 But we see Jesus, who was made a little lower than the angels for the suffering of death, crowned with glory and honor; that he by the grace of God should taste death for every man.

10 For it became him, for whom are all things, and by whom are all things, in bringing many sons unto glory, to make the captain of their salvation perfect through sufferings.

11 For both he that sanctifieth and they who are sanctified are all of one; for which cause he is not ashamed to call them brethren,

12 Saying, I will declare thy name unto my brethren, in the midst of the church will I sing praise unto thee.

13 And again, I will put my trust in him. And again, Behold I and the children which God hath given me.

14 Forasmuch then as the children are partakers of flesh and blood, he also himself likewise took part of the same; that through death he might destroy him that had the power of death, that is, the devil;

15 And deliver them, who through fear of death were all their lifetime subject to bondage.

16 For verily, he took not on him the likeness of angels; but he took on him the seed of Abraham.

17 Wherefore in all things it behooved him to be made like unto his brethren, that he might be a merciful and faithful high priest in things pertaining to God, to make reconciliation for the sins of the people.

18 For in that he himself hath suffered being tempted, he is able to succor them that are tempted.

## CHAPTER 3
*Christ more worthy than Moses.*

1 Wherefore, holy brethren, partakers of the heavenly calling, consider the Apostle and High Priest of our profession, Christ Jesus;

2 Who was faithful to him that appointed him, as also Moses was faithful in all his house.

3 For he was counted worthy of more glory than Moses, inasmuch as he who hath builded the house hath more honor than the house.

4 For every house is builded by some man; but he that built all things is God.

5 And Moses verily was faithful in all

his house as a servant, for a testimony of those things which were to be spoken after;

6 But Christ as a son over his own house; whose house are we, if we hold fast the confidence and the rejoicing of the hope firm unto the end.

7 Wherefore as the Holy Ghost saith, Today if ye will hear his voice,

8 Harden not your hearts, as in the provocation, in the day of temptation in the wilderness;

9 When your fathers tempted me, proved me, and saw my works forty years.

10 Wherefore I was grieved with that generation, and said, They do always err in their heart; and they have not known my ways.

11 So I sware in my wrath, They shall not enter into my rest.

12 Take heed, brethren, lest there be in any of you an evil heart of unbelief, in departing from the living God.

13 But exhort one another daily, while it is called Today; lest any of you be hardened through the deceitfulness of sin.

14 For we are made partakers of Christ, if we hold the beginning of our confidence steadfast unto the end;

15 While it is said, Today if ye will hear his voice, harden not your hearts, as in the provocation.

16 For some, when they had heard, did provoke; howbeit not all that came out of Egypt by Moses.

17 But with whom was he grieved forty years? was it not with them that had sinned, whose carcasses fell in the wilderness?

18 And to whom sware he that they should not enter into his rest, but to them that believed not?

19 So we see that they could not enter in because of unbelief.

## CHAPTER 4
*The rest of saints attained by faith—The power of God's word—Our high priest, Jesus, the Son of God.*

1 Let us therefore fear, lest, a promise being left us by entering into his rest, any of you should seem to come short of it.

2 For unto us was the rest preached, as well as unto them; but the word preached did not profit them, not being mixed with faith in them that heard it.

3 For we who have believed do enter into rest, as he said, As I have sworn in my wrath, If they harden their hearts they shall not enter into my rest; also, I have sworn, If they will not harden their hearts, they shall enter into my rest; although the works of God were prepared, (or finished,) from the foundation of the world.

4 For he spake in a certain place of the seventh day on this wise, And God did rest the seventh day from all his works.

5 And in this place again, If they harden not their hearts they shall enter into my rest.

6 Seeing therefore it remaineth that some must enter therein, and they to whom it was first preached entered not in because of unbelief;

7 Again, he limiteth a certain day, saying in David, Today, after so long a time; as it is said, Today if ye will hear his voice, harden not your hearts.

8 For if Jesus had given them rest, then would he not afterward have spoken of another day.

9 There remaineth therefore a rest to the people of God.

10 For he that is entered into his rest, he also hath ceased from his own works, as God did from his.

11 Let us labour therefore to enter into that rest, lest any man fall after the same example of unbelief.

12 For the word of God is quick, and powerful, and sharper than any two-edged sword, piercing even to the dividing asunder of body and spirit, and of the joints and marrow, and is a discerner of the thoughts and intents of the heart.

13 Neither is there any creature that is not manifest in his sight; but all things are naked and opened unto the eyes of him with whom we have to do.

14 Seeing then that we have a great high priest, that is passed into the heavens, Jesus the Son of God, let us hold fast our profession.

15 For we have not a high priest which cannot be touched with the feeling of our infirmities; but was on all points tempted like as we are, yet without sin.

16 Let us therefore come boldly unto the throne of grace, that we may obtain mercy, and find grace to help in time of need.

## CHAPTER 5

*Of the priesthood.*

1 For every high priest taken from among men is ordained for men in things pertaining to God, that he may offer both gifts and sacrifices for sins;

2 Who can have compassion on the ignorant, and on them that are out of the way; for that he himself also is compassed with infirmity.

3 And by reason hereof he ought, as for the people, so also for himself to offer for sins.

4 And no man taketh this honor unto himself, but he that is called of God, as was Aaron.

5 So also Christ glorified not himself to be made a high priest; but he that said unto him, Thou art my Son, today have I begotten thee.

6 As he saith also in another place, Thou art a priest for ever after the order of Melchizedek.

*7 (Who in the days of his flesh, when he had offered up prayers and supplications with strong crying and tears unto him that was able to save him from death, and was heard in that he feared;

8 Though he were a son, yet learned he obedience by the things which he suffered.)

9 And being made perfect, he became the author of eternal salvation unto all them that obey him;

10 Called of God a high priest after the order of Melchizedek.

11 Of whom we have many things to say, and hard to be uttered, seeing ye are dull of hearing.

12 For when for the time ye ought to be teachers, ye have need that one teach you again which be the first principles of the oracles of God; and are become such as have need of milk, and not of strong meat.

13 For every one that useth milk is unskillful in the word of righteousness; for he is a babe.

14 But strong meat belongeth to them that are of full age, even those who by reason of use have their senses exercised to discern both good and evil.

---

*The 7th and 8th verses allude to Melchizedek, and not to Christ.—I.V.MS.

## CHAPTER 6

*Principles of the doctrine of Christ—*
*The restitution—The surety of God's*
*promise.*

1 Therefore not leaving the principles of the doctrine of Christ, let us go on unto perfection; not laying again the foundation of repentance from dead works, and of faith toward God.

2 Of the doctrine of baptisms, of laying on of hands, and of the resurrection of the dead, and of eternal judgment.

3 And we will go on unto perfection if God permit.

4 For he hath made it impossible for those who were once enlightened, and have tasted of the heavenly gift, and were made partakers of the Holy Ghost,

5 And have tasted the good word of God, and the powers of the world to come,

6 If they shall fall away, to be renewed again unto repentance; seeing they crucify unto themselves the Son of God afresh, and put him to an open shame.

7 For the day cometh that the earth which drinketh in the rain that cometh oft upon it, and bringeth forth herbs meet for them who dwelleth thereon, by whom it is dressed, who now receiveth blessings from God, shall be cleansed with fire.

8 For that which beareth thorns and briers is rejected, and is nigh unto cursing; therefore they who bring not forth good fruits, shall be cast into the fire; for their end is to be burned.

9 But, beloved, we are persuaded of better things of you, and things that accompany salvation, though we thus speak.

10 For God is not unrighteous, therefore he will not forget your work and labor of love, which ye have showed toward his name, in that ye have ministered to the saints, and do minister.

11 And we desire that every one of you do show the same diligence to the full assurance of hope unto the end;

12 That ye be not slothful, but followers of them who through faith and patience inherit the promises.

13 For when God made promise to Abraham, because he could swear by no greater, he sware by himself,

14 Saying, Surely blessing I will bless thee, and multiplying I will multiply thee.

15 And so, after he had patiently endured, he obtained the promise.

16 For men verily swear by the greater; and an oath for confirmation is to them an end of all strife.

17 Wherein God, willing more abundantly to show unto the heirs of promise the immutability of his counsel, confirmed it by an oath;

18 That by two immutable things, in which it was impossible for God to lie, we might have a strong consolation, who have fled for refuge to lay hold upon the hope set before us;

19 Which hope we have as an anchor of the soul, both sure and steadfast, and which entereth into that within the veil;

20 Whither the forerunner is for us entered, even Jesus, made an high priest for ever after the order of Melchizedek.

## CHAPTER 7

*Of the Melchizedek and Aaronic priesthood.*

1 For this Melchizedek, king of Salem, priest of the most high God, who met Abraham returning from the slaughter of the kings, and blessed him;

2 To whom also Abraham gave a tenth part of all; first being by interpretation King of righteousness, and after that also King of Salem, which is, King of peace;

3 For this Melchizedek was ordained a priest after the order of the Son of God, which order was without father, without mother, without descent, having neither beginning of days, nor end of life. And all those who are ordained unto this priesthood are made like unto the Son of God, abiding a priest continually.

4 Now consider how great this man was, unto whom even the patriarch Abraham gave the tenth of the spoils.

5 And verily they that are of the sons of Levi, who receive the office of the priesthood, have a commandment to take tithes of the people according to the law, that is, of their brethren, though they come out of the loins of Abraham;

6 But he whose descent is not counted from them received tithes of

Abraham, and blessed him that had the promises.

7 And without all contradiction the less is blessed of the better.

8 And here men that die receive tithes; but there he receiveth them, of whom it is witnessed that he liveth.

9 And as I may so say, Levi also, who receiveth tithes, paid tithes in Abraham.

10 For he was yet in the loins of his father, when Melchizedek met him.

11 If therefore perfection were by the Levitical priesthood, (for under it the people received the law,) what further need was there that another priest should rise after the order of Melchizedek, and not be called after the order of Aaron?

12 For the priesthood being changed, there is made of necessity a change also of the law.

13 For he of whom these things are spoken pertaineth to another tribe, of which no man gave attendance at the altar.

14 For it is evident that our Lord sprang out of Juda; of which tribe Moses spake nothing concerning priesthood.

15 And it is yet far more evident; for that after the similitude of Melchizedek there ariseth another priest,

16 Who is made, not after the law of a carnal commandment, but after the power of an endless life.

17 For he testifieth, Thou art a priest for ever after the order of Melchizedek.

18 For there is verily a disannulling of the commandment going before, for the weakness and unprofitableness thereof.

19 For the law was administered without an oath and made nothing perfect, but was only the bringing in of a better hope; by the which we draw nigh unto God.

20 Inasmuch as this high priest was not without an oath, by so much was Jesus made the surety of a better testament.

21 (For those priests were made without an oath; but this with an oath by him that said unto him, The Lord sware and will not repent, Thou art a priest for ever after the order of Melchizedek;)

22 And they truly were many priests, because they were not suffered to continue by reason of death;

23 But this man, because he continueth ever, hath an unchangeable priesthood.

24 Wherefore he is able also to save them to the uttermost that come unto God by him, seeing he ever liveth to make intercession for them.

25 For such an high priest became us, who is holy, harmless, undefiled, separate from sinners, and made ruler over the heavens;

26 And not as those high priests who offered up sacrifice daily, first for their own sins, and then for the sins of the people; for he needeth not offer sacrifice for his own sins, for he knew no sins; but for the sins of the people. And this he did once, when he offered up himself.

27 For the law maketh men high priests which have infirmity; but the word of the oath, which was since the law, maketh the Son, who is consecrated for evermore.

## CHAPTER 8

*Of the priesthood—The new covenant.*

1 Now of the things which we have spoken this is the sum; we have such an high priest, who is set on the right hand of the throne of the Majesty in the heavens;

2 A minister of the sanctuary, and of the true tabernacle, which the Lord pitched, and not man.

3 For every high priest is ordained to offer gifts and sacrifices; wherefore it is of necessity that this man have somewhat also to offer.

4 Therefore while he was on the earth, he offered for a sacrifice his own life for the sins of the people. Now every priest under the law, must needs offer gifts, or sacrifices, according to the law.

5 Who serve unto the example and shadow of heavenly things, as Moses was admonished of God when he was about to make the tabernacle; for, See, saith he, that thou make all things according to the pattern showed to thee in the mount.

6 But now hath he obtained a more excellent ministry, by how much also he is the mediator of a better covenant, which was established upon better promises.

7 For if that first covenant had been faultless, then should no place have been sought for the second.

8 For finding fault with them, he saith, Behold, the days come, saith the Lord, when I will make a new covenant with the house of Israel and with the house of Judah;

9 Not according to the covenant that I made with their fathers, in the day when I took them by the hand to lead them out of the land of Egypt; because they continued not in my covenant, and I regarded them not, saith the Lord.

10 For this is the covenant that I will make with the house of Israel after those days, saith the Lord; I will put my laws into their mind, and write them in their hearts; and I will be to them a God, and they shall be to me a people;

11 And they shall not teach every man his neighbor, and every man his brother, saying, Know the Lord; for all shall know me, from the least to the greatest.

12 For I will be merciful to their unrighteousness, and their sins and their iniquities will I remember no more.

13 In that he saith, A new covenant, he hath made the first old. Now that which decayeth and waxeth old is ready to vanish away.

## CHAPTER 9

*Ordinances of the first covenant—Man perfected by the new covenant.*

1 Then verily the first covenant had also ordinances of divine service, and a worldly sanctuary.

2 For there was a tabernacle made; the first, wherein was the candlestick, and the table, and the showbread; which is called the sanctuary.

3 And after the second veil, the tabernacle which is called the holiest of all;

4 Which had the golden censer, and the ark of the covenant overlaid round about with gold, wherein was the golden pot that had manna, and Aaron's rod that budded, and the tables of the covenant;

5 And over it the cherubim of glory shadowing the mercy seat; of which we cannot now speak particularly.

6 Now when these things were thus ordained, the priests went always into the first tabernacle, accomplishing the service of God.

7 But into the second went the high priest alone once every year, not with-

out blood, which he offered for himself, and for the errors of the people;

8 The Holy Ghost signifying this that the way into the holiest of all was not yet made manifest, while as yet the first tabernacle was standing;

9 Which was a figure for the time then present, in which were offered both gifts and sacrifices, that could not make him that did the service perfect, as pertaining to the conscience;

10 Which consisted only in meats and drinks, and divers washings, and carnal ordinances, imposed on them until the time of reformation.

11 But Christ being come a high priest of good things to come, by a greater and more perfect tabernacle, not made with hands, that is to say, not of this building;

12 Neither by the blood of goats and calves, but by his own blood he entered in once into the holy place, having obtained eternal redemption for us.

13 For if the blood of bulls and of goats, and the ashes of an heifer sprinkling the unclean, sanctifieth to the purifying of the flesh;

14 How much more shall the blood of Christ, who through the eternal Spirit offered himself without spot to God, purge your conscience from dead works to serve the living God?

15 And for this cause he is the mediator of the new covenant, that by means of death, for the redemption of the transgressions that were under the first covenant, they which are called might receive the promise of eternal inheritance.

16 For where a covenant is, there must also of necessity be the death of the victim.

17 For a covenant is of force after the victim is dead; otherwise it is of no strength at all while the victim liveth.

18 Whereupon neither the first covenant was dedicated without blood.

19 For when Moses had spoken every precept to all the people according to the law, he took the blood of calves and of goats, with water, and scarlet wool, and hyssop, and sprinkled both the book and all the people,

20 Saying, This is the blood of the covenant which God hath enjoined unto you.

21 Moreover he sprinkled likewise with blood both the tabernacle, and all the vessels of the ministry.

22 And almost all things are by the law purged with blood; and without shedding of blood is no remission.

23 It was therefore necessary that the patterns of things in the heavens should be purified with these; but the heavenly things themselves with better sacrifices than these.

24 For Christ is not entered into the holy places made with hands, which are the figures of the true; but into heaven itself, now to appear in the presence of God for us;

25 Nor yet that he should offer himself often, as the high priest entereth into the holy place every year with blood of others;

26 For then must he often have suffered since the foundation of the world; but now once in the meridian of time hath he appeared to put away sin by the sacrifice of himself.

27 And as it is appointed unto men once to die, but after this the judgment;

28 So Christ was once offered to bear the sins of many; and he shall appear the second time, without sin unto salvation unto them that look for him.

## CHAPTER 10

*The weakness of the law—The sacrifice of Christ—An exhortation to hold fast the faith.*

1 For the law having a shadow of good things to come, and not the very image of the things, can never with those sacrifices, which they offered continually year by year make the comers thereunto perfect.

2 For then would they not have ceased to be offered? because that the worshipers once purged should have had no more conscience of sins.

3 But in those sacrifices there is a remembrance again made of sins every year.

4 For it is not possible that the blood of bulls and of goats should take away sins.

5 Wherefore, when he cometh into the world, he saith, Sacrifice and offering thou wouldst not, but a body hast thou prepared me;

6 In burnt offerings and sacrifices for sin thou hast had no pleasure.

7 Then said I, Lo, I come (in the volume of the book it is written of me) to do thy will, O God.

8 Above when he said, Sacrifice and offering and burnt offerings and offer-

ing for sin thou wouldest not, neither hadst pleasure therein; which are offered by the law;

9 Then said he, Lo, I come to do thy will, O God. He taketh away the first, that he may establish the second.

10 By which will we are sanctified through the offering once of the body of Jesus Christ.

11 And every priest standeth daily ministering and offering oftentimes the same sacrifices, which can never take away sins;

12 But this man, after he had offered one sacrifice for sins for ever, sat down on the right hand of God;

13 From henceforth to reign until his enemies be made his footstool.

14 For by one offering he hath perfected for ever them that are sanctified.

15 Whereof the Holy Ghost also is a witness to us; for after that he had said before,

16 This is the covenant that I will make with them after those days, saith the Lord; I will put my laws into their hearts, and in their minds will I write them;

17 And their sins and iniquities will I remember no more.

18 Now where remission of these is, there is no more offering for sin.

19 Having therefore, brethren, boldness to enter into the holiest by the blood of Jesus,

20 By a new and living way, which he hath consecrated for us, through the veil, that is to say, his flesh;

21 And having such an high priest over the house of God;

22 Let us draw near with a true heart in full assurance of faith, having our hearts sprinkled from an evil conscience, and our bodies washed with pure water.

23 Let us hold fast the profession of our faith without wavering; for he is faithful that promised;

24 And let us consider one another to provoke unto love and to good works;

25 Not forsaking the assembling of ourselves together, as the manner of some is; but exhorting one another; and so much the more, as ye see the day approaching.

26 For if we sin willfully after that we have received the knowledge of the truth, there remaineth no more sacrifice for sins,

27 But a certain fearful looking for of judgment and fiery indignation, which shall devour the adversaries.

28 He that despised Moses' law died without mercy under two or three witnesses;

29 Of how much sorer punishment, suppose ye, shall he be thought worthy, who hath trodden underfoot the Son of God, and hath counted the blood of the covenant, wherewith he was sanctified, an unholy thing, and hath done despite unto the Spirit of grace?

30 For we know him that hath said, Vengeance belongeth unto me, I will recompense, saith the Lord. And again, The Lord shall judge his people.

31 It is a fearful thing to fall into the hands of the living God.

32 But call to remembrance the former days, in which, after ye were illuminated, ye endured a great fight of afflictions;

33 Partly, whilst ye were made a gazingstock both by reproaches and afflictions; and partly, whilst ye became companions of them that were so used.

34 For ye had compassion of me in my bonds, and took joyfully the spoiling of your goods, knowing in yourselves that ye have in heaven a better and an enduring substance.

35 Cast not away therefore your confidence, which hath great recompense of reward.

36 For ye have need of patience, that, after ye have done the will of God, ye might receive the promise.

37 For yet a little while, and he that shall come will come, and will not tarry.

38 Now the just shall live by faith; but if any man draw back, my soul shall have no pleasure in him.

39 But we are not of them who draw back unto perdition; but of them that believe to the saving of the soul.

## CHAPTER 11

*Faith and the fruits thereof.*

1 Now faith is the assurance of things hoped for, the evidence of things not seen.

2 For by it the elders obtained a good report.

3 Through faith we understand that the worlds were framed by the word of God, so that things which are seen were not made of things which do appear.

4 By faith Abel offered unto God a more excellent sacrifice than Cain, by which he obtained witness that he was righteous, God testifying of his gifts; and by it he being dead yet speaketh.

5 By faith Enoch was translated that he should not see death; and was not found, because God had translated him; for before his translation he had this testimony, that he pleased God.

6 But without faith it is impossible to please him; for he that cometh to God must believe that he is, and that he is a rewarder of them that diligently seek him.

7 By faith Noah, being warned of God of things not seen as yet, moved with fear, prepared an ark to the saving of his house; by the which he condemned the world, and became heir of the righteousness which is by faith.

8 By faith Abraham, when he was called to go out into a place which he should after receive for an inheritance, obeyed; and he went out, not knowing whither he went.

9 By faith he sojourned in the land of promise, as in a strange country, dwelling in tabernacles with Isaac and Jacob, the heirs with him of the same promise;

10 For he looked for a city which hath foundations, whose builder and maker is God.

11 Through faith also Sarah herself received strength to conceive seed, and was delivered of a child when she was past age, because she judged him faithful who had promised.

12 Therefore sprang there even of one, and him as good as dead, as many as the stars of the sky in multitude, and as the sand which is by the seashore innumerable.

13 These all died in faith, not having received the promises, but having seen them afar off, and were persuaded of them, and embraced them, and confessed that they were strangers and pilgrims on the earth.

14 For they that say such things declare plainly that they seek a country.

15 And truly, if they had been mindful of that country from whence they came out, they might have had opportunity to have returned.

16 But now they desire a better country, that is, a heavenly; wherefore

God is not ashamed to be called their God; for he hath prepared for them a city.

17 By faith Abraham, when he was tried, offered up Isaac; and he that had received the promises offered up his only begotten son,

18 Of whom it was said, That in Isaac shall thy seed be called;

19 Accounting that God was able to raise him up, even from the dead; from whence also he received him in a figure.

20 By faith Isaac blessed Jacob and Esau concerning things to come.

21 By faith Jacob, when he was a-dying, blessed both the sons of Joseph; and worshiped, leaning upon the top of his staff.

22 By faith Joseph, when he died, made mention of the departing of the children of Israel; and gave commandment concerning his bones.

23 By faith Moses, when he was born, was hid three months of his parents, because they saw that he was a peculiar child; and they were not afraid of the king's commandment.

24 By faith Moses, when he was come to years of discretion, refused to be called the son of Pharaoh's daughter;

25 Choosing rather to suffer affliction with the people of God, than to enjoy the pleasures of sin for a season;

26 Esteeming the reproach of Christ greater riches than the treasures in Egypt; for he had respect unto the recompense of the reward.

27 By faith he forsook Egypt, not fearing the wrath of the king; for he endured, as seeing him who is invisible.

28 Through faith he kept the passover, and the sprinkling of blood, lest he that destroyed the firstborn should touch them.

29 By faith they passed through the Red sea as by dry land; which the Egyptians assaying to do were drowned.

30 By faith the walls of Jericho fell down, after they were compassed about seven days.

31 By faith the harlot Rahab perished not with them that believed not, when she had received the spies with peace.

32 And what shall I say more? for the time would fail me to tell of Gideon, and of Barak, and of Samson, and of Jephthah; of David also, and Samuel, and of the prophets;

33 Who through faith subdued kingdoms, wrought righteousness, obtained promises, stopped the mouths of lions,

34 Quenched the violence of fire, escaped the edge of the sword, out of weakness were made strong, waxed valiant in fight, turned to flight the armies of the aliens.

35 Women received their dead raised to life again; and others were tortured, not accepting deliverance; that they might obtain the first resurrection;

36 And others had trial of cruel mockings and scourgings, yea, moreover of bonds and imprisonment;

37 They were stoned, they were sawn asunder, were tempted, were slain with the sword; they wandered about in sheepskins and goatskins; being destitute, afflicted, tormented;

38 Of whom the world was not worthy; they wandered in deserts, and in mountains, and in dens and caves of the earth.

39 And these all, having obtained a good report through faith, received not the promises;

40 God having provided some better things for them through their sufferings, for without sufferings they could not be made perfect.

## CHAPTER 12

*An exhortation to constant faith, patience, and godliness—The new covenant better than the old.*

1 Wherefore, seeing we also are compassed about with so great a cloud of witnesses, let us lay aside every weight, and the sin which doth so easily beset us, and let us run with patience the race that is set before us,

2 Looking unto Jesus the author and finisher of our faith; who for the joy that was set before him endured the cross, despising the shame, and is set down at the right hand of the throne of God.

3 For consider him that endured such contradiction of sinners against himself, lest ye be wearied and faint in your minds.

4 Ye have not yet resisted unto blood, striving against sin.

5 And ye have forgotten the exhortation which speaketh unto you as unto children, My son, despise not thou the

chastening of the Lord, nor faint when thou art rebuked of him;

6 For whom the Lord loveth he chasteneth, and scourgeth every son whom he receiveth.

7 If ye endure chastening, God dealeth with you as with sons; for what son is he whom the father chasteneth not?

8 But if ye be without chastisement, whereof all are partakers, then are ye bastards, and not sons.

9 Furthermore, we have had fathers of our flesh which corrected us, and we gave them reverence; shall we not much rather be in subjection unto the Father of spirits, and live?

10 For they verily for a few days chastened us after their own pleasure; but he for our profit, that we might be partakers of his holiness.

11 Now no chastening for the present seemeth to be joyous, but grievous; nevertheless, afterward it yieldeth the peaceable fruit of righteousness unto them which are exercised thereby.

12 Wherefore lift up the hands which hang down, and strengthen the feeble knees;

13 And make straight paths for your feet, lest that which is lame be turned out of the way; but let it rather be healed.

14 Follow peace with all men, and holiness, without which no man shall see the Lord;

15 Looking diligently lest any man fail of the grace of God; lest any root of bitterness springing up trouble you, and thereby many be defiled;

16 Lest there be any fornicator, or profane person, as Esau, who for one morsel of meat sold his birthright.

17 For ye know how that afterward, when he would have inherited the blessing, he was rejected; for he found no place of repentance, though he sought it carefully with tears.

18 For ye are not come unto the mount that might be touched, and that burned with fire, nor unto blackness, and darkness, and tempest,

19 And the sound of a trumpet, and the voice of words; which voice they that heard entreated that the word should not be spoken to them any more;

20 (For they could not endure that which was commanded, And if so much as a beast touch the mountain, it shall be stoned, or thrust through with a dart;

21 And so terrible was the sight, that Moses said, I exceedingly fear and quake;)

22 But ye are come unto mount Sion, and unto the city of the living God, the heavenly Jerusalem, and to an innumerable company of angels,

23 To the general assembly and church of the firstborn, which are written in heaven, and to God the Judge of all, and to the spirits of just men made perfect,

24 And to Jesus the mediator of the new covenant, and to the blood of sprinkling, that speaketh better things than that of Abel.

25 See that ye refuse not him that speaketh; for if they escaped not who refused him that spake on earth, much more shall not we escape, if we turn away from him that speaketh from heaven;

26 Whose voice then shook the earth; but now he hath promised, saying, Yet once more I shake not the earth only, but also heaven.

27 And this word, Yet once more, signifieth the removing of those things that are shaken, as of things that are made, that those things which cannot be shaken may remain.

28 Wherefore we receiving a kingdom which cannot be moved, should have grace, whereby we may serve God acceptably with reverence and godly fear;

29 For our God is a consuming fire.

## CHAPTER 13

*Admonitions as to charity, honesty, covetousness; in regard to preachers, to confess Christ, to give alms.*

1 Let brotherly love continue.

2 Be not forgetful to entertain strangers; for thereby some have entertained angels unawares.

3 Remember them that are in bonds, as bound with them; and them which suffer adversity, as being yourselves also of the body.

4 Marriage is honorable in all, and the bed undefiled; but whoremongers and adulterers God will judge.

5 Let your consecrations be without covetousness; and be content with giving such things as ye have; for he hath said, I will never leave thee, nor forsake thee.

6 So that we may boldly say, The Lord is my helper, and I will not fear what man shall do unto me.

7 Remember them which have the rule over you, who have spoken unto you the word of God; whose faith follow, considering the end of their conversation.

8 Jesus Christ the same yesterday, and today, and for ever.

9 Be not carried about with divers and strange doctrines; for it is a good thing that the heart be established with grace; not with meats, which have not profited them that have been occupied therein.

10 We have an altar, whereof they have no right to eat which serve the tabernacle.

11 For the bodies of those beasts, whose blood is brought into the sanctuary by the high priest for sin, are burned without the camp.

12 Wherefore Jesus also, that he might sanctify the people with his own blood, suffered without the gate.

13 Let us go forth therefore unto him without the camp, bearing his reproach.

14 For here have we no continuing city, but we seek one to come.

15 By him therefore let us offer the sacrifice of praise to God continually, that is, the fruit of our lips, giving thanks to his name.

16 But to do good and to communicate forget not; for with such sacrifices God is well pleased.

17 Obey them that have the rule over you, and submit yourselves; for they watch for your souls, as they that must give account, that they may do it with joy, and not with grief; for that is unprofitable for you.

18 Pray for us; for we trust we have a good conscience, in all things willing to live honestly.

19 But I beseech you the rather to do this, that I may be restored to you the sooner.

20 Now the God of peace, that brought again from the dead our Lord Jesus, that great Shepherd of the sheep, through the blood of the everlasting covenant,

21 Make you perfect in every good work to do his will, working in you that which is well pleasing in his sight, through Jesus Christ; to whom be glory for ever and ever. Amen.

22 And I beseech you, brethren, suffer the word of exhortation; for I have written a letter unto you in few words.

23 Know ye that our brother Timothy is set at liberty; with whom, if he come shortly, I will see you.

24 Salute all them that have the rule over you, and all the saints. They of Italy salute you.

25 Grace be with you all. Amen.

Written to the Hebrews from Italy by Timothy.

## The General Epistle of
# James

### CHAPTER 1

*We are to rejoice under the cross, to exercise patience—To ask wisdom of God— The law of liberty.*

1 James, a servant of God and of the Lord Jesus Christ, to the twelve tribes which are scattered abroad, greeting.

2 My brethren, count it all joy when ye fall into many afflictions;

3 Knowing this, that the trying of your faith worketh patience.

4 But let patience have its perfect work, that ye may be perfect and entire, wanting nothing.

5 If any of you lack wisdom, let him ask of God, that giveth to all men liberally, and upbraideth not; and it shall be given him.

6 But let him ask in faith, nothing wavering; for he that wavereth is like a wave of the sea driven with the wind and tossed.

7 For let not that man think that he shall receive any thing of the Lord.

8 A double-minded man is unstable in all his ways.

9 Let the brother of low degree rejoice in that he is exalted;

10 But the rich, in that he is made low; because as the flower of the grass he shall pass away.

11 For the sun is no sooner risen with a burning heat, but it withereth

the grass, and the flower thereof falleth, and the grace of the fashion of it perisheth; so also shall the rich man fade away in his ways.

12 Blessed is the man that resisteth temptation; for when he is tried, he shall receive the crown of life, which the Lord hath promised to them that love him.

13 Let no man say when he is tempted, I am tempted of God; for God cannot be tempted with evil, neither tempteth he any man;

14 But every man is tempted, when he is drawn away of his own lust, and enticed.

15 Then when lust hath conceived, it bringeth forth sin; and sin, when it is finished, bringeth forth death.

16 Do not err, my beloved brethren.

17 Every good gift and every perfect gift is from above, and cometh down from the Father of lights, with whom is no variableness, neither shadow of turning.

18 Of his own will begat he us with the word of truth, that we should be a kind of firstfruits of his creatures.

19 Wherefore, my beloved brethren, let every man be swift to hear, slow to speak, slow to wrath;

20 For the wrath of man worketh not the righteousness of God.

21 Wherefore lay aside all filthiness and superfluity of naughtiness, and receive with meekness, the engrafted word, which is able to save your souls.

22 But be ye doers of the word, and not hearers only, deceiving your own selves.

23 For if any be a hearer of the word, and not a doer, he is like unto a man beholding his natural face in a glass;

24 For he beholdeth himself, and goeth his way, and straightway forgetteth what manner of man he was.

25 But whoso looketh into the perfect law of liberty, and continueth therein, he being not a forgetful hearer, but a doer of the work, this man shall be blessed in his deed.

26 If any man among you seem to be religious, and bridleth not his tongue, but deceiveth his own heart, this man's religion is vain.

27 Pure religion and undefiled before God and the Father is this, To visit the fatherless and widows in their affliction, and to keep himself unspotted from the vices of the world.

## CHAPTER 2

*Faith to be held without a respect to persons—Of faith and works.*

1 My brethren, ye cannot have the faith of our Lord Jesus Christ, the Lord of glory, and yet have respect to persons.

2 Now if there come unto your assembly a man with a gold ring, in goodly apparel, and there come in also a poor man in vile raiment;

3 And ye have respect to him that weareth the gay clothing, and say unto him, Sit thou here in a good place; and say to the poor, Stand thou there, or sit here under my footstool;

4 Are ye not then in yourselves partial judges, and become evil in your thoughts?

5 Hearken, my beloved brethren, Hath not God chosen the poor of this world rich in faith, and heirs of the kingdom which he hath promised to them that love him?

6 But ye have despised the poor. Do not rich men oppress you, and draw you before the judgment seats?

7 Do not they blaspheme that worthy name by the which ye are called?

8 If ye fulfill the royal law according to the scripture, Thou shalt love thy neighbor as thyself, ye do well;

9 But if ye have respect to persons, ye commit sin, and are convinced of the law as transgressors.

10 For whosoever shall, save in one point, keep the whole law, he is guilty of all.

11 For he that said, Do not commit adultery, said also, Do not kill. Now if thou commit no adultery, yet if thou kill, thou art become a transgressor of the law.

12 So speak ye, and so do, as they that shall be judged by the law of liberty.

13 For he shall have judgment without mercy, that hath showed no mercy; and mercy rejoiceth against judgment.

14 What profit is it, my brethren, for a man to say he hath faith, and hath not works? can faith save him?

15 Yea, a man may say, I will show thee I have faith without works; but I say, Show me thy faith without works, and I will show thee my faith by my works.

16 For if a brother or sister be naked and destitute, and one of you say, Depart in peace, be warmed and filled; notwithstanding he give not those things which are needful to the body; what profit is your faith unto such?

17 Even so faith, if it have not works is dead, being alone.

18 Therefore wilt thou know, O vain man, that faith without works is dead and cannot save you?

19 Thou believest there is one God; thou doest well; the devils also believe, and tremble; thou hast made thyself like unto them, not being justified.

20 Was not Abraham our father justified by works, when he had offered Isaac his son upon the altar?

21 Seest thou how works wrought with his faith, and by works was faith made perfect?

22 And the scripture was fulfilled which saith, Abraham believed God, and it was imputed unto him for righteousness; and he was called the friend of God.

23 Ye see then that by works a man is justified, and not by faith only.

24 Likewise also Rahab the harlot was justified by works, when she had received the messengers and sent them out another way.

25 For, as the body without the spirit is dead, so faith without works is dead.

## CHAPTER 3

*Of care in speech—Tongue to be bridled—The truly wise are pure, peaceable and gentle.*

1 My brethren, strive not for the mastery, knowing that in so doing we shall receive the greater condemnation.

2 For in many things we offend all. If any man offend not in word, the same is a perfect man, and able also to bridle the whole body.

3 Behold, we put bits in the horses' mouths, that they may obey us; and we turn about their whole body.

4 Behold also the ships, which though they be so great, and are driven of fierce winds, yet are they turned about with a very small helm, whithersoever the governor listeth.

5 Even so the tongue is a little member, and boasteth great things. Behold, how great a matter a little fire kindleth!

6 And the tongue is a fire, a world of iniquity; so is the tongue among our members, that it defileth the whole body, and setteth on fire the course of nature; and it is set on fire of hell.

7 For every kind of beasts, and of birds, and of serpents, and of things in the sea, is tamed, and hath been tamed of mankind;

8 But the tongue can no man tame; it is an unruly evil, full of deadly poison.

9 Therewith bless we God, even the Father; and therewith curse we men, which are made after the similitude of God.

10 Out of the same mouth proceedeth blessing and cursing. My brethren, these things ought not so to be.

11 Doth a fountain send forth at the same place sweet water and bitter?

12 Can the fig tree, my brethren, bear olive berries? either a vine, figs? so can no fountain both yield salt water and fresh.

13 Who is a wise man and endued with knowledge among you? let him show out of a good conversation his works with meekness of wisdom.

14 But if ye have bitter envying and strife in your hearts, glory not, and lie not against the truth.

15 This wisdom descendeth not from above, but is earthly, sensual, devilish.

16 For where envying and strife is, there is confusion and every evil work.

17 But the wisdom that is from above is first pure, then peaceable, gentle, and easy to be entreated, full of mercy and good fruits, without partiality, and without hypocrisy.

18 And the fruit of righteousness is sown in peace of them that make peace.

## CHAPTER 4

*Against covetousness, intemperance, pride, detraction, and rash judgment of others—We are to commit ourselves and all our affairs to God's providence.*

1 From whence come wars and fightings among you? come they not hence, even of your lusts that war in your members?

2 Ye lust, and have not; ye kill, and desire to have, and cannot obtain; ye fight and war; yet ye have not, because ye ask not.

3 Ye ask, and receive not, because ye ask amiss, that ye may consume it upon your lusts.

4 Ye adulterers and adulteresses,

know ye not that the friendship of the world is enmity with God? whosoever therefore will be a friend of the world is the enemy of God.

5 Do ye think that the scripture saith in vain, The spirit that dwelleth in us lusteth to envy?

6 But he giveth more grace. Wherefore he saith, God resisteth the proud, but giveth grace unto the humble.

7 Submit yourselves therefore to God. Resist the devil, and he will flee from you.

8 Draw nigh to God, and he will draw nigh to you. Cleanse your hands, ye sinners; and purify your hearts, ye doubleminded.

9 Be afflicted, and mourn, and weep; let your laughter be turned to mourning, and your joy to heaviness.

10 Humble yourselves in the sight of the Lord, and he shall lift you up.

11 Speak not evil one of another, brethren. He that speaketh evil of his brother, and judgeth his brother, speaketh evil of the law, and judgeth the law; but if thou judge the law, thou art not a doer of the law, but a judge.

12 There is one lawgiver, who is able to save and to destroy; who art thou that judgest another?

13 Go to now, ye that say, Today or tomorrow we will go into such a city, and continue there a year, and buy and sell, and get gain;

14 Whereas ye know not what shall be on the morrow. For what is your life? It is even a vapor, that appeareth for a little time, and then vanisheth away.

15 For that ye ought to say, If the Lord will, we shall live, and do this, or that.

16 But now ye rejoice in your boastings; all such rejoicing is evil.

17 Therefore to him that knoweth to do good, and doeth it not, to him it is sin.

## CHAPTER 5

*Rich men are to fear God's vengeance—Patience in afflictions.*

1 Go to now, ye rich men, weep and howl for your miseries that shall come upon you.

2 Your riches are corrupted, and your garments are moth-eaten.

3 Your gold and silver is cankered; and the rust of them shall be a witness against you, and shall eat your flesh as it were fire. Ye have heaped treasure together for the last days.

4 Behold, the hire of the laborers who have reaped down your fields, which is of you kept back by fraud, crieth; and the cries of them which have reaped are entered into the ears of the Lord of Sabaoth.

5 Ye have lived in pleasure on the earth, and been wanton; ye have nourished your hearts, as in a day of slaughter.

6 Ye have condemned and killed the just; and he doth not resist you.

7 Be patient therefore, brethren, unto the coming of the Lord. Behold, the husbandman waiteth for the precious fruit of the earth, and hath long patience for it, until he receive the early and latter rain.

8 Be ye also patient; stablish your hearts; for the coming of the Lord draweth nigh.

9 Grudge not one against another, brethren, lest ye be condemned; behold, the judge standeth before the door.

10 Take, my brethren, the prophets, who have spoken in the name of the Lord, for an example of suffering affliction, and of patience.

11 Behold, we count them happy which endure. Ye have heard of the patience of Job, and have seen the end of the Lord; that the Lord is very pitiful, and of tender mercy.

12 But above all things, my brethren, swear not, neither by heaven, neither by the earth, neither by any other oath; but let your yea be yea; and your nay, nay; lest ye fall into condemnation.

13 Is any among you afflicted? let him pray. Is any merry? let him sing psalms.

14 Is any sick among you? let him call for the elders of the church; and let them pray over him, anointing him with oil in the name of the Lord;

15 And the prayer of faith shall save the sick, and the Lord shall raise him up; and if he have committed sins, they shall be forgiven him.

16 Confess your faults one to another, and pray one for another, that ye may be healed. The effectual fervent prayer of a righteous man availeth much.

17 Elias was a man subject to like passions as we are, and he prayed ear-

nestly that it might not rain; and it rained not on the earth by the space of three years and six months.

18 And he prayed again, and the heaven gave rain, and the earth brought forth her fruit.

19 Brethren, if any of you do err from the truth, and one convert him;

20 Let him know, that he which converteth the sinner from the error of his way shall save a soul from death, and shall hide a multitude of sins.

## The First Epistle General of
# Peter

### CHAPTER 1
*Salvation in Christ prophesied of old—The new birth—Godly walk and conversation enjoined.*

1 Peter, an apostle of Jesus Christ, to the strangers scattered throughout Pontus, Galatia, Cappadocia, Asia, and Bithynia,

2 Elect according to the foreknowledge of God the Father, through sanctification of the Spirit, unto obedience and sprinkling of the blood of Jesus Christ; Grace unto you, and peace, be multiplied.

3 Blessed be the God and Father of our Lord Jesus Christ, which according to his abundant mercy hath begotten us again unto a lively hope by the resurrection of Jesus Christ from the dead,

4 To an inheritance incorruptible, and undefiled, and that fadeth not away, reserved in heaven for you,

5 Who are kept by the power of God through faith unto salvation ready to be revealed in the last time.

6 Wherein ye greatly rejoice, though now for a season, if need be, ye are in heaviness through manifold temptations;

7 That the trial of your faith, being much more precious than of gold that perisheth, though it be tried with fire, might be found unto praise and honor and glory at the appearing of Jesus Christ;

8 Whom having not seen, ye love; in whom, though now ye see him not, yet believing, ye rejoice with joy unspeakable and full of glory;

9 Receiving the object of your faith, even the salvation of your souls.

10 Concerning which salvation the prophets who prophesied of the grace bestowed upon you, inquired and searched diligently;

11 Searching what time, and what manner of salvation the Spirit of Christ which was in them did signify, when it testified beforehand the sufferings of Christ, and the glory which should follow.

12 Unto whom it was revealed, that not unto themselves, but unto us they did minister the things, which are now reported unto you by them that have preached the gospel unto you with the Holy Ghost sent down from heaven; which things the angels desire to look into.

13 Wherefore gird up the loins of your mind, be sober, and hope to the end for the grace that is to be brought unto you at the revelation of Jesus Christ;

14 As obedient children, not fashioning yourselves according to the former lusts in your ignorance;

15 But as he which hath called you is holy, so be ye holy in all manner of conversation;

16 Because it is written, Be ye holy; for I am holy.

17 And if ye call on the Father, who without respect of persons judgeth according to every man's work, pass the time of your sojourning here in fear;

18 Forasmuch as ye know that ye were not redeemed with corruptible things, as silver and gold, from your vain conversation received by tradition from your fathers;

19 But with the precious blood of Christ, as of a lamb without blemish and without spot;

20 Who verily was foreordained before the foundation of the world, but was manifest in these last times for you,

21 Who by him do believe in God, that raised him up from the dead, and gave him glory; that your faith and hope might be in God.

22 Seeing ye have purified your souls

in obeying the truth through the Spirit unto unfeigned love of the brethren, see that ye love one another with a pure heart fervently;

23 Being born again, not of corruptible seed, but of incorruptible, by the word of God, which liveth and abideth for ever.

24 For all flesh is as grass, and all the glory of man as the flower of grass. The grass withereth, and the flower thereof falleth away;

25 But the word of the Lord endureth for ever. And this is the word which by the gospel is preached unto you.

## CHAPTER 2

*Obedience to rulers in patience and well-doing.*

1 Wherefore laying aside all malice, and all guile, and hypocrisies, and envies, and all evil speakings,

2 As newborn babes, desire the sincere milk of the word, that ye may grow thereby;

3 If so be ye have tasted that the Lord is gracious.

4 To whom coming, as unto a living stone, disallowed indeed of men, but chosen of God, and precious,

5 Ye also, as lively stones, are built up a spiritual house, an holy priesthood, to offer up spiritual sacrifices, acceptable to God by Jesus Christ.

6 Wherefore also it is contained in the scripture, Behold, I lay in Sion a chief cornerstone, elect, precious; and he that believeth on him shall not be confounded.

7 Unto you therefore who believe, he is precious; but unto them who are disobedient, who stumble at the word, through disobedience, whereunto they were appointed, a stone of stumbling, and a rock of offense.

8 For the stone which the builders disallowed, is become the head of the corner.

9 But ye are a chosen generation, a royal priesthood, a holy nation, a peculiar people; that ye should show forth the praises of him who hath called you out of darkness into his marvelous light;

10 Which in time past were not a people, but are now the people of God; which had not obtained mercy, but now have obtained mercy.

11 Dearly beloved, I beseech you as strangers and pilgrims, abstain from fleshly lusts, which war against the soul;

12 Having your conduct honest among the Gentiles; that, whereas they speak against you as evildoers, they may by your good works, which they shall behold, glorify God in the day of visitation.

13 Submit yourselves to every ordinance of man for the Lord's sake; whether it be to the king, as supreme;

14 Or unto governors, as unto them that are sent by him for the punishment of evildoers, and for the praise of them that do well.

15 For so is the will of God, that with well doing ye may put to silence the ignorance of foolish men;

16 As free, and not using your liberty for a cloak of maliciousness, but as the servants of God.

17 Honor all men. Love the brotherhood. Fear God. Honor the king.

18 Servants, be subject to your masters with all fear; not only to the good and gentle, but also to the froward.

19 For this is thankworthy, if a man for conscience toward God endure grief, suffering wrongfully.

20 For what glory is it, if, when ye be buffeted for your faults, ye shall take it patiently? but if, when ye do well, and suffer for it, ye take it patiently, this is acceptable with God.

21 For even hereunto were ye called; because Christ also suffered for us, leaving us an example, that ye should follow his steps;

22 Who did no sin, neither was guile found in his mouth;

23 Who, when he was reviled, reviled not again; when he suffered, he threatened not; but committed himself to him that judgeth righteously;

24 Who his own self bare our sins in his own body on the tree, that we, being dead to sins, should live unto righteousness; by whose stripes ye were healed.

25 For ye were as sheep going astray; but are now returned unto the Shepherd and Bishop of your souls.

## CHAPTER 3

*Duty of wives and husbands—Unity and love enjoined.*

1 Likewise, ye wives, be in subjection to your own husbands; that, if any obey not the word, they also may with-

out the word be won by the conduct of the wives;

2 While they behold your chaste conduct coupled with fear.

3 Let your adorning be not that outward adorning of plaiting the hair, and wearing of gold, or putting on of apparel;

4 But let it be the hidden man of the heart, in that which is not corruptible, even the ornament of a meek and quiet spirit, which is in the sight of God of great price.

5 For after this manner in old times the holy women, who trusted in God, adorned themselves, being in subjection unto their own husbands;

6 Even as Sarah obeyed Abraham, calling him lord; whose daughters ye are, as long as ye do well, and are not afraid with any amazement.

7 Likewise, ye husbands, dwell with them according to knowledge, giving honor unto the wife, as unto the weaker vessel, and as being heirs together of the grace of life; that your prayers be not hindered.

8 Finally, be ye all of one mind, having compassion one of another; love as brethren, be pitiful, be courteous;

9 Not rendering evil for evil, or railing for railing; but contrariwise blessing; knowing that ye are thereunto called, that ye should inherit a blessing.

10 For he that will love life, and see good days, let him refrain his tongue from evil, and his lips that they speak no guile;

11 Let him eschew evil, and do good; let him seek peace, and ensue it.

12 For the eyes of the Lord are over the righteous, and his ears are open unto their prayers; but the face of the Lord is against them that do evil.

13 And who is he that will harm you, if ye be followers of that which is good?

14 But and if ye suffer for righteousness' sake, happy are ye; and be not afraid of their terror, neither be troubled;

15 But sanctify the Lord God in your hearts; and be ready always to give an answer with meekness and fear to every man that asketh of you a reason for the hope that is in you:

16 Having a good conscience; that, whereas they speak evil of you, as of evildoers, they may be ashamed that

falsely accuse your good conduct in Christ.

17 For it is better, if the will of God be so, that ye suffer for well doing, than for evil doing.

18 For Christ also once suffered for sins, the just for the unjust, being put to death in the flesh, but quickened by the Spirit, that he might bring us to God.

19 For which cause also, he went and preached unto the spirits in prison;

20 Some of whom were disobedient in the days of Noah, while the longsuffering of God waited, while the ark was preparing, wherein few, that is, eight souls were saved by water.

21 The like figure whereunto even baptism doth also now save us, (not the putting away of the filth of the flesh, but the answer of a good conscience toward God,) by the resurrection of Jesus Christ;

22 Who is gone into heaven, and is on the right hand of God; angels and authorities and powers being made subject unto him.

## CHAPTER 4
*The gospel preached to the dead—Of persecution.*

1 Forasmuch then as Christ hath suffered for us in the flesh, arm yourselves likewise with the same mind;

2 For you who have suffered in the flesh should cease from sin, that you no longer the rest of your time in the flesh, should live to the lusts of men, but to the will of God.

3 For the time past of life may suffice to have wrought the will of the Gentiles, when ye walked in lasciviousness, lusts, excess of wine, revellings, banquetings, and abominable idolatries;

4 Wherein they speak evil of you, thinking it strange that you run not with them to the same excess of riot;

5 Who shall give account to him that is ready to judge the quick and the dead.

6 Because of this, is the gospel preached to them who are dead, that they might be judged according to men in the flesh, but live in the spirit according to the will of God.

7 But to you, the end of all things is at hand; be ye therefore sober, and watch unto prayer.

8 And above all things have fervent

charity among yourselves; for charity preventeth a multitude of sins.

9 Use hospitality one to another without grudging.

10 As every man hath received the gift, even so minister the same one to another, as good stewards of the manifold grace of God.

11 If any man speak, let him speak as an oracle of God; if any man minister, let him do it as of the ability which God giveth; that God in all things may be glorified through Jesus Christ; to whom be praise and dominion for ever and ever. Amen.

12 Beloved, think it not strange concerning the fiery trial which is to try you, as though some strange thing happened unto you;

13 But rejoice, inasmuch as ye are partakers of Christ's sufferings; that, when his glory shall be revealed, ye may be glad also with exceeding joy.

14 If ye be reproached for the name of Christ, happy are ye; for the Spirit of glory and of God resteth upon you; on their part he is evil spoken of, but on your part he is glorified.

15 But let none of you suffer as a murderer or as a thief, or as an evildoer, or as a busybody in other men's matters.

16 Yet if any man suffer as a Christian, let him not be ashamed; but let him glorify God on this behalf.

17 For the time is come that judgment must begin at the house of God; and if it first begin at us, what shall the end be of them that obey not the gospel of God?

18 And if the righteous scarcely be saved, where shall the ungodly and the sinner appear?

19 Wherefore, let them that suffer according to the will of God commit the keeping of their souls to him in well doing, as unto a faithful Creator.

## CHAPTER 5

*Peter exhorteth the elders to feed their flocks.*

1 The elders which are among you I exhort, who am also an elder, and a witness of the sufferings of Christ, and also a partaker of the glory that shall be revealed;

2 Feed the flock of God which is among you, taking the oversight thereof, not by constraint, but willingly; not for filthy lucre, but of a ready mind;

3 Neither as being lords over God's heritage, but being ensamples to the flock.

4 And when the chief Shepherd shall appear, ye shall receive a crown of glory that fadeth not away.

5 Likewise, ye younger, submit yourselves unto the elder. Yea, all of you be subject one to another, and be clothed with humility; for God resisteth the proud, and giveth grace to the humble.

6 Humble yourselves therefore under the mighty hand of God, that he may exalt you in due time.

7 Casting all your care upon him; for he careth for you.

8 Be sober, be vigilant; because your adversary the devil, as a roaring lion, walketh about, seeking whom he may devour;

9 Whom resist steadfast in the faith, knowing that the same afflictions are accomplished in your brethren that are in the world.

10 But the God of all grace, who hath called us unto his eternal glory by Christ Jesus, after that ye have suffered a while, make you perfect, stablish, strengthen, settle you.

11 To him be glory and dominion for ever and ever. Amen.

12 By Sylvanus, a faithful brother unto you, as I suppose, I have written briefly, exhorting, and testifying that this is the true grace of God wherein ye stand.

13 They at Babylon, elected together with you, salute you; and so doth Marcus my son.

14 Greet ye one another with a kiss of charity. Peace be with you all that are in Christ Jesus. Amen.

# The Second Epistle General of
# Peter

## CHAPTER 1

*He exhorteth them, by faith, and good works, to make their calling sure—His death is at hand—He warneth them to be constant in the faith of Christ—Use of prophecy.*

1 Simon Peter, a servant and an apostle of Jesus Christ, to them that have obtained like precious faith with us through the righteousness of God and our Savior Jesus Christ;

2 Grace and peace be multiplied unto you through the knowledge of God, and of Jesus our Lord,

3 According as his divine power hath given unto us all things that pertain unto life and godliness, through the knowledge of him that hath called us to glory and virtue;

4 Whereby are given unto us exceeding great and precious promises; that by these ye might be partakers of the divine nature, having escaped the corruption that is in the world through lust.

5 And besides this, giving all diligence, add to your faith virtue; and to virtue, knowledge;

6 And to knowledge, temperance; and to temperance, patience; and to patience, godliness;

7 And to godliness, brotherly kindness; and to brotherly kindness, charity.

8 For if these things be in you, and abound, they make you that ye shall neither be barren nor unfruitful in the knowledge of our Lord Jesus Christ.

9 But he that lacketh these things is blind, and cannot see afar off, and hath forgotten that he was purged from his old sins.

10 Wherefore the rather, brethren, give diligence to make your calling and election sure; for if ye do these things, ye shall never fall;

11 For so an entrance shall be ministered unto you abundantly into the everlasting kingdom of our Lord and Savior Jesus Christ.

12 Wherefore I will not be negligent to put you always in remembrance of these things, though ye know them, and be established in the present truth.

13 Yea, I think it meet, as long as I am in this tabernacle, to stir you up by putting you in remembrance;

14 Knowing that shortly I must put off this my tabernacle, even as our Lord Jesus Christ hath showed me.

15 Moreover I will endeavor that ye may be able after my decease to have these things always in remembrance.

16 For we have not followed cunningly devised fables, when we made known unto you the power and coming of our Lord Jesus Christ, but were eyewitnesses of his majesty.

17 For he received from God the Father honor and glory, when there came such a voice to him from the excellent glory, This is my beloved Son, in whom I am well pleased.

18 And this voice which came from heaven we heard, when we were with him in the holy mount.

19 We have therefore a more sure knowledge of the word of prophecy, to which word of prophecy ye do well that ye take heed, as unto a light which shineth in a dark place, until the day dawn, and the day star arise in your hearts;

20 Knowing this first, that no prophecy of the scriptures is given of any private will of man.

21 For the prophecy came not in old time by the will of man; but holy men of God spake as they were moved by the Holy Ghost.

## CHAPTER 2

*He foretelleth of false teachers, showing the impiety and punishment both of them and their followers.*

1 But there were false prophets also among the people, even as there shall be false teachers among you, who privily shall bring in abominable heresies, even denying the Lord that bought them, and bring upon themselves swift destruction.

2 And many shall follow their pernicious ways; by reason of whom the way of truth shall be evil spoken of.

3 And through covetousness shall they with feigned words make merchandise of you; whose judgment now of a long time lingereth not, and their destruction slumbereth not.

4 For if God spared not the angels that sinned, but cast them down to hell, and delivered them into chains of darkness, to be reserved unto judgment;

5 And spared not the old world, but saved Noah the eighth person, a preacher of righteousness, bringing in the flood upon the world of the ungodly;

6 And turning the cities of Sodom and Gomorrah into ashes condemned them with an overthrow, making them an ensample unto those that after should live ungodly;

7 And delivered just Lot, vexed with the filthy conversation of the wicked;

8 (For that righteous man dwelling among them, in seeing and hearing, vexed his righteous soul from day to day with their unlawful deeds;)

9 The Lord knoweth how to deliver the godly out of temptation, and to reserve the unjust unto the day of judgment to be punished;

10 But chiefly them that walk after the flesh in the lust of uncleanness, and despise government. Presumptuous are they, self-willed, they are not afraid to speak evil of dignities.

11 Whereas angels, which are greater in power and might, bring not railing accusation against them before the Lord.

12 But these, as natural brute beasts made to be taken and destroyed, speak evil of the things that they understand not; and shall utterly perish in their own corruption;

13 And shall receive the reward of unrighteousness, as they that count it pleasure to riot in the daytime. Spots they are and blemishes, sporting themselves with their own deceivings while they feast with you;

14 Having eyes full of adultery, and that cannot cease from sin; beguiling unstable souls; a heart they have exercised with covetous practices; cursed children;

15 Which have forsaken the right way, and are gone astray, following the way of Balaam the son of Bosor, who loved the wages of unrighteousness;

16 But was rebuked for his iniquity; the dumb ass speaking with man's voice forbade the madness of the prophet.

17 These are wells without water, clouds that are carried with a tempest; to whom the mist of darkness is reserved for ever.

18 For when they speak great swelling words of vanity, they allure through the lusts of the flesh, through much wantonness, those that were clean escaped from them who live in error.

19 While they promise them liberty, they themselves are the servants of corruption; for of whom a man is overcome, of the same is he brought into bondage.

20 For if after they have escaped the pollutions of the world through the knowledge of the Lord and Savior Jesus Christ, they are again entangled therein, and overcome, the latter end is worse with them than the beginning.

21 For it had been better for them not to have known the way of righteousness, than, after they had known it, to turn from the holy commandment delivered unto them.

22 But it is happened unto them according to the true proverb, The dog is turned to his own vomit again; and, The sow that was washed to her wallowing in the mire.

## CHAPTER 3

*Christ's second coming—The world shall be destroyed; exhorting them, from the expectation thereof, to all holiness of life.*

1 This second epistle, beloved, I now write unto you; in which I stir up your pure minds by way of remembrance;

2 That ye may be mindful of the words which were spoken before by the holy prophets, and of the commandments of us, the apostles of the Lord and Savior;

3 Knowing this first, that in the last days there shall come scoffers, walking after their own lusts.

4 Denying the Lord Jesus Christ, and saying, Where is the promise of his coming? for since the fathers fell asleep, all things must continue as they are, and have continued as they are from the beginning of the creation.

5 For this they willingly are ignorant of, that of old the heavens, and the earth standing in the water and out of the water, were created by the word of God;

6 And by the word of God, the world that then was, being overflowed with water, perished;

7 But the heavens, and the earth which are now, are kept in store by the same word, reserved unto fire against

253

the day of judgment and perdition of ungodly men.

8 But concerning the coming of the Lord, beloved, I would not have you ignorant of this one thing, that one day is with the Lord as a thousand years, and a thousand years as one day.

9 The Lord is not slack concerning his promise and coming, as some men count slackness; but long-suffering toward us, not willing that any should perish, but that all should come to repentance.

10 But the day of the Lord will come as a thief in the night, in the which the heavens shall shake, and the earth also shall tremble, and the mountains shall melt, and pass away with a great noise, and the elements shall be filled with fervent heat; the earth also shall be filled, and the corruptible works which are therein shall be burned up.

11 If then all these things shall be destroyed, what manner of persons ought ye to be in holy conduct and godliness,

12 Looking unto, and preparing for the day of the coming of the Lord wherein the corruptible things of the heavens being on fire, shall be dissolved, and the mountains shall melt with fervent heat?

13 Nevertheless, if we shall endure, we shall be kept according to his promise. And we look for new heavens, and a new earth wherein dwelleth righteousness.

14 Wherefore, beloved, seeing that ye look for such things, be diligent, that ye may be found of him in peace, without spot and blameless;

15 And account, even as our beloved brother Paul also, according to the wisdom given unto him, hath written unto you, the long-suffering and waiting of our Lord, for salvation.

16 As also in all his epistles, speaking in them of these things, in which are some things hard to be understood, which they who are unlearned and unstable wrest, as they do also the other scriptures, unto their own destruction.

17 Ye therefore, beloved, seeing ye know before the things which are coming, beware lest ye also being led away with the error of the wicked, fall from your own steadfastness.

18 But grow in grace and the knowledge of our Lord and Savior Jesus Christ. To him be glory both now and for ever. Amen.

## The First Epistle General of
# John

### CHAPTER 1
*John testifieth of the gospel*

1 Brethren, this is the testimony which we give of that which was from the beginning, which we have heard, which we have seen with our eyes, which we have looked upon, and our hands have handled, of the Word of life;

2 (For the life was manifested, and we have seen it, and bear witness, and show unto you that eternal life, which was with the Father, and was manifested unto us;)

3 That which we have seen and heard declare we unto you, that ye also may have fellowship with us; and truly our fellowship is with the Father, and with his Son Jesus Christ.

4 And these things write we unto you, that your joy may be full.

5 This then is the message which we have heard of him, and declare unto you, that God is light, and in him is no darkness at all.

6 If we say that we have fellowship with him, and walk in darkness, we lie, and do not the truth.

7 But if we walk in the light, as he is in the light, we have fellowship one with another, and the blood of Jesus Christ his Son cleanseth us from all sin.

8 If we say that we have no sin, we deceive ourselves, and the truth is not in us.

9 If we confess our sins, he is faithful and just to forgive us our sins, and to cleanse us from all unrighteousness.

10 If we say that we have not sinned, we make him a liar, and his word is not in us.

### CHAPTER 2
*Christ our advocate—Vices of the world to be avoided—The unction of the Spirit.*

1 My little children, these things write I unto you, that ye sin not. But if any man sin and repent, we have an advocate with the Father, Jesus Christ the righteous;

2 And he is the propitiation for our sins; and not for ours only, but also for the sins of the whole world.

3 And hereby we do know that we know him, if we keep his commandments.

4 He that saith, I know him, and keepeth not his commandments, is a liar, and the truth is not in him.

5 But whoso keepeth his word, in him verily is the love of God perfected; hereby know we that we are in him.

6 He that saith he abideth in him ought himself also so to walk, even as he walked.

7 Brethren, I write a new commandment unto you, but it is the same commandment which ye had from the beginning. The old commandment is the word which ye have heard from the beginning.

8 Again, a new commandment I write unto you, which thing was of old ordained of God; and is true in him, and in you; because the darkness is past in you, and the true light now shineth.

9 He that saith he is in the light, and hateth his brother, is in darkness even until now.

10 He that loveth his brother abideth in the light, and there is none occasion of stumbling in him.

11 But he that hateth his brother is in darkness, and walketh in darkness, and knoweth not whither he goeth, because that darkness hath blinded his eyes.

12 I write unto you, little children, because your sins are forgiven you for his name's sake.

13 I write unto you, fathers, because ye have known him that is from the beginning. I write unto you, young men, because ye have overcome the wicked one. I write unto you, little children, because ye have known the Father.

14 I have written unto you, fathers, because ye have known him that is from the beginning. I have written unto you, young men, because ye are strong, and the word of God abideth in you, and ye have overcome the wicked one.

15 Love not the world, neither the things that are of the world. If any man love the world, the love of the Father is not in him.

16 For all in the world that is of the lusts of the flesh, and the lust of the eyes, and the pride of life, is not of the Father, but is of the world.

17 And the world passeth away, and the lust thereof; but he that doeth the will of God abideth for ever.

18 Little children, it is the last time; and as ye have heard that antichrist shall come, even now are there many antichrists; whereby we know that it is the last time.

19 They went out from us, but they were not of us; for if they had been of us, they would no doubt have continued with us; but they went out, that they might be made manifest that they were not all of us.

20 But ye have an unction from the Holy One, and ye know all things.

21 I have not written unto you because ye know not the truth, but because ye know it, and that no lie is of the truth.

22 Who is a liar but he that denieth that Jesus is the Christ? He is antichrist, that denieth the Father and the Son.

23 Whosoever denieth the Son, the same hath not the Father; but he that acknowledgeth the Son hath the Father also.

24 Let that therefore abide in you, which ye have heard from the beginning. If that which ye have heard from the beginning shall remain in you, ye shall continue in the Son, and also in the Father.

25 And this is the promise that he hath promised us, even eternal life.

26 These things have I written unto you concerning them that seduce you.

27 But the anointing which ye have received of him abideth in you, and ye need not that any man teach you; but as the same anointing teacheth you of all things, and is truth, and is no lie, and even as it hath taught you, ye shall abide in him.

28 And now, little children, abide in him; that, when he shall appear, we may have confidence, and not be ashamed before him at his coming.

29 If ye know that he is righteous, ye know that every one that doeth righteousness is born of him.

## CHAPTER 3

*The love of God to the saints—The new birth—The love of Christ.*

1 Behold, what manner of love the Father hath bestowed upon us, that we should be called the sons of God; therefore the world knoweth us not, because it knew him not.

2 Beloved, now are we the sons of God, and it doth not yet appear what we shall be; but we know that, when he shall appear, we shall be like him; for we shall see him as he is.

3 And every man that hath this hope in him purifieth himself, even as he is pure.

4 Whosoever committeth sin transgresseth also the law; for sin is the transgression of the law.

5 And ye know that he was manifested to take away our sins; and in him is no sin.

6 Whosoever abideth in him sinneth not; whosoever continueth in sin hath not seen him, neither known him.

7 Little children, let no man deceive you; he that doeth righteousness is righteous, even as he is righteous.

8 He that continueth in sin is of the devil; for the devil sinneth from the beginning. For this purpose the Son of God was manifested, that he might destroy the works of the devil.

9 Whosoever is born of God doth not continue in sin; for the Spirit of God remaineth in him; and he cannot continue in sin, because he is born of God, having received that holy Spirit of promise.

10 In this the children of God are manifest, and the children of the devil; whosoever doeth not righteousness is not of God, neither he that loveth not his brother.

11 For this is the message that ye heard from the beginning, that we should love one another.

12 Not as Cain, who was of that wicked one, and slew his brother. And wherefore slew he him? Because his own works were evil, and his brother's righteous.

13 Marvel not, my brethren, if the world hate you.

14 We know that we have passed from death unto life, because we love the brethren. He that loveth not his brother abideth in death.

15 Whosoever hateth his brother is a murderer; and ye know that no murderer hath eternal life abiding in him.

16 Hereby perceive we the love of Christ, because he laid down his life for us; and we ought to lay down our lives for the brethren.

17 But whoso hath this world's good, and seeth his brother have need, and shutteth up his bowels of compassion from him, how dwelleth the love of God in him?

18 My little children, let us not love in word, neither in tongue only; but in deed and in truth.

19 And hereby we know that we are of the truth, and shall assure our hearts before him.

20 For if our heart condemn us, God is greater than our heart, and knoweth all things.

21 Beloved, if our heart condemn us not, then have we confidence toward God.

22 And whatsoever we ask, we receive of him, because we keep his commandments, and do those things that are pleasing in his sight.

23 And this is his commandment, That we should believe on the name of his Son Jesus Christ, and love one another, as he gave us commandment.

24 And he that keepeth his commandments dwelleth in him, and he in him. And hereby we know that he abideth in us, by the Spirit which he hath given us.

## CHAPTER 4

*Try the spirits—The excellency of love—God is love.*

1 Beloved, believe not every spirit, but try the spirits whether they are of God; because many false prophets are gone out into the world.

2 Hereby know ye the Spirit of God; Every spirit that confesseth that Jesus Christ is come in the flesh is of God;

3 And every spirit that confesseth not that Jesus Christ is come in the flesh is not of God; and this is that spirit of antichrist, whereof ye have heard that it should come; and even now it is already in the world.

4 Ye are of God, little children, and have overcome them; because greater is he that is in you, than he that is in the world.

5 They are of the world; therefore speak they of the world, and the world heareth them.

6 We are of God; he that knoweth God heareth us; he that is not of God heareth not us. Hereby know we the spirit of truth, and the spirit of error.

7 Beloved, let us love one another; for love is of God; and every one that loveth is born of God, and knoweth God.

8 He that loveth not, knoweth not God; for God is love.

9 In this was manifested the love of God toward us, because that God sent his only begotten Son into the world, that we might live through him.

10 Herein is love, not that we loved God, but that he loved us, and sent his Son to be the propitiation for our sins.

11 Beloved, if God so loved us, we ought also to love one another.

12 No man hath seen God at any time, except them who believe. If we love one another, God dwelleth in us, and his love is perfected in us.

13 Hereby know we that we dwell in him, and he in us, because he hath given us of his Spirit.

14 And we have seen and do testify that the Father sent the Son to be the Savior of the world.

15 Whosoever shall confess that Jesus is the Son of God, God dwelleth in him, and he in God.

16 And we have known and believed the love that God hath to us. God is love; and he that dwelleth in love dwelleth in God, and God in him.

17 Herein is our love made perfect, that we may have boldness in the day of judgment; because as he is, so are we in this world.

18 There is no fear in love; but perfect love casteth out fear; because fear hath torment. He that feareth is not made perfect in love.

19 We love him, because he first loved us.

20 If a man say, I love God, and hateth his brother, he is a liar; for he that loveth not his brother whom he hath seen, how can he love God whom he hath not seen?

21 And this commandment have we from him, That he who loveth God love his brother also.

## CHAPTER 5

*The new birth—The witnesses which bear record of eternal life.*

1 Whosoever believeth that Jesus is the Christ is born of God; and every one that loveth him that begat loveth him also that is begotten of him.

2 By this we know that we love the children of God, when we love God, and keep his commandments.

3 For this is the love of God, that we keep his commandments; and his commandments are not grievous.

4 For whatsoever is born of God overcometh the world; and this is the victory that overcometh the world, even our faith.

5 Who is he that overcometh the world, but he that believeth that Jesus is the Son of God?

6 This is he that came by water and blood, even Jesus Christ; not by water only, but by water and blood. And it is the Spirit that beareth witness, because the Spirit is truth.

7 For there are three that bear record in heaven, the Father, the Word, and the Holy Ghost; and these three are one.

8 And there are three that bear witness in earth, the Spirit, and the water, and the blood; and these three agree in one.

9 If we receive the witness of men, the witness of God is greater; for this is the witness of God which he hath testified of his Son.

10 He that believeth on the Son of God hath the witness in himself; he that believeth not God hath made him a liar; because he believeth not the record that God gave of his Son.

11 And this is the record, that God hath given to us eternal life, and this life is in his Son.

12 He that hath the Son hath life; and he that hath not the Son of God hath not life.

13 These things have I written unto you that believe on the name of the Son of God; that ye may know that ye have eternal life, and that ye may continue to believe on the name of the Son of God.

14 And this is the confidence that we have in him, that, if we ask any thing according to his will, he heareth us;

15 And if we know that he hear us, whatsoever we ask, we know that we have the petitions that we desired of him.

16 If any man see his brother sin a sin which is not unto death, he shall ask, and he shall give him life for them that sin not unto death. There is a sin

unto death; I do not say that he shall pray for it.

17 All unrighteousness is sin; and there is a sin not unto death.

18 We know that whosoever is born of God continueth not in sin; but he that is begotten of God and keepeth himself, that wicked one overcometh him not.

19 And we know that we are of God, and the whole world lieth in wickedness.

20 And we know that the Son of God is come, and hath given us an understanding, that we may know him that is true; and we are in him that is true, even in his Son Jesus Christ. This is the true God, and eternal life.

21 Little children, keep yourselves from idols. Amen.

## The Second Epistle of
# John

*Walk in love—The antichrist—The doctrine of Christ.*

1 The elder unto the elect lady and her children, whom I love in the truth; and not I only, but also all they that have known the truth;

2 For the truth's sake, which dwelleth in us, and shall be with us for ever.

3 Grace be with you, mercy, and peace, from God the Father, and from the Lord Jesus Christ, the Son of the Father, in truth and love.

4 I rejoiced greatly that I found of thy children walking in truth, as we have received a commandment from the Father.

5 And now I beseech thee, lady, not as though I wrote a new commandment unto thee, but that which we had from the beginning, that we love one another.

6 And this is love, that we walk after his commandments. This is the commandment, That, as ye have heard from the beginning, ye should walk in it.

7 For many deceivers are entered into the world, who confess not that Jesus Christ is come in the flesh. This is a deceiver and an antichrist.

8 Look to yourselves, that we lose not those things which we have wrought, but that we receive a full reward.

9 Whosoever transgresseth, and abideth not in the doctrine of Christ, hath not God. He that abideth in the doctrine of Christ, he hath both the Father and the Son.

10 If there come any unto you, and bring not this doctrine, receive him not into your house, neither bid him Godspeed;

11 For he that biddeth him Godspeed is partaker of his evil deeds.

12 Having many things to write unto you, I would not write with paper and ink; but I trust to come unto you, and speak face to face, that our joy may be full.

13 The children of thy elect sister greet thee. Amen.

## The Third Epistle of
# John

*He commendeth Gaius.*

1 The elder unto the well beloved Gaius, whom I love in the truth.

2 Beloved, I wish above all things that thou mayest prosper and be in health, even as thy soul prospereth.

3 For I rejoiced greatly, when the brethren came and testified of the truth that is in thee, even as thou walkest in the truth.

4 I have no greater joy than to hear that my children walk in truth.

5 Beloved, thou doest faithfully whatsoever thou doest to the brethren, and to strangers;

6 Which have borne witness of thy charity before the church; whom if thou

bring forward on their journey after a godly sort, thou shalt do well;

7 Because that for his name's sake they went forth, taking nothing of the Gentiles.

8 We therefore ought to receive such, that we might be fellow helpers to the truth.

9 I wrote unto the church; but Diotrephes, who loveth to have the preeminence among them, receiveth us not.

10 Wherefore, if I come, I will remember his deeds which he doeth, prating against us with malicious words; and not content therewith, neither doth he himself receive the brethren, and forbiddeth them that would, and casteth them out of the church.

11 Beloved, follow not that which is evil, but that which is good. He that doeth good is of God; but he that doeth evil hath not seen God.

12 Demetrius hath good report of all men, and of the truth itself; yea, and we also bare record; and ye know that our record is true.

13 I had many things to write, but I will not with ink and pen write unto thee;

14 But I trust I shall shortly see thee, and we shall speak face to face. Peace be to thee. Our friends salute thee. Greet the friends by name.

## The General Epistle of
# Jude

*Saints to contend for the faith—False teachers reproved—Satan reproved by Michael—Mockers foretold.*

1 Jude, the servant of God, called of Jesus Christ, and brother of James; to them who are sanctified of the Father; and preserved in Jesus Christ;

2 Mercy unto you, and peace, and love, be multiplied.

3 Beloved, when I gave all diligence to write unto you of the common salvation, it was needful for me to write unto you, and exhort you that ye should earnestly contend for the faith which was once delivered unto the saints.

4 For there are certain men crept in unawares, who were before of old ordained to this condemnation, ungodly men, turning the grace of our God into lasciviousness, and denying the only Lord God, and our Lord Jesus Christ.

5 I will therefore put you in remembrance, though ye once knew this, how that the Lord, having saved the people out of the land of Egypt, afterward destroyed them that believed not.

6 And the angels which kept not their first estate, but left their own habitation, he hath reserved in everlasting chains under darkness unto the judgment of the great day.

7 Even as Sodom and Gomorrah, and the cities about them in like manner, giving themselves over to fornication, and going after strange flesh, are set forth for an example, suffering the vengeance of eternal fire.

8 Likewise also these filthy dreamers defile the flesh, despise dominion, and speak evil of dignities.

9 Yet Michael the archangel, when contending with the devil he disputed about the body of Moses, durst not bring against him a railing accusation, but said, The Lord rebuke thee.

10 But these speak evil of those things which they know not; but what they know naturally, as brute beasts, in those things they corrupt themselves.

11 Woe unto them! for they have gone in the way of Cain, and ran greedily after the error of Balaam for reward, and shall perish in the gainsaying of Core.

12 These are spots in your feasts of charity, when they feast with you, feeding themselves without fear; clouds they are without water, carried about of winds; trees whose fruit withereth, without fruit, twice dead, plucked up by the roots;

13 Raging waves of the sea, foaming out their own shame; wandering stars, to whom is reserved the blackness of darkness for ever.

14 And Enoch also, the seventh from Adam, prophesied of these, saying, Behold, the Lord cometh with ten thousand of his saints,

15 To execute judgment upon all, and to convince all that are ungodly among them of all their ungodly deeds which they have ungodly committed, and of all their hard speeches which ungodly sinners have spoken against him.

16 These are murmurers, complainers, walking after their own lusts; and their mouth speaketh great swelling words, having men's persons in admiration because of advantage.

17 But, beloved, remember ye the words which were spoken before of the apostles of our Lord Jesus Christ;

18 How that they told you there should be mockers in the last time, who should walk after their own ungodly lusts.

19 These be they who separate themselves, sensual, having not the Spirit.

20 But ye, beloved, building up yourselves on your most holy faith, praying in the Holy Ghost,

21 Keep yourselves in the love of God, looking for the mercy of our Lord Jesus Christ unto eternal life.

22 And of some have compassion, making a difference;

23 And others save with fear, pulling them out of the fire; hating even the garment spotted by the flesh.

24 Now unto him that is able to keep you from falling, and to present you faultless before the presence of his glory with exceeding joy,

25 To the only wise God our Savior, be glory and majesty, dominion and power, both now and ever. Amen.

# The Revelation
## of St. John the Divine

### CHAPTER 1

1 The Revelation of John, a servant of God, which was given unto him of Jesus Christ, to show unto his servants things which must shortly come to pass, that he sent and signified by his angel unto his servant John,

2 Who bore record of the word of God, and of the testimony of Jesus Christ, and of all things that he saw.

3 Blessed are they who read, and they who hear and understand the words of this prophecy, and keep those things which are written therein, for the time of the coming of the Lord draweth nigh.

4 Now this is the testimony of John to the seven servants who are over the seven churches in Asia. Grace unto you, and peace from him who is, and who was, and who is to come; before his throne, to testify unto those who are the seven servants over the seven churches.

5 Therefore, I, John, the faithful witness, bear record of the things which were delivered me of the angel, and from Jesus Christ the first begotten of the dead, and the Prince of the kings of the earth.

6 And unto him who loved us, be glory; who washed us from our sins in his own blood, and hath made us kings and priests unto God, his Father. To him be glory and dominion, for ever and ever. Amen.

7 For behold, he cometh in the clouds with ten thousands of his saints in the kingdom, clothed with the glory of his Father. And every eye shall see him; and they who pierced him, and all kindreds of the earth shall wail because of him. Even so, Amen.

8 For he saith, I am Alpha and Omega, the beginning and the ending, the Lord, who is, and who was, and who is to come, the Almighty.

9 I John, who also am your brother, and companion in tribulation, and in the kingdom and patience of Jesus Christ, was in the isle that is called Patmos, for the word of God, and for the testimony of Jesus Christ.

10 I was in the Spirit on the Lord's day, and heard behind me a great voice, as of a trumpet,

11 Saying, I am Alpha and Omega, the first and the last; and, What thou seest, write in a book, and send it unto the seven churches which are in Asia; unto Ephesus, and unto Smyrna, and unto Pergamos, and unto Thyatira, and unto Sardis, and unto Philadelphia, and unto Laodicea.

12 And I turned to see from whence

the voice came that spake to me; and being turned, I saw seven golden candlesticks;

13 And in the midst of the seven candlesticks one like unto the Son of man, clothed with a garment down to the foot, and girt about the paps with a golden girdle.

14 His head and his hairs were white like wool, as white as snow; and his eyes were as a flame of fire;

15 And his feet like unto fine brass, as if they burned in a furnace; and his voice as the sound of many waters.

16 And he had in his right hand seven stars; and out of his mouth went a sharp two-edged sword; and his countenance was as the sun shining in his strength.

17 And when I saw him, I fell at his feet as dead. And he laid his right hand upon me, saying unto me, Fear not; I am the first and the last;

18 I am he that liveth, and was dead; and, behold, I am alive for evermore, Amen; and have the keys of hell and of death.

19 Write the things which thou hast seen, and the things which are, and the things which shall be hereafter.

20 This is the mystery of the seven stars which thou sawest in my right hand, and the seven golden candlesticks. The seven stars are the servants of the seven churches; and the seven candlesticks which thou sawest are the seven churches.

## CHAPTER 2
*Charges to the elders of Ephesus, Smyrna, Pergamos and Thyatira.*

1 Unto the servant of the church of Ephesus write; These things saith he that holdeth the seven stars in his right hand, who walketh in the midst of the seven golden candlesticks;

2 I know thy works, and thy labour, and thy patience, and how thou canst not bear them which are evil; and thou hast tried them which say they are apostles, and are not, and hast found them liars;

3 And hast borne, and hast patience, and for my name's sake hast laboured, and hast not fainted.

4 Nevertheless I have somewhat against thee, because thou hast left thy first love.

5 Remember therefore from whence thou art fallen, and repent, and do the first works; or else I will come unto thee quickly, and will remove thy candlestick out of his place, except thou repent.

6 But this thou hast, that thou hatest the deeds of the Nicolaitans, which I also hate.

7 He that hath an ear, let him hear what the Spirit saith unto the churches; To him that overcometh will I give to eat of the tree of life, which is in the midst of the paradise of God.

8 And unto the servant of the church in Smyrna write; These things saith the first and the last, which was dead, and is alive;

9 I know thy works, and tribulation, and poverty, (but thou art rich) and I know the blasphemy of them which say they are Jews, and are not, but are the synagogue of Satan.

10 Fear none of those things which thou shalt suffer; behold, the devil shall cast some of you into prison, that ye may be tried; and ye shall have tribulation ten days; be thou faithful unto death and I will give thee a crown of life.

11 He that hath an ear, let him hear what the Spirit saith unto the churches; He that overcometh shall not be hurt of the second death.

12 And to the servant of the church in Pergamos write; These things saith he which hath the sharp sword with two edges;

13 I know thy works, and where thou dwellest, even where Satan's seat is; and thou holdest fast my name, and hast not denied my faith, even in those days wherein Antipas was my faithful martyr, who was slain among you, where Satan dwelleth.

14 But I have a few things against thee, because thou hast there them that hold the doctrine of Balaam, who taught Balak to cast a stumbling block before the children of Israel, to eat things sacrificed unto idols, and to commit fornication.

15 So hast thou also them that hold the doctrine of the Nicolaitans, which thing I hate.

16 Repent; or else I will come unto thee quickly, and will fight against them with the sword of my mouth.

17 He that hath an ear, let him hear what the Spirit saith unto the churches; To him that overcometh will I give to eat of the hidden manna, and will give

him a white stone, and in the stone a new name written, which no man knowest saving he that receiveth it.

18 And unto the servant of the church in Thyatira write; These things saith the Son of God, who hath his eyes like unto a flame of fire, and his feet are like fine brass;

19 I know thy works, and charity, and service, and faith, and thy patience, and thy works; and the last to be more than the first.

20 Notwithstanding I have a few things against thee, because thou sufferest that woman Jezebel, which calleth herself a prophetess, to teach and to seduce my servants to commit fornication, and to eat things sacrificed unto idols.

21 And I gave her space to repent of her fornications; and she repented not.

22 Behold, I will cast her into hell, and them that commit adultery with her into great tribulation, except they repent of their deeds.

23 And I will kill her children with death; and all the churches shall know that I am he which searcheth the reins and hearts; and I will give unto every one of you according to your works.

24 But unto you I say, and unto the rest in Thyatira, as many as have not this doctrine, and which have not known the depths of Satan, as they speak; I will put upon you none other burden.

25 But that which ye have already, hold fast till I come.

26 And to him who overcometh, and keepeth my commandments unto the end, will I give power over many kingdoms;

27 And he shall rule them with the word of God; and they shall be in his hands as the vessels of clay in the hands of a potter, and he shall govern them by faith, with equity and justice, even as I received of my Father.

28 And I will give him the morning star.

29 He that hath an ear, let him hear what the Spirit saith unto the churches.

## CHAPTER 3

*Charge to the elders of Sardis, Philadelphia, and Laodicea.*

1 And unto the servant of the church in Sardis, write; These things saith he who hath the seven stars, which are the seven servants of God; I know thy

works, that thou hast a name that thou livest, and art not dead.

2 Be watchful therefore, and strengthen those who remain, who are ready to die; for I have not found thy works perfect before God.

3 Remember therefore how thou hast received and heard, and hold fast, and repent. If therefore thou shalt not watch, I will come on thee as a thief, and thou shalt not know what hour I will come upon thee.

4 Thou hast a few names even in Sardis which have not defiled their garments; and they shall walk with me in white; for they are worthy.

5 He that overcometh, the same shall be clothed in white raiment; and I will not blot out his name out of the book of life, but I will confess his name before my Father, and before his angels.

6 He that hath an ear, let him hear what the Spirit saith unto the churches.

7 And to the servant of the church in Philadelphia write; These things saith he that is holy, he that is true, he that hath the key of David, he that openeth, and no man shutteth; and shutteth, and no man openeth;

8 I know thy works; behold, I have set before thee an open door, and no man can shut it; for thou hast a little strength, and hast kept my word, and hast not denied my name.

9 Behold, I will make them of the synagogue of Satan, which say they are Jews, and are not, but do lie; behold, I will make them to come and worship before thy feet, and to know that I have loved thee.

10 Because thou hast kept the word of my patience, I also will keep thee from the hour of temptation, which shall come upon all the world, to try them that dwell upon the earth.

11 Behold, I come quickly; hold that fast which thou hast, that no man take thy crown.

12 Him that overcometh will I make a pillar in the temple of my God, and he shall go no more out; and I will write upon him the name of my God, and the name of the city of my God, this is New Jerusalem, which cometh down out of heaven from my God; and I will write upon him my new name.

13 He that hath an ear, let him hear what the Spirit saith unto the churches.

14 And unto the servant of the church of the Laodiceans write; These

things saith the Amen, the faithful and true witness, the beginning of the creation of God;

15 I know thy works, that thou art neither cold nor hot; I would thou wert cold or hot.

16 So then because thou art lukewarm, and neither cold nor hot, I will spew thee out of my mouth.

17 Because thou sayest, I am rich, and increased with goods, and have need of nothing; and knowest not that thou art wretched, and miserable, and poor, and blind, and naked;

18 I counsel thee to buy of me gold tried in the fire, that thou mayest be rich; and white raiment, that thou mayest be clothed, and that the shame of thy nakedness do not appear; and anoint thine eyes with eye salve, that thou mayest see.

19 As many as I love, I rebuke and chasten; be zealous therefore, and repent.

20 Behold, I stand at the door, and knock; if any man hear my voice, and open the door, I will come in to him, and will sup with him, and he with me.

21 To him that overcometh will I grant to sit with me in my throne, even as I also overcame, and am set down with my Father in his throne.

22 He that hath an ear, let him hear what the Spirit saith unto the churches.

## CHAPTER 4

*John seeth the throne of God—The four and twenty elders—The four beasts.*

1 After this I looked, and behold, a door was opened into heaven; and the first voice which I heard was as it were of a trumpet talking with me; which said, Come up hither, and I will show thee things which must be hereafter.

2 And immediately I was in the Spirit; and, behold, a throne was set in heaven, and one sat on the throne.

3 And he that sat there was to look upon like a jasper and a sardine stone; and there was a rainbow round about the throne, in sight like unto an emerald.

4 And in the midst of the throne were four and twenty seats; and upon the seats I saw four and twenty elders sitting, clothed in white raiment, and they had on their heads crowns like gold.

5 And out of the throne proceeded

lightnings and thunderings and voices; and there were seven lamps of fire burning before the throne, which are the seven servants of God.

6 And before the throne there was a sea of glass like unto crystal; and in the midst of the throne were the four and twenty elders; and round about the throne, were four beasts full of eyes before and behind.

7 And the first beast was like a lion, and the second beast like a calf, and the third beast had a face as a man, and the fourth beast was like a flying eagle.

8 And the four beasts had each of them six wings about him; and they were full of eyes within; and they rest not day and night, saying, Holy, holy, holy, Lord God Almighty, which was, and is, and is to come.

9 And when those beasts give glory and honor and thanks to him that sits on the throne, who liveth for ever and ever,

10 The four and twenty elders fall down before him that sits on the throne, and worship him that liveth for ever and ever, and cast their crowns before the throne, saying,

11 Thou art worthy, O Lord, to receive glory and honor and power; for thou hast created all things, and for thy pleasure they are and were created.

## CHAPTER 5

*The book sealed with seven seals—The Lion of the tribe of Juda.*

1 And I saw in the right hand of him that sits on the throne a book written within and on the back side, sealed with seven seals.

2 And I saw a strong angel, and heard him proclaiming with a loud voice, Who is worthy to open the book, and loose the seals thereof?

3 And no man in heaven, nor in earth, neither under the earth, was able to open the book, neither to look thereon.

4 And I wept much, because no man was found worthy to open and to read the book, neither to look thereon.

5 And one of the elders saith unto me, Weep not; behold, the Lion of the tribe of Juda, the Root of David, hath prevailed to open the book, and to loose the seven seals thereof.

6 And I beheld, and, lo, in the midst

of the throne and of the four beasts, and in the midst of the elders, stood a Lamb as it had been slain, having twelve horns and twelve eyes, which are the twelve servants of God, sent forth into all the earth.

7 And he came and took the book out of the right hand of him that sat upon the throne.

8 And when he had taken the book, the four beasts and four and twenty elders fell down before the Lamb, having every one of them harps, and golden vials full of odors, which are the prayers of saints.

9 And they sung a new song, saying, Thou art worthy to take the book, and to open the seals thereof; for thou wast slain, and hast redeemed us to God by thy blood out of every kindred, and tongue, and people, and nation;

10 And hast made us unto our God kings and priests; and we shall reign on the earth.

11 And I beheld, and I heard the voice of many angels round about the throne, and the beasts, and the elders; and the number of them was ten thousand times ten thousand, and thousands of thousands;

12 Saying with a loud voice, Worthy is the Lamb that was slain to receive power, and riches, and wisdom, and strength, and honor, and glory, and blessing.

13 And every creature which is in heaven, and on the earth, and under the earth, and such as are in the sea, and all that are in them, heard I saying, Blessing, and honor, and glory, and power, be unto him that sitteth upon the throne, and unto the Lamb for ever and ever.

14 And the four beasts said, Amen. And the four and twenty elders fell down and worshiped him that liveth for ever and ever.

## CHAPTER 6

*The opening of the seals.*

1 And I saw when the Lamb opened one of the seals, one of the four beasts, and I heard, as it were, the noise of thunder, saying, Come and see.

2 And I saw, and behold a white horse; and he that sat on him had a bow; and a crown was given unto him; and he went forth conquering; and to conquer.

3 And when he had opened the sec-

ond seal, I heard the second beast say, Come and see.

4 And there went out another horse that was red; and power was given to him that sat thereon to take peace from the earth, and that they should kill one another; and there was given unto him a great sword.

5 And when he had opened the third seal, I heard the third beast say, Come and see. And I beheld, and lo a black horse; and he that sat on him had a pair of balances in his hand.

6 And I heard a voice in the midst of the four beasts say, A measure of wheat for a penny, and three measures of barley for a penny; and hurt not thou the oil and the wine.

7 And when he had opened the fourth seal, I heard the voice of the fourth beast say, Come and see.

8 And I looked, and behold a pale horse; and his name that sat on him was Death, and Hell followed with him. And power was given unto them over the fourth part of the earth, to kill with sword, and with hunger, and with death, and with the beasts of the earth.

9 And when he had opened the fifth seal, I saw under the altar the souls of them that were slain for the word of God, and for the testimony which they held;

10 And they cried with a loud voice, saying, How long, O Lord, holy and true, dost thou not judge and avenge our blood on them that dwell on the earth?

11 And white robes were given unto every one of them; and it was said unto them, that they should rest yet for a little season, until their fellow servants also and their brethren, that should be killed as they were, should be fulfilled.

12 And I beheld when he had opened the sixth seal, and, lo, there was a great earthquake; and the sun became black as sackcloth of hair, and the moon became as blood;

13 And the stars of heaven fell unto the earth, even as a fig tree casteth her untimely figs, when she is shaken of a mighty wind.

14 And the heavens opened as a scroll is opened when it is rolled together; and every mountain, and island, was moved out of its place.

15 And the kings of the earth, and the

great men, and the rich men, and the chief captains, and the mighty men, and every bondman, and every free man, hid themselves in the dens and in the rocks of the mountain;

16 And said to the mountains and rocks, Fall on us, and hide us from the face of him that sitteth on the throne, and from the wrath of the Lamb;

17 For the great day of his wrath is come; and who shall be able to stand?

## CHAPTER 7

*The servants of God sealed—The innumerable multitude.*

1 And after these things I saw four angels standing on the four corners of the earth, holding the four winds of the earth, that the wind should not blow on the earth, nor on the sea, nor on any tree.

2 And I saw another angel ascending from the east, having the seal of the living God; and I heard him cry with a loud voice to the four angels, to whom it was given to hurt the earth and the sea,

3 Saying, Hurt not the earth, neither the sea, nor the trees, till we have sealed the servants of our God in their foreheads.

4 And the number of them who were sealed, were an hundred and forty and four thousand of all the tribes of the children of Israel.

5 Of the tribe of Juda were sealed twelve thousand. Of the tribe of Reuben were sealed twelve thousand. Of the tribe of Gad were sealed twelve thousand.

6 Of the tribe of Aser were sealed twelve thousand. Of the tribe of Nephthalim were sealed twelve thousand. Of the tribe of Manasses were sealed twelve thousand.

7 Of the tribe of Simeon were sealed twelve thousand. Of the tribe of Levi were sealed twelve thousand. Of the tribe of Issachar were sealed twelve thousand.

8 Of the tribe of Zabulon were sealed twelve thousand. Of the tribe of Joseph were sealed twelve thousand. Of the tribe of Benjamin were sealed twelve thousand.

9 After this I beheld, and, lo, a great multitude, which no man could number, of all nations, and kindreds, and people, and tongues, stood before the throne, and before the Lamb, clothed with white robes, and palms in their hands;

10 And cried with a loud voice, saying, Salvation to our God which sitteth upon the throne, and unto the Lamb.

11 And all the angels stood round about the throne, and about the elders and the four beasts, and fell before the throne on their faces, and worshiped God,

12 Saying, Amen; Blessing, and glory, and wisdom, and thanksgiving, and honor, and power, and might, be unto our God for ever and ever. Amen.

13 And one of the elders answered, saying unto me, What are these which are arrayed in white robes? and whence came they?

14 And I said unto him, Sir, thou knowest. And he said to me, These are they which came out of great tribulation, and have washed their robes, and made them white in the blood of the Lamb.

15 Therefore are they before the throne of God, and serve him day and night in his temple; and he that sitteth on the throne shall dwell among them.

16 They shall hunger no more, neither thirst any more; neither shall the sun light on them, nor any heat.

17 For the Lamb which is in the midst of the throne shall feed them, and shall lead them unto living fountains of waters; and God shall wipe away all tears from their eyes.

## CHAPTER 8

*Seven angels, seven trumpets—Four sound, and great plagues follow.*

1 And when he had opened the seventh seal, there was silence in heaven about the space of half an hour.

2 And I saw the seven angels which stood before God; and to them were given seven trumpets.

3 And another angel came and stood at the altar, having a golden censer; and there was given unto him much incense, that he should offer it with the prayers of all saints upon the golden altar which was before the throne.

4 And the smoke of the incense, which came with the prayers of the saints, ascended up before God out of the angel's hand.

5 And the angel took the censer, and filled it with fire of the altar, and cast it into the earth; and there were voices,

and thunderings, and lightnings, and an earthquake.

6 And the seven angels which had the seven trumpets prepared themselves to sound.

7 The first angel sounded, and there followed hail and fire mingled with blood, and they were cast upon the earth; and the third part of trees was burnt up, and all green grass was burnt up.

8 And the second angel sounded, and as it were a great mountain burning with fire was cast into the sea; and the third part of the sea became blood.

9 And the third part of the creatures which were in the sea, and had life, died; and the third part of the ships were destroyed.

10 And the third angel sounded, and there fell a great star from heaven, burning as it were a lamp, and it fell upon the third part of the rivers, and upon the fountains of waters;

11 And the name of the star is called Wormwood; and the third part of the waters became wormwood; and many men died of the waters, because they were made bitter.

12 And the fourth angel sounded, and the third part of the sun was smitten, and the third part of the moon, and the third part of the stars; so that the third part of them was darkened, and the day shone not for a third part of it, and the night likewise.

13 And I beheld, and heard an angel flying through the midst of heaven, saying with a loud voice, Woe, woe, woe, to the inhabiters of the earth by reason of the other voices of the trumpet of the three angels, which are yet to sound!

## CHAPTER 9

*Opening of the bottomless pit.*

1 And the fifth angel sounded, and I saw a star fall from heaven unto the earth; and to the angel was given the key of the bottomless pit.

2 And he opened the bottomless pit; and there arose a smoke out of the pit, as the smoke of a great furnace; and the sun and the air were darkened by reasons of the smoke of the pit.

3 And there came out of the smoke locusts upon the earth; and unto them was given power, as the scorpions of the earth have power.

4 And it was commanded them that they should not hurt the grass of the earth, neither any green thing, neither any tree; but only those men which have not the seal of God in their foreheads.

5 And to them it was given that they should not kill them, but that they should be tormented five months; and their torment was as the torment of a scorpion, when he striketh a man.

6 And in those days shall men seek death, and shall not find it; and shall desire to die, and death shall flee from them.

7 And the shapes of the locusts were like unto horses prepared unto battle; and on their heads were as it were crowns like gold, and their faces were as the faces of men.

8 And they had hair as the hair of women, and their teeth were as the teeth of lions.

9 And they had breastplates, as it were breastplates of iron; and the sound of their wings was as the sound of chariots of many horses running to battle.

10 And they had tails like unto scorpions, and there were stings in their tails; and their power was to hurt men five months.

11 And they had a king over them, which is the angel of the bottomless pit, whose name in the Hebrew tongue is Abaddon, but in the Greek tongue hath his name Apollyon.

12 One woe is past; and, behold, there come two woes more hereafter.

13 And the sixth angel sounded, and I heard a voice from the four horns of the golden altar which is before God,

14 Saying to the sixth angel which had the trumpet, Loose the four angels which are bound in the bottomless pit.

15 And the four angels were loosed, which were prepared for an hour, and a day, and a month, and a year, for to slay the third part of men.

16 And the number of the army of the horsemen were two hundred thousand thousand; and I saw the number of them.

17 And thus I saw the horses in the vision, and them that sat on them, having breastplates of fire, and of jacinth, and brimstone; and the heads of the horses were as the heads of lions; and out of their mouths issued fire and smoke and brimstone.

18 By these three was the third part

of men killed, by the fire, and by the smoke, and by the brimstone, which issued out of their mouths.

19 For their power is in their mouth, and in their tails; for their tails were like unto serpents, and had heads, and with them they do hurt.

20 And the rest of the men which were not killed by these plagues yet repented not of the works of their hands, that they should not worship devils, and idols of gold, and silver, and brass, and stone, and of wood; which neither can see, nor hear, nor walk;

21 Neither repented they of their murders, nor of their sorceries, nor of their fornication, nor of their thefts.

## CHAPTER 10
*The angel with an open book—The end of time declared—John eats the book.*

1 And I saw another mighty angel come down from heaven, clothed with a cloud; and a rainbow was upon his head, and his face was as it were the sun, and his feet as pillars of fire;

2 And he had in his hand a little book open and he set his right foot upon the sea, and his left foot on the earth,

3 And cried with a loud voice, as when a lion roareth; and when he had cried, seven thunders uttered their voices.

4 And when the seven thunders had uttered their voices, I was about to write; and I heard a voice from heaven saying unto me, Those things are sealed up which the seven thunders uttered, and write them not.

5 And the angel which I saw stand upon the sea and upon the earth lifted up his hand to heaven,

6 And sware by him that liveth for ever and ever, who created heaven, and the things that therein are, and the earth, and the things that therein are, and the sea, and the things which are therein, that there should be time no longer;

7 But in the days of the voice of the seventh angel, when he shall begin to sound, the mystery of God should be finished, as he hath declared to his servants the prophets.

8 And the voice which I heard from heaven spake unto me again, and said, Go and take the little book which is open in the hand of the angel which standeth upon the sea and upon the earth.

9 And I went unto the angel, and said unto him, Give me the little book. And he said unto me, Take it, and eat it up; and it shall make thy belly bitter, but it shall be in thy mouth sweet as honey.

10 And I took the little book out of the angel's hand, and ate it up; and it was in my mouth sweet as honey; and as soon as I had eaten it, my belly was bitter.

11 And he said unto me, Thou must prophesy again before many peoples, and nations, and tongues, and kings.

## CHAPTER 11
*The two witnesses prophesy—They have power to shut heaven, that it rain not— The beast shall fight against them, and kill them—They lie unburied—After three days and a half rise again—The second woe is past—The seventh trumpet soundeth.*

1 And there was given me a reed like unto a rod; and the angel stood, saying, Rise, and measure the temple of God, and the altar, and them that worship therein.

2 But the court which is without the temple, leave out, and measure it not; for it is given unto the Gentiles; and the holy city shall they tread under foot forty and two months.

3 And I will give power unto my two witnesses, and they shall prophesy a thousand two hundred and threescore days, clothed in sackcloth.

4 These are the two olive trees, and the two candlesticks standing before the God of the earth.

5 And if any man will hurt them, fire proceedeth out of their mouth, and devoureth their enemies; and if any man will hurt them, he must in this manner be killed.

6 These have power to shut heaven, that it rain not in the days of their prophecy; and have power over waters to turn them to blood, and to smite the earth with all plagues, as often as they will.

7 And when they shall have finished their testimony, the beast that ascendeth out of the bottomless pit shall make war against them, and shall overcome them, and kill them.

8 And their dead bodies shall lie in the street of the great city, which spiritually is called Sodom and Egypt, where also our Lord was crucified.

9 And they of the people and kin-

dreds and tongues and nations shall see their dead bodies three days and a half, and shall not suffer their dead bodies to be put in graves.

10 And they that dwell upon the earth shall rejoice over them, and make merry, and shall send gifts one to another; because these two prophets tormented them that dwelt on the earth.

11 And after three days and a half the Spirit of life from God entered into them, and they stood upon their feet; and great fear fell upon them which saw them.

12 And they heard a great voice from heaven, saying unto them, Come up hither. And they ascended up to heaven in a cloud; and their enemies beheld them.

13 And the same hour was there a great earthquake, and the tenth part of the city fell, and in the earthquake were slain of men seven thousand; and the remnant were affrighted, and gave glory to the God of heaven.

14 The second woe is past; and, behold, the third woe cometh quickly.

15 And the seventh angel sounded; and there were great voices in heaven, saying, The kingdoms of this world are become the kingdom of our Lord, and of his Christ; and he shall reign for ever and ever.

16 And the four and twenty elders, which sat before God on their seats, fell upon their faces, and worshiped God,

17 Saying, We give thee thanks, O Lord God Almighty, which art, and wast, and art to come: because thou hast taken to thee thy great power, and hast reigned.

18 And the nations were angry, and thy wrath is come, and the time of the dead, that they should be judged, and that thou shouldest give reward unto thy servants the prophets, and to the saints, and them that fear thy name, small and great; and shouldest destroy them which destroy the earth.

19 And the temple of God was opened in heaven, and there was seen in his temple the ark of his testament; and there were lightnings, and voices, and thunderings and an earthquake, and great hail.

## CHAPTER 12

*The woman clothed with the sun—The*

*red dragon—The woman fleeth—Fight with the dragon.*

1 And there appeared a great sign in heaven, in the likeness of things on the earth; a woman clothed with the sun, and the moon under her feet, and upon her head a crown of twelve stars.

2 And the woman being with child, cried, travailing in birth, and pained to be delivered.

3 And she brought forth a man child, who was to rule all nations with a rod of iron; and her child was caught up unto God and his throne.

4 And there appeared another sign in heaven; and behold, a great red dragon, having seven heads and ten horns, and seven crowns upon his heads. And his tail drew the third part of the stars of heaven, and did cast them to the earth. And the dragon stood before the woman which was delivered, ready to devour her child after it was born.

5 And the woman fled into the wilderness, where she had a place prepared of God, that they should feed her there a thousand two hundred and threescore years.

6 And there was war in heaven; Michael and his angels fought against the dragon; and the dragon and his angels fought against Michael;

7 And the dragon prevailed not against Michael, neither the child, nor the woman which was the church of God, who had been delivered of her pains, and brought forth the kingdom of our God and his Christ.

8 Neither was there place found in heaven for the great dragon, who was cast out; that old serpent called the devil, and also called Satan, which deceiveth the whole world; he was cast out into the earth; and his angels were cast out with him.

9 And I heard a loud voice saying in heaven, Now is come salvation, and strength, and the kingdom of our God, and the power of his Christ;

10 For the accuser of our brethren is cast down, which accused them before our God day and night.

11 For they have overcome him by the blood of the Lamb, and by the word of their testimony; for they loved not their own lives, but kept the testimony even unto death. Therefore, rejoice O heavens, and ye that dwell in them.

12 And after these things I heard another voice saying, Woe to the in-

habiters of the earth, yea, and they who dwell upon the islands of the sea! for the devil is come down unto you, having great wrath, because he knoweth that he hath but a short time.

13 For when the dragon saw that he was cast unto the earth, he persecuted the woman which brought forth the man-child.

14 Therefore, to the woman were given two wings of a great eagle, that she might flee into the wilderness, into her place, where she is nourished for a time, and times, and half a time, from the face of the serpent.

15 And the serpent casteth out of his mouth water as a flood after the woman, that he might cause her to be carried away of the flood.

16 And the earth helpeth the woman, and the earth openeth her mouth, and swalloweth up the flood which the dragon casteth out of his mouth.

17 Therefore, the dragon was wroth with the woman, and went to make war with the remnant of her seed, which keep the commandments of God, and have the testimony of Jesus Christ.

## CHAPTER 13

*The beast with seven heads and ten horns—Another beast—Men compelled to worship the beast.*

1 And I saw another sign, in the likeness of the kingdoms of the earth; a beast rise up out of the sea, and he stood upon the sand of the sea, having seven heads and ten horns; and upon his horns ten crowns; and upon his heads the name of blasphemy.

2 And the beast which I saw was like unto a leopard, and his feet were as the feet of a bear, and his mouth as the mouth of a lion; and the dragon gave him his power, and his seat, and great authority.

3 And I saw one of his heads as it were wounded to death; and his deadly wound was healed; and all the world wondered after the beast.

4 And they worshiped the dragon which gave power unto the beast; and they worshiped the beast, saying, Who is like unto the beast? who is able to make war with him?

5 And there was given unto him a mouth speaking great things and blasphemies; and power was given unto him to continue forty and two months.

6 And he opened his mouth in blasphemy against God, to blaspheme his name, and his tabernacle, and them that dwell in heaven.

7 And it was given unto him to make war with the saints, and to overcome them; and power was given him over all kindreds, and tongues, and nations.

8 And all that dwell upon the earth shall worship him, whose names are not written in the book of life of the Lamb slain from the foundation of the world.

9 If any man have an ear, let him hear.

10 He that leadeth into captivity shall go into captivity; he that killeth with the sword must be killed with the sword. Here is the patience and the faith of the saints.

11 And I beheld another beast coming up out of the earth; and he had two horns like a lamb, and he spake as a dragon.

12 And he exerciseth all the power of the first beast before him, and causeth the earth and them which dwell therein to worship the first beast, whose deadly wound was healed.

13 And he doeth great wonders, so that he maketh fire come down from heaven on the earth in the sight of men,

14 And deceiveth them that dwell on the earth by the means of those miracles which he had power to do in the sight of the beast; saying to them that dwell on the earth, that they should make an image to the beast, which had the wound by a sword, and did live.

15 And he had power to give life unto the image of the beast, that the image of the beast should both speak, and cause that as many as would not worship the image of the beast should be killed.

16 And he causeth all, both small and great, rich and poor, free and bond, to receive a mark in their right hand, or in their foreheads;

17 And that no man might buy or sell, save he that had the mark, or the name of the beast, or the number of his name.

18 Here is wisdom. Let him that hath understanding count the number of the beast; for it is the number of a man; and his number is Six hundred threescore and six.

## CHAPTER 14

*The Lamb on mount Sion—An angel restoreth the gospel—The fall of Babylon—The harvest of the world.*

1 And I looked, and, lo, a Lamb stood on the mount Sion, and with him a hundred forty and four thousand, having his Father's name written in their foreheads.

2 And I heard a voice from heaven, as the voice of many waters, and as the voice of a great thunder; and I heard the voice of harpers harping with their harps;

3 And they sung as it were a new song before the throne, and before the four beasts, and the elders; and no man could learn that song but the hundred and forty and four thousand, which were redeemed from the earth.

4 These are they which were not defiled with women; for they are virgins. These are they which follow the Lamb whithersoever he goeth. These were redeemed from among men, being the firstfruits unto God and to the Lamb.

5 And in their mouth was found no guile; for they are without fault before the throne of God.

6 And I saw another angel fly in the midst of heaven, having the everlasting gospel to preach unto them that dwell on the earth, and to every nation, and kindred, and tongue, and people,

7 Saying with a loud voice, Fear God, and give glory to him; for the hour of his judgment is come; and worship him that made heaven, and earth, and the sea, and the fountains of waters.

8 And there followed another angel, saying, Babylon is fallen, is fallen, that great city, because she made all nations drink of the wine of the wrath of her fornication.

9 And the third angel followed them, saying with a loud voice, If any man worship the beast and his image, and receive his mark in his forehead or in his hand,

10 The same shall drink of the wine of the wrath of God, which is poured out without mixture into the cup of his indignation; and he shall be tormented with fire and brimstone in the presence of the holy angels, and in the presence of the Lamb;

11 And the smoke of their torment ascendeth up for ever and ever; and they have no rest day nor night, who worship the beast and his image, and whosoever receiveth the mark of his name.

12 Here is the patience of the saints; here are they that keep the commandments of God, and the faith of Jesus.

13 And I heard a voice from heaven saying unto me, Write, Blessed are the dead which die in the Lord from henceforth; Yea, saith the Spirit, that they may rest from their labours; and their works do follow them.

14 And I looked, and behold a white cloud, and upon the cloud one sat like unto the Son of man, having on his head a golden crown, and in his hand a sharp sickle.

15 And another angel came out of the temple, crying with a loud voice to him that sat on the cloud, Thrust in thy sickle, and reap; for the time is come for thee to reap; for the harvest of the earth is ripe.

16 And he that sat on the cloud thrust in his sickle on the earth; and the earth was reaped.

17 And another angel came out of the temple which is in heaven, he also having a sharp sickle.

18 And another angel came out from the altar, which had power over fire; and cried with a loud cry to him that had the sharp sickle, saying, Thrust in thy sharp sickle, and gather the clusters of the vine of the earth; for her grapes are fully ripe.

19 And the angel thrust in his sickle into the earth, and gathered the vine of the earth, and cast it into the great winepress of the wrath of God.

20 And the winepress was trodden without the city, and blood came out of the winepress, even unto the horses' bridles, by the space of a thousand and six hundred furlongs.

## CHAPTER 15

*The seven last plagues—The song of them that overcome—The seven vials of wrath.*

1 And I saw another sign in heaven, great and marvelous, seven angels having the seven last plagues; for in them is filled up the wrath of God.

2 And I saw as it were a sea of glass mingled with fire; and them that had gotten the victory over the beast, and over his image, and over his mark, and over the number of his name, stand on

the sea of glass, having the harps of God.

3 And they sing the song of Moses the servant of God, and the song of the Lamb, saying, Great and marvelous are thy works, Lord God Almighty; just and true are thy ways, thou King of saints.

4 Who shall not fear thee, O Lord, and glorify thy name? for thou only art holy; for all nations shall come and worship before thee; for thy judgments are made manifest.

5 And after that I looked, and, behold, the temple of the tabernacle of the testimony in heaven was opened;

6 And the seven angels came out of the temple, having the seven plagues, clothed in pure and white linen, and having their breasts girded with golden girdles.

7 And one of the four beasts gave unto the seven angels seven golden vials full of the wrath of God, who liveth for ever and ever.

8 And the temple was filled with smoke from the glory of God, and from his power; and no man was able to enter into the temple, till the seven plagues of the seven angels were fulfilled.

## CHAPTER 16

*The angels pour out their vials—The plagues that follow—Christ cometh as a thief—Blessed are they that watch—Spirits of devils.*

1 And I heard a great voice out of the temple saying to the seven angels, Go your ways, and pour out the vials of the wrath of God upon the earth.

2 And the first went, and poured out his vial upon the earth; and there fell a noisome and grievous sore upon the men which had the mark of the beast, and upon them which worshiped his image.

3 And the second angel poured out his vial upon the sea; and it became as the blood of a dead man; and every living soul died in the sea.

4 And the third angel poured out his vial upon the rivers and fountains of waters; and they became blood.

5 And I heard the angel of the waters say, Thou art righteous, O Lord, which art, and wast, and shalt be, because thou hast judged thus.

6 For they have shed the blood of saints and prophets, and thou hast

given them blood to drink; for they are worthy.

7 And I heard another angel who came out from the altar saying, Even so, Lord God Almighty, true and righteous are thy judgments.

8 And the fourth angel poured out his vial upon the sun; and power was given unto him to scorch men with fire.

9 And men were scorched with great heat, and blasphemed the name of God, which hath power over these plagues; and they repented not to give him glory.

10 And the fifth angel poured out his vial upon the seat of the beast; and his kingdom was full of darkness; and they gnawed their tongues for pain,

11 And blasphemed the God of heaven because of their pains and their sores, and repented not of their deeds.

12 And the sixth angel poured out his vial upon the great river Euphrates; and the water thereof was dried up, that the way of the kings of the east might be prepared.

13 And I saw three unclean spirits like frogs come out of the mouth of the dragon, and out of the mouth of the beast, and out of the mouth of the false prophet.

14 For they are the spirits of devils, working miracles, which go forth unto the kings of the earth and of the whole world, to gather them to the battle of that great day of God Almighty.

15 Behold, I come as a thief. Blessed is he that watcheth, and keepeth his garments, lest he walk naked and they see his shame.

16 And he gathered them together into a place called in the Hebrew tongue Armageddon.

17 And the seventh angel poured out his vial into the air; and there came a great voice out of the temple of heaven, from the throne, saying, It is done.

18 And there were voices, and thunders, and lightnings; and there was a great earthquake, such as was not since men were upon the earth, so mighty an earthquake, and so great.

19 And the great city was divided into three parts, and the cities of the nations fell; and great Babylon came in remembrance before God, to give unto her the cup of the wine of the fierceness of his wrath.

20 And every island fled away, and the mountains were not found.

21 And there fell upon men a great hail out of heaven, every stone about the weight of a talent; and men blasphemed God because of the plague of the hail; for the plague thereof was exceeding great.

## CHAPTER 17

*A woman sitting upon the beast—The interpretation of the seven heads, and the ten horns—The punishment of the whore—The victory of the Lamb.*

1 And there came one of the seven angels which had the seven vials, and talked with me, saying unto me, Come hither; I will show unto thee the judgment of the great whore that sitteth upon many waters;

2 With whom the kings of the earth have committed fornication, and the inhabitants of the earth have been made drunk with the wine of her fornication.

3 So he carried me away in the spirit into the wilderness; and I saw a woman sit upon a scarlet colored beast, full of names of blasphemy, having seven heads and ten horns.

4 And the woman was arrayed in purple and scarlet color, and decked with gold and precious stones and pearls, having a golden cup in her hand full of abominations and filthiness of her fornication;

5 And upon her forehead was a name written, MYSTERY, BABYLON THE GREAT, THE MOTHER OF HARLOTS AND ABOMINATIONS OF THE EARTH.

6 And I saw the woman drunken with the blood of the saints, and with the blood of the martyrs of Jesus; and when I saw her, I wondered with great admiration.

7 And the angel said unto me, Wherefore didst thou marvel? I will tell thee the mystery of the woman, and of the beast that carrieth her, which hath the seven heads and ten horns.

8 The beast that thou sawest was, and is not; and shall ascend out of the bottomless pit, and go into perdition; and they that dwell on the earth shall wonder, whose names were not written in the book of life from the foundation of the world, when they behold the beast that was, and is not, and yet is.

9 And here is the mind which hath wisdom. The seven heads are seven mountains, on which the woman sitteth.

10 And there are seven kings; five are fallen, and one is, and the other is not yet come; and when he cometh, he must continue a short space.

11 And the beast that was, and is not, even he is the eighth, and is of the seven, and goeth into perdition.

12 And the ten horns which thou sawest are ten kings, which have received no kingdom as yet; but receive power as kings one hour with the beast.

13 These have one mind, and shall give their power and strength unto the beast.

14 These shall make war with the Lamb, and the Lamb shall overcome them; for he is Lord of lords, and King of kings; and they that are with him are called, and chosen, and faithful.

15 And he saith unto me, The waters which thou sawest, where the whore sitteth, are peoples, and multitudes, and nations, and tongues.

16 And the ten horns which thou sawest upon the beast, these shall hate the whore, and shall make her desolate and naked, and shall eat her flesh, and burn her with fire.

17 For God hath put in their hearts to fulfill his will, and to agree, and give their kingdom unto the beast, until the words of God are fulfilled.

18 And the woman which thou sawest is that great city, which reigneth over the kings of the earth.

## CHAPTER 18

*Babylon is fallen—Voice from heaven to the saints—The destruction of the wicked—The saints rejoice.*

1 And after these things I saw another angel come down from heaven, having great power; and the earth was lightened with his glory.

2 And he cried mightily with a strong voice, saying, Babylon the great is fallen, is fallen, and is become the habitation of devils, and the hold of every foul spirit, and a cage of every unclean and hateful bird.

3 For all nations have drunk of the wine of the wrath of her fornication, and the kings of the earth have committed fornication with her, and the merchants of the earth are waxed rich through the abundance of her delicacies.

4 And I heard another voice from heaven, saying, Come out of her, my people, that ye be not partakers of her sins, and that ye receive not of her plagues.

5 For her sins have reached unto heaven, and God hath remembered her iniquities.

6 Reward her even as she rewarded you, and double unto her double according to her works; in the cup which she hath filled, fill to her double.

7 How much she hath glorified herself, and lived deliciously, so much torment and sorrow give her; for she saith in her heart, I sit a queen, and am no widow, and shall see no sorrow.

8 Therefore shall her plagues come in one day, death, and mourning, and famine; and she shall be utterly burned with fire; for strong is the Lord God who judgeth her.

9 And the kings of the earth, who have committed fornication and lived deliciously with her, shall bewail her, and lament for her, when they shall see the smoke of her burning,

10 Standing afar off for the fear of her torment, saying, Alas, alas, that great city Babylon, that mighty city! for in one hour is thy judgment come.

11 And the merchants of the earth shall weep and mourn over her; for no man buyeth their merchandise any more;

12 The merchandise of gold, and silver, and precious stones, and of pearls, and fine linen, and purple, and silk, and scarlet, and all thyine wood, and all manner of vessels of ivory, and all manner of vessels of most precious wood, and of brass, and iron, and marble,

13 And cinnamon, and odors, and ointments, and frankincense, and wine, and oil, and fine flour, and wheat, and beasts, and sheep, and horses, and chariots, and slaves, and souls of men.

14 And the fruits that thy soul lusted after are departed from thee, and all things which were dainty and goodly are departed from thee, and thou shalt find them no more at all.

15 The merchants of these things, which were made rich by her, shall stand afar off for the fear of her torment, weeping and wailing,

16 And saying, Alas, alas, that great city, that was clothed in fine linen, and purple, and scarlet, and decked with gold, and precious stones, and pearls!

17 For in one hour so great riches is come to naught. And every shipmaster, and all the company in ships, and sailors, and as many as trade by sea, stood afar off.

18 And cried when they saw the smoke of her burning, saying, What city is like unto this great city!

19 And they cast dust on their heads, and cried, weeping and wailing, saying, Alas, alas, that great city, wherein were made rich all that had ships in the sea by reason of her costliness! for in one hour is she made desolate.

20 Rejoice over her, thou heaven, and ye holy apostles and prophets; for God hath avenged you on her.

21 And a mighty angel took up a stone like a great millstone, and cast it into the sea, saying, Thus with violence shall that great city Babylon be thrown down, and shall be found no more at all.

22 And the voice of harpers, and musicians, and of pipers, and trumpeters, shall be heard no more at all in thee; and no craftsman, of whatsoever craft he be, shall be found any more in thee; and the sound of a millstone shall be heard no more at all in thee;

23 And the light of a candle shall shine no more at all in thee; and the voice of the bridegroom and of the bride shall be heard no more at all in thee; for thy merchants were the great men of the earth; for by thy sorceries were all nations deceived.

24 And in her was found the blood of prophets, and of saints, and of all that were slain upon the earth.

## CHAPTER 19
*Joy in heaven—Blood of saints avenged—Marriage of the Lamb—Beast and false prophet destroyed.*

1 And after these things I heard a great voice of much people in heaven, saying, Alleluia; Salvation, and glory, and honor, and power, unto the Lord our God;

2 For true and righteous are his judgments; for he hath judged the great whore, which did corrupt the earth with her fornication, and hath avenged the blood of his saints at her hand.

3 And again they said, Alleluia. And her smoke rose up for ever and ever.

4 And the four and twenty elders and the four beasts fell down and worshiped God that sat on the throne, saying, Amen; Alleluia.

5 And a voice came out of the throne, saying, Praise our God, all ye his saints, and ye that fear him, both small and great.

6 And I heard as it were the voice of a great multitude, and as the voice of many waters, and as the voice of mighty thunderings, saying, Alleluia; for the Lord God omnipotent reigneth.

7 Let us be glad and rejoice, and give honor to him; for the marriage of the Lamb is come, and his wife hath made herself ready.

8 And to her was granted that she should be arrayed in fine linen, clean and white; for the fine linen is the righteousness of saints.

9 And he saith unto me, Write, Blessed are they which are called unto the marriage supper of the Lamb. And he saith unto me, These are the true sayings of God.

10 And I fell at his feet to worship him. And he said unto me, See that thou do it not; I am thy fellow servant, and of thy brethren that have the testimony of Jesus; worship God; for the testimony of Jesus is the spirit of prophecy.

11 And I saw heaven opened, and behold a white horse; and he that sat upon him is called Faithful and True, and in righteousness he doth judge and make war;

12 His eyes as a flame of fire; and he had on his head many crowns; and a name written, that no man knew, but himself.

13 And he is clothed with a vesture dipped in blood; and his name is called The Word of God.

14 And the armies which were in heaven followed him upon white horses, clothed in fine linen, white and clean.

15 And out of his mouth proceedeth the word of God, and with it he will smite the nations; and he will rule them with the word of his mouth; and he treadeth the winepress in the fierceness and wrath of Almighty God.

16 And he hath on a vesture, and on his thigh a name written, KING OF KINGS, AND LORD OF LORDS.

17 And I saw an angel standing in the sun; and he cried with a loud voice, saying to all the fowls that fly in the midst of heaven, Come and gather yourselves together unto the supper of the great God;

18 That ye may eat the flesh of kings, and the flesh of captains, and the flesh of mighty men, and the flesh of horses, and of them that sit on them, and the flesh of all who fight against the Lamb, both bond and free, both small and great.

19 And I saw the beast, and the kings of the earth, and their armies, gathered together to make war against him that sat on the horse, and against his army.

20 And the beast was taken, and with him the false prophet that wrought miracles before him, with which he deceived them that had received the mark of the beast, and them that worshiped his image. These both were cast alive into a lake of fire burning with brimstone.

21 And the remnant were slain with the word of him that sat upon the horse, which word proceeded out of his mouth; and all the fowls were filled with their flesh.

## CHAPTER 20

*Satan bound for a thousand years— The first resurrection—Satan let loose again—Gog and Magog—The last and general resurrection.*

1 And I saw an angel come down out of heaven, having the key of the bottomless pit and a great chain in his hand.

2 And he laid hold on the dragon, that old serpent, which is the Devil, and Satan, and bound him a thousand years,

3 And cast him into the bottomless pit, and shut him up, and set a seal upon him, that he should deceive the nations no more, till the thousand years should be fulfilled; and after that he must be loosed a little season.

4 And I saw thrones, and they sat upon them, and judgment was given unto them; and I saw the souls of them that were beheaded for the witness of Jesus, and for the word of God, and which had not worshiped the beast, neither his image, neither had received his mark upon their foreheads, or in their hands: and they lived and reigned with Christ a thousand years.

5 But the rest of the dead lived not

again until the thousand years were finished. This is the first resurrection.

6 Blessed and holy are they who have part in the first resurrection; on such the second death hath no power, but they shall be priests of God and of Christ, and shall reign with him a thousand years.

7 And when the thousand years are expired, Satan shall be loosed out of his prison,

8 And shall go out to deceive the nations which are in the four quarters of the earth, Gog and Magog, to gather them together to battle; the number of whom is as the sand of the sea.

9 And they went up on the breadth of the earth, and compassed the camp of the saints about, and the beloved city; and fire came down from God out of heaven, and devoured them.

10 And the devil that deceived them was cast into the lake of fire and brimstone, where the beast and the false prophet are, and shall be tormented day and night for ever and ever.

11 And I saw a great white throne, and him that sat on it, from whose face the earth and the heaven fled away; and there was found no place for them.

12 And I saw the dead, small and great, stand before God; and the books were opened; and another book was opened, which is the book of life; and the dead were judged out of those things which were written in the books, according to their works.

13 And the sea gave up the dead which were in it; and death and hell delivered up the dead which were in them; and they were judged every man according to their works.

14 And death and hell were cast into the lake of fire. This is the second death.

15 And whosoever was not found written in the book of life was cast into the lake of fire.

## CHAPTER 21

*A new heaven and a new earth—The New Jerusalem.*

1 And I saw a new heaven and a new earth; for the first heaven and the first earth were passed away; and there was no more sea.

2 And I John saw the holy city, new Jerusalem, coming down from God out of heaven, prepared as a bride adorned for her husband.

3 And I heard a great voice out of heaven saying, Behold, the tabernacle of God is with men, and he will dwell with them, and they shall be his people, and God himself shall be with them, and be their God.

4 And God shall wipe away all tears from their eyes; and there shall be no more death, neither sorrow, nor crying, neither shall there be any more pain; for the former things are passed away.

5 And he that sat upon the throne said, Behold, I make all things new. And he said unto me, Write; for these words are true and faithful.

6 And he said unto me, It is done. I am Alpha and Omega, the beginning and the end. I will give unto him that is athirst of the fountain of the water of life freely.

7 He that overcometh shall inherit all things; and I will be his God, and he shall be my son.

8 But the fearful, and unbelieving, and the abominable, and murderers, and whoremongers, and sorcerers, and idolaters, and all liars, shall have their part in the lake which burneth with fire and brimstone; which is the second death.

9 And there came unto me one of the seven angels which had the seven vials full of the seven last plagues, and talked with me, saying, Come hither, I will show thee the bride, the Lamb's wife.

10 And he carried me away in the Spirit to a great and high mountain, and showed me that great city, the holy Jerusalem, descending out of heaven from God,

11 Having the glory of God; and her light was like unto a stone most precious, even like a jasper stone, clear as crystal;

12 And had a wall great and high, and had twelve gates, and at the gates twelve angels, and names written thereon, which are the names of the twelve tribes of the children of Israel;

13 On the east three gates; on the north three gates; on the south three gates; and on the west three gates.

14 And the wall of the city had twelve foundations, and in them names of the twelve apostles of the Lamb.

15 And he that talked with me had a

golden reed to measure the city, and the gates thereof, and the wall thereof.

16 And the city lieth foursquare, and the length is as large as the breadth; and he measured the city with the reed, twelve thousand furlongs. The length and the breadth and the height of it are equal.

17 And he measured the wall thereof, a hundred and forty and four cubits, according to the measure of a man, that is, of the angel.

18 And the building of the wall of it was of jasper; and the city was pure gold, like unto clear glass.

19 And the foundations of the wall of the city were garnished with all manner of precious stones. The first foundation was jasper; the second, sapphire; the third, a chalcedony; the fourth, an emerald;

20 The fifth, sardonyx; the sixth, sardius; the seventh, chrysolite; the eighth, beryl; the ninth, a topaz; the tenth, a chrysoprasus; the eleventh, a jacinth; the twelfth, an amethyst.

21 And the twelve gates were twelve pearls; every several gate was of one pearl; and the street of the city was pure gold, as it were transparent glass.

22 And I saw no temple therein; for the Lord God Almighty and the Lamb are the temple of it.

23 And the city had no need of the sun, neither of the moon, to shine in it; for the glory of God did lighten it, and the Lamb is the light thereof.

24 And the nations of them which are saved shall walk in the light of it; and the kings of the earth do bring their glory and honor into it.

25 And the gates of it shall not be shut at all by day; for there shall be no night there.

26 And they shall bring the glory and honor of the nations into it.

27 And there shall in no wise enter into it anything that defileth, neither whatsoever worketh abomination, or maketh a lie; but they which are written in the Lamb's book of life.

## CHAPTER 22

*The river of the water of life—The tree of life—The light of the city—Nothing may be added to the words of this book of prophecy, nor taken therefrom.*

1 And he showed me a pure river of water of life, clear as crystal, proceeding out of the throne of God and of the Lamb.

2 In the midst of the street of it, and on either side of the river, was there the tree of life, which bare twelve manner of fruits, and yielded her fruit every month; and the leaves of the tree were for the healing of the nations.

3 And there shall be no more curse; but the throne of God and of the Lamb shall be in it; and his servants shall serve him;

4 And they shall see his face; and his name shall be in their foreheads.

5 And there shall be no night there; and they need no candle, neither light of the sun; for the Lord God giveth them light; and they shall reign for ever and ever.

6 And he said unto me, These sayings are faithful and true; and the Lord God of the holy prophets sent his angel to show unto his servants the things which must shortly be done.

7 Behold, I come quickly; blessed is he that keepeth the sayings of the prophecy of this book.

8 And I John saw these things, and heard them. And when I had heard and seen, I fell down to worship before the feet of the angel which showed me these things.

9 Then saith he unto me, See that thou do it not; for I am thy fellowservant, and of thy brethren the prophets, and of them which keep the sayings of this book; worship God.

10 And he saith unto me, Seal not the sayings of the prophecy of this book; for the time is at hand.

11 He that is unjust, let him be unjust still; and he which is filthy, let him be filthy still; and he that is righteous, let him be righteous still; and he that is holy, let him be holy still.

12 And, behold, I come quickly; and my reward is with me to give every man according as his work shall be.

13 I am Alpha and Omega, the beginning and the end, the first and the last.

14 Blessed are they that do his commandments, that they may have right to the tree of life, and may enter in through the gates into the city.

15 For without are dogs, and sorcerers, and whoremongers, and murderers, and idolaters, and whosoever loveth and maketh a lie.

16 I Jesus have sent mine angel to

testify unto you these things in the churches. I am the root and the off-spring of David, and the bright and morning star.

17 And the Spirit and the bride say, Come. And let him that heareth say, Come. And let him that is athirst come. And whosoever will, let him take the water of life freely.

18 For I testify unto every man that heareth the words of the prophecy of this book, If any man shall add unto these things, God shall add unto him the plagues that are written in this book;

19 And if any man shall take away from the words of the book of this prophecy, God shall take away his part out of the book of life, and out of the holy city, and from the things which are written in this book.

20 He which testifieth these things saith, Surely I come quickly; Amen. Even so, come, Lord Jesus.

21 The grace of our Lord Jesus Christ be with you all. Amen.

THE END OF THE NEW TESTAMENT.

# The
# Book of
# Psalms

# The Book of Psalms

## PSALM 1

*The happiness of the godly.*

1 Blessed is the man that walketh not in the counsel of the ungodly, nor standeth in the way of sinners, nor sitteth in the seat of the scornful.

2 But his delight is in the law of the Lord; and in his law doth he meditate day and night.

3 And he shall be like a tree planted by the rivers of water, that bringeth forth his fruit in his season; his leaf also shall not wither; and whatsoever he doeth shall prosper.

4 The ungodly are not so; but are like the chaff which the wind driveth away.

5 Therefore the ungodly shall not stand in the judgment, nor sinners in the congregation of the righteous.

6 For the Lord knoweth the way of the righteous; but the way of the ungodly shall perish.

## PSALM 2

*Kings told to accept Christ.*

1 Why do the heathen rage, and the people imagine a vain thing?

2 The kings of the earth set themselves, and the rulers take counsel together, against the Lord, and against his Anointed, saying,

3 Let us break their bands asunder, and cast away their cords from us.

4 He that sitteth in the heavens shall laugh; the Lord shall have them in derision.

5 Then shall he speak unto them in his wrath, and vex them in his sore displeasure.

6 Yet have I set my king upon my holy hill of Zion.

7 I will declare the decree; the Lord hath said unto me, Thou art my Son; this day have I begotten thee.

8 Ask of me, and I shall give thee the heathen for thine inheritance, and the uttermost parts of the earth for thy possession.

9 Thou shalt break them with a rod of iron; thou shalt dash them in pieces like a potter's vessel.

10 Be wise now therefore, O ye kings; be instructed, ye judges of the earth.

11 Serve the Lord with fear, and rejoice with trembling.

12 Kiss the Son, lest he be angry, and ye perish from the way, when his wrath is kindled but a little. Blessed are all they that put their trust in him.

## PSALM 3

*The security of God's protection.*

A Psalm of David, when he fled from Absalom his son.

1 Lord, how are they increased that trouble me! many are they that rise up against me.

2 Many there be which say of my soul, There is no help for him in God. Selah.

3 But thou, O Lord, art a shield for me; my glory, and the lifter up of mine head.

4 I cried unto the Lord with my voice, and he heard me out of his holy hill. Selah.

5 I laid me down and slept; I awaked; for the Lord sustained me.

6 I will not be afraid of ten thousands of people, that have set themselves against me round about.

7 Arise, O Lord; save me, O my God; for thou hast smitten all mine enemies upon the cheek bone; thou hast broken the teeth of the ungodly.

8 Salvation belongeth unto the Lord; thy blessing is upon thy people. Selah.

## PSALM 4

*David reproveth his enemies.*

To the chief Musician on Neginoth.

1 Hear me when I call, O God of my righteousness; thou hast enlarged me when I was in distress; have mercy upon me, and hear my prayer.

2 O ye sons of men, how long will ye turn my glory into shame? how long will ye love vanity, and seek after leasing? Selah.

3 But know that the Lord hath set apart him that is godly for himself; the Lord will hear when I call unto him.

4 Stand in awe, and sin not; commune with your own heart upon your bed, and be still. Selah.

5 Offer the sacrifices of righteousness, and put your trust in the Lord.

6 There be many that say, Who will show us any good? Lord, lift thou up the light of thy countenance upon us.

7 Thou hast put gladness in my heart, more than in the time that their corn and their wine increased.

8 I will both lay me down in peace, and sleep; for thou, Lord, only makest me dwell in safety.

## PSALM 5

*God favoreth not the wicked.*

To the chief Musician upon Nehiloth, A Psalm of David.

1 Give ear to my words, O Lord, consider my meditation.

2 Hearken unto the voice of my cry, my King, and my God; for unto thee will I pray.

3 My voice shalt thou hear in the morning, O Lord; in the morning will I direct my prayer unto thee, and will look up.

4 For thou art not a God that hath pleasure in wickedness; neither shall evil dwell with thee.

5 The foolish shall not stand in thy sight; thou hatest all workers of iniquity.

6 Thou shalt destroy them that speak leasing; the Lord will abhor the bloody and deceitful man.

7 But as for me, I will come into thy house in the multitude of thy mercy; and in thy fear will I worship toward thy holy temple.

8 Lead me, O Lord, in thy righteousness because of mine enemies; make thy way straight before my face.

9 For there is no faithfulness in their mouth; their inward part is very wickedness; their throat is an open sepulcher; they flatter with their tongue.

10 Destroy thou them, O God; let them fall by their own counsels; cast them out in the multitude of their transgressions; for they have rebelled against thee.

11 But let all those that put their trust in thee rejoice; let them ever shout for joy, because thou defendest them; let them also that love thy name be joyful in thee.

12 For thou, Lord, wilt bless the righteous; with favor wilt thou compass him as with a shield.

## PSALM 6

*David, by faith, triumpheth.*

To the chief Musician on Neginoth upon Sheminith, A Psalm of David.

1 O Lord, rebuke me not in thine anger, neither chasten me in thy hot displeasure.

2 Have mercy upon me, O Lord; for I am weak; O Lord, heal me; for my bones are vexed.

3 My soul is also sore vexed; but thou, O Lord, how long?

4 Return, O Lord, deliver my soul; oh save me for thy mercies' sake.

5 For in death there is no remembrance of thee; in the grave who shall give thee thanks?

6 I am weary with my groaning; all the night make I my bed to swim; I water my couch with my tears.

7 Mine eye is consumed because of grief; it waxeth old because of all mine enemies.

8 Depart from me, all ye workers of iniquity; for the Lord hath heard the voice of my weeping.

9 The Lord hath heard my supplication; the Lord will receive my prayer.

10 Let all mine enemies be ashamed and sore vexed; let them return and be ashamed suddenly.

## PSALM 7

*David prayeth against the malice of his enemies, professing his innocency.*

Shiggaion of David, which he sang unto the Lord, concerning the words of Cush the Benjamite.

1 O Lord my God, in thee do I put my trust; save me from all them that persecute me, and deliver me;

2 Lest he tear my soul like a lion, rending it in pieces, while there is none to deliver.

3 O Lord my God, if I have done this; if there be iniquity in my hands;

4 If I have rewarded evil unto him that was at peace with me; (yea, I have delivered him that without cause is mine enemy;)

5 Let the enemy persecute my soul, and take it; yea, let him tread down my life upon the earth, and lay mine honor in the dust. Selah.

6 Arise, O Lord, in thine anger, lift up thyself because of the rage of mine enemies; and awake for me to the judgment that thou hast commanded.

7 So shall the congregation of the people compass thee about; for their sakes therefore return thou on high.

8 The Lord shall judge the people; judge me, O Lord, according to my righteousness, and according to mine integrity that is in me.

9 Oh let the wickedness of the wicked come to an end; but establish

the just; for the righteous God trieth the hearts and reins.

10 My defense is of God, which saveth the upright in heart.

11 God judgeth the righteous, and God is angry with the wicked every day.

12 If he turn not, he will whet his sword; he hath bent his bow, and made it ready.

13 He hath also prepared for him the instruments of death; he ordaineth his arrows against the persecutors.

14 Behold, he travaileth with iniquity, and hath conceived mischief, and brought forth falsehood.

15 He made a pit, and digged it, and is fallen into the ditch which he made.

16 His mischief shall return upon his own head, and his violent dealing shall come down upon his own pate.

17 I will praise the Lord according to his righteousness; and will sing praise to the name of the Lord most high.

## PSALM 8
*God's glory magnified by his works and love to man.*
To the chief Musician upon Gittith, A Psalm of David.

1 O Lord, our Lord, how excellent is thy name in all the earth! who hast set thy glory above the heavens.

2 Out of the mouth of babes and sucklings hast thou ordained strength because of thine enemies, that thou mightest still the enemy and the avenger.

3 When I consider thy heavens, the work of thy fingers, the moon and the stars, which thou hast ordained;

4 What is man, that thou art mindful of him? and the son of man, that thou visitest him?

5 For thou hast made him a little lower than the angels, and hast crowned him with glory and honor.

6 Thou madest him to have dominion over the works of thy hands; thou hast put all things under his feet;

7 All sheep and oxen, yea, and the beasts of the field;

8 The fowl of the air, and the fish of the sea, and whatsoever passeth through the paths of the seas.

9 O Lord our Lord, how excellent is thy name in all the earth!

## PSALM 9
*David praiseth God for executing of judgment.*
To the chief Musician upon Muthlabben, A Psalm of David.

1 I will praise thee, O Lord, with my whole heart; I will show forth all thy marvelous works.

2 I will be glad and rejoice in thee; I will sing praise to thy name, O thou Most High.

3 When mine enemies are turned back, they shall fall and perish at thy presence.

4 For thou hast maintained my right and my cause; thou satest in the throne judging right.

5 Thou hast rebuked the heathen, thou hast destroyed the wicked, thou hast put out their name for ever and ever.

6 O thou enemy, destructions are come to a perpetual end; and thou hast destroyed cities; their memorial is perished with them.

7 But the Lord shall endure for ever; he hath prepared his throne for judgment.

8 And he shall judge the world in righteousness, he shall minister judgment to the people in uprightness.

9 The Lord also will be a refuge for the oppressed, a refuge in times of trouble.

10 And they that know thy name will put their trust in thee; for thou, Lord, hast not forsaken them that seek thee.

11 Sing praises to the Lord, which dwelleth in Zion; declare among the people his doings.

12 When he maketh inquisition for blood, he remembereth them; he forgetteth not the cry of the humble.

13 Have mercy upon me, O Lord; consider my trouble which I suffer of them that hate me, thou that liftest me up from the gates of death;

14 That I may show forth all thy praise in the gates of the daughter of Zion; I will rejoice in thy salvation.

15 The heathen are sunk down in the pit that they made; in the net which they hid is their own foot taken.

16 The Lord is known by the judgment which he executeth; the wicked is snared in the work of his own hands. Higgaion. Selah.

17 The wicked shall be turned into hell, and all the nations that forget God.

18 For the needy shall not always be forgotten; the expectation of the poor shall not perish for ever.

19 Arise, O Lord; let not man prevail; let the heathen be judged in thy sight.

20 Put them in fear, O Lord; that the nations may know themselves to be but men. Selah.

## PSALM 10
*David professeth his faith in God.*

1 Why standest thou afar off, O Lord? why hidest thou thyself in times of trouble?

2 The wicked in his pride doth persecute the poor; let them be taken in the devices that they have imagined.

3 For the wicked boasteth of his heart's desire, and blesseth the covetous, whom the Lord abhorreth.

4 The wicked, through the pride of his countenance, will not seek after God; God is not in all his thoughts.

5 His ways are always grievous; thy judgments are far above out of his sight; as for all his enemies, he puffeth at them.

6 For he hath said in his heart, I shall not be moved; never in adversity.

7 His mouth is full of cursing and deceit; and his heart is full of fraud; and under his tongue is mischief and vanity.

8 He sitteth in the lurking places of the villages; in the secret places doth he murder the innocent; his eyes are privily set against the poor.

9 He lieth in wait secretly as a lion in his den; he lieth in wait to catch the poor; he doth catch the poor, when he draweth him into his net.

10 He croucheth to the strong ones, and humbleth himself, that the poor may fall by his devices.

11 He hath said in his heart, God hath forgotten; he hideth his face; he will never see it.

12 Arise, O Lord; O God, lift up thine hand; forget not the humble.

13 The wicked condemn God; wherefore he doth say in his heart, Thou wilt not require iniquity at my hand.

14 O Lord, thou hast seen all this, for thou beholdest mischief and spite, to requite it with thy hand. The poor committeth himself unto thee; thou art the helper of the fatherless.

15 O Lord, thou wilt break the arm of the wicked, and the evil; and seek out his wickedness until thou find none that remain.

16 And the Lord shall be king for ever and ever over his people; for the wicked shall perish out of his land.

17 Lord, thou hast heard the desire of the humble; thou wilt prepare their heart, thou wilt cause thine ear to hear;

18 To judge the fatherless and the oppressed, that the man of the earth may no more oppress.

## PSALM 11
*The providence and justice of God.*
To the chief Musician, A Psalm of David.

1 In that day thou shalt come, O Lord; and I will put my trust in thee. Thou shalt say unto thy people, for mine ear hath heard thy voice; thou shalt say unto every soul, Flee unto my mountain; and the righteous shall flee like a bird that is let go from the snare of the fowler.

2 For the wicked bend their bow; lo, they make ready their arrow upon the string, that they may privily shoot at the upright in heart, to destroy their foundation.

3 But the foundations of the wicked shall be destroyed, and what can they do?

4 For the Lord, when he shall come into his holy temple, sitting upon God's throne in heaven, his eyes shall pierce the wicked.

5 Behold his eyelids shall try the children of men, and he shall redeem the righteous, and they shall be tried. The Lord loveth the righteous, but the wicked, and him that loveth violence, his soul hateth.

6 Upon the wicked he shall rain snares, fire, and brimstone, and a horrible tempest, the portion of their cup.

7 For the righteous Lord loveth righteousness; his countenance doth behold the upright.

## PSALM 12
*David is comforted with God's tried promises.*

1 In that day thou shalt help, O Lord, the poor and the meek of the earth. For the godly man shall cease to be found, and the faithful fail from among the children of men.

2 They shall speak vanity every one

with his neighbor; with flattering lips, with a double heart do they speak.

3 But the Lord shall cut off all flattering lips, the tongue that speaketh proud things,

4 Who have said, With our tongue will we prevail, our lips are our own, who shall be Lord over us?

5 Therefore, thus saith the Lord, I will arise in that day, I will stand upon the earth, and I will judge the earth for the oppression of the poor, for the sighing of the needy; and their cry hath entered into mine ear.

6 Therefore the Lord shall sit in judgment upon all those who say in their hearts, We all sit in safety; and puffeth at him. These are the words of the Lord; yea, pure words, like silver tried in a furnace of earth, purified seven times.

7 Thou shalt save thy people, O Lord; thou shalt keep them; thou shalt preserve them from the wickedness of their generation for ever.

8 The wicked walk on every side, and the vilest men are exalted; but in the day of their pride thou shalt visit them.

## PSALM 13

*The grace and mercy of God.*

1 How long, O Lord, wilt thou withdraw thyself from me? How long wilt thou hide thy face from me, that I may not see thee? Wilt thou forget me, and cast me off from thy presence for ever?

2 How long shall I take counsel in my soul, sorrowing in my heart daily? How long shall mine enemy be exalted over me?

3 Consider me, O Lord; and hear my cry, O my God; and lighten mine eyes, lest I sleep the death of the ungodly; lest mine enemy say, I have prevailed against him.

4 Those that trouble me, rejoice when I am moved;

5 But I have trusted in thy mercy, my heart shall rejoice in thy salvation.

6 I will sing unto the Lord, because he hath dealt bountifully with me.

## PSALM 14

*Corruption of man—Light of conscience.*

To the chief Musician, A Psalm of David.

1 The fool hath said in his heart, There is no man that hath seen God.

Because he showeth himself not unto us, therefore there is no God. Behold, they are corrupt; they have done abominable works, and none of them doeth good.

2 For the Lord looked down from heaven upon the children of men, and by his voice said unto his servant, Seek ye among the children of men, to see if there are any that do understand God. And he opened his mouth unto the Lord, and said, Behold, all these who say they are thine.

3 The Lord answered, and said, They are all gone aside, they are together become filthy, thou canst behold none of them that are doing good, no, not one.

4 All they have for their teachers are workers of iniquity, and there is no knowledge in them. They are they who eat up my people. They eat bread and call not upon the Lord.

5 They are in great fear, for God dwells in the generation of the righteous. He is the counsel of the poor, because they are ashamed of the wicked, and flee unto the Lord for their refuge.

6 They are ashamed of the counsel of the poor because the Lord is his refuge.

7 Oh that Zion were established out of heaven, the salvation of Israel. O Lord, when wilt thou establish Zion? When the Lord bringeth back the captivity of his people, Jacob shall rejoice, Israel shall be glad.

## PSALM 15

*The righteousness of Zion's children.*

A Psalm of David.

1 Lord, who shall abide in thy tabernacle? who shall dwell in thy holy hill of Zion?

2 He that walketh uprightly, and worketh righteousness, and speaketh the truth in his heart.

3 He that backbiteth not with his tongue, nor doeth evil to his neighbor, nor taketh up a reproach against his neighbor.

4 In whose eyes a vile person is contemned; but he honoreth them that fear the Lord; sweareth not falsely to hurt any man, and changeth not.

5 He that putteth not out his money to usury, nor taketh reward against the innocent. He that doeth these things shall never be moved.

## PSALM 16

*David showeth the hope of life everlasting.*

Michtam of David.

1 Preserve me, O God; for in thee do I put my trust.

2 Thou hast said unto me, that thou art the Lord my God, and, My goodness is extended unto thee;

3 And to all the saints that dwell in the earth, and the excellent, in whom is all my delight.

4 And the wicked, there is no delight in them; their sorrows shall be multiplied upon all those who hasten for to seek another god; their drink offerings of blood will I not accept, nor take up their names into my lips.

5 Therefore thou, Lord, art the portion of mine inheritance, and of my cup; thou maintainest my lot.

6 The lines are fallen unto me in pleasant places; yea, I have a goodly heritage.

7 I will bless the Lord, who hath given me counsel; my reins also instruct me in the night seasons.

8 I have set the Lord always before me; because he is at my right hand, I shall not be moved.

9 Therefore my heart is glad, and my glory rejoiceth; my flesh also shall rest in hope.

10 For thou wilt not leave my soul in hell; neither wilt thou suffer thine Holy One to see corruption.

11 Thou wilt show me the path of life; in thy presence is fullness of joy; at thy right hand there are pleasures for evermore.

## PSALM 17

*God the defense of the righteous.*

A Prayer of David.

1 Give me right words, O Lord; speak, and thy servant shall hear thee; attend unto my cry, give ear unto my prayer. I come not unto thee out of feigned lips.

2 Let my sentence come forth from thy presence; let thine eyes behold the things that are equal.

3 Thou hast proved mine heart; thou hast visited me in the night; thou hast tried me; thou shalt find nothing evil in me, for I am purposed my mouth shall not transgress concerning the works of men.

4 By the word of thy lips I have kept out of the paths of the destroyer.

5 Hold up my goings in thy paths, that my footsteps slip not.

6 I have called upon thee, for thou wilt hear, O God, my speech, and incline thine ear unto me.

7 Show thy marvelous loving-kindness, O thou that savest them which put their trust in thee, by thy right hand from those that rise up.

8 Keep me as the apple of the eye. Hide me under the shadow of thy wings from the wicked that oppress me.

9 My deadly enemies compass me about;

10 They are enclosed in their own fat; with their mouth they speak proudly.

11 They have now compassed us in our steps; they have set their eyes, bowing down to the earth;

12 Like as a lion that is greedy of his prey, and as it were a young lion lurking in secret places.

13 Arise, O Lord, disappoint him, cast him down.

14 Deliver my soul from the wicked by thy sword; from men by thy strong hand. Yea, O Lord, from men of the world; for their portion is in their life, and whose belly thou fillest with thy good things; they are full of children, and they die and leave the rest of their inheritance to their babes.

15 As for me, I will behold thy face in righteousness; I shall be satisfied, when I awake, with thy likeness.

## PSALM 18

*The manifold blessings of God.*

To the chief Musician, A Psalm of David, the servant of the Lord, who spake unto the Lord the words of this song in the day that the Lord delivered him from the hand of all his enemies, and from the hand of Saul; And he said,

1 I will love thee, O Lord, my strength.

2 The Lord is my rock, and my fortress, and my deliverer; my God, my strength, in whom I will trust; my buckler, and the horn of my salvation, and my high tower.

3 I will call upon the Lord, for he is worthy to be praised; so shall I be saved from mine enemies.

4 The sorrows of death compassed

me, and the floods of ungodly men made me afraid.

5 The sorrows of hell compassed me about; the snares of death prevented me.

6 In my distress I called upon the Lord, and cried unto my God; he heard my voice out of his temple, and my cry came before him, even into his ears.

7 Then the earth shook and trembled; the foundations also of the hills moved and were shaken, because he was wroth.

8 There went up a smoke out of his nostrils, and fire out of his mouth devoured; coals were kindled by it.

9 He bowed the heavens also, and came down; and darkness was under his feet.

10 And he rode upon a cherub, and did fly; yea, he did fly upon the wings of the wind.

11 He made darkness his secret place; his pavilion round about him were dark waters and thick clouds of the skies.

12 At the brightness that was before him his thick clouds passed, hailstones and coals of fire.

13 The Lord also thundered in the heavens, and the Highest gave his voice; hailstones and coals of fire.

14 Yea, he sent out his arrows, and scattered them; and he shot out lightnings, and discomfited them.

15 Then the channels of waters were seen, and the foundations of the world were discovered at thy rebuke, O Lord, at the blast of the breath of thy nostrils.

16 He sent from above, he took me, he drew me out of many waters.

17 He delivered me from my strong enemy, and from them which hated me; for they were too strong for me.

18 They prevented me in the day of my calamity; but the Lord was my stay.

19 He brought me forth also into a large place; he delivered me, because he delighted in me.

20 The Lord rewarded me according to my righteousness; according to the cleanness of my hands hath he recompensed me.

21 For I have kept the ways of the Lord, and have not wickedly departed from my God.

22 For all his judgments were before

me, and I did not put away his statutes from me.

23 I was also upright before him, and I kept myself from mine iniquity.

24 Therefore hath the Lord recompensed me according to my righteousness, according to the cleanness of my hands in his eyesight.

25 With the merciful thou wilt show thyself merciful; with an upright man thou wilt show thyself upright;

26 With the pure thou wilt show thyself pure; and with the froward thou wilt show thyself froward.

27 For thou wilt save the afflicted people; but wilt bring down high looks.

28 For thou wilt light my candle; the Lord my God will enlighten my darkness.

29 For by thee I have run through a troop; and by my God have I leaped over a wall.

30 O God, thy ways are perfect; the word of the Lord is tried; he is a buckler to all those who trust in him.

31 For who is God save the Lord? or who is a rock save our God,

32 Our God that girdeth me with strength, and maketh my way perfect?

33 He maketh my feet like hinds' feet, and setteth me upon my high places.

34 He teacheth my hands to war, so that a bow of steel is broken by mine arms.

35 Thou hast also given me the shield of thy salvation; and thy right hand hath holden me up, and thy gentleness hath made me great.

36 Thou hast enlarged my steps under me, that my feet did not slip.

37 I have pursued mine enemies, and overtaken them; neither did I turn again till they were consumed.

38 I have wounded them that they were not able to rise; they are fallen under my feet.

39 For thou hast girded me with strength unto the battle; thou hast subdued under me those that rose up against me.

40 Thou hast also given me the necks of mine enemies; that I might destroy them that hate me.

41 They cried, but found none to save; unto the Lord, but he answered them not.

42 Then did I beat them small as the dust before the wind; I did cast them out as the dirt in the streets.

43 Thou hast delivered me from the strivings of the people; and thou hast made me the head of the heathen; a people whom I have not known shall serve me.

44 As soon as they hear of me, they shall obey me; the strangers shall submit themselves unto me.

45 The strangers shall fade away, and be afraid out of their close places.

46 The Lord liveth; and blessed be my Rock; and let the God of my salvation be exalted.

47 It is God that avengeth me, and subdueth the people under me.

48 He delivereth me from mine enemies; yea, thou liftest me up above those that rise up against me: thou hast delivered me from the violent man.

49 Therefore will I give thanks unto thee, O Lord, among the heathen, and sing praises unto thy name.

50 Great deliverance giveth he to his king; and showeth mercy to his anointed, to David, and to his seed for evermore.

## PSALM 19

*The creation showeth God's glory—Prayer for grace.*

To the chief Musician, A Psalm of David.

1 The heavens declare the glory of God; and the firmament showeth his handiwork.

2 Day unto day uttereth speech, and night unto night showeth knowledge.

3 No speech nor language can be, if their voice is not heard.

4 Their line is gone out through all the earth, and their words to the end of the world. In them hath he set a tabernacle for the sun,

5 Which is as a bridegroom coming out of his chamber, and rejoiceth as a strong man to run a race.

6 His going forth is from the end of the heaven, and his circuit unto the ends of it; and there is nothing hid from the heat thereof.

7 The law of the Lord is perfect, converting the soul; the testimony of the Lord is sure, making wise the simple.

8 The statutes of the Lord are right, rejoicing the heart; the commandment of the Lord is pure, enlightening the eyes.

9 The fear of the Lord is clean, enduring for ever; the judgments of the

Lord are true and righteous altogether.

10 More to be desired are they than gold, yea, than much fine gold; sweeter also than honey and the honeycomb.

11 Moreover by them is thy servant warned; and in keeping of them there is great reward.

12 Who can understand his errors? cleanse thou me from secret faults.

13 Keep back thy servant also from presumptuous acts; let them not have dominion over me; then shall I be upright, and I shall be innocent from the great transgression.

14 Let the words of my mouth, and the meditation of my heart, be acceptable in thy sight, O Lord, my strength, and my redeemer.

## PSALM 20

*Confidence in God's succor.*

To the chief Musician, A Psalm of David.

1 The Lord hear thee in the day of trouble; the name of the God of Jacob defend thee;

2 Send thee help from the sanctuary, and strengthen thee out of Zion;

3 Remember all thy offerings, and accept thy burnt sacrifice; Selah.

4 Grant thee according to thine own heart, and fulfill all thy counsel.

5 We will rejoice in thy salvation, and in the name of our God we will set up our banners; the Lord fulfill all thy petitions.

6 Now know I that the Lord saveth his anointed; he will hear him from his holy heaven with the saving strength of his right hand.

7 Some trust in chariots, and some in horses; but we will remember the name of the Lord our God.

8 They are brought down and fallen; but we are risen, and stand upright.

9 Save, Lord; let the king hear us when we call.

## PSALM 21

*A thanksgiving for blessings.*

To the chief Musician, A Psalm of David.

1 The king shall joy in thy strength, O Lord; and in thy salvation how greatly shall he rejoice!

2 Thou hast given him his heart's desire, and hast not withholden the request of his lips. Selah.

3 For thou preventest him with the

blessings of goodness; thou settest a crown of pure gold on his head.

4 He asked life of thee, and thou gavest it him, even length of days for ever and ever.

5 His glory is great in thy salvation; honor and majesty hast thou laid upon him.

6 For thou hast made him most blessed for ever; thou hast made him exceeding glad with thy countenance.

7 For the king trusteth in the Lord, and through the mercy of the Most High he shall not be moved.

8 Thine hand shall find out all thine enemies; thy right hand shall find out those that hate thee.

9 Thou shalt make them as a fiery oven in the time of thine anger; the Lord shall swallow them up in his wrath, and the fire shall devour them.

10 Their fruit shalt thou destroy from the earth, and their seed from among the children of men.

11 For they intended evil against thee; they imagined a mischievous device, which they are not able to perform.

12 Therefore shalt thou make them turn their back, when thou shalt make ready thine arrows upon thy strings against the face of them.

13 Be thou exalted, Lord, in thine own strength; so will we sing and praise thy power.

## PSALM 22

*David prayeth in great distress, yet he praiseth God.*

To the chief Musician upon Aijeleth Shahar, A Psalm of David.

1 My God, why hast thou forsaken me? My God, hear the words of my roaring; thou art far from helping me.

2 O my God, I cry in the daytime, but thou answerest not; and in the night season, and am not silent.

3 But thou art holy that inhabitest the heavens; thou art worthy of the praises of Israel.

4 Our fathers trusted in thee; they trusted, and thou didst deliver them.

5 They cried unto thee, and were delivered; they trusted in thee, and were not confounded.

6 But I, a worm, am loved of no man; a reproach of men, and despised of the people.

7 All they that see me laugh me to scorn; they shoot out the lip, they shake the head, saying,

8 He trusted on the Lord that he would deliver him; let him deliver him, seeing he delighted in him.

9 But thou art he that took me out of the womb; thou didst make me hope when I was upon my mother's breasts.

10 I was cast upon thee from the womb; thou wast my God from my mother's breasts.

11 Be not far from me; for trouble is near; for there is none to help.

12 Many armies have compassed me; strong armies of Bashan have beset me around.

13 They gaped upon me with their mouths, like a ravening and a roaring lion.

14 I am poured out like water, and all my bones are out of joint; my heart is like wax; it is melted in the midst of my bowels.

15 My strength is dried up like a potsherd; and my tongue cleaveth to my jaws; and thou hast brought me into the dust of death.

16 For dogs have compassed me; the assembly of the wicked have enclosed me; they pierced my hands and my feet.

17 I may tell all my bones; they look and stare upon me.

18 They part my garments among them, and cast lots upon my vesture.

19 But be not thou far from me, O Lord; O my strength, haste thee to help me.

20 Deliver my soul from the sword; my darling from the power of the dog.

21 Save me from the lion's mouth, for thou hast heard me speak from the secret places of the wilderness through the horns of the unicorns.

22 I will declare thy name unto my brethren; in the midst of the congregation will I praise thee.

23 Ye that fear the Lord, praise him; all ye the seed of Jacob, glorify him; and fear him, all ye the seed of Israel.

24 For he hath not despised nor abhorred the affliction of the afflicted; neither hath he hid his face from him; but when he cried unto him, he heard.

25 My praise shall be of thee in the great congregation; I will pay my vows before them that fear him.

26 The meek shall eat and be satisfied; they shall praise the Lord that seek him; your heart shall live for ever.

27 All the ends of the world shall remember and turn unto the Lord; and

all the kindreds of the nations shall worship before thee.

28 For the kingdom is the Lord's; and he is the governor among the nations.

29 All they that be fat upon earth shall eat and worship; all they that go down to the dust shall bow before him; and none can keep alive his own soul.

30 A seed shall serve him; it shall be accounted to the Lord for a generation.

31 They shall come, and shall declare his righteousness unto a people that shall be born, what he hath done.

## PSALM 23

*Confidence in God's grace.*
A Psalm of David.

1 The Lord is my shepherd; I shall not want.

2 He maketh me to lie down in green pastures; he leadeth me beside the still waters.

3 He restoreth my soul; he leadeth me in the paths of righteousness for his name's sake.

4 Yea, though I walk through the valley of the shadow of death, I will fear no evil; for thou art with me; thy rod and thy staff they comfort me.

5 Thou preparest a table before me in the presence of mine enemies; thou anointest my head with oil; my cup runneth over.

6 Surely goodness and mercy shall follow me all the days of my life; and I will dwell in the house of the Lord for ever.

## PSALM 24

*Of the kingdom of God.*
A Psalm of David.

1 The earth is the Lord's, and the fullness thereof; the world, and they that dwell therein.

2 For he hath founded it upon the seas, and established it upon the floods.

3 Who shall ascend into the hill of the Lord? or who shall stand in his holy place?

4 He that hath clean hands, and a pure heart; who hath not lifted up his soul unto vanity, nor sworn deceitfully.

5 He shall receive the blessing from the Lord, and righteousness from the God of his salvation.

6 This is the generation of them that seek him, that seek thy face, O Jacob. Selah.

7 Lift up your heads, O ye genera-

tions of Jacob; and be ye lifted up; and the Lord strong and mighty; the Lord mighty in battle, who is the king of glory, shall establish you for ever.

8 And he will roll away the heavens; and will come down to redeem his people; to make you an everlasting name; to establish you upon his everlasting rock.

9 Lift up your heads, O ye generations of Jacob; lift up your heads, ye everlasting generations, and the Lord of hosts, the king of kings;

10 Even the king of glory shall come unto you; and shall redeem his people, and shall establish them in righteousness. Selah.

## PSALM 25

*David's prayer for remission of sins and for help in affliction.*
A Psalm of David.

1 Unto thee, O Lord, do I lift up my soul.

2 O my God, I trust in thee; let me not be ashamed, let not mine enemies triumph over me.

3 Yea, let none that wait on thee be ashamed; let them be ashamed which transgress without cause.

4 Show me thy ways, O Lord; teach me thy paths.

5 Lead me in thy truth, and teach me; for thou art the God of my salvation; on thee do I wait all the day.

6 Remember, O Lord, thy tender mercies and thy loving-kindnesses; for they have been ever of old.

7 Remember not the sins of my youth, nor my transgressions; according to thy mercy remember thou me for thy goodness' sake, O Lord.

8 Good and upright is the Lord; therefore will he teach sinners in the way.

9 The meek will he guide in judgment; and the meek will he teach his way.

10 All the paths of the Lord are mercy and truth unto such as keep his covenant and his testimonies.

11 For thy name's sake, O Lord, pardon mine iniquity; for it is great.

12 What man is he that feareth the Lord? him shall he teach in the way that he shall choose.

13 His soul shall dwell at ease; and his seed shall inherit the earth.

14 The secret of the Lord is with them that fear him; and he will show them his covenant.

15 Mine eyes are ever toward the Lord; for he shall pluck my feet out of the net.

16 Turn thee unto me, and have mercy upon me; for I am desolate and afflicted.

17 The troubles of my heart are enlarged; O bring thou me out of my distresses.

18 Look upon mine affliction and my pain; and forgive all my sins.

19 Consider mine enemies; for they are many; and they hate me with cruel hatred.

20 O keep my soul, and deliver me; let me not be ashamed; for I put my trust in thee.

21 Let integrity and uprightness preserve me; for I wait on thee.

22 Redeem Israel, O God, out of all his troubles.

## PSALM 26

*David professeth unto God his integrity.*
A Psalm of David.

1 Judge me, O Lord; for I have walked in mine integrity; I have trusted also in the Lord; therefore I shall not slide.

2 Examine me, O Lord, and prove me; try my reins and my heart.

3 For thy loving-kindness is before mine eyes; and I have walked in thy truth.

4 I have not sat with vain persons, neither will I go in with dissemblers.

5 I have hated the congregation of evildoers; and will not sit with the wicked.

6 I will wash mine hands in innocency; so will I compass thine altar, O Lord;

7 That I may publish with the voice of thanksgiving, and tell of all thy wondrous works.

8 Lord, I have loved the habitation of thy house, and the place where thine honor dwelleth.

9 Gather not my soul with sinners, nor my life with bloody men;

10 In whose hands is mischief, and their right hand is full of bribes.

11 But as for me, I will walk in mine integrity; redeem me, and be merciful unto me.

12 My foot standeth in an even place; in the congregations will I bless the Lord.

## PSALM 27

*David sustaineth his faith by prayer.*

A Psalm of David.

1 The Lord is my light and my salvation; whom shall I fear? the Lord is the strength of my life; of whom shall I be afraid?

2 When the wicked, even mine enemies and my foes, came upon me to eat up my flesh, they stumbled and fell.

3 Though a host should encamp against me, my heart shall not fear; though war should rise against me, in this I am confident.

4 One thing have I desired of the Lord, that will I seek after; that I may dwell in the house of the Lord all the days of my life, to behold the beauty of the Lord, and to inquire in his temple.

5 For in the time of trouble he shall hide me in his pavilion; in the secret of his tabernacle shall he hide me; he shall set me up upon a rock.

6 And now shall mine head be lifted up above mine enemies round about me; therefore will I offer in his tabernacle sacrifices of joy; I will sing, yea, I will sing praises unto the Lord.

7 Hear, O Lord, when I cry with my voice; have mercy also upon me, and answer me.

8 When thou saidst, Seek ye my face; my heart said unto thee, Thy face, Lord, will I seek.

9 Hide not thy face far from me; put not thy servant away in anger; thou hast been my help; leave me not, neither forsake me, O God of my salvation.

10 When my father and my mother forsake me, then the Lord will take me up.

11 Teach me thy way, O Lord, and lead me in a plain path, because of mine enemies.

12 Deliver me not over unto the will of mine enemies; for false witnesses are risen up against me, and such as breathe out cruelty.

13 Unless I had believed to see the goodness of the Lord in the land of the living, thou wouldst deliver my soul into hell.

14 Thou didst say unto me, Wait on the Lord, be of good courage, and he shall strengthen thy heart; wait, I say, on the Lord.

## PSALM 28

*David prayeth for the people.*
A Psalm of David.

1 Unto thee will I cry, O Lord, my

rock; be not silent to me; lest, if thou be silent to me, I become like them that go down into the pit.

2 Hear the voice of my supplications, when I cry unto thee, when I lift up my hands toward thy holy oracle.

3 Draw me not away with the wicked, and with the workers of iniquity, which speak peace to their neighbors, but mischief is in their hearts.

4 Give them according to their deeds, and according to the wickedness of their endeavors; give them after the work of their hands; render to them their desert.

5 Because they regard not the works of the Lord, nor the operation of his hands, he shall destroy them, and not build them up.

6 Blessed be the Lord, because he hath heard the voice of my supplications.

7 The Lord is my strength and my shield; my heart trusted in him, and I am helped; therefore my heart greatly rejoiceth; and with my song will I praise him.

8 The Lord is their strength, and he is the saving strength of his anointed.

9 Save thy people, and bless thine inheritance; feed them also, and lift them up for ever.

## PSALM 29

*Princes exhorted to give glory to God.*
A Psalm of David.

1 Give unto the Lord, O ye mighty, give unto the Lord glory and strength.

2 Give unto the Lord the glory due unto his name; worship the Lord in the beauty of holiness.

3 The voice of the Lord is upon the waters; the God of glory thundereth; the Lord is upon many waters.

4 The voice of the Lord is powerful; the voice of the Lord is full of majesty.

5 The voice of the Lord breaketh the cedars; yea, the Lord breaketh the cedars of Lebanon.

6 He maketh them also to skip like a calf; Lebanon and Sirion like a young unicorn.

7 The voice of the Lord divideth the flames of fire.

8 The voice of the Lord shaketh the wilderness; the Lord shaketh the wilderness of Kadesh.

9 The voice of the Lord maketh the hinds to calve, and discovereth the for-

ests; and in his temple doth every one speak of his glory.

10 The Lord sitteth upon the flood; yea, the Lord sitteth King for ever.

11 The Lord will give strength unto his people; the Lord will bless his people with peace.

## PSALM 30

*David praiseth God for his deliverance.*
A Psalm and Song at the dedication of the house of David.

1 I will extol thee, O Lord; for thou hast lifted me up, and hast not made my foes to rejoice over me.

2 O Lord my God, I cried unto thee, and thou hast healed me.

3 O Lord, thou hast brought up my soul from the grave; thou hast kept me alive, that I should not go down to the pit.

4 Sing unto the Lord, O ye saints of his, and give thanks at the remembrance of his holiness.

5 For his anger kindleth against the wicked; they repent, and in a moment it is turned away, and they are in his favor, and he giveth them life; therefore, weeping may endure for a night, but joy cometh in the morning.

6 And in my prosperity I said, I shall never be moved.

7 Lord, by thy favor thou hast made my mountain to stand strong; thou didst hide thy face, and I was troubled.

8 I cried to thee, O Lord; and unto the Lord I made supplication.

9 When I go down to the pit, my blood shall return to the dust. I will praise thee; my soul shall declare thy truth; for what profit am I, if I do it not?

10 Hear, O Lord, and have mercy upon me; Lord, be thou my helper.

11 Thou hast turned for me my mourning into dancing; thou hast put off my sackcloth, and girded me with gladness;

12 To the end that my soul may give glory to thy name, and sing praise to thee, and not be silent. O Lord my God, I will give thanks unto thee for ever.

## PSALM 31

*David rejoiceth in God's mercy, and praiseth him for his goodness.*
To the chief Musician, A Psalm of David.

1 In thee, O Lord, do I put my trust;

let me never be ashamed; deliver me in thy righteousness.

2 Bow down thine ears to me; deliver me speedily; be thou my strong rock, for a house of defense to save me.

3 For thou art my rock and my fortress; therefore for thy name's sake, lead me, and guide me.

4 Pull me out of the net that they have laid privily for me; for thou art my strength.

5 Into thine hand I commit my spirit; thou hast redeemed me, O Lord God of truth.

6 I have hated them that regard lying vanities; but I trust in the Lord.

7 I will be glad and rejoice in thy mercy; for thou hast considered my trouble; thou hast known my soul in adversities;

8 And hast not shut me up into the hand of the enemy; thou hast set my feet in a large room.

9 Have mercy upon me, O Lord, for I am in trouble; mine eye is consumed with grief, yea, my soul and my belly.

10 For my life is spent with grief, and my years with sighing; my strength faileth because of mine iniquity, and my bones are consumed.

11 I was a reproach among all mine enemies, but especially among my neighbors, and a fear to mine acquaintance; they that did see me without fled from me.

12 I am forgotten as a dead man out of mind; I am like a broken vessel.

13 For I have heard the slander of many; fear was on every side; while they took counsel together against me, they devised to take away my life.

14 But I trusted in thee, O Lord; I said, Thou art my God.

15 My times are in thy hand; deliver me from the hand of mine enemies, and from them that persecute me.

16 Make thy face to shine upon thy servant; save me for thy mercies' sake.

17 Let me not be ashamed, O Lord; for I have called upon thee; let the wicked be ashamed, and let them be silent in the grave.

18 Let the lying lips be put to silence; which speak grievous things proudly and contemptuously against the righteous.

19 Oh how great is thy goodness, which thou hast laid up for them that fear thee; which thou hast wrought for them that trust in thee before the sons of men!

20 Thou shalt hide them in the secret of thy presence from the pride of man; thou shalt keep them secretly in a pavilion from the strife of tongues.

21 Blessed be the Lord; for he hath showed me his marvelous kindness in a strong city.

22 For I said in my haste, I am cut off from before thine eyes; nevertheless thou heardest the voice of my supplications when I cried unto thee.

23 O love the Lord, all ye his saints; for the Lord preserveth the faithful, and plentifully rewardeth the proud doer.

24 Be of good courage, and he shall strengthen your heart, all ye that hope in the Lord.

## PSALM 32

*Confession and remission of sins.*

A Psalm of David, Maschil.

1 Blessed are they whose transgressions are forgiven, and who have no sins to be covered.

2 Blessed is the man unto whom the Lord imputeth not iniquity, and in whose spirit there is no guile.

3 When I kept silence, my spirit failed within me; when I opened my mouth, my bones waxed old through my speaking all the day long.

4 For day and night thy Spirit was heavy upon me; my moisture is turned into the drought of summer. Selah.

5 I acknowledge my sin unto thee, and mine iniquity have I not hid. I said, I will confess my transgressions unto the Lord; and thou forgavest the iniquity of my sin. Selah.

6 For this shall every one that is godly pray unto thee in a time when thou mayest be found; surely in the floods of great waters they shall not come nigh unto him.

7 Thou art my hiding place; thou shalt preserve me from trouble; thou shalt compass me about with songs of deliverance. Selah.

8 Thou hast said, I will instruct thee and teach thee in the way which thou shalt go; I will guide thee with mine eye.

9 Be ye not as the horse, or as the mule, which have no understanding; whose mouth must be held in with bit and bridle, lest they come near unto thee.

10 Many sorrows shall be to the wicked; but he that trusteth in the Lord, mercy shall compass him about.

11 Be glad in the Lord, and rejoice, ye righteous; and shout for joy, all ye that are upright in heart.

## PSALM 33

*God's goodness, power, and providence.*

1 Rejoice in the Lord, O ye righteous; to praise the Lord is comely for the upright in heart.

2 Praise the Lord with thy voice; sing unto him with the psaltery and harp, an instrument with ten strings.

3 Sing unto him a new song; play skillfully with a loud noise.

4 For the word of the Lord is given to the upright, and all his works are done in truth.

5 He loveth righteousness and judgment; the earth is full of the goodness of the Lord.

6 By the word of the Lord were the heavens made; and all the host of them by the breath of his mouth.

7 He gathereth the waters of the sea together as a heap; he layeth up the depth in storehouses.

8 Let all the earth fear the Lord; let all the inhabitants of the world stand in awe of him.

9 For he spake, and it was finished; he commanded, and it stood fast.

10 The Lord bringeth the counsel of the heathen to naught; he maketh the devices of the people of none effect.

11 The counsel of the Lord standeth for ever, the thoughts of his heart to all generations.

12 Blessed are the nations and the people whom the Lord God hath chosen for his own inheritance.

13 The Lord looketh from heaven; he beholdeth all the sons of men.

14 From the place of his habitation he looketh upon all the inhabitants of the earth.

15 He fashioneth their hearts alike; he considereth all their works.

16 There is no king saved by the multitude of a host; a mighty man is not delivered by much strength.

17 A horse is a vain thing for safety; neither shall he deliver any by his great strength.

18 Behold, the eye of the Lord is upon them that fear him, upon them that hope in his mercy;

19 To deliver their soul from death, and to keep them alive in a time of famine.

20 Our soul waiteth for the Lord; he is our help and our shield.

21 For our heart shall rejoice in him, because we have trusted in his holy name.

22 Let thy mercy, O Lord, be upon us, according as we hope in thee.

## PSALM 34

*David's experience—Trust in God—The fear of God.*

A Psalm of David, when he changed his behavior before Abimelech; who drove him away, and he departed.

1 I will bless the Lord at all times; his praise shall continually be in my mouth.

2 My soul shall make her boast in the Lord; the humble shall hear thereof, and be glad.

3 O magnify the Lord with me, and let us exalt his name together.

4 I sought the Lord, and he heard me, and delivered me from all my fears.

5 They looked unto him, and were lightened; and their faces were not ashamed.

6 This poor man cried, and the Lord heard him, and saved him out of all his troubles.

7 The angel of the Lord encampeth round about them that fear him, and delivereth them.

8 O taste and see that the Lord is good; blessed is the man that trusteth in him.

9 O fear the Lord, ye his saints; for there is no want to them that fear him.

10 The young lions do lack, and suffer hunger; but they that seek the Lord shall not want any good thing.

11 Come, ye children, hearken unto me; I will teach you the fear of the Lord.

12 What man is he that desireth life, and loveth many days, that he may see good?

13 Keep thy tongue from evil, and thy lips from speaking guile.

14 Depart from evil, and do good; seek peace, and pursue it.

15 The eyes of the Lord are upon the righteous, and his ears are open unto their cry.

16 The face of the Lord is against them that do evil, to cut off the remembrance of them from the earth.

17 The righteous cry, and the Lord heareth, and delivereth them out of all their troubles.

18 The Lord is nigh unto them that are of a broken heart; and saveth such as be of a contrite spirit.

19 Many are the afflictions of the righteous; but the Lord delivereth him out of them all.

20 He keepeth all his bones; not one of them is broken.

21 Evil shall slay the wicked; and they that hate the righteous shall be desolate.

22 The Lord redeemeth the soul of his servants; and none of them that trust in him shall be desolate.

## PSALM 35

*David prayeth for safety.*

1 Plead my cause, O Lord, with them that strive with me; fight against them that fight against me.

2 Take hold of shield and buckler, and stand up for mine help.

3 Draw out also the spear, and stop the way against them that persecute me; say unto my soul, I am thy salvation.

4 Let them be confounded and put to shame that seek after my soul; let them be turned back and brought to confusion that devise my hurt.

5 Let them be as chaff before the wind; and let the angel of the Lord chase them.

6 Let their way be dark and slippery; and let the angel of the Lord persecute them.

7 For without cause have they hid for me their net in a pit, which without cause they have digged for my soul.

8 Let destruction come upon him at unawares; and let his net that he hath hid catch himself; into that very destruction let him fall.

9 And my soul shall be joyful in the Lord; it shall rejoice in his salvation.

10 All my bones shall say, Lord, who is like unto thee, which deliverest the poor from him that is too strong for him, yea, the poor and the needy from him that spoileth him?

11 False witnesses did rise up; they laid to my charge things that I knew not.

12 They rewarded me evil for good, for the purpose of the spoiling of my soul.

13 But as for me, when they were sick, my clothing was sackcloth; I humbled my soul with fasting; and my prayer returned into mine own bosom.

14 I behaved myself as though he had been my friend or brother; I bowed down heavily, as one that mourneth for his mother.

15 But in mine adversity they rejoiced, and gathered themselves together; yea, the abjects gathered themselves together against me, and I knew it not; they did tear me, and ceased not;

16 With hypocritical mockers in feasts, they gnashed upon me with their teeth.

17 Lord, how long wilt thou look on? rescue my soul from their destructions, my darling from the lions.

18 I will give thee thanks in the great congregation; I will praise thee among much people.

19 Let not them that are mine enemies wrongfully rejoice over me; neither let them wink with the eye that hate me without a cause.

20 For they speak not peace; but they devise deceitful matters against them that are quiet in the land.

21 Yea, they opened their mouth wide against me, and said, Aha, ah , our eye hath seen it.

22 This thou hast seen, O Lord; keep not silence; O Lord, be not far from me.

23 Stir up thyself, and awake to my judgment, even unto my cause, my God and my Lord.

24 Judge me, O Lord my God, according to thy righteousness; and let them not rejoice over me.

25 Let them not say in their hearts, Ah, so would we have it; let them not say, We have swallowed him up.

26 Let them be ashamed and brought to confusion together that rejoice at mine hurt; let them be clothed with shame and dishonor that magnify themselves against me.

27 Let them shout for joy, and be glad, that favor my righteous cause; yea, let them say continually, Let the Lord be magnified, which hath pleasure in the prosperity of his servant.

28 And my tongue shall speak of thy righteousness and of thy praise all the day long.

## PSALM 36

*Estate of the wicked—Excellency of God's mercy.*

To the chief Musician, A Psalm of David the servant of the Lord.

1 The wicked, who live in transgres-

sion, saith in their hearts, There is no condemnation; for there is no fear of God before their eyes.

2 For they flattereth themselves in their own eyes, until their iniquities are found to be hateful.

3 The words of their mouth are full of iniquity and deceit. The wicked man hath left off to be wise, and to do good;

4 He deviseth mischief upon his bed; he setteth himself in a way that is not good.

5 O Lord, thou art in the heavens; they are full of thy mercy. And the thoughts of a righteous man ascendeth up unto thee whose throne is far above the clouds.

6 He is filled with thy righteousness like the great mountains, and with thy judgments like a great deep. O Lord, thou preservest man and beast.

7 How excellent is thy loving-kindness, O God! therefore the children of men put their trust under the shadow of thy wings.

8 They shall be abundantly satisfied with the fatness of thy house; and thou shalt make them drink of the river of thy pleasures.

9 For with thee is the fountain of life; in thy light shall we see light.

10 O continue thy loving-kindness unto them that know thee; and thy righteousness to the upright in heart.

11 Let not the foot of pride come against me, and let not the hand of the wicked remove me.

12 They are the workers of iniquity and shall fall; they shall be cast down, and shall not be able to rise.

## PSALM 37

*David persuadeth to patience and confidence in God, by the different estate of the godly and the wicked.*
A Psalm of David.

1 Fret not thyself because of evildoers, neither be thou envious against the workers of iniquity.

2 For they shall soon be cut down like the grass, and wither as the green herb.

3 Trust in the Lord, and do good; so shalt thou dwell in the land, and verily thou shalt be fed.

4 Delight thyself also in the Lord; and he shall give thee the desires of thine heart.

5 Commit thy way unto the Lord; trust also in him; and he shall bring it to pass.

6 And he shall bring forth thy righteousness as the light, and thy judgment as the noonday.

7 Rest in the Lord, and wait patiently for him; fret not thyself because of him who prospereth in his way, because of the man who bringeth wicked devices to pass.

8 Cease from anger, and forsake wrath; fret not thyself in any wise to do evil.

9 For evildoers shall be cut off; but those that wait upon the Lord, they shall inherit the earth.

10 For yet a little while, and the wicked shall not be; yea, thou shalt diligently consider his place, and it shall not be.

11 But the meek shall inherit the earth; and shall delight themselves in the abundance of peace.

12 The wicked plotteth against the just, and gnasheth upon him with his teeth.

13 The Lord shall laugh at him; for he seeth that his day is coming.

14 The wicked have drawn out the sword, and have bent their bow, to cast down the poor and needy, and to slay such as be of upright conversation.

15 Their sword shall enter into their own heart, and their bows shall be broken.

16 A little that a righteous man hath is better than the riches of many wicked.

17 For the arms of the wicked shall be broken; but the Lord upholdeth the righteous.

18 The Lord knoweth the days of the upright; and their inheritance shall be for ever.

19 They shall not be ashamed in the evil time; and in the days of famine they shall be satisfied.

20 But the wicked shall perish, and the enemies of the Lord shall be as the fat of lambs; they shall consume; into smoke shall they consume away.

21 The wicked borroweth, and payeth not again; but the righteous showeth mercy, and giveth.

22 For such as be blessed of him shall inherit the earth; and they that be cursed of him shall be cut off.

23 The steps of a good man are ordered by the Lord; and he delighteth in his way.

24 Though he fall, he shall not be utterly cast down; for the Lord upholdeth him with his hand.

25 I have been young, and now am old; yet have I not seen the righteous forsaken, nor his seed begging bread.

26 He is ever merciful, and lendeth; and his seed is blessed.

27 Depart from evil, and do good; and dwell for evermore.

28 For the Lord loveth judgment, and forsaketh not his saints; they are preserved for ever; but the seed of the wicked shall be cut off.

29 The righteous shall inherit the land, and dwell therein for ever.

30 The mouth of the righteous speaketh wisdom, and his tongue talketh of judgment.

31 The law of his God is in his heart; none of his steps shall slide.

32 The wicked watcheth the righteous, and seeketh to slay him.

33 The Lord will not leave him in his hand, nor condemn him when he is judged.

34 Wait on the Lord, and keep his way, and he shall exalt thee to inherit the land; when the wicked are cut off, thou shalt see it.

35 I have seen the wicked in great power, and spreading himself like a green bay tree.

36 Yet he passed away, and, lo, he was not; yea, I sought him, but he could not be found.

37 Mark the perfect man, and behold the upright; for the end of that man is peace.

38 But the transgressors shall be destroyed together; the end of the wicked shall come, and they will be cut off.

39 But the salvation of the righteous is of the Lord; he is their strength in the time of trouble.

40 And the Lord shall help them, and deliver them; he shall deliver them from the wicked, and save them, because they trust in him.

## PSALM 38

*David moveth God to compassion.*

A Psalm of David, to bring to remembrance.

1 O Lord, rebuke me not in thy wrath; neither chasten me in thy hot displeasure.

2 For thine arrows stick fast in me, and thy hand presseth me sore.

3 There is no soundness in my flesh because of thine anger; neither is there any rest in my bones because of my sin.

4 For mine iniquities are gone over mine head; as a heavy burden they are too heavy for me.

5 My wounds stink and are corrupt because of my foolishness.

6 I am troubled; I am bowed down greatly; I go mourning all the day long.

7 For my loins are filled with a loathsome distress; and no soundness is found in in my flesh.

8 I am feeble, and broken, and very sore. I have wept by reason of the disquietness of my heart.

9 Lord, all my desire is before thee; and my groaning is not hid from thee.

10 My heart panteth, my strength faileth me; as for the light of mine eyes, it also is gone from me.

11 My lovers and my friends stand aloof because of my sore; and my kinsmen stand afar off.

12 They also that seek after my life lay snares for me; and they that seek my hurt speak mischievous things, and imagine deceits all the day long.

13 But I, as a deaf man, heard not; and I was as a dumb man that openeth not his mouth.

14 Thus I was as a man that heareth not, and in whose mouth are no reproofs.

15 For in thee, O Lord, do I hope; thou wilt hear, O Lord my God.

16 For I said, Hear me, lest otherwise they should rejoice over me; when my foot slippeth, they magnify themselves against me.

17 For I am ready to halt, and my sorrow is continually before me.

18 For I will declare mine iniquity; I will be sorry for my sin.

19 But mine enemies are lively, and they are strong; and they that hate me wrongfully are multiplied.

20 They also that render evil for good are mine adversaries; because I follow the thing that good is.

21 Forsake me not, O Lord; O my God, be not far from me.

22 Make haste to help me, O Lord my salvation.

## PSALM 39

*David's care of his thoughts.*

To the chief Musician, even to Jeduthun, A Psalm of David.

1 I said, I will take heed to my ways, that I sin not with my tongue; I will

keep my mouth with a bridle, while the wicked is before me.

2 I was dumb with silence, I held my peace, even from good; and my sorrow was stirred.

3 My heart was hot within me; while I was musing the fire burned; then spake I with my tongue,

4 Lord, make me to know mine end, and the measure of my days, what it is; that I may know how frail I am.

5 Behold, thou hast made my days as an handbreadth; and mine age is as nothing before thee; verily every man at his best state is altogether vanity. Selah.

6 Surely every man walketh in a vain show; surely they are disquieted in vain; he heapeth up riches, and knoweth not who shall gather them.

7 And now, Lord, what wait I for? my hope is in thee.

8 Deliver me from all my transgressions; make me not the reproach of the foolish.

9 I was dumb, and opened not my mouth; because thou didst chasten me.

10 Remove thy stroke away from me, or I shall be consumed by the blow of thy hand.

11 When thou with rebukes dost correct man for iniquity, thou makest his beauty to consume away like a moth; surely every man is vanity. Selah.

12 Hear my prayer, O Lord, and give ear unto my cry; hold not thy peace at my tears; for I am a stranger with thee, and a sojourner, as all my fathers were.

13 O spare me, that I may recover strength, before I go hence, and be no more.

## PSALM 40

*Obedience the best sacrifice.*

To the chief Musician, A Psalm of David.

1 I waited patiently for the Lord; and he inclined unto me, and heard my cry.

2 He brought me up also out of a horrible pit, out of the miry clay, and set my feet upon a rock, and established my doings.

3 And he hath put a new song in my mouth, even praise unto our God; many shall see it, and fear, and shall trust in the Lord.

4 Blessed is that man that maketh the Lord his trust, and respecteth not the proud, nor such as turn aside to lies.

5 Many, O Lord my God, are thy wonderful works which thou hast done, and thy thoughts which are to us-ward; they cannot be reckoned up in order unto thee; if I would declare and speak of them, they are more than can be numbered.

6 Sacrifice and offering thou didst not desire; mine ears hast thou opened; burnt offering and sin offering hast thou not required.

7 Then said I, Lo, I come; in the volume of the book it is written of me,

8 I delight to do thy will, O my God; yea, thy law is within my heart.

9 I have preached righteousness in the great congregation; lo, I have not refrained my lips, O Lord, thou knowest.

10 I have not hid thy righteousness within my heart; I have declared thy faithfulness and thy salvation; I have not concealed thy loving-kindness and thy truth from the great congregation.

11 Withhold not thou thy tender mercies from me, O Lord: let thy loving-kindness and thy truth continually preserve me.

12 For innumerable evils have compassed me about; mine iniquities have taken hold upon me, so that I am not able to look up; they are more than the hairs of mine head; therefore my heart faileth me.

13 Be pleased, O Lord, to deliver me; O Lord, make haste to help me.

14 Let them be ashamed and confounded together that seek after my soul to destroy it; let them be driven backward and put to shame that wish me evil.

15 Let them be desolate for a reward of their shame that say unto me, Aha, aha.

16 Let all those that seek thee rejoice and be glad in thee; let such as love thy salvation say continually, The Lord be magnified.

17 But I am poor and needy; yet the Lord thinketh upon me; thou art my help and my deliverer; make no tarrying, O my God.

## PSALM 41

*God's care of the poor—David fleeth to God for succor.*

To the chief Musician, A Psalm of David.

1 Blessed is he that considereth the poor; the Lord will deliver him in time of trouble.

2 The Lord will preserve him, and keep him alive; and he shall be blessed upon the earth; and thou wilt not deliver him unto the will of his enemies.

3 The Lord will strengthen him upon the bed of languishing; thou wilt make all his pains to cease, when he is laid in his bed of sickness.

4 I said, Lord, be merciful unto me; heal my soul; for I have sinned against thee.

5 Mine enemies speak evil of me, When shall he die, and his name perish?

6 And if he come to see me, he speaketh vanity; his heart gathereth iniquity to itself; when he goeth abroad, he telleth it.

7 All that hate me whisper together against me; against me do they devise my hurt.

8 An evil disease, say they, cleaveth fast unto him; and now that he lieth he shall rise up no more.

9 Yea, mine own familiar friend, in whom I trusted, which did eat of my bread, hath lifted up his heel against me.

10 But thou, O Lord, be merciful unto me, and raise me up, that I may requite them.

11 By this I know that thou favorest me, because mine enemy doth not triumph over me.

12 And as for me, thou upholdest me in mine integrity, and settest me before thy face for ever.

13 Blessed be the Lord God of Israel from everlasting, and to everlasting. Amen, and Amen.

## PSALM 42

*David's zeal to serve God—His trust in God.*

To the chief Musician, Maschil, for the sons of Korah.

1 As the hart panteth after the water brooks, so panteth my soul after thee, O God.

2 My soul thirsteth for to see God, for to see the living God; when shall I come and appear before thee, O God?

3 My tears have been poured out unto thee day and night, while mine enemies continually say unto me, Where is thy God?

4 When I remember these mine enemies, I pour out my soul unto thee; for I had gone with the multitude, I also went with them to the house of God, with the voice of joy and praise, with the multitude that kept holyday.

5 Why art thou cast down, O my soul? and why art thou disquieted in me? hope thou in God; for I shall yet praise him for the help of his countenance.

6 O my God, my soul is cast down within me; therefore will I remember thee from the land of Jordan, and of the Hermonites, from the hill Mizar.

7 Deep calleth unto deep at the noise of thy waterspouts; all thy waves and thy billows are gone over me.

8 Yet the Lord will command his loving-kindness in the daytime, and in the night his song shall be with me and my prayer unto the God of my life.

9 I will say unto God my rock, Why hast thou forgotten me? why go I mourning because of the oppression of the enemy?

10 As with a sword in my bones, mine enemies reproach me; while they say daily unto me, Where is thy God?

11 Why art thou cast down, O my soul? and why art thou disquieted within me? hope thou in God; for I shall yet praise him, who is the health of my countenance, and my God.

## PSALM 43

*David promiseth to serve God.*

1 Judge me, O God, and plead my cause against an ungodly nation; O deliver me from the deceitful and unjust man.

2 For thou art the God of my strength; why dost thou cast me off? why go I mourning because of the oppression of the enemy?

3 O send out thy light and thy truth; let them lead me; let them bring me unto thy holy hill, and to thy tabernacles.

4 Then will I go unto the altar of God, unto God my exceeding joy; yea, upon the harp will I praise thee, O God my God.

5 Why art thou cast down, O my soul? and why art thou disquieted within me? hope in God; for I shall yet praise him, who is the health of my countenance, and my God.

## PSALM 44

*Favor and evils contrasted.*

To the chief Musicians, for the sons of Korah, Maschil.

1 We have heard with our ears, O God, our fathers have told us, what work thou didst in their days, in the times of old.

2 How thou didst drive out the heathen with thy hand, and plantedst them; how thou didst afflict the people, and cast them out.

3 For they got not the land in possession by their own sword, neither did their own arm save them; but thy right hand, and thine arm, and the light of thy countenance, because thou hadst a favor unto them.

4 Thou art my King, O God; command deliverances for Jacob.

5 Through thee will we push down our enemies; through thy name will we tread them under that rise up against us.

6 For I will not trust in my bow, neither shall my sword save me.

7 But thou hast saved us from our enemies, and hast put them to shame that hated us.

8 In God we boast all the day long, and praise thy name for ever. Selah.

9 But thou hast cast off, and put us to shame; and goest not forth with our armies.

10 Thou makest us to turn back from the enemy; and they which hate us spoil for themselves.

11 Thou hast given us like sheep appointed for meat; and hast scattered us among the heathen.

12 Thou sellest thy people for naught, and dost not increase thy wealth by their price.

13 Thou makest us a reproach to our neighbors, a scorn and a derision to them that are round about us.

14 Thou makest us a byword among the heathen, a shaking of the head among the people.

15 My confusion is continually before me, and the shame of my face hath covered me,

16 For the voice of him that reproacheth and blasphemeth; by reason of the enemy and avenger.

17 All this is come upon us; yet have we not forgotten thee, neither have we dealt falsely in thy covenant.

18 Our heart is not turned back, neither have our steps declined from thy way;

19 Though thou hast sore broken us in the place of dragons, and covered us with the shadow of death.

20 If we have forgotten the name of our God, or stretched out our hands to a strange god;

21 Shall not God search this out? for he knoweth the secrets of the heart.

22 Yea, for thy sake are we killed all the day long; we are counted as sheep for the slaughter.

23 Awake, why sleepest thou, O Lord? arise, cast us not off for ever.

24 Wherefore hidest thou thy face, and forgettest our affliction and our oppression?

25 For our soul is bowed down to the dust; our belly cleaveth unto the earth.

26 Arise for our help, and redeem us for thy mercies' sake.

## PSALM 45

*Christ and his kingdom described.*

To the chief Musician upon Shoshannim, for the sons of Korah, Maschil, A Song of loves.

1 My heart is inditing a good matter; I speak of the things which I have made touching the King; my tongue is the pen of a ready writer.

2 Thou art fairer than the children of men; grace is poured into thy lips; therefore God hath blessed thee for ever.

3 Gird thy sword upon thy thigh, O most Mighty, with thy glory and thy majesty.

4 And in thy majesty ride prosperously because of truth and meekness and righteousness; and thy right hand shall teach thee terrible things.

5 Thine arrows are sharp in the heart of the king's enemies; whereby the people fall under thee.

6 Thy throne, O God, is for ever and ever; the scepter of thy kingdom is a right scepter.

7 Thou lovest righteousness, and hatest wickedness; therefore God, thy God, hath anointed thee with the oil of gladness above thy fellows.

8 All thy garments smell of myrrh, and aloes, and cassia, out of the ivory palaces, whereby they have made thee glad.

9 Kings' daughters were among thy honorable women; upon thy right hand did stand the queen in gold of Ophir.

10 Hearken, O daughter, and consider, and incline thine ear; forget also thine own people, and thy father's house;

11 So shall the King greatly desire

thy beauty; for he is thy Lord; and worship thou him.

12 And the daughter of Tyre shall be there with a gift; even the rich among the people shall entreat thy favor.

13 The King's daughter is all glorious within; her clothing is of wrought gold.

14 She shall be brought unto the King in raiment of needlework; the virgins her companions that follow her shall be brought unto thee.

15 With gladness and rejoicing shall they be brought; they shall enter into the King's palace.

16 Instead of thy fathers shall be thy children, whom thou mayest make princes in all the earth.

17 I will make thy name to be remembered in all generations; therefore shall the people praise thee for ever and ever.

## PSALM 46
*God the refuge of his people.*
To the chief Musician for the sons of Korah, A Song upon Alamoth.

1 God is our refuge and strength, a present help in trouble.

2 Therefore we will not fear, though the earth shall be removed, and though the mountains shall be carried into the midst of the sea;

3 And the waters thereof roar, being troubled, and the mountains shake with the swelling thereof.

4 Yet there shall be a river, the streams whereof shall make glad the city of God, the holy place of the tabernacle of the Most High.

5 For Zion shall come, and God shall be in the midst of her; she shall not be moved; God shall help her right early.

6 The heathen shall be enraged, and their kingdoms shall be moved, and the Lord shall utter his voice, and the earth shall be melted;

7 The Lord of hosts who shall be with us, the God of Jacob our refuge. Selah.

8 Come, behold the works of the Lord, what desolations he shall make in the earth in the latter days.

9 He maketh wars to cease unto the end of the earth; he breaketh the bow, and cutteth the spear in sunder; he burneth the chariot in the fire, and saith unto the nations,

10 Be still, and know that I am God; I will be exalted among the heathen, I will be exalted in the earth.

11 The Lord of hosts shall be with us, the God of Jacob our refuge. Selah.

## PSALM 47
*Christ's reign on earth.*
To the chief Musician, A Psalm for the sons of Korah.

1 O clap your hands, all ye people; shout unto God with the voice of triumph.

2 For the Lord most high is terrible; he is a great King over all the earth.

3 He shall subdue the people under us, and the nations under our feet.

4 He shall choose our inheritance for us, the excellency of Jacob whom he loved. Selah.

5 God is gone up with a shout, the Lord with the sound of a trumpet.

6 Sing praises to God, sing praises; sing praises unto our King, sing praises.

7 For God is the King of all the earth; sing ye praises with understanding.

8 God reigneth over the heathen; God sitteth upon the throne of his holiness.

9 The princes of the people are gathered together, even the people of the God of Abraham; for the shields of the earth belong unto God; he is greatly exalted.

## PSALM 48
*The situation and glory of Zion.*
A Song and Psalm for the sons of Korah.

1 Great is the Lord, and greatly to be praised in the city of our God, in the mountain of his holiness.

2 Beautiful for situation, the joy of the whole earth, is mount Zion, on the sides of the north, the city of the great King.

3 God is known in her palaces for a refuge.

4 For, lo, the kings were assembled, they passed by together.

5 They saw it, and so they marveled; they were troubled, and hasted away.

6 Fear took hold upon them there, and pain, as of a woman in travail.

7 Thou breakest the ships of Tarshish with an east wind.

8 As we have heard, so have we seen in the city of the Lord of hosts, in the city of our God; God will establish it for ever. Selah.

9 We have thought of thy loving-kindness, O God, in the midst of thy temple.

10 According to thy name, O God, so is thy praise unto the ends of the earth; thy right hand is full of righteousness.

11 Let mount Zion rejoice, let the daughters of Judah be glad, because of thy judgments.

12 Walk about Zion, and go round about her; tell the towers thereof.

13 Mark ye well her bulwarks, consider her palaces; that ye may tell it to the generation following.

14 For this God is our God for ever and ever; he will be our guide even unto death.

## PSALM 49

*Resurrection of the dead.*

To the chief Musician, A Psalm for the sons of Korah.

1 Hear this, all ye people; give ear, all ye inhabitants of the world;

2 Both low and high, rich and poor, together.

3 My mouth shall speak of wisdom; and the meditation of my heart shall be of understanding.

4 I will incline mine ear to a parable; I will open my dark saying upon the harp.

5 Wherefore should I fear in the days of evil, when the iniquity of my heels shall compass me about?

6 They that trust in their wealth, and boast themselves in the multitude of their riches;

7 None can by any means redeem his brother;

8 Nor give to God a ransom for him that he should still live for ever, that it ceaseth not for ever to see corruption.

9 For the redemption of their souls is through God, and precious.

10 For he seeth wise men die; likewise the fool and the brutish person perish, and leave their wealth to others;

11 Their inward thought of their houses for ever; their dwelling places, to all generations. Lands they called after their own names, and they are honorable.

12 Nevertheless, man in honor abideth not, he is also like the beasts that perish.

13 This I speak of them who walk in their way, and forsaketh the Almighty in their folly; yet their posterity approve their sayings. Selah.

14 Like sheep they are laid in the grave; death shall feed on them; and the upright shall have dominion over them in the morning; and their beauty shall consume in the grave from their dwelling.

15 But God will redeem my soul from the power of the grave, for he shall receive me. Selah.

16 Be not thou afraid when one is made rich; when the glory of his house is increased;

17 For when he dieth he shall carry nothing away; his glory shall not descend after him.

18 Though while he lived he blessed his soul, (and men will praise thee, when thou doest well to thyself,)

19 He shall go to the generation of his fathers; they shall never see light.

20 Man that is in honor, and understandeth not, is like the beasts that perish.

## PSALM 50

*The gathering of the saints—Obedience enjoined.*

A Psalm of Asaph.

1 The mighty God, even the Lord, hath spoken, and called the earth from the rising of the sun unto the going down thereof.

2 Out of Zion, the perfection of beauty, God hath shined.

3 Our God shall come, and shall not keep silence; a fire shall devour before him, and it shall be very tempestuous round about him.

4 He shall call to the heavens from above, and to the earth, that he may judge his people.

5 Gather my saints together unto me; those that have made a covenant with me by sacrifice.

6 And the heavens shall declare his righteousness; for God is judge himself. Selah.

7 Hear, O my people, and I will speak; O Israel, and I will testify against thee; I am God, even thy God.

8 I will not reprove thee for thy sacrifices or thy burnt offerings, to have been continually before me.

9 I will take no bullock out of thy house, nor he goats out of thy folds.

10 For every beast of the forest is mine, and the cattle upon a thousand hills.

11 I know all the fowls of the mountains; and the wild beasts of the field are mine.

12 If I were hungry, I would not tell

thee; for the world is mine, and the fullness thereof.

13 Will I eat the flesh of bulls, or drink the blood of goats?

14 Offer unto God thanksgiving, and pay thy vows unto the Most High;

15 And call upon me in the day of trouble; I will deliver thee, and thou shalt glorify me.

16 But unto the wicked God saith, What hast thou to do to declare my statutes, or that thou shouldest take my covenant in thy mouth?

17 Seeing thou hatest instruction, and casteth my words behind thee.

18 When thou sawest a thief, then thou consentedst with him, and hast been partaker with adulterers.

19 Thou givest thy mouth to evil, and thy tongue frameth deceit.

20 Thou sittest and speakest against thy brother; thou slanderest thine own mother's son.

21 These things hast thou done, and I kept silence; thou thoughtest that I was altogether such a one as thyself; but I will reprove thee, and set covenants in order before thine eyes.

22 Now consider this, ye that forget God, lest I tear you in pieces, and there be none can deliver.

23 Whoso offereth praise glorifieth me; and to him that ordereth his conversation aright will I show the salvation of God.

## PSALM 51

*Prayer for remission of sins.*

To the chief Musician, A Psalm of David, when Nathan the prophet came unto him, after he had gone into Bath-sheba.

1 Have mercy upon me, O God, according to thy loving-kindness; according unto the multitude of thy tender mercies, blot out my transgressions.

2 Wash me throughly from mine iniquity, and cleanse me from my sin.

3 For I acknowledge my transgressions; and my sin is ever before me.

4 Against thee, thee only, have I sinned, and done this evil in thy sight; that thou mightest be justified when thou speakest, and be clear when thou judgest.

5 Behold, I was shapen in iniquity; and in sin did my mother conceive me.

6 Behold, thou desirest truth in the inward parts; and in the hidden part thou shalt make me to know wisdom.

7 Purge me with hyssop, and I shall be clean; wash me, and I shall be whiter than snow.

8 Make me to hear joy and gladness; that the bones which thou hast broken may rejoice.

9 Hide thy face from my sins, and blot out all mine iniquities.

10 Create in me a clean heart, O God; and renew a right spirit within me.

11 Cast me not away from thy presence; and take not thy Holy Spirit from me.

12 Restore unto me the joy of thy salvation; and uphold me with thy free Spirit.

13 Then will I teach transgressors thy ways; and sinners shall be converted unto thee.

14 Deliver me from bloodguiltiness, O God, thou God of my salvation; and my tongue shall sing aloud of thy righteousness.

15 O Lord, open thou my lips; and my mouth shall show forth thy praise.

16 For thou desirest not sacrifice; else would I give it; thou delightest not in burnt offering.

17 The sacrifices of God are a broken spirit; a broken and a contrite heart, O God, thou wilt not despise.

18 Do good in thy good pleasure unto Zion; build thou the walls of Jerusalem.

19 Then shalt thou be pleased with the sacrifices of righteousness, with burnt offering and whole burnt offering; then shall they offer bullocks upon thine altar.

## PSALM 52

*David prophesieth the destruction of Doeg.*

To the chief Musician, Maschil, A Psalm of David, when Doeg the Edomite came and told Saul, and said unto him, David is come to the house of Ahimelech.

1 Why boastest thou thyself in mischief, O mighty man? the goodness of God endureth continually.

2 Thy tongue deviseth mischiefs; like a sharp razor, working deceitfully.

3 Thou lovest evil more than good; and lying rather than to speak righteousness. Selah.

4 Thou lovest all devouring words, O thou deceitful tongue.

5 God shall likewise destroy thee for ever, he shall take thee away, and pluck thee out of thy dwelling place,

and root thee out of the land of the living. Selah.

6 The righteous also shall see, and fear, and shall laugh at him.

7 Lo, the man who made not God his strength; but trusted in the abundance of his riches, and strengthened himself in his wickedness.

8 But I am like a green olive tree in the house of God; I trust in the mercy of God for ever and ever.

9 I will praise thee for ever, because thou hast done wonderful works; I will wait on thy name; for thou art good before thy saints.

## PSALM 53

*The corruption of natural man.*
To the chief Musician upon Mahalath, Maschil, A Psalm of David.

1 The fool hath said in his heart, There is no God. Such are corrupt, and they have done abominable iniquity. There is none that doeth good.

2 God looked down from heaven upon the children of men, to see if there were any that did understand, that did seek God.

3 Every one of them is gone back; they are altogether become filthy.

4 The workers of iniquity have no knowledge; they eat up my people as they eat bread; they have not called upon God.

5 There is none that doeth good, no not one. They were in great fear, for God hath scattered the bones of him that encampeth against him.

6 O Lord, thou hast put to shame those who have said in their hearts there was no fear, because thou hast despised them.

7 Oh that Zion were come, the salvation of Israel; for out of Zion shall they be judged, when God bringeth back the captivity of his people. And Jacob shall rejoice; Israel shall be glad.

## PSALM 54

*Praying for salvation, we promise sacrifice.*
To the chief Musician on Neginoth, Maschil, A Psalm of David, when the Ziphim came and said to Saul, Doth not David hide himself with us?

1 Save me, O God, by thy name, and judge me by thy strength.

2 Hear my prayer, O God; give ear to the words of my mouth.

3 For strangers are risen up against me, and oppressors seek after my soul; they have not set God before them. Selah.

4 Behold, God is mine helper; the Lord is with them that uphold my soul.

5 He shall reward evil unto mine enemies; cut them off in thy truth.

6 I will freely sacrifice unto thee; I will praise thy name, O Lord; for it is good.

7 For he hath delivered me out of all trouble; and mine eye hath seen his desire upon mine enemies.

## PSALM 55

*David's prayer for preservation.*
To the chief Musician on Neginoth, Maschil, A Psalm of David.

1 Give ear to my prayer, O God, and hide not thyself from my supplication.

2 Attend unto me, and hear me; I mourn in my complaint, and make a noise;

3 Because of the voice of the enemy, because of the oppression of the wicked; for they cast iniquity upon me, and in wrath they hate me.

4 My heart is sore pained within me; and the terrors of death are fallen upon me.

5 Fearfulness and trembling are come upon me, and horror hath overwhelmed me.

6 And I said, Oh that I had wings like a dove! for then would I fly away, and be at rest.

7 Lo, then would I wander far off, and remain in the wilderness. Selah.

8 I would hasten my escape from the windy storm and tempest.

9 Destroy, O Lord, and divide their tongues; for I have seen violence and strife in the city.

10 Day and night they go about it upon the walls thereof; mischief also and sorrow are in the midst of it.

11 Wickedness is in the midst thereof; deceit and guile depart not from her streets.

12 For it was not an enemy that reproached me, neither he that hated me that did magnify himself against me; if so, then I could have borne it; I would have hid myself from him;

13 But it was a man mine equal, my guide, and mine acquaintance.

14 We took sweet counsel together, and walked unto the house of God in company.

15 Let death seize upon them, and let them go down quick into hell; for

wickedness is in their dwellings, and among them.

16 As for me, I will call upon God; and the Lord shall save me.

17 Evening, and morning, and at noon, will I pray, and cry aloud; and he shall hear my voice.

18 He hath delivered my soul in peace from the battle that was against me; for there were many with me.

19 God shall hear, and afflict them, even he that abideth of old. Selah. Because they have no changes, therefore they fear not God.

20 They have put forth their hands against such as be at peace with them; they have broken the Lord's covenant.

21 The words of their mouth were smoother than butter, but war was in their heart. Their words were softer than oil, yet they have drawn swords.

22 Cast thy burden upon the Lord, and he shall sustain thee; he shall never suffer the righteous to be moved.

23 But thou, O God, shalt bring them down into the pit of destruction; bloody and deceitful men shall not live out half their days; but I will trust in thee.

## PSALM 56
*David complaineth of his enemies—His confidence in God's word.*
To the chief Musician upon Jonathelem-rechokim, Michtam of David, when the Philistines took him in Gath.

1 Be merciful unto me, O God; for man would swallow me up; he fighting daily oppresseth me.

2 Mine enemies would daily swallow me up; for they be many that fight against me, O thou Most High.

3 What! am I afraid? I will trust in thee.

4 In God I will praise his word, in God I have put my trust; I will not fear what flesh can do unto me.

5 Every day they wrest my words; all their thoughts are against me for evil.

6 They gather themselves together, they hide themselves, they mark my steps, when they wait for my soul.

7 Shall they escape by iniquity? in thine anger cast down the people, O God.

8 Thou tellest my wanderings; put thou my tears into thy bottle; are they not in thy book?

9 When I cry unto thee, then shall mine enemies turn back; this I know; for God is for me.

10 In God will I praise his word; in the Lord will I praise his word.

11 In God have I put my trust; I will not be afraid what man can do unto me.

12 Thy vows are upon me, O God; I will render praises unto thee.

13 For thou hast delivered my soul from death; wilt not thou deliver my feet from falling, that I may walk before God in the light of the living?

## PSALM 57
*David's trust in God.*
To the chief Musician, Al-taschith, Michtam of David, when he fled from Saul in the cave.

1 Be merciful unto me, O God, be merciful unto me, for my soul trusteth in thee; yea, in the shadow of thy wings will I make my refuge, until these calamities be overpast.

2 I will cry unto God most high; unto God that performeth all things for me.

3 He shall send from heaven, and save me from the reproach of him that would swallow me up. Selah. God shall send forth his mercy and his truth.

4 My soul is among lions; and I lie even among them that are set on fire, even the sons of men, whose teeth are spears and arrows, and their tongue a sharp sword.

5 Be thou exalted, O God, above the heavens; let thy glory be above all the earth.

6 They have prepared a net for my steps; my soul is bowed down; they have digged a pit before me, into the midst whereof they are fallen themselves. Selah.

7 My heart is fixed, O God, my heart is fixed; I will sing and give praise.

8 Awake up, my glory; awake, psaltery and harp; I myself will awake early.

9 I will praise thee, O Lord, among the people; I will sing unto thee among the nations.

10 For thy mercy is great unto the heavens, and thy truth unto the clouds.

11 Be thou exalted, O God, above the heavens; let thy glory be above all the earth.

## PSALM 58
*Wicked judges reproved—Judgment of the wicked.*
To the chief Musician, Al-taschith, Michtam of David.

1 Do ye indeed speak righteousness,

O congregation? do ye judge uprightly, O ye sons of men?

2 Yea, in heart ye work wickedness; ye weigh the violence of your hands in the earth.

3 The wicked are estranged from the womb; they go astray as soon as they be born, speaking lies.

4 Their poison is like the poison of a serpent; they are like the deaf adder that stoppeth her ear;

5 Which will not hearken to the voice of charmers, charming never so wisely.

6 Break their teeth, O God, in their mouth; break out the great teeth of the young lions, O Lord.

7 Let them melt away as waters which run continually; when he bendeth his bow to shoot his arrows, let them be as cut in pieces.

8 As a snail which melteth, let every one of them pass away; like the untimely birth of a woman, that they may not see the sun.

9 Before your pots can feel the thorns, he shall take them away as with a whirlwind, both living, and in his wrath.

10 The righteous shall rejoice when he seeth the vengeance; he will wash his feet in the blood of the wicked.

11 So that a man shall say, Verily there is a reward for the righteous; verily he is a God that judgeth in the earth.

## PSALM 59

*David prayeth to be delivered from his enemies.*

To the chief Musician, Al-taschith, Michtam of David; when Saul sent, and they watched the house to kill him.

1 Deliver me from mine enemies, O my God; defend me from them that rise up against me.

2 Deliver me from the workers of iniquity, and save me from bloody men.

3 For, lo, they lie in wait for my soul; the mighty are gathered against me; not for my transgression, nor for my sin, O Lord.

4 They run and prepare themselves without my fault; awake to help me, and behold.

5 Thou therefore, O Lord God of hosts, the God of Israel, awake to visit all the heathen; be not merciful to any wicked transgressors. Selah.

6 They return at evening; they make a noise like a dog, and go round about the city.

7 Behold, they belch out with their mouth; swords are in their lips; for who, say they, doth hear?

8 But thou, O Lord, shalt laugh at them; thou shalt have all the heathen in derision.

9 Because of his strength will I wait upon thee; for God is my defense.

10 The God of my mercy shall prevent me; God shall let me see my desire upon mine enemies.

11 Slay them not, lest my people forget; scatter them by thy power; and bring them down, O Lord our shield.

12 For the sin of their mouth and the words of their lips let them even be taken in their pride; and for cursing and lying which they speak.

13 Consume them in wrath, consume them, that they may not be; and let them know that God ruleth in Jacob unto the ends of the earth. Selah.

14 And at evening let them return; and let them make a noise like a dog, and go round about the city.

15 Let them wander up and down for meat, and grudge if they be not satisfied.

16 But I will sing of thy power; yea, I will sing aloud of thy mercy in the morning; for thou hast been my defense and refuge in the day of my trouble.

17 Unto thee, O my strength, will I sing; for God is my defense, and the God of my mercy.

## PSALM 60

*David, upon better hope, prayeth for deliverance.*

To the chief Musician upon Sushane-duth, Michtam of David, to teach; when he strove with Aram-naharaim and with Aram-zobah, when Joab returned, and smote of Edom in the valley of salt twelve thousand.

1 O God, thou hast cast us off, thou hast scattered us, thou hast been displeased; O turn thyself to us again.

2 Thou hast made the earth to tremble; thou hast broken it; heal the breaches thereof; for it shaketh.

3 Thou hast showed thy people hard things; thou hast made us to drink the wine of astonishment.

4 Thou hast given a banner to them that fear thee, that it may be displayed because of the truth. Selah.

5 That thy beloved may be delivered; save with thy right hand, and hear me.

6 God hath spoken in his holiness; I will rejoice, I will divide Shechem, and mete out the valley of Succoth.

7 Gilead is mine, and Manasseh is mine; Ephraim also is the strength of mine head; Judah is my lawgiver;

8 Moab is my washpot; over Edom will I cast out my shoe; Philistia, triumph thou because of me.

9 Who will bring me into the strong city? who will lead me into Edom?

10 Wilt not thou, O God, which hadst cast us off? and thou, O God, which didst not go out with our armies?

11 Give us help from trouble; for vain is the help of man.

12 Through God we shall do valiantly; for he it is that shall tread down our enemies.

## PSALM 61

*David's service to God based upon his experience in the promises.*

To the chief Musician upon Neginah.

1 Hear my cry, O God; attend unto my prayer.

2 From the end of the earth will I cry unto thee, when my heart is overwhelmed; lead me to the rock that is higher than I.

3 For thou hast been a shelter for me, and a strong tower from the enemy.

4 I will abide in thy tabernacle for ever; I will trust in the covert of thy wings. Selah.

5 For thou, O God, hast heard my vows; thou hast given me the heritage of those that fear thy name.

6 Thou wilt prolong the king's life; and his years as many generations.

7 He shall abide before God for ever; O prepare mercy and truth, which may preserve him.

8 So will I sing praise unto thy name for ever, that I may daily perform my vows.

## PSALM 62

*In God only is salvation.*

To the chief Musician, to Jeduthum, A Psalm of David.

1 Truly my soul waiteth upon God; from him cometh my salvation.

2 He only is my rock and my salvation; he is my defense; I shall not be greatly moved.

3 How long will ye imagine mischief against a man? ye shall be slain all of you; as a bowing wall shall ye be, and as a tottering fence.

4 They only consult to cast him down from his excellency; they delight in lies; they bless with their mouth, but they curse inwardly. Selah.

5 My soul, wait thou only upon God; for my expectation is from him.

6 He only is my rock and my salvation; he is my defense; I shall not be moved.

7 In God is my salvation and my glory; the rock of my strength, and my refuge, is in God.

8 Trust in him at all times; ye people, pour out your heart before him; God is a refuge for us. Selah.

9 Surely men of low degree are vanity, and men of high degree are a lie; to be laid in the balance, they are altogether lighter than vanity.

10 Trust not in oppression, and become not vain in robbery; if riches increase, set not your heart upon them.

11 God hath spoken once; twice have I heard this; that power belongeth unto God.

12 Also unto thee, O Lord, belongeth mercy; for thou renderest to every man according to his work.

## PSALM 63

*David's desire for God.*

David's Psalm in the wilderness of Judah.

1 O God, thou art my God; early will I seek thee; my soul thirsteth for thee, my flesh longeth for thee in a dry and thirsty land, where no water is;

2 To see thy power and thy glory, so as I have seen thee in the sanctuary.

3 Because thy loving-kindness is better than life, my lips shall praise thee.

4 Thus will I bless thee while I live; I will lift up my hands in thy name.

5 My soul shall be satisfied as with marrow and fatness; and my mouth shall praise thee with joyful lips;

6 When I remember thee upon my bed, and meditate on thee in the night watches.

7 Because thou hast been my help, therefore in the shadow of thy wings will I rejoice.

8 My soul followeth hard after thee; thy right hand upholdeth me.

9 But those that seek my soul, to destroy it, shall go into the lower parts of the earth.

10 They shall fall by the sword; they shall be a portion for foxes.

11 But the king shall rejoice in God; every one that sweareth by him shall glory; but the mouth of them that speak lies shall be stopped.

## PSALM 64

*David's prayer for deliverance and trust in God.*

To the chief Musician, A Psalm of David.

1 Hear my voice, O God, in my prayer; preserve my life from fear of the enemy.

2 Hide me from the secret counsel of the wicked; from the insurrection of the workers of iniquity;

3 Who whet their tongue like a sword, and bend their bows to shoot their arrows, even bitter words:

4 That they may shoot in secret at the perfect; suddenly do they shoot at him, and fear not.

5 They encourage themselves in an evil matter; they commune of laying snares privily; they say, Who shall see them?

6 They search out iniquities; they accomplish a diligent search; both the inward thought of every one of them, and the heart, is deep.

7 But God shall shoot at them with an arrow; suddenly shall they be wounded.

8 So they shall make their own tongue to fall upon themselves; all that see them shall flee away.

9 And all men shall fear, and shall declare the work of God; for they shall wisely consider of his doing.

10 The righteous shall be glad in the Lord, and shall trust in him; and all the upright in heart shall glory.

## PSALM 65

*The blessedness of God's chosen.*

To the chief Musician, A Psalm and Song of David.

1 Praise waiteth for thee, O God, in Zion; and unto thee shall the vow be performed.

2 O thou that hearest prayer, unto thee shall all flesh come.

3 Iniquities prevail against me; as for our transgressions, thou shalt purge them away.

4 Blessed is the man whom thou choosest, and causest to approach unto thee, that he may dwell in thy courts;

we shall be satisfied with the goodness of thy house, even of thy holy temple.

5 By terrible things in righteousness wilt thou answer us, O God of our salvation; who art the confidence of all the ends of the earth, and of them that are afar off upon the sea;

6 Which by his strength setteth fast the mountains; being girded with power;

7 Which stilleth the noise of the seas, the noise of their waves, and the tumult of the people.

8 They also that dwell in the uttermost parts are afraid at thy tokens; thou makest the outgoings of the morning and evening to rejoice.

9 Thou visitest the earth, and waterest it; thou greatly enrichest it with the river of God, which is full of water; thou preparest them corn, when thou hast so provided for it.

10 Thou waterest the ridges thereof abundantly; thou settlest the furrows thereof; thou makest it soft with showers; thou blessest the springing thereof.

11 Thou crownest the year with thy goodness; and thy paths drop fatness.

12 They drop upon the pastures of the wilderness; and the little hills rejoice on every side.

13 The pastures are clothed with flocks; the valleys also are covered over with corn; they shout for joy, they also sing.

## PSALM 66

*God to be praised—Reasons therefor.*

To the chief Musician, A Song or Psalm.

1 Make a joyful noise unto God, all ye lands;

2 Sing forth the honor of his name; make his praise glorious.

3 Say unto God, How terrible art thou in thy works! through the greatness of thy power shall thine enemies submit themselves unto thee.

4 All the earth shall worship thee, and shall sing unto thee; they shall sing to thy name. Selah.

5 Come and see the works of God; he is terrible in his doing toward the children of men.

6 He turned the sea into dry land; they went through the flood on foot; there did we rejoice in him.

7 He ruleth by his power for ever; his eyes behold the nations; let not the rebellious exalt themselves. Selah.

8 O bless our God, ye people, and make the voice of his praise to be heard;

9 Which holdeth our soul in life, and suffereth not our feet to be moved.

10 For thou, O God, hast proved us; thou hast tried us, as silver is tried.

11 Thou broughtest us into the net; thou laidst affliction upon our loins.

12 Thou hast caused men to ride over our heads; we went through fire and through water; but thou broughtest us out into a wealthy place.

13 I will go into thy house with burnt offerings; I will pay thee my vows,

14 Which my lips have uttered, and my mouth hath spoken, when I was in trouble.

15 I will offer unto thee burnt sacrifices of fatlings, with the incense of rams; I will offer bullocks with goats. Selah.

16 Come and hear, all ye that fear God, and I will declare what he hath done for my soul.

17 I cried unto him with my mouth, and he was extolled with my tongue.

18 If I regard iniquity in my heart, the Lord will not hear me;

19 But verily God hath heard me; he hath attended to the voice of my prayer.

20 Blessed be God, which hath not turned away my prayer, nor his mercy from me.

## PSALM 67

*A prayer for the universal establishment of God's kingdom.*

To the chief Musician on Neginoth, A Psalm or Song.

1 God be merciful unto us, and bless us; and cause his face to shine upon us; Selah;

2 That thy way may be known upon earth, thy saving health among all nations.

3 Let the people praise thee, O God; let all the people praise thee.

4 O let the nations be glad and sing for joy; for thou shalt judge the people righteously, and govern the nations upon earth. Selah.

5 Let the people praise thee, O God; let all the people praise thee.

6 Then shall the earth yield her increase; and God, even our own God, shall bless us.

7 God shall bless us; and all the ends of the earth shall fear him.

## PSALM 68

*An exhortation to praise God for his mercies, and his great works.*

To the chief Musician, A Psalm or Song of David.

1 Let God arise, let his enemies be scattered; let them also that hate him flee before him.

2 As smoke is driven away, so drive them away; as wax melteth before the fire, so let the wicked perish at the presence of God.

3 But let the righteous be glad; let them rejoice before God; yea, let them exceedingly rejoice.

4 Sing unto God, sing praises to his name; extol him that rideth upon the heavens by his name JÄH, and rejoice before him.

5 A father of the fatherless, and a judge of the widows, is God in his holy habitation.

6 God setteth the solitary in families; he bringeth out those which are bound with chains; but the rebellious dwell in a dry land.

7 O God, when thou wentest forth before thy people, when thou didst march through the wilderness; Selah;

8 The earth shook, the heavens also dropped at the presence of God; even Sinai itself was moved at the presence of God, the God of Israel.

9 Thou, O God, didst send a plentiful rain, whereby thou didst confirm thine inheritance, when it was weary.

10 Thy congregation hath dwelt therein; thou, O God, hast prepared of thy goodness for the poor.

11 The Lord gave the word; great was the company of those that published it.

12 Kings of armies did flee apace; and she that tarried at home divided the spoil.

13 Though ye have lain among the pots, yet shall ye be as the wings of a dove covered with silver, and her feathers with yellow gold.

14 When the Almighty scattered kings in it, it was white as snow in Salmon.

15 The hill of God is as the hill of Bashan; a high hill as the hill of Bashan.

16 Why leap ye, ye high hills? this is the hill which God desireth to dwell in; yea, the Lord will dwell in it for ever.

17 The chariots of God are twenty thousand, even thousands of angels;

the Lord is among them, as in Sinai, in the holy place.

18 Thou hast ascended on high, thou hast led captivity captive; thou hast received gifts for men; yea, for the rebellious also, that the Lord God might dwell among them.

19 Blessed be the Lord, who daily loadeth us with benefits, even the God of our salvation. Selah.

20 He that is our God is the God of salvation; and unto God the Lord belong the issues from death.

21 But God shall wound the head of his enemies, and the hairy scalp of such a one as goeth on still in his trespasses.

22 The Lord said, I will bring again from Bashan, I will bring my people again from the depths of the sea;

23 That thy foot may be dipped in the blood of thine enemies, and the tongue of thy dogs in the same.

24 They have seen thy goings, O God; even the goings of my God, my King, in the sanctuary.

25 The singers went before, the players on instruments followed after; among them were the damsels playing with timbrels.

26 Bless ye God in the congregations, even the Lord, from the fountain of Israel.

27 There is little Benjamin with their ruler, the princes of Judah and their council, the princes of Zebulun, and the princes of Naphtali.

28 Thy God hath commanded thy strength; strengthen, O God, that which thou hast wrought for us.

29 Because of thy temple at Jerusalem shall kings bring presents unto thee.

30 Rebuke the company of spearmen, the multitude of the bulls, with the calves of the people, till every one submit himself with pieces of silver; scatter thou the people that delight in war.

31 Princes shall come out of Egypt; Ethiopia shall soon stretch out her hands unto God.

32 Sing unto God, ye kingdoms of the earth; O sing praises unto the Lord; Selah.

33 To him that rideth upon the heavens of heavens, which were of old; lo, he doth send out his voice, and that a mighty voice.

34 Ascribe ye strength unto God; his excellency is over Israel, and his strength is in the clouds.

35 O God, thou art terrible out of thy holy places; the God of Israel is he that giveth strength and power unto his people. Blessed be God.

## PSALM 69

*David's affliction—His prayer for deliverance.*

To the chief Musician upon Shoshannim, A Psalm of David.

1 Save me, O God; for the waters are come in unto my soul.

2 I sink in deep mire, where there is no standing; I am come into deep waters, where the floods overflow me.

3 I am weary of my crying; my throat is dried; mine eyes fail while I wait for my God.

4 They that hate me without a cause are more than the hairs of mine head; they that would destroy me, being mine enemies wrongfully, are mighty; then I restored that which I took not away.

5 O God, thou knowest my foolishness; and my sins are not hid from thee.

6 Let not them that wait on thee, O Lord God of hosts, be ashamed for my sake; let not those that seek thee be confounded for my sake, O God of Israel.

7 Because for thy sake I have borne reproach; shame hath covered my face.

8 I am become a stranger unto my brethren, and an alien unto my mother's children.

9 For the zeal of thine house hath eaten me up; and the reproaches of them that reproached thee are fallen upon me.

10 When I wept, and chastened my soul with fasting, that was to my reproach.

11 I made sackcloth also my garment; and I became a proverb to them.

12 They that sit in the gate speak against me; and I was the song of the drunkards.

13 But as for me, my prayer is unto thee, O Lord, in an acceptable time; O God, in the multitude of thy mercy hear me, in the truth of thy salvation.

14 Deliver me out of the mire, and let me not sink; let me be delivered from them that hate me, and out of the deep waters.

15 Let not the waterflood overflow

8 Let my mouth be filled with thy praise and with thy honor all the day.

9 Cast me not off in the time of old age; forsake me not when my strength faileth.

10 For mine enemies speak against me; and they that lay wait for my soul take counsel together;

11 Saying, God hath forsaken him: persecute and take him; for there is none to deliver him.

12 O God, be not far from me: O my God, make haste for my help.

13 Let them be confounded and consumed that are adversaries to my soul; let them be covered with reproach and dishonor that seek my hurt.

14 But I will hope continually, and will yet praise thee more and more.

15 My mouth shall show forth thy righteousness and thy salvation all the day; for I know not the numbers thereof.

16 I will go in the strength of the Lord God: I will make mention of thy righteousness, even of thine only.

17 O God, thou hast taught me from my youth; and hitherto have I declared thy wondrous works.

18 Now also when I am old and gray-headed, O God, forsake me not; until I have showed thy strength unto this generation, and thy power to every one that is to come.

19 Thy righteousness also, O God, is very high, who hast done great things: O God, who is like unto thee!

20 Thou, which hast showed me great and sore troubles, shalt quicken me again, and shalt bring me up again from the depths of the earth.

21 Thou shalt increase my greatness, and comfort me on every side.

22 I will also praise thee with the psaltery, even thy truth, O my God: unto thee will I sing with the harp, O thou Holy One of Israel.

23 My lips shall greatly rejoice when I sing unto thee; and my soul, which thou hast redeemed.

24 My tongue also shall talk of thy righteousness all the day long; for they are confounded, for they are brought unto shame, that seek my hurt.

## PSALM 72

*David showeth the glory of Christ's kingdom.*

A Psalm for Solomon.

1 Give the king thy judgments, O God, and thy righteousness unto the king's son.

2 He shall judge thy people with righteousness, and thy poor with judgment.

3 The mountains shall bring peace to the people, and the little hills, by righteousness.

4 He shall judge the poor of the people, he shall save the children of the needy, and shall break in pieces the oppressor.

5 They shall fear thee as long as the sun and moon endure, throughout all generations.

6 He shall come down like rain upon the mown grass; as showers that water the earth.

7 In his days shall the righteous flourish; and abundance of peace so long as the moon endureth.

8 He shall have dominion also from sea to sea, and from the river unto the ends of the earth.

9 They that dwell in the wilderness shall bow before him; and his enemies shall lick the dust.

10 The kings of Tarshish and of the isles shall bring presents: the kings of Sheba and Seba shall offer gifts.

11 Yea, all kings shall fall down before him: all nations shall serve him.

12 For he shall deliver the needy when he crieth; the poor also, and him that hath no helper.

13 He shall spare the poor and needy, and shall save the souls of the needy.

14 He shall redeem their soul from deceit and violence: and precious shall their blood be in his sight.

15 And he shall live, and to him shall be given of the gold of Sheba: prayer also shall be made for him continually; and daily shall he be praised.

16 There shall be a handful of corn in the earth upon the top of the mountains; the fruit thereof shall shake like Lebanon: and they of the city shall flourish like grass of the earth.

17 His name shall endure for ever: his name shall be continued as long as the sun: and men shall be blessed in him: all nations shall call him blessed.

18 Blessed be the Lord God, the God of Israel, who only doeth wondrous things.

19 And blessed be his glorious name for ever: and let the whole earth be filled with his glory. Amen, and Amen.

me, neither let the deep swallow me up, and let not the pit shut her mouth upon me.

16 Hear me, O Lord; for thy loving-kindness is good; turn unto me according to the multitude of thy tender mercies.

17 And hide not thy face from thy servant; for I am in trouble; hear me speedily.

18 Draw nigh unto my soul, and redeem it; deliver me because of mine enemies.

19 Thou hast known my reproach, and my shame, and my dishonor; mine adversaries are all before thee.

20 Reproach hath broken my heart; and I am full of heaviness; and I looked for some to take pity, but there was none; and for comforters, but I found none.

21 They gave me also gall for my meat; and in my thirst they gave me vinegar to drink.

22 Let their table become a snare before them; and that which should have been for their welfare, let it become a trap.

23 Let their eyes be darkened, that they see not; and make their loins continually to shake.

24 Pour out thine indignation upon them, and let thy wrathful anger take hold of them.

25 Let their habitation be desolate; and let none dwell in their tents.

26 For they persecute him whom thou hast smitten; and they talk to the grief of those whom thou hast wounded.

27 Add iniquity unto their iniquity; and let them not come into thy righteousness.

28 Let them be blotted out of the book of the living, and not be written with the righteous.

29 But I am poor and sorrowful; let thy salvation, O God, set me up on high.

30 I will praise the name of God with a song, and will magnify him with thanksgiving.

31 This also shall please the Lord better than an ox or bullock that hath horns and hooves.

32 The humble shall see this, and be glad; and your heart shall live that seek God.

33 For the Lord heareth the poor, and despiseth not his prisoners.

34 Let the heaven and earth praise him, the seas, and every thing that moveth therein.

35 For God will save Zion, and will build the cities of Judah; that they may dwell there, and have it in possession.

36 The seed also of his servants shall inherit it; and they that love his name shall dwell therein.

## PSALM 70

*David prayeth God for the speedy destruction of the wicked, and preservation of the godly.*

To the chief Musician, A Psalm of David, to bring to remembrance.

1 Make haste, O God, to deliver me; make haste to help me, O Lord.

2 Let them be ashamed and confounded that seek after my soul; let them be turned backward, and put to confusion, that desire my hurt.

3 Let them be turned back for a reward of their shame that say, Aha, aha.

4 Let all those that seek thee rejoice and be glad in thee; and let such as love thy salvation say continually, Let God be magnified.

5 But I am poor and needy; make haste unto me, O God; thou art my help and my deliverer; O Lord, make no tarrying.

## PSALM 71

*David, in faith, prayeth for himself, and against the enemies of his soul— He promiseth constancy.*

1 In thee, O Lord, do I put my trust; let me never be put to confusion.

2 Deliver me in thy righteousness, and cause me to escape; incline thine ear unto me, and save me.

3 Be thou my strong habitation, whereunto I may continually resort; thou hast given commandment to save me; for thou art my rock and my fortress.

4 Deliver me, O my God, out of the hand of the wicked, out of the hand of the unrighteous and cruel man.

5 For thou art my hope, O Lord God; thou art my trust from my youth.

6 By thee have I been holden up from the womb; thou art he that took me out of my mother's bowels; my praise shall be continually of thee.

7 I am as a wonder unto many; but thou art my strong refuge.

20 The prayers of David the son of Jesse are ended.

## PSALM 73

*The prophet's deliverance from temptation—God's purpose in destroying the wicked.*

A Psalm of Asaph.

1 Truly God is good to Israel, even to such as are of a clean heart.

2 But as for me, my feet were almost gone; my steps had well-nigh slipped.

3 For I was envious at the foolish, when I saw the prosperity of the wicked.

4 For there are no bands in their death; but their strength is firm.

5 They are not in trouble as other men; neither are they plagued like other men.

6 Therefore pride compasseth them about as a chain; violence covereth them as a garment.

7 Their eyes stand out with fatness; they have more than heart could wish.

8 They are corrupt, and speak wickedly concerning oppression; they speak loftily.

9 They set their mouth against the heavens, and their tongue walketh through the earth.

10 Therefore his people return hither; and waters of a full cup are wrung out to them.

11 And they say, How doth God know? and is there knowledge in the Most High?

12 Behold, these are the ungodly, who prosper in the world; they increase in riches.

13 Verily I have cleansed my heart in vain, and washed my hands in innocency.

14 For all the day long have I been plagued, and chastened every morning.

15 If I say, I will speak thus; behold, I should offend against the generation of thy children.

16 When I thought to know this, it was too painful for me;

17 Until I went into the sanctuary of God; then understood I their end.

18 Surely thou didst set them in slippery places; thou castedst them down into destruction.

19 How are they brought into desolation, as in a moment! they are utterly consumed with terrors.

20 As a dream when one awaketh; so, O Lord, when thou awakest, thou shalt despise their image.

21 Thus my heart was grieved, and I was pricked in my reins.

22 So foolish was I, and ignorant; I was as a beast before thee.

23 Nevertheless I am continually with thee; thou hast holden me by my right hand.

24 Thou shalt guide me with thy counsel, and afterward receive me to glory.

25 Whom have I in heaven but thee? and there is none upon earth that I desire besides thee.

26 My flesh and my heart faileth; but God is the strength of my heart, and my portion for ever.

27 For, lo, they that are far from thee shall perish; thou hast destroyed all them that go a whoring from thee.

28 But it is good for me to draw near to God; I have put my trust in the Lord God, that I may declare all thy works.

## PSALM 74

*The prophet complaineth of the desolation of the sanctuary—He moveth God to help.*

Maschil of Asaph.

1 O God, why hast thou cast us off for ever? why doth thine anger smoke against the sheep of thy pasture?

2 Remember thy congregation, which thou hast purchased of old; the rod of thine inheritance, which thou hast redeemed; this mount Zion, wherein thou hast dwelt.

3 Lift up thy feet unto the perpetual desolations; even all that the enemy hath done wickedly in the sanctuary.

4 Thine enemies roar in the midst of thy congregations; they set up their ensigns for signs.

5 A man was famous according as he had lifted up axes upon the thick trees.

6 But now they break down the carved work thereof at once with axes and hammers.

7 They have cast fire into thy sanctuary, they have defiled by casting down the dwelling place of thy name to the ground.

8 They said in their hearts, Let us destroy them together; they have burned up all the synagogues of God in the land.

9 We see not our signs; there is no more any prophet; neither is there among us any that knoweth how long.

10 O God, how long shall the adversary reproach? shall the enemy blaspheme thy name for ever?

11 Why withdrawest thou thy hand, even thy right hand? pluck it out of thy bosom.

12 For God is my King of old, working salvation in the midst of the earth.

13 Thou didst divide the sea by thy strength; thou brakest the heads of the dragons in the waters.

14 Thou brakest the heads of leviathan in pieces, and gavest him to be meat to the people inhabiting the wilderness.

15 Thou didst cleave the fountain and the flood; thou driedst up mighty rivers.

16 The day is thine, the night also is thine; thou hast prepared the light and the sun.

17 Thou hast set all the borders of the earth; thou hast made summer and winter.

18 Remember this, that the enemy hath reproached, O Lord, and that the foolish people have blasphemed thy name.

19 O deliver not the soul of thy turtledove unto the multitude of the wicked; forget not the congregation of thy poor for ever.

20 Have respect unto the covenant; for the dark places of the earth are full of the habitations of cruelty.

21 O let not the oppressed return ashamed; let the poor and needy praise thy name.

22 Arise, O God, plead thine own cause; remember how the foolish man reproacheth thee daily.

23 Forget not the voice of thine enemies; the tumult of those that rise up against thee increaseth continually.

## PSALM 75

*The prophet praiseth God, and promiseth to execute justice.*

To the chief Musician, Al-taschith, A Psalm or Song of Asaph.

1 Unto thee, O God, do we give thanks, unto thee do we give thanks; for that thy name is near thy wondrous works declare.

2 When I shall receive the congregation I will judge uprightly.

3 The earth and all the inhabitants thereof are dissolved; I bear up the pillars of it. Selah.

4 I said unto the fools, Deal not fool-ishly; and to the wicked, Lift not up the horn;

5 Lift not up your horn on high; speak not with a stiff neck.

6 For promotion cometh neither from the east, nor from the west, nor from the south.

7 But God is the judge; he putteth down one, and setteth up another.

8 For in the hand of the Lord there is a cup, and the wine is red; it is full of mixture; and he poureth out of the same; but the dregs thereof, all the wicked of the earth shall wring them out, and drink them.

9 But I will declare for ever; I will sing praises to the God of Jacob.

10 All the horns of the wicked also will I cut off; but the horns of the righteous shall be exalted.

## PSALM 76

*God's majesty in the church—Exhortation to serve him reverently.*

To the chief Musician on Neginoth, A Psalm or Song of Asaph.

1 In Judah is God known; his name is great in Israel.

2 In Salem also is his tabernacle, and his dwelling place in Zion.

3 There brake he the arrows of the bow, the shield, and the sword, and the battle. Selah.

4 Thou art more glorious and excellent than the mountains of prey.

5 The stouthearted are spoiled, they have slept their sleep; and none of the men of might have found their hands.

6 At thy rebuke, O God of Jacob, both the chariot and horse are cast into a dead sleep.

7 Thou, even thou, art to be feared; and who may stand in thy sight when once thou art angry?

8 Thou didst cause judgment to be heard from heaven; the earth feared, and was still,

9 When God arose to judgment, to save all the meek of the earth. Selah.

10 Surely the wrath of man shall praise thee; the remainder of wrath shalt thou restrain.

11 Vow, and pay unto the Lord your God; let all that be round about him bring presents unto him that ought to be feared.

12 He shall cut off the spirit of princes; he is terrible to the kings of the earth.

## PSALM 77

*The meditations of the psalmist—God's great and gracious works.*

To the chief Musician, to Jeduthun, A Psalm of Asaph.

1 I cried unto God with my voice, even unto God with my voice; and he gave ear unto me.

2 In the day of my trouble I sought the Lord; my sore ran in the night, and ceased not; my soul refused to be comforted.

3 I remembered God, and was troubled; I complained, and my spirit was overwhelmed. Selah.

4 Thou holdest mine eyes waking; I am so troubled that I cannot speak.

5 I have considered the days of old, the years of ancient times.

6 I call to remembrance my song in the night; I commune with mine own heart; and my spirit made diligent search.

7 Will the Lord cast off for ever? and will he be favorable no more?

8 Is his mercy clean gone for ever? doth his promise fail for evermore?

9 Hath God forgotten to be gracious? hath he in anger shut up his tender mercies? Selah.

10 And I said, This is my infirmity; but I will remember the years of the right hand of the Most High.

11 I will remember the works of the Lord; surely I will remember thy wonders of old.

12 I will meditate also of all thy work, and talk of thy doings.

13 Thy way, O God, is in the sanctuary; who is so great a God as our God?

14 Thou art the God that doest wonders; thou hast declared thy strength among the people.

15 Thou hast with thine arm redeemed thy people, the sons of Jacob and Joseph. Selah.

16 The waters saw thee, O God, the waters saw thee; they were afraid; the depths also were troubled.

17 The clouds poured out water; the skies sent out a sound; thine arrows also went abroad.

18 The voice of thy thunder was in the heaven; the lightnings lightened the world; the earth trembled and shook.

19 Thy way is in the sea, and thy path in the great waters, and thy footsteps are not known.

20 Thou leddest thy people like a flock by the hand of Moses and Aaron.

## PSALM 78

*An exhortation to learn and teach the law of God—God's wrath against the disobedient.*

Maschil of Asaph.

1 Give ear, O my people, to my law; incline your ears to the words of my mouth.

2 I will open my mouth in a parable; I will utter dark sayings of old;

3 Which we have heard and known, and our fathers have told us.

4 We will not hide them from their children, showing to the generation to come the praises of the Lord, and his strength, and his wonderful works that he hath done.

5 For he established a testimony in Jacob, and appointed a law in Israel, which he commanded our fathers, that they should make them known to their children;

6 That the generation to come might know them, even the children which should be born; who should arise and declare them to their children;

7 That they might set their hope in God, and not forget the works of God, but keep his commandments;

8 And might not be as their fathers, a stubborn and rebellious generation; a generation that set not their heart aright, and whose spirit was not steadfast with God.

9 The children of Ephraim, being armed, and carrying bows, turned back in the day of battle.

10 They kept not the covenant of God, and refused to walk in his law;

11 And forgat his works, and his wonders that he had showed them.

12 Marvelous things did he in the sight of their fathers, in the land of Egypt, in the field of Zoan.

13 He divided the sea, and caused them to pass through; and he made the waters to stand as a heap.

14 In the daytime also he led them with a cloud, and all the night with a light of fire.

15 He clave the rocks in the wilderness, and gave them drink as out of the great depths.

16 He brought streams also out of the rock, and caused waters to run down like rivers.

17 And they sinned yet more against

him by provoking the Most High in the wilderness.

18 And they tempted God in their heart by asking meat for their lust.

19 Yea, they spake against God; they said, Can God furnish a table in the wilderness?

20 Behold, he smote the rock, that the waters gushed out, and the streams overflowed; can he give bread also? can he provide flesh for his people?

21 Therefore the Lord heard this, and was wroth; so a fire was kindled against Jacob, and anger also came up against Israel;

22 Because they believed not in God, and trusted not in his salvation;

23 Though he had commanded the clouds from above, and opened the doors of heaven,

24 And had rained down manna upon them to eat, and had given them of the corn of heaven.

25 Man did eat angels' food; he sent them meat to the full.

26 He caused an east wind to blow in the heaven; and by his power he brought in the south wind.

27 He rained flesh also upon them as dust, and feathered fowls like as the sand of the sea;

28 And he let it fall in the midst of their camp, round about their habitations.

29 So they did eat, and were well filled; for he gave them their own desire;

30 They were not estranged from their lust; but while their meat was yet in their mouths,

31 The wrath of God came upon them, and slew the fattest of them, and smote down the chosen men of Israel.

32 For all this they sinned still, and believed not for his wondrous works.

33 Therefore their days did he consume in vanity, and their years in trouble.

34 When he slew them, then they sought him; and they returned and inquired early after God.

35 And they remembered that God was their Rock, and the high God their Redeemer.

36 Nevertheless they did flatter him with their mouth, and they lied unto him with their tongues.

37 For their heart was not right with him, neither were they steadfast in his covenant.

38 But he, being full of compassion, forgave their iniquity, and destroyed them not; yea, many a time turned he his anger away, and did not stir up all his wrath.

39 For he remembered that they were but flesh; a wind that passeth away, and cometh not again.

40 How oft did they provoke him in the wilderness, and grieve him in the desert!

41 Yea, they turned back and tempted God, and limited the Holy One of Israel.

42 They remembered not his hand, nor the day when he delivered them from the enemy;

43 How he had wrought his signs in Egypt, and his wonders in the field of Zoan;

44 And had turned their rivers into blood; and their floods, that they could not drink.

45 He sent divers sorts of flies among them, which devoured them; and frogs, which destroyed them.

46 He gave also their increase unto the caterpillar, and their labour unto the locust.

47 He destroyed their vines with hail, and their sycamore trees with frost.

48 He gave up their cattle also to the hail, and their flocks to hot thunderbolts.

49 He cast upon them the fierceness of his anger, wrath, and indignation, and trouble, by sending evil angels among them.

50 He made a way to his anger; he spared not their soul from death, but gave their life over to the pestilence;

51 And smote all the firstborn in Egypt; the chief of their strength in the tabernacles of Ham;

52 But made his own people to go forth like sheep, and guided them in the wilderness like a flock.

53 And he led them on safely, so that they feared not; but the sea overwhelmed their enemies.

54 And he brought them to the border of his sanctuary, even to this mountain, which his right hand had purchased.

55 He cast out the heathen also before them, and divided them an inheri-

tance by line, and made the tribes of Israel to dwell in their tents.

56 Yet they tempted and provoked the most high God, and kept not his testimonies;

57 But turned back, and dealt unfaithfully like their fathers; they were turned aside like a deceitful bow.

58 For they provoked him to anger with their high places, and moved him to jealousy with their graven images.

59 When God heard this, he was wroth, and greatly abhorred Israel:

60 So that he forsook the tabernacle of Shiloh, the tent which he placed among men;

61 And delivered his strength into captivity, and his glory into the enemy's hand.

62 He gave his people over also unto the sword; and was wroth with his inheritance.

63 The fire consumed their young men; and their maidens were not given to marriage.

64 Their priests fell by the sword; and their widows made no lamentation.

65 Then the Lord awaked as one out of sleep, and like a mighty man that shouteth by reason of wine.

66 And he smote his enemies in the hinder parts; he put them to a perpetual reproach.

67 Moreover he refused the tabernacle of Joseph, and chose not the tribe of Ephraim;

68 But chose the tribe of Judah, the mount Zion which he loved.

69 And he built his sanctuary like high palaces, like the earth which he hath established for ever.

70 He chose David also his servant, and took him from the sheepfolds;

71 From following the ewes great with young he brought him to feed Jacob his people, and Israel his inheritance.

72 So he fed them according to the integrity of his heart; and guided them by the skillfulness of his hands.

## PSALM 79

*The desolation of Jerusalem.*

A Psalm of Asaph.

1 O God, the heathen are come into thine inheritance; thy holy temple have they defiled; they have laid Jerusalem on heaps.

2 The dead bodies of thy servants have they given to be meat unto the fowls of the heaven, the flesh of thy saints unto the beasts of the earth.

3 Their blood have they shed like water round about Jerusalem; and there was none to bury them.

4 We are become a reproach to our neighbors, a scorn and derision to them that are round about us.

5 How long, Lord? wilt thou be angry for ever? shall thy jealousy burn like fire?

6 Pour out thy wrath upon the heathen that have not known thee, and upon the kingdoms that have not called upon thy name.

7 For they have devoured Jacob, and laid waste his dwelling place.

8 O remember not against us former iniquities; let thy tender mercies speedily prevent us; for we are brought very low.

9 Help us, O God of our salvation, for the glory of thy name; and deliver us, and purge away our sins, for thy name's sake.

10 Wherefore should the heathen say, Where is their God? let him be known among the heathen in our sight by the revenging of the blood of thy servants which is shed.

11 Let the sighing of the prisoner come before thee; according to the greatness of thy power preserve thou those that are appointed to die;

12 And render unto our neighbors sevenfold into their bosom their reproach, wherewith they have reproached thee, O Lord.

13 So we thy people and sheep of thy pasture will give thee thanks for ever; we will show forth thy praise to all generations.

## PSALM 80

*A complaint for Israel—David prayeth for deliverance.*

To the chief Musician upon Shoshannim-Eduth, A Psalm of Asaph.

1 Give ear, O Shepherd of Israel, thou that leadest Joseph like a flock; thou that dwellest between the cherubim, shine forth.

2 Before Ephraim and Benjamin and Manasseh stir up thy strength, and come and save us.

3 Turn us again, O God, and cause thy face to shine; and we shall be saved.

4 O Lord God of hosts, how long wilt

thou be angry against the prayer of thy people?

5 Thou feedest them with the bread of tears; and givest them tears to drink in great measure.

6 Thou makest us a strife unto our neighbors; and our enemies laugh among themselves.

7 Turn us again, O God of hosts, and cause thy face to shine; and we shall be saved.

8 Thou hast brought a vine out of Egypt; thou hast cast out the heathen, and planted it.

9 Thou preparedst room before it, and didst cause it to take deep root, and it filled the land.

10 The hills were covered with the shadow of it, and the boughs thereof were like the goodly cedars.

11 She sent out her boughs unto the sea, and her branches unto the river.

12 Why hast thou then broken down her hedges, so that all they which pass by the way do pluck her?

13 The boar out of the wood doth waste it, and the wild beast of the field doth devour it.

14 Return, we beseech thee, O God of hosts; look down from heaven, and behold, and visit this vine;

15 And the vineyard which thy right hand hath planted, and the branch that thou madest strong for thyself.

16 It is burned with fire, it is cut down; they perish at the rebuke of thy countenance.

17 Let thy hand be upon the man of thy right hand, upon the son of man whom thou madest strong for thyself.

18 So will not we go back from thee; quicken us, and we will call upon thy name.

19 Turn us again, O Lord God of hosts, cause thy face to shine; and we shall be saved.

## PSALM 81

*An exhortation to praise God.*

To the chief Musician upon Gittith, A Psalm of Asaph.

1 Sing aloud unto God our strength; make a joyful noise unto the God of Jacob.

2 Take a psalm, and bring hither the timbrel, the pleasant harp with the psaltery.

3 Blow up the trumpet in the new moon, in the time appointed, on our solemn feast day.

4 For this was a statute for Israel, and a law of the God of Jacob.

5 This he ordained in Joseph for a testimony, when he went out through the land of Egypt; where I heard a language that I understood not.

6 I removed his shoulder from the burden; his hands were delivered from the pots.

7 Thou calledst in trouble, and I delivered thee; I answered thee in the secret place of thunder; I proved thee at the waters of Meribah. Selah.

8 Hear, O my people, and I will testify unto thee; O Israel, if thou wilt hearken unto me;

9 There shall no strange god be in thee; neither shalt thou worship any strange god.

10 I am the Lord thy God, which brought thee out of the land of Egypt; open thy mouth wide, and I will fill it.

11 But my people would not hearken to my voice; and Israel would none of me.

12 So I gave them up unto their own hearts' lust; and they walked in their own counsels.

13 Oh that my people had hearkened unto me, and Israel had walked in my ways!

14 I should soon have subdued their enemies, and turned my hand against their adversaries.

15 The haters of the Lord should have submitted themselves unto him; but their time should have endured for ever.

16 He should have fed them also with the finest of the wheat; and with honey out of the rock should I have satisfied thee.

## PSALM 82

*A prayer for judgment.*

A Psalm of Asaph.

1 God standeth in the congregation of the mighty; he judgeth among the gods.

2 How long will ye suffer them to judge unjustly, and accept the persons of the wicked? Selah.

3 Defend the poor and fatherless; do justice to the afflicted and needy.

4 Deliver the poor and needy; rid them out of the hand of the wicked.

5 They know not, neither will they understand; they walk on in darkness; all the foundations of the earth are out of course.

6 I have said, Ye are gods; and all of you are children of the Most High.

7 But ye shall die like men, and fall like one of the princes.

8 Arise, O God, judge the earth; for thou shalt inherit all nations.

## PSALM 83

*A prayer against them that oppress.*

A Song or Psalm of Asaph.

1 Keep not thou silence, O God; hold not thy peace, and be not still, O God.

2 For, lo, thine enemies make a tumult; and they that hate thee have lifted up the head.

3 They have taken crafty counsel against thy people, and consulted against thy hidden ones.

4 They have said, Come, and let us cut them off from being a nation; that the name of Israel may be no more in remembrance.

5 For they have consulted together with one consent; they are confederate against thee;

6 The tabernacles of Edom, and the Ishmaelites; of Moab, and the Hagarenes;

7 Gebal, and Ammon, and Amalek; the Philistines with the inhabitants of Tyre;

8 Assur also is joined with them; they have holpen the children of Lot. Selah.

9 Do unto them as unto the Midianites; as to Sisera, as to Jabin, at the brook of Kishon;

10 Which perished at En-dor; they became as dung for the earth.

11 Make their nobles like Oreb, and like Zeeb; yea, all their princes as Zebah, and as Zalmunna;

12 Who said, Let us take to ourselves the houses of God in possession.

13 O my God, make them like a wheel; as the stubble before the wind.

14 As the fire burneth a wood, and as the flame setteth the mountains on fire;

15 So persecute them with thy tempest, and make them afraid with thy storm.

16 Fill their faces with shame; that they may seek thy name, O Lord.

17 Let them be confounded and troubled for ever; yea, let them be put to shame, and perish;

18 That men may know that thou, whose name alone is JEHOVAH, art the Most High over all the earth.

## PSALM 84

*Blessedness of communion with God.*

To the chief Musician upon Gittith, A Psalm for the sons of Korah.

1 How amiable are thy tabernacles, O Lord of hosts!

2 My soul longeth, yea, even fainteth for the courts of the Lord; my heart and my flesh crieth out for the living God.

3 Yea, the sparrow hath found a house, and the swallow a nest for herself, where she may lay her young, even thine altars, O Lord of hosts, my King, and my God.

4 Blessed are they that dwell in thy house; they will be still praising thee. Selah.

5 Blessed is the man whose strength is in thee; in whose heart are the ways of them.

6 Who passing through the valley of Baca make it a well; the rain also filleth the pools.

7 They go from strength to strength, every one of them in Zion appeareth before God.

8 O Lord God of hosts, hear my prayer; give ear, O God of Jacob. Selah.

9 Behold, O God our shield, and look upon the face of thine anointed.

10 For a day in thy courts is better than a thousand. I had rather be a doorkeeper in the house of my God, than to dwell in the tents of wickedness.

11 For the Lord God is a sun and shield; the Lord will give grace and glory; no good thing will he withhold from them that walk uprightly.

12 O Lord of hosts, blessed is the man that trusteth in thee.

## PSALM 85

*Return from captivity foretold—Reign of righteousness.*

To the chief Musician, a Psalm for the sons of Korah.

1 Lord, thou hast been favorable unto thy land; thou hast brought back the captivity of Jacob.

2 Thou hast forgiven the iniquity of thy people, thou hast covered all their sin. Selah.

3 Thou hast taken away all thy wrath; thou hast turned thyself from the fierceness of thine anger.

4 Turn us, O God of our salvation,

and cause thine anger toward us to cease.

5 Wilt thou be angry with us for ever? wilt thou draw out thine anger to all generations?

6 Wilt thou not revive us again; that thy people may rejoice in thee?

7 Show us thy mercy, O Lord, and grant us thy salvation.

8 I will hear what God the Lord will speak; for he will speak peace unto his people, and to his saints; but let them not turn again to folly.

9 Surely his salvation is nigh them that fear him; that glory may dwell in our land.

10 Mercy and truth are met together; righteousness and peace have kissed each other.

11 Truth shall spring out of the earth; and righteousness shall look down from heaven.

12 Yea, the Lord shall give that which is good; and our land shall yield her increase.

13 Righteousness shall go before him; and shall set us in the way of his steps.

## PSALM 86

*Final triumph of God's government.*
A Prayer of David.

1 Bow down thine ear, O Lord, hear me; for I am poor and needy.

2 Preserve my soul; for I am holy; O thou my God, save thy servant that trusteth in thee.

3 Be merciful unto me, O Lord; for I cry unto thee daily.

4 Rejoice the soul of thy servant; for unto thee, O Lord, do I lift up my soul.

5 For thou, Lord, art good, and ready to forgive; and plenteous in mercy unto all them that call upon thee.

6 Give ear, O Lord, unto my prayer; and attend to the voice of my supplications.

7 In the day of my trouble I will call upon thee; for thou wilt answer me.

8 Among the gods there is none like unto thee, O Lord; neither are there any works like unto thy works.

9 All nations whom thou hast made shall come and worship before thee, O Lord; and shall glorify thy name.

10 For thou art great, and doest wondrous things; thou art God alone.

11 Teach me thy way, O Lord; I will walk in thy truth; unite my heart to fear thy name.

12 I will praise thee, O Lord my God, with all my heart; and I will glorify thy name for evermore.

13 For great is thy mercy toward me; and thou hast delivered my soul from the lowest hell.

14 O God, the proud are risen against me, and the assemblies of violent men have sought after my soul; and have not set thee before them.

15 But thou, O Lord, art a God full of compassion, and gracious, longsuffering, and plenteous in mercy and truth.

16 O turn unto me, and have mercy upon me; give thy strength unto thy servant, and save the son of thine handmaid.

17 Show me a token for good; that they which hate me may see it, and be ashamed; because thou, Lord, hast holpen me, and comforted me.

## PSALM 87

*The glory of Zion.*
A Psalm or Song for the sons of Korah.

1 His foundation is in the holy mountains.

2 The Lord loveth the gates of Zion more than all the dwellings of Jacob.

3 Glorious things are spoken of thee, O city of God. Selah.

4 I will make mention of Rahab and Babylon to them that know me; behold Philistia, and Tyre, with Ethiopia; this man was born there.

5 And of Zion it shall be said, This and that man was born in her; and the highest himself shall establish her.

6 The Lord shall count, when he writeth up the people, that this man was born there. Selah.

7 As well the singers as the players on instruments shall be there; all my springs are in thee.

## PSALM 88

*A prayer of complaint.*
A Song or Psalm for the sons of Korah, to the chief Musician upon Mahalath Leannoth, Maschil of Heman the Ezrahite.

1 O Lord God of my salvation, I have cried day and night before thee;

2 Let my prayer come before thee; incline thine ear unto my cry;

3 For my soul is full of troubles; and my life draweth nigh unto the grave.

4 I am counted with them that go down into the pit; I am as a man that hath no strength;

5 Free among the dead, like the

slain that lie in the grave, whom thou rememberest no more; and they are cut off from thy hand.

6 Thou hast laid me in the lowest pit, in darkness, in the deeps.

7 Thy wrath lieth hard upon me, and thou hast afflicted me with all thy waves. Selah.

8 Thou hast put away mine acquaintance far from me; thou hast made me an abomination unto them; I am shut up, and I cannot come forth.

9 Mine eye mourneth by reason of affliction; Lord, I have called daily upon thee, I have stretched out my hands unto thee.

10 Wilt thou show wonders to the dead? shall the dead arise and praise thee? Selah.

11 Shall thy loving-kindness be declared in the grave? or thy faithfulness in destruction?

12 Shall thy wonders be known in the dark? and thy righteousness in the land of forgetfulness?

13 But unto thee have I cried, O Lord; and in the morning shall my prayer prevent thee.

14 Lord, why castest thou off my soul? why hidest thou thy face from me?

15 I am afflicted and ready to die from my youth up; while I suffer thy terrors I am distracted.

16 Thy fierce wrath goeth over me; thy terrors have cut me off.

17 They came round about me daily like water; they compassed me about together.

18 Lover and friend hast thou put far from me, and mine acquaintance into darkness.

## PSALM 89

*God praised for the establishment of his covenant.*

Maschil of Ethan the Ezrahite.

1 I will sing of the mercies of the Lord for ever, with my mouth will I make known thy faithfulness to all generations.

2 For I have said, Mercy shall be built up for ever; thy faithfulness shalt thou establish in the very heavens.

3 I have made a covenant with my chosen, I have sworn unto David my servant,

4 Thy seed will I establish for ever, and build up thy throne to all generations. Selah.

5 And the heavens shall praise thy wonders, O Lord; thy faithfulness also in the congregation of the saints.

6 For who in the heaven can be compared unto the Lord? who among the sons of the mighty can be likened unto the Lord?

7 God is greatly to be feared in the assembly of the saints, and to be had in reverence of all them that are about him.

8 O Lord God of hosts, who is a strong Lord like unto thee? or to thy faithfulness round about thee?

9 Thou rulest the raging of the sea; when the waves thereof arise, thou stillest them.

10 Thou hast broken Rahab in pieces, as one that is slain; thou hast scattered thine enemies with thy strong arm.

11 The heavens are thine, the earth also is thine; as for the world and the fullness thereof, thou hast founded them.

12 The north and the south thou hast created them; Tabor and Hermon shall rejoice in thy name.

13 Thou hast a mighty arm; strong is thy hand, and high is thy right hand.

14 Justice and judgment are the habitation of thy throne; mercy and truth shall go before thy face.

15 Blessed is the people that know the joyful sound; they shall walk, O Lord, in the light of thy countenance.

16 In thy name shall they rejoice all the day; and in thy righteousness shall they be exalted.

17 For thou art the glory of their strength; and in thy favor our horn shall be exalted.

18 For the Lord is our defense; and the Holy One of Israel is our King.

19 Then thou spakest in vision to thy Holy One, and saidst, I have laid help upon one that is mighty; I have exalted one chosen out of the people.

20 I have found David my servant; with my holy oil have I anointed him;

21 With whom my hand shall be established; mine arm also shall strengthen him.

22 The enemy shall not exact upon him; nor the son of wickedness afflict him.

23 And I will beat down his foes before his face, and plague them that hate him.

24 But my faithfulness and my

mercy shall be with him; and in my name shall his horn be exalted.

25 I will set his hand also in the sea, and his right hand in the rivers.

26 He shall cry unto me, Thou art my Father, my God, and the Rock of my salvation.

27 Also I will make him my first-born, higher than the kings of the earth.

28 My mercy will I keep for him for evermore, and my covenant shall stand fast with him.

29 His seed also will I make to endure for ever, and his throne as the days of heaven.

30 If his children forsake my law, and walk not in my judgments;

31 If they break my statutes, and keep not my commandments;

32 Then will I visit their transgression with the rod, and their iniquity with stripes.

33 Nevertheless my loving-kindness will I not utterly take from him, nor suffer my faithfulness to fail.

34 My covenant will I not break, nor alter the thing that is gone out of my lips.

35 Once have I sworn by my holiness that I will not lie unto David.

36 His seed shall endure for ever, and his throne as the sun before me.

37 It shall be established for ever as the moon, and as a faithful witness in heaven. Selah.

38 But thou hast cast off and abhorred, thou hast been wroth with thine anointed.

39 Thou hast made void the covenant of thy servant; thou hast profaned his crown by casting it to the ground.

40 Thou hast broken down all his hedges; thou hast brought his strongholds to ruin.

41 All that pass by the way spoil him; he is a reproach to his neighbors.

42 Thou hast set up the right hand of his adversaries; thou hast made all his enemies to rejoice.

43 Thou hast also turned the edge of his sword, and hast not made him to stand in the battle.

44 Thou hast made his glory to cease, and cast his throne down to the ground.

45 The days of his youth hast thou shortened; thou hast covered him with shame. Selah.

46 How long, Lord? wilt thou hide thyself for ever? shall thy wrath burn like fire?

47 Remember how short my time is; wherefore hast thou made all men in vain?

48 What man is he that liveth, and shall not see death? shall he deliver his soul from the hand of the grave? Selah.

49 Lord, where are thy former loving-kindnesses, which thou swarest unto David in thy truth?

50 Remember, Lord, the reproach of thy servants; how I do bear in my bosom the reproach of all the mighty people;

51 Wherewith thine enemies have reproached, O Lord; wherewith they have reproached the footsteps of thine anointed.

52 Blessed be the Lord for evermore. Amen, and Amen.

## PSALM 90

*The prayer of Moses.*

A Prayer of Moses the man of God.

1 Lord, thou hast been our dwelling place in all generations.

2 Before the mountains were brought forth, or ever thou hadst formed the earth and the world, even from everlasting to everlasting, thou art God.

3 Thou turnest man to destruction; and sayest, Return, ye children of men.

4 For a thousand years in thy sight are but as yesterday when it is past, and as a watch in the night.

5 Thou carriest them away as with a flood; they are as a sleep; in the morning they are like grass which groweth up.

6 In the morning it flourisheth, and groweth up; in the evening it is cut down, and withereth.

7 For we are consumed by thine anger, and by thy wrath are we troubled.

8 Thou hast set our iniquities before thee, our secret sins in the light of thy countenance.

9 For all our days are passed away in thy wrath; we spend our years as a tale that is told.

10 The days of our years are threescore years and ten; and if by reason of strength they be fourscore years, yet is their strength labour and sorrow; for it is soon cut off, and we fly away.

11 Who knoweth the power of thine

anger? even according to thy fear, so is thy wrath.

12 So teach us to number our days, that we may apply our hearts unto wisdom.

13 Return us, O Lord. How long wilt thou hide thy face from thy servants? and let them repent of all their hard speeches they have spoken concerning thee.

14 O satisfy us early with thy mercy; that we may rejoice and be glad all our days.

15 Make us glad according to the days wherein thou hast afflicted us, and the years wherein we have seen evil.

16 Let thy work appear unto thy servants, and thy glory unto their children.

17 And let the beauty of the Lord our God be upon us; and establish thou the work of our hands upon us; yea, the work of our hands establish thou it.

## PSALM 91

*The security of the Godly.*

1 He that dwelleth in the secret place of the Most High shall abide under the shadow of the Almighty.

2 I will say of the Lord, He is my refuge and my fortress; my God; in him will I trust.

3 Surely he shall deliver thee from the snare of the fowler, and from the noisome pestilence.

4 He shall cover thee with his feathers, and under his wings shalt thou trust; his truth shall be thy shield and buckler.

5 Thou shalt not be afraid for the terror by night; nor for the arrow that flieth by day;

6 Nor for the pestilence that walketh in darkness; nor for the destruction that wasteth at noonday.

7 A thousand shall fall at thy side, and ten thousand at thy right hand; but it shall not come nigh thee.

8 Only with thine eyes shalt thou behold and see the reward of the wicked.

9 Because thou hast made the Lord, which is my refuge, even the Most High, thy habitation;

10 There shall no evil befall thee, neither shall any plague come nigh thy dwelling.

11 For he shall give his angels charge over thee, to keep thee in all thy ways.

12 They shall bear thee up in their hands, lest thou dash thy foot against a stone.

13 Thou shalt tread upon the lion and adder; the young lion and the dragon shalt thou trample under feet.

14 Because he hath set his love upon me, therefore will I deliver him; I will set him on high, because he hath known my name.

15 He shall call upon me, and I will answer him; I will be with him in trouble; I will deliver him, and honor him.

16 With long life will I satisfy him, and show him my salvation.

## PSALM 92

*God's goodness portrayed.*

A Psalm or Song for the Sabbath day.

1 It is a good thing to give thanks unto the Lord, and to sing praises unto thy name, O Most High;

2 To show forth thy loving-kindness in the morning, and thy faithfulness every night,

3 Upon an instrument of ten strings, and upon the psaltery; upon the harp with a solemn sound.

4 For thou, Lord, hast made me glad through thy work; I will triumph in the works of thy hands.

5 O Lord, how great are thy works! and thy thoughts are very deep.

6 A brutish man knoweth not; neither doth a fool understand this.

7 When the wicked spring as the grass, and when all the workers of iniquity do flourish; it is that they shall be destroyed for ever;

8 But thou, Lord, art most high for evermore.

9 For, lo, thine enemies, O Lord, for, lo, thine enemies shall perish; all the workers of iniquity shall be scattered.

10 But my horn shalt thou exalt like the horn of a unicorn; I shall be anointed with fresh oil.

11 Mine eye also shall see my desire on mine enemies, and mine ears shall hear my desire of the wicked that rise up against me.

12 The righteous shall flourish like the palm tree; he shall grow like a cedar in Lebanon.

13 Those that he planted in the house of the Lord shall flourish in the courts of our God.

14 They shall still bring forth fruit in old age; they shall be fat and flourishing;

15 To show that the Lord is upright; he is my rock, and there is no unrighteousness in him.

## PSALM 93

*The majesty and power of God.*

1 The Lord reigneth, he is clothed with majesty; the Lord is clothed with strength, wherewith he hath girded himself; the world also is stablished, that it cannot be moved.

2 Thy throne is established of old; thou art from everlasting.

3 The floods have lifted up, O Lord, the floods have lifted up their voice; the floods lift up their waves.

4 The Lord on high is mightier than the noise of many waters, yea, than the mighty waves of the sea.

5 Thy testimonies are very sure; holiness becometh thine house, O Lord, for ever.

## PSALM 94

*The prophet, calling for justice, teacheth God's providence.*

1 O Lord God, to whom vengeance belongeth; O God, to whom vengeance belongeth, show thyself.

2 Lift up thyself, thou Judge of the earth; render a reward to the proud.

3 Lord, how long shall the wicked, how long shall the wicked triumph?

4 How long shall they utter and speak hard things? and all the workers of iniquity boast themselves?

5 They break in pieces thy people, O Lord, and afflict thine heritage.

6 They slay the widow and the stranger, and murder the fatherless.

7 Yet they say, The Lord shall not see, neither shall the God of Jacob regard it.

8 Understand, ye brutish among the people; and ye fools, when will ye be wise?

9 He that planted the ear, shall he not hear? he that formed the eye, shall he not see?

10 He that chastiseth the heathen, shall not he correct? he that teacheth man knowledge, shall not he know?

11 The Lord knoweth the thoughts of man, that they are vanity.

12 Blessed is the man whom thou chastenest, O Lord, and teachest him out of thy law;

13 That thou mayest give him rest from the days of adversity, until the pit be digged for the wicked.

14 For the Lord will not cast off his people; neither will he forsake his inheritance.

15 But judgment shall return unto righteousness; and all the upright in heart shall follow it.

16 Who will rise up for me against the evildoers? or who will stand up for me against the workers of iniquity?

17 Unless the Lord had been my help, my soul had almost dwelt in silence.

18 When I said, My foot slippeth; thy mercy, O Lord, held me up.

19 In the multitude of my thoughts within me thy comforts delight my soul.

20 Shall the throne of iniquity have fellowship with thee, which frameth mischief by a law?

21 They gather themselves together against the soul of the righteous, and condemn the innocent blood.

22 But the Lord is my defense; and my God is the rock of my refuge.

23 And he shall bring upon them their own iniquity, and shall cut them off in their own wickedness; yea, the Lord our God shall cut them off.

## PSALM 95

*An exhortation to praise God.*

1 O come, let us sing unto the Lord; let us make a joyful noise to the rock of our salvation.

2 Let us come before his presence with thanksgiving, and make a joyful noise unto him with psalms.

3 For the Lord is a great God, and a great King above all gods.

4 In his hand are the deep places of the earth; the strength of the hills is his also.

5 The sea is his, and he made it; and his hands formed the dry land.

6 O come, let us worship and bow down; let us kneel before the Lord our maker.

7 For he is our God; and we are the people of his pasture, and the sheep of his hand. Today if ye will hear his voice,

8 Harden not your heart, as in the provocation, and as in the day of temptation in the wilderness;

9 When your fathers tempted me, proved me, and saw my work.

10 Forty years long was I grieved

with this generation, and said, It is a people that do err in their heart, and they have not known my ways;

11 Unto whom I sware in my wrath that they should not enter into my rest.

## PSALM 96

*An exhortation to praise God.*

1 O sing unto the Lord a new song; sing unto the Lord, all the earth.

2 Sing unto the Lord, bless his name; show forth his salvation from day to day.

3 Declare his glory among the heathen, his wonders among all people.

4 For the Lord is great, and greatly to be praised; he is to be feared above all gods.

5 For all the gods of the nations are idols; but the Lord made the heavens.

6 Honor and majesty are before him; strength and beauty are in his sanctuary.

7 Give unto the Lord, O ye kindreds of the people, give unto the Lord glory and strength.

8 Give unto the Lord the glory due unto his name; bring an offering, and come into his courts.

9 O worship the Lord in the beauty of holiness; fear before him, all the earth.

10 Say among the heathen that the Lord reigneth; the world also shall be established that it shall not be moved; he shall judge the people righteously.

11 Let the heavens rejoice, and let the earth be glad; let the sea roar, and the fullness thereof.

12 Let the field be joyful, and all that is therein; then shall all the trees of the wood rejoice

13 Before the Lord; for he cometh, for he cometh to judge the earth; he shall judge the world with righteousness, and the people with his truth.

## PSALM 97

*The majesty of God's power.*

1 The Lord reigneth; let the earth rejoice; let the multitude of isles be glad thereof.

2 Clouds and darkness are round about him; righteousness and judgment are the habitation of his throne.

3 A fire goeth before him, and burneth up his enemies round about.

4 His lightnings enlightened the world; the earth saw, and trembled.

5 The hills melted like wax at the presence of the Lord, at the presence of the Lord of the whole earth.

6 The heavens declare his righteousness, and all the people see his glory.

7 Confounded be all they that serve graven images, that boast themselves of idols; worship him, all ye gods.

8 Zion heard, and was glad; and the daughters of Judah rejoiced because of thy judgments, O Lord.

9 For thou, Lord, art high above all the earth; thou art exalted far above all gods.

10 Ye that love the Lord, hate evil; he preserveth the souls of his saints; he delivereth them out of the hand of the wicked.

11 Light is sown for the righteous, and gladness for the upright in heart.

12 Rejoice in the Lord, ye righteous; and give thanks at the remembrance of his holiness.

## PSALM 98

*All creatures exhorted to praise God.*

A Psalm.

1 O sing unto the Lord a new song; for he hath done marvelous things; his right hand, and his holy arm, hath gotten him the victory.

2 The Lord hath made known his salvation; his righteousness hath he openly shown in the sight of the heathen.

3 He hath remembered his mercy and his truth toward the house of Israel; all the ends of the earth have seen the salvation of our God.

4 Make a joyful noise unto the Lord, all the earth; make a loud noise, and rejoice, and sing praise.

5 Sing unto the Lord with the harp; with the harp, and the voice of a psalm.

6 With trumpets and sound of cornet make a joyful noise before the Lord, the King.

7 Let the sea roar, and the fullness thereof; the world, and they that dwell therein.

8 Let the floods clap their hands; let the hills be joyful together

9 Before the Lord; for he cometh to judge the earth; with righteousness shall he judge the world, and the people with equity.

## PSALM 99

*God to be praised in Zion.*

1 The Lord reigneth; let the people tremble; he sitteth between the cherubim; let the earth be moved.

2 The Lord is great in Zion; and he is high above all the people.

3 Let them praise thy great and terrible name; for it is holy.

4 The king's strength also loveth judgment; thou dost establish equity, thou executest judgment and righteousness in Jacob.

5 Exalt ye the Lord our God, and worship at his footstool; for he is holy.

6 Moses and Aaron among his priests, and Samuel among them that call upon his name; they called upon the Lord, and he answered them.

7 He spake unto them in the cloudy pillar; they kept his testimonies, and the ordinance that he gave them.

8 Thou answeredst them, O Lord our God; thou wast a God that forgavest them, though thou tookest vengeance of their inventions.

9 Exalt the Lord our God, and worship at his holy hill; for the Lord our God is holy.

## PSALM 100

*An exhortation to praise God with gladness.*

A Psalm of praise.

1 Make a joyful noise unto the Lord, all ye lands.

2 Serve the Lord with gladness; come before his presence with singing.

3 Know ye that the Lord he is God; it is he that hath made us, and not we ourselves; we are his people, and the sheep of his pasture.

4 Enter into his gates with thanksgiving, and into his courts with praise; be thankful unto him, and bless his name.

5 For the Lord is good; his mercy is everlasting; and his truth endureth to all generations.

## PSALM 101

*David maketh a profession of godliness.*

A Psalm of David.

1 I will sing of mercy and judgment; unto thee, O Lord, will I sing.

2 I will behave myself wisely in a perfect way. O when wilt thou come unto me? I will walk within my house with a perfect heart.

3 I will set no wicked thing before mine eyes; I hate the work of them that turn aside; it shall not cleave to me.

4 A froward heart shall depart from me; I will not know a wicked person.

5 Whoso privily slandereth his neighbor, him will I cut off; him that hath a high look and a proud heart will not I suffer.

6 Mine eyes shall be upon the faithful of the land, that they may dwell with me; he that walketh in a perfect way, he shall serve me.

7 He that worketh deceit shall not dwell within my house; he that telleth lies shall not tarry in my sight.

8 I will early destroy all the wicked of the land; that I may cut off all wicked doers from the city of the Lord.

## PSALM 102

*Comfort in the eternity and mercy of God.*

A prayer of the afflicted, when he is overwhelmed, and poureth out his complaint before the Lord.

1 Hear my prayer, O Lord, and let my cry come unto thee.

2 Hide not thy face from me in the day when I am in trouble; incline thine ear unto me; in the day when I call answer me speedily.

3 For my days are consumed like smoke, and my bones are burned as an hearth.

4 My heart is smitten, and withered like grass; so that I forget to eat my bread.

5 By reason of the voice of my groaning my bones cleave to my skin.

6 I am like a pelican of the wilderness; I am like an owl of the desert.

7 I watch, and am as a sparrow alone upon the housetop.

8 Mine enemies reproach me all the day; and they that are mad against me are sworn against me.

9 For I have eaten ashes like bread, and mingled my drink with weeping,

10 Because of thine indignation and thy wrath; for thou hast lifted me up, and cast me down.

11 My days are like a shadow that declineth; and I am withered like grass.

12 But thou, O Lord, shalt endure for ever; and thy remembrance unto all generations.

13 Thou shalt arise, and have mercy

upon Zion; for the time to favor her, yea, the set time, is come.

14 For thy servants take pleasure in her stones, and favor the dust thereof.

15 So the heathen shall fear the name of the Lord, and all the kings of the earth thy glory.

16 When the Lord shall build up Zion, he shall appear in his glory.

17 He will regard the prayer of the destitute, and not despise their prayer.

18 This shall be written for the generation to come; and the people which shall be gathered shall praise the Lord.

19 For he hath looked down from the height of his sanctuary; from heaven did the Lord behold the earth;

20 To hear the groaning of the prisoner; to loose those that are appointed to death;

21 To declare the name of the Lord in Zion, and his praise in Jerusalem;

22 When the people are gathered together, and the kingdoms, to serve the Lord.

23 He weakened my strength in the way; he shortened my days.

24 I said, O my God, take me not away in the midst of my days; thy years are throughout all generations.

25 Of old hast thou laid the foundation of the earth; and the heavens are the work of thy hands.

26 They shall perish, but thou shalt endure; yea, all of them shall wax old like a garment; as a vesture shalt thou change them, and they shall be changed;

27 But thou art the same, and thy years shall have no end.

28 The children of thy servants shall continue, and their seed shall be established before thee.

## PSALM 103

*An exhortation to praise God for his mercy.*

A Psalm of David.

1 Bless the Lord, O my soul; and all that is within me, bless his holy name.

2 Bless the Lord, O my soul, and forget not all his benefits;

3 Who forgiveth all thine iniquities; who healeth all thy diseases;

4 Who redeemeth thy life from destruction; who crowneth thee with loving-kindness and tender mercies;

5 Who satisfieth thy mouth with good things; so that thy youth is renewed like the eagle's.

6 The Lord executeth righteousness and judgment for all that are oppressed.

7 He made known his ways unto Moses, his acts unto the children of Israel.

8 The Lord is merciful and gracious, slow to anger, and plenteous in mercy.

9 He will not always chide; neither will he keep his anger for ever.

10 He hath not dealt with us after our sins; nor rewarded us according to our iniquities.

11 For as the heaven is high above the earth, so great is his mercy toward them that fear him.

12 As far as the east is from the west, so far hath he removed our transgressions from us.

13 Like as a father pitieth his children, so the Lord pitieth them that fear him.

14 For he knoweth our frame; he remembereth that we are dust.

15 As for man, his days are as grass; as a flower of the field, so he flourisheth.

16 For the wind passeth over it, and it is gone, and the place thereof shall know it no more.

17 But the mercy of the Lord is from everlasting to everlasting upon them that fear him, and his righteousness unto children's children;

18 To such as keep his covenant, and to those that remember his commandments to do them.

19 The Lord hath prepared his throne in the heavens; and his kingdom ruleth over all.

20 Bless the Lord, ye his angels, that excel in strength, that do his commandments, hearkening unto the voice of his word.

21 Bless ye the Lord, all ye his hosts; ye ministers of his that do his pleasure.

22 Bless the Lord, all his works in all places of his dominion; bless the Lord, O my soul.

## PSALM 104

*Meditations upon the power, providence, and glory of God.*

1 Bless the Lord, O my soul. O Lord my God, thou art very great; thou art clothed with power and majesty;

2 Who coverest thyself with light as

with a garment; who stretchest out the heavens like a curtain;

3 Who layeth the beams of his chambers in the waters; who maketh the clouds his chariot; who walketh upon the wings of the wind;

4 Who maketh his angels spirits; his ministers a flaming fire;

5 Who laid the foundations of the earth, that it should not be removed for ever.

6 Thou coveredst it with the deep as with a garment; the waters stood above the mountains.

7 At thy rebuke they fled; at the voice of thy thunder they hasted away.

8 They go up by the mountains; they go down by the valleys unto the place which thou hast founded for them.

9 Thou hast set a bound that they may not pass over; that they turn not again to cover the earth.

10 He sendeth the springs into the valleys, which run among the hills.

11 They give drink to every beast of the field; the wild asses quench their thirst.

12 By them shall the fowls of the heaven have their habitation, which sing among the branches.

13 He watereth the hills from his chambers; the earth is satisfied with the fruit of thy works.

14 He causeth the grass to grow for the cattle, and herb for the service of man; that he may bring forth food out of the earth;

15 And wine that maketh glad the heart of man, and oil to make his face to shine, and bread which strengtheneth man's heart.

16 The trees of the Lord are full of sap; the cedars of Lebanon, which he hath planted;

17 Where the birds make their nests; as for the stork, the fir trees are her house.

18 The high hills are a refuge for the wild goats; and the rocks for the conies.

19 He appointed the moon for seasons; the sun knoweth his going down.

20 Thou makest darkness, and it is night; wherein all the beasts of the forest do creep forth.

21 The young lions roar after their prey, and seek their meat from God.

22 The sun ariseth, they gather themselves together, and lay them down in their dens.

23 Man goeth forth unto his work and to his labour until the evening.

24 O Lord, how manifold are thy works! in wisdom hast thou made them all; the earth is full of thy riches.

25 So is this great and wide sea, wherein are things creeping innumerable, both small and great beasts.

26 There go the ships; and thou hast made leviathan to play therein.

27 These wait all upon thee; that thou mayest give them their meat in due season.

28 That thou givest them they gather; thou openest thine hand, they are filled with good.

29 Thou hidest thy face, they are troubled; thou takest away their breath, they die, and return to their dust.

30 Thou sendest forth thy Spirit, they are created; and thou renewest the face of the earth.

31 The glory of the Lord shall endure for ever; the Lord shall rejoice in his works.

32 He looketh on the earth, and it trembleth; he toucheth the hills, and they smoke.

33 I will sing unto the Lord as long as I live; I will sing praise to my God while I have my being.

34 My meditation of him shall be sweet; I will be glad in the Lord.

35 Let the sinners be consumed out of the earth, and let the wicked be no more. Bless thou the Lord, O my soul. Praise ye the Lord.

## PSALM 105

*God's providence over Israel.*

1 O give thanks unto the Lord; call upon his name; make known his deeds among the people.

2 Sing unto him, sing psalms unto him; talk ye of all his wondrous works.

3 Glory ye in his holy name; let the heart of them rejoice that seek the Lord.

4 Seek the Lord, and his strength; seek his face evermore.

5 Remember his marvelous works that he hath done; his wonders, and the judgments of his mouth;

6 O ye seed of Abraham his servant, ye children of Jacob his chosen.

7 He is the Lord our God; his judgments are in all the earth.

8 He hath remembered his covenant

for ever, the word which he commanded to a thousand generations.

9 Which covenant he made with Abraham, and his oath unto Isaac;

10 And confirmed the same unto Jacob for a law, and to Israel for an everlasting covenant;

11 Saying, Unto thee will I give the land of Canaan, the lot of your inheritance;

12 When they were but a few men in number; yea, very few, and strangers in it.

13 When they went from one nation to another, from one kingdom to another people;

14 He suffered no man to do them wrong; yea, he reproved kings for their sakes;

15 Saying, Touch not mine anointed, and do my prophets no harm.

16 Moreover he called for a famine upon the land; he brake the whole staff of bread.

17 He sent a man before them, even Joseph, who was sold for a servant;

18 Whose feet they hurt with fetters; he was laid in iron;

19 Until the time that his word came; the word of the Lord tried him.

20 The king sent and loosed him; even the ruler of the people, and let him go free.

21 He made him lord of his house, and ruler of all his substance;

22 To bind his princes at his pleasure; and teach his senators wisdom.

23 Israel also came into Egypt; and Jacob sojourned in the land of Ham.

24 And he increased his people greatly; and made them stronger than their enemies.

25 He turned their heart to hate his people, to deal subtilely with his servants.

26 He sent Moses his servant; and Aaron whom he had chosen.

27 They showed his signs among them, and wonders in the land of Ham.

28 He sent darkness, and made it dark; and they rebelled not against his word.

29 He turned their waters into blood, and slew their fish.

30 Their land brought forth frogs in abundance, in the chambers of their kings.

31 He spake, and there came divers sorts of flies, and lice in all their coasts.

32 He gave them hail for rain, and flaming fire in their land.

33 He smote their vines also and their fig trees; and brake the trees of their coasts.

34 He spake, and the locusts came, and caterpillars, and that without number,

35 And did eat up all the herbs in their land, and devoured the fruit of their ground.

36 He smote also all the firstborn in their land, the chief of all their strength.

37 He brought them forth also with silver and gold; and there was not one feeble person among their tribes.

38 Egypt was glad when they departed; for the fear of them fell upon them.

39 He spread a cloud for a covering; and fire to give light in the night.

40 The people asked, and he brought quails, and satisfied them with the bread of heaven.

41 He opened the rock, and the waters gushed out; they ran in the dry places like a river.

42 For he remembered his holy promise unto Abraham his servant.

43 And he brought forth his people with joy, and his chosen with gladness;

44 And gave them the lands of the heathen; and they inherited the labour of the people;

45 That they might observe his statutes, and keep his laws. Praise ye the Lord.

## PSALM 106

*The story of Israel's rebellion, and God's mercy.*

1 Praise ye the Lord. O give thanks unto the Lord; for he is good; for his mercy endureth for ever.

2 Who can utter the mighty acts of the Lord? who can show forth all his praise?

3 Blessed are they that keep judgment, and he that doeth righteousness at all times.

4 Remember me, O Lord, with the favor of thy people; O visit me with thy salvation;

5 That I may see the good of thy chosen, that I may rejoice in the gladness of thy nation, that I may glory with thine inheritance.

6 We have sinned with our fathers,

we have committed iniquity, we have done wickedly.

7 Our fathers understood not thy wonders in Egypt; they remembered not the multitude of thy mercies; but provoked thee at the sea, at the Red sea.

8 Nevertheless he saved them for his name's sake, that he might make his mighty power to be known.

9 He rebuked the Red sea also, and it was dried up; so he led them through the depths, as through the wilderness.

10 And he saved them from the hand of him that hated them, and redeemed them from the hand of the enemy.

11 And the waters covered their enemies; there was not one of them left.

12 Then believed they his words; they sang his praise.

13 They soon forgat his works; they waited not for his counsel;

14 But lusted exceedingly in the wilderness, and tempted God in the desert.

15 And he gave them their request; but sent leanness into their soul.

16 They envied Moses also in the camp, and Aaron the saint of the Lord.

17 The earth opened and swallowed up Dathan and covered the company of Abiram.

18 And a fire was kindled in their company; the flame burned up the wicked.

19 They made a calf in Horeb, and worshiped the molten image.

20 Thus they changed their glory into the similitude of an ox that eateth grass.

21 They forgat God their savior, which had done great things in Egypt;

22 Wondrous works in the land of Ham, and terrible things by the Red sea.

23 Therefore he said that he would destroy them, had not Moses his chosen stood before him in the breach, to turn away his wrath, lest he should destroy them.

24 Yea, they despised the pleasant land, they believed not his word;

25 But murmured in their tents, and hearkened not unto the voice of the Lord.

26 Therefore he lifted up his hand against them, to overthrow them in the wilderness;

27 To overthrow their seed also among the nations, and to scatter them in the lands.

28 They joined themselves also unto Baal-peor, and ate the sacrifices of the dead.

29 Thus they provoked him to anger with their inventions; and the plague brake in upon them.

30 Then stood up Phinehas, and executed judgment; and so the plague was stayed.

31 And that was counted unto him for righteousness unto all generations for evermore.

32 They angered him also at the waters of strife, so that it went ill with Moses for their sakes;

33 Because they provoked his spirit, so that he spake unadvisedly with his lips.

34 They did not destroy the nations, concerning whom the Lord commanded them;

35 But were mingled among the heathen, and learned their works.

36 And they served their idols; which were a snare unto them.

37 Yea, they sacrificed their sons and their daughters unto devils,

38 And shed innocent blood, even the blood of their sons and of their daughters, whom they sacrificed unto the idols of Canaan; and the land was polluted with blood.

39 Thus were they defiled with their own works, and went a whoring with their own inventions.

40 Therefore was the wrath of the Lord kindled against his people, insomuch that he abhorred his own inheritance.

41 And he gave them into the hand of the heathen; and they that hated them ruled over them.

42 Their enemies also oppressed them, and they were brought into subjection under their hand.

43 Many times did he deliver them; but they provoked him with their counsel, and were brought low for their iniquity.

44 Nevertheless he regarded their affliction, when he heard their cry;

45 And he remembered for them his covenant, and spared his people according to the multitude of his mercies.

46 He made them also to be pitied of all those that carried them captive.

47 Save us, O Lord our God, and gather us from among the heathen, to

give thanks unto thy holy name, and to triumph in thy praise.

48 Blessed be the Lord God of Israel from everlasting to everlasting; and let all the people say, Amen. Praise ye the Lord.

## PSALM 107

*God's providence illustrated.*

1 O give thanks unto the Lord, for he is good; for his mercy endureth for ever.

2 Let the redeemed of the Lord say so, whom he hath redeemed from the hand of the enemy;

3 And gathered them out of the lands, from the east, and from the west, from the north, and from the south.

4 They wandered in the wilderness in a solitary way; they found no city to dwell in.

5 Hungry and thirsty, their soul fainted in them.

6 Then they cried unto the Lord in their trouble, and he delivered them out of their distresses.

7 And he led them forth by the right way, that they might go to a city of habitation.

8 Oh that men would praise the Lord for his goodness, and for his wonderful works to the children of men!

9 For he satisfieth the longing soul, and filleth the hungry soul with goodness.

10 Such as sit in darkness and in the shadow of death, being bound in affliction and iron;

11 Because they rebelled against the words of God, and contemned the counsel of the Most High;

12 Therefore he brought down their heart with labour; they fell down, and there was none to help.

13 Then they cried unto the Lord in their trouble, and he saved them out of their distresses.

14 He brought them out of darkness and the shadow of death, and brake their bands in sunder.

15 Oh that men would praise the Lord for his goodness, and for his wonderful works to the children of men!

16 For he hath broken the gates of brass, and cut the bars of iron in sunder.

17 Fools, because of their transgression, and because of their iniquities, are afflicted.

18 Their soul abhorreth all manner of meat; and they draw near unto the gates of death.

19 Then they cry unto the Lord in their trouble, and he saveth them out of their distresses.

20 He sent his word, and healed them, and delivered them from their destructions.

21 Oh that men would praise the Lord for his goodness, and for his wonderful works to the children of men!

22 And let them sacrifice the sacrifices of thanksgiving, and declare his works with rejoicing.

23 They that go down to the sea in ships, that do business in great waters;

24 These see the works of the Lord, and his wonders in the deep.

25 For he commandeth, and raiseth the stormy wind, which lifteth up the waves thereof.

26 They mount up to the heaven, they go down again to the depths; their soul is melted because of trouble.

27 They reel to and fro, and stagger like a drunken man, and are at their wit's end.

28 Then they cry unto the Lord in their trouble, and he bringeth them out of their distresses.

29 He maketh the storm a calm, so that the waves thereof are still.

30 Then are they glad because they be quiet; so he bringeth them unto their desired haven.

31 Oh that men would praise the Lord for his goodness, and for his wonderful works to the children of men!

32 Let them exalt him also in the congregation of the people, and praise him in the assembly of the elders.

33 He turneth rivers into a wilderness, and the watersprings into dry ground;

34 A fruitful land into barrenness, for the wickedness of them that dwell therein.

35 He turneth the wilderness into a standing water, and dry ground into watersprings.

36 And there he maketh the hungry to dwell, that they may prepare a city for habitation;

37 And sow the fields, and plant vineyards, which may yield fruits of increase.

38 He blesseth them also, so that

they are multiplied greatly; and suffereth not their cattle to decrease.

39 Again, they are minished and brought low through oppression, affliction, and sorrow.

40 He poureth contempt upon princes, and causeth them to wander in the wilderness, where there is no way.

41 Yet setteth he the poor on high from affliction, and maketh him families like a flock.

42 The righteous shall see it, and rejoice; and all iniquity shall stop her mouth.

43 Whoso is wise, and will observe these things, even they shall understand the loving-kindness of the Lord.

## PSALM 108

*David's confidence in God's help.*
A Song or Psalm of David.

1 O God, my heart is fixed; I will sing and give praise, even with my glory.

2 Awake, psaltery and harp; I myself will awake early.

3 I will praise thee, O Lord, among the people; and I will sing praises unto thee among the nations.

4 For thy mercy is great above the heavens; and thy truth reacheth unto the clouds.

5 Be thou exalted, O God, above the heavens; and thy glory above all the earth;

6 That thy beloved may be delivered; save with thy right hand, and answer me.

7 God hath spoken in his holiness; I will rejoice, I will divide Shechem, and mete out the valley of Succoth.

8 Gilead is mine; Manasseh is mine; Ephraim also is the strength of mine head; Judah is my lawgiver;

9 Moab is my washpot; over Edom will I cast out my shoe; over Philistia will I triumph.

10 Who will bring me into the strong city? who will lead me into Edom?

11 Wilt not thou, O God, who hast cast us off? and wilt not thou, O God, go forth with our hosts?

12 Give us help from trouble; for vain is the help of man.

13 Through God we shall do valiantly; for he it is that shall tread down our enemies.

## PSALM 109

*David complaineth of God's enemies—
Prayeth against them.*
To the chief Musician, A Psalm of David.

1 Hold not thy peace, O God of my praise;

2 For the mouth of the wicked and the mouth of the deceitful are opened against me; they have spoken against me with a lying tongue.

3 They compassed me about; they spake against me also, with words of hatred; and fought against me without a cause.

4 And, notwithstanding my love, they are my adversaries; yet I will continue in prayer for them.

5 And they have rewarded me evil for good, and hatred for my love.

6 Set thou a wicked man over them; and let Satan stand at his right hand.

7 When they shall be judged, let them be condemned; and let their prayer become sin.

8 Let their days be few; let another take their office.

9 Let their children be fatherless, and their wives widows.

10 Let their children be continually vagabonds, and beg; let them seek also out of their desolate places.

11 Let the extortioner catch all that they have; and let the stranger spoil their labour.

12 Let there be none to extend mercy unto them, neither let there be any to favor their fatherless children.

13 Let their posterity be cut off in the generation following; let their names be blotted out.

14 Let the iniquity of their fathers be remembered before the Lord; and let not the sin of their mothers be blotted out.

15 Let them be before the Lord continually, that he may cut off the memory of them from the earth.

16 Because they remembered not to show mercy, but persecuted the poor and needy man, that they might even slay the broken in heart.

17 As they loved cursing, so let it come upon them; as they delighted not in blessing, so let it be far from them.

18 As they clothed themselves with cursing like as with their garments, so let it come into their bowels like water, and like oil into their bones.

19 Let it be unto them as a garment

which covereth them, and for a girdle wherewith they are girded continually.

20 This shall be the reward of mine adversaries, from the Lord; and of them who speak evil against my soul.

21 But do thou deliver me, O Lord my God, for thy name's sake; because thy mercy is good, therefore deliver thou me.

22 For I am poor and needy, and my heart is wounded within me.

23 I am gone like the shadow when it declineth; I am tossed up and down as the locust.

24 My knees are weak through fasting; and my flesh faileth of fatness.

25 I became also a reproach unto them; when they looked upon me they shaked their heads.

26 Help me, O Lord my God; O save me according to thy mercy;

27 That they may know that this is thy hand; that thou, Lord, hast done it.

28 Let them curse, but bless thou; when they arise, let them be ashamed; but let thy servant rejoice.

29 Let mine adversaries be clothed with shame, and let them cover themselves with their own confusion, as with a mantle.

30 I will greatly praise the Lord with my mouth; yea, I will praise him among the multitude.

31 For he shall stand at the right hand of the poor, to save him from those that condemn his soul.

## PSALM 110

*The kingdom, priesthood, and conquest of Christ.*

A Psalm of David.

1 The Lord said unto my Lord, Sit thou at my right hand, until I make thine enemies thy footstool.

2 The Lord shall send the rod of thy strength out of Zion; rule thou in the midst of thine enemies.

3 Thy people shall be willing in the day of thy power, in the beauties of holiness from the womb of the morning; thou hast the dew of thy youth.

4 The Lord hath sworn, and will not repent, Thou art a priest for ever after the order of Melchizedek.

5 The Lord at thy right hand shall strike through kings in the day of his wrath.

6 He shall judge among the heathen, he shall fill their streets with their dead bodies; he shall wound the heads over many countries.

7 He shall drink of the brook in the way; therefore shall he lift up the head.

## PSALM 111

*Men should praise God for his glorious and gracious works.*

1 Praise ye the Lord. I will praise the Lord with my whole heart, in the assembly of the upright, and in the congregation.

2 The works of the Lord are great, sought out of all them that have pleasure therein.

3 His work is honorable and glorious; and his righteousness endureth for ever.

4 He hath made his wonderful works to be remembered; the Lord is gracious and full of compassion.

5 He hath given meat unto them that fear him; he will ever be mindful of his covenant.

6 He hath showed his people the power of his works, that he may give them the heritage of the heathen.

7 The works of his hands are verity and judgment; all his commandments are sure.

8 They stand fast for ever and ever, and are done in truth and uprightness.

9 He sent redemption unto his people; he hath commanded his covenant for ever; holy and reverend is his name.

10 The fear of the Lord is the beginning of wisdom; a good understanding have all they that do his commandments; his praise endureth for ever.

## PSALM 112

*Godliness hath the promises of life.*

1 Praise ye the Lord. Blessed is the man who feareth the Lord, and delighteth greatly in his commandments.

2 His seed shall be mighty upon earth; the generation of the upright shall be blessed.

3 Wealth and riches shall be in his house; and his righteousness endureth for ever.

4 Unto the upright there ariseth light in the darkness; he is gracious, and full of compassion, and righteous.

5 A good man showeth favor, and

lendeth; he will guide his affairs with discretion.

6 Surely he shall not be moved for ever; the righteous shall be in everlasting remembrance.

7 He shall not be afraid of evil tidings; his heart is fixed, trusting in the Lord.

8 His heart is established, he shall not be afraid, until he see judgment executed upon his enemies.

9 He hath dispersed, he hath given to the poor; his righteousness endureth for ever; his horn shall be exalted with honor.

10 The wicked shall see it, and be grieved; he shall gnash with his teeth, and melt away; the desire of the wicked shall perish.

## PSALM 113

*An exhortation to praise God for his excellency.*

1 Praise ye the Lord. Praise, O ye servants of the Lord, praise the name of the Lord.

2 Blessed be the name of the Lord from this time forth and for evermore.

3 From the rising of the sun unto the going down of the same the Lord's name is to be praised.

4 The Lord is high above all nations, and his glory above the heavens.

5 Who is like unto the Lord our God, who dwelleth on high,

6 Who humbleth himself to behold the things that are in heaven, and in the earth!

7 He raiseth up the poor out of the dust, and lifteth the needy out of the dunghill;

8 That he may set him with princes, even with the princes of his people.

9 He maketh the barren woman to keep house, and to be a joyful mother of children. Praise ye the Lord.

## PSALM 114

*An exhortation to fear God.*

1 When Israel went out of Egypt, the house of Jacob from a people of strange language;

2 Judah was his sanctuary, and Israel his dominion.

3 The sea saw it, and fled; Jordan was driven back.

4 The mountains skipped like rams, and the little hills like lambs.

5 What ailed thee, O thou sea, that thou fleddest? thou Jordan, that thou wast driven back?

6 Ye mountains, that ye skipped like rams; and ye little hills, like lambs?

7 Tremble, thou earth, at the presence of the Lord, at the presence of the God of Jacob;

8 Which turned the rock into a standing water, the flint into a fountain of waters.

## PSALM 115

*God is truly glorious, and idols are vanity.*

1 Not unto us, O Lord, not unto us, but unto thy name be glory, for thy mercy, and for thy truth's sake.

2 Wherefore should the heathen say, Where is now their God?

3 But our God is in the heavens; he hath done whatsoever he hath pleased.

4 Their idols are silver and gold, the work of men's hands.

5 They have mouths, but they speak not; eyes have they, but they see not;

6 They have ears, but they hear not; noses have they, but they smell not;

7 They have hands, but they handle not; feet have they, but they walk not; neither speak they through their throat.

8 They that make them are like unto them; so is every one that trusteth in them.

9 O Israel, trust thou in the Lord; he is their help and thy shield.

10 O house of Aaron, trust in the Lord; he is thy help and thy shield.

11 Ye that fear the Lord, trust in the Lord; he is your help and your shield.

12 The Lord hath been mindful of us; he will bless us; he will bless the house of Israel; he will bless the house of Aaron.

13 He will bless them that fear the Lord, both small and great.

14 The Lord shall increase you more and more, you and your children.

15 Ye are blessed of the Lord which made heaven and earth.

16 The heaven, even the heavens, are the Lord's; but the earth hath he given to the children of men.

17 The dead praise not the Lord, neither any that go down into silence.

18 But we will bless the Lord from this time forth and for evermore. Praise the Lord.

## PSALM 116

*The psalmist professeth his love and duty to God for his deliverance.*

1 I love the Lord, because he hath heard my voice and my supplications.

2 Because he hath inclined his ear unto me, therefore will I call upon him as long as I live.

3 The sorrows of death compassed me, and the pains of hell gat hold upon me; I found trouble and sorrow.

4 Then called I upon the name of the Lord; O Lord, I beseech thee, deliver my soul.

5 Gracious is the Lord, and righteous; yea, our God is merciful.

6 The Lord preserveth the simple; I was brought low, and he helped me.

7 Return unto thy rest, O my soul; for the Lord hath dealt bountifully with thee.

8 For thou hast delivered my soul from death, mine eyes from tears, and my feet from falling.

9 I will walk before the Lord in the land of the living.

10 I believed, therefore have I spoken; I was greatly afflicted;

11 I said in my haste, All men are liars.

12 What shall I render unto the Lord for all his benefits toward me?

13 I will take the cup of salvation, and call upon the name of the Lord.

14 I will pay my vows unto the Lord now in the presence of all his people.

15 Precious in the sight of the Lord is the death of his saints.

16 O Lord, truly I am thy servant; I am thy servant, and the son of thine handmaid; thou hast loosed my bonds.

17 I will offer to thee the sacrifice of thanksgiving, and will call upon the name of the Lord.

18 I will pay my vows unto the Lord now in the presence of all his people,

19 In the courts of the Lord's house, in the midst of thee, O Jerusalem. Praise ye the Lord.

## PSALM 117

*An exhortation to praise God.*

1 O praise the Lord, all ye nations; praise him all ye people.

2 For his merciful kindness is great toward us; and the truth of the Lord endureth for ever. Praise ye the Lord.

## PSALM 118

*The psalmist showeth how good it is to trust in God—The coming of Christ.*

1 O give thanks unto the Lord; for he is good; because his mercy endureth for ever.

2 Let Israel now say, that his mercy endureth for ever.

3 Let the house of Aaron now say, that his mercy endureth for ever.

4 Let them now that fear the Lord say, that his mercy endureth for ever.

5 I called upon the Lord in distress; the Lord answered me, and set me in a large place.

6 The Lord is on my side; I will not fear; what can man do unto me?

7 The Lord taketh my part with them that help me; therefore shall I see my desire upon them that hate me.

8 It is better to trust in the Lord than to put confidence in man.

9 It is better to trust in the Lord than to put confidence in princes.

10 All nations compassed me about; but in the name of the Lord will I destroy them.

11 They compassed me about; yea, they compassed me about; but in the name of the Lord I will destroy them.

12 They compassed me about like bees; they are quenched as the fire of thorns; for in the name of the Lord I will destroy them.

13 Thou hast thrust sore at me that I might fall; but the Lord helped me.

14 The Lord is my strength and song, and is become my salvation.

15 The voice of rejoicing and salvation is in the tabernacles of the righteous; the right hand of the Lord doeth valiantly.

16 The right hand of the Lord is exalted; the right hand of the Lord doeth valiantly.

17 I shall not die, but live, and declare the works of the Lord.

18 The Lord hath chastened me sore; but he hath not given me over unto death.

19 Open to me the gates of righteousness; I will go into them, and I will praise the Lord;

20 This gate of the Lord, into which the righteous shall enter.

21 I will praise thee; for thou hast heard me, and art become my salvation.

22 The stone which the builders re-

fused has become the headstone of the corner.

23 This is the Lord's doing; it is marvelous in our eyes.

24 This is the day which the Lord hath made; we will rejoice and be glad in it.

25 Save now, I beseech thee, O Lord; O Lord, I beseech thee, send now prosperity.

26 Blessed be he that cometh in the name of the Lord; we have blessed you out of the house of the Lord.

27 God is the Lord, which hath showed us light; bind the sacrifice with cords, even unto the horns of the altar.

28 Thou art my God, and I will praise thee; thou art my God, I will exalt thee.

29 O give thanks unto the Lord; for he is good; for his mercy endureth for ever.

## PSALM 119

*Sundry prayers, praises, and professions of obedience.*

### ALEPH

1 Blessed are the undefiled in the way, who walk in the law of the Lord.

2 Blessed are they that keep his testimonies, and that seek him with the whole heart.

3 They also do no iniquity; they walk in his ways.

4 Thou hast commanded us to keep thy precepts diligently.

5 O that my ways were directed to keep thy statutes!

6 Then shall I not be ashamed, when I have respect unto all thy commandments.

7 I will praise thee with uprightness of heart, when I shall have learned thy righteous judgments.

8 I will keep thy statutes; O forsake me not utterly.

### BETH

9 Wherewithal shall a young man cleanse his way? by taking heed thereto according to thy word.

10 With my whole heart have I sought thee; O let me not wander from thy commandments.

11 Thy word have I hid in mine heart, that I might not sin against thee.

12 Blessed art thou, O Lord; teach me thy statutes.

13 With my lips have I declared all the judgments of thy mouth.

14 I have rejoiced in the way of thy testimonies, as much as in all riches.

15 I will meditate upon thy precepts, and have respect unto thy ways.

16 I will delight myself in thy statutes; I will not forget thy word.

### GIMEL

17 Deal bountifully with thy servant, that I may live, and keep thy word.

18 Open thou mine eyes, that I may behold wondrous things out of thy law.

19 I am a stranger in the earth; hide not thy commandments from me.

20 My heart breaketh, for my soul longeth after thy judgments at all times.

21 Thou hast rebuked the proud; they are cursed who do err from thy commandments.

22 Remove from me reproach and contempt; for I have kept thy testimonies.

23 Princes also did sit and speak against me; but thy servant did meditate in thy statutes.

24 Thy testimonies also are my delight and my counselors.

### DALETH

25 My soul cleaveth unto the dust; quicken thou me according to thy word.

26 I have declared my ways, and thou heardest me; teach me thy statutes.

27 Make me to understand the way of thy precepts; so shall I talk of thy wondrous works.

28 My soul melteth for heaviness; strengthen thou me according unto thy word.

29 Remove from me the way of lying; and grant me thy law graciously.

30 I have chosen the way of truth; thy judgments have I laid before me.

31 I have stuck unto thy testimonies; O Lord, put me not to shame.

32 I will run the way of thy commandments, when thou shalt enlarge my heart.

### HE

33 Teach me, O Lord, the way of thy statutes; and I shall keep it to the end.

34 Give me understanding, and I shall keep thy law; yea, I shall observe it with my whole heart.

35 Make me to go in the path of thy commandments; for therein do I delight.

36 Incline my heart unto thy testimonies, and not to covetousness.

37 Turn away mine eyes from beholding vanity; and quicken thou me in thy way.

38 Stablish thy word unto thy servant, who is devoted to thy fear.

39 Turn away my reproach which I fear; for thy judgments are good.

40 Behold, I have longed after thy precepts; quicken me in thy righteousness.

VAU

41 Let thy mercies come also unto me, O Lord, even thy salvation, according to thy word.

42 So shall I have wherewith to answer him that reproacheth me; for I trust in thy word.

43 And take not the word of truth utterly out of my mouth; for I have hoped in thy judgments.

44 So shall I keep thy law continually for ever and ever.

45 And I will walk at liberty; for I seek thy precepts.

46 I will speak of thy testimonies also before kings, and will not be ashamed.

47 And I will delight myself in thy commandments, which I have loved.

48 My hands also will I lift up unto thy commandments, which I have loved; and I will meditate upon thy statutes.

ZAIN

49 Remember the word unto thy servant, upon which thou hast caused me to hope.

50 This is my comfort in my affliction; for thy word hath quickened me.

51 The proud have had me greatly in derision; yet have I not declined from thy law.

52 I remembered thy judgments of old, O Lord; and have comforted myself.

53 Horror hath taken hold upon me because of the wicked that forsake thy law.

54 Thy statutes have been my songs in the house of my pilgrimage.

55 I have remembered thy name, O Lord, in the night, and have kept thy law.

56 This I had, because I kept thy precepts.

CHETH

57 Thou art my portion, O Lord; I have said that I would keep thy words.

58 I entreated thy favor with my whole heart; be merciful unto me according to thy word.

59 I thought on my ways, and turned my feet unto thy testimonies.

60 I made haste, and delayed not to keep thy commandments.

61 The bands of the wicked have robbed me; but I have not forgotten thy law.

62 At midnight I will rise to give thanks unto thee because of thy righteous judgments.

63 I am a companion of all them that fear thee, and of them that keep thy precepts.

64 The earth, O Lord, is full of thy mercy; teach me thy statutes.

TETH

65 Thou hast dealt well with thy servant, O Lord, according unto thy word.

66 Teach me good judgment and knowledge; for I have believed thy commandments.

67 Before I was afflicted I went astray; but now have I kept thy word.

68 Thou art good, and doest good; teach me thy statutes.

69 The proud have forged a lie against me; but I will keep thy precepts with my whole heart.

70 Their heart is as fat as grease; but I delight in thy law.

71 It is good for me that I have been afflicted; that I might learn thy statutes.

72 The law of thy mouth is better unto me than thousands of gold and silver.

JOD

73 Thy hands have made me and fashioned me; give me understanding, that I may learn thy commandments.

74 They that fear thee will be glad when they see me; because I have hoped in thy word.

75 I know, O Lord, that thy judgments are right, and that thou in faithfulness hast afflicted me.

76 Let, I pray thee, thy merciful kindness be for my comfort, according to thy word unto thy servant.

77 Let thy tender mercies come unto me, that I may live; for thy law is my delight.

78 Let the proud be ashamed; for they dealt perversely with me without a cause; but I will meditate upon thy precepts.

79 Let those that fear thee turn unto

me, and those that have known thy testimonies.

80 Let my heart be sound in thy statutes; that I be not ashamed.

CAPH

81 My soul fainteth for thy salvation; but I hope in thy word.

82 Mine eyes fail for thy word, saying, When wilt thou comfort me?

83 For I am become like a bottle in the smoke; yet do I not forget thy statutes.

84 How many are the days of thy servant? when wilt thou execute judgment on them that persecute me?

85 The proud have digged pits for me, which are not after thy law.

86 All thy commandments are faithful; they persecute me wrongfully; help thou me.

87 They had almost consumed me upon earth; but I forsook not thy precepts.

88 Quicken me after thy loving-kindness; so shall I keep the testimony of thy mouth.

LAMED

89 For ever, O Lord, thy word is settled in heaven.

90 Thy faithfulness is unto all generations; thou hast established the earth, and it abideth.

91 They continue this day according to thine ordinances; for all are thy servants.

92 Unless thy law had been my delight, I should then have perished in mine affliction.

93 I will never forget thy precepts; for with them thou hast quickened me.

94 I am thine, save me; for I have sought thy precepts.

95 The wicked have waited for me to destroy me; but I will consider thy testimonies.

96 I have seen an end of all perfection; but thy commandment is exceeding broad.

MEM

97 O how I love thy law! it is my meditation all the day.

98 Thou through thy commandments hast made me wiser than mine enemies; for they are ever with me.

99 I have more understanding than all my teachers; for thy testimonies are my meditation.

100 I understand more than the ancients, because I keep thy precepts.

101 I have refrained my feet from every evil way, that I might keep thy word.

102 I have not departed from thy judgments; for thou hast taught me.

103 How sweet are thy words unto my taste! yea, sweeter than honey to my mouth.

104 Through thy precepts I get understanding; therefore I hate every false way.

NUN

105 Thy word is a lamp unto my feet, and a light unto my path.

106 I have sworn and I will perform it, that I will keep thy righteous judgments.

107 I am afflicted very much; quicken me, O Lord, according unto thy word.

108 Accept, I beseech thee, the free-will offerings of my mouth, O Lord, and teach me thy judgments.

109 My soul is continually in thy hand; and I do not forget thy law.

110 The wicked have laid a snare for me; yet I erred not from thy precepts.

111 Thy testimonies have I taken as a heritage for ever; for they are the rejoicing of my heart.

112 I have inclined mine heart to perform thy statutes always, even unto the end.

SAMECH

113 I hate vain thoughts; but thy law do I love.

114 Thou art my hiding place and my shield; I hope in thy word.

115 Depart from me, ye evildoers; for I will keep the commandments of my God.

116 Uphold me according unto thy word, that I may live; and let me not be ashamed of my hope.

117 Hold thou me up, and I shall be safe; and I will have respect unto thy statutes continually.

118 Thou hast trodden down all them that err from thy statutes; for their deceit is falsehood.

119 Thou puttest away all the wicked of the earth like dross; therefore I love thy testimonies.

120 My flesh trembleth for fear of thee; and I am afraid of thy judgments.

AIN

121 I have done judgment and justice; leave me not to mine oppressors.

122 Be surety for thy servant for good; let not the proud oppress me.

123 Mine eyes fail for thy salvation, and for the word of thy righteousness.

124 Deal with thy servant according unto thy mercy, and teach me thy statutes.

125 I am thy servant; give me understanding, that I may know thy testimonies,

126 And the time, O Lord, for me to work; for they have made void thy law.

127 Therefore I love thy commandments above gold; yea, above fine gold.

128 Therefore I esteem all thy precepts concerning all things to be right; and I hate every false way.

PE

129 Thy testimonies are wonderful; therefore doth my soul keep them.

130 The entrance of thy words giveth light; they give understanding unto the simple.

131 I opened my mouth, and panted; for I longed for thy commandments.

132 Look thou upon me, and be merciful unto me, as thou usest to do unto those that love thy name.

133 Order my steps in thy word; and let not any iniquity have dominion over me.

134 Deliver me from the oppression of man; so will I keep thy precepts.

135 Make thy face to shine upon thy servant; and teach me thy statutes.

136 Rivers of waters run down mine eyes, because they keep not thy law.

TZADDI

137 Righteous art thou, O Lord, and upright are thy judgments.

138 Thy testimonies that thou hast commanded are righteous and very faithful.

139 My zeal hath consumed me, because mine enemies have forgotten thy words.

140 Thy word is very pure; therefore thy servant loveth it.

141 I am small and despised; yet do not I forget thy precepts.

142 Thy righteousness is an everlasting righteousness, and thy law is the truth.

143 Trouble and anguish have taken hold on me; yet thy commandments are my delights.

144 The righteousness of thy testimonies is everlasting; give me understanding, and I shall live.

KOPH

145 I cried with my whole heart; hear me, O Lord; I will keep thy statutes.

146 I cried unto thee; save me, and I shall keep thy testimonies.

147 I prevented the dawning of the morning, and cried; I hoped in thy word.

148 Mine eyes prevent the night watches, that I might meditate in thy word.

149 Hear my voice according unto thy loving-kindness; O Lord, quicken me according to thy judgment.

150 They draw nigh that follow after mischief; they are far from thy law.

151 Thou art near, O Lord; and all thy commandments are truth.

152 Concerning thy testimonies, I have known of old that thou hast founded them for ever.

RESH

153 Consider mine affliction, and deliver me; for I do not forget thy law.

154 Plead my cause, and deliver me; quicken me according to thy word.

155 Salvation is far from the wicked; for they seek not thy statutes.

156 Great are thy tender mercies, O Lord; quicken me according to thy judgments.

157 Many are my persecutors and mine enemies; yet do I not decline from thy testimonies.

158 I beheld the transgressors, and was grieved; because they kept not thy word.

159 Consider how I love thy precepts; quicken me, O Lord, according to thy loving-kindness.

160 Thy word is true from the beginning; and every one of thy righteous judgments endureth for ever.

SCHIN

161 Princes have persecuted me without a cause; but my heart standeth in awe of thy word.

162 I rejoice at thy word, as one that findeth great spoil.

163 I hate and abhor lying; but thy law do I love.

164 Seven times a day do I praise thee because of thy righteous judgments.

165 Great peace have they which love thy law; and nothing shall offend them.

166 Lord, I have hoped for thy salvation, and done thy commandments.

167 My soul hath kept thy testimonies; and I love them exceedingly.

168 I have kept thy precepts and thy testimonies; for all my ways are before thee.

169 Let my cry come near before thee, O Lord; give me understanding according to thy word.

170 Let my supplication come before thee; deliver me according to thy word.

171 My lips shall utter praise, when thou hast taught me thy statutes.

172 My tongue shall speak of thy word; for all thy commandments are righteousness.

173 Let thine hand help me; for I have chosen thy precepts.

174 I have longed for thy salvation, O Lord; and thy law is my delight.

175 Let my soul live, and it shall praise thee; and let thy judgments help me.

176 I have gone astray like a lost sheep; seek thy servant; for I do not forget thy commandments.

## PSALM 120

*David prayeth for deliverance.*

A Song of degrees.

1 In my distress I cried unto the Lord, and he heard me.

2 Deliver my soul, O Lord, from lying lips, and from a deceitful tongue.

3 What shall be given unto thee? or what shall be done unto thee, thou false tongue?

4 Sharp arrows of the mighty, with coals of juniper.

5 Woe is me, that I sojourn in Mesech, that I dwell in the tents of Kedar!

6 My soul hath long dwelt with him that hateth peace.

7 I am for peace; but when I speak, they are for war.

## PSALM 121

*The great safety of the godly.*

A Song of degrees.

1 I will lift up mine eyes unto the hills, from whence cometh my help.

2 My help cometh from the Lord, which made heaven and earth.

3 Behold, he that keepeth Israel shall neither slumber nor sleep.

4 He will not suffer thy foot to be moved; he that keepeth thee will not slumber.

5 The Lord is thy keeper; the Lord is thy shade upon thy right hand.

6 The sun shall not smite thee by day, nor the moon by night.

7 The Lord shall preserve thee from all evil; he shall preserve thy soul.

8 The Lord shall preserve thy going out and thy coming in from this time forth, and even for evermore.

## PSALM 122

*David prayeth for peace.*

A Song of degrees of David.

1 I was glad when they said unto me, Let us go into the house of the Lord.

2 Our feet shall stand within thy gates, O Jerusalem.

3 Jerusalem is builded as a city that is compact together;

4 Whither the tribes go up, the tribes of the Lord, unto the testimony of Israel, to give thanks unto the name of the Lord.

5 For there are set thrones of judgment, the thrones of the house of David.

6 Pray for the peace of Jerusalem; they shall prosper that love thee.

7 Peace be within thy walls, and prosperity within thy palaces.

8 For my brethren and companions' sakes, I will now say, Peace be within thee.

9 Because of the house of the Lord our God I will seek thy good.

## PSALM 123

*Prayer for mercy.*

A Song of degrees.

1 Unto thee lift I up mine eyes, O thou that dwellest in the heavens.

2 Behold, as the eyes of servants look unto the hand of their masters, and as the eyes of a maiden unto the hand of her mistress; so our eyes wait upon the Lord our God, until that he have mercy upon us.

3 Have mercy upon us, O Lord, have mercy upon us; for we are exceedingly filled with contempt.

4 Our soul is exceedingly filled with the scorning of those that are at ease, and with the contempt of the proud.

## PSALM 124

*Israel praiseth God for deliverance.*

A Song of degrees of David.

1 Now may Israel say, If the Lord was not on our side when men rose up against us, then they had swallowed us up quick when their wrath was kindled against us.

2 Then the waters had overwhelmed us, the stream had gone over our soul;

3 Then the proud waters had gone over our soul.

4 Blessed be the Lord, who hath not given us as a prey to their teeth.

5 Our soul is escaped as a bird out of the snare of the fowlers; the snare is broken, and we are escaped.

6 Our help is in the name of the Lord, who made heaven and earth.

## PSALM 125

*The safety of trust in God.*

A Song of degrees.

1 They that trust in the Lord in mount Zion, cannot be removed, but abide for ever.

2 As the mountains are round about Jerusalem, so the Lord is round about his people from henceforth even for ever.

3 For the rod of the wicked shall not rest upon the lot of the righteous; lest the righteous put forth their hands unto iniquity.

4 Do good, O Lord, unto the good, and unto the upright in their hearts.

5 As for such as turn aside unto their crooked ways, the Lord shall lead them forth with the workers of iniquity; but peace shall be upon Israel.

## PSALM 126

*Glory of Zion declared.*

A Song of degrees.

1 When the Lord turned again the captivity of Zion, we were like them that dream.

2 Then was our mouth filled with laughter, and our tongue with singing; then said they among the heathen, The Lord hath done great things for them.

3 The Lord hath done great things for us; whereof we are glad.

4 Turn again our captivity, O Lord, as the streams in the south.

5 They that sow in tears shall reap in joy.

6 He that goeth forth and weepeth, bearing precious seed, shall doubtless come again with rejoicing, bringing his sheaves with him.

## PSALM 127

*Virtue of God's blessing.*

A Song of degrees for Solomon.

1 Except the Lord build the house, they labour in vain that build it; ex-cept the Lord keep the city, the watch-man waketh but in vain.

2 It is vain for you to rise up early, to sit up late, to eat the bread of sorrows; for so he giveth his beloved sleep.

3 Lo, children are a heritage of the Lord; and the fruit of the womb is his reward.

4 As arrows are in the hand of a mighty man; so are children of the youth.

5 Happy is the man that hath his quiver full of them; they shall not be ashamed, but they shall speak with the enemies in the gate.

## PSALM 128

*Sundry blessings which follow them that fear God.*

A Song of degrees.

1 Blessed is every one that feareth the Lord; that walketh in his ways.

2 For thou shalt eat the labour of thine hands; happy shalt thou be, and it shall be well with thee.

3 Thy wife shall be as a fruitful vine by the sides of thine house; thy chil-dren like olive plants round about thy table.

4 Behold, that thus shall the man be blessed that feareth the Lord.

5 The Lord shall bless thee out of Zion; and thou shalt see the good of Je-rusalem all the days of thy life.

6 Yea, thou shalt see thy children's children, and peace upon Israel.

## PSALM 129

*The security of Israel.*

A Song of degrees.

1 Many a time have they afflicted me from my youth, may Israel now say;

2 Many a time have they afflicted me from my youth; yet they have not prevailed against me.

3 The ploughers ploughed upon my back; they made long their furrows.

4 The Lord is righteous; he hath cut asunder the cords of the wicked.

5 Let them all be confounded and turned back that hate Zion.

6 Let them be as the grass upon the housetops, which withereth afore it groweth up;

7 Wherewith the mower filleth not his hand; nor he that bindeth sheaves his bosom.

8 Neither do they which go by say,

The blessing of the Lord be upon you; we bless you in the name of the Lord.

## PSALM 130

*Patient hope—Redemption sure.*

A Song of degrees.

1 Out of the depths have I cried unto thee, O Lord.

2 Lord, hear my voice; let thine ears be attentive to the voice of my supplications.

3 If thou, Lord, shouldest mark iniquities, O Lord, who shall stand?

4 But there is forgiveness with thee, that thou mayest be feared.

5 I wait for the Lord, my soul doth wait, and in his word do I hope.

6 My soul waiteth for the Lord more than they that watch for the morning; I say, more than they that watch for the morning.

7 Let Israel hope in the Lord; for with the Lord there is mercy, and with him is plenteous redemption.

8 And he shall redeem Israel from all his iniquities.

## PSALM 131

*Humility the surety of hope.*

A Song of degrees of David.

1 Lord, my heart is not haughty, nor mine eyes lofty; neither do I exercise myself in great matters, or in things too high for me.

2 Surely I have behaved and quieted myself, as a child that is weaned of his mother; my soul is even as a weaned child.

3 Let Israel hope in the Lord from henceforth and for ever.

## PSALM 132

*David's covenant—God's promises to his people.*

A Song of degrees.

1 Lord, remember David, and all his afflictions;

2 How he sware unto the Lord, and vowed unto the mighty God of Jacob;

3 Surely I will not come into the tabernacle of my house, nor go up into my bed;

4 I will not give sleep to mine eyes, or slumber to mine eyelids,

5 Until I find out a place for the Lord, a habitation for the mighty God of Jacob.

6 Lo, we heard of it at Ephratah; we found it in the fields of the wood.

7 We will go into his tabernacles; we will worship at his footstool.

8 Arise, O Lord, into thy rest; thou, and the ark of thy strength.

9 Let thy priests be clothed with righteousness; and let thy saints shout for joy.

10 For thy servant David's sake turn not away the face of thine anointed.

11 The Lord hath sworn in truth unto David; he will not turn from it; Of the fruit of thy body will I set upon thy throne.

12 If thy children will keep my covenant and my testimony that I shall teach them, their children shall also sit upon thy throne for evermore.

13 For the Lord hath chosen Zion; he hath desired it for his habitation.

14 This is my rest for ever; here will I dwell; for I have desired it.

15 I will abundantly bless her provision; I will satisfy her poor with bread.

16 I will also clothe her priests with salvation; and her saints shall shout aloud for joy.

17 There will I make the horn of David to bud; I have ordained a lamp for mine anointed.

18 His enemies will I clothe with shame; but upon himself shall his crown flourish.

## PSALM 133

*The communion of saints.*

A Song of degrees of David.

1 Behold, how good and how pleasant it is for brethren to dwell together in unity!

2 It is like the precious ointment upon the head, that ran down upon the beard, even Aaron's beard; that went down to the skirts of his garments;

3 As the dew of Hermon, and as the dew that descended upon the mountains of Zion; for there the Lord commanded the blessing, even life for evermore.

## PSALM 134

*An exhortation to praise God.*

A Song of degrees.

1 Behold, bless ye the Lord, all ye servants of the Lord, which by night stand in the house of the Lord.

2 Lift up your hands in the sanctuary, and bless the Lord.

3 The Lord that made heaven and earth bless thee out of Zion.

## PSALM 135

*An exhortation to praise God—The vanity of idols.*

1 Praise ye the Lord. Praise ye the name of the Lord; praise him, O ye servants of the Lord.

2 Ye that stand in the house of the Lord, in the courts of the house of our God,

3 Praise the Lord; for the Lord is good; sing praises unto his name; for it is pleasant.

4 For the Lord hath chosen Jacob unto himself, and Israel for his peculiar treasure.

5 For I know that the Lord is great, and that our Lord is great, and that our Lord is above all gods.

6 Whatsoever the Lord pleased, that did he in heaven, and in earth, in the seas, and all deep places.

7 He causeth the vapors to ascend from the ends of the earth; he maketh lightnings for the rain; he bringeth the wind out of his treasuries.

8 Who smote the firstborn of Egypt, both of man and beast.

9 Who sent tokens and wonders into the midst of thee, O Egypt, upon Pharaoh, and upon all his servants.

10 Who smote great nations, and slew mighty kings;

11 Sihon king of the Amorites, and Og king of Bashan, and all the kingdoms of Canaan;

12 And gave their land for a heritage, a heritage unto Israel his people.

13 Thy name, O Lord, endureth for ever; and thy memorial, O Lord, throughout all generations.

14 For the Lord will judge his people, and he will not repent himself concerning his servants.

15 The idols of the heathen are silver and gold, the work of men's hands.

16 They have mouths, but they speak not; eyes have they, but they see not;

17 They have ears, but they hear not; neither is there any breath in their mouths.

18 They that make them are like unto them; so is every one that trusteth in them.

19 Bless the Lord, O house of Israel; bless the Lord, O house of Aaron;

20 Bless the Lord, O house of Levi; ye that fear the Lord, bless the Lord.

21 Blessed be the Lord out of Zion; Blessed be the Lord out of Jerusalem. Praise ye the Lord.

## PSALM 136

*Thanks to God for his mercies.*

1 O give thanks unto the Lord; for he is good; for his mercy endureth for ever.

2 O give thanks unto the God of gods; for his mercy endureth for ever.

3 O give thanks to the Lord of lords; for his mercy endureth for ever.

4 To him who alone doeth great wonders; for his mercy endureth for ever.

5 To him that by wisdom made the heavens; for his mercy endureth for ever.

6 To him that stretched out the earth above the waters; for his mercy endureth for ever.

7 To him that made great lights; for his mercy endureth for ever;

8 The sun to rule by day; for his mercy endureth for ever;

9 The moon and stars to rule by night; for his mercy endureth for ever.

10 To him that smote Egypt in their firstborn; for his mercy endureth for ever;

11 And brought out Israel from among them; for his mercy endureth for ever;

12 With a strong hand, and with a stretched-out arm; for his mercy endureth for ever.

13 To him which divided the Red sea into parts; for his mercy endureth for ever;

14 And made Israel to pass through the midst of it; for his mercy endureth for ever;

15 But overthrew Pharaoh and his host in the Red sea; for his mercy endureth for ever.

16 To him which led his people through the wilderness; for his mercy endureth for ever.

17 To him which smote great kings; for his mercy endureth for ever;

18 And slew famous kings; for his mercy endureth for ever;

19 Sihon king of the Amorites; for his mercy endureth for ever;

20 And Og the king of Bashan; for his mercy endureth for ever;

21 And gave their land for a heritage; for his mercy endureth for ever;

22 Even a heritage unto Israel his servant; for his mercy endureth for ever.

23 Who remembered us in our low estate; for his mercy endureth for ever;

24 And hath redeemed us from our enemies; for his mercy endureth for ever.

25 Who giveth food to all flesh; for his mercy endureth for ever.

26 O give thanks unto the God of heaven; for his mercy endureth for ever.

## PSALM 137

*Constancy in captivity.*

1 By the rivers of Babylon, there we sat down, yea, we wept, when we remembered Zion.

2 We hanged our harps upon the willows in the midst thereof.

3 For there they that carried us away captive required of us a song; and they that wasted us required of us mirth, saying, Sing us one of the songs of Zion.

4 How shall we sing the Lord's song in a strange land?

5 If I forget thee, O Jerusalem, let my right hand forget its cunning.

6 If I do not remember thee, let my tongue cleave to the roof of my mouth; if I prefer not Jerusalem above my chief joy.

7 Remember, O Lord, the children of Edom in the day of Jerusalem; who said, Rase it, even to the foundation thereof.

8 O daughter of Babylon, who art to be destroyed; happy shall he be, that rewardeth thee as thou hast served us.

9 Happy shall he be, that taketh and dasheth thy little ones against the stones.

## PSALM 138

*David praiseth God for the truth of his word.*

1 I will praise thee with my whole heart; before the gods will I sing praise unto thee.

2 I will worship toward thy holy temple, and praise thy name for thy loving-kindness and for thy truth; for that hast magnified thy word above all thy name.

3 In the day when I cried thou answeredst me, and strengthenedst me with strength in my soul.

4 All the kings of the earth shall praise thee, O Lord, when they hear the words of thy mouth.

5 Yea, they shall sing in the ways of the Lord; for great is the glory of the Lord.

6 Though the Lord be high, yet hath he respect unto the lowly; but the proud he knoweth afar off.

7 Though I walk in the midst of trouble, thou wilt revive me; thou shalt stretch forth thine hand against the wrath of mine enemies, and thy right hand shall save me.

8 The Lord will perfect me in knowledge, concerning his kingdom. I will praise thee O Lord, for ever; for thou art merciful, and wilt not forsake the works of thine own hands.

## PSALM 139

*God's power and knowledge everywhere present.*

To the chief Musician, A Psalm of David.

1 O Lord, thou hast searched me, and known me.

2 Thou knowest my downsitting and mine uprising; thou understandest my thought afar off.

3 Thou compassest my path and my lying down, and art acquainted with all my ways.

4 For there is not a word in my tongue, but, lo, O Lord, thou knowest it altogether.

5 Thou hast beset me behind and before, and laid thine hand upon me.

6 Such knowledge is too wonderful for me; it is high, I cannot attain unto it.

7 Whither shall I go from thy Spirit? or whither shall I flee from thy presence?

8 If I ascend up into heaven, thou art there; if I make my bed in hell, behold, thou art there.

9 If I take the wings of the morning, and dwell in the uttermost parts of the sea;

10 Even there shall thy hand lead me, and thy right hand shall hold me.

11 If I say, Surely the darkness shall cover me; even the night shall be light about me.

12 Yea, the darkness hideth not from thee; but the night shineth as the day; the darkness and the light are both alike to thee.

13 For thou hast possessed my reins; thou hast covered me in my mother's womb.

14 I will praise thee; for I am fearfully and wonderfully made; marvelous

are thy works; and that my soul knoweth right well.

15 My substance was not hid from thee, when I was made in secret, and curiously wrought in the lowest parts of the earth.

16 Thine eyes did see my substance, yet being unperfect; and in thy book all my members were written, which in continuance were fashioned, when as yet I knew none of them.

17 How precious also are thy thoughts unto me, O God! how great is the sum of them!

18 If I should count them, they are more in number than the sand; when I awake, I am still with thee.

19 Surely thou wilt slay the wicked, O God; depart from me therefore, ye bloody men.

20 For they speak against thee wickedly, and thine enemies take thy name in vain.

21 Do not I hate them, O Lord, that hate thee? and am not I grieved with those that rise up against thee?

22 I hate them with perfect hatred; I count them mine enemies.

23 Search me, O God, and know my heart; try me, and know my thoughts;

24 And see if there be any wicked way in me, and lead me in the way everlasting.

## PSALM 140

*David prayeth to be delivered from the wicked.*

To the chief Musician, A Psalm of David.

1 Deliver me, O Lord, from the evil man; preserve me from the violent man;

2 Which imagine mischiefs in their heart; continually are they gathered together for war.

3 They have sharpened their tongues like a serpent; adders' poison is under their lips. Selah.

4 Keep me, O Lord, from the hands of the wicked; preserve me from the violent man; who have purposed to overthrow my goings.

5 The proud have hid a snare for me, and cords; they have spread a net by the wayside; they have set gins for me. Selah.

6 I said unto the Lord, Thou art my God; hear the voice of my supplications, O Lord.

7 O God the Lord, the strength of my

salvation, thou hast covered my head in the day of battle.

8 Grant not, O Lord, the desires of the wicked; further not his wicked device; lest they exalt themselves. Selah.

9 As for the head of those that compass me about, let the mischief of their own lips cover them.

10 Let burning coals fall upon them; let them be cast into the fire; into deep pits, that they rise not up again.

11 Let not an evil speaker be established in the earth; evil shall hunt the violent man to overthrow him.

12 I know that the Lord will maintain the cause of the afflicted, and the right of the poor.

13 Surely the righteous shall give thanks unto thy name; the upright shall dwell in thy presence.

## PSALM 141

*A prayer for sincerity, and for safety from snares.*

A Psalm of David.

1 Lord, I cry unto thee; make haste unto me; give ear unto my voice, when I cry unto thee.

2 Let my prayer be set forth before thee as incense; and the lifting up of my hands as the evening sacrifice.

3 Set a watch, O Lord, before my mouth; keep the door of my lips.

4 Incline not my heart to any evil thing, to practice wicked works with men that work iniquity; and let me not eat of their dainties.

5 When the righteous smite me with the word of the Lord it is a kindness; and when they reprove me, it shall be an excellent oil, and shall not destroy my faith; for yet my prayer also shall be for them. I delight not in their calamities.

6 When their judges are overthrown in stony places, they shall hear my words; for they are sweet.

7 Our bones are scattered at the grave's mouth, as when one cutteth and cleaveth wood upon the earth.

8 But mine eyes are unto thee, O God the Lord; in thee is my trust; leave not my soul destitute.

9 Keep me from the snares which they have laid for me, and the gins of the workers of iniquity.

10 Let the wicked fall into their own nets, whilst that I withal escape.

## PSALM 142

*There is comfort in prayer.*

Maschil of David; A prayer when he was in the cave.

1 I cried unto the Lord with my voice; with my voice unto the Lord did I make my supplication.

2 I poured out my complaint before him; I showed before him my trouble.

3 When my spirit was overwhelmed within me, then thou knewest my path. In the way wherein I walked have they privily laid a snare for me.

4 I looked on my right hand, and behold, but there was no man that would know me; refuge failed me; no man cared for my soul.

5 I cried unto thee, O Lord; I said, Thou art my refuge and my portion in the land of the living.

6 Attend unto my cry; for I am brought very low; deliver me from my persecutors; for they are stronger than I.

7 Bring my soul out of prison, that I may praise thy name; the righteous shall compass me about; for thou shalt deal bountifully with me.

## PSALM 143

*Faith strengthened by meditation and prayer.*

A Psalm of David.

1 Hear my prayer, O Lord, give ear to my supplications; in thy faithfulness answer me, and in thy righteousness.

2 And enter not into judgment with thy servant; for in thy sight shall no man living be justified.

3 For the enemy hath persecuted my soul; he hath smitten my life down to the ground; he hath made me to dwell in darkness, as those that have long been dead.

4 Therefore is my spirit overwhelmed within me; my heart within me is desolate.

5 I remember the days of old; I meditate on all thy works; I muse on the work of thy hands.

6 I stretch forth my hands unto thee; my soul thirsteth after thee, as a thirsty land. Selah.

7 Hear me speedily, O Lord; my spirit faileth; hide not thy face from me, lest I be like unto them that go down into the pit.

8 Cause me to hear thy loving-kindness in the morning; for in thee do I trust; cause me to know the way wherein I should walk; for I lift up my soul unto thee.

9 Deliver me, O Lord, from mine enemies; I flee unto thee to hide me.

10 Teach me to do thy will; for thou art my God; thy Spirit is good; lead me into the land of uprightness.

11 Quicken me, O Lord, for thy name's sake; for thy righteousness' sake bring my soul out of trouble.

12 And of thy mercy cut off mine enemies, and destroy all them that afflict my soul; for I am thy servant.

## PSALM 144

*A prayer for sundry blessings.*

A Psalm of David.

1 Blessed be the Lord my strength which teacheth my hands to war, and my fingers to fight;

2 My goodness, and my fortress; my high tower, and my deliverer; my shield, and he in whom I trust; who subdueth my people under me.

3 Lord, what is man, that thou takest knowledge of him! or the son of man, that thou makest account of him!

4 Man is like to vanity; his days are as a shadow that passeth away.

5 Bow thy heavens, O Lord, and come down; touch the mountains, and they shall smoke.

6 Cast forth lightning, and scatter them; shoot out thine arrows, and destroy them.

7 Send thine hand from above; rid me, and deliver me out of great waters, from the hand of strange children;

8 Whose mouth speaketh vanity, and their right hand is a right hand of falsehood.

9 I will sing a new song unto thee, O God; upon a psaltery and an instrument of ten strings will I sing praises unto thee.

10 It is he that giveth salvation unto kings; who delivereth David his servant from the hurtful sword.

11 Rid me, and deliver me from the hand of strange children, whose mouth speaketh vanity, and their right hand is a right hand of falsehood;

12 That our sons may be as plants grown up in their youth; that our daughters may be as cornerstones, polished after the similitude of a palace;

13 That our garners may be full, affording all manner of store; that our

sheep may bring forth thousands and ten thousands in our streets;

14 That our oxen may be strong to labour; that there be no breaking in, nor going out; that there be no complaining in our streets.

15 Happy is that people, that is in such a case; yea, happy is that people, whose God is the Lord.

## PSALM 145

*David's psalm of praise.*

1 I will extol thee, my God, O King; and I will bless thy name for ever and ever.

2 Every day will I bless thee; and I will praise thy name for ever and ever.

3 Great is the Lord, and greatly to be praised; and his greatness is unsearchable.

4 One generation shall praise thy works to another, and shall declare thy mighty acts.

5 I will speak of the glorious honor of thy majesty, and of thy wondrous works.

6 And men shall speak of the might of thy terrible acts; and I will declare thy greatness.

7 They shall abundantly utter the memory of thy great goodness, and shall sing of thy righteousness.

8 The Lord is gracious, and full of compassion; slow to anger, and of great mercy.

9 The Lord is good to all; and his tender mercies are over all his works.

10 All thy works shall praise thee, O Lord; and thy saints shall bless thee.

11 They shall speak of the glory of thy kingdom, and talk of thy power;

12 To make known to the sons of men his mighty acts, and the glorious majesty of his kingdom.

13 Thy kingdom is an everlasting kingdom, and thy dominion endureth throughout all generations.

14 The Lord upholdeth all that fall, and raiseth up all those that be bowed down.

15 The eyes of all wait upon thee; and thou givest them their meat in due season.

16 Thou openest thine hand, and satisfiest the desire of every living thing.

17 The Lord is righteous in all his ways, and holy in all his works.

18 The Lord is nigh unto all them that call upon him, to all that call upon him in truth.

19 He will fulfill the desire of them that fear him; he also will hear their cry, and will save them.

20 The Lord preserveth all them that love him; but all the wicked will he destroy.

21 My mouth shall speak the praise of the Lord; and let all flesh bless his holy name for ever and ever.

## PSALM 146

*God alone worthy to be praised, and trusted.*

1 Praise ye the Lord. Praise the Lord, O my soul.

2 While I live will I praise the Lord; I will sing praises unto my God while I have any being.

3 Put not your trust in princes, nor in the son of man, in whom there is no help.

4 His breath goeth forth, he returneth to his earth; in that very day his thoughts perish.

5 Happy is he that hath the God of Jacob for his help, whose hope is in the Lord his God:

6 Which made heaven, and earth, the sea, and all that therein is; which keepeth truth for ever:

7 Which executeth judgment for the oppressed; which giveth food to the hungry. The Lord looseth the prisoners;

8 The Lord openeth the eyes of the blind; the Lord raiseth them that are bowed down; the Lord loveth the righteous;

9 The Lord preserveth the strangers; he relieveth the fatherless and widow; but the way of the wicked he turneth upside down.

10 The Lord shall reign for ever, even thy God, O Zion, unto all generations. Praise ye the Lord.

## PSALM 147

*Recounts many reasons for praising God.*

1 Praise ye the Lord; for it is good to sing praises unto our God; for it is pleasant; and praise is comely.

2 The Lord doth build up Jerusalem; he gathereth together the outcasts of Israel.

3 He healeth the broken in heart, and bindeth up their wounds.

4 He telleth the number of the stars; he calleth them all by their names.

5 Great is our Lord, and of great power; his understanding is infinite.

6 The Lord lifteth up the meek; he casteth the wicked down to the ground.

7 Sing unto the Lord with thanksgiving; sing praise upon the harp unto our God;

8 Who covereth the heaven with clouds, who prepareth rain for the earth, who maketh grass to grow upon the mountains.

9 He giveth to the beast his food, and to the young ravens which cry.

10 He delighteth not in the strength of the horse; he taketh not pleasure in the legs of a man.

11 The Lord taketh pleasure in them that fear him, in those that hope in his mercy.

12 Praise the Lord, O Jerusalem; praise thy God, O Zion.

13 For he hath strengthened the bars of thy gates; he hath blessed thy children within thee.

14 He maketh peace in thy borders, and filleth thee with the finest of the wheat.

15 He sendeth forth his commandment upon earth; his word runneth very swiftly.

16 He giveth snow like wool; he scattereth the hoarfrost like ashes.

17 He casteth forth his ice like morsels; who can stand before his cold?

18 He sendeth out his word, and melteth them; he causeth his wind to blow, and the waters flow.

19 He showeth his word unto Jacob, his statutes and his judgments unto Israel.

20 He hath not dealt so with any nation; and as for his judgments, they have not known them. Praise ye the Lord.

## PSALM 148
*All creation exhorted to praise God.*

1 Praise ye the Lord. Praise ye the Lord from the heavens; praise him in the heights.

2 Praise ye him, all his angels; praise ye him, all his hosts.

3 Praise ye him, sun and moon; praise him, all ye stars of light.

4 Praise him, ye heavens of heavens, and ye waters that be above the heavens.

5 Let them praise the name of the Lord; for he commanded, and they were created.

6 He hath also stablished them for ever and ever; he hath made a decree which shall not pass.

7 Praise the Lord from the earth, ye dragons, and all deeps.

8 Fire, and hail; snow, and vapors; stormy wind fulfilling his word;

9 Mountains, and all hills; fruitful trees, and all cedars;

10 Beasts, and all cattle; creeping things, and flying fowl;

11 Kings of the earth, and all people; princes, and all judges of the earth;

12 Both young men, and maidens; old men, and children;

13 Let them praise the name of the Lord; for his name alone is excellent; his glory is above the earth and heaven.

14 He also exalteth the horn of his people, the praise of all his saints; even of the children of Israel, a people near unto him. Praise ye the Lord.

## PSALM 149
*God to be praised.*

1 Praise ye the Lord. Sing unto the Lord a new song, and his praise in the congregation of saints.

2 Let Israel rejoice in him that made him; let the children of Zion be joyful in their King.

3 Let them praise his name in the dance; let them sing praises unto him with the timbrel and harp.

4 For the Lord taketh pleasure in his people; he will beautify the meek with salvation.

5 Let the saints be joyful in glory; let them sing aloud upon their beds.

6 Let the high praises of God be in their mouth, and a two-edged sword in their hand;

7 To execute vengeance upon the heathen, and punishments upon the people;

8 To bind their kings with chains, and their nobles with fetters of iron;

9 To execute upon them the judgment written; this honor have all his saints. Praise ye the Lord.

## PSALM 150
*An exhortation to praise God with instrumental music.*

1 Praise ye the Lord. Praise God in

his sanctuary; praise him in the firmament of his power.

2 Praise him for his mighty acts; praise him according to his excellent greatness.

3 Praise him with the sound of the trumpet; praise him with the psaltery and harp.

4 Praise him with the timbrel and dance; praise him with stringed instruments and organs.

5 Praise him upon the loud cymbals; praise him upon the high-sounding cymbals.

6 Let every thing that hath breath praise the Lord. Praise ye the Lord.